# Teaching Science
# for All Children
## Third Edition

**Ralph Martin**
Ohio University

**Colleen Sexton**
Ohio University

**Jack Gerlovich**
Drake University

**Allyn and Bacon**
Boston    London    Toronto    Sydney    Tokyo    Singapore

Editor: Traci Mueller
Editorial Assistant: Bridget Keane
Senior Marketing Manager: Brad Parkins
Cover Administrator: Linda Knowles
Composition Buyer: Linda Cox
Manufacturing Buyer: Megan Cochran
Production Coordinator: Deborah Brown
Photo Researcher: Kate Cook
Text Designer: Glenna Collett
Electronic Composition: Omegatype Typography, Inc.

The material in this book is based upon work supported by the National Science Foundation under grant number 91–47392. Any opinions, findings, conclusions, or recommendations expressed in this publication are those of the authors and do not necessarily reflect the views of the Foundation.

Internet: www.abacon.com

Between the time Web site information is gathered and then published, it is not unusual for some sites to have closed. Also, the transcription of URLs can result in unintended typographical errors. The publisher would appreciate being notified of any problems with URLs so that they may be corrected in subsequent editions.

**Library of Congress Cataloging-in-Publication Data**
Martin, Ralph E., 1951-
    Teaching science for all children.—3rd ed. / Ralph Martin, Colleen Sexton, Jack Gerlovich.
        p. cm.
    Rev. ed. of: Teaching science for all children / Ralph Martin . . . [et al.]. 2nd ed. c1997.
    Includes bibliographical references and index.
    ISBN 0-205-32533-5
    1. Science—Study and teaching. 2. Science—Study and teaching (Elementary) 3. Activity programs in education. I. Sexton, Colleen M. II. Gerlovich, Jack A. III. Teaching science for all children. IV. Title
    Q181 M17783 2001
    3732.3'5044–dc21                                                    00–040595

*Photo Credits*
**Will Hart:** pp. 2, 36, 46, 50, 72, 76, 90, 104, 138, 187, 210, 313, 346, 369, 398, 404; **Courtesy of William E. Mills:** pp. 40, 56, 59, 63, 69, 100, 114, 116, 144, 151, 165, 167, 192, 226, 233, 262, 308, 315, 324, 325, 331, 350, 379, 383, 388, 389; **Gloria Schlaepfer:** p. 51; **Robert Harbison:** pp. 86, 124; **Russell D. Curtis/Photo Researchers:** p. 94; **Corbis:** p. 113; **Will Faller:** pp. 157, 173, 176; **Dave Shaefer/Picture Cube:** p. 182; **Brian Smith:** pp. 201, 354, 392, 397; **Jim Pickerell:** pp. 268, 278, 289; **Stephen Marks:** p. 285; **Michael Dwyer/Stock Boston:** p. 298; **Gale Zucker/Stock Boston:** p. 310; **Courtesy of H. L. Bouton Co., Inc.:** p. 315; **Courtesy of Boekel Industries, Inc.:** p. 318 (top); **Courtesy of Eagle Manufacturing Company:** p. 318 (bottom); **Courtesy of Lab Safety Supply:** p. 319 (top); **Courtesy of Amerex:** p. 319 (bottom); **Courtesy of Sellstrom Manufacturing Co.:** p. 320; **Modern Curriculum Press:** p. 400.

Printed in the United States of America

10 9 8 7 6 5 4                     03 04 05 06

## DEDICATION

For Marilyn—in celebration of our twenty-sixth anniversary.
I cannot imagine a better friend or more dedicated mother.

R. M.

To my parents, Colette and Bill Athans,
who continually told all six of their children
"you can do anything you set your mind to,"
and to my daughters, Sarah and Celeste,
who are a source of encouragement and inspiration.

C. S.

To the Elementary Science Methods students at Drake University,
who have been and continue to be inspirations for my science activity ideas,
as well as enthusiastic supporters of hands-on,
and often electronically delivered, quality science teaching.

J. G.

# Contents

iv

## PART II    The Explanation: Modern Science Teaching Benefits from Inquiry-Based, Interactive Approaches to Learning    75

### 3    What Is Science?    77

### 4    How Do Children Learn Science?    105

### 5    How Can You Teach Science for All Children?    139

### 6    What Goals Promote Scientific Literacy?    183

---

## PART III    The Expansion: Continuing Our Learning, Developing Skills, and Using the Tools of Science    209

### How Can You Plan Constructivist Science Lessons and Assess Student Performance?    211

### How Can You Use Questions to Promote Science Inquiry?    263

### How Can You Create a Safe, Efficient, Inquiry-Based Science Classroom?    299

## PART IV   Lessons, Activities, and Teaching Materials to Meet the Goals of Elementary and Middle School Science   423

### SECTION I   Life Science Activities   424

**SECTION II**   Physical Science Lessons   490

**SECTION III**   Earth and Space Science Activities   559

# Preface

## FOR WHOM IS THIS BOOK DESIGNED AND WHAT DOES IT STRIVE TO DO?

Designed for preservice and inservice teachers, this book helps users develop scientific literacy among learners of school science. "Scientific literacy implies that a person can identify scientific issues underlying national and local decisions and express positions that are scientifically and technologically informed" (NRC, 1996, 23). While many conditions and standards yield the synergetic factors necessary for establishing scientific literacy, the National Science Education Standards (NSES) advocate teaching and learning through inquiry—a key to learner scientific literacy and the dominate theme of our third edition of *Teaching Science for All Children.*

## WHAT IS NEW TO THIS EDITION?

We have reorganized and revised our strong chapters into a format that immerses users immediately into teaching and doing science through inquiry. We use our popular 4-E learning cycle approach for organizing this text. While there are many effective ways to teach and learn science, one of the most effective and enduring is the learning cycle: *Explore, Explain, Expand, Evaluate.* Experience is an important foundation for the processes of inquiry if a learner is to be successful in making meaning out of the unique experiences that science can provide. We offer you an opportunity to accumulate science teaching experiences by testing the methods and techniques described in this book. For example, you will be immersed in teaching methods and experiences in Part I.

Part I of our book offers opportunities to *Explore* the teaching of science. Chapters 1 and 2 illustrate several methods for teaching science. While we use the 4-E learning cycle as a preferred teaching method and as an organizer for this text, we do encourage you to fully explore many different science teaching methods. The 4-E learning cycle method is used in each of the lessons located in Part IV of our text and is presented first among the methods offered in Chapter 1.

Part II helps teachers to understand the *Explanation* that undergirds the processes of scientific inquiry. The chapters in Part II help to construct a foundation for understanding science, how children learn science, how to meet the needs of all learners, and the goals for attaining scientific literacy.

Part III of our book helps you to *Expand* your understanding of basic principles of science teaching. In this part you will develop selected skills in areas such as concept mapping and planning, assessing learning, questioning, practicing science safety and managing classrooms, and using technology, texts and instructional supplements effectively.

As previously mentioned, our science lessons or activities are located in Part IV and are designed to help you strengthen your own conceptual understanding of science as you guide children's learning. Each lesson is keyed to the National Science Education Standards.

*Evaluation*, the fourth E and an essential function of a learning cycle, is interspersed throughout the text. We provide several opportunities for a teacher to "Build a Portfolio" that demonstrates what you know and can do.

For those who may prefer to use an eclectic or customized approach, you will find each chapter is written to stand alone so that you may easily choose how you wish to use this text; we often reorder the text when we use it for our own classes. Users of our past texts will find familiar material in all of these new parts. In addition, we offer the following new items:

- Chapter 1 is refocused on inquiring teaching methods; it includes problem-based learning and more emphasis on early childhood learning.
- Chapter 4 includes the latest brain research while it maintains a constructivist teaching and learning approach.
- Chapter 5 gives greater attention to the exceptional learner and builds a foundation for scientific literacy.
- Chapter 6 provides more emphasis on science content standards.
- Chapter 7 celebrates more opportunities and examples for authentic assessment.
- Chapter 9 integrates safe science and classroom management; safety is expanded.
- Chapter 11 is completely new and illustrates how technology and multimedia resources can be used to address numerous standards and learning outcomes.
- Part IV contains numerous new lessons and all lessons are keyed to the National Science Education Standards.
- All appendices are thoroughly revised and support the reform efforts advocated by the National Science Education Standards.

## COMPANION WEB SITE

Our new companion Web site is located at *www.abacon.com/martin* and contains several helpful learning and teaching aids such as:

- *Chapter objectives* for a quick summary of each chapter's mission.
- *Concept maps* that provide a visual graphic story of each chapter's important concepts.
- *Practice tests* that support study and preparation for examinations by giving instant feedback.

- *Additional readings* that contain annotations for further reading and study on the important topics of each chapter.
- *Teachers on Science Teaching*, written by teachers to give an applied view on each chapter's topics, with classroom uses described by some of our country's finest teachers.
- *Digital Videos* that demonstrate safe and effective teaching approaches.
- *PowerPoint* slides for teaching and learning about the main features in each chapter.
- *Safe Science*, in which our text is a leader, is supported by numerous links to safety Web sites and by state-of-the-art, authoritative, special safety software—*The Total Science Safety System*—available from co-author Dr. Jack Gerlovich. Contact via e-mail: *jakel@netins.net* or *http://www.netins.net/showcase/jakel*

## ALLYN & BACON "SCIENCE ZONE" WEB SITE

Browse around *www.abacon.com/C&I* to pick up helpful hints and discover resources for your science lessons.

- *In the News*—a monthly report of current issues in science education
- *Discussion Forum*—a monthly discussion of an important issue in science education
- *Teaching Resources*—sources of materials, teaching aids, teaching guidelines for science educators
- *Classroom Activities*—specific lessons, investigations, applications, and assignments that teachers can use with their students
- *Web Links in Science Education*—a wealth of valuable links relating to science and science education
- *Allyn & Bacon Professional Books*—a listing of education resources for in-service science educators

## BELIEFS ABOUT LEARNING AND TEACHING

Learners may believe what they see, but they actually *understand* what they do. Understanding is rather simple to describe in theoretical terms, but is difficult to achieve with the limits and daily pressures of the classroom. "Hands-on" learning is a teaching concept often expressed and supported by teachers and school administrators. However, it may be misinterpreted or misused. It is important that the children's hands stimulate their senses, but it is perhaps more important that children's minds be strongly connected to what their hands *do*. Hands-on, minds-on learning can be effective, but only if *both* occur. Inquiry teaching and learning processes connect the mind's thinking with what the hands do. Similar to our previous editions, this edition helps you to learn how to assure that what children's senses "see" helps them create understanding from what they *do*. Our book expands its long-standing constructivist approach to help you to help learners to make important learning connections by stimulating and guiding their thinking through science inquiry processes.

## OUR MISSION

Our text's mission is to offer effective ways to help learners construct their own understanding by connecting their many ideas into a fabric of concepts, attitudes, and skills that carries meaning for them personally and academically. Additional goals of this mission are to fulfill the National Science Education Standards (NSES); the NSES are fully integrated and addressed throughout this text. Most notably, you will find our science lessons consist of carefully constructed activities with a specific focus on the concepts recommended by the NSES. As well, each lesson addresses the new science content dimensions recommended by the NSES, such as helping learners to develop an awareness of the history and nature of science, an understanding of the influence of science in personal and social perspectives, skills in using science inquiry processes, and an understanding of the complex interrelationships between science and technology.

## OUR PHILOSOPHY

The philosophy that guides our book is one of promoting the concept of "whole science" by making certain that the ideas, skills, and attitudes of science all are included in the experiences teachers offer learners. Whole science is based on the *constructivist* belief that knowledge exists only in the minds of learners, and that they must create those understandings from their own experiences. The whole science approach was developed in our preservice teachers' courses at our universities several years ago. The methods were refined and expanded with funding from the National Science Foundation during the Lead Teacher Project at Ohio University. The project involved dozens of practicing elementary, middle school, and special education teachers who taught science. The Lead Teachers tested in their own classrooms and helped to improve the ideas and activities that are in this book. As leaders in science education reform, the teachers shared these same ideas and methods with hundreds of other teachers. All of the ideas, methods, and activities have been tested extensively; they can and do work if you are willing to accept as evidence significant and substantial gains in pupil science achievement, skills, and attitudes.

## THE RESEARCH BASE THAT UNDERGIRDS OUR BOOK

We have constructed our book to help you connect the important parts of science, first by helping you to understand the holistic nature of science teaching, and later by helping you to develop your own impression about how learners construct their understanding. The science goals, planning techniques, and teaching approaches provided in our book support this conception of constructivism. Dorothy Gabel, editor of the *Handbook of Research on Science Teaching and Learning* (Macmillan, 1994), identified the most promising and effective research-based teaching strategies and practices for science. Our text incorporates these strategies and practices into its chapters and science lessons. For example, you learn how use the practice of *wait time,* and the strategies of a *learning cycle* and *cooperative learning. Analogies* are used within our chapters to assist conceptual understanding, and the tool of *concept mapping* is illustrated and used as a lesson design, teaching, and assessment tool. Teaching for *conceptual understanding* is emphasized throughout, and *problem solving* is a common technique emphasized in our science lessons' assessment tools. *Science-technology-society* is included in each lesson, and the technique of using *discrepant events* is featured as a special teaching method. *Real-life situations* and uses are emphasized where they logically fit within the chapter narrative and science lessons.

## OUR PEDAGOGY

Each chapter begins with a *scenario,* which is a story that sets a visual context for the chapter's message. The scenarios are all factual, but have been changed for rather obvious reasons. Each scenario helps to create a vicarious experience through a short story related to the chapter. This experience, when combined with the concept maps available on our companion Web site, should give you an advanced organizer (a mental framework) for understanding parts of the chapter that may be new or difficult for you. We hope these features help you to construct your own understanding of the material in our book.

Within each chapter we have added visual aids—figures, tables and photographs—to reinforce the ideas presented. Sometimes we include relevant exercises that you might want to try. One different feature is *What Research Says.* This material supplements the chapters with a brief authoritative report taken from the recent research. Of course we close each chapter with a customary summary, which complements the concept map. *Discussion questions* and ideas for *authentic evaluation* are included; many of these are field-based to complement any early field experience or internship that instructors may prefer. The *Build a Portfolio* feature is offered to help preservice teachers build a professional portfolio that celebrates their science teaching. Future editions to our companion Web site should lend support for building and managing individual portfolios, and for marketing and promoting one's entry into the profession.

## ACKNOWLEDGMENTS

In addition to our author team, many important persons supported the project and turned the dreams and ideas into a reality. Indeed, it is an understatement to say we are grateful to those many talented persons. For example:

We are indebted to Traci Mueller, education editor, whose vision and quick-study shaped the project into a comprehensive product, and her able assistant Bridget Keane, who assured first-class treatment at every stage of the publishing process. Deborah Brown, as production administrator, steered us through the complexity of publishing and capably assumed additional duties during times of changing personnel for a seamless march through deadlines, and packager Barbara Gracia assured the book's accuracy and completion.

Other support has been provided by Amy Stevens, a dedicated, persistent, and talented researcher. Without her, the task would have been much more difficult for the author team.

Our special thanks go to the reviewers who offered substantial suggestions that helped to shape this third edition. They are: Bonnie Bailey, Ohio University, Lancaster; C. David Christensen, University of Northern Iowa; Ravider Koul, Pennsylvania State University; and Debby Todd, Ohio University.

Finally, we are grateful to our spouses and children for their encouragement, support, and understanding, especially during the tense moments that always accompany the deadlines for such a large project. Knowing that we could help our children's teachers gave inspiration and helped to shape our mission. There will always be a special place in our hearts for Marilyn, Jennifer, Jessica, Jonathan, Sarah, Celeste, Pat, Jacque, and Kelly.

**PART I**

# The Exploration

## Methods and Best Practices for Effective Science Teaching

Children are naturally curious and eager to learn. They desire to wrap their hands and minds around objects of interest quickly. Similarly, throughout Part I we provide a quick entry into the methods of science teaching.

Although there are many effective ways to teach and learn, we have chosen to base our book on a *learning cycle* approach, one of the most effective and enduring inquiry methods for teaching and learning modern science. This learning cycle follows the 4-E processes of learning: Exploration, Explanation, Expansion, and Evaluation.

Part I offers opportunities to Explore the teaching of science. We know that children must have concrete materials and experiences if they are to learn concrete concepts. Adults, too, benefit from concrete experiences. Therefore, the first two chapters describe several methods for teaching science and encourage you to try these methods in order to build a concrete base for mastering the concepts of effective science teaching and for developing essential teaching skills. We use the 4-E learning cycle as a preferred teaching method and as an organizer for this text because the method recognizes the importance of experiences. It is used in each of the lessons located in Part IV and is presented first among the methods described in Chapter 1. Please explore all of Chapter 1's methods in order to obtain a quick entry into science teaching.

Learning cycles are potent in part because they focus on helping students to learn essential concepts and skills. A concept must be identified clearly in order to plan lessons, and a concept provides a clear focus for a teacher while the teacher is teaching and evaluating learning. Concepts also provide the grist for constructing story lines, the glue that holds together planning, teaching, and learning. Each story line is supported by concepts that emerge from studying specific chapters. The story lines and chapter concepts for Part I are as follows:

### Story Line

Effective science programs nurture the spirit and skills of inquiry among children.

### Concepts

*Chapter 1:* Many teaching methods promote inquiry. Some are child-centered while others are teacher-guided. All inquiry methods help children to experience the puzzles and thrills of scientific enterprise.

*Chapter 2:* Some learning experiences benefit from explicit presentation or from teacher demonstration, as in the case of safe rule protocols that must be followed. It is best not to use these methods exclusively. It is important to promote interaction between the teacher and students and among students whenever possible.

## CHAPTER OUTLINE

# How Can We Help Learners to Inquire and Construct Scientific Meaning?

## INTRODUCTION

Some researchers and educators imply that *what* we teach may be less important than *how* we teach. This emerging belief is based on changing attitudes toward science. For example, children ages five to nine most often reply that their favorite subject is science, yet this is no longer the case when upper-grade learners (ages thirteen to eighteen) are asked (Solomon, 1997). So, if *how* we teach contributes to this difference, what is the best way to teach science? Although the National Science Education Standards (National Research Council, 1996) and other authoritative publications emphasize the importance and benefits of inquiry-based teaching and learning, no single method of teaching has been found exclusively to meet all needs all the time. However, effective teachers do develop a repertoire of methods they can draw on for maximum effect and to fit their preferred teaching and student-learning styles. To help you to explore science teaching and to develop your repertoire, the purposes of this chapter are as follows:

- to introduce you to the complications, problems, and current directions of science teaching,

- to encourage you to explore several teaching methods that use inquiry to promote student discovery and concept constructions,
- to describe techniques that promote student cooperation,
- to recommend conditions that enhance students' learning of science.

Let us share with you a scenario in order that we may help you to explore the complications, problems, and current directions of science teaching.

## COMPLICATIONS, PROBLEMS, AND CURRENT DIRECTIONS

### A Scenario

Mrs. Todd is an elementary teacher who also instructs a university science methods course as a part of a local professional development school-university teacher preparation partnership. Let's listen in on a discussion during one of her early class sessions. Mrs. Todd assigned her university science methods students to interview people about science teaching and learning. Her students had to determine their questions and design a survey in order to collect the perceptions of those interviewed. We pick up the conversation midstream, just as her students are offering summary comments about their findings.

**Karen:** "When I asked college students, teachers, and school administrators what they recall about science when they were in elementary school, most said they remembered very little, but what they did remember consisted of reading about science in a book and answering questions. Some offered that they remembered making leaf collections and growing flowers, but I couldn't clearly 'see the science.' It seems as if these things were done for other reasons, such as an art project or a gift for Mother's Day. Two of my interviewees did describe some hands-on activities, such as completing science fair projects, working with magnets, and caring for an aquarium."

**Charles:** "When I interviewed the teachers in my sample, I was really encouraged because I heard language about doing science and devoting considerable effort to science, but when I visited the classrooms, I wasn't sure the class activity matched the teachers' descriptions. Some of what I saw seemed like a modern version of what Karen just described."

**Mrs. Todd:** "Would you please tell me more about what you mean?"

**Charles:** "OK. The teachers talked about doing all of these neat activities, and I did see some of that, especially from two teachers in the school I visited. I guess my concern is difficult to put into words. It's as if the teachers are clear about what they think the students are learning, but when I spoke with some of the students they weren't thinking about the same things; the students just seemed to regard what they were doing as fun, kind of like playtime. And that bothers me. It's not that the students shouldn't enjoy science, but shouldn't they be able to, to. . . ."

**Mrs. Todd:** ". . . to have a hands-on, minds-on connection stimulated by teachers who guide students through the activity and inquiry, and continually assess student understanding at appropriate times?"

**Charles:** "Yes! It seems that things needed to be handled a bit differently for the students to really benefit from the lesson. I also wonder if all students benefit from being treated alike all the time. And another thing: I did overhear in the lounge some teachers questioning the benefit of hands-on learning because of a perception that test scores are not as strong as they could be if more direct teaching methods were used."

**Mrs. Todd:** "Did anyone happen to explore the beliefs about how children learn and how to teach them?"

**Alicia:** "My group did. Many students said they have to 'see it' and 'do it' in order to learn. Teachers' opinions were mixed. Many stated that it's important for children to manipulate objects—hands-on learning—and yet when my teammates and I made our classroom observations we noticed that when students were asked to show what they know and can do, they were expected to write, fill in worksheets, and fill in blanks on tests. The emphasis was on 'testing' factual science information, usually at the end of a unit or chapter. We think this seems to be a bit of a mismatch between what teachers may believe and actually practice. Maybe this helps to explain the concern that Charles just expressed."

**Jim:** "Yes, and when we sampled the community's perspectives and asked about how people think children learn and should be taught, some described active and interactive teaching and learning in which students are guided, and where a teacher might be a co-investigator along with the children. But most emphasized the importance of acquiring information such as memorizing, giving definitions, stating theories and laws and giving the information back to the teacher. They expect the teacher to be the sole authority—in charge—and for the teacher to respond to the class as a whole. There was almost no support for reorganizing the school structure so that teachers could work together. No wonder teachers who want to make a change feel pressure!"

**Sara:** "When we interviewed school principals and superintendents, one principal said that he believed that if only his school could get a grant or a donation from a power company to build a nature trail that would make all the difference in the science program. I wasn't sure I understood the point until I interviewed the principal's superintendent. The superintendent defined 'good science' as when students win the regional science fair, and many of the recent winning projects have been outdoor, environmental and wildlife-types of studies. The superintendent also spent a lot of time describing the district average scores on tests like the ACT, SAT, and state science proficiency tests. When these scores improve, the superintendent infers that the science program is good and that the teaching and learning is strong. He described the essential teaching methods as lecture or demonstration and using separate facilities for doing labs. He described the labs as completing the procedures in a manual. I heard no mention of science as a priority for young learners. Discussion only seemed to mention the middle grades on up."

**Mrs. Todd:** "And what do you make of all that?"

**Sara:** "To me it seems as if an emphasis is placed on competition, contests, and trying to figure out what will be tested so that the curriculum can be realigned to be sure those topics are included, and so that the teachers give explicit attention to those topics. It may also be that it's believed young children can't do these things—on their own level, of course. Yet, to me, the whole effort of trying to focus on tests seem futile. How can a teacher know enough about a secure test to 'teach' to it? It seemed the teachers were frustrated trying to guess about what they should teach. And, when students reported that the rock and water cycles were on the state test, some teachers thought the entire science program needed to be changed so all teachers focused their teaching on those topics. Aren't there guidelines to limit the need to guess?"

**Mrs. Todd:** "Those are fair questions. If you examine the state science tests closely, you'll see that they are given for certain benchmark grade levels, and although the tests do require students to know some facts and information about some science topics and processes, much of the focus is on application, such as using information contained in a scenario to solve a problem, to critique an experimental design, or to make inferences about cause-and-effect relationships. Many of the things all of you have described tend to fall into the categories in this table. [At this point Mrs. Todd showed a transparency of the "Changing Emphases" found in Table 1.1 of this chapter.] This information comes from the *National Science Education Standards*. The 'Standards' were developed by hundreds of experts and are published by the National Research Council. The information is quite consistent with the recommendations offered by other prestigious science organizations. The Standards provide clear information about what should be done: promote scientific literacy and provide science experiences that benefit all learners. Consider that our lives are becoming increasingly complex. We are confronted with questions that require us to think about and use scientific information so that we are able to make informed decisions. Also, the collective judgment of our representatives and lawmakers determine how we'll manage our planet's resources. Certainly our leaders need to be well informed and our citizens need to be literate so they will select well-prepared leaders. So, out of necessity, our mission as educators is changing. We must now work to enhance the capability of all learners so they will be able to gain meaningful employment when they enter the workforce. At the same time, our economy is becoming ever more closely linked to the world's economy, and this brings the stresses of global competition. Science, with mathematics, is centrally important to the preparation for that competition. And, more to the point of Sara's questions, the Standards and other documents from respected organizations do provide recommendations about what children should know and be able to do with science.

"Please understand that the Standards aren't a prescription, but they do provide us teachers with criteria we can use to judge the quality of our science programs, teaching, learning, and the system that supports science education. Unlike past education standards, these science standards don't place all of the burden on teachers. Rather, the standards describe systemic changes that are necessary if we teachers are to be empowered and supported in order to do our jobs.

## TABLE 1.1   Changing Emphases

The *National Science Education Standards* envision change throughout the system. The teaching standards encompass the following changes in emphases:

| *Less Emphasis On* | *More Emphasis On* |
|---|---|
| Treating all students alike and responding to the group as a whole | Understanding and responding to individual student's interests, strengths, experiences, and needs |
| Rigidly following curriculum | Selecting and adapting curriculum |
| Focusing on student acquisition of information | Focusing on student understanding and use of scientific knowledge, ideas, and inquiry processes |
| Presenting scientific knowledge through lecture, text, and demonstration | Guiding students in active and extended scientific inquiry |
| Asking for recitation of acquired knowledge | Providing opportunities for scientific discussion and debate among students |
| Testing students for factual information at the end of the unit or chapter | Continuously assessing student understanding |
| Maintaining responsibility and authority | Sharing responsibility for learning with students |
| Supporting competition | Supporting a classroom community with cooperation, shared responsibility, and respect |
| Working alone | Working with other teachers to enhance the science program |

*Source:* National Research Council (NRC). (1996). *National Science Education Standards.* Washington, DC: National Academy Press, p. 52.

Author's note: Our purpose here is to inform that Standards exist and may be used to inform the decisions that influence teaching and learning. More information about the National Science Education Standards may be found in Chapter 6 and Appendix A.

"The Teaching Standards that are described within the National Science Education Standards do give us some explicit guidance, and it seems your surveys and interviews have uncovered some things that really need to be emphasized less in schools. Table 1.1 show those, and in their place more emphasis needs to be shifted toward attending to individual learners, adapting the curriculum, focusing on a different type of student understanding, fostering learning through active methods, providing opportunities for students to construct and strengthen their understanding, assessing learning in authentic forms, sharing with students so they assume more responsibility for their learning, establishing and nurturing classroom cooperation, and finding ways to work with other teachers in order to build the science program."

### The Importance of Scientific Inquiry

The National Science Education Standards (NSES) (National Research Council, 1996, p. 32) list among the specific Teaching Standards several points that encourage teachers to

- focus and support inquiries while interacting with students;

- orchestrate discourse among students about scientific ideas;
- challenge students to accept and share responsibility for their own learning;
- recognize and respond to student diversity and encourage all students to participate fully in science learning;
- encourage and model the skills of scientific inquiry, as well as the curiosity, openness to new ideas and data, and skepticism that characterize science.

Inquiry is the cornerstone of these standards for teaching, and according to the NSES (1996, p. 4) good teachers at all age and grade levels are expected to be able to plan inquiry-based science lessons and science programs, take proper actions to guide and facilitate learning, assess teaching and learning, and develop and maintain classroom environments and learning communities that enable children to learn science. Even so, teachers hold diverse views about what inquiry is (Bybee et al., 1997), and many teachers report familiarity with inquiry, yet their actual teaching practices suggest they do not understand deeply the purposes and processes of inquiry (Lederman & Neiss, 1997; Mullis et al., 1997).

We strive to help you understand the new expectations that face teachers of elementary and middle school science. These expectations are based on beliefs that science is important and appropriate for all ages of learners, and that active processes are necessary for learning science. These active processes are encouraged through the methods of inquiry. For children, our guidance helps them to experience some of the diverse ways that scientists study the natural world and propose explanations based on evidence gathered through research. Studies report several benefits that may be expected for all learners through inquiry, including student science attitude and science achievement improvements (Dalton et al., 1997; Flick, 1995; Haury, 1993; Jarrett, 1997; Scruggs et al., 1993).

For children, inquiry refers to the activities—the processes—that children experience in which they develop testable ideas and construct understandings of real-world scientific ideas. Inquiry activities usually involve

- pondering and posing questions,
- using tools to make and classify observations,
- examining sources of information,
- investigating, analyzing, forming answers, and explanations,
- communicating outcomes and conclusions.

Hands-on activities alone do not guarantee inquiry. Inquiry is dependent on a set of interrelated processes guided by questions. Inquiry is a process of interrelationships between the object of the inquiry and those who do the inquiring. Inquiry refers to the process of the effort used to explore questions, ideas, and phenomena. The result of the effort is a discovery that is new to the child in school science, but already known by scientists and teachers. Children are able to inquire when they are given hands-on learning opportunities, appropriate materials to manipulate, puzzling circumstances or problems for motivation, enough structure to help them focus or maintain a productive direction, and enough freedom to compare ideas and make personal learning discoveries.

# METHODS THAT USE INQUIRY TO PROMOTE STUDENT CONCEPT FORMATION AND DISCOVERY

## A Scenario

Mrs. Myers has loved science since she was very young, and her love is communicated to her students through her positive attitude and enthusiasm. She tries to connect each lesson with her students' experiences by involving each child in a personal way. Her third-grade classroom is an active place. Sometimes her lessons are mistaken by visitors as play. When queried she always refers to the "play" as a way to make an important point. In fact, her young scientists can be overheard asking each other about "the point" because they have become accustomed to looking for a focus in each lesson. A "minds-on" focus guides each "hands-on" lesson. Mrs. Myers' classroom consists of individual desks clustered into "research" groups of four. Her classroom walls are alive with brilliant colors, usually the children's artwork and projects, but also commercial posters carefully selected to illustrate a variety of careers and diverse role models for the young scientists as well as illustrate various forms and uses of technology. Plants and small mammals are positioned in the research corner near the aquarium and the desert climate terrarium.

Mrs. Myers begins the day's science lesson by asking the children to count off from 1 to 4 and reminds each child to remember his or her number. Being of small frame, Mrs. Myers often safely joins the children in the physical activities. She asks:

"OK, scientists. Today we are going to begin an investigation of a very important idea. Would you all please gather in a circle around me?"

In no particular order, Mrs. Myers gently directs the twenty-four children into a tight circle, each standing shoulder-to-shoulder. Humor and gentle prodding accomplish the task and provide a nice link to the geometry lesson learned in math class last week.

"Where are the number 'one's' standing?" asks Mrs. Myers. "All of the 'one's' will represent 'food' during our activity. What does the number 'one' mean for us?"

"Food!" answer the scientists with enthusiasm.

"All of you will represent a special role. Who are the 'two's'?"

Exuberant "me's" identify most of the "two's" and a few gentle jostles of classmates remind the other "two's" to identify themselves.

"The 'two's' will be 'water' " informs Mrs. Myers.

"The 'three's' will be 'shelter.' "

"The 'four's' will be 'space.' " A brief practice session ensures that everyone understands her or his role. Some tightening of the circle and turning in a common direction places all children appropriately, with hands grasping the shoulders of the scientist in front.

"Now for the physical challenge. When I count to 3 our mission is to hold our positions, bend our legs, and gently sit on the knees of the scientist behind us." Mrs. Myers takes some time to offer assurance and make the process clear. The 1-2-3 count is given and success happens fleetingly until pandemonium breaks out as the seated circle breaks apart and children do a controlled fall with enthusiastic exaggeration.

"Everybody up! Let's talk about this. Why do you suppose we had trouble keeping our circle together?"

"I couldn't find Sasha's knees!" quips Sachiko.

"Brent fell down and so did I," offers Jon.

"So what happened to the rest of us when Brent fell?" asks Mrs. Myers.

"We all fell!" responds a chorus of voices.

"That's right. We depend on one another. We have a system of parts, and when one part falls the others also soon fall. Let's try this again and see whether we can set a record. What do you suppose we could do to make it easier for us to keep our circle together when we sit?"

A number of suggestions are offered and after incorporating them into the arrangement, Mrs. Myers gives the physical challenge again. The children count to 30 before Mrs. Myers gives the signal to stand. Not one child drops out of the circle. Mrs. Myers continues her lesson:

"All animals need a habitat in order to survive, and all habitats contain the food, water, shelter, and space unique for the animal. In today's activity we each play an important role—food, water, shelter, space—and when we keep our circle together we provide a 'pretend' habitat for an animal." Mrs. Myers continues the discussion by asking the children to identify the parts of a habitat needed for a common animal such as a robin, fish, cow, dog, or squirrel.

"What's a habitat?" she asks, testing the young scientists. The children put into their own words their operational definition and descriptions of food, water, shelter and space as examples for some other animals familiar to them.

"Let's do our activity again, and this time let's pretend we have a drought," offers Mrs. Myers. The children are told that each of the "waters" will leave the circle, one at a time, while all are seated, and try to keep the circle together as long as possible. Some of the children predict all of the "waters" can leave and they can still keep the circle together, while the skeptics don't think any "waters" can leave without the circle falling.

"What do you think we might have to do to keep our circle together?" asks Mrs. Myers. After some discussion, the children offer that they might be able to "adapt" by scooching together to take up the empty space and avoid falling.

The lap sit is repeated. After the first "water" slips out, the strain of the void can be felt around the entire circle, but all adapt and manage to keep the circle together. Mrs. Myers asks the children to think about the effort before the next "water" is invited to leave. Barely successful after the next departure, the circle collapses when the third "water" slips aside.

## Processing the Scenario

The discussion that followed was rich with understanding about the importance of a habitat with all components available in sufficient supply and suitable arrangement. Children were asked to think about how common wild animals and outdoor domestic animals could be affected by a drought or a loss of other essential components of their habitats. Other variations were attempted to simulate stresses placed on human habitats, including famine, overcrowding and shelter lost to natural disasters. Notions of interdependence and the need to adapt or relocate emerged from the ideas. In the days that followed, books were read, videos were viewed, Internet searches were conducted, and information was organized to help the children observe the habitats of local animals and plan suitable habitats for crickets, ants, and earthworms to be placed in classroom terraria.

Mrs. Myers understands that each of her individual students must integrate a complex mental structure of many types of information in order to construct his or her own understandings of science. She encourages each child to explore the ideas of science—looking for relationships among ideas and the reasons for those relationships. Children are encouraged to use their formative ideas to explain natural phenomena and to solve problems. Each lesson is multifaceted and requires each child to make observations, ponder and pose questions, examine books and other sources of information to discern what is already known about a topic, plan investigations, gather data and analyze and interpret it, and suggest explanations and answers for problems and experimental outcomes. Mrs. Myers encourages her learners to be active inquirers.

Inquiry methods can take several forms, yet all strive to promote a healthy dynamic between hands-on, minds-on learning processes. This dynamic has been found to improve the spatial ability of children and help to reduce early differences between genders respective to imagining and manipulating objects with moving parts (Solomon, 1997). In this section of the chapter we invite you to explore a learning cycle method, scientific experimental method, Suchman's Inquiry method, playful discovery, problem-based learning, and techniques for using children's own questions to stimulate inquiry. All of these methods make use of inquiry techniques to stimulate conceptualization and discovery of meaning. As simple as each method appears, you will benefit from cumulative experiences, reflection and self-evaluation, and revision in using these methods.

## The 4-E Science Learning Cycle

A learning cycle is a method for planning lessons, teaching, learning, and developing curricula. This teaching method was originally designed for the Science Curriculum Improvement Study and has produced the largest achievement gains of the experimental elementary science programs of the 1960s. These increases are largely a result of the learning cycle as an inquiry teaching and learning method.

In science, a learning cycle is a way of thinking and acting that is consistent with how pupils learn. It provides an excellent approach for planning effective science instruction. The science learning cycle originally consisted of three phases: exploration, concept invention, and application. With today's goals emphasizing new dimensions of science and accountability, we recommend a 4-E learning cycle: exploration, explanation, expansion, and evaluation. Each phase, when followed in sequence (see Figure 1.1), has sound theoretical support from the cognitive development theory of Jean Piaget (Renner & Marek, 1988; Marek & Cavallo, 1997) and applies constructivist learning procedures (see Chapter 4).

*Phase One: Exploration.*   The exploration phase is student centered, stimulates learner mental disequilibrium, and fosters mental assimilation. (You might review the section in Chapter 4 devoted to Jean Piaget if these ideas are unclear.) The teacher is responsible for giving students sufficient directions and materials that interact in ways that are related to the concept. The teacher's directions *must not tell* students what they should learn and *must not explain* the concept. The teacher's role is to

- answer students' questions,
- ask questions to guide student observations and to cause students to engage in science processes or thinking skills (see Figure 1.2),
- give hints and cues to keep the exploration going.

### FIGURE 1.1   The 4-E Science Learning Cycle

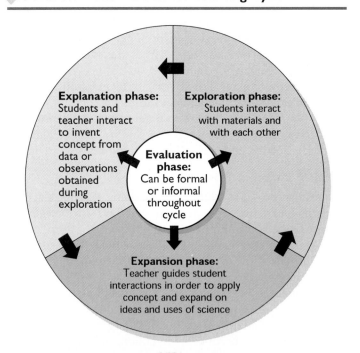

*Source:* Adapted from a figure by Charles Barman, "The Learning Cycle: Making It Work," *Science Scope* (February 1989) 28–31.

**FIGURE 1.2　Using Questions During a Learning Cycle**

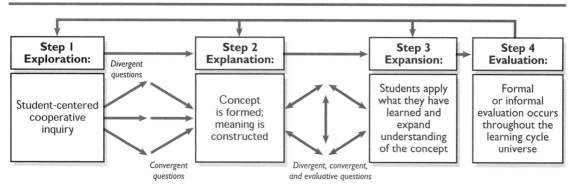

Students are responsible for exploring the materials and for gathering and recording their own information. Teachers rely on questioning skills such as those shown in Figure 1.2 to guide learning.

Children must have concrete materials and experiences too if they are to construct science concepts for themselves. Use these guiding questions to help you begin your planning process:

- What is the precise concept the students will explore?
- What activities must the children do to become familiar with the concept?
- What kinds of observations or records should the children keep?
- What kinds of instructions will the children need? How can I give the instructions without telling the concept?

This last question directly transforms into verbal or written instructions you will give the children. Instructions need to direct the children's activities, suggest what kinds of records they should keep, and *not tell or explain the concept.* Instructions may be stated succinctly, perhaps in the form of an objective. What questions will you ask to encourage student exploration?

*Phase Two: Explanation.*　The explanation phase is less student centered and provides for learner mental accommodation. The purpose of this phase is for teachers to guide student thinking so the concept of the lesson is constructed cooperatively, not merely given by the teacher. To accomplish this, the teacher selects and sets the desired class environment. The teacher asks students to give the information they have collected and helps students to process and mentally organize the information. Once the information is organized, the teacher introduces the specific language needed for the concept, much as Mrs. Myers did *after* her students had observed and explored what happened to them during the lap sit when different variables were introduced. Teachers help students to construct and attach meaning to these new science words—the concepts.

This phase helps to lead to mental accommodation, as described by Piaget's theory. Here students must focus on their primary findings from their firsthand explorations. The teacher must introduce language or concept labels to assist mental accommodation. These questions can help teachers guide students so they construct their own explanations of the concept:

- What kinds of information or findings should the students talk about?
- How can I help students summarize their findings?
- How can I guide the students and refrain from telling them what they should have found, even if their understanding is incomplete? How can I help them use their information to construct the concept correctly?
- What labels or descriptions should the students attach to the concept?
- What reasons can I give the students if they ask me why the concept is important? This question automatically leads to the next phase, expansion.

***Phase Three: Expansion.***    The expansion phase should be student centered as much as possible and organized to encourage group cooperation. The purpose of this phase is to help learners mentally organize the experiences they have acquired by forming connections with similar previous experiences and by discovering new applications for what they have learned. Constructed concepts must be linked to other related ideas or experiences. The purpose is to take the students' thinking beyond where it is presently. You must require students to use the language or labels of the new concept so that they add depth to their understanding. This is a proper place to help students apply what they learned by expanding examples or by providing additional exploratory experiences for stimulating students' science inquiry skills, encouraging them to investigate science-technology-society interrelationships, and for understanding the history and nature of science. (See goals in Chapter 6.) The expansion phase can automatically lead to the exploration phase of the next lesson; hence a continuing cycle for teaching and learning is established. Exhibit 1.1 shows how to do this in a sample lesson.

Teachers help students organize their thinking by relating what they have learned to other ideas or experiences that relate to the constructed concept. It is very important to use the language of the concept during this phase to add depth to the concept's meaning and to expand the range of the children's vocabulary. Consider these questions:

- What previous experiences have the students had that relate to the concept? How can I connect the concept to those experiences?
- What are some examples of how the concept encourages the students to see science's benefits to themselves? to help them understand the relationships among science, technology, and society? to help them develop science inquiry skills? to help them be informed about the history and nature of science?
- What questions can I ask to encourage students to discover the concept's importance? to apply the concept? to appreciate the problems it solves? to

*(text continues on page 18)*

## Make a Sinker Float: Clay Boats

**GRADE**
**4–6**
**DISCIPLINE**
**Physical**
**Science**

### Concept/statement

Buoyancy: If the upward force of the liquid is greater than the downward force of an object, the object will float because it is buoyed (lifted up or supported) by the water. This concept is called *buoyancy*, and it explains why some heavy objects, such as steel ships, will float in water.

### Additional concepts that are important to expansion

Displacement, flotation, Archimedes' principle, specific gravity

### Materials needed

Small tubs or buckets to hold water, small objects that will sink or float in water, modeling clay (plasticene), small uniform objects to use as cargo (weights, such as ceramic tiles or marbles) in the clay boats, a container modified like the illustration shown in phase 3 (expansion), a small container to catch the water that spills from the modified container, and a scale or balance to measure the weight of the spilled water.

➥ **Safety precautions:** Have students notify you in case of spills. Use a room with a nonslip floor surface if possible.

## 1. EXPLORATION

*Instructions:* Have the students examine the variety of objects given to them and predict whether each object will sink or float in the water. Have the students write their predictions on an organized data sheet that you provide. Use as one of the objects a lump of clay about the size of a tennis ball. Provide time for the students to test their predictions and then gather the students together to explore what their predictions reveal.

## 2. EXPLANATION

*Concept:* Buoyancy. If objects of different sizes and weights are used in the exploration phase, students will discover that heaviness is not the factor that determines whether an object will sink or float. For example, a large piece of 2-by-4-inch wood will be heavier than a glass marble or a metal washer, but it will float while the marble and washer will sink. Explain that Archimedes, a Greek philosopher, is credited with discovering that an object immersed in a liquid (water) will appear to lose some of its weight. Ask students to speculate why this seems to be. A suitable explanation may be: "If the upward force of

*(continued)*

**EXHIBIT 1.1  A Sample Lesson Plan Based on the 4-E Science Learning Cycle**

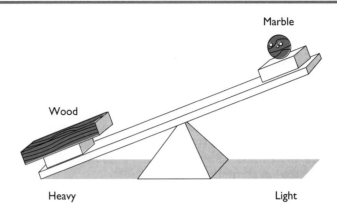

the liquid is greater than the downward force of the object, it will float because the object is buoyed (lifted up or supported) by the water." This factor is called *buoyancy*, and it explains why some heavy objects, such as steel ships, will float in water when it can be easily illustrated that steel sinks. Steel has been given a special shape (the ship) that gives it a greater volume, which helps to spread its weight across a larger amount (volume) of the water, making it possible for the buoyant upward force of the water to be greater than the downward force of the ship's weight. How might buoyancy be affected by the amount of cargo a ship carries? Why is it important to keep a ship from taking on water?

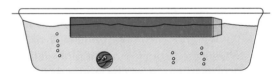

## 3. EXPANSION

Weigh the lump of dry clay and the smaller container to be used to catch the water spill; record the measures. Take the lump of clay and use the device as illustrated. Carefully lower the clay into the container of water and measure its weight while it is submerged. Catch the water that spills out of the container and weigh the container again; subtract the dry container weight to determine the weight of the water displaced by the sinking clay. The weight of the submerged clay should be less than the dry weight because of the upward (buoyant) force of the water. Challenge the students to find a way to change the shape of the clay so that it will float in water. Challenge them to see who can make the clay boat that will carry the largest amount of cargo before it sinks. Have students draw pictures of their boats' shapes and/or measure the size of the boats'

**EXHIBIT 1.1    *(continued)***

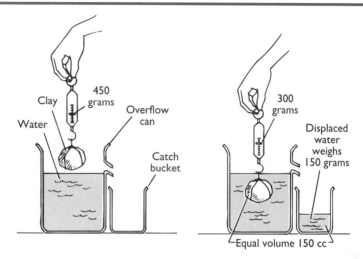

bottoms. Capable students could calculate the surface area of the boats' bottoms and graph the amount of cargo carried (before sinking) as a function of area. Ask them to observe carefully what happens to make their clay boats sink and to describe later what they observe.

### Science in Personal and Social Perspectives

Ask the students why the Coast Guard requires flotation devices on boats and why these devices make it possible for a person who otherwise might sink to float. Why does the Coast Guard set passenger limits on pleasure craft?

### Science and Technology

Ask the students to search for other inventions that apply the buoyancy principle. Ask how these uses have had an impact on people. Examples might include floats connected to switches or valves that control pumps or appliances, seat cushions on airliners that are removable and can be used as flotation devices, channel buoys for navigation or to mark danger zones.

### Science as Inquiry

Ask the students to identify other examples of buoyancy in liquids and to describe differences. As examples, ask the students to redo their sink-or-float tests in denatured or isopropyl alcohol, or a mixture of alcohol and water, or water with different amounts of salt added. (This can lead to another concept and another lesson: specific gravity.)

Ask the students to explain why a submarine can sink and float, and how it is possible for a submarine or a SCUBA diver to remain at a particular depth.

Construct a Cartesian diver using a 2-liter soft drink container filled with water. Place a glass medicine dropper in the container and put the cap on tightly. Squeeze the sides of the container, release, and watch what happens to

*(continued)*

the dropper. Why does the dropper sink and rise? What is necessary to keep the submarine dropper at a constant depth in the container?

Ask students to explain why it is easier to swim and float in salt water than in fresh water.

### History and Nature of Science

As an expansion assignment, have the students search for pictures and examples of careers that require some knowledge of the buoyancy concept. Examples may include ship builders, navy and marine personnel, fishermen, marine salvage crews, plumbers, SCUBA divers. How have the inventions used by these changed over time?

Read Pamela Allen's *Mr. Archimedes' Bath* (1991) to the class and discuss what the author needed to know about science to write this children's book.

## 4. EVALUATION

- Using the ball of clay and/or Cartesian diver, the students will demonstrate and explain the concept of buoyancy.
- The students will draw a picture of what happens when their clay ball is placed in water and when its shape is changed. They will write a paragraph in their own words that explains why and how the clay floats.
- The students will demonstrate proper use of the balance when weighing the clay dry and submerged.
- The advanced students will measure and calculate the area of the clay boats and graph the maximum cargo carried as a function of the surface area of the boats.
- Students will research the buoyancy inventions used by a single career over a period of time (perhaps fifty years) and explain how different understandings of buoyancy and technical advancement influenced persons in those careers.

**EXHIBIT 1.1**   *(continued)*

understand the problems it causes? to identify the careers influenced by it? to understand how the concept has been viewed or used throughout history?
- What new experiences are needed to apply or expand the concept?
- What is the next concept related to the present one? How can I encourage exploration of the next concept?

*Phase Four: Evaluation.*   The purpose of this phase is to overcome the limits of standard types of testing. Learning often occurs in small increments before larger mental leaps of insight are possible. Therefore, evaluation should be continuous, not a typical end-of-chapter or -unit approach. Several types of measures are necessary to form a wholistic evaluation of the students' learning and to encourage mental construction of concepts and process skills. Evaluation can be included in each phase of the learning cycle, not just held for the end. Ask yourself:

- What appropriate learning outcomes should I expect?
- What types of hands-on evaluation techniques can the students do to demonstrate the basic skills of observation, classification, communication, measurement, prediction, and inference?
- What techniques are appropriate for students to demonstrate the integrated science process skills of identifying and controlling variables, defining operationally, forming hypotheses, experimenting, interpreting data, and forming models?
- How can I use pictures to help students demonstrate how well they can think through problems that require understanding fundamental concepts and the integration of ideas?
- What types of questions can I ask students to help them reflect and to indicate how well they recall and understand what has been learned?

### Scientific Method: How Can You Use Principles of Scientific Experimentation While Teaching?

> Scientific method is defined as the systematic pursuit of knowledge involving the recognition and formulation of a problem, the collection of data through observation and experimentation (the experiential element), the formulation of a hypothesis, and the testing and confirmation (or rejection) of that hypothesis. (Fields, 1989, p. 15)

What went through your mind as you read the definition? When and if a scientific method was taught to you, it was probably taught in a high school science class separately from actually doing science. Some scientists and educators object to the notion of a scientific method and, justifiably, cite that all scientists do not think or investigate in such a linear way. Often a method is memorized as a series of steps like these:

Step 1: Define the problem.

Step 2: Find out what is already known about the problem.

Step 3: Form a hypothesis or educated guess.

Step 4: Conduct an experiment to test the hypothesis.

Step 5: Use the results to reach a conclusion.

Unfortunately, many textbooks and teachers have treated these steps as a recipe for doing and learning science. The new vision presented by the National Science Education Standards (NSES) encourages inquiry beyond the "science as a process" approach. The principles of scientific experimentation encourage learners to combine science skills (such as observing, classifying, predicting, and experimenting) and scientific knowledge by reasoning and thinking to develop their understanding of science. According to the NSES, students who inquire through scientific experimentation

- construct understanding of science concepts
- "know how we know" in science
- develop an understanding of the nature of science
- develop many skills necessary to become independent inquirers about their natural world
- develop mental habits of using their skills and abilities (NRC, 1996)

The principles of scientific inquiry and experimentation offer ways to form cooperative problem-solving groups, particularly when the principles are used flexibly to help learners design a procedure they wish to follow. Most children need structure and considerable guidance until they develop the mental habits of thinking like a scientist. Begin simply, perhaps by saying that science deals with answering questions or solving mysteries, or as Fields (1989), says, "Science invents stories and then sees if they are true" (p. 15). Use thoughtful questions to guide classroom discussions and pursue answers to those questions and soon you will find students asking their own questions, inventing their own stories, and pursuing those stories to see whether they are true. These questions usually serve to define the problem and point out what needs to be known and implies how the inquiry ought to occur.

### The Principles of Scientific Inquiry as a Teaching Method

The teaching strategy can have five steps that parallel those listed above. Steven Fields's fine article in *Science and Children* (Fields, 1989) provides many practical examples of how the steps you have memorized can be turned into a motivating, interactive, and effective teaching method. We paraphrase his ideas as follows:

**Step I. Have students conclude that experimenting will provide the best answer to the science question.**

If a child shows interest in a topic by asking a question, or if children become curious about a topic after you ask a question, look for a way to discover the answer by acting on it. For example, how can you discover the answer to a question like, "If rudders (and flaps) steer an airplane in flight, which rudders steer it in which direction?" (See Figure 1.3.) Problem questions such as this can make good challenges for cooperative group investigations in which each learner has a specific duty to fulfill.

**Step 2. Focus the science question to seek a specific answer.**

Try a brainstorming session. Accept all ideas related to the question, then limit the question to the kernel of the problem it poses. Identify a hypothesis from the ideas offered. Help the student groups find out all they can about the prob-

**FIGURE 1.3   Paper Airplane Illustration**   On this paper airplane, the wing rudders and vertical stabilizer rudder are located as shown. Of course, creating various models of airplanes is a scientific endeavor in its own right. Let students experiment with making planes and rudders themselves.

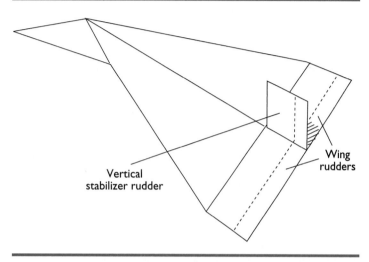

*Source:* Steve Fields, "The Scientific *Teaching* Method," *Science and Children* (April 1989): 15. Reprinted with permission from NSTA publications, 1840 Wilson Boulevard, Arlington, Virginia 22201–3000.

lem; then encourage them to make and test predictions. Continuing with Steve Fields's airplane example, some predictions could include:

- Wing rudders control up-and-down movement.
- Tail rudders control movement to the left and right.
- When rudders are set in any given way, the plane will fly up and down or side to side.

**Step 3. Guess the answer to the science question and use references to try to find out if the answer is already known.**

Individual students and groups can brainstorm and decide the best way to find out the answer. Guiding questions can steer their thinking. Examples include

- "Can you find the answer in a book?" If "yes," what kind of book?
- "Whom do you know who might already know the answer?" (Other children, teachers, outside resources, experts, and so on.)

### The Science Learning Cycle

The learning cycle is an approach to teaching and learning that ensures that students are involved in the types of thinking (inquiry) that constructivists argue is necessary for production learning. Jean Piaget's research on cognitive development helped to establish the first two phases of the learning cycle: exploration and explanation (concept invention). Mental activities in these phases promote what Piaget called *assimilation* and *accommodation*. Imagine the mind as a file cabinet: faced with information, the mind seeks a place to put it. Placing new information in an existing file with similar information would be an example of assimilation, as the mind adds to what already exists. However, when it does not find a file with information similar to that to be stored away, the mind must create a new file.

Robert Karplus, director of the Science Curriculum Improvement Study (SCIS), is credited with adding a third phase to the learning cycle. He named this phase *discovery* and then later changed the name to concept *implementation*. Some science educators prefer to call this the *application phase*. John Renner and Edmund Marek have made improvements and call the third phase *expansion of the idea*. There is con-siderable research to support uses of the learning cycle for improving children's science achievement and process skill development.

Renner and Marek note that the SCIS program relies on the learning cycle to organize its materials and to guide its teaching methods. Consequently, they have used the SCIS materials to conduct their own research.

Renner and Marek have used Piagetian mental conservation tasks to design experimental studies that indicate what effect the learning cycle may have on the intellectual development of young children. They found that when the learning cycle was used, children in an experimental group significantly outperformed other children who learned within a traditional textbook control group. Number, weight, liquid amount, solid amount, length, and area were the measures of conservation. The researchers believe "the data support the conclusion that the rate of attainment of conservation reasoning is significantly enhanced by the experiences made possible by [the first graders who learned through a learning cycle]." They also claim that the learning cycle enhances the intellectual development of young learners.

- If these questions do not help, try "How can you (we) design a test to find out the answer?" For older children, this a good place to discuss variables that can affect the outcome and reliability of an experiment.

Step 4. Follow the procedures suggested by the guiding questions in Step 3 to find the answer to the science question raised in Step 2.

Help children during this stage by limiting their temptation to overgeneralize. For example, if the wing rudders are set up and the plane flies up, guide the students to the conclusion that these settings *probably* affect all planes the same way. One could not know for certain that larger planes are affected the same way unless they also are tested.

Step 5. After experimenting, interpreting, and concluding, have the students use what they have learned.

Focus on everyday experiences and have the children apply the main ideas they have learned—the concepts—to things they can understand. The rudder exam-

◆◆◆

The learning cycle has also been used to test the ability of children to use science processes. In a study that investigated fifth graders who were controlled (via a matched-pairs design) for intellectual development, chronological age, gender, and socioeconomic level, Renner and Marek found that all differences in the performance of science process skills favored the group that used the learning cycle. They concluded that the learning cycle helped children learn to use the processes of science much better than did a traditional program using a conventional science textbook.

In still another study, Renner and Marek investigated the influence of the learning cycle in a science program on student achievement in mathematics, reading, and social studies. They discovered that children learned *just as much and just as well* from the learning cycle as those who learned from a traditional program on understanding mathematics concepts, learning mathematics skills, learning social studies content, and understanding word meaning. However, they conclude that the *learning cycle was superior* for helping children apply mathematics; master social studies skills that involve interpreting graphs, tables, and posters and assimilation of

data for problem solving; and determine paragraph meaning. In yet another study, Renner and Marek discovered that the learning cycle used in the SCIS first-grade program helped children outperform other children in a reading program on reading readiness skills.

The researchers maintain that the learning cycle is a natural way to learn and that it fulfills the major purpose of education: helping children learn how to think. Furthermore, Renner and Marek state that their research provides a rebuttal to school people who say, "We just don't have time or cannot afford to invest in the resources to teach science." They conclude: "The truth of the matter is that any school that teaches science using the learning cycle model is teaching much more than good science; it is also teaching reading, mathematics, and social science. In fact, schools cannot afford *not* to teach science using [the learning cycle model]."

*Source:* Adapted and quoted from J. W. Renner and E. Marek, *The Learning Cycle and Elementary Science Teaching* (Portsmouth, NH: Heinemann, 1988), pp. 185–199. See also E. A. Marek and A. M. L. Cavallo, *The Learning Cycle: Elementary Science and Beyond* (Portsmouth, NH: Heinemann, 1997).

ple applies to paper airplanes as well as kites, model rockets and planes, spoilers on racing cars, and rudder steering on conventional boats and swamp or airboats.

### Limitations and Benefits

Like most other inquiry approaches, this method requires more time and planning to cover concepts. Equipment is needed, although often simple and inexpensive materials will do. Certain concepts lend themselves to experimentation more easily than others. The emphasis on concepts, however, is precisely what makes student comprehension greater and retention last longer. The cooperative group problem investigation approach helps to leverage the students' ideas by stimulating new approaches to the problem.

### Suchman's Inquiry: How Can You Get Students to Think and Question?

**Science Magic?**  Dressed in cape and top hat, Mr. Martinez was ready to deliver his promised special treat to the fourth-grade class. With the theatrical flair of an amateur magician, he proposed to take his very sharp magic wand (the straight steel shank cut out of a coat hanger and filed to a pin-sharp point on one end) and pass it through a balloon without bursting it. Mr. Martinez played the crowd. He blew up a balloon, tied it off, and enlisted the aid of the audience by having them chant, "I believe! I believe!" and then on his signal say the magic words. As the magic wand of a super-sharp pin was about to touch the stretched side of the balloon, several children furrowed their brows and covered their ears. And with good reason: Pop!

The giggles were meant to tell Mr. Martinez "I told you so," but he persisted with jabs about not all of them believing or not selecting the right magic words. "Let's try again," he said as he began working the crowd again. Martinez blew up another balloon, tied it, and then remembered that he should add a drop of elixir from an oil can to his magic wand. Through the routine they all went, again, and this time, to the amazement of the children, the wand pierced one end of the balloon and slowly came out the other—a perfect axis through the top of the balloon and at the bottom near the knot (Figure 1.4). The children clapped and immediately wanted to know how he did it.

Mr. Martinez explained that he was not aware of any magic that really worked and that part was only an act. He emphasized that there are usually scientific explanations for the discrepancies we observe. But he assured the children that the balloon trick was no illusion. To convince them, he passed the balloon around for the children to inspect and then said: "You usually expect for me to ask *you* questions, but today is a special opportunity for *you* to ask the questions. Let's pretend you are super sleuths who are going to find out the explanation for this balloon trick. You can ask me all the questions you want, but there are some special rules you must follow. First, you can only ask me questions I can answer with a 'Yes' or 'No.' Second, begin by asking questions to establish the facts of what you have just seen. Don't take anything for granted: Verify that it was done as you *think* you saw it. Finally, after you think you have all the facts you need, tell me the reason you think this trick was possible. Let's begin. Lucinda?"

"Did you do anything special to the second balloon, like make it stronger?"
"No."
Then other children asked:
"Were they the same kind of balloons?"
"Yes."
"Were they the same size? I mean when you blew them up?"
"Yes—I *tried* to have them the same."
"Did you let a little air out of each one?"
"Yes."
"Does the oil make it work?"
"That sounds like an explanation type of question to me. Let's hold that one a while until after we uncover some more facts," said Mr. Martinez. Then the lesson continued until eventually the children discovered the *real* answer, and it wasn't because of the oil. The answer was related to the position, thickness, and strength of the balloon's fabric.

**FIGURE 1.4    Balloon Discrepant Event**

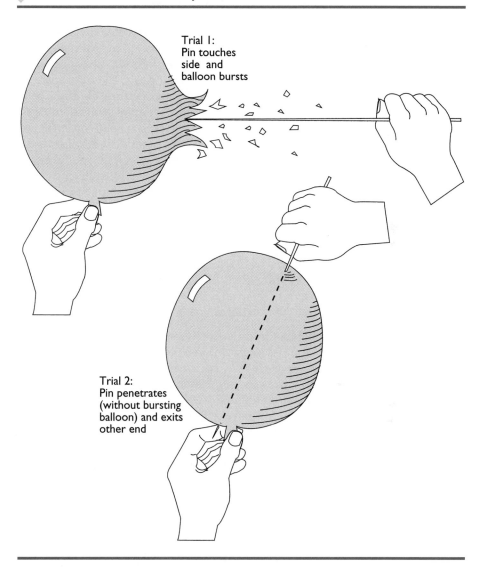

Trial 1:
Pin touches
side and
balloon bursts

Trial 2:
Pin penetrates
(without bursting
balloon) and exits
other end

*Discrepant Events.*    This inquiry technique, developed by J. Richard Suchman (1962), relies on the use of discrepant events. *Discrepancies* are differences from what we normally expect, like the sharp pin's penetrating the balloon without bursting it. It is believed that the human mind is intolerant of discrepancies and needs to maintain consistency. This belief refers to an inconsistency between two cognitions—cognitive dissonance—between what one observes and what one believes. The balloon is a good example: Everyone knows sharp objects cause them to pop, but that one didn't!

***The Method.***   Your students' needs for cerebral consistency can motivate even those who are less alert and attentive. Why not use it to your advantage and teach science concepts with it? Suchman's method uses inquiry to help children construct theories (best explanations) for the discrepancies they observe. The approach is student centered and requires children to ask the questions—possibly a difficult task, because it requires considerable thought to ask useful questions and to build the answers into some order that will explain the discrepancy. The approach can be cooperative if the class is divided into detective teams to organize questions, conduct research, and form scientific explanations. The questions to use are convergent and must be answered with either a *yes* or a *no*. (See Figure 1.5 for a visual map of how the inquiry is structured.) These are the phases of Suchman's method:

1. Present the discrepant event.
2. Students ask yes/no questions to verify the events and collect information.
3. Students discuss ideas and do library research or further investigations to gather additional information to help them form explanations or theories.
4. The teacher reconvenes the class and leads a discussion to help students give and test their explanations or theories.

Suchman's approach is successful with intermediate and middle school children, but younger children need more teacher guidance. With K–2 children we have successfully used versions of the game Twenty Questions to accomplish the same outcome. Familiar objects placed in mystery boxes work well with younger children.

The need to know is the powerful force of motivation with this type of method. However, this power can lead to student frustration and unproductive activity. Robert Shrigley suggests bringing closure or resolution to the discrepant event at least by the end of the class period; otherwise, the discrepancy can lead to an overload of frustration.

> At an inservice meeting . . . teachers had sat through a lengthy inference demonstration using a mystery box with objects sealed inside. Announcing that they should learn to live with the unknown, the science educator refused to open the box for inspection or tell the participants what its contents were. During the break, one teacher, who until that point had been poised and cooperative, bolted to the table on which the box had been left, and ripped off the lid to see what was inside. (Shrigley, 1987, p. 25)

### Can Children Learn Science through Play?

Young children are natural scientists and their time spent at play with common objects helps to reveal their intuitive grasp of simple scientific processes. Sand, water, and block play areas are in demand, suggesting that children usually do

**FIGURE 1.5   Discrepant Event Map**

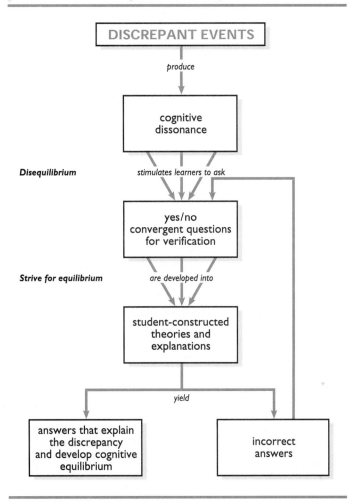

not need external motivation to probe into nature. However, teachers and adult helpers can encourage exploratory play and help to nurture a solid foundation of scientific inquiry by providing children with time, place, and simple equipment needed for investigating the natural world. Ross (1997, p. 35) offers teachers and adult helpers play-based tips that consist of

- supporting open-ended inquiry;
- supplying instruments of play;
- supervising to ensure safety;
- seizing the moment to capitalize on natural interest;

- offering inviting places for discovery to occur;
- providing access to relevant information through tapes, video, picture books and computer programs;
- sharing respect for life (even the small, innocent insect!);
- seeking to develop a community for involvement;
- celebrating wonder.

The method of playful discovery helps to illustrate how these principles can be put into a simple teaching model based on children's play.

Playful discovery is a method based on the innate curiosity of very young children, in which play becomes the method for learning science. The method uses some of the elements of inquiry, but it is much more open ended. Children are natural investigators. Combine a child's interest with some adult encouragement and opportunities to play around with interesting materials, and playful discovery becomes a method that is useful for helping very young children begin to form fundamental science concepts they can build on for the rest of their lives (Lind, 1999; McIntyre, 1984). The method also encourages cooperation among very young learners.

Playful discovery is based on the theories of John Dewey and Jean Piaget, who stated that young children learn best through active involvement with interesting and meaningful materials. Dewey and Piaget, however, reminded us that we as teachers must go beyond simply passing out interesting materials and letting children play with them. Both believed that teachers should direct the hands-on learning through encouragement and guiding questions. Dewey was most concerned about the quality of this hands-on experience, about which he wrote, "Everything depends upon the quality of the experience which is had. The quality of the experience has two aspects. There is an immediate aspect of agreeableness or disagreeableness, and there is an influence upon later experiences" (Dewey, 1937, p. 27).

Versions of playful discovery strive to provide young children with a variety of rich and immediately agreeable experiences. The method is used in child care centers and preschools with three- to five-year-old children and in progressive kindergarten classrooms. Playful discovery is stimulated initially by teacher-planned experiments that are based on phenomena, substances, and/or materials that are interesting and familiar to the children. For science, the learning activities can promote positive attitudes, lay the foundation for learning simple science concepts, and stimulate development of such process skills as observation, comparison, classification, prediction, and interpretation. The following scenario (Rogers, Martin, & Kousaleos, 1988, p. 21) helps to illustrate the method. Figure 1.6 briefly describes its six stages.

***Christopher: A Blossoming Scientist.***   Mrs. Kousaleos invited her group of four- and five-year-olds to gather by her and experiment with ice cubes in hot

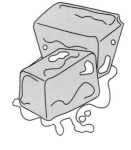

### ◆ FIGURE 1.6  Six Stages of Playful Discovery

**Stage 1:** Self-selected teacher-proposed experiment.
Encourage children to discover if ice cubes melt at the same rate in hot and cold water.

**Stage 2:** Repeat experiment with slight variation.
Encourage children to
- Vary amount of water used.
- Vary size of containers used.
- Determine if stirring the water makes a difference.
- Vary number of ice cubes placed in water.

**Stage 3:** Elaborate further on completed experiment.
Encourage children to discover how many ways you can break up ice cubes (with hands, feet, teeth, hammer, and so on).

**Stage 4:** Provide opportunities for and actively encourage children's self-initiated experiments.
Make a variety of materials accessible, read books, use teacher questioning. For example:
- Child makes ice cubes in a variety of containers (egg carton, muffin tin, plastic bottle, small bucket).
- Child also explores ways to remove ice from container and uses knowledge from Stage 1 to solve problems.
- Child discovers whether or not magic markers melt in hot water.

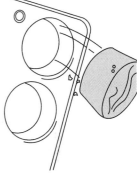

**Stage 5:** Communicate with parents and inform them of child's interest.
- Parent encourages child to experiment at home and while on vacation (exploring ice cubes in bath water, mixing sand and water, discovering effect of jumping in water).
- Parent provides materials as child expresses interest.

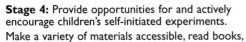

**Stage 6:** Conduct a new experiment.
Encourage
- Children to explore the effect of pressure or force on water.
- Children to explore the effects of adding sand to container of water (e.g., displacement).

*Source:* D. L. Rogers, R. E. Martin, Jr., and S. Kousaleos. "Encouraging Science through Playful Discovery," *Day Care and Early Education* 16 (1988): 1, 23. Reprinted with permission.

and cold water. Five small bodies were arched over the two containers of water observing and comparing the effects. Christopher suddenly announced with obvious excitement, "Look! The ones in hot water are really getting small." At Mrs. K's suggestion to check the water with their fingers, the children were surprised to discover how very cold the formerly hot water had become.

A week later, after repeating the ice activity, Mrs. K suggested another experiment to find out how to melt an ice cube quickly. Eager children generated ideas, then tested them by several methods. Putting ice cubes into mouths and breaking ice cubes into smaller pieces were by far the most popular methods. Midway through the experiment, however, Christopher, eyes wide open and a "Eureka" tone in his voice, proclaimed, "Let's try hot water!"

After duplicating the ice experiments with slight variations (such as exploring effects of amounts of water, numbers of ice cubes, and sizes of containers), the children began to ask permission to conduct their own experiments, Christopher in particular. These requests usually meant making ice in some uniquely shaped container, mixing various ingredients together, or adding a variety of materials to water.

During one of Christopher's self-initiated experiments, he noted that pouring salt into a container of water made the water "lift out." Since Christopher seemed intrigued with this phenomenon, Mrs. K planned some activities on displacement.

Later, when Christopher took a vacation, his parents sent a postcard that said, "Christopher is spending much time on the beach experimenting with water, observing changes as he adds shells and sand." Christopher had become fascinated by how the water "came out" when he and his dad jumped into their vacation swimming pool.

When Christopher returned, his class did a displacement experiment, using different sizes of containers and different amounts of water with marbles to assess and extend some of his vacation learning. After exploring the effect of adding marbles to water in narrow and wide containers, Christopher observed, "When the water's up high, the marbles lift the water out." He later concluded in response to a question about the difference between the narrow and wide containers, "In a fat one the water spreads out. In a thin one it goes up to the top."

*The Playful Science Classroom.* Christopher's response is an example of what can happen when sensitive teacher guidance and well-planned experiences are combined to set the stage for the high-quality "later experiences" John Dewey wrote about. Numerous and different ongoing experiments will be evident in the playful discovery classroom. Many experiences will be based on common activities that use ordinary materials such as sand, water, and blocks.

Playful discovery gives young children opportunities to explore freely and to begin to understand the nature of materials before more structured lessons try to teach them concepts. Figure 1.6 outlines the stages Mrs. K followed to guide the children and improve the quality of their experiences. First she stimulated interest by proposing class experiments; later she stimulated sustained learning and experiential elaboration by permitting children to self-select experiments. Children will function at different stages at different times. For example,

> Some children may not go beyond Stage 1 because of lack of interest or under-standing, and the teacher must proceed to Stage 6 for them. Others may spend a great deal of time on Stages 1 and 2, but not be able to make the leap to Stages 3 and 4. In this case it may help to skip these stages and go to Stage 5, so as to pro-mote elaboration and self-initiation [by] suggesting that parents provide experiences in "science experiments" at home. (Rogers, Martin, & Kousaleos, 1988, p. 23)

Is this approach worth the effort? How long do the experiences endure? Perhaps you will find the answer here:

> Even months after the [first ice] experiment, a mother of one of the children [said] that when she was trying to figure out how to get ice cubes in a small-necked thermos, her four-year-old daughter suggested she could melt them a little in hot water first so they would fit. (Rogers, Martin, & Kousaleos, 1988, p. 23)

Playful discovery works best when the experiments chosen deal with phenomena and substances that the children encounter every day. The everyday environment adds a practical aspect to science by showing its usefulness, and it helps the children to construct a better understanding of their own world.

Objects from the everyday environment can be assembled into simple tools or explorer kits. These kits should be built on topics that interest the children and serve the science content recommendations offered by the National Science Education Standards (see Appendix A). Kit materials can be stored in plastic tubs; color-coordinated stickers help children learn to clean up after themselves. Management and storage ideas may be found in Chapter 9. Ross (1997) offers kit ideas such as the following:

- Exploring light with prisms, crystals, sheets of Mylar or chrome tubes, lenses, kaleidoscopes, and spectroscopes;
- Creating a disassembly line while wearing goggles and using screwdrivers and pliers to remove loosened screws from broken appliances (electric plugs removed) such as old clocks, radios, computers and modems, VCRs, cassette players, and irons;
- Digging soil in outdoor or indoor designated areas with various sizes of food containers, cookie cutters, molds, magnets, strainers, trowels, small shovels, or spoons;
- Investigating (with a respect for life) roly-poly insects—commonly called pill bugs—typically found under rotting logs or leaf litter by using magnifying lenses, soil tubs, watercolor brushes, toothpicks, or pipe cleaners;
- Seizing the moment by exploring playground puddles and windy days with pinwheels, kites, and vessels made from paper, straws, aluminum foil, or common craft supplies.

## Problem-Based Learning

The new age of science teaching recognizes that basic skills are important, yet reformers argue that future citizens must also have a command of key scientific ideas, be able to solve problems, and think critically (National Research Council, 1996). An emphasis on inquiry-based learning methods and student construction of understanding takes time, vision and cooperation, and often interdisciplinary treatment of school subjects. The National Science Education Standards suggest that desirable long-term inquiry activities include formation of arguments, explanation, and communication of ideas to others while using a wide range of procedural, manipulative and cognitive skills (Marx et al., 1997). Problem-based learning approaches are useful for

- enhancing students' abilities to attend to and store information in closer proximity to what they already know with potential for avoiding misconceptions;
- situating newly constructed understanding within a realistic experiential context;
- promoting productive social interaction and learning through collaboration;
- stimulating the uses of cognitive tools such as videodisks, web sites, microcomputer simulations, concept maps, and problem-posing/decision-making structures. (Marx et al., 1997)

Marx, Blumenfeld, Krajcik, and Soloway (1997, pp. 344–346) report five important features of their Project-Based Science model, which is exemplary of many problem-based learning approaches in science. They recommend that teachers

1. Help students form a *driving question* in order that projects have a focus. Driving questions should be worthwhile (connected to a curriculum framework); pose real-world problems that students find meaningful and feel ownership over; and be feasible and within the learners' realms of experience, knowledge, and skills.
2. Engage students in *investigation*—the real work of science—which consists of planning and designing the investigations and conducting real-world research to collect and analyze information so that the students may form inferences and conclusions about the driving question.
3. Guide students toward the collection and creation of *artifacts*, which are tangible, real results of an investigation. Artifacts can consist of air- and water-quality samples, documents from corporations and science agencies, multimedia materials obtained from internet searches, and so on.
4. Help students to *collaborate.* When students labor together to plan and complete tasks, they benefit from the collective intelligence of all group members and learn to value the ideas of others.
5. Expose learners to *technological tools.* Investigations become more authentic when students use tools to measure, gather, and process information by themselves. The entire classroom environment becomes more authentic and

inquiry becomes more serious through real-time data collection. Students learn to make models and extend their inquiry and collaboration to other groups outside the home base of their classroom.

Figures 1.7 and 1.8 illustrate some of the tools used to nurture the students' cognitive skills and to encourage the formation and analysis of driving questions. A teacher using these tools could consult the National Science Education Standards for content and curriculum framework ideas. The Standards help to

**FIGURE 1.7  Spider Map for Investigating Technology's Influence on Our Daily Lives**   A spider map can be used to help students list and organize the various ideas they have about a topic. You could draw the basic sketch of the spider and add the legs (we have used just four, but more could be added). You might also suggest the labels for the legs and then ask the children to offer examples, which you list. From the ideas and examples, driving questions may emerge, which can be organized into a framework for investigating a problem as shown in Figure 1.7.

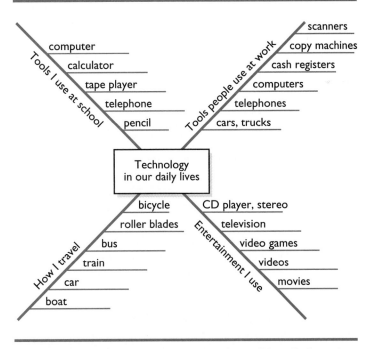

*Source:* The idea of the spider map is used in the *Breakthroughs: Strategies for Thinking* series. Columbus, OH: Zaner-Bloser, 1992.

**FIGURE 1.8    Problem-Based Learning Decision-Making Framework**

| | |
|---|---|
| **Question Box** | What is technology?<br><br>How does technology affect me?<br><br>What kinds of problems or solutions does technology create?<br><br>How can I use technology? |
| **Important Information Box** | Technology helps people to make new tools.<br><br>People have used technology for a long time.<br><br>Technology can help to keep me healthy.<br><br>Technology can be misused and cause harmful things to happen to people and animals.<br><br>All kinds of people use technology.<br><br>You do not have to be a scientist to use and understand technology.<br><br>Technology can make work easier.<br><br>Sometimes technology can help people to do more work in less time. |
| **Decisions or Solutions Box** | The students' decisions or problem solutions should reflect their understanding about science and technology and a balance among positive and negative effects. |

guide learners in the direction of worthwhile questions and applications to their daily lives. The figures illustrate the investigation of technology, a new science content area included in the Standards.

## How Can You Turn Students' Questions into an Inquiry Teaching Method?

Fred Biddulph and Roger Osborne (1984) provide an inquiry approach to teaching that involves children in science investigations that are based on *their* own questions. They believe children's questions ought to be central to the process of inquiry because they show the extent of the ideas children have about a science topic, and they can be used to generate interest. Basing inquiry on student's questions

- helps them gain understanding,
- provides them a powerful incentive to improve their own information-processing skills,
- helps them learn to interact with ideas and construct meanings for themselves from an interesting situation or topic,
- gives them occasional opportunities to learn from their own mistakes.

The teacher's role in this approach is to

- encourage students to ask questions about their encounters,
- encourage students to seek more information and rely less on teachers and others,
- help students find ways to test their ideas,
- help students construct well-reasoned explanations for their questions. (Biddulph & Osborne, 1984, p. 2)

Table 1.2 provides a quick visual outline of the method. We paraphrase Biddulph and Osborne's work in the following steps.

### Step 1. Elicit and record the students' questions.

Time required is perhaps one lesson. It is easier for students to ask questions if they already know something about the topic from prior experience. If experience is lacking, provide a demonstration, perhaps a discrepant event; show a film, poster, photograph, or slides; give descriptions of situations, encounters, or examples of the topic; read them a relevant story; or give them time for free exploration with materials.

These opportunities may spark a wide range of questions; it may be necessary to help the children focus the points of their questions. Students may be reluctant or uncertain about how to form good questions if they have not had practice.

### ◆ TABLE 1.2    Students' Questions as an Inquiry Approach

| | |
|---|---|
| *Step 1: Provision of initiating activities.*   Provide your students with experiences that will enable them to ask questions. Record their questions. | *Step 4: Assistance with investigations.*   Provide assistance to the students during their investigations. |
| *Step 2: Decision about questions.*   Decide which questions are to be investigated. | *Step 5: Help with findings.*   Help the students to record, interpret, and report their findings. |
| *Step 3: Guidance with planning.*   Assist the students to plan their investigations. | |

*Source:* Fred Biddulph and Roger Osborne, "Children's Questions and Science Teaching: An Alternative Approach," *Learning in Science Project* (Primary), working paper 117 (Hamilton, New Zealand: Waikato University, 1984). (ERIC Reproduction Document no. ED 252400), p. 4.

*Questions from children help motivate further inquiry and encourage discovery.*

Teacher modeling of proper question-asking behavior can help; so can using divergent questions to stimulate thoughtfulness and multiple possibilities. After a while, eliciting questions is not a great matter of concern; deciding *when* to stop is.

### Step 2. Decide which questions to investigate.

The time needed may be as much as one lesson. Once you have obtained genuine questions to which students do not know the answers, selection must occur. These are some possible ways to proceed:

- Have individual students select questions for independent projects, or have groups choose a question of interest and work on it collectively.
- When separate questions may be related, let the students group them in ways that make sense to them.
- Refine the selection process by classifying the questions according to which ones may be investigated by practical activities or by consultation with books or people. Eliminate or defer questions that are outside the range of the science topic or that may be too difficult conceptually for the students.

### Step 3. Help students plan their investigations.

Time required may be one or more class periods. Encourage practical hands-on investigations as well as consultations with resources. Guide the students so that they learn to

- identify and use appropriate materials,
- carry out fair and accurate tests of their ideas,
- select and consult suitable print, media, and human resources,
- collect useful information,
- have realistic expectations for how long they will need to test their ideas,
- show concern for the environment and treatment of people.

Intermediate and middle grade students may benefit from a written framework to help organize their investigation, such as the one in Table 1.3.

**Step 4. Monitor the students' investigations and provide assistance.**

Several class periods will be needed. Young or inexperienced older students will need considerable help as they concurrently develop research and thinking skills while they pursue science learning. You can encourage students by showing empathy for their frustrations and providing sympathetic challenges to strengthening their ideas. You can support students' inquiry by directing their attention to factors they may have overlooked or by suggesting alternatives.

**Step 5. Help the students record, interpret, and report their findings.**

Several class periods may be necessary. Consider that children probably will need help with

- knowing what to record and learning that several tests (repeated measures) will provide more accuracy than a single measure;
- organizing information to record it in chart, table, graph, or narrative form (this is a good place to integrate mathematics and language arts skills);
- knowing what meaning is or is not possible to take from certain information; meaning can be enhanced if children are encouraged to use analogies;
- forming a succinct, clear conceptual understanding, free of misconceptions, which becomes the focal point of their reports;
- reporting the results in an organized format such as posters, charts, models, film, video, and so on.

**TABLE 1.3   Organization Framework**

1. Name
2. Science topic
3. My question
4. My investigation
   - (a) What do I want to ask someone?
   - (b) Whom can I ask?
   - (c) What should I read about?
   - (d) What could I do to find out?

# TECHNIQUES FOR PROMOTING STUDENT COOPERATION

Science inquiry encourages learners to construct their understanding from direct physical experiences and guided thinking. The methods have risks and potential difficulties. If all teachers were responsible for only one student at a time, these constructivist, inquiry approaches to science education would be rather simple to manage. Problems arise when two or more learners independently attempt to inquire. That students or a group may pursue several different questions and work on various projects at the same time presents management and organization difficulties for most teachers. Sufficient resources may also be in short supply. Postponing or even canceling lessons are options if the initial difficulties become too much to risk. With encouragement and time to develop the needed skills, students can grow into the role of posing questions and need less help researching their answers. With practice, you too will become more skilled at managing the busy class activity and will know what questions and needs to anticipate. You will also learn many fascinating things about science that you probably never had a chance to investigate. One procedure that can help you manage the inquiry from children's questions is associated with learning teams or cooperative groups.

## Cooperative Learning in Science

Science teachers frequently group students during science activities to manage crowded classes and stretch precious materials that always seem to be in short supply. Cooperative learning, even if used mostly for science management, is more than asking students to group their desks together, however. F. James Rutherford and Andrew Ahlgren, writing in *Science for All Americans*, tell us

> The collaborative nature of scientific and technological work should be strongly reinforced by frequent group activity in the classroom. Scientists and engineers work mostly in groups and less often as isolated investigators. Similarly, students should gain experience in sharing responsibility for learning with each other. In the process of coming to common understandings, students in a group must frequently inform each other about procedures and meaning, argue over findings, and assess how the task is progressing. In the context of team responsibility, feedback and communication become more realistic and of a character very different from the usual individualistic textbook-homework-recitation approach. (Rutherford & Alhgren, 1990, p. 189)

Scientists and engineers work in an environment that is more cooperative than competitive. Roger Johnson and David Johnson (1991) and Robert Slavin (1995), well-known promoters of cooperative learning methods, maintain that the research base for cooperative learning (in its many forms) indicates that students would learn more science, like it more, and feel more positive about their performance if more of their science experiences were obtained through cooperative learning. In their extensive review of the research on instructional strategies for teaching science, Tobin, Tippins, and Gallard (1994) remind us that cooperative learning should not be viewed as a panacea. Rather, it is valuable because of the potential for students to clarify, defend, elaborate, evaluate, and argue their constructed thoughts with one another. Table 1.4 compares the advantages of cooperative learning teaching and management techniques over those of customary small groups. This comparison illustrates that clear learning outcomes and systematic management procedures are keys to success.

### Cooperative Inquiry Groups

Three to five is a functional number for inquiry groups or cooperative learning groups. When each group member has a special job, the group inquiry process can be both effective and functional. The research on this management approach shows that "students who work in groups learn concepts just as well as those who work individually, with the added bonus that students who work together can develop both interpersonal skills and a sense of group responsibility" (Jones, 1985, p. 21).

Form groups, assign roles, and give each child a job description. The *principal investigator* (PI) is in charge of managing the group. Duties are to check the assignment and ask the teacher any clarifying questions, then lead the group by conducting the activity for the rest of the group or by assigning duties to the other group members. The PI is also in charge of safety.

The *materials manager* is in charge of picking up and passing out all equipment and materials that are necessary. Inside the classroom, the materials manager is usually the only student who has a reason to be moving around.

### ◥ TABLE 1.4    Benefits of Cooperative Science Groups

| Cooperative Groups | Small Groups |
| --- | --- |
| Positive interdependence; students sink or swim together; face-to-face verbal communication | No interdependence; students work on their own, often or occasionally checking their answers with other students |
| Individual accountability; each pupil must master the material | Hitchhiking; some students let others do most or all of the work, then copy |
| Teachers teach social skills needed for successful group work | Social skills are not systematically taught |
| Teacher monitors students' behavior | Teacher does not directly observe student behavior; often works with a few students or works on other tasks |
| Feedback and discussion of students' behavior are integral parts of ending the activity before moving on | No discussion of how well students worked together, other than general comments such as "Nice job," or "Next time, try to work more quietly." |

*Source:* P. E. Blosser, "Using Cooperative Learning in Science Education." Columbus, OH: ERIC Clearinghouse for Science, Mathematics, and Environmental Education, 1993, ERIC Reproduction Document No. ED 351 207, p. 4.

*Children learn responsibility by sharing tasks in cooperative groups.*

The *recorder* is in charge of collecting the necessary information and recording it in the proper form: graph, table, tape recorder, and so on. The recorder works with the principal investigator and the materials manager to verify the accuracy of the data.

The *reporter* is in charge of reporting the results, orally or in writing, back to the teacher or the entire class.

The *maintenance director* is in charge of cleanup and has the power to involve others in this group responsibility. Equipment must be returned and consumables must be cleaned up.

Recorder and reporter can be combined, as can materials manager and maintenance director for groups as small as three. Badges, sashes, headbands, photo IDs, or other role-identifying management devices can be used to limit confusion. Rotate the roles and form different groups often to promote fairness and group responsibility. This group technique can be used with any inquiry method in which groups are used. Robert Jones provides further tricks of the trade in Table 1.5.

Successful, problem-free science lessons can occur if each member of the group understands the importance of his or her role. In a cooperative learning environment, the groups purposely comprise boys and girls of different ability levels. Each student realizes that on any given day, he or she could serve in any capacity as a member of the cooperative group. Therefore, each member is responsible for learning the material. The grade earned by participating in the lesson is a reflection of the group effort, not an individual. The group is interdependent; its members will sink or swim together. The students within a group need to communicate to one another problems, observations, and successes before they go to the teacher with them. Courtesy, respect, and encouragement are interpersonal skills needed by each member of the cooperative group.

One useful cooperative method is known as a *jigsaw approach* (Watson, 1992). Use it, for example, when you are teaching third-grade students about the state tree, flower, and bird. Within each cooperative group, a different member will be assigned one of the following tasks:

- to determine the criteria for becoming the official state tree,
- to determine the criteria for becoming the official state flower,
- to determine the criteria for becoming the official state bird,

## TABLE 1.5    Tricks of the Trade for Cooperative Group Inquiry Activities

- Let each group choose a name for itself. It is a good social activity, and the names will help you identify the different groups.
- Change group members from time to time. Try out introvert-extrovert or boy-girl teams; experiment with cultural and racial mixes; form academically heterogeneous groups.
- Talk only to the principal investigators about the activity. This will set up a chain of command and prevent a repetition of questions. The students should discuss questions and problems among themselves so that it will only be necessary for you to clarify points with the principal investigator.
- Employ both indoor and outdoor activities. Badges work well indoors; armbands and headbands are more visible on school grounds. Hand-held walkie-talkies (inexpensive children's type) are also useful and (if they are available) should be used by the principal investigators.
- Use groups of three when working outdoors or on a field trip. This size group is better for safety.
- To ensure clear communication, post class rules, group names, job descriptions, and any other important information on a bulletin board in the classroom.
- Develop a system for rotating roles.
- Use job descriptions for classroom management and discipline. Most of the time you will simply need to ask which person has which role to resolve problems.
- Develop a worksheet, data recording sheet, or some other instrument for each activity.
- Make yourself a badge and join in the fun.

*Source:* R. M. Jones, "Teaming Up," *Science and Children* (May 1985): 23.

- to find out who suggested the state tree, bird, or flower, and where these are found in the state,
- to learn what the state tree, bird, and flower are in one bordering state.

The students in the cooperative groups should decide which student will take on each of the five tasks. Once these students are determined, then all of the students in the class assigned to task 1 should get together to find answers to that task, those assigned to task 2 should do the same, and so on. After a sufficient amount of time has passed (for this topic with third graders, two or three 35- to 40-minute class periods should be enough time) the students should have found answers for their task. They must now return to their original cooperative groups to share their information. The success of the cooperative group will depend on how well the expert gets his or her information across to the members of the group. After two class periods of sharing information from the five tasks, it is time for the quiz. This can be done by student experts for task 1 moving to different cooperative groups. Those experts will then quiz each member of a different cooperative group individually on task 1 information. After task 1 experts quiz the students and record their results, then task 2 experts will do the same, and so on. The success of each student will be reflected by how well his or her cooperative group expert prepared the group for the quiz.

## RECOMMENDATIONS FOR ENHANCING STUDENTS' LEARNING OF SCIENCE

All of the inquiry methods we have presented are student centered to various degrees. They engage children in active thinking and learning and differ only in approach, but despite these procedural differences, each method guides children through inquiry toward making discoveries. The methods are successful when teachers help students to construct understanding. What elements unite these different procedures, which lead to a common outcome (Rakow, 1986)?

**1.** Successful constructivist teachers *model scientific attitudes.* The scientific attitudes we most wish to develop in children must be evident in the people who teach them. Successful inquiry teachers must be curious, open minded, tolerant of different viewpoints, skeptical at times, willing to admit it when they do not know answers to all questions, and able to view those occasions as opportunities to expand their learning.

**2.** Successful constructivist teachers are *creative.* Effective teachers find ways to make deficient materials effective. They are masters at adapting others' ideas, and they become comfortable taking risks with the unknown. They encourage creativity in students by being creative themselves.

**3.** Successful constructivist teachers are *flexible.* Inquiry takes time. Students need time to explore, think, and ask questions. Successful constructivist teachers are patient and use time flexibly to afford children the time they need for effective inquiry learning.

**4.** Successful constructivist teachers use effective *questioning strategies.* Types of questions used, wait-time, and proper uses of praise, reinforcement, and encouragement are the fodder of inquiry learning.

**5.** Successful constructivist teachers *focus* their efforts on preparing students to *think* in order to construct meaning. The constructivist teacher most wants students to develop an ability to solve problems. Successful problem solving depends on numerous thinking skills that arise from the processes of science that guide all phases of the inquiry. The end result of the inquiry process is the construction of scientific concepts. The end justifies the means, but exclusive focus on the end product does not provide the means for future problem solving.

Take the first step by beginning small. Trying to adapt all lessons into a constructivist approach is an overwhelming task and can be frustrating. If yours is a conventional textbook science program, focus on only one or two chapters at first by mapping the concepts (see Chapter 7). Then develop the material into good inquiry activities or find other supplementing resources. Each year add more, and soon you will develop an effective collection of material. Combine your efforts with those of other teachers (particularly those who teach the same grade level), pool your materials, improve them, and help your program become more effective. Read such journals as *Science and Children* for elementary teachers and *Science Scope* for middle and junior high teachers. These journals, available from the National Science Teachers Association, contain activities reported by experienced teachers and describe new materials available through government-sponsored programs and commercial publishers.

## CHAPTER SUMMARY

Inquiry-based science teaching methods are interactive: Students and teachers investigate together and share many responsibilities that are carried only by the teacher in conventional classrooms. Construction of understanding is encouraged by a family of science teaching methods that promote student inquiry in a hands-on, minds-on way. Inquiry is a process, a way of pursuing learning. The outcomes of its methods are students' discoveries. Discoveries are mental constructions. All constructivist methods are based on a belief about the power of experience. The methods rely on effective questioning to promote concept development.

Several inquiry-based science teaching methods are described in this chapter. The science

learning cycle is appropriate for concept development in all grades and is particularly well suited for implementing the new goals in science education described in Chapter 6. A sample plan is included in this chapter.

Principles of scientific inquiry help us develop an approach for turning what once were memory exercises into a powerful teaching and learning method. This approach is most suitable for the intermediate through middle school grades and lends itself to cooperative inquiry groups.

Suchman's inquiry makes use of puzzling phenomena—discrepant events—that permit teachers to build on intrinsic motivation and turn children into questioners and pursuers of explanations. Playful discovery is a little-known inquiry method that was developed for very young children. Preschool and kindergarten children benefit from its playful atmosphere, accumulating agreeable and valuable experiences that help them build concept structures for later study. Problem-based learning revolves around children forming and pursuing solutions to meaningful problems. Inquiry with children's questions is another approach for turning children's questions into a teaching and learning method. With so many possible different questions children may wish to pursue, classroom management can become a night-mare; therefore, we offer practical recommendations for using cooperative learning groups.

Effective teachers who use inquiry methods demonstrate several common attributes: They model science attitudes, are creative in their approaches to science material and flexible in classroom management, and tend to focus more on developing children's abilities to think than on mere acquisition of subject matter. Research verifies the superior effects of student-centered constructivist approaches over traditional text-based teaching methods for science achievement, and the attitudes and skills of scientific inquiry.

## DISCUSSION QUESTIONS

**1.** What arguments support using inquiry science teaching methods? What barriers seem to limit inquiry's acceptance and use in elementary classrooms? Will you use some of the methods described in this chapter? Why?

**2.** What are the similarities and differences in the approaches described in this chapter? Under what circumstances would you favor any one approach over the others?

**3.** Why is it that as children get older and presumably more capable of thinking independently, they appear to rely more on an authority figure for information than on their own experiences for discovering it?

**4.** Inquiry methods tend to promote greater independence among learners. What are several things you can do to help students become more independent learners?

**5.** Inquiry teaching strives to accommodate individual student differences. Individual differences do, however, tend to complicate teaching. What are some things you could do to manage the diversity of individuality without losing your cooperative focus?

**6.** How do inquiry methods help slow and fast learners?

## BUILD A PORTFOLIO

**1.** Select a teaching method described in this section and prepare a lesson for it. Teach the lesson, videotape it, analyze it, and evaluate the effects of the method.

**2.** How could you modify the method to make it more effective or a better fit for the needs of your learners? Prepare a brief essay describing your experience and your thoughts.

**3.** Try teaching science lessons a conventional way and then with one of the methods described in this section. Determine the extent to which learners obtain and retain the points of the lesson. What does your analysis reveal? Write a summary that describes your "experiment" and your conclusions.

**4.** Edit a videotape of your teaching to a brief length that highlights the prime features of the method, or prepare still photos showing yourself in action and the reactions of the children as they experience the wonders of science. Share your tape with your supervisor, professor, or prospective employer.

**5.** Investigate the ways you use questioning during your science lessons and the types of questions that children ask and your responses to them. Report the frequency and types of questions. What patterns do you detect? What improvements could you make in your skills to make your inquiry lessons more effective? Write a summary and include it in your portfolio.

**6.** Develop original lessons for each of the methods described in this chapter. How do these lessons vary? What aspects of planning are emphasized more and less as the instruction becomes more cooperative among students?

# CHAPTER 2

# How Can You Use Demonstrations, Direct Instruction, and Textbooks Effectively?

Ms. Ramirez's classroom is in the same pod as Mrs. Todd (of the Chapter 1 scenario). Although they often share their unit plans, Ms. Ramirez prefers a different teaching approach. Her style reflects, in part, her philosophy and provides a glimpse of her confidence level in teaching science. She believes science is important, but especially enjoys teaching reading.

Ms. Ramirez' classroom is arranged in rows, and posters on the wall feature award-winning books and travel posters from the many countries she has visited. Classroom rules are clearly posted, and all students share in the important duties.

"We will learn a new word in our science reading today," she begins. Ms. Ramirez writes the word "habitat" on the flip chart. "This word is 'habitat.' A habitat is like a location that contains all of the things needed for survival. All animals must have a suitable habitat if they are to survive. A suitable habitat contains all of the food, water, shelter and space that an animal needs in order to survive. For example, look at our fish bowl. The bowl contains all of the things our goldfish needs: the bowl provides the space, water is in the bowl, and we feed the fish. Let's read today's lesson. Please open your science books to page 36. Alicia, would you please begin reading?"

"Many animals live together in the forest. Some of the animals eat plants. A rabbit eats clover. Some animals eat other animals. A fox will eat a rabbit if it can catch the rabbit. Other animals eat both plants and animals."

"Thank you Alicia. Sean, would you continue, please?"

"All animals need water. All animals need a space. In order to live safely animals must also have shelter. An animal can survive if it has all of these things. All of these things make an animal's hab . . . habit. . . ."

"Hab-i-tat," says Ms. Ramirez, pronouncing each syllable for the class.

"Habitat!" beams Sean.

"Nice job, Sean."

The children finish reading the section and learn about different types of habitats and the unique needs of several animals. Then Ms. Ramirez asks them to indicate what they remember by completing a worksheet. She promises them a chance to watch a video from the Discovery Channel and to play a habitat game if they cooperate. ◆

## INTRODUCTION

### *Avoiding Authoritarianism and the Exclusive Use of Textbooks*

Ms. Ramirez's approach is typical of most traditional science lessons, which rely on teacher-centered methods consisting of lectures, reading, and questions and answers. These approaches are often limited to the information provided by the adopted textbook and assume that students should mainly pay attention to the teacher. However, this way of learning gives students a mainly passive role as receivers and memorizers of information rather than as active seekers of answers to important scientific questions.

Texts and lectures are *not* all bad. They do present important science information that is useful in addressing *some* of the National Science Education Standards content. Complete reliance upon textbooks, however, usually means students will be deprived of other worthy science education goals relevant to understanding the history and nature of science, developing science inquiry skills, and understanding personal, technological, and societal issues.

Reliance on a single science textbook can promote an authoritarian approach to teaching and learning. The text or the teacher becomes *the* authority, with the textbook becoming the principal determiner of what is taught. The science topic usually is selected because it is "in the book" (Staver & Bay, 1987). Furthermore, textbooks by themselves, without teacher modification, usually do not promote or encourage the development of scientific thinking or attitudes; nor do they engage students in applying the cognitive processes that are basic to understanding the content covered. If teachers use these programs to teach science without drawing on supplementary resources, students will understand science mainly as a collection of conclusions to be memorized: They will not be brought to an adequate understanding of the nature and methods of science nor will they be afforded sufficient opportunities to explore the relationship of science to technology and to the problems of living in the modern world (Elliott & Carter, 1986, p. 11).

Constructing science knowledge in the classroom depends on the interplay of various factors such as personal experience, language, and socialization and the involvement of learners in the problematic relationships of compilations of scientific information (a.k.a. textbooks), learning processes, and teaching methods (Driver, 1994). As von Glaserfeld (1993) reminds us,

> Knowledge is always the result of a constructive activity and, therefore it cannot be transferred to a passive receiver. [Knowledge] has to be actively built up by each individual knower. A teacher, however, can orient a learner in a general direction, and constraints can be arranged that prevent the learner from constructing in directions that seem unsuitable to the teacher. (p. 26)

The National Science Education Standards make a compelling case for helping learners develop scientific ways of knowing. Yet, there are no simple rules or recipes to follow for foolproof teaching and learning. Instead, there are many guiding principles that a well-informed, reflective teacher can use to create effective learning conditions. According to Rosalind Driver and associates (1994), "If students are to adopt scientific ways of knowing, then intervention and negotiation with an authority figure, usually the teacher, is essential" (p. 11).

As science teacher authority figures, we have important functions: to introduce new ideas or cultural tools where they are necessary; provide support and guidance to students so that they can make sense for themselves; listen to learners' responses so that we can determine the ways that our learning activities are being interpreted; and form diagnoses that inform the further actions we choose to take (Driver, 1994). Classrooms require successful interaction between and among teachers and students if the new vision of science learning is to occur.

### Why Is an Interactive Classroom Important?

*Interactive* teaching approaches are recommended in elementary science. Interactive approaches encourage young children to think and reason. Mary Willert and Constance Kamii also remind us that authoritative teacher-centered forms of direct instruction are "based on the erroneous assumption that children are like empty glasses who learn by having bits of knowledge poured into them, and that the sooner we start to fill the glasses, the sooner this process will be completed" (Willert & Kamii, 1985, p. 3).

Interactive classrooms are places where teachers and students exchange ideas and observations. Classrooms of this type develop learners who are intrinsically motivated and who will go much further than those who wait to be told what to learn (Willert & Kamii, 1985). The purpose of this chapter is to help you to

1. explore ways of making a teacher-centered classroom more interactive,
2. develop skills in using effective teacher demonstrations that encourage constructed learning,

*Interaction is an important tool that helps learners to construct meaning from materials and experiences.*

3. teach more effectively those lessons when you may choose to use exposition as a method to support other constructivist efforts,
4. become informed about how to select and use science textbooks and trade-books that support constructive learning.

## HOW CAN YOU USE TEACHER DEMONSTRATIONS TO FOSTER CONSTRUCTED LEARNING?

With most demonstrations, a central figure stands before a class and shows something and then tells what happened. The central authority figure, often a teacher, usually is the only individual actually involved with the demonstration. Students' reactions to demonstrations may range from wide-eyed excitement to sleepy apathy (Wolfinger, 1984). How can you conduct a demonstration that stimulates curiosity and motivates the children so they actually *want* to hear an explanation? Clara Guerra (1988) succeeds nicely, combining a bit of showmanship with the magic of science. She describes an exciting demonstration that can be done safely with sufficient planning and safety protection. We recommend that the demonstrator wear approved safety goggles, have a fire blanket on hand, and seat the front row of students at least 10 feet from the demonstration table; the observers should wear goggles as required by state law. We recommend that you review the safety and management recommendations found in Chapter 9 before trying the demonstration. Let's read Guerra's (1988, pp. 23–24) approach and learn about her techniques.

> "A Bit of Science—A Bit of Magic" is a presentation I do for the elementary schools. It is nothing more than simple science dressed up as magic. I am the magician and the children are my dutifully amazed audience. I explode cans based on the rapid oxidation principle, I turn liquids blue with chemical reactions, and I pull the tablecloth out from under dishes, thanks to Newton's law of inertia. While many in the audience may remember only the razzle-dazzle, the pops and bangs of the show, every so often one of their parents will tell me later that their son or daughter wants to be a scientist. That's when I know that a spark has been ignited. Someone has taken the first step toward discovering the real magic of science.
>
> "Ladies and gentlemen, boys and girls, I am a scientist!" I begin, standing in front of the students in a sorcerer's hat. "I am someone who sees things a little differently." As I talk, the house lights go out and black lights come on. My hat, decorated with stars and crayoned with fluorescent colors, catches the light and

*Increase interaction and discovery by directly involving children in demonstrations.*

seems to stand alone on the stage. Without a drum roll or a more formal fanfare, the show begins.

Nothing quite catches the attention of a young audience like a big bang does. And a big bang is what they get with the exploding dust can trick.

To perform this, I use a candle and candle holder, lycopodium powder (flour will also work) and a small metal doll's cup, a clean paint can with the cup inside, and an air hose leading into the cup.

First, I fill the cup half full of the lycopodium powder and place it in the paint can. Then, I place a lit candle in its holder inside the paint can and put the lid back on. The air hose has been inserted through a hole in the side of the paint can and sits in the cup. I take a deep breath, blow deeply into the air hose, and stand back quickly. (See Figure 2.1.)

Within seconds, the top explodes off the can. Then I explain. When I blew into the can, I made the dust spread throughout it. The candle then ignited the mixture, causing the gases in the air to expand. When the gases expanded, they needed more space than the inside of the can had. There was only one place for the gases to go—out of that can. I tell the children this sometimes happens in grain dust elevators or flour mills or even in the family woodworking shop.

After the explosion, I set the lit candle on the table. I sprinkle a small amount of lycopodium dust onto the lid of the paint can. Holding the lid, I sprinkle some of the dust directly into the candle's flame. This shows the children what happened inside the can. A word of caution, if you try this: Wear goggles, move away from the candle quickly, and don't wear flowing sleeves.

### Tips for Effective Demonstrations

Guerra's (1988) technique provides a vivid illustration of several effective tips for planning and delivering classroom demonstrations. We do not suggest that

**FIGURE 2.1   The Exploding Can Demonstration**

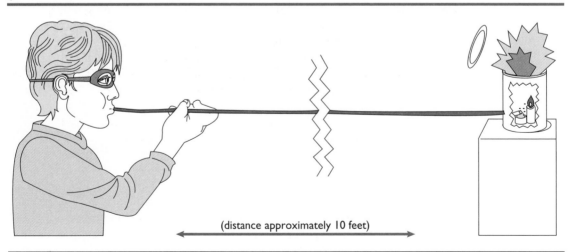

(distance approximately 10 feet)

you must always be an entertainer. However, a little panache does enliven the class. Demonstrations can be effective teaching tools if you follow these suggestions:

**1.** The demonstration should have a *specific purpose,* and this purpose must *be clear* to all learners. Focus on the point to be learned, and make it evident in the demonstration. Also discuss how it relates to past or future lessons. If it is intended only to entertain and not teach a concept, the demonstration has little value.

**2.** *Plan carefully.* Collect all the necessary materials and practice the demonstration in advance. Follow the instructions and inspect them for inaccuracies. Modify the demonstration, if necessary, for safety. Remember, we recommend that you use goggles, distance, and fire protection if you try Guerra's demonstration. Sometimes a substitution may be useful; a safer but still exciting alternative to explosion is implosion. For example, try a clean, empty metal can with a top (like a rinsed Ditto fluid can or rinsed camp fuel container). Add 70 mL water (about a quarter cup) and heat it to a boil on a hotplate (without the cap). Wearing oven mitts, remove the can from the heat, replace the cap, cool it under a faucet or in a bucket of cold water, and watch what happens. (The can is crushed by a greater air pressure outside the can than inside.)

**3.** *Involve the students when possible.* Let the students participate in the demonstrations or permit them to conduct the demonstration. Interactive teaching techniques such as questions and guess-making stimulate thinking, enthusiasm, and participation.

**4.** *Stimulate thinking and discussion.* "What do you think will happen if . . . ?" questions help stimulate original thinking and bring forth children's ideas for productive discussion. This technique also releases you from giving away too much information before the demonstration and running the risk of destroying interest. Refer to Chapter 8 for additional questioning ideas.

**5.** *Repeat the demonstration.* A rapid flash, a loud bang, or an imploding can is sure to get attention and will demand a repeat performance. During the repeat, students will pay closer attention, and their powers of observation will be keener. Also, they will be given chances to acquire ideas or form mental connections that seem simple for us but are difficult for them because of their limited experiences.

**6.** *Use simple materials.* Unfamiliar equipment may distract the students' attention. Familiar objects and equipment will help them focus on the cause of the action or the purpose of the demonstration rather than on the gadgets being used. Students may also choose to try the demonstrations for themselves. Importation of high school equipment for elementary classroom use should be selective and always screened for safety (see Chapter 9).

**7.** *Keep the demonstration easily visible.* A cluttered demonstration table will distract children from seeing what you intend. Similarly, objects that are too small to be seen by those sitting beyond the first row will frustrate viewers and cause them to lose interest. Use a tall table or counter, gather the students around when feasible (and when safe), or consider using such projection devices as the overhead projector or computer.

**8.** *Connect* with the students' environment. Interact in order to connect the point of the demonstration with the children's personal interests, community, or social issues to expand the benefits of the demonstration and the scientific concepts or principles. Guerra did this when referring to the grain elevator, flour mill, and family wood shop.

**9.** *Rely on quality, not quantity.* Avoid a large number of demonstrations hoping the students learn *something*. A single well-designed, timely demonstration can communicate powerful ideas more effectively than an overwhelming number of entertaining shows. Focus on a central concept.

### When Should You Use a Demonstration?

"To keep the room neat" and "to prevent the kids from tearing things up" are not good reasons for doing demonstrations. These reasons only prevent learners from gaining necessary experience with the materials and also prevent them from learning how to interact appropriately with learning aids. Nevertheless, there are some reasons for teachers to do demonstrations:

- to avoid putting students in danger by using a demonstration as a safer alternative;
- to help students learn such skills as the proper ways to use equipment or the proper way to handle and care for plants and animals;
- to stop the class action so it can be focused on an important event for concept development;
- to overcome equipment shortages when there is not enough equipment for all children to benefit firsthand from the exercise;
- to arouse student interest, raise important questions, or pose learning problems that require critical and creative thinking;
- to help solve academic problems;
- to apply what has been studied to new situations by expanding experiences;
- to encourage slow learners and challenge rapid learners.

### When Should the Students Do a Demonstration?

Student demonstrations may also be helpful. Proper times for children to demonstrate for their peers include

- when the child has designed an original activity and should receive recognition for the effort;
- when a child's demonstration and explanation will help other students understand better;
- when a child cannot otherwise tell in words what has been done;
- to help children build self-confidence by speaking before others, to help build verbal communication skills, to help the rapid learner gain new insights.

Demonstrations inevitably open the door for questions. Along with questions come children who are intrinsically motivated and who want more information. These interaction-rich moments provide opportunities to guide students' knowledge construction.

## HOW CAN YOU USE EXPOSITION EFFECTIVELY?

Exposition, or lecture, is an efficient way to convey information. Although it may be time efficient, exposition is not necessarily effective when used with young children unless certain steps are taken that enable students to form conceptual constructions and connections. Exposition consists of verbal teaching by an authority such as a teacher, textbook, speaker, film, or video. Information is presented, usually without planned interaction between the authority and the student. Teacher lecture and textbook reading are the most common forms of exposition. The way to use exposition most effectively is rather simple: Plan for interaction to occur often between the authority and the student, and relate the interaction to student science experiences.

### Problems and Uses

Exposition carries several problems when used in elementary classrooms. Young children need concrete experiences during most of the elementary grades: verbal presentations of information are difficult for them to follow, and their attention span is limited; generally, the younger the child, the shorter the attention span. The logic of the adult mind may not match well with that of the younger mind, and textbook-ordered information has this same problem. Two other problems are related to exposition: Under the best circumstances the most capable learners only retain about half or less of what they hear, and what is said is not always what is heard or remembered.

Expository teaching does have several appropriate uses: to provide necessary background information before the lesson, to provide important instructions for an activity, to summarize, to bring a lesson to a close, and, most important, to make mental connections.

**Before the Lesson.**   The *advance organizer* is an effective verbal device to use before an expository method. According to David Ausubel (1963), its purpose is to provide a mental structure or framework for thinking before the lesson begins and the actual material is taught. Advance organizers "are broadly defined as bridges from the [learner's] previous knowledge to whatever is to be learned; they are supposed to be more abstract and inclusive than the more specific material to be learned, and to provide a means of organizing the new material" (Stone, 1982, p. 1). The lesson then may progress with a teacher presentation, reading, film, or video program; the students already know which important points they should attend to. Use of the advance organizer promotes more active mental participation during the presentation and has contributed to significantly

*What can you do before the lesson to help the children understand the concept?*

greater pupil learning and retention because presentations are made more meaningful to learners through conceptual connections (Stone, 1982).

There are two types of advance organizers. *Expository* organizers are used with unfamiliar material, often at the beginning of a unit or lesson. For example, a teacher may begin a lesson by saying: "Today we are going to begin a study of animal habitats with an activity. At the end of the activity you should be able to define 'habitat' by describing its parts and how they are related. A habitat consists of five main parts: food, water, shelter, space, and arrangement. Look for examples of these as we do the activity and then read about habitats in our textbooks."

*Comparative* organizers work well when the children are going to learn new material but already are familiar with the topic in other ways. Comparative organizers help to link new information with what is already known. A lesson with a comparative organizer may begin this way: "Doors and gates open and close. A switch is like a door or a gate. It opens and closes a circuit. When the switch is open the circuit is open and will *not* permit the electrical device to operate. When the switch is closed, the electricity can pass through the circuit and the devices connected to it *will* work. Today we are going to make switches and construct different types of circuits to see how they operate."

***To Provide Instructions or Give Directions.***   Exposition is always used when a teacher gives instructions to the class. Effective steps for giving directions include: read, review, and question. It is incorrect to assume that the children will read and follow the directions by themselves if given printed instructions. Instead, read the directions to them or invite a student to read to the class or for a cooperative group, and then review with the children what should be done first, second, and so on. Next, answer their questions. If the children have no questions, offer some of your own that they may think of later, and be prepared to review the answers again. All of this should be done *before* the children receive the materials to ensure safe, orderly completion of the learning activity.

*For Summary or Closure.*   Exposition can be a useful tool for review at the end of the lesson or the activity if modified from a teacher-centered approach into one that is more student centered. The teacher can review for the pupils the important points by linking them with specific experiences and by redefining or reexplaining. Ask review questions to encourage the children to construct the summary for themselves. These techniques can help the important concepts to be developed in the same order of the lesson and to be linked with what the children have experienced.

These three uses of expository teaching complement parts of a deductive teaching method. They may be used within a larger framework of deductive teaching and thinking for effective exposition.

### Using Deduction

Exposition often follows a deductive approach and is organized from the general idea of the lesson to the specific participation of the learners. Figure 2.2 shows a general deductive model, with four steps proceeding from the broad, general base to the specific learner experiences provided by the lesson. Simple enhancements can be added to make the teaching more interactive. Using a deductive approach, Ms. Ramirez (of our chapter scenario) proceeded along the following steps during a subsequent lesson.

#### Step 1. Give the generalization.

"Predators and prey are part of the life cycle of all living things. Our lesson today is about predators and prey."

#### Step 2. Clarify key terms.

"Pred-a-tor [written on the chalkboard and carefully pronounced for the class, and then with class participation in its spelling and pronunciation] refers to animals that hunt other animals for food. Prey [written, spelled, and pronounced] is the name given to the animals that are hunted and eaten by other animals."

#### Step 3. Give examples.

"Some examples include hawks that catch and eat mice, spiders that catch other insects in their webs, foxes that prey on a farmer's young chickens, and big fish, like a largemouth bass, that eat smaller fish." Textbook reading can also help to give examples.

**FIGURE 2.2    Deductive Science Teaching**    In deductive teaching, the lesson progresses from the general (a rule, concept, or formula) to the specific student experience (a learning activity, seat work, problem solving).

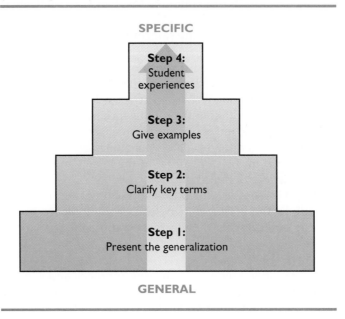

SPECIFIC

**Step 4:**
Student experiences

**Step 3:**
Give examples

**Step 2:**
Clarify key terms

**Step 1:**
Present the generalization

GENERAL

Step 4. Students gain experiences by working with and/or by giving specific examples.

"Here is a list of animal names. I'd like you to look at it and tell which are the predators and which are the prey: lion, skunk, insect, frog, human, cow, pig, deer, rabbit, fish, bear." After a while the children classify the animals into a predator and prey list, but with difficulty since some animals may be both predator and prey. The children also learn that a single predator may prey upon more than one type of animal and that humans are predators too, an idea that many students had not recognized but now think about as they eat and help parents shop.

"Now please add to our list of predators and prey." Ideas are obtained from the children until two long lists are constructed with a wide variety of animals represented. The teacher then groups the children, has them draw pictures of the animals, and adds them to a mural of an outdoor scene constructed during a previous lesson on habitat. Children then take string or yarn and use tape or thumbtacks to connect the predators with their prey, noting the multiple connections between several and the web of life that is a part of the life cycle of all living things. A discussion about what happens to predators when their preferred prey is not available could close the lesson, or the students could identify the relationships found in popular videos, such as Disney's *The Lion King*.

For expansion or for pupil evaluation, the children could write stories to describe or perform skits to demonstrate the relationship between predator and prey, including stalking and hiding habits. Students can also research what happens when predators hunt *not* to eat, such as poachers who prey on the rhino for its horn or on elephants for their ivory tusks. Their research can lead to position statements on ethics and any responsibility governments may have for regulation of commerce, export, or import. Research is also useful for comprehending the difference between preservation and conservation and possessing a better understanding of wildlife protection careers.

## Teaching Explicit Material

Science textbooks may introduce more new words or phrases than are introduced in first-year foreign language textbooks (Yager, 1983). This type of treatment assumes explicit material must be learned and that it is the teacher's job to present it so learners can master it. Exclusively treating science material in this fashion does a disservice to the learners and misrepresents the nature of science. However, there are occasions when a body of information or well-defined skills must be taught. Science facts, some concepts, selected laboratory skills,

*Explicit teaching requires teacher guidance.*

and science vocabulary may be taught effectively with explicit teaching methods. Barak Rosenshine (1986) identifies the actions of effective teachers when they teach facts, concepts, or skills explicitly:

1. Begin a lesson with a brief statement of goals.
2. Begin teaching with a brief review of the previous lesson in order to lay a foundation for the connections.
3. Present new material in small steps with practice after each step to make connections.
4. Give clear and detailed instructions and explanations.
5. Provide active practice for all children to strengthen connections.
6. Ask many questions to check for learner understanding; obtain responses from all children and correct misconceptions.
7. Guide children when they start to practice.
8. Provide systematic feedback for all children, and correct their mistakes.
9. Provide explicit instruction and practice for seatwork and monitor learner progress.
10. Continue practice until all children are independent and confident.

Rosenshine clusters the major parts of this method into several small steps, as shown in Table 2.1. He concedes that this approach does not apply to all students or for all teaching situations. Used with discretion, the method can support constructivist efforts.

The method is based on information processing research that recognizes the limits of human memory, the importance of practice, and the elements of task mastery. Learners can only attend to and process effectively small amounts of information at any one time. Abstract learners can process only seven unrelated items at a time without confusion; learners whose cognitive development has not reached that level (which includes most elementary children) can process even fewer than seven. Material must be processed (connected to what is understood) before it can be remembered and used. Active mental processing such as reviewing, summarizing, and rehearsing moves material into long-term memory. Teacher questions, student summaries, and active supervision assist this processing. Finally, if learning is to appear automatic through effortless recall, extensive practice and frequent review are necessary.

Interaction is a constructivist tool that can unite the methods presented in this chapter. Interaction can be used to make teacher-centered methods less authoritarian, less reliant on a textbook, and more effective by

- stimulating students' interests;
- more actively involving children in the lesson;
- promoting more thinking, information processing, and connection making;
- providing relevant learning experiences.

Teacher-centered methods work well with science textbooks. Aside from the teacher, the single most dominant factor in most elementary science programs

## TABLE 2.1    Explicit Teaching Functions

1. Teach for review.
   - Review homework.
   - Review previous learning important to the present lesson.
   - Review prerequisite skills and information needed for the present lesson.

2. Present the lesson.
   - State the lesson goals and/or outline the lesson.
   - Teach in small steps.
   - Model the skills and procedures children are to follow.
   - Provide concrete positive and negative examples to assist comprehension and connection making.
   - Use clear language.
   - Check for student understanding.
   - Avoid digressions or tangents.

3. Guide the practice.
   - Use many questions to help guide practice, to clarify, and to overcome misconceptions.
   - Ensure that all students respond and receive feedback about their learning.
   - Strive for a high success rate; optimal is 75–80 percent correct answers during guided practice.
   - Continue guided practice until all students are competent.

4. Make corrections and give feedback.
   - Give process feedback when children are correct but hesitant.
   - When children are incorrect, give them clues or encouragement.
   - Reteach when necessary.

5. Provide for independent practice.
   - Actively supervise to give children help.
   - Continue practice until students can respond automatically (when this applies).
   - Use routines to help slower pupils; this may include peers helping peers.

6. Use weekly and monthly reviews to strengthen learning and to form multiple connections.
   - Select a special day to review the previous week's concepts.
   - Use a TV show format.
   - Involve children in constructing questions.
   - Develop a special monthly format and promote it like a coming big event on television.

*Source:* Adapted from B. V. Rosenshine, "Synthesis of Research on Explicit Teaching," *Educational Leadership* (April 1986): 65.

may be a textbook. Selection of an appropriate textbook and effective use of it can improve your students' achievement, skills, attitudes, and help you encourage learners to make progress toward the national standards.

## HOW CAN YOU USE SCIENCE TEXTBOOKS EFFECTIVELY?

Reams of research reports support the superiority of activity-based science programs and teaching methods (Meyer, Greer, & Crummey, 1986). Unfortunately, "what was intended to be joyful discovery for students too often turned out to be a lost sojourn into the abstract and difficult" (Mechling & Oliver, 1983a, p. 43) because teachers returned to textbooks even though textbooks continue to be criticized for their shortcomings.

### Be Aware of Shortcomings and Differences

Although authors and publishers have made dramatic improvements over recent years, science textbooks vary considerably on such factors as readability, reading and study aids, treatment of race and gender, and emphasis given to vocabulary versus concepts. Readability studies show greater levels of difference mostly for the upper elementary and the middle grades. Students' science achievements decline when they use textbooks written above their reading ability levels. Reading and study aids, such as chapter headings, help pupils comprehend and recall, particularly when children are taught to use these features. Gender bias has been reduced recently, with more balance now seen toward male and female representation. However, persons who have disabilities and nonwhites often do not receive substantial recognition in textbooks. Science vocabulary is emphasized much more than science concepts, although researchers report that emphasis on concepts rather than vocabulary results in *increased* science achievement (Meyer, Greer, & Crummey, 1986). In contrast to this finding, Paul D. Hurd (1982) has found science texts often introduce "as many as 2,500 technical terms and unfamiliar words" (p. 12). He notes that a beginning foreign language course attempts to cover only half as many new words.

Who decides what material science textbooks will include and how they will be organized? Recommendations from credible sources such as the National Research Council, the National Science Teachers Association, or the American Association for the Advancement of Science do not always drive the development or revision of printed materials like school textbooks. Authors, teachers, editors, marketing staffs in publishing houses, boards of education, and textbook censors have less influence than you may imagine. A single large state that adopts one or two science textbook series for use by all schools, carries a tremendous influence because of its large market. What one large state wants in a textbook, it usually receives, and therefore it can influence what the books contain for the rest of the country. Approaches and material that appear radical or unconventional stand little chance despite their academic merits, origin, or proven effects.

*Student activities can enhance the use of a textbook.*

If it seems unlikely that textbooks will be dramatically improved, what options do you have? You *do* have a choice of programs. The choice you make will influence the amount of teacher direction you use to guide your students and the extent of the positive impact on their interactive learning experience. You can

- enhance the textbook in use,
- change the sequence of topics to reflect better the concepts to be learned,
- select the textbook that most closely represents the needs of your students and fulfills the recommendations for effective science teaching and learning.

### Enhancing the Textbook

Each teacher can enhance the textbook to include more effective learning activities and interesting information, rather than wait for authors and publishers to do it. You can add enhancements that are timely and that match learner interests and abilities. There are some other ways you can use textbooks to foster constructivism. You can

**1.** Combine the best elements from published programs. Use old editions or the most interesting materials from unadopted examination copies of textbooks.

Cut out pictures, information, and activities to make mini-books or a resource file by topic.

**2.** Select relevant supplements from laboratory programs and web-based materials. Experimental programs may have been used by your school in the past and then discarded. Remnants may be found stored away. Conduct an inventory of equipment and teaching materials from the past, and select useful materials relevant to the concepts you are teaching.

**3.** Identify local resources. School and community professionals, local businesses, parks and recreation facilities, libraries, and museums all provide rich resources for classroom speakers and field trips. These enhancement resources also help to demonstrate the relationship of science and everyday life as well as update or fill in gaps not covered by dated textbooks. (See Chapter 8 for more ideas.)

**4.** Check with your state's department of education. Some states compare commercial materials and keep on file survey-style coverage of important science findings and laboratory programs that make fine enhancements for standard textbook programs.

**5.** Screen supplementary materials for the appropriate reading level. Deemphasize use of a textbook written on a reading level too high by substituting suitable materials. Use accelerated material if the writing is too simple.

**6.** Select evaluation devices that reflect the preferred outcomes. If your desire is development of a particular process skill, select performance-based evaluation tasks that require the children to demonstrate the skill. Carefully screen all textbook questions and written exercises and select those that match the intended level of thinking and skills. Adapt project ideas and improve the types of questions used in the textbook or teacher's guide.

**7.** Work to organize building- or district-level committees in which teachers form supplement teams. More hands make lighter work, and more heads generate a greater number of effective ideas. Teams of teachers can share the research and swap ideas.

**8.** Attend professional conferences. States have affiliates of the National Science Teachers Association, and large cities have their own science education organizations. Attend their annual conferences and listen to other teachers to get ideas for your own classroom. Adapt these ideas to your science program. Remember, your ideas are just as important as those of others. Why not make your own presentation at a conference or provide a workshop for other teachers?

**9.** Relearn the concepts and processes of science. Take workshops or courses to learn about the most recent ideas in science and its teaching. This continues your education and professional development; both can help you enhance the science textbook. Request a staff development program for yourself and for helping the other school staff members relearn and elevate their own levels of scientific literacy. Other teachers will be more likely to enhance the textbook if they feel more confident and informed.

**WHAT** RESEARCH **SAYS**

## How Are Scientists Portrayed in Children's Literature?

Allen Evans, assistant professor and fifth-grade teacher at the Ackerman Lab School at Eastern Oregon State College in La Grande, investigated popular children's literature to uncover the ways scientists are portrayed to children. His research was stimulated by his students' stereotypical images of scientists. Children's literature is rapidly replacing a single text in classrooms where whole language approaches and tradebooks are favored. Therefore, it is important to expand our concerns about textbooks to the collection of literature used with children. We use many of Evans's words to report what he found.

Elementary classroom teachers have long been aware that books influence children's perceptions of the world. Characters found in children's books provide inspiration, consolation, and motivation. They entertain, inform, and encourage, and they can provide positive examples for overcoming adversity.

Sadly, however, not all characters in children's books present accurate depictions of their real-life counterparts, and teachers must be vigilant in looking out for stereotypes in order to make informed and appropriate choices of instructional materials.

With recent trends of "reading-across-the-curriculum," classroom teachers, and science teachers in particular, need to know how scientists are portrayed in children's books. Is the image of the scientist an accurate one? Or, do children's books reinforce the absentminded, bubbling-pot, blow-up-the-laboratory stereotype? Furthermore, as teachers encourage their students to consider careers in science, knowledge of the scientists in children's books becomes more important. If children's books do in fact depict scientists in stereotypical ways, children may be less likely to view science as a desirable career choice. To answer these questions, I decided to investigate the portrayal of scientists and science-oriented characters in seventeen selected children's fiction books.

The selection criteria resulted in books that had either a science-oriented plot or at least one science-oriented character, were written for upper elementary or middle school children, had been published within the last twenty years (the majority were published during the last ten), were realistic fiction or science-fiction books, and had been cited and reviewed in at least one major professional journal devoted to children's literature.

Twenty-five science-oriented characters were found, and 88 percent were male. Eleven of the seventeen books were written by females. Sixty percent of the science-oriented characters were adults, 20 percent were teenagers, and 20 percent were children. Science teachers, professors, and laboratory researchers represented 52 percent of the characters; 20 percent had a personal interest in science, perhaps as a hobby; 4 percent were involved in school science activities; the rest had an unclear orientation toward science. Evans's report sums up the portrait of a scientist in children's literature this way:

Scientists are adult males whose orientation is due to a professional relationship. They are generally ordinary in their actions and mannerisms, as well as ordinary in their physical appearance, and are of above-average intelligence. For concerned science teachers, the news is good—the image of the scientists appearing in these books is one that is reasonably free of the typical stereotypes.

There does, however, appear to be room for improvement. While it is true that the sciences are currently a white-male-dominated field, more and more women and minorities are pursuing science as a viable career option. Therefore, the inclusion of female and minority science-oriented characters in children's books must be encouraged.

Science teachers in particular should benefit from an increased awareness of how scientists and science-oriented characters are portrayed in children's books. With that understanding, teachers can work more closely with other nonscience professionals, such as reading teachers and librarians, in identifying and selecting children's books depicting scientists in positive, nonstereotypical roles.

*Source:* A. Evans, "A Look at the Scientists Portrayed in Children's Literature," *Science and Children* (March, 1992): 35–37.

*Changing the Sequence*

The textbook's chapter order and the organization of the information within chapters may not be what is best for your students. Perhaps some simple re-sequencing will bring improvements in science achievement, attitudes, and interest and help you to help learners make clearer and stronger conceptual connections.

Cognitive scientists emphasize the importance of anchoring ideas to the learner's mental structure. New information becomes more meaningful when it can be attached to concepts already in the children's minds. Science material is better understood when it interrelates "in such a way as to make sense to the learner" (Hamrick & Harty, 1987, p. 16). Resequencing material so ideas relate in ways that make more sense to the children adds meaning. In a study of sixth graders,

> the findings revealed that students for whom content structure was clarified through resequencing general science chapters exhibited significantly higher science achievement, significantly more positive attitudes toward science, and significantly greater interest in science than students for whom general science content was not resequenced. (Hamrick & Harty, 1987, p. 15)

Concept mapping is a method of sequencing the ideas of a lesson, and a version of it can be used to sequence the text effectively. A concept map shows ideas graphically according to their relationships. (See Chapter 7 for more information.) The relationships communicate important connections that show an intended mental structure to be formed about the map's topic. Consider the following when resequencing:

**1.** Proceed from the smallest to the largest ideas, or from the simple to the complex, when resequencing a text. Researchers recommend that rearrangements first be made into an interrelated pattern based on the size of the ideas (Hamrick & Harty, 1987). A hierarchy of ideas is formed; perhaps physical science leads to life science topics, which progress to earth and space science concepts. See Table 2.2 for an example of a typical textbook sequence of topics with a revised sequence. You can determine the children's hierarchical views of the material by doing a webbing exercise in which they refer to the table of contents or chapter titles of the text and connect them in a web that makes sense to them. Begin at the chalkboard with a single word such as *science* and have the children refer to the ideas in the chapter titles and sections within chapters to add the ideas of science to the chalkboard. Engage the children in a discussion of how they see these ideas of science connected; ask for their reasons. Your prompts can help them to order material from the simple to the more complex in a way that is more understandable. At the same time, you will be reinforcing higher levels of thinking.

**2.** Convey the interrelated structure to the students. An overview of the re-structured material can be made on a student handout, placed in a notebook, and used for clarification, reinforcement, and review throughout the year. Children can check off the major concepts as they are studied. This serves as a struc-

**TABLE 2.2    A Sample Comparison of Unrevised and Revised Textbook Content Sequence**

| Textbook Sequence | Revised Content Sequence |
|---|---|
| Animals with backbones | Matter (elements and compounds) |
| Classifying animals without backbones | Sources of energy |
| Plants | Light |
| Life cycles | Electricity and magnetism |
| Matter (elements and compounds) | Communications |
| Electricity and magnetism | Energy outcomes and the future |
| Sources of energy | Energy for living things |
| Light | Plants |
| Communications | Life cycles |
| Climates of the world | Classifying animals without backbones |
| Energy for living things | Animal with backbones |
| Energy outcomes and the future | Climates of the world |

*Source:* L. Hamrick and H. Harty, "Influence of Resequencing General Science Content on the Science Achievement, Attitudes Toward Science, and Interests in Science of Sixth Grade Students," *Journal of Research in Science Teaching* 24(1) (1987): 20.

ture of information for learners, gives you an opportunity to teach for concepts, and provides a ready guide for reinforcement. Figure 2.3 shows an example of a student handout with text overview.

**3.** Help learners to clarify the content structure. They will not absorb all the ideas of the resequencing overview at once. Take advantage of any opportunity to discuss the structure of the material you have chosen for your class. Help learners to paint the big picture and to see how the smaller ideas fit into a pattern with the larger ideas.

### Selecting the Best Textbook

Teachers are becoming more selective, and it may be that their efforts to identify the best textbooks are having effects on changes. Textbooks are often selected because they offer many activities, worksheets, tests, and programmed teacher's guides. They appear busy or glitzy and may require little more than reading and writing exercises. Such textbooks may fall short of meeting recommendations for effective science instruction and do not support inquiry-based, constructivist learning. What can you do to select a better textbook or to use the one you have in ways that improve the experience for students? As a starting point for screening textbooks, ask yourself:

- What does the textbook expect my students to do?
- What should my students be able to do after they study the textbook that they could not do before?

**FIGURE 2.3    A Sample Student Overview of Resequenced Material with Chapter Numbers**

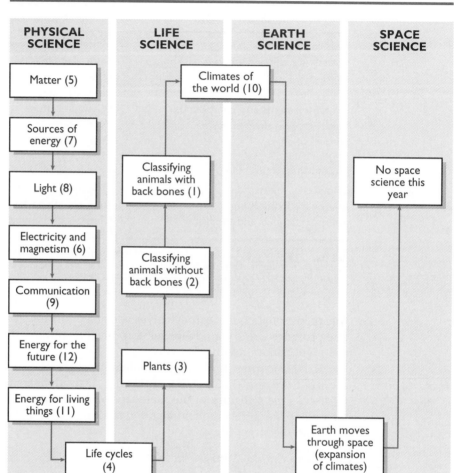

*Source:* Linda Hamrick and Harold Harty, "Influence of Resequencing General Science Content on the Science Achievement, Attitudes Toward Science, and Interest in Science of Sixth Grade Students," *Journal of Research in Science Teaching* 24, no. 1 (1987), p. 19.

- For every student activity, project, or question, ask, "What kind of thinking is required?" "How does this address the National Standards?"
- Examine the textbooks for inclusion of the science content standards (Chapter 6) and ask, "To what extent is each new dimension emphasized?" and "How is it included in the textbook?"

- Consider the goals of Project 2061 or the National Science Education Standards (Chapter 6), especially conceptual science content emphasis, and ask, "How well do the textbook's concepts represent those recommendations?"
- Summarize your initial screening by asking, "Will this textbook really help my students reach the goals I have set for them—or is it going to waste their time?"

Look again at those textbooks that pass your initial screening. Now is the time to be more critical. An effective textbook should involve children in the processes of science by guiding them toward making discoveries. How does the textbook help students to experience the history and nature of science? The activities should not be cookbook recipes that encourage learners to follow the steps mindlessly. Focus on the student activities, sample several from each book, and ask these questions:

- Are students required to make careful observations?
- Are students encouraged to make inferences?

*The best science textbook will challenge children to improve their thinking.*

- Is classification a skill used in the experiments?
- How often are students asked to make a prediction based on observation or data?
- How often are students encouraged to display data in a systematic way that will enhance their ability to communicate?

These questions will help you select a textbook that delivers a strong blend of expository information and productive interaction through sound activity-based learning. Table 2.3 provides a brief instrument for screening textbooks and printed curriculum materials. All the information in this section of the

## TABLE 2.3   Screening Texts and Other Printed Curriculum Materials

You can learn about the science program by examining the textbooks and other written curriculum materials available.

| | Yes | No | ? |
|---|---|---|---|
| ***Science Content*** | | | |
| 1. Is there a balanced emphasis among the life sciences, earth sciences, and physical sciences? | ___ | ___ | ___ |
| 2. Do the materials include study of problems that are important to us now and in the future? Examples: acid rain, air and water pollution, technology's impact, energy production and availability, medical research, world hunger, population, deforestation, ozone depletion. | ___ | ___ | ___ |
| 3. Do materials require students to apply major science concepts to everyday life situations? | ___ | ___ | ___ |
| 4. Are the materials accurate? | ___ | ___ | ___ |
| 5. Do the materials encourage an in-depth examination of concepts and issues? | ___ | ___ | ___ |
| 6. Other | ___ | ___ | ___ |
| ***Science Processes*** | | | |
| 1. Do the materials include liberal amounts of hands-on investigations and activities that the children can do in order to experience the nature of science? | ___ | ___ | ___ |
| 2. Is scientific inquiry an important part of the materials the children will read? Examples: observing, measuring, predicting, inferring, classifying, recording and analyzing data, etc. | ___ | ___ | ___ |
| 3. Do the materials encourage children to explore, discover, and construct answers for themselves rather than tell them how things should turn out? | ___ | ___ | ___ |
| 4. Do the materials require children to use scientific reasoning, to apply science processes to problem-solving situations, and to construct conclusions? | ___ | ___ | ___ |
| 5. To what extent do the materials help learners to build thinking skills? | ___ | ___ | ___ |
| 6. Other: | ___ | ___ | ___ |

*Source:* Originally adapted from Kenneth R. Mechling and Donna L. Oliver, *Characteristics of a Good Elementary Science Program* (Washington, DC: National Science Teachers Association, 1983) and updated by the authors of this text to reflect contemporary expectations and the *National Science Education Standards* (NRC, 1996).

chapter can be developed into your own customized form for rating and selecting textbooks or other printed curriculum materials.

We cannot force students to learn. We can help them make discoveries and form connections for themselves, and our guidance is an important factor. Go slowly and guide with purpose. Avoid merely covering information without ensuring student understanding. Strive for quality rather than quantity. Remember the maxim: Less is more. Listen to students more and talk less. Try to emphasize student cooperation instead of competition. Blend learning activities to include discovery opportunities, group work, and learning that requires different types of information processing—thinking. Try to concentrate on

|  | Yes | No | ? |
|---|---|---|---|

*Other Considerations*

1. Are the materials consistent with the science goals of your school? (Or, in the absence of such goals, those of the National Science Education Standards or your state framework of science goals.) ___ ___ ___

2. Are the materials well designed, clearly written, accurate, up to date, and easy to use? ___ ___ ___

3. Do the materials proceed from the simple to the complex and are they designed for the children's appropriate developmental levels? ___ ___ ___

4. Is the information written at the proper grade level? ___ ___ ___

5. Do the materials for children appear interesting and relevant to their levels? ___ ___ ___

6. Are there opportunities for children to learn about the history and nature of science and science-related careers? ___ ___ ___

7. Are valid evaluation materials used or included? Examples: performance demonstrations, pictorial assessment. ___ ___ ___

8. Is a teacher's guide included and is it helpful for using the materials? ___ ___ ___

9. Do the materials include enough application of science content and processes to make science meaningful to students? ___ ___ ___

10. Is technology included and do children have to use appropriate forms of technology to access or process the science material? ___ ___ ___

11. Are different cultures, races, genders, social groups, ages included with respect and equity? ___ ___ ___

12. Do the materials promote teaching methods that promote an effective, interactive learning environment? ___ ___ ___

13. Other: ___ ___ ___

students doing right thinking rather than getting right answers. If you must use a textbook and teacher-centered approaches, incorporate several of the suggestions offered in this chapter to make your classroom more interactive. Chances for effective teaching will be greater through your efforts, and your reward will be improved student achievement, positive attitudes toward science, and greater interest in school through more student-centered, constructivist teaching practices.

### Using Trade Books

Trade books use children's literature as another way to bring content-focused science material to class. The trade book is not a substitute for skills-directed instruction in reading or for teaching science concepts, but is a vehicle that can be used to introduce concepts or to complement a lesson that has been taught. Science trade books usually offer an applied setting for learning or reinforcing material. Trade books may include biographies of scientists; reference books on particular types of animals, plants, or environmental issues; natural science concepts; or specifically focused single publications on physical science topics, science theories, or natural causes, such as volcanoes and tornadoes. Trade books may contain fictional characters, but illustrate specific science concepts. The annual March issue of *Science and Children,* published by the National

*Trade books for children help to expand conceptualization and to support habits of scientific literacy.*

Science Teachers Association, lists the most outstanding science trade books for children. Those books selected to make the list pass scrutiny for having substantial science content; clarity, accuracy and timeliness of information; presentation of significant concepts; and freedom from gender, ethnic and socio-economic bias (Madrazo, 1997, p. 20).

## CHAPTER SUMMARY

Some studies suggest that about 90 percent of science classrooms use a single textbook the majority of the time for instruction. The teaching methods used are often teacher centered and authoritarian, even though considerable evidence reveals the limits of these approaches and more effective methods are available. Teacher-centered methods can be made more effective by using interactive techniques that enhance the children's learning experiences and help meet the goals of an effective science education.

The interactive techniques described in this chapter include demonstrations, exposition, deductive teaching, explicit teaching, and uses of science textbooks and trade books. Used with care, these techniques can support constructivist learning. Exposition includes use of advance organizers, giving directions, and summary techniques for lessons. Deductive teaching organizes lessons from science generalizations to specific learner experiences. Explicit teaching is a technique of interactive lecture, student recitation, feedback, misconception correction, and practice. It is based on the effective teaching research.

The quality and features of textbooks may vary considerably, although important improvements have been made recently. The last section of this chapter acquaints readers with the shortcomings and differences of textbooks. Positive actions teachers can take to use textbooks more effectively include enhancing the text, changing the instructional sequence of textbook topics, mapping the chapter concepts, and exercising discretion when selecting a textbook.

## DISCUSSION QUESTIONS

**1.** Why do most teachers revert to teacher-centered methods and authoritarian treatment of science through extensive use of the textbook even though they may know about more effective alternatives?

**2.** What can be done to motivate teachers to use more interactive teaching methods with young children?

**3.** How does the planning that teachers must do to use the methods recommended in this chapter compare with the constructivist methods described in Chapter 9?

**4.** What characteristics do you think a science textbook must have in order to address *all* of the National Science Education Standards?

**5.** Why do you think something as simple as resequencing the topics of a textbook is related to increased student science achievement?

**6.** What signs indicate that a textbook should be considered or avoided?

**7.** How can teachers evaluate process skills and higher thinking? To what extent are these promoted by teacher-centered methods and textbooks?

**8.** How can reading enhancements (such as bold print for special words) found in textbooks interfere with the goals of science education? Do you believe the goals for scientific literacy run counter to the goals of general literacy? Why?

## BUILD A PORTFOLIO

**1.** Plan a lesson (or a unit) using an advance organizer, demonstration, and techniques of deductive and/or explicit teaching with a textbook. Teach the lesson and have it recorded (video preferred). Compare your skills with the ideal requirements for each method described in this chapter. How do your skills compare? What can you do to become more effective? Which methods made it possible for you to be more interactive with the children?

**2.** Examine a school's science program for inclusion of the methods of effective teacher-centered teaching. To what extent is each method encouraged? Write a summary and offer recommendations for improving the program.

**3.** Analyze several science textbooks written for the same grade level. What are their advantages and shortcomings? Which textbook do you prefer? Why? What is needed to overcome the shortcomings of your choice?

**4.** Analyze your preferred science textbook (or textbooks from different publishers) across grade levels. Use the criteria for selecting the best textbook given in this chapter. Which textbook series do you prefer, and why?

**5.** Examine a school district's course of study, and compare it with the actual science program or textbook used. Which was done first, the writing of the course of study or the selection of the science program? To what extent does the course of study reflect the organization of the program or textbook? Compare your findings with those of your classmates. What do you conclude about the extent to which a program relates to a course of study?

**6.** Use the ideas provided in this chapter to develop your own form for science textbook and curriculum materials analysis. What are the main categories you feel must be included to yield a useful form? Try your form and ask others to try it. What revisions may be necessary and why?

**7.** Write to your state's department of education and ask what information it provides to help teachers and school districts improve science programs. Does your state have recommended programs or textbooks? If yes, determine how they were selected for recommendation. If no, determine why your state takes no position and what services it does provide to teachers and schools seeking assistance.

**8.** Select a textbook, read one of its chapters, and record the science words emphasized in the titles, headings, and bold or italicized print. Develop a strategy for mapping the concepts of these words and for helping students understand the connections between and among the concepts.

## PART II

# The Explanation

## Modern Science Teaching Benefits from Inquiry-Based, Interactive Approaches to Learning

Exploring science teaching likely helped you to raise several important questions. The purpose of the learning cycle's Explanation phase is to help you to use your experiences in order to construct understanding: to make meaning from your ideas and experiences. The chapters of Part II help you to

- comprehend the meaning and possibilities of science,
- understand and use perspectives on learning and brain research for designing high-impact lessons for children,
- conceptualize the differences among learners and to celebrate diversity in your classroom,
- see the big picture painted on the canvas of scientific literacy and comprehend the specific national teaching goals that nurture literacy.

The details of Chapters 3–6 will help you to construct the following story line:

### Story Line

Science is a human enterprise and must be fully experienced if students are to understand it. Inquiry is consistent with the natural processes of children's learning. The interactive methods of science match well with the needs and learning style preferences of all children. Children bring to the classroom many differences, limitations, and potentials. The goals of modern science include discipline-based content that should be linked with real-world experiences. A well-prepared teacher will address the goals of modern science in order to meet the children's needs.

### Concepts

*Chapter 3:* Children are naturally interested in science and benefit from acquiring the essential attitudes, processes, and knowledge of it. When learned holistically, science helps to prepare children to learn well in other school subject and skill areas, such as reading.

*Chapter 4:* Children are biologically driven to reason explanations from their experiences. This construction of understanding fills many needs, including the development of self-esteem, social skills, and problem-solving skills. The emerging science of brain research helps us to understand children's needs and limitations and offers specific insight for achieving best practice.

*Chapter 5:* Each child's uniqueness enriches the classroom. Science is a medium for helping to fulfill children's unique needs, such as development of language, overcoming stereotypes, disabilities, and gifted and talented potential.

*Chapter 6:* The National Science Education Standards and the goals of hallmark science reform projects advocate specific goals for attaining scientific literacy. It is important that all children learn essential concepts in the life, earth/space and physical sciences, as well as learn and develop skills that will help them to sustain inquiry, understand the interrelationships between science and technology, understand the history and nature of science, and understand and appreciate the role of science in our personal lives.

## CHAPTER OUTLINE

# CHAPTER 3

# What Is Science?

$O$ne of Jessica's first assignments was to observe at least two different grade levels of children. Her science methods course was designed to immerse Jessica into teaching and to use her direct experiences as a platform for constructing the main concepts of the course. Jessica had selected Dawn in the prekindergarten class and Jorgé in the fourth-grade class. She decided to shadow the two students and to record her observations about the types of things the children did while learning science. She also had discussions with the children and used her field notes to write a summary for her methods course portfolio. Here is her account:

"Today Dawn played with a small plastic boat at the water table. I observed her push the boat down into the water until it filled and sank. Dawn did this several times and then the teacher suggested that Dawn try some experiments with marbles and wooden buttons of a uniform size. Dawn spent about five minutes putting the marbles and buttons into the water watching the marbles sink immediately and the buttons float. She pushed the buttons down into the water and released them, noting that they floated to the surface each time. I suggested she put the objects into the boat to see what would happen. Dawn put six buttons and six marbles into the boat and the boat slowly began to take on water until it sank to the bottom with the buttons floating to the surface.

Dawn persisted by piling six marbles into the dry boat. The boat began to take on water and Dawn quickly added the buttons. The marbles went down with the boat and the buttons floated to the top. 'Pop!' exclaimed Dawn for each button that jetted to the surface: 'Pop! Pop! Pop! Pop! Pop!' Dawn continued to investigate the boat's sinking and floating with different numbers of marbles and buttons, and she returned to the water table after snack time to try different objects in the boat."

"Jorgé had missed some school because of illness and the teacher asked me to 'tutor' him in electricity so he could catch up with the rest of the class. I could feel my heart race because I knew nothing about electricity, but had observed earlier classes, so I gave it a try. Jorgé did remember the concept of 'circuit' from a prior class, but today's challenge was to use a variety of materials to construct a flashlight: a cardboard tube, a bottle cap, metal paper fasteners, a metal paper clip, batteries, a couple of short wires, and a flashlight bulb. Jorgé had to construct the flashlight using these materials and what he knew about circuits and demonstrate that it worked at least one time. Jorgé seemed pretty happy and dived right in, but I felt the pressure. To me, it seemed as if the minutes turned into hours and I wondered if 'we' would succeed. By now the task became 'our' project because Jorgé was teaching me about conductors, insulators, and a series circuit. Jorgé needed help fixing the bulb in place and was a little frustrated because the parts kept slipping and loosening connections. Finally, when all was hooked up, Jorgé turned the paper clip switch and the bulb lit. 'You did it!' I shouted, attracting the attention of the whole class, and I immediately turned scarlet. I couldn't help myself. The shouting just came as a natural release for me and a nice reinforcement for Jorgé. He beamed a smile. The teacher didn't frown or scold us as I expected. Instead, she gave me a wink and a nod as if that kind of stuff happened all the time in her class."

"Before this early field experience, I really dreaded having to take this teaching of science course. I am sorry to write that science was not one of my favorite subjects, but I think I can already see that it is important and the children seem to like it, and I am not writing this to gain your favor. I am wondering, though, what kind of difference can I make? I don't feel confident or competent in science. What kinds of things should I do or teach in order to help children have a better impression of science than I had before I started this course?"                 ◆

## INTRODUCTION

Jessica's prior experience in science (or lack of experience) influenced her perspective, attitude, and self-confidence. Our perceptions, attitudes, and confidence influence our teaching decisions and what we choose to expect from our students. Our expectations also influence how students will perform. Jessica's two questions are very fair. What kind of difference can one teacher make in a science program? What things should be emphasized in science classes?

From Jessica's notes we can get the impression that the teachers in Dawn and Jorgé's classes made a difference, because each child in her or his own way demonstrated interest and persisted with the task. Four-year-old Dawn explored the concepts of floating and sinking—at her own pace—and she demonstrated several important skills such as observing, comparing, and investigating. These early skills helped her to form rudimentary conceptions of cause and effect as she began to accumulate some factual knowledge through play. Curiosity drove her to experiment on her own developmental level, which was not systematic in our adult eyes. However, with repeated encouragement and appropriate teacher intervention Dawn learned to use several scientific processes, such as observing, comparing, classifying, using numbers, etc. (Van Horn et al., 1993). In Jorgé's case, he appeared more systematic, had a firmer grasp on cause-and-effect relationships, and had a repertoire of scientific attitudes to help him persist with thorny problems. Most likely Jorgé acquired and developed his attitudes and skills from an early science program and teachers who had a clear vision of what students should know and be able to do in science. Both children benefited from teacher expectations and programs that were built upon a strong foundation of science teaching. In this chapter we help you to develop a similar foundation by introducing you to

1. Children's perceptions of science and scientists, as well as their science achievement
2. The nature of science
3. The essential aspects of a holistic science experience and the importance of hands-on, minds-on, inquiry-based science experiences
4. The aims of modern science education

## HOW DO CHILDREN PERCEIVE SCIENCE?

Jessica's professor assigned her to interview children in the next school on her field experience rotation. She was to find out what they thought about science and scientists. Jessica's professor suggested that the insights she gained would help her understand the readiness and needs of the children and prepare her for the challenges that lay ahead.

### Science Is . . .

Jessica obtained permission to interview children of different ages. She used this question: "What is science?" Some children simply shrugged off the question or chose to talk about something else. Jessica presumed that was because they were unfamiliar with "real" science since she observed that little time seemed to be devoted to it. She reported to her professor a sample of her findings*:

> "Real hard. Harder than reading. We aren't allowed to have it in kindergarten." (Antonio—kindergarten)

> "The weatherman. He gets to choose the weather each day and he gets to color on the wall." (Mary Beth—kindergarten)

*These replies are direct quotations from a sample of children (distributed across race and socioeconomic status) in urban and suburban settings when asked the question, "What is science?" (Wagner, K., 1988) and from children interviewed by the authors' preservice teachers.

"It (science) is what brainy people who know a lot do." (first grader)

"After lunch sometimes when there is nothing else to do." (Shawna—grade 1)

"I don't think we have science yet. I'm not a good reader." (Jeremy—grade 1)

"Mostly rocks and leaves. We put them on a table." (Lyn—grade 1)

"Computers and moving things with buttons you push. Also, anything with batteries or that plugs in. Rockets are my favorite part of science." (Carl—grade 1)

"When you smoke cigarettes and get cancer it is because of science." (Nancy—grade 1)

"Children can't be scientists until they are older." (first grader)

"On TV sometimes. *NOVA* is my favorite." (Alex—grade 2)

"When you go up in the space shuttle and you are an astronaut. Girls can be astronauts too, you know. I'm going to be in science when I grow up. The only thing is—I don't know if I will have enough money to buy a space shuttle. You have to be rich to be an astronaut." (Andrea—grade 3)

"The opposite of social studies." (Luanne—grade 3)

"Children can be scientists, and *really* good ones, too!" (third grader)

"We just read a book. I think you get it (science) in junior high. My brother is in junior high, and he has science." (William—grade 3)

"The same old stuff. I've seen the same filmstrip on erosion three years in a row." (Joshua—grade 4)

"It depends on what grade you're in and who your teacher is. If a teacher doesn't like science, then you don't get it very much. Once when the principal was coming Mrs. ——— did this experiment with a tin can and a candle and a balloon—but that was the only time." (Greg—grade 5)

"Supposed to be about learning how we learn about the world and how to use the scientific method in thinking. I know because my dad is a scientist and he keeps asking me when we're going to learn that in science. I just tell him that we haven't gotten to it yet." (Doreen—grade 6)

Jessica pored over the messages and wrote a summary to report back to her methods class. Jessica was not certain how much she could generalize from the interviews, but nevertheless the children seemed to describe science as something that usually was not given much time in the primary grades, but rather was reserved for the more advanced grades, at least when the children could read well. Children also seemed to have several misconceptions about what science is and isn't; for example, one child opined that science is responsible for causing disease or illness. Overall, the children seemed not to value science much or perceive it as useful. Some thought it was repetitive or something to be watched, and implied that teachers used it as a time filler when nothing else more important was waiting to be done; or perhaps the teachers might not have felt comfortable or prepared to teach it adequately. On the positive side, Jessica noted that some children viewed science as a career opportunity for women, though access to science careers was believed to be limited, and that some parents expected the science curriculum to help the children develop important cognitive skills.

*Scientists Are . . .*

When Jessica's professor urged her to probe a bit more into the values and stereotypes that children might reveal, Jessica decided to try the Draw-A-Scientist Test (Barman, 1996), which she had read about in several articles used in her classes. This test was simple; it required only that Jessica ask students to draw a picture of a scientist without prompting the students to do the drawing in any particular way. Judging that her earlier interview question could be considered a prompt, Jessica selected a new sample of students and hoped to get a fresh, unbiased perception. She collected dozens of drawings and compared them to find similarities. Then she selected two to put into her science methods class portfolio.

The first drawing (Figure 3.1 on page 82) illustrated a composite and was a rather common perception that most of the drawings seemed to share. She then wrote in her summary, "Scientists are middle-aged white males who wear lab coats and glasses. Their peculiar facial features are indicative of their generally deranged behavior. They work indoors, alone, perhaps underground, surrounded by smoking test tubes and other pieces of technology. An air of secrecy and danger surrounds their work" (Flick, 1989, p. 8; Barman and Ostlund, 1996).

Jessica based her summary on the fact that most of the scientists were depicted as white males (Barman, 1997). Overall, only about 8 percent of the scientists were drawn as female—close to the reality of the 6 percent women in the engineering and scientific workforce (Kahle, 1983). Only 1 percent of the students drew minority scientists, mostly African Americans; in reality, Asians "make up 5 percent of the scientists and engineers (in comparison to 2 percent of the population)" (Fort & Varney, 1989, p. 9). When they drew the scientists, the children reached back into their own experiences. Some drew the scientist by race and gender as a self-image; some took their images from television and movies; some were honoring a significant person who had affected them; and, of course, some knew only the general stereotype that is perceived to fit the look of most scientists (Sumrall, 1995). However, only a small number were drawn as fictional characters (Barman, 1997).

Jessica was now curious about why the children held these particular attitudes and beliefs about science and scientists and how the children's perceptions might reflect the beliefs of others, such as teachers. As she reflected on her findings, she decided to try to see a snapshot of the field of science teaching. Given all of the research and attention placed on improving science programs and teaching over the past several years, Jessica was motivated to ask . . .

◆**FIGURE 3.1   Children's Perception of a Scientist**

## WHAT IS THE STATUS OF ELEMENTARY SCIENCE?

For more than twenty-five years the National Assessment of Educational Progress (NAEP) has been the only continuing assessment of U.S. children's achievement in grades K–12. This test has been mandated by the U.S. Congress and has attempted to measure what students know and can do against widely agreed on expectations in science and other subject areas. NAEP scores have shown the levels of student performance: (1) *Basic*—denoting partial mastery of knowledge and skills that are fundamental for performing proficient work at each grade; (2) *Proficient*—revealing solid academic performance over challenging subject matter, application to real world situations, and ability to use appropriate analytical skills; and (3) *Advanced*—signifying superior performance. NAEP science tests use multiple-choice, and constructed-response questions, and hands-on tasks to measure knowledge and performance of three science themes: systems, models, and patterns of change. In addition, the Third International Mathematics and Science Study (TIMSS) provided an international comparison of U.S. students' performances to their counterparts in other participating countries. Both NAEP and TIMSS tested at grades 4, 8, and 12. Both tests have been scrutinized and used by other researchers to conduct additional studies in order to gauge the conditions and progress of elementary science education. These are some of the findings:

*Achievement*

- In grades 4 and 8, the performances of males and females were not significantly different, yet by grade 12 males outperformed females in the science NAEP test. The science performance differences reveal some improvement in closing a prior gap between the genders (O'Sullivan et al., 1997).
- Whites and Asian/Pacific Islanders have higher average science scale scores than African American and Hispanic students at all three grades. This remains consistent with past NAEP assessments (O'Sullivan et al., 1997).
- In all three grades, children of parents with higher levels of education scored higher than children of parents with lower levels of education on the NAEP (O'Sullivan et al., 1997).
- On the NAEP, students in grades 4 and 8 currently participating in Title I and free/reduced lunch programs, scored lower on average than classmates who were not participating (O'Sullivan et al., 1997).
- At all three NAEP grade levels, 3 percent of the students reached the Advanced level; 26 percent of the fourth and eighth graders performed within the Proficient level; while 30 percent and 32 percent scored at the Basic level for grades 4 and 8, respectively (O'Sullivan et al., 1997). However, ". . . more than 70 percent of the students in each of the three grades demonstrated an understanding of science below the proficient level. Indeed, 33 percent of the fourth graders, 39 percent of the eighth graders, and 43 percent of the twelfth graders never even reached the basic level" (Johnson, 1997, p. 12).
- The number of college science degrees granted to all students, minorities, and females increased between 1991 and 1995 (National Education Goals Panel, 1997).
- Only Korea outperformed the United States in the fourth-grade science international assessment, and only Singapore, Czech Republic, Japan, Korea, and Hungary outperformed U.S. eighth-grade students (National Research Council, 1997).

*Science Teaching*

- Approximately 75 percent of the teachers in grades 4 and 8 state that hands-on activities should be a part of science teaching and learning. However, 50 percent of the fourth-grade classes and nearly 67 percent of the eighth-grade classes emphasize terms and facts, and devote the largest portion of class time to lecture and discussion (National Research Council, 1997).
- Uses of hands-on activities have increased since the mid-1980s. (Hands-on activities require students to use firsthand experiences with science materials and phenomena to construct an understanding of science concepts and principles.)

- Seventy-five percent of the elementary classrooms and 95 percent of the middle school classrooms use commercially available textbooks or a single science program (Willis, 1995b).

## Goals
- The following percentages of teachers report that their teaching goals contain these emphases: basic science concepts, 83 percent; awareness and importance of science to daily life, 77 percent; and developing inquiry skills that are helpful for problem solving, 74 percent.
- Nearly 20 percent of the science classes in each grade put considerable emphasis on preparing students to take standardized tests.
- Teachers with high proportions of students who are minorities are more likely to emphasize preparation for standardized science tests rather than preparation for further study in science (Willis, 1995b).

## Time
- About 30 minutes is devoted to science each day in elementary schools, a slight increase over 15 years ago (Willis, 1995b). (What does this seem to suggest about how much science is valued?)

## Diversity
- Non-Asian minority students are most likely to discontinue taking science courses in high school.
- Only about 11 percent of the elementary and middle school science teachers belong to minority groups, whereas about 30 percent of students belong to such groups (Willis, 1995b).

Jessica now turned her attention to the second drawing of a scientist that she put in her portfolio; it appealed to her for its special message (Figure 3.2). An older sister had drawn her younger brother and added this explanation: "This is my brother and I think he is a scientist. He is very curious, like this time when he threw our cat down the stairs. He always wants to know why things work and what will happen when he tries a new idea." Jessica doubted that the sister was advocating violence or cruelty toward animals. Rather, her remarks seem to suggest that the brother was following his natural curiosity. This caused Jessica to ponder what science is and what it means to "do" science.

# THE NATURE OF SCIENCE

The word *science* originates from the Latin word *scientia,* meaning "knowledge," as in possessing knowledge instead of misunderstanding or being ignorant. In fact, one of the authors distinctly remembers having to memorize a definition from a junior high textbook (long since forgotten, along with almost everything else in it!) that defined science as an "organized body of knowledge." Following that were the steps of the scientific method, also to be mem-

**FIGURE 3.2   Children as Scientists**   Children are great examples of scientists. Their curiosity motivates them to act on their ideas.

orized: (1) identify the problem, (2) examine the data, (3) form a hypothesis, (4) experiment, and (5) make a conclusion. Textbook definitions and memory exercises are helpful only to a point in learning *about* how some of the ideas of science were developed, a process that was often the subject of large posters adorning walls in science classrooms.

Eventually most science classrooms abandoned the posters and the scientific method as something to be memorized, perhaps because the mechanistic

*Science naturally stimulates positive attitudes, enhances inquiry skills, and elevates understanding of our natural world.*

certainty of the steps did not reveal the true nature of science, its history, and its implications for society. For example, George deMestral did not set out to invent Velcro. However, his mind was specially prepared to be curious about why some burrs stuck so tightly to his clothing (Roberts, 1989). By recognizing that the commonplace provided an important insight, deMestral developed a product that has a wide range of uses. Charles Townes too saw the commonplace in a special way, and his vision helped him to invent the laser. He said: "The laser was born one beautiful spring morning on a park bench in Washington, D.C. As I sat in Franklin Square, musing and admiring the azaleas, an idea came to me for a practical way to obtain a very pure form of electromagnetic waves from molecules" (Roberts, 1989, p. 82). Who among us does not use Velcro in some way? And consider how greatly the laser has changed whole fields: medicine, electronics, merchandising, and defense and warfare, among many others. These examples of serendipities—accidental discoveries made possible by a mind receptive to scientific thinking—are typical of many sudden breakthroughs in science and help us to understand that not all of what is learned through science is orderly and predictable. Robert Hazen and James Trefil help us to see this a bit more clearly:

> There is a temptation, when presenting a subject as complex as the natural sciences, to present topics in a rigid, mathematical outline. . . . In the first place, it does not reflect the way science is actually performed. Real science, like any

human activity, tends to be a little messy around the edges. More important, the things you need to know to be scientifically literate tend to be a somewhat mixed bag. You need to know some facts, to be familiar with some general concepts, to know a little about how science works and how it comes to conclusions, and to know a little about scientists as people. All of these things may affect how you interpret the news of the day. . . . Finally, . . . [science] is just plain fun—not just "good for you" like some foul-tasting medicine. It grew out of observations of everyday experience by thousands of our ancestors, most of whom actually enjoyed what they were doing. (Hazen & Trefil, 1991, p. xix)

A definition or a description does not always give a sufficient impression of what and how science should be taught for maximum effect. Consider Jessica's recollections of her classroom experiences with science and the influences made on her. It seems fair to assume that Jessica's teachers carried an image and feeling about science that contributed to their beliefs and affected their teaching of science. This teaching then influenced Jessica's beliefs. And when Jessica teaches, she will continue the cycle by influencing her own students' beliefs. Perhaps this is not a desirable picture when you consider the influence Jessica could have on children—that is, *before* she acquired new impressions about science.

How does a child receive information, construct knowledge, and gain meaning from what is experienced? Hazen and Trefil's view of science offers some useful clues for answering this question. From their description, we may infer that human curiosity is important and that certain types of mental and physical skills are needed for learning: skills for acquiring useful information that has practical value and carries real meaning for learners, meaning that is constructed from the learner's experiences. Therefore, science

- is a human construct and human activity,
- is bound by history,
- changes over time,
- has theories that are underdetermined by empirical evidence,
- has a knowledge base that is not absolute,
- has methods and methodology that change over time,
- deals in abstractions and ideals,
- has research agendas that are influenced by social interests and ideology,
- in order to be learned, requires that children be attentive and intellectually engaged. (Matthews, 1998, p. 166)

Children are naturally curious (remember the brother who threw the cat down the stairs). Their curiosity motivates them to discover new ways to use this powerful key for unlocking the mysteries of their world. Therefore, when we consider what science is and make decisions about what to teach children and how to teach them, three parts of what science actually is must be remembered and put to use:

1. *Attitudes.* Science encourages humans to develop positive attitudes, including their powerful curiosity.

2. *Skills.* Science stimulates humans to use their curiosity to construct new ways of investigating and understanding.

3. *Knowledge.* Science consists of what humans learn—knowledge for practical learning and everyday living—the meaning humans construct for themselves (Flick, 1993, pp. 3–4).

The new things children learn tend to stimulate curiosity and motivate them to investigate further. When children are given a complete experience with all that science is—whole science—a cycle is established that continues to build under its own momentum (Figure 3.3). Whole science thus consists of three parts: development of children's *attitudes* and *skills* and children's construction of useful ideas—*knowledge*. Children's experiences can stimulate their curiosity (*attitudes*), which can motivate them to develop new ways of processing ideas or solving problems (*skills*); these are used to construct the *knowledge* of science. Successful learning enriches the experience universe of children and stimulates further inquiry. Teachers provide children with a whole science experience when they are immersed in all of science's parts.

**FIGURE 3.3   The Science Cycle**   Children receive a whole science experience when they are immersed in *all* of science's parts. The synergy among the parts makes science whole.

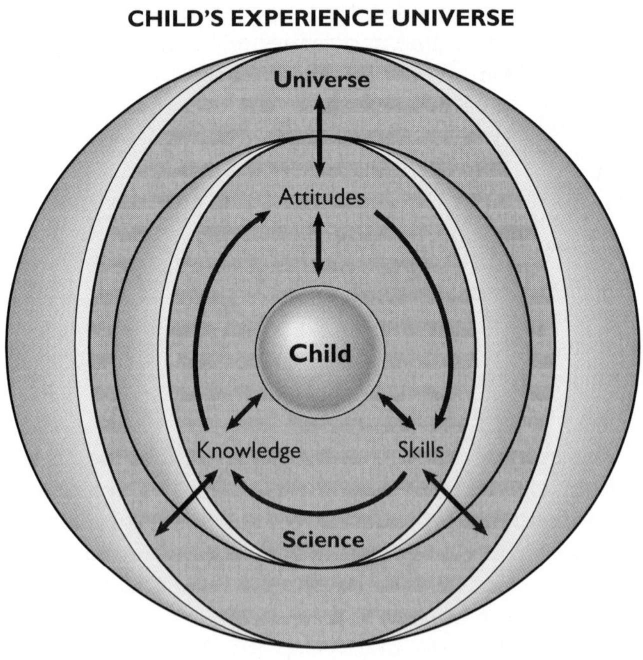

CHILD'S EXPERIENCE UNIVERSE

# THREE PARTS OF SCIENCE

Three aspects of science are necessary for a wholesome, productive learning experience: development of children's attitudes, development of their thinking and kinesthetic skills (gross, fine motor, and eye–hand coordination, as well as training of the senses), and development of knowledge that is constructed from experiences in natural settings.

## Science Attitudes

***What Are Attitudes?***   Attitudes are mental predispositions toward people, objects, subjects, events, and so on. In science, attitudes are important because of three primary factors (Martin, 1984, pp. 13–14). First, a child's attitude carries a mental state of readiness with it. With a positive attitude, a child will perceive science objects, topics, activities, and people positively. A child who is unready or hesitant, for whatever reason, will be less willing to interact with people and things associated with science. Realize, though, that this readiness factor occurs unconsciously in a child, without prior thought or overt consent.

Second, attitudes are not innate or inborn. Contemporary psychologists maintain that attitudes are learned and are organized through experiences as children develop (Halloran, 1970; Oskamp, 1977). Furthermore, a child's attitude can be changed through experience. Teachers and parents have the greatest influence on science attitudes (George & Kaplan, 1998).

Third, attitudes are dynamic results of experiences that act as directive factors when a child enters into new experiences. As a result, attitudes carry an emotional and an intellectual tone, both of which lead to making decisions and forming evaluations. These decisions and evaluations can cause a child to set priorities and hold different preferences. In our chapter scenario, Jessica is an example. Her attitude toward science and the way she values it appear to shift from a negative to a neutral or perhaps even a positive viewpoint. In time, with continued positive experiences and adjustments in her attitude, Jessica may become more open to science, think differently about it, and accumulate more useful ideas and skills—all products of her learning. But all of this begins with her attitude. Attitudes influence how people choose to respond.

***Emotional Attitudes.***   Young children's attitudes, so it seems, are more emotional than intellectual. Curiosity, the natural start of it all, may be accompanied by perseverance, a positive approach to failure (or accepting not getting one's own way all the time), and openness to new experiences or even other people's points of view (such as tolerance for other children's ways of playing a favorite game). These are fundamental attitudes, useful for building the other specific scientific attitudes that are necessary for success and the continuation of the science cycle.

***Intellectual Attitudes.***   Attitudes based on intellect or rational thought develop simultaneously with science process skill development (the second part of science) and with the discovery or construction of useful science ideas (the

*Positive attitudes help children succeed in science.*

third part of science). Teacher guidance, learning materials that can be manipulated, and interactive teaching methods help encourage formation of intellectual attitudes. Examples include skepticism and the development of a desire to follow procedures that increase objectivity. (See Table 3.1.)

***Importance of Attitudes.***   Young children have positive attitudes toward science and display many of these attitudes as they explore and interact with age-mates. However, over time these initial positive attitudes may decline.

One way to maintain and improve attitudes is to help children develop appreciation for the role science plays in their daily lives. They can realize the value of science when attitudes and practical value become teaching goals. Consider, for example, the influence science has on the food we eat, the clothing we wear, our use of leisure time, the forms of entertainment we enjoy, and the higher quality of life its technology provides us. Is there any career that is unaffected by science? Appreciation for science and recognition of its value accumulate as the intellectual attitudes of science are emphasized. Guide children through the science process skills—ways of doing and learning science—to stimulate and develop the intellectual attitudes.

### Science Process Skills

Perhaps you remember hearing about something called the "scientific method" in your science classes. Some people once believed that scientists used a spe-

**TABLE 3.1 Attitudes of Young Scientists**

| *Emotional* | *Intellectual* |
|---|---|
| From children's natural curiosity for learning and acquiring new experiences, we can encourage them to develop <ul><li>more curiosity</li><li>perseverance</li><li>a positive approach to failure</li><li>open-mindedness</li><li>cooperation with others</li></ul> | From children's positive learning experiences we can encourage them to develop <ul><li>a desire for reliable sources of information</li><li>skepticism; a desire to be shown or to have alternative points of view proven</li><li>avoidance of broad generalizations when evidence is limited</li><li>tolerance for other opinions, explanations, or points of view</li><li>willingness to withhold judgment until all evidence or information is found or examined</li><li>refusal to believe in superstitions or to accept claims without proof</li><li>openness to changing their minds when evidence for change is given and openness to questions about their own ideas</li></ul> |

cific, step-by-step method in their research. But when scientists were questioned about how they actually went about their work, it soon became clear that there were numerous ways that they approach problems. It was also obvious that there are several processes that are common to most forms of inquiry, and these soon became known as the *science process skills*. Those processes are applicable to other subjects of study as well as science, and you probably have been using some of them most of your life. What sets professional scientists aside from you might be little more than the skill with which they have learned to use those processes to solve problems. We think you will recognize the process skills as you review them, and we also think you will quickly realize how important it is that children learn to use them to solve their own problems.

The mission of elementary and middle school science is not to persuade all children to become scientists. The mission is to help make science more accessible to *all* children. One way this can be done is to help children discover how science can be important to them. Therefore, let us consider the process skills rooted in science that young children must develop and the ways children can use these skills to solve their own problems of learning and life.

***Learning How to Learn.*** Some people refer to developing process skills as "learning how to learn." Children learn how to learn by thinking critically and using information creatively. Children continue to learn how to learn

> when making discriminating observations, when organizing and analyzing facts and concepts, when giving reasons for expecting particular outcomes, when eval-

## WHAT RESEARCH SAYS

### Attitudes and Science Teaching

The importance of attitudes was recognized in science teaching and learning in the 1960s. The Educational Policies Commission issued a document titled *Education and the Spirit of Science*. The writers urged schools to promote "understanding of the values on which science is everywhere based. . . . We believe that the following values underlie science:

1. Longing to know and to understand
2. Questioning of all things
3. Search for data and their meaning
4. Demand for verification
5. Respect for logic
6. Consideration for premises
7. Consideration of consequences

"Commission members believed that the values of science are the most complete expression of one of the deepest of human values—the belief applies today, but assumes a lower level of rigor for elemen-

tary children, this is one way to justify the importance of developing a scientific attitude in children. Other reasons have been offered during more recent years: such attitudes help students have a better understanding of the nature of science by encouraging them to act out roles similar to those of scientists, and it is important for all students to become rational thinkers. What does this imply for science teachers?

"First, the science teacher is the key person for successful promotion of positive attitudes and affective attributes in children. Therefore, the science teacher must have a good knowledge of the nature of science and must be a good role model. Students must be enabled to perform experiments and solve problems that require use of the thinking skills involved in scientific inquiry."

*Source:* Compiled from Patricia Blosser, Bulletin Editor, Attitude Research in Science Education, Columbus, OH: ERIC/SMEAC, 1984, pp. 2–3.

---

uating and interpreting the results of experiments, and when drawing justifiable conclusions. [Also, children] . . . should be able to predict what will happen when the conditions of a phenomenon in nature are changed. (Victor, 1985, p. 47)

***Types of Process Skills.*** In science, the ways of thinking, measuring, solving problems, and using thoughts are called *processes. Process skills* describe the types of thinking and reasoning required. Science process skills may be divided into two types: basic skills and integrated skills (Arena, 1996). Table 3.2 suggests the grade levels at which these skills are appropriate.

*Basic Skills.* If children show that they can observe, classify, communicate, measure, estimate, predict, and infer, they are showing understanding of basic science processes.

*Observation* is the primary way children obtain information. This does not mean that they benefit solely from watching someone else and listening to what others think. Children observe by using all their senses. For example, how do you observe a concert? Can you close your eyes now and recreate a concert you have attended by recalling how your senses were stimulated? Can you see the lights and special effects? Can you smell the odors unique to the crowd and

**TABLE 3.2  Science Process Skills**

Basic skills can be emphasized at the primary grades and then serve as a foundation for using the integrated skills at the intermediate grades and higher.

| Basic Skills | Grades | | | | | | | | | |
|---|---|---|---|---|---|---|---|---|---|---|
| | *PreK* | *K* | *1* | *2* | *3* | *4* | *5* | *6* | *7* | *8* |
| Observation | X | X | X | X | X | X | X | X | X | X |
| Classification | X | X | X | X | X | X | X | X | X | X |
| Communication | X | X | X | X | X | X | X | X | X | X |
| Measurement | X | X | X | X | X | X | X | X | X | X |
| Estimation | X | X | X | X | X | X | X | X | X | X |
| Prediction | X | X | X | X | X | X | X | X | X | X |
| Inference | | X | X | X | X | X | X | X | X | X |
| **Integrated Skills** | | *K* | *1* | *2* | *3* | *4* | *5* | *6* | *7* | *8* |
| Identifying | | | | | X | X | X | X | X | X |
| Controlling variables | | | | | X | X | X | X | X | X |
| Defining operationally | | | | | X | X | X | X | X | X |
| Hypothesizing | | | | | X | X | X | X | X | X |
| Experimenting | | | | | X | X | X | X | X | X |
| Graphing | | | | | X | X | X | X | X | X |
| Interpreting | | | | | X | X | X | X | X | X |
| Modeling | | | | | X | X | X | X | X | X |
| Investigating | | | | | X | X | X | X | X | X |

those special effects? Can you feel the vibrations of the bass and drums? Can you hear the music and vocals—really hear them with all of their rhythm? Can you taste the popcorn or the Junior Mints? Teachers stimulate useful observation through the five senses when they ask children questions that cause them to identify properties of objects, changes, and similarities and differences; and to determine the difference between an observation and an inference. An example of an observation could be: *The object is hard, gray, round, and the size of a baseball.* Instruments such as thermometers, volt meters, balances, and computers help to add precision to observations.

*Classification* requires that children organize their observations in ways that carry special meaning. Teachers can encourage children to classify when they ask them to group objects by their observed properties and/or to arrange objects or events in a particular order. An example is: *Placing all rocks of the same size, color, and hardness into the same group.*

When *communication* is emphasized, children use language (spoken, written, and symbolic in many forms) to express their thoughts in ways that others

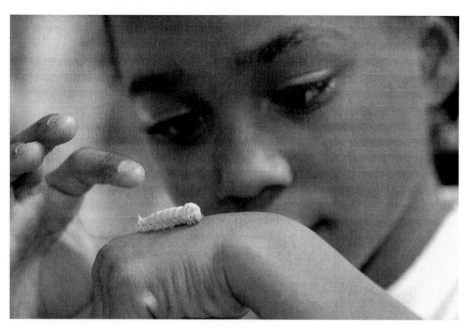

*Observation is a basic science process.*

can understand. Development of useful communication skills is encouraged by teachers who ask children to define words and terms operationally, to describe objects and events as they are perceived, and to record information and make data tables, graphs, and models to show what they have found. An example is: *Describing an observed change in a river over time by speaking, writing, or showing in a graph or data table.*

*Measurement* adds precision to observations, classifications, and communications. Children can be encouraged to measure by using standard tools like rulers, meter sticks, balances, graduated cylinders, calibrated liquid containers, clocks, calculators, computers, electrical instruments, and even arbitrary units such as marbles, paper clips, and so on to measure quantity or distance. An example is: *Using a meter stick to describe the height of a child.* (Note: The metric system is *the* measurement system in science.)

*Estimation* involves using judgment to approximate an amount or a value. The estimate is based on knowledge of measurement, but not direct measure. Estimation is useful for quick observations for which precision is not necessary. An example of an estimate could be: *I think the chair is about 1 meter high,* or *the glass looks as if it has about 300 milliliters of water in it.*

*Predictions* refer to types of thinking that require our best guesses based on the information available to us. Meteorologists, for example, predict the weather. Their predictions are made in advance of the weather's actual occurrence and are based on accumulated observations, analysis of information, and prior experience. Similarly, children can be encouraged to make predictions before they carry out an act, such as grouping different objects into classifications based on a prediction concerning whether they will float when placed in water. A teacher can stimulate predictive thinking by asking children to review the observed properties of objects or events and asking them to tell what they think will happen when a change of some sort is made, such as our sink-or-float example. Another example is: *Predicting the size and shape of an ice cube after heating it for 10 minutes.*

*Inferences* are conclusions about the cause of an observation. Consider the sink-or-float example again. Children may observe that all lightweight objects from their collections float in water and infer that light weight was the cause of floating. Of course, this could be disproved by items not included in the children's limited collection of objects. Therefore, it is necessary to help children make better inferences by guiding their thinking in ways that (1) help them make conclusions (2) about an observation (3) based on the prior knowledge they have. Another example of an inference is: *Saying a person is happy because she smiles and hums a song.*

*Integrated Skills.*   Integrated science process skills rely on the students' capabilities to think at a higher level and to consider more than one thought at a time. Just as the word *integrated* implies, several of the basic process skills can be combined for greater power to form the tools used to solve problems. The basic skills are prerequisites for integrated skills—those necessary to do science experiments. These skills consist of identifying and controlling variables, defining operationally, forming hypotheses, experimenting, interpreting data, forming models, making graphs, and investigating.

*Identifying and controlling variables* requires students to identify aspects of an experiment that can affect its outcome and to keep constant as many as possible, while manipulating only the aspects or factors (variables) that are independent. Example: *Varying only the amount of fertilizer used on similar plants while keeping soil type, amount of sunlight, water, and temperature the same.*

*Defining operationally* occurs when children use observations and other information gained through experience to describe or label an object or event. Example: *An acid is a substance that changes bromethymol blue indicator from blue to yellow.*

*Forming hypotheses* is important for designed investigations and is similar to prediction, but more controlled and formal. Hypothesizing is using information to make a best educated guess about the expected outcome of an experiment. An example could be: *The more fertilizer is added to plants, the greater their growth.*

*Experimenting* requires using many thinking skills to design and conduct a controlled scientific test. This consists of asking a research question, forming a hypothesis, identifying and controlling variables, using operational definitions, conducting the experiment, and interpreting the data. An example could be: *The entire operational process of investigating the effects of amounts of fertilizer added to plants of the same type.*

*Graphing* makes it necessary for students to convert measurements into a diagram to show the relationships among and between the measures. An example could be from the experiment above: *Constructing a graph to show the heights of the plants, experimental and control, for each day (or week) of the experiment.*

*Interpreting data* requires that students collect observations and measurements (data) in an organized way and that they draw conclusions from the information obtained by reading tables, graphs and diagrams. An example: *Reading information in a table or graph about the growth of plants in the experiment described above and forming conclusions based on the interpretation of the data.* The interpretation could help to "prove" that *more fertilizer added to plants causes greater growth.*

*Forming models* requires that students create an abstract (mental) or concrete (physical) illustration of an object or event. An example could be: *A model that shows the best amount of fertilizer to use on a plant and the consequences of using too little or too much.*

*Investigating* is a complex process skill that requires students to use observations, to collect and analyze data, and to draw conclusions in order to solve a problem. Applying our plant experiment example further: *Complete an investigation to evaluate the fertilizer dosage model as a way of deciding on a plant feeding routine for the class's garden.*

***Importance of Process Skills.*** Basic science skills help children to expand their learning through experience. They begin with simple ideas, and then those ideas compound and form new, more complex ideas. All ideas are valuable because they have the potential to help children to become better decision makers, consumers, citizens, and problem solvers. Emphasis on science process skills helps them discover meaningful information and accumulate knowledge by constructing understanding within and beyond the science classroom.

The skills used in science are remarkably similar to those used in other subjects, especially reading (Table 3.3 on pages 98–99). When children are doing science, following scientific procedures, and thinking as scientists, they are developing skills that are necessary for effective reading and understanding (Padilla, Muth, & Lund Padilla, 1991). A creative lesson planner can have students working on science and developing the skills useful to other subjects simultaneously. Science experiences can help preschool children develop their intellect and get an early start on fundamental reading and thinking skills. Primary students can become motivated through science activities and their natural interests to work on vocabulary development, word discrimination, and comprehension. Intermediate and middle school youth develop their abilities to identify and control variables, make meaningful conclusions, and communicate ideas clearly.

## Science Knowledge

***Importance of Science Knowledge.***   Children construct important ideas and discover much for themselves when they use the skills of science. They gain knowledge by accumulating and processing information and by forming concepts about their natural world, human use of natural resources, and the impact of this use on society. Children also discover, in time, that knowledge provides power and carries with it a responsibility for its proper use. Perhaps most important, children can understand that much of science is tentative, has changed over time, and is subject to future change. Knowledge in science is not absolute, and research findings may be interpreted differently by different people, depending on their values and experiences.

***Examples of Science Knowledge.***   The information and ideas of science that compose its knowledge base are often referred to as *products*. That is because new discoveries that add to the base of scientific information are the products of curiosity and experimentation. An interesting thing about science knowledge is that new discoveries often lead to more questions, more experiments, and more new discoveries. Indeed, the solutions to scientific problems can create new problems. The science cycle moves under its own momentum, propelled initially and again later sustained by human curiosity and a desire to explain natural phenomena. The effect is an exploding accumulation of new information that is added to the knowledge base. Scientific knowledge consists primarily of facts, concepts, principles, and theories.

*Facts* are specific, verifiable pieces of information obtained through observation and measurement. For example, let us say that during a class project Jessica observes over the course of two weeks that she produces an average of 1 kilogram of solid waste each day: cans, bottles, paper, plastic, and so on—a fact of her living habits.

*Concepts* are abstract ideas that are generalized from facts or specific relevant experiences. Jessica's class project may help her form the concept that her habits of consumption yield considerable solid waste over time. Since she believes her habits are typical of other young adults, she also forms a conception of how much solid waste a number of people generate within a specific amount of time. Concepts are single ideas that may become linked to form more complex ideas.

*Principles* are more complex ideas based on several related concepts. To continue with Jessica's example, she might declare, "The reason people recycle solids is because they create a lot of waste." Jessica's principle is based on three concepts: creation, waste, and recycling.

*Theories* consist of broadly related principles that provide an explanation for a phenomenon. The purpose of a theory is to provide a best explanation based on evidence. Theories are used to explain, relate, and predict. After some added observation and consideration, Jessica may theorize that commercial marketing

**TABLE 3.3   Relationship of Science and Reading Skills**

| Science Skills | Reading Skills | Examples |
| --- | --- | --- |
| Observation | Discriminating shapes, sounds, syllables, and word accents | Break words in syllables and list on chalkboard. Class pronounces new words aloud. Teacher mispronounces some words and rewards students who make corrections. |
| Identification | Recognizing letters, words, prefixes, suffixes, and base words | Select a common science prefix, suffix, or base word, define it, and list several words in which it may be used. Example: *kilo* (1,000): *kilometer, kilogram, kiloliter.* |
| Description | Isolating important attributes and characteristics Enumerating ideas Using appropriate terminology and synonyms | Ask students to state the purpose of an activity. Construct keys for student rock collections, etc. Play vocabulary games. Use characteristics to identify an object or animal. |
| Classification | Comparing and contrasting characteristics Arranging ideas and ordering and sequencing information Considering multiple attributes | List in order the steps of a mealworm's metamorphosis. Construct charts that compare and contrast characteristics. Put concepts in order. |
| Investigation design | Question asking Investigating possible relationships Following organized procedures | Use library resources and design an experiment from an outline. Write original lab reports. Outline facts and concepts. |

*Source:* The comparisons are drawn from Glenda S. Carter and Ronald D. Simpson's "Science and Reading: A Basic Duo," *Science Teacher* (March 1978): 20, and from Ronald Simpson and Norman Anderson's *Science, Students and Schools: A Guide for the Middle and Secondary School Teacher* (New York: Wiley, 1980). Padilla, Muth, and Lund Padilla (1991) continue to clarify the similarities between science process skills and reading comprehension skills.

practices and convenience packaging are responsible for much of the eastern United States' landfill problems. She may use her theory to urge lawmakers to develop regulations and to persuade city leaders to establish recycling programs to ease the pressures on their landfills.

Throughout history, scientific thinkers have found that the hierarchy of facts and ideas that they have accepted over the years cannot answer certain important questions. As scientists struggle to refine the theories and principles in an effort to answer those questions, they sometimes come up with a radical new idea that seems to solve the problem better. If the new idea appears to answer

| Science Skills | Reading Skills | Examples |
|---|---|---|
| Data collection | Note taking<br>Using reference materials<br>Using different parts of a book<br>Recording information in an organized way<br>Being precise and accurate | Prepare bibliographies from library information.<br>Use tables of contents, indexes, and organizational features of chapters.<br>Use quantitative skills in lab activities.<br>Have students compare and discuss notes. |
| Interpretation of data | Recognizing cause-and-effect relationships<br>Organizing facts<br>Summarizing new information<br>Varying reading rate<br>Thinking inductively and deductively | Discuss matters that could affect the health of an animal.<br>Teach students to preview and scan printed text.<br>Have students organize notes in an outline.<br>Have students construct concept maps, flowcharts, and new arrangements of facts. |
| Communication of results | Using graphs<br>Arranging information logically<br>Sequencing ideas<br>Describing clearly | List discoveries through a time line.<br>Ask for conclusions from graphed data or tables and figures.<br>Describe chronological events. |
| Conclusion formation | Generalizing<br>Critically analyzing<br>Identifying main ideas<br>Establishing relationships<br>Using information in other situations | Ask "What if?" questions.<br>Have students scrutinize conclusions for errors.<br>Use case studies to develop conclusions through critical thinking. |

the old questions as well as the old way of thinking did, the scientific community will eventually throw out the old hierarchy of ideas in favor of what Thomas Kuhn (1970) called a *new paradigm*. The work of Copernicus is a good example of what Kuhn called a *scientific revolution*. Copernicus was trying to explain the orbit of Mars using Ptolemy's geocentric theory of the structure of the universe, but he was having no success. As he tried to refine Ptolemy's system, it occurred to him that it would be a much simpler problem to solve if only the sun were in the center rather than the Earth. In a moment of serendipity, he came up with an idea that, on further examination, seemed to explain the orbits

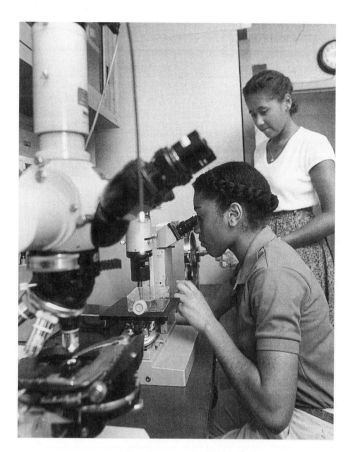

*Children construct science knowledge for themselves.*

of the other planets as well as Ptolemy's theory did, and a new paradigm was born. It was many years before Copernicus's heliocentric theory was widely accepted by the scientific community as the basis for a new hierarchy of theories about the relationship of the Earth to the sun and the other planets (Prather, 1991).

It is important for science teachers to help learners realize that scientific theories are based on the best information that scientists have been able to collect, but that many theories have been discarded as the result of new ideas that provide greater problem-solving power. Therefore, many of the theories and principles that scientists believe today may be discarded as new and better ideas are discovered in the future. At first, this concept may seem confusing to learners. They may ask why they should bother to learn about such things as Newton's laws or the theory of evolution if it might be imperfect and replaced by another view in the future. At this point, a teacher might use the history of science to help learners gain an appreciation of the nature of science and its worth. For example, Ptolemy's system was used for navigation for centuries, and Arabic camel drivers used it with confidence to navigate the otherwise intolerably hot deserts in the cool of night. Also, it was Ptolemy's astronomy that Magellan's sailors used to sail safely around the Earth—nearly a quarter of a century before Copernicus published his new astronomical theory (Prather, 1991).

Scientists are very aware of the limitations of their knowledge, but they are also aware that it represents the best information available to them at the time. Therefore, it is useful to learn about the theories of science, even if they might be replaced later. Theories are best explanations that scientists have, and they are based on the strength of evidence that is available to scientists at that time. Scientists possess a holistic view of science: They use scientific attitudes to identify and define problems and scientific skills to inquire, and they contribute what they learn to the knowledge base of science, which makes it possible for the scientific community to attempt solutions to many important problems that can benefit us all.

## THE AIMS OF MODERN SCIENCE EDUCATION

The aims of modern science education exceed the simplicity of understanding the three parts of science. The primary aim is to provide pupils with experiences that will help them become *scientifically literate.* Literacy is more than commanding a list of ideas and demonstrating selected skills. Modern views of scientific literacy include mathematics as well as technology and the social sciences as well as the natural sciences.

*Science for All Americans–Project 2061* (Rutherford & Ahlgren, 1990) and the National Science Education Standards (National Research Council, 1996) are significant reports, and *Benchmarks* (AAAS, 1993) is a curriculum effort based on many years of collaboration among several hundred scientists, mathematicians, engineers, physicians, philosophers, historians, and educators. These efforts offer a comprehensive and valid view of modern scientific literacy, the prime aim of science teaching. We learn from them that

> the scientifically literate person is one who is aware that science, mathematics, and technology are interdependent human enterprises with strengths and limitations; understands key concepts and principles of science; is familiar with the natural world and recognizes both its diversity and unity; and uses scientific knowledge and scientific ways of thinking for individual and social purposes. (Rutherford & Ahlgren, 1990, p. ix)

We must expand our vision of science when we take on this aim. Our national vision is to make our students first in the world in math and science achievement, and to develop a system of science education that prepares them to be informed and active participants in civic life, citizens who are productive workers and lifelong learners. The vision sees in the future a better informed citizenry that helps to maintain a strong democracy, strengthens our country's economy, and maintains excellent standing in science and technology.

The National Science Education Standards (NSES) (coordinated by the National Research Council of the National Academy of Sciences and the National Academy of Engineering) provides direction toward our national vision. NSES advocates a less-is-more philosophy for developing science curriculum, teaching approaches, and appropriate forms of assessment. These standards support practical learning experiences and problem-solving opportunities for children. The standards are based on a holistic view of science. These standards can help us progress toward our national aims and to do our part, as teachers, to fulfill the national vision.

## CHAPTER SUMMARY

The nature of science must be viewed holistically, and whole science is more than knowledge and scientific names and facts. This chapter has shown that assumptions about science that focus only on treating it as a body of knowledge are incomplete and incorrect. Science *is* possible because it is inherently human. Human *attitudes* provide the curiosity to begin its study, the perseverance to continue, and the necessary qualities for making informed judgments. Science *process skills* make it possible for children to accumulate the factual *information* they use to construct concepts, form scientific principles, and comprehend theories. Children

are able to construct their own understanding when encouraged to inquire by exploring, questioning, and seeking.

Science has the most impact on children when they value it and learn it holistically. Children value science when they find uses for it and enjoy its pleasures. Science programs, science teaching practices, and assessment techniques must provide experiences that will help children to value and use science by making important discoveries for themselves. How children construct ideas and learn is a topic explored in Chapter 4.

## DISCUSSION QUESTIONS

**1.** Think back to your elementary and middle school years. What do you remember about your science classes? How do your memories compare with those of your classmates? In what ways do your recollections represent whole science?

**2.** To what extent did your teachers teach science according to our definition? What do you remember about the emphasis given to attitudes, thinking skills, and science information? Why do you think your teachers emphasized (or did not emphasize) each of these parts?

**3.** Think about developmental differences observed between first-, third-, and sixth-grade students. In each grade, how much emphasis do you think should be given to emotional and intellectual attitude development? Give reasons for your answer.

**4.** Review the differences between basic and integrated science process skills. Describe the connection between these skills and the types of science information children are expected to learn.

**5.** The attitudes we carry with us are linked to experiences we have accumulated over time. Both help us form images that we treat as our independent sense of reality. Sometimes these images represent widely recognized stereotypes. For example, when you hear the word *scientist,* what image comes to mind? Draw a picture of a scientist.

**6.** Compare your picture of a scientist with other class members' pictures. Classify them according to such features as age, gender, amount and types of hair, eyeglasses, lab coat, laboratory apparatus, appearance (weird, out of control, and so on), and other factors. Tally the features and compute percentages to develop a class profile of a scientist. Treat this as a pretest and do the exercise again at the end of the course to look for any possible differences in stereotypes.

## BUILD A PORTFOLIO

**1.** Try a version of the projects described in the Discussion Questions at the end of the chapter with elementary school children. How do their pictures compare with your own or those of your college class? Develop a summary of the children's views and speculate about reasons.

**2.** Interview children using these questions:
  (a) What do you think science is?
  (b) Is science important? Why?
  (c) What is the most important thing you have learned in science?
  (d) What sort of people (children included) make good scientists?
  (e) Are you a scientist? Why? or Can you be a scientist? Why?

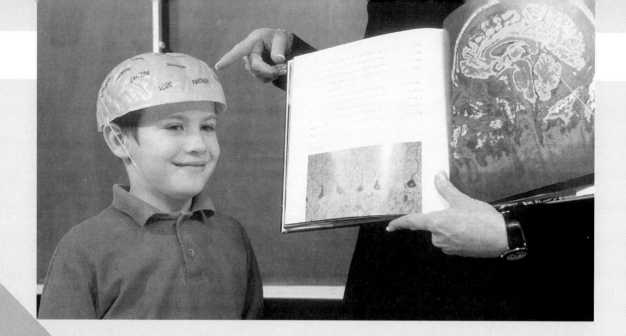

## CHAPTER OUTLINE

# CHAPTER 4

# How Do Children Learn Science?

When we revisit Jessica (of Chapter 3) after teaching for some years, we see that she has developed helpful routines to manage her classroom duties. Her teaching methods are consistent. In math, she presents the topic, demonstrates models, explains the functions and steps to follow by giving examples, and involves some of the children in board work. Drill and practice come next and are followed by assigned seatwork, which is reviewed at the start of math time the following day.

In science, Jessica explains the point, provides a demonstration, and gives her pupils step-by-step instructions for completing the corresponding activity. She always uses visual models to help students understand complicated concepts. Each learner follows her recipe, and her methods are similar for all subjects.

Jessica is regarded as an outstanding teacher and has received several commendations, yet although her students perform well on the school district's standardized tests, they do not fare as well as she would hope on the obligatory statewide performance assessments. Jessica is frustrated. Her fifth graders seem to do well only at memorization. In addition, they seem to return to their own ideas when confronted with problems or questions that are not an exact replica of what they have studied in class. Their learning appears to be superficial, and idea retention is elusive. What can Jessica do to develop deeper, lasting understanding?

Jessica was pondering this question during her vacation as she supervised the play of her two children. Her daughter, the older child, was experiencing some difficulty using a pump to inflate her bicycle tires. As her daughter struggled with the handle and plunger of the pump, she exclaimed: "Ouch! Why is this so hot?" She had touched the long plunger that she had been rapidly moving up and down to inflate the tire. Jessica's nine-year-old son, Jonathan, was close by, riding his skateboard, and stopped to offer an explanation: "It's hot because of friction."

"What's that?" inquired his sister.

Jonathan attempted to explain: "See the wheels on my skateboard? Listen as I turn them quickly. Hear this one squeak? Now let me put a little oil on it like Uncle Frank showed me." Jonathan retrieved the oil can from the garage workbench to put a few drops of oil on the bearings of the squeaking wheel. "What do you hear now?" he asked.

"I hear the wheel turning, but I don't hear the squeak," his sister replied.

"Exactly. The wheel squeaked because of too much friction. I put on some oil to take away some of it. I think there is still some friction here. That is why we hear this rolling sound of the little balls in the wheel," hypothesized Jonathan. "Let's try something. Feel the back wheel on your bike to see how cool it feels. Then hold up your bike so the back wheel is off the floor so I can turn the pedal really fast. Then hang on but drop it so the wheel hits the floor." This was done with a skidding sound and jerking motion that left a black mark on the concrete floor. "Now quick, feel the tire. How does it feel now?"

"I think its hotter, but I'm not sure," ventured his sister.

"Yes, that's because the tire rubbed against the floor and the friction heated it. Now try this. Press your hands together so the palms are flat. Press a little and then rub them back and forth. How do they feel now?"

"A little warm," replied his sister.

"Yes. Now press harder and move them faster. How do they feel now?" asked Jonathan.

"Hot!" exclaimed his sister.

Jessica was intrigued by this conversation and startled that her young son seemed to understand deeply the idea of friction, although he did not exactly define it. She knew this was a difficult concept and asked: "Jon, how do you know about friction? Did Ms. Glock teach you about it in school?"

"Well, I think she tried," offered Jonathan. "We studied machines in third grade, and I remember reading about friction in the book. Ms. Glock talked about it, but I couldn't remember much."

"Then how did you learn so much about friction?" persisted Jessica.

"Uncle Frank taught me."

Jessica encouraged Jonathan to explain and eventually uncovered his story. Jonathan had been helping his uncle to build a storage shed for lawn tools. His uncle had put a board in place with long screws as a temporary support, then rapidly removed the screws with his cordless drill when the support was no longer needed.

Jonathan's job was to pick up the screws and put them away. His uncle had warned that the screws would be hot and that Jonathan should let them cool for a few moments. Jonathan did not understand. The screws had been cool to the touch when he had handed them to his uncle, *before they were driven into the board*. Instead of explaining, Jonathan's uncle had helped him to drive some cool screws into a board and then remove them quickly. They carefully touched the screws and noticed that they were quite warm. Uncle Frank then explained that the surface of the screw threads rubbed quickly against the wood and that the rubbing heated the screw. He showed Jonathan how to understand what happened by rubbing his hands together, as Jonathan had done with his sister.

Uncle Frank used the word *friction* to represent the idea they were investigating. He had also demonstrated the same idea with a sabre saw. Jonathan carefully touched the blade of the unplugged saw and felt that it was cool to the touch. Then Uncle Frank cut a board, unplugged the saw, and touched a piece of tissue paper to the blade. The hot saw blade scorched the paper. Uncle Frank asked Jonathan to explain what happened by using the idea of friction. He also asked Jonathan to get his Cub Scout book, and they looked at ways to make campfires with primitive methods that used a bow and friction. They continued their discussion of friction by trying to stand on marbles in a box and noticed that it was difficult to do since friction between their shoes and the floor was reduced, and they speculated what it would be like to try to run on slick, wet concrete with smooth-soled shoes. They discussed why oil and coolants are important to an automobile by reducing friction and removing excess heat from the motor that is caused by friction and why cars skid off rain-slicked highway curves or on snow and ice. Jonathan and his uncle worked together to identify times when friction is helpful, such as a fast-moving biker's trying to cycle around a sharp curve, or a basketball player's making a cut and driving to the basket. The firsthand experiences and discussions had helped Jonathan understand the basic idea of friction and expanded his understanding by applying the idea in new situations, such as with his sister and the bicycle pump.

The story was a serendipity for Jessica. Her prepared mind made a connection with her teaching. She decided to try a new learning opportunity for herself and developed a vision of how to present lessons during the upcoming school year. Jessica resolved to use her college texts and professional journals to review the principles of child and brain development. She changed her metaphor of learning from teacher-explainer/student-receiver to teacher-guide/student-constructor. Jessica was determined to view her learners through new eyes and considered different perspectives on how children learn and how to help them form mental connections. She resolved to try different teaching approaches that would help her guide her students' learning—helping them learn how to learn rather than telling them what they needed to know.                                                                ◆

## INTRODUCTION

How did you learn science? Was it similar to Jessica's typical way of teaching it? Was your experience based on the teacher's instructions and explanations, vocabulary development, and memorization? Or was your experience more like an adventure, where the exact steps to follow were as unknown as the consequences of your decisions? Did your teachers emphasize the facts, symbols, labels, and formulas of science? Or were the general ideas—concepts—developed in a way that helped you to discover the connections among the many ideas and fields of science?

How you view science and how children learn share related consequences. If you view science as a discrete body of information to be learned, you will probably bring that assumption to your teaching, which will be much like Jessica's routine. If, after reading Chapter 3, you view science as a dynamic opportunity to help children develop essential attitudes, skills, and knowledge that can benefit each of them, you will likely bring that assumption to your teaching, which may resemble Jessica's new vision. Your view of how children learn has been shaped by your teachers, and in turn your beliefs will affect the children you teach. With a little imagination you can see the repeating cycle.

Jessica's routine methods did not produce the results she wanted. She decided to experiment with her methods and in doing so challenged and adapted her beliefs about learning. In this chapter we challenge you to

1. Consider the brain's unique structure and the function it plays in learning.
2. Consider the role that children's prior ideas and misconceptions play in their learning.
3. Identify what children need to help them become self-motivated and to sustain independent learning.
4. Examine the dominant contemporary perspective on science learning.
5. Explore essential techniques important for constructivist teaching.

## WHAT ROLE DOES BRAIN DEVELOPMENT AND PROCESSING PLAY IN LEARNING?

### Simplified Brain Anatomy

Your adult brain is about the size of an oblong grapefruit, weighs about 3 pounds, consists of about 78 percent water (10 percent fat and 8 percent protein), and is covered with a ¼-inch-thick wrinkled covering resembling an orange peel, called the cerebral cortex. If unfolded, the cerebral cortex would be about the size of a sheet of newspaper. The cortex is divided into lobes. Each of the lobes has a specific task with some functional overlap between lobes (see Figure 4.1). The occipital lobes process visual stimuli; the temporal lobes process auditory stimuli; the parietal lobes interpret and integrate sensory stimuli; the frontal lobes process high-level thinking such as problem solving and future planning; and, deep within the cortex's lobes somewhere exists the capability to reflect and have awareness about what one thinks and does (Wolfe in D'Arcangelo, 1998). The human brain also contains the largest area of cortex (out of all animals) that has no specifically assigned function, giving humans extraordinary flexibility for processing information and learning. To assist in

**FIGURE 4.1   Lobes of the Brain**   The cerebral cortex, a wrinkled ¼-inch-thick structure, covers the brain. Its regions are divided into lobes, each with specific functions.

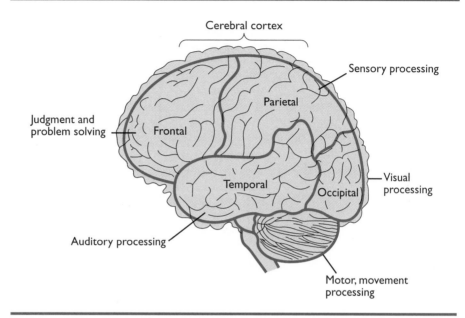

rapid and thorough processing, the brain's nerve cells are connected by about 1 million miles of nerve fibers (Jensen, 1998).

### Simplified Brain Development and Function

Although your brain is about 2 percent of your body's weight, it consumes 20 percent of your energy (enough to light a 25-watt lightbulb). Brain energy comes from nutrients in your blood, and people need eight to twelve glasses of water each day to assure optimal electrolytic balance of brain chemicals. Dehydration is a common problem in schools and can impair learning (Hannaford, 1995). Your brain uses 20 percent of your body's oxygen. Air quality and lack of exercise can affect the oxygen richness of your blood, which can impair learning. Many worry that schoolchildren lack sufficient exercise to ensure oxygen-rich blood (Jensen, 1998).

About 10 percent of your brain's cells are neurons, and these are used for thinking and learning (see Figure 4.2 on page 110). As an adult, you have about 100 billion neurons, plenty to get you through your lifetime, though the number is about half that found in a two year old (Howard, 1994). Young children's brains are like sponges, thriving on enriched stimulation. Human newborns begin to form synapses at rates far in excess of adults, so that by about age four

◆**FIGURE 4.2   Neurons Make Connections; Connections
Define Learning**   Neurons connect to other neurons via
multiple pathways. Axons trail outward from neurons and connect with dendrites from other neurons. The connecting point is
called a synapse—a space gap—across which electrochemical
signals travel. Learning is believed to exist at these connections.
A single neuron can connect with many other neurons.

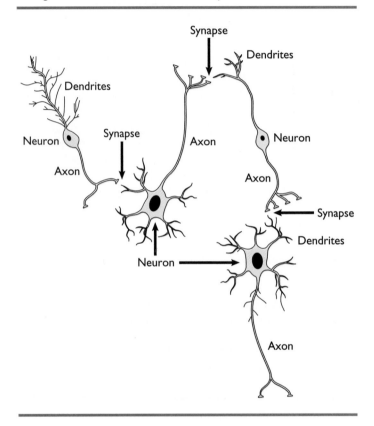

synaptic densities have peaked and are about 50 percent greater than adults.
Around puberty a process that prunes away excess synapses and continues
through adulthood begins, in which cell neuron and synapse losses occur every
day through attrition, decay, and disuse (Bruer, 1998).

## Signal Processing

Neurons have a compact cell body. They process information by converting
chemicals into electrical signals and conveying the signals back and forth be-

tween other neurons; normal neurons constantly receive and send signals. Dendrites and axons are attached to the body of the neuron cell. Dendrites are like branches and extend outward from the neuron. Enriched learning environments stimulate the growth and number of dendrites, helping to afford each neuron multiple pathways for processing signals. Similar to alternative traffic routes used as detours around clogged highways or closed bridges, multiple pathways provide bypasses for each neuron; this helps learning. Axons grow out from each neuron and connect with the dendrites of other cells. Each axon helps to transport the brain's chemicals and conducts the electrical signals received by the neuron (see Figure 4.3 on page 112). Each neuron can receive signals from thousands of other brain cells, depending on the number of branches grown.

Electrical signals speed along at about 200 miles per hour. Each of our brain cells behave like a very small battery, generating electrical impulses from the potassium and sodium concentrated in the cell membranes located at the synaptic gap—the small space located between the end of the axon and the tip of a dendrite. Some of these electrical signals may be new stimuli, which require larger, less efficient, numbers of neurons to be involved in processing. These new stimuli encourage the growth of new synapses, which are regarded as evidence that the brain grows new connections as a consequence of learning. When the transmitted signals are related to what we already know or we can do, they move along previously established neural pathways. This allows the processing to be more efficient and uses fewer of our brain's neurons, but it also reinforces and makes connections stronger (Jensen, 1998). In brief, we can say that "learning" occurs when synaptic efficiency is enhanced.

## Making Connections Makes Learning

Jensen (1998) distinguishes between learning, which is what we have described so far, and behavior, which is more likely governed by our emotional states and memories. It seems our brain has a soup of floating chemicals, mostly peptides, and Pert (1997) estimates that at least 98 percent of our brain and body's internal communications occur through peptides and control behavior such as attention span, levels of stress, and drowsiness.

Experienced educators today often remark that children seem different and less well prepared for learning in school. There is some evidence to suggest this is true. A developing fetus is extremely sensitive to stress from chemical and emotional effects and from poor nutrition. The effects can be huge if these stresses occur during embryonic development, at a time when brain cells develop at a rate of 250,000 a minute.

Researchers report that emotional intelligence begins very early, and the early school grades may be a last opportunity to nurture emotional literacy (Goleman, 1995). Troubled early relationships can cause the brain to consume nutrients essential to cognitive functions and divert them to dealing with stress or violence. The brain can become reorganized, and the child more impulsive or aggressive in school or social relationships (Kotulak, 1996)

**FIGURE 4.3** **The Synaptic Gap** An electrical charge is received by a neuron and travels to the tip of the axon, where electrical energy is converted to chemical energy by chemicals called neurotransmitters, which send a signal across the synaptic gap to the receptors on the dendrite of another neuron. The chemical signal is converted to electricity and travels through the axon of different neurons to the receptors of other neurons' dendrites. A network is established with multiple pathways for signals that travel at speeds of about 200 miles per hour.

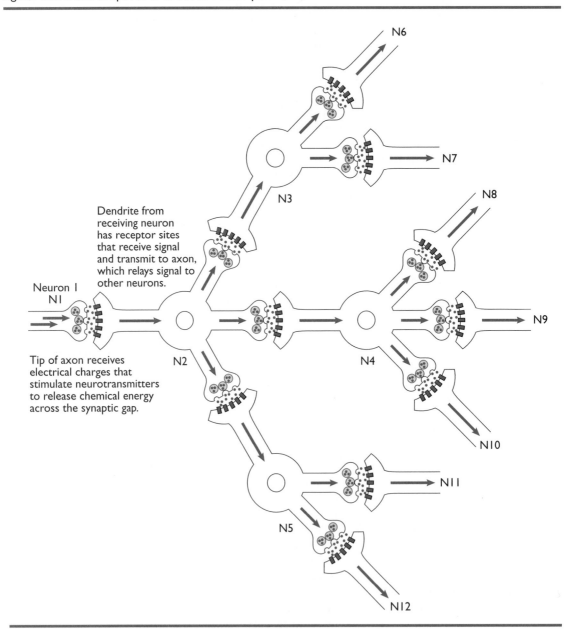

*Experiences using tools help to develop and strengthen neural pathways.*

Less-stimulating playgrounds, car seats that limit visual stimulation, sedentary activity while in day care, and lengthy exposure to television can impede the development of early motor skills by restricting vestibular stimulation, which can impact the brain's readiness for reading, writing, and attention (Hannaford, 1995). Restricted stimulation has been linked to learning problems such as dyslexia (Cleeland, 1984). Early stimulation in enriched environments can help the brain develop visualization (Kotulak, 1996), thinking skills (Greenfield, 1995), auditory skills (Begley, 1996), and language (Kotulak, 1993). Inadequate sleep, poor nutrition, and dehydration also impact the developing (and the developed) brain's ability to function properly in school (Jensen, 1998).

What does brain research suggest we can do to improve learning? One thing we can do is to focus our efforts on helping learners to grow more synaptic connections between brain cells and to strengthen, rather than lose, existing connections. Connection-making is central to learning, and it is believed that brain cell connections help learners problem solve, a key to modern scientific literacy. Connections are made among and between ideas and experiences. We can help children learn science more effectively if we consider their prior ideas and nurture their connection-making through constructivist principles of learning.

## WHERE DO CHILDREN'S IDEAS COME FROM AND HOW DO THEY INFLUENCE LEARNING?

Rosalind Driver (Driver, Guensne & Tiberghien, 1985) and her fellow researchers have studied this question extensively. Consider the following classroom example involving two 11-year-old students.

Tim and Ricky are studying the way a spring extends as they add ball bearings to a plastic drinking cup that is attached to and hangs from the spring, which is suspended from a clamp on a stand. Ricky carefully adds the bearings one at a time and measures the change in the length of the spring after each addition. Tim watches and inquires, "Wait a moment. What happens if we lift up the spring?" Ricky clamps the spring higher on the stand, measures its stretched length, and continues after he is satisfied that the length of the spring is the same as before the change in position. An observer asks Tim for the reasons behind his suggestion. Tim picks up two bearings, pretends they are pebbles, and explains his idea about weight changing as objects are lifted higher:

> This is farther up and gravity is pulling it down harder the farther away. The higher it gets the more effect gravity will have on it because if you just stood over there and someone dropped a pebble on him, it would just sting him, it wouldn't hurt him. But if I dropped it from an aeroplane it would be accelerating faster and

*Children form their own science ideas through direct experience.*

faster and when it hit someone on the head it would kill him. (Driver, Guensne, & Tiberghien, 1985, pp. 1–2)

Tim's idea is not scientifically correct. The object's weight decreases as height increases. However, the idea is not irrational if you consider Tim's reasoning: He seems to be referring to what scientists call gravitational potential energy. The ideas children bring with them often influence what and how they learn.

## Preconceptions

The ideas from prior experiences that children bring with them have been called a variety of names: alternative frameworks, children's science, naive theories, and preconceptions. We prefer to call them *preconceptions* because children's ideas are often incomplete preliminary understandings of the fundamental science concepts that can be used to explain their everyday world. These preconceptions are influenced by hands-on, minds-on experiences, such as direct physical experiences, emotional experiences through social processes, and thoughtful efforts to make sense of the various things that exist in a child's world. These preconceptions that are brought to a new learning opportunity are important, even for adults, because the process of learning is the human activity of making connections in the brain. Adults and children can be infected by a type of bias that is influenced by expectations that seem to fit patterns formed in our brains through prior experiences. The problem is that young children often have limited or incomplete experiences. Bias is inherent in preconceptions and can influence concept formation. A well-known paleoanthropologist, Donald Johanson, recognized the importance of this when he wrote: "There is no such thing as total lack of bias. . . . The fossil hunter in the field has it. If he is interested in hippo teeth, that is what he is going to find, and that will bias his collection because he will walk right by other fossils without noticing them" (Kinnear, 1994, p. 3). Another scientist, David Pilbeam, illustrates this point by explaining how his original interpretation of a particular fossil was affected by his prior expectations: "I knew . . . [the fossil], being a hominid, would have a short face and rounded jaw—so that's what I saw" (Kinnear, 1994, p. 3). Additional discoveries and further investigation revealed that the fossil did not possess the features that Pilbeam described and that it was not a hominid.

## Misconceptions

*Misconceptions* are alternative understandings about phenomena that learners have formed. They are scientifically incorrect interpretations that learners believe or responses to problems that learners provide. "Misconceptions do not simply signify a lack of knowledge, factual errors, or incorrect definitions. Instead, misconceptions represent explanations of phenomena constructed by a student in response to the student's prior knowledge and experience" (Munson, 1994, pp. 30–31). For example, through reading and participation in class activities, including gamelike simulations, a learner may form the misconception that the top of a food chain has the most energy because it accumulates up the food chain (Adeniyi, 1985), whereas a correct scientific conception maintains the opposite: Available energy decreases as one progresses up a food chain (Munson, 1994). Students commonly believe that gravity results from air pressure (Minstrell, 1982) or that light from a candle travels further at night than during the day (Stead & Osborne, 1980).

William Philips, an earth science teacher, discovered some interesting but depressing facts about what his students knew about science—or rather, what they really did not understand. What was most troublesome was what his students thought they knew without realizing they were incorrect: their misconceptions. These are his words:

> Misconceptions are rarely expressed aloud or in writing and, therefore, often go undetected. Twenty years ago, shortly after I began teaching science, I encountered an outrageous misconception (or so it seemed at the time). While I was using a globe to explain seasonal changes, one very attentive eighth grader raised

*Guided direct experiences help to reduce misconceptions.*

her hand and asked, "Where are we?" Thinking she wanted to know the location of our school, I pointed to Delaware and resumed my lecture. She immediately stopped me with another question. "No. I don't mean that. I mean, do we live inside the Earth or outside it?" The question caused several students to laugh, but most appeared to be waiting for an answer. It was all I could do to hide my astonishment. (Philips, 1991, p. 21)

Philips cites a survey in which second-grade teachers estimated that 95 percent of their students knew the earth is a sphere. Later the teachers conducted interviews with the children and discovered that the students actually believed the earth is flat. Misconceptions are common, and once formed, they are held a long while. Misconceptions are linked to intuitive ideas, beliefs, or preconceptions. It is not unusual for students to progress through school providing correct answers when the teachers ask for them but believing otherwise, much like the second graders mentioned above. When students give science facts correctly to questions and on tests, it does not mean they have replaced the misconceptions they formed much earlier.

Examples of misconceptions Philips uncovered are given in Table 4.1. Misconceptions seem to occur as students construct knowledge; they may be linked to incomplete or insufficient experiences, faulty explanations, and misperceived meanings. Joseph Novak (1991), a professor of science and education, reminds us that students must construct new meaning from the foundation of the knowledge they already possess. This means that teachers cannot afford to overlook student misconceptions, because of the negative learning cycle caused

### TABLE 4.1   Common Earth Science Misconceptions

More than ten years' worth of research on misconceptions yielded the following list for children. Adults often harbor the same misconceptions.

| | |
|---|---|
| The earth is sitting on something. | Rain comes from holes in clouds. |
| The earth is larger than the sun. | Rain comes from clouds' sweating. |
| The earth is round like a pancake. | Rain falls from funnels in the clouds. |
| We live on the flat middle of a sphere. | Rain occurs when clouds are shaken. |
| There is a definite up and down in space. | God and angels cause thunder and lightning. |
| Astrology is able to predict the future. | Clouds move because we move. |
| Gravity increases with height. | Clouds come from somewhere above the sky. |
| Gravity cannot exist without air. | Empty clouds are refilled by the sea. |
| Any crystal that scratches glass is a diamond. | Clouds are formed by vapors from kettles. |
| Coral reefs exist throughout the Gulf of Mexico and the North Atlantic. | The sun boils the sea to create water vapor. |
| Dinosaurs and cavemen lived at the same time. | Clouds are made of cotton, wool, or smoke. |
| | Clouds are bags of water. |

*Source:* Excerpted from the list provided by William C. Philips, "Earth Science Misconceptions," *Science Teacher* (February 1991): 21–23.

by misunderstanding the simplest point. Novak also states that students can create new meaning only by constructing new propositions, linked concepts that are usually formed through discovery learning. This requires expansions of their neural networks.

### What Do We Know About Children's Ideas?

Children bring many ideas to class. Their ideas represent the interpretations they have formed about the dilemmas and phenomena they have encountered, as in examples given earlier in this chapter. Many of these experiences occur out of school and are not connected to formal teaching. Children's ideas arise from everyday experiences, including play, conversations, and events observed through the media. The recent research on children's ideas reveals three important factors: (1) Children's ideas are very personal constructions, (2) the ideas may seem incomplete or contradictory, and (3) the ideas are often very stable and highly resistant to change (Driver et al., 1985).

**Children's Ideas Are Personal.**   Have you ever been with a group of your friends and witnessed a remarkable event such as a concert, athletic event, or auto accident? Or have you participated in a heated debate about a topic important to you? How did your perceptions of the facts or the event compare with those of your friends? Was there complete agreement on each detail? "No" is not an unusual answer. Consider the children in a class, each participating in the same science activity. It is likely that the children will report diverse perceptions of what happened during the activity. Each child has seen and experienced the activity, but each has internalized the experiences in his or her own way. Our perceptions and descriptions depend as much on our original ideas as they do on the nature of the new experience or lesson. All readers do not receive exactly the same message, even from written words.

Learners construct their own meanings. *Constructed meanings* are based on new experiences that are accumulated and compared with and processed from old ideas. Constructed meanings arise from the expanded and cross-referenced neural networks formed in the brain. The preexisting ideas are the basis for observing, classifying, and interpreting new experiences. In this way, each learner, even a very young one, continually forms and reforms hypotheses and theories about natural phenomena. We call on the mind's existing ideas to help us understand new experiences (Harlen, 1992, p. 11). What is remarkable is that although ideas are constructed independently, the general interpretations and conclusions are often shared by many (Driver, 1983).

**A Child's Individual Ideas May Seem Contradictory.**   Natural science is blessed with many intriguing discrepancies. Touch the flat bottom of an uncoated paper cup with a candle flame, and predictably, the paper burns after a brief time. But add water to a cup and the cup will not burn even when heated by a stronger source for a much longer time. This result challenges the mature mind to identify a coherent reason that explains the behavior of the candle and cup under all circumstances. The younger mind may see no problem and simply use another, even contradictory, explanation, unconcerned that the explanation is inconsistent with what was previously said. As Driver (1983) reminds us:

> The same child may have different conceptions of a particular type of phenomenon, sometimes using different arguments leading to opposite predictions in situations which are equivalent from a scientist's point of view, and even switching from one sort of explanation to another for the same phenomenon. (p. 3)

A child does not have the same need for coherence as an adult or a scientist, nor does a child have a mental model to use to unify a range of different perceptions that relate to the same event. Furthermore, a child usually does not see the need for a consistent view. The constructed ideas work quite well for the child in his or her classroom practice, even though the ideas may be based on prior false conclusions.

*Children's Ideas Often Resist Change.*   It is not simple for teachers to change children's incomplete or flawed ideas about scientific events and phenomena. Additional activities, comparative discussions, and even direct teacher explanations may not cause children to modify their ideas. Changing ideas is a slow process, and the necessary changes may never be complete. Children may simply realize that they are to provide a certain correct answer to a teacher's questions but choose to turn off the academically correct in favor of the previous independent ideas once the test is over. Counter evidence presented to the child seems to make no difference. Interpretations often are based on prior ideas. Personal, if contradictory, ideas have tremendous stability and endurance (Driver, 1983, p. 4).

## WHAT DO CHILDREN NEED TO HELP THEM LEARN?

We must concern ourselves with more than what happens in the learner's mind. Stimulating learning in science, or any other subject, is a complex mission. Compare two age groups of children, primary and middle school. The physical, intellectual, social, and emotional differences are obvious. Younger children tend to be much smaller with less-developed muscle structures, are less social, and are more prone to spontaneous emotional outbursts. As children become older and more experienced, their interest in their peers increases, they become less reliant on concrete objects and more capable of abstract reasoning, and their speech and language patterns become more complex.

Change and development happen over time. The changes are physical and mental with the brain reorganizing itself and shaping emotions and behaviors. While their bodies are maturing and becoming stronger through exercise, children's minds, emotions, and self-confidence also develop through the exercise afforded by useful experiences. Children need experiences that will help develop their thinking, afford considerable activity, stimulate language, and help them develop social skills and self-confidence. Children need *time* for all of these changes to occur and an enriched learning environment if their brains are to develop well (Jensen, 1988).

## Thinking

Younger children benefit from using their five senses extensively. Talking about and showing children pictures of mammals, for example, provides less stimulation than giving them time to smell, touch, hear, and observe the movements of classroom pets. Imagine teaching children about foods that are salty, sweet, sour, or bitter without letting them taste! Stimulate many of the senses to overcome the limits imposed on children by just listening. Older youths benefit from the stimulation too, even though they are more capable of mental reasoning. Do you recall the difficulties prior ideas bring to new learning?

## Physical Activity

Middle school children may be able to sit still for rather long periods of time, but young children cannot. Indeed, very young children may actually get more tired if they have to sit still for long. Martha Denckla (1989), a professor of neurology and pediatrics, explains that this difference is related to development of the brain: "The frontal lobe, the part of the brain that applies the brakes to children's natural energy and curiosity, is still maturing in six to nine year olds. As the lobe develops, so does 'boredom tolerance' " (pp. 53–54). Purposeful physical activity helps to provide the experiences that are essential for thinking and language development.

## Language

Children learn to develop and use language by talking, not by learning isolated skills. Reasoning and expression are developed through child–child and child–adult conversations. Encourage communication of ideas first; then worry over spelling and grammar. Again, class experience affords abundant opportunities to develop language and thinking patterns. Acquire the experience first; then develop the language from it.

## Socialization

Social development is related to academic success. Children who are socially maladjusted and cannot get along with their peers often do poorly in school and may eventually drop out. Children tend to do better in school when they work in groups and cooperate with others. Some educators claim that *relationships* should be the first of the three Rs (Katz, 1989). Science provides abundant opportunities for children to cooperate and develop relationships through group activities and projects.

## Self-Esteem

Younger and older children struggle to meet the teacher's adult expectations and in doing so learn to judge themselves in relation to others. The unfortunate aspect to this is that young children have not yet learned to distinguish between effort and ability. If trying hard to accomplish a task results in failure, a child is likely to conclude that he or she will never be able to succeed. Cooperation, rather than competition, may inflate self-esteem while it deflates feelings of incompetence.

### Time

We cannot create more time. But we can decide how to allot the time we have. The fact is that young children need time to grow, mature, and develop the thinking and communication skills, socialization, and self-esteem they need for productive learning. Appropriate challenge stimulates the brain. However, piling on excessive challenges for younger children or accelerating the classroom pace will not help them develop into well-adjusted, creative, and critically thinking youth. Developmental differences observed during the primary years often wash out around the fourth grade if the children have been exposed to useful experiences through heterogeneous groups during their early years.

The many needs of children are a part of their learning environment. Attend to the needs, and the learning will follow as children become self-motivated and confident and as they develop the capability to think more abstractly and to communicate their ideas. Successes that arise from fulfilled needs help children to develop and sustain the capability to learn more independently.

## WHAT IS THE DOMINANT PERSPECTIVE ABOUT HOW CHILDREN LEARN SCIENCE?

*Constructivism* is the general name given to the dominant perspective on learning in science education. A constructivist perspective on teaching and learning is very different from traditional views. A teacher who embraces constructivism supports a different view of science, regards the roles of teacher and learner very differently, and selects and organizes teaching materials with particular care. A constructivist perspective emphasizes the role of the learner, regarding the role as active—physically, mentally, and socially—rather than passive. The constructivist teacher seeks ways to challenge and stimulate mental connection-making in order to enhance the active participation of learners in lessons and encourage learners to construct their own understanding from their sense of reality, which arises from their experiences. Let us visit Jessica again to see how her efforts toward change may illustrate a constructivist approach.

### Jessica: A Constructivist Attempt

Based on her experience with her son, Jessica determined to avoid her usual demonstration and recipe instructions. Now she distributed the materials for the science lesson *first*: clay, scissors, cardboard, rulers, string, and so on. She asked small groups of children to work together in teams to design and construct a landscape—any type of landscape *they* chose. Jessica wanted to avoid mimicry and to encourage the students not to get fixed on the definitions of a

## WHAT RESEARCH SAYS

### Brain-Based Learning

Much has been written about hemispheric brain dominance, and these ideas have influenced our views on learning and teaching even though they do not apply to normal learners. Although it is true that our brains benefit from abundant varieties of stimulation, prescriptions are difficult and risky because we are still learning how our brains function. Researchers Renate and Geoffrey Caine and Marian Diamond have summarized important principles from the brain-based research on teaching and learning that may help you to find effective ways to stimulate learning:

- We should stimulate all of the senses, but not necessarily all at once.
- Previous experiences and meaning affect how the brain processes new experiences and organizes new knowledge.
- Our emotions and our learning share an important relationship.
- Learning is more than exercising the brain like a muscle. It is a true physiological experience that involves a sophisticated set of systems.
- Our brain processes and organizes many stimuli and ideas at the same time, even though we may focus on only one thing at a time.

- The significance of subject matter content depends on how our experiences are arranged and fit into patterns.
- We should present a series of novel challenges that are appropriate for development.
- Our brains process peripheral stimuli consciously and unconsciously.
- Parts and wholes are processed simultaneously by our brains, not separately or in isolation in a particular hemisphere.
- We possess spatial memories that help us to retrieve experiences rapidly and easily; for example, we might have a detailed memory of an important event even though we made no special attempt to memorize details.
- We need more practice to recall facts and to establish a level of skill when these facts are not embedded in our spatial memories.
- Our brains respond positively to problems and challenges but are less effective under duress.
- We should allow social interaction for a significant percentage of activities.

Ernst von Glaserfeld, philosopher and regarded leader of the constructivist movement in science

---

landscape, since that was not the point of the lesson. Therefore she did not define "landscape," nor did she show particular examples. When students questioned her about the task, she encouraged them to use their intuitive understanding about landscapes—their preconceptions—to think about their experiences and use what they already knew.

The groups did not begin smoothly, perhaps because the children were not accustomed to vague instructions. However, the puzzled expressions and occasional off-task behavior associated with the newfound freedom quickly subsided as Jessica maintained consistent contact with each group and challenged their thinking by asking guiding questions: "How else could you do that?" "What other features could you add?" "Where have you seen landscapes like this?" Jessica also lifted up the unique examples from single groups for all of the other groups to examine. These examples stimulated many to say: "Oh, now I see!"

education, provides the following implications for teaching and learning:

- Whatever a student provides as an answer to a question or problem is based on what made sense to the student at that time. The response must be taken seriously, regardless of how odd or "wrong" it might seem to the teacher. Otherwise the student will be discouraged and inhibited. Also, understand that the answer may be a good one depending on how the student interpreted the question.
- A teacher who wishes to modify a student's concepts and conceptual structures must try to build a mental model of the student's individual thinking. Never assume that a student's way of thinking is simple or transparent.
- Asking students how they arrived at their given answer is a good way of discovering something about their thinking, and it opens the way to explaining why a particular answer may not be useful under different circumstances.
- If you want to motivate students to delve further into questions that they say are of no particular interest to them, create situations in which the students have an opportunity to experience the plea-sure inherent in solving a problem. Simply being told "good" or "correct" does not help a learner's conceptual development.
- Successful thinking is more than "correct" answers; it should be rewarded even if it is based on unacceptable premises.
- A teacher must have an almost infinitely flexible mind to understand and appreciate students' thinking because students sometimes start from premises that seem inconceivable to teachers.
- Constructivist teachers can never justify what they teach by claiming it is true. In science, they cannot say more than that it is the best way of conceiving the situation because it is the most effective way at the moment of dealing with it.

*Sources:* Renate Nummela Caine and Geoffrey Caine, *Teaching and the Human Brain* (Alexandria, VA: Association for Supervision and Curriculum Development, 1991); Diamond, M. & Hopson, J. (1998). *Magic trees of the mind: How to nurture your child's intelligence, creativity, and healthy emotions from birth through adolescence.* New York: Dutton (pp. 107–108). Ernst von Glaserfeld, "Questions and Answers about Radical Constructivism," in Kenneth Tobin (Ed.), *The Practice of Constructivism in Science Education* (Washington, DC: AAAS Press, 1993), pp. 32–33.

After a bit more exploration, Jessica challenged each group to draw two-dimensional maps of their three-dimensional landscapes. This proved difficult until the concepts of contour and interval were constructed. Jessica guided her class in defining what these words meant and figuring out how the ideas were important to the lesson. Soon each group was applying basic math and measurement skills to construct a contour map of their own landscapes to scale. Later, the children took actual contour maps and recreated different landscapes they had never visited, again to scale.

Jessica continued to use traditional testing methods and seemed to notice a deeper understanding of the children's learning. When she asked questions or when the children wrote answers to her tests, the responses were more detailed and appeared to be more thoughtful, and the children seemed able to use their ideas in new situations. The children seemed happier and excited about science, and this satisfied Jessica—for now.

## Constructivism

Jessica appears to be guided by the notion of constructivism, an emerging consensus among psychologists, science educators, philosophers of science, scientists, and others who are interested in improving children's learning. This view of learning maintains that learners (young and old, and professionals such as scientists) must construct and reconstruct their own meaning for ideas about how the world works (Good, Wandersee, & St. Julien, 1993). In a very simplified way, an ancient Chinese proverb encapsulates the intent of constructivism: "I hear and I forget; I see and I remember; I *do* and I *understand*." A lot of wisdom is packed into these three phrases. One type of sensory experience alone is insufficient when we strive for understanding. Experience requires substantial stimulation of all senses and each child's mental processes if meaningful learning is to happen.

Childhood educators Connie Williams and Constance Kamii (1986) recommend that we strive to accomplish three things when we encourage children toward understanding:

1. Use or create learning circumstances that are indeed meaningful to the learners.
2. Encourage children to make real decisions.
3. Provide children opportunities to refine their thinking and deepen their understanding by exchanging views with their peers.

*Constructivism enables each learner to build understanding.*

Williams and Kamii (1986) remind us that what is important is "the mental action that is encouraged when children act on objects themselves" (p. 26). The prevailing view of how children learn captures this intent: How can teachers stimulate the mental action necessary for children to construct ideas?

***Constructivism Defined.*** Constructivism is a theory that assumes knowledge cannot exist outside the minds of thinking persons. This theory capitalizes on the brain's natural curiosity as it constantly seeks to make connections between the new and the known (Wolfe & Brandt, 1998). Joseph Novak (Novak & Gowin 1986) defines constructivism as the notion that humans construct or build meaning into their ideas and experiences as a result of an effort to understand or to make sense of them. Novak explains that this construction

> involves at times recognition of new regularities in events or objects, inventing new concepts or extending old concepts, recognition of new relationships (propositions) between concepts, and . . . major restructuring of conceptual frameworks to see new higher order relationships. (p. 356)

Constructivism emphasizes the importance of each pupil's active construction of knowledge through the interplay of prior learning and newer learning. "Learning is a process of active construction by the learner, and an enriched environment gives the students the opportunity to relate what they are learning to what they already know" (Wolfe & Brandt, 1998, p. 11). Connections are sought between the prior and newer learning; the connections are constructed by the learners for themselves. Researchers and theorists maintain that the key element of constructivist theory is that people learn by actively constructing their own knowledge, comparing new information with their previous understanding and using all of this to work through discrepancies to come to a new understanding (Loucks-Horsley, 1990; Harlen, 1992; Peterson & Knapp, 1993; Yager, 1991). For example:

> In their early experiences of the world, pupils develop ideas which enable them to make sense of the things that happen around them. They bring these informal ideas into the classroom and the aim of science education is to give pupils more explanatory power so that their ideas can become useful concepts. Viewed from this perspective, it is important that we should take a pupil's initial ideas seriously so as to ensure that any change or development of these ideas . . . becomes "owned" by the pupil. (National Curriculum Council, 1989, p. 6.2)

Consider the possible vast difference between a scientist's ideas and those of a child. A scientist's perspective might be, "A plant is a producer." In contrast, a child's perspective might be:

> A plant is something that grows in a garden. Carrots and cabbage from the garden are not plants; they are vegetables. Trees are not plants; they are plants when they are little, but when they grow up they are not plants. Seeds are not plants. Dandelions are not plants; they are weeds. Plants . . . have multiple sources of food. Photosynthesis is not important to plants. (Osborne & Freyberg, 1990, p. 49)

Some concepts are correct but not inclusive. Other concepts are incorrect and merit thoughtful attention and eventual correction.

Constructivism is a synthesis of several dominant perspectives on learning. It is not entirely new. Contemporary researchers from Great Britain, Australia, New Zealand, and the United States have updated the theories and methods to capture the synergy of legendary psychologists, philosophers, and researchers.

The constructivist perspective is grounded in the research and theories of Jean Piaget, Lev Vygotsky, the Gestalt psychologists, Jerome Bruner, and the philosophy of John Dewey and is a natural extension of applied brain research. As you may imagine, the very nature and meaning of constructivism is open to interpretation; there is no one constructivist theory of learning. For example, some perspectives embrace the social nature of learning (Vygotsky); radical constructivists do not believe the world is knowable (Ernst von Glaserfeld); and more conservative views advocate using constructivist principles to help learners construct accurate and useful conceptions and webs of conceptual understanding. The continuum in Figure 4.4 implies degrees of difference in viewpoints among constructivists and positions the constructivist views respective to traditional views on teaching and learning (Shapiro, 1994). Radical constructivists place greater emphasis on the individual's active participation in knowledge construction and are located at the farthest point on the active/passive continuum. Conservative constructivists use activity-based and problem-based learning experiences and teacher intervention to promote conceptual constructions, yet they attempt to correct student misconceptions by helping learners construct understanding based on concepts embraced by the scientific community. Traditionalists, at the extreme right of the continuum, assume more passive learning roles for students.

Jean Piaget's research and cognitive development theory is regarded as the foundation of conservative constructivist's views. His contributions to the modern theory of constructivism are summarized for your convenience. Let us review some of his fundamental ideas.

**FIGURE 4.4   Teaching/Learning Continuum of Mental Operations**

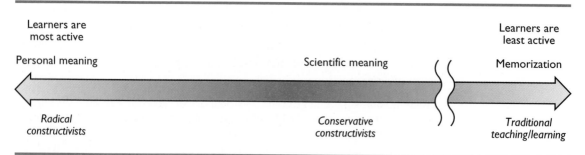

## Jean Piaget

Trained as a biologist, Jean Piaget (1896–1980) developed a theory of cognitive development that for several decades dominated our view of how children learn science. Not a learning theorist, Piaget described a process by which knowledge accumulates in a learner's mind when mental structures are formed.

If you have completed a course in educational psychology or child development, you may be familiar with Piaget's developmental stage theory. The stages are linked to probable age ranges and are labeled sensorimotor, preoperational, concrete operational, and formal operational. Young school children usually fit the preoperational stage description, while most elementary and middle school youngsters fit the descriptions of the concrete and formal operations stages, with many affected by the gradual transition between the two stages.

*Preoperational Stage.*    Children who think preoperationally may be five to seven years old and not capable of reversing their thinking. In Piaget's classic experiment, a child believes that a ball of clay patted into a sausage shape has more or less clay than the original ball. Children have difficulty seeing that there is no difference in the amount. Young children tend to be intuitive, egocentric, not rational, and not logical; they may confuse play with reality.

*Concrete Operations.*    Thought becomes internal, rational, and reversible during this stage. Children at this stage interact well with real objects, not abstract ideas. Children who process events concretely develop the ability to classify and conserve, and they develop some ability to engage in if-then hypothetical thinking.

*Formal Operations.*    During early adolescence, perhaps from age eleven onward, children tend to develop the capability to think more formally, more abstractly. They can consider many alternatives to a problem and can begin to identify the important variables that influence the outcomes of science activities and experiments. The ability to think about one's own thinking—*metacognition*—opens wonderful worlds of self-reliance and creativity.

The different stages are used to describe developmental differences among learners and to show progressive mental maturation through the experiences that each learner must process in his or her own mind. For educators, Piaget's work has been helpful in designing learning experiences that are most developmentally appropriate and that afford abundant opportunities for pupil success.

The stage progression portion of Piaget's theory implies that no person skips a stage and that learning is developmental; individuals may take different lengths of time and need different experiences to complete their development. Mental development does not merely click into place with a passing birthday. Indeed, learners differ in capability, most likely due to variations in their physical and mental experiences. Researchers in the United Kingdom and the United States report experimental results that cause them to question the absolute validity of the stage development and progression portion of Piaget's theory (Driver, 1983, pp. 52–58). Perhaps Piaget's most important contribution to our quest to understand learning is his description of a process through which each individual experiences stimuli and uses them to produce meaning.

*Physical Knowledge.*   Physical knowledge is formed from external observations and interactions with the physical world. Referring back to the Tim and Ricky scenario, each child observed a change in the length of the spring as each ball bearing was added to the cup. They could not have known the stretchiness of the spring and the firm, rolling weight of the bearings except through physical contact with the objects.

*Logicomathematical Knowledge.*   A more sophisticated type of knowledge, logicomathematical knowledge, is created when a learner establishes mental relationships between objects. Tim observed a type of cause-and-effect relationship about the length of the spring as more bearings were added; he formed a connection, albeit not completely correct, between the weight of the bearings and the distance the spring stretched away from the cup. Tim's mistake may have been due to a mental assumption that the bearing-and-spring experience was like pebbles being dropped first from the room's ceiling and then from an aircraft. The relationship existed in Tim's mind and was not based on direct physical knowledge.

*External and Internal Knowledge.*   In Piaget's theory, knowledge comes from two sources: external and internal. Physical knowledge is often external, and logicomathematical knowledge is internal. These sources of knowledge help each learner to form mental schemes or constructions: mental images constructed by organizing observations, behaviors, or thoughts into patterns. Piaget offers three other concepts to help us understand the complexity of forming schemes while learning: equilibration, assimilation, and accommodation.

*Equilibration.*   According to Piaget's theory, learning is an active mental process in which each learner must construct knowledge by interacting with the environment and by resolving the cognitive conflicts that arise between what is expected and what is observed (Driver, 1983, p. 52). Each new interaction or conflict creates a dilemma in each learner's mind about how to maintain mental equilibrium.

Equilibration is a process by which each learner compensates mentally for each dilemma. Each new attempt at restoring equilibrium helps to create a higher level of functional equilibration; higher mental structures are formed. (See Figure 4.5.) However, equilibrium is not a static point at which the mind

**FIGURE 4.5    Equilibrium Model Based on Piaget's Theory**   Disequilibrium
occurs in each learner's universe of experiences and causes an attempt to restore
equilibrium through assimilation and accommodation.

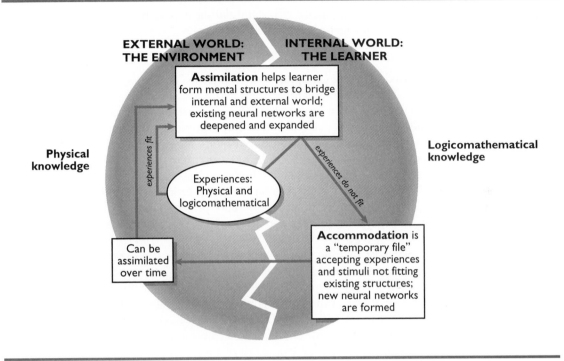

rests as if on a balance beam. Instead, equilibration is like a cyclist's maintaining
dynamic balance with each new challenge on the touring course. "The brain is
continually seeking to impose order on incoming stimuli and to generate models that lead to adaptive behavior and useful predictions" (Yager, 1991, p. 54).

*Assimilation.*    Assimilation is one way the mind may adapt to the learning
challenge and restore equilibrium. If the stimulus is not too different from previous experiences and mental actions, it may be combined with or added to existing mental structures, like filing a new letter into a preexisting folder
containing the same or similar information.

*Accommodation.*   On those occasions when no preexisting mental structures
(or file folders) are available to assimilate, the mind must adapt by changing or
adding to its mental structures. This process of adaptation is called accommodation. The learner's thinking is adapted to accommodate the dilemma.

In practice, assimilation and accommodation are related and do not occur in isolation; each process complements the other. A rational, thinking learner is mentally active. Always losing equilibrium and trying to restore it, the learner develops structures through the continuous interaction between the person and the external world. Again, rich, stimulating experiences—physical and mental—feed the learner's development.

### Jessica: The Novelty Wore Off

Jessica used learning groups to undertake the class's new approach to science learning. The students were very excited and cooperative—for about a week. Soon what had been discussion, sharing and playing roles, and collective searches for meaning degenerated into arguments and stalemates over who would get materials and clean up. Normally the class time devoted to positive human relations, genuine regard, and time management would not concern Jessica. As the weeks passed, what bothered Jessica most was the growing number of students who seemed to have persistent ideas and misconceptions unchanged by the effort of problem- and project-based group work. Several individual students complained that they preferred to work by themselves rather than be a part of a group.

Concurrent reading that Jessica was doing as she experimented with her new class arrangements led her into a deeper investigation of cooperative group learning processes, constructivism, and learning models. Students wanted a flexible grouping arrangement and job assignments; they also wanted opportunities to leave a group structure. Poring over how to structure and manage all of the requests for changes, Jessica became mildly embarrassed by the sudden realization that the true spirit of constructivism would be for her to let the *students* decide how to solve their problem. The class decided to vary the number of persons in groups; some contained only two, while others usually consisted of three to five students. Most realized that working with others was a better way to form understandings because ideas and explanations always had to be tested; cases had to be presented and pass the scrutiny of other group members.

When ideas did not fit with existing conceptions, there seemed to be four options.

**1.** The uneasiness many group individuals experienced became a source of motivation as students attempted to create minitheories to help them include the new experiences into their conceptual structures.

**2.** When some fit was constructed, students achieved a level of learning that was meaningful to them by regaining their equilibrium and changing previous ideas by adjusting their schema through a process of accommodation; this was regarded as the preferred learning outcome (see Figure 4.6, Exit 2). Jessica realized that a single successful experience was not enough to cause major changes in student thinking. Recalling the story of her son, Jonathan, and his learning about friction, Jessica determined that multiple experiences in a vari-

**FIGURE 4.6    Science Education Learning Model**

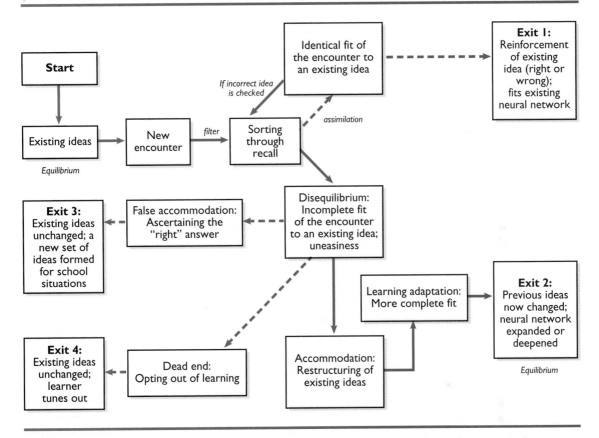

*Source:* Adapted from K. Appleton, "Using Theory to Guide Practice: Teaching Science from a Constructivist Perspective," *School Science and Mathematics* 93 (5) (1993): 270.

ety of situations were helpful, and she used this notion to plan many opportunities for her students to expand their understanding of science concepts. She discovered that her role was important. At times she became the source of information and explanation, although she usually functioned as a guide and questioner.

3. Despite Jessica's best efforts, some learners preferred to wait for the answer to be given—by a book, a search on the Internet, other students, or Jessica. These few students seemed to prefer to learn the answer by rote (see Figure 4.6, Exit 3). As unsatisfying as this was to Jessica, she realized that it was a beginning for these youngsters, so she resolved to help them by challenging the students to use the answer in other contexts, much like Jonathan's uncle had encouraged him to do when constructing an understanding of friction.

**4.** Jessica was most disappointed by the two or three children who opted out of the learning experience (see Figure 4.6, Exit 4). These learners were not only the isolated, surly types who did not consider the science topic interesting or the effort worthwhile; they also included the happy social types who were present in group activities, yet—perhaps because of prior poor experiences in science or repeated failures—chose to avoid further failure by opting out of the learning situation (Appleton, 1993, p. 270). This disconcerting student behavior motivated Jessica to seek teaching guidelines and intervention strategies that would serve all learners.

## WHAT TECHNIQUES AND ROLES SUPPORT CONSTRUCTIVIST LEARNING?

### A Constructivist Learning and Teaching Model

*A Constructivist Model.*   Constructivism strives toward a deeper understanding and is served by the inquiry teaching methods described in Chapter 1. Frontal teaching—telling and showing students all kinds of things—is minimized. According to Eleanor Duckworth (1989), all people ever have is their own understanding, and you cannot make them believe anything unless they construct it for themselves. Students can be encouraged to learn by reinventing the wheel for themselves—not a particularly time-efficient approach, but it *is* effective: retention is greater and understanding is deeper. The learner does the discovering by forming mental connections; the teacher mediates the learning environment.

There is a downside of which we must be aware: Not all student conceptual constructions are correct, and simply voting on what is right does not make it so. At times like this, a teacher may feel compelled to step in and correct the record. This can be fine, but beware the tendency to do too much telling. Instead, try an approach like the one shown in Figure 4.7. Provide an opportunity for children to explore and be directly involved in manipulating objects; ask questions and encourage children to ask useful and productive questions themselves. Help children to construct best explanations from their direct experiences by finding out their ideas and encouraging them to reflect on similarities and differences, to construct connections among and between their ideas. Encourage children to expand on their ideas by using them in other settings, such as the natural world and technology, and to develop process skills to enhance their thinking. Try to evaluate children's thinking by assessing any change in their ideas and process skills. Also encourage children to evaluate ideas by helping them to become interested in the explanations of others.

### Constructivist Teaching Roles

*Constructivism* is becoming a popular catchword in education. Teachers may mistakenly believe they are already using constructivism. (Try your hand at Figure 4.8 on page 134 to be certain.) While it is true that hands-on science, mathematics manipulatives, and process writing share some common inten-

**FIGURE 4.7   A Constructivist Learning and Teaching Model**

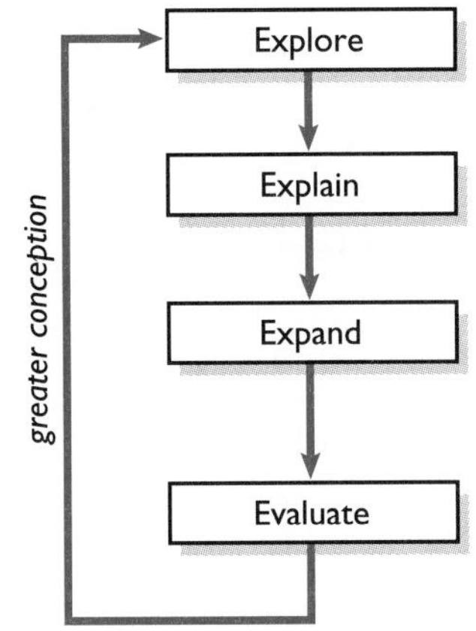

**TEACHER'S ACTIVITY**

| | |
|---|---|
| *greater conception* → **Explore** | Provides opportunities for students to explore through all appropriate senses and to be fully involved. Encourage group cooperation during investigations; encourage questions. |
| **Explain** | Interact with children to discover their ideas. Question to cause them to reflect. Help them use ideas formed from exploration to "construct" concepts and meaning sensible to them. |
| **Expand** | Help chidren develop their ideas further through additional physical and mental activity. Help them refine their ideas and expand their repertoire of science process skills. Encourage communication through group cooperation and broaden experience of nature and technology. |
| **Evaluate** | Evaluate conception by examining changes in children's ideas and by their mastery of science process skills. Use hands-on assessment, pictorial problem-solving, and reflective questioning. Encourage children's interest in the ideas and reasoning of others. Frequent evaluation improves each of the prior steps. |

tions with constructivism, applying constructivist research is much more difficult. The constructivist teacher must fill many roles but largely functions as a facilitator of knowledge construction. Young children can be encouraged to construct their own understanding if you perform these roles (Chaille & Britain, 1991, p. 54):

- *Presenter*—not a lecturer but one who demonstrates, models, and presents activities to groups of children and options to individuals so that direct pupil experiences are encouraged in an ongoing fashion.
- *Observer*—one who works in formal and informal ways to identify children's ideas, to interact appropriately, and to provide learning options.
- *Question asker and problem poser*—one who stimulates idea formation, idea testing, and concept construction by asking questions and posing problems that arise from observation.
- *Environment organizer*—one who organizes carefully and clearly what children are to do, while allowing sufficient freedom for true exploration; one who organizes from the child's perspective.
- *Public relations coordinator*—one who encourages cooperation, development of human relations, and patience with diversity within the class, and who defends this practice and educates others outside the class about the benefits for children of this approach.
- *Documenter of learning*—one who satisfies the accountability expectations and gauges the impact of these practices on each learner in terms of knowledge construction and science skill development.

◆ **FIGURE 4.8   Does Your Teaching Support Constructivism?**   Use this
continuum to determine the extent to which you are supporting constructivism.

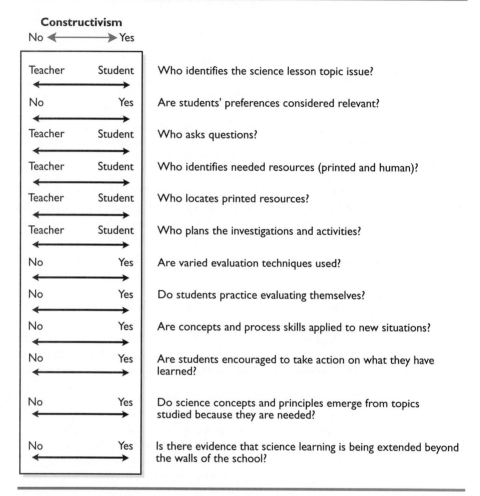

**Constructivism**
No ←——→ Yes

| | | |
|---|---|---|
| Teacher | Student | Who identifies the science lesson topic issue? |
| No | Yes | Are students' preferences considered relevant? |
| Teacher | Student | Who asks questions? |
| Teacher | Student | Who identifies needed resources (printed and human)? |
| Teacher | Student | Who locates printed resources? |
| Teacher | Student | Who plans the investigations and activities? |
| No | Yes | Are varied evaluation techniques used? |
| No | Yes | Do students practice evaluating themselves? |
| No | Yes | Are concepts and process skills applied to new situations? |
| No | Yes | Are students encouraged to take action on what they have learned? |
| No | Yes | Do science concepts and principles emerge from topics studied because they are needed? |
| No | Yes | Is there evidence that science learning is being extended beyond the walls of the school? |

*Source:* Adapted from Robert E. Yager, "The Constructivist Learning Model," *Science Teacher*
(September 1991): 56.

- *Theory builder*—one who helps children to form connections between and among their ideas and to construct meaningful patterns that represent their constructed knowledge.

Intermediate and middle school children can benefit from these same roles, particularly if cognition is elevated to a stimulating and challenging level that is developmentally appropriate.

## Jessica's Knowledge Construction

Throughout this chapter we have seen how Jessica wrestled with her own learning as she attempted to reconceptualize learning and teaching. When this happens to a professional or even a student, there are often several recurring actions that are important to recognize. First, Jessica was dissatisfied with her teaching and what children were learning. This dissatisfaction perturbed her and motivated her to seek change. Shaw and Etchberger (1993) claim that change cannot occur without some *perturbation*. Jessica's perturbation stimulated considerable thought about how children learn and how she could teach more effectively. Students too must become perturbed in order to stimulate learning.

Perturbation often encourages *commitment*—a personal decision to make a change. Commitment and progress toward change often cause additional perturbations. If you commit to a course of constructivism in your science classroom, you are likely to encounter many such perturbations that disrupt your "mental state of equilibrium" (Shaw & Etchberger, 1993, p. 264). When this happens, say Shaw and Jakubowski (1991), there are three likely pathways for you to deal with when experiencing this disequilibrium: (1) you may block the perturbation and reduce the opportunity for meaningful change; (2) you may rationalize excuses for not dealing with the perturbation; or (3) you will form an active plan for making a change. To which pathway are you likely to commit?

A *vision* may help you keep your commitments and steer the course toward meaningful change. This vision should be a clear, personal view of what the teaching and learning in your classroom should look like. You should be able to describe clearly to parents, supervisors, and visitors what you are trying to accomplish and the reasons for your choices. Figure 4.9 on page 136 summarizes the differences between traditional and constructivist classrooms. Perhaps it will help you to construct and maintain your vision.

*Reflection* will help you to evaluate and improve your vision, strengthen your commitment, and construct options to overcome your perturbations. Thinking reflectively means to give serious and frequent consideration to the factors associated with your vision. The following questions illustrate a reflective process and can help bring congruence to your desires, beliefs, and teaching practices: "What do students know about this topic? How are students thinking about what I am presenting to them? How do they come to think this way? How can they learn to value new ways of thinking about things? How can I help them to grasp scientific ideas? How do learners feel uncomfortable with science?" (Shapiro, 1994, p. xv).

For successful constructivist teaching and learning to occur, the teacher must become perturbed, commit to change, envision the type of change preferred, plan for change, garner the support for pursuing the vision, and reflect consistently about the progress and perturbations encountered along the path toward change. Change is a slow and deliberate process; for students, constructivist learning requires patience, persistence and respect for another's thinking (Shaw & Etchberger, 1993).

◆ **FIGURE 4.9   Traditional Versus Constructivist Classrooms**

| TRADITIONAL CLASSROOMS | CONSTRUCTIVIST CLASSROOMS |
| --- | --- |
| Curriculum<br>• Presented part to whole; emphasis on basic skills<br>• Fixed curriculum<br>• Relies heavily on textbooks and workbooks | • Presented whole to part; emphasis on big concepts and thinking skills<br>• Responsive to student questions and interest<br>• Relies heavily on primary sources of data and manipulative materials |
| Role of students<br>• "Blank slates" onto which information is etched by the teacher<br>• Work alone | • Thinkers with emerging theories about the world<br>• Work in groups |
| Role of teacher<br>• Generally behaves in a didactic manner; disseminates information to students<br>• Seeks the correct anwer to validate student learning | • Generally behaves in an interactive manner; mediates the environment for students<br>• Seeks the students' point of view in order to understand students' present conceptions for use in subsequent lessons |
| Assessment<br>• Viewed as separate from teaching: occurs almost entirely through testing | • Interwoven with teaching; occurs through teacher observations of students at work and through student exhibitions and portfolios |

*Source:* Cantrell, D. C. & Barron, P. A. (Eds.). (1994). *Integrating environmental education and science.* Newark, OH: Environmental Education Council of Ohio, p. 148.

## CHAPTER SUMMARY

Our approach in this chapter is different from what you might find in typical textbooks on teaching science. We assume you have completed a prior course in psychology or educational psychology, maybe even a course in child development. Therefore, rather than revisit the depths of some theories you may have studied, we visit the emergent findings from brain research and the fundamental ideas behind the dominant belief about learning science from the perspective of a practicing teacher. How can we take some of this dominant perspective on learning and use it to teach science better?

No perspective on learning is complete without considering the potential of neural networks that arise through experiences and represent the prior ideas of children. These ideas represent preconceptions—conceptual understanding in the early stages of development—and misconceptions—conceptual understandings that do not agree with the concepts of the scientific community. These ideas are personal, may be contradictory when examined under a variety of circumstances, and are stubbornly rooted in children's minds. That their ideas are resistant to change poses a big challenge for teachers.

Children's learning benefits from enriching experiences that helps to fulfill needs and must be considered and assimilated into a perspective on learning. As children develop over time, their needs change, and their exact cognitive capabilities are dynamic rather than static. Children need extensive experiences to stimulate their senses and to affect thinking. Physical activity is especially important for younger children, with mental and physical activity being interrelated in learning. Language has no automatic meaning for children since words have no inherent value, making an emphasis on word recognition and memorization meaningless. However, language constructed from experience has meaning that represents the physical and mental action understood by children. A child's social development is related to academic success. Group work and tasks that require cooperation help a child learn. Self-esteem is another need for effective learning. All of these needs must be attended to over time. The factor of time is variable for children since maturation and development occur at different rates.

Experience is the one factor that unites the dominant perspectives on how children learn science. But not all experiences are equivalent, and experience alone is insufficient. Constructivists advocate several approaches for stimulating mental action and learning in conjunction with experience.

Constructivism is the contemporary concept we use to think about a child's learning. This perspective focuses on the child and what the child does during learning. It holds that knowledge cannot exist outside the mind of a learner, it cannot be directly transferred, and it must be each learner's construction of reality. The teaching recommendations offered should help you construct appropriate roles for yourself. If you follow these recommendations, you will find yourself covering less and guiding more, and your students will learn more in the deepest sense of the word. The chapter ends with discussion of the relationship of dissatisfaction, commitment, vision, and reflection as a process for becoming the type of science teacher you wish to be. We challenge you to envision the type of learning you wish for children and to construct a classroom that supports this vision.

## DISCUSSION QUESTIONS

**1.** In what ways do children benefit from learning through experience? What types of materials or problems do you think are developmentally appropriate for young children? for the intermediate grades? for middle school youth? What similarities and differences do you detect when you compare the materials and problems you favor for each group?

**2.** As may be revealed by their prior ideas, how might children's science misconceptions affect how you teach? What could you do to learn about these prior ideas and to identify misconceptions?

## BUILD A PORTFOLIO

**1.** Select several science concepts. Interview several children, perhaps from different age groups, to determine their ideas about the concepts. What are their misconceptions? What similarities or differences do you detect across the age groups you have selected? How do you think you could attempt to correct those misconceptions? What perspectives on learning could you use to help you with this task? You might try using Suchman's Inquiry Method (Chapter 1) and science discrepant events to encourage children to reveal their understanding.

**2.** Prepare a lesson designed to teach a particular science concept. What teaching and learning recommendations do you plan to use to help your learners be successful? Videotape your lesson as you teach it. Analyze the tape. How consistent were you in using the recommendations you selected? What do you plan to do to become the type of science teacher you prefer? What are your specific goals and action plan for accomplishing your goals?

## CHAPTER OUTLINE

# CHAPTER 5
# How Can You Teach Science for All Children?

Julie B., a recent graduate from a liberal arts teacher preparation program, exuded confidence and passion for her first teaching position. Prior to the school year she decorated her classroom with colorful and interesting displays. Her first primary class was a dream come true after four and a half years of preservice teacher preparation and a semester of substitute teaching.

The list of children's names and a review of records suggested she would have an enriched class. Julie's first-day meeting with parents and children proved her hypothesis: several ethnic groups and races were representative of the school's diverse community, some spoke English as a second language, and a number of children were placed in her class with Individual Education Plans (IEPs) to help them overcome learning disabilities, proving the school's commitment to the concept of inclusion. A few of the children's records suggested potential for giftedness, which was supported by their precocious behavior and mature uses of language.

The excitement of the new school year and a novelty of a having a new teacher began to subside after the first week. Toward the end of the first month Julie took note of tensions among the children, which she suspected were related to differences in culture, language, gender and social class, and the children's self-perceived shortcomings in academic ability.

The autumn outdoor science projects did not progress as smoothly as Julie had planned; some children remarked that science was too difficult for them, and some of the boys stated with derision that girls couldn't do science. The children who had learning disabilities especially concerned her. Julie had been taught and passionately believed that all children could learn. She shared her concern with a veteran teacher: How can you teach all children when the class is so diverse? Many of the children exhibited low self-perceptions, language was a barrier for some, those who had gifted talents were impatient and constantly asked questions that seemed to take her plans off track, and she had concluded that three students who were included probably ought to be placed in a special class. Julie sought the advice of an experienced colleague who had befriended her. Mrs. Rice, the resource teacher, offered several practical suggestions, which were based on her many years of experience. She gave further encouragement by sharing the following story from her earlier years of teaching.

It had been at least seven years since my school had a science fair. Late in the fall I asked my principal if I could organize and sponsor a school science fair for my class and the other students in grades four through six. My main concern would be to get as many students as possible to follow a project through to completion so they could experience the reward of displaying their work. She immediately gave her permission and support.

My sixteen boys and one girl, aged eleven to thirteen, have reading abilities ranging from beginning first grade to high third grade. Their math skills are somewhat higher, while handwriting and spelling skills vary but are generally low.

According to intelligence test scores, these students have at least average potential, but they have not achieved at the same rate as most of their peers. They have been placed in my class in order to receive special and individualized instruction.

The behavior and attitudes of children with learning disabilities have been described as impulsive, distractible, frustrated, stubborn, disruptive, defiant, obstinate, and extremely disorganized. One word I would never use to characterize my students, though, is "unmotivated." Of course their motivation varies according to the activity at hand, but when their interest has been roused, they really get into gear. Fortunately, my explanation of a science fair induced every member of the class to decide to enter a project.

During the three months our school was involved in the science fair, I noticed some important changes in my own students and in other students and the faculty.

Learning-disabled children have difficulty getting along with one another in group situations. They are easily frustrated and tend to argue and become angry. Much to my surprise, however, this did not occur when my students worked on their science fair projects. I must stress the significance of this change in behavior. Naturally it improved the quality of their work for the science fair, but it also demonstrated to me—and to them—that they could control themselves and cooperate to solve difficult problems.

While my students' perceptions of what they could do were changing, the attitudes of other students towards my class were also shifting. At the beginning, most of the other students in the school had little information about learning-disabled children. They only knew that my students were somehow different, and they usually called ours the "dummy class." I, of course, was the "dummies' teacher." But during preparations for the science fair, the perceptions of some of these other students began to change. They found it difficult to understand how a "dummy teacher" could run a science fair and why she'd want to. The fact that I seemed to be doing a good job created a halo effect that was important: As my image began to improve among students throughout the school, so did the image of my students. For the first time, members of my class began to develop friendships with other students.

Many teachers were as uninformed as their students about the limitations and the capabilities of learning-disabled children. These colleagues often viewed students in my class simply as behavior problems. This misapprehension is not necessarily the fault of the teachers, since many of them finished college before courses in special education and learning disabilities had become part of the curriculum.

I initiated our science fair with one goal—to have my students complete and display science projects. However, as preparations for the fair progressed, it became clear that my students were learning more than I had originally imagined possible. I was curious about their perceptions of what they were accomplishing, so I asked them.

My students had no doubt that they'd learned some valuable lessons by participating in the science fair and neither had I. In fact, it seems to me that several important academic and personal goals can be accomplished by involving learning-disabled children in a science fair.

For me and my students, the school science fair was an extremely satisfying experience. Of the nine winners chosen by outside judges, four were from my learning-disabled class. And while getting prizes was exciting, equally important for my students were the intangible rewards of embarking on a joint enterprise with others, and discovering within themselves capabilities of which they had not been aware. (Rice, 1983, pp. 15–16) ◆

## INTRODUCTION

Have you ever heard someone reason like this: "If you can't walk, talk, or hear, or if you look or sound different, you must be intellectually and socially inferior." Most physical differences have no connection to one's intellect or mental capability. The biases of our hypothetical conversationalist are based on two important factors: stereotypes and a lack of information. Stereotypes caused the learners without disabilities in Ms. Rice's school to refer to her students as "dummies." The uninformed teacher can insufficiently stimulate the intellect by holding low expectations for children with learning disabilities. Without realizing just how unfairly their expectations may treat the children, teachers may actually reinforce the wider perception that learners who have disabilities or are different in some other way are dummies, and this type of teacher behavior may tend to reinforce the prejudices held by others. Julie's desire to reach for help was wise. The challenges for teachers in knowing the right things to do increase as classrooms become more diverse.

Children with learning disabilities are only one example of students who have special needs. Each child is a special case and deserves special attention and encouragement. You will be in a better position to teach, to strike down unfair stereotypes, and to serve the needs of *all* learners if you become informed about the special needs many school children have. This will be a great service for all of your students and will especially benefit those who need special assistance.

This chapter is about teaching science to serve *all* children's needs. Technically, of course, all students are culturally different; each family is unique and has its own identity. The multicultural focus of this chapter explores the special needs of culturally diverse populations (groups of students with home environments very different from society's mainstream in terms of economics, ethnicity, religion, race, and/or language) and learners who have distinct exceptionalities (children with differences in vision, hearing, speech, emotions, giftedness, and so on). In both instances, the science teaching techniques we recommend to help the few students in your class who may have special needs will better serve the needs of all learners.

The chapter begins with an investigation of several general factors that impede science learning and provides teaching recommendations beneficial for all children. After reading the first part of this chapter, you should be able to

1. Describe the special needs of children who are members of minority groups, culturally different, and/or multilingual.
2. Practice techniques that help meet their special needs.
3. Promote gender equality in your classroom.
4. Identify the different learning styles.
5. Discuss management and teaching practices that encourage all learners.

The second part of this chapter should help you to

1. Identify characteristics of the exceptional students who will enrich your classes.
2. Practice classroom techniques that help meet these special needs.

The third part of this chapter explores ways to include parents in science teaching.

## SCIENCE FOR ALL

Not all children come to school able to function effectively within a school's culture. Some children lack the skills necessary to cope with the routines or rigors of schooling. These children often feel hostile toward school and toward any authority figure, especially a teacher.

Being different carries liabilities. The price of being different may be exclusion from social groups at school and prejudiced treatment from those who appear not to be different. Cultural differences can contribute to the difficulties and problems of school children. The principles of multicultural education can help us meet the special needs of all children.

## Celebrating Diversity

All children are culturally different. Multicultural education strives to promote the often-overlooked contributions made by less-dominant cultures. Children who are culturally different may include those of minority races or children with special needs, as well as children who come from home environments out of the mainstream of society. Cultural differences include those of race, religion, economic level, ethnic background, the primary language used by the child, and in some instances gender. Different backgrounds often offer rich heritages beneficial to all. Cultural pluralism brings the perspectives of many cultures to our schools. The history of our nation is strong as a result of the contributions of this heritage.

The importance of cultural pluralism is recognized and supported in the 1991 Position Statement on Multicultural Science Education from the National Science Teachers Association. This statement encourages teachers to seek resources to ensure effective science learning for culturally diverse populations. The position statement urges that teachers

- provide access to high-quality science education experiences so that culturally diverse populations can become successful participants in our democratic society,
- select and use curriculum materials and teaching strategies that reflect and incorporate diversity,
- become aware of children's learning styles and instructional preferences,
- expose culturally diverse children to career opportunities in science, engineering, and technology (NSTA, 1991).

Although the challenge can be great, preparation in science can lead to higher paying careers, more critical thinkers, and a greater number of future technical workers who can fill vital vacancies and support our nation's economy (Linn, 1994).

**Who Makes Up Culturally Diverse Populations?**    Often the African American child who lives in poverty is envisioned as a typical example of one who is culturally different. This is an inaccurate stereotype of African Americans. Although the example does apply, culturally different children are as likely to come from the hills and mountains of Appalachia, Spanish-speaking communities of the Southwest, French settlements of the northernmost regions of Maine, or Asian communities of the West Coast. Let us not overlook the Native Americans who once were the majority on this land. They, too, are now culturally different from a changed mainstream society. In fact, each of us can become culturally different when we enter a community or region where our identity is not among the majority of the residents.

*All children benefit from learning science.*

***How Can You Use Cultural Differences to Promote Greater Science Under-
standing?***   Your science classes can reflect greater cultural diversity if your instruction reflects contributions made by people all over the world. Often our
print materials and media leave the impression that science is a recent white
European construct. In fact this impression is very wrong. Consider that

> over 5000 years ago in Egypt and Mesopotamia copper was being extracted from
> its ores, glass was made, and fabrics were dyed with natural colors. . . . Iron
> swords are known to have been produced over 3000 years ago. . . . Distillation
> was used in Mesopotamia as far back as 1200 B.C. for the production of
> perfumes. . . . Many of the techniques and much of the terminology of modern
> chemistry derives from ancient times; for example, *alkali* from the Arabic *al
> qality*—the roasted ashes; *soda* from Arabic *studa*—a splitting headache. (Williams,
> 1984, pp. 133–146)

You can promote diversity education in your science class by

- *Developing science themes related to conservation and pollution, disease, food and health, and population growth and teaching with consideration for humankind as a whole.* Develop an understanding among your students about the interdependence of people and unequal distribution of natural resources.
- *Selecting classroom teaching examples that address the contributions and participation of people from a range of backgrounds, cultures, and genders.*
- *Considering carefully any issues of race, gender, and human origins by exploring the myths that surround them* (Antonouris, 1989, p. 98).
- *Challenging inaccurate statements students make about ethnic minority communities and people.* Statements may refer to different physical features, countries of origin, religion, language, and customs (Antonouris, 1989). For example, we have all heard myths about the strengths and weaknesses of blacks, Asians, women, and so on. As educated adults, we understand that these alleged qualities cannot be applied to all members of a group and that beliefs like these arise from ignorance. We know that human beings are much more alike than they are different. Use science teaching as an opportunity to refute these myths when children repeat them.

***How Can You Meet the Needs of Children from Diverse Backgrounds?*** Although they come from different backgrounds and ways of life, culturally different children seem to share some characteristics. Here are some tips for meeting their needs:

*Children with different experiences.* What most of us take for granted may be completely lacking from the childhoods of children who are culturally different, minority, low income, or disabled. For example, herds of domestic animals, menageries of pets, and/or wild animals that roam at will may be as foreign to a city dweller as the piles of wind-tossed convenience packaging, crowds of densely packed people, and clouds of smog are to the rancher. Classroom activities, videos, and field trips with planned comparative discussions help to build awareness about and tolerance for differences by adding new experiences. Yet real experiences are a better choice. Activity-based science learning has long proven to help the students who are culturally different reach higher levels of science achievement, develop better process skills, and develop more logical thought processes (Bredderman, 1982).

*Children with a desire for action rather than words.* Few children who are multilingual or multicultural will be patient enough to listen to long instructions or descriptions. Get to the point. Provide simple, direct demonstrations and concrete experiences. Indeed, all children benefit from clarity and directness.

*Children who need a better vocabulary.* The rough, blunt street talk or backwoods language of some children can cause quite a culture shock. In the same way, the child with limited English proficiency who speaks haltingly may have difficulty following a normal conversation. Children need a vocabulary suited to the mainstream if they are to become competitive in the workplace. Science offers abundant opportunities for developing vocabulary and effective communication skills.

*Children who are disorganized.* Children can become frustrated and misunderstand the purpose of an activity if there are too many choices or if your instructions are too flexible. Some children may live in cultures in which they are not encouraged to make many of their own decisions. Be definite and clear with your instructions.

*Children who need genuine (rather than patronizing) relationships.* Be empathetic rather than sympathetic. Looking down on the students' different social or economic standing is demeaning despite your best intentions.

*Children who cannot easily control their own destinies.* Poverty tends to produce feelings of hopelessness and desperation. Children who are culturally different, minority, low income, or disabled may feel that they have little or no control over their lives and may look for immediate gratification. Fate control is defined as the belief that you can control what happens to you. Many children from culturally different backgrounds believe that what happens to them happens by chance or that their future lies in the hands of others who are more powerful and beyond influence. Science experiments help children to learn that variables can be manipulated to produce different outcomes. Educators have realized for decades that children can apply this understanding about variables to themselves and eventually use their understanding to help shift the locus of fate control to a point where they perceive the power to control their own lives (Rowe, 1974).

### How Can You Help Non-English-Speaking Students?

Lack of familiarity with the dominant spoken language can cause students to believe their fate is beyond their control. However, a shortcoming in using the dominant spoken language may not indicate a lack of intelligence. It is possible that the non-English-speaking student possesses what Howard Gardner calls "linguistic intelligences," the capacity to use native language to express thinking and to understand other people (Checkley, 1997). Therefore, children can be helped if your efforts and focused upon helping them to use the second language proficiently. The following tips can assist non-English speakers in your classes.

**Help Students to Help Themselves.**   Ideally, students should learn to help themselves learn. Try these approaches:

*Distribute a vocabulary list and/or copy of the curriculum guide at the beginning of each unit.* This material helps students know exactly what will be expected of them and will give them additional time to master the difficult terms.

*Ask students who are readers of their native language to carry pocket dictionaries (English-to-native language and vice versa).* At times simple words create communication barriers. Pocket dictionaries can solve the problem and help create the self-sufficient habit of looking up unfamiliar words. English-speaking students can be encouraged to do the same as a way of learning words in another language.

*Invite the students who are uncomfortable with English to ask questions.* This personal invitation, in a nonthreatening environment, will help students to overcome fear of using the new language. The joy of being successful at expressing opinions or asking questions becomes a positive reinforcer.

*Be patient.* Wait-time is particularly important for multilingual speakers, to allow them to form their questions or answers.

*Encourage the children to write their own translations of words in their notes.* As you examine lab notebooks and see translations, you will be aware that the student has looked up the words and probably understands them better.

*Encourage students to read science articles and books in their own languages.* Additional supplemental readings such as those available from *Scholastic* provide brief, popular articles and photographs that encourage additional practice with the language.

*I Hear and I Forget.* For those times when you feel you must lecture, try the following to help students remember:

*Speak slowly and enunciate clearly.* All students benefit from this because the technical words of science at times seem like a foreign language.

*On the chalkboard or overhead projector, display an outline or definitions, descriptions, or figures to add meaning to your spoken words.*

*Add emphasis to the main ideas.* Underline concepts or highlight the important meanings. Non-English speakers will remember to look them up later, while other students will treat the emphasis as a study cue.

*I See and I Remember.* A picture really is worth a thousand words. It provides another mode for learning, and it is helpful for memory retention. Try these suggestions:

*Use visual aids as often as possible.* The problem in science education is deciding what to teach and what materials to use, not the availability of interesting, useful materials. Check the school district's resource center or curriculum library or the education resource co-op that serves your school. There is a wealth of films, videos, film strips, bulletin board ideas, computer programs, models, posters, and charts. Old, discarded science textbooks or magazines can be salvaged for useful visual aids.

*Nurture animals and plants.* They add excitement and can also make superior visual aids.

*Use artwork.* Add your own artwork and invite talented student artists to contribute to your notes, transparencies, learning activity illustrations, and lab activities. Stick figures with details are fine too.

*I Do and I Understand.* All three learning approaches—hearing, seeing, and doing—are important, especially when all five senses are stimulated. Combined approaches provide better opportunities for understanding than a single approach. The power of activity learning stimulates improved communication as well as greater levels of science achievement, process skill development, scientific attitudes, and logical thinking than traditional teaching, in which teacher talk and student reading dominate (Shymansky, Kyle & Allport, 1982). Keep these suggestions in mind while working with non-English speakers:

*Try the "demonstrate–group investigate–individual investigate" teaching model.*   You can demonstrate the concept and create interest as well as stimulate curiosity. A demonstration also gives students an opportunity to listen and observe before having to produce any language. Group investigation can help learners comprehend and practice communication skills with peers. Language skills are developed naturally as students observe and communicate with others. Independent individual investigation helps students to explore questions that are related to the concept but already familiar to them. Table 5.1 provides some examples of this teaching and learning model.

*Have students do hands-on, lab-type learning activities often.* The minds-on experiences that accompany hands-on learning can contribute to language and

### TABLE 5.1   Language Development Model

| Teacher Demonstration | Group Investigation | Individual Investigation |
|---|---|---|
| *Concept:* **Electrical energy causes motion.** | | |
| Use an inflated balloon to pick up small pieces of paper. | Use an inflated balloon to cause another balloon to move. | Use an inflated balloon to test what objects it will pick up. |
| *Concept:* **Rapid motion causes the temperature of objects to rise.** | | |
| Rub a wooden block over sandpaper to show how the temperature of the block goes up. | Bend paper clip rapidly back and forth, and use cheeks to test for temperature change. | Find other objects (e.g., saw, chisel, file) outside the classroom that change temperature after rapid motion, and test them for temperature change. |
| *Concept:* **Animals move in different ways; some animals move by stretching.** | | |
| Use earthworms to show how they move by stretching because they have no legs. | Observe earthworm activity when these are placed in a carton of soil. | Find examples of other animals without legs outside the classroom or in pictures. Name and classify them according to how they move. |
| *Concept:* **Rapidly moving air causes some objects to rise.** | | |
| Hold a long piece of paper to the bottom lip and blow hard across the top of the paper to show how it moves up. | Blow hard across the top of a balloon, and then try to explain why it rises and what makes airplanes rise into the air. | Use a fan to see what objects you can lift up into the air. |

*Source:* A. K. Fathman, M. E. Quinn, and C. Kessler, *Teaching Science to English Learners, Grades 4–8* (Washington, DC: National Clearinghouse for Bilingual Education, 1992), p. 13 (ERIC Document Reproduction Service No. ED 349 844).

reading development. Some non-English-speaking students may not understand a lecture, discussion, or teacher demonstration, but once they have done it themselves, the experience is easier for them to link with the language. You can assist language development by focusing on one or two language functions that are particularly appropriate for the planned activities. "Language functions are specific uses of language for accomplishing certain functions. . . . For example, *directing* (giving and following directions) may be emphasized in an activity where the teacher first gives directions on how to build a rocket" (Fathman, Quinn, & Kessler, 1992, p. 16) and then has students work in groups to direct each other in building their own paper rockets. Table 5.2 shows several language functions that are commonly used in science classrooms.

*Coordinate your teaching with the English as a Second Language (ESL) teacher.* Blend the grammar and vocabulary used in both classes so the students have a double exposure to the science vocabulary.

*Link science concepts with the students' background experiences.* Learn what you can about the children's countries of origin and refer to geographical locations, climate conditions, fauna and flora, and so on to link the new science concepts with what the students already know. Why is it always necessary to mention the Rocky Mountains or the Mississippi? The rest of the class will benefit from the geography enrichment.

*Use guest speakers and field trips.* These are good ways to help multilingual students become more accepted and feel at home in their new environment and with science. Be aware of the linguistic and cultural differences and include all children in the full range of activities. Invite speakers from the students' countries of origin to help classmates become familiar with people from other cultures.

---

### TABLE 5.2   Language Functions

Language functions are specific uses of language for accomplishing certain purposes. Teachers can help students develop an understanding of these functions by building them into their lessons. Verbal ("What to Discuss") and written ("What to Record") exercises can be included in teacher demonstrations and student group and individual investigations.

| | | |
|---|---|---|
| Directing | Requesting | Questioning |
| Praising | Cautioning | Encouraging |
| Advising | Suggesting | Disagreeing |
| Agreeing | Describing | Expressing opinions |
| Refusing | Accepting | Defining |

*Source:* A. K. Fathman, M. E. Quinn, C. Kessler, *Teaching Science to English Learners, Grades 4–8* (Washington, DC: National Clearinghouse for Bilingual Education, 1992), p. 13 (ERIC Document Reproduction Service No. ED 349 844).

*Try to Reduce Test Anxiety.* Children from other countries often attach more importance to testing and achievement than native-born American children might. The mere mention of a test can evoke much anxiety because of its importance in determining children's academic futures in other countries, and a test in the English language can pump anxiety to counterproductive levels. The following suggestions offer some ideas for reducing test anxiety:

*Try puzzles.* Crossword puzzles assist spelling and provide additional cues for correct answers. Students seem to do better when they know how many letters to expect in an answer. A list of words helps, too, for crosswords and fill-in-the-blank questions.

*Encourage children to draw.* Invite children to draw answers rather than write. This is a good way to communicate ideas as the child gets around the temporary language barriers.

*Encourage students to check their work.* At the end of each test, consider allotting 3 to 5 minutes for students to check answers. Permit them to use books, notes, and class handouts.

*Try bonus points for extra credit.* Offer bonus points for student creations. Science-oriented jokes, riddles, poems, and songs that use the concepts and vocabulary being studied can be a great way to encourage review and creativity. Permitted as homework, this can also be a good way to promote language study between the child and parents.

### Is Gender Equality a Special Need?

Females do not have equal access to nor do they receive equal encouragement to pursue careers in science. This appears to be a cultural problem linked to how females are socialized in the mainstream of society; it is not a women's problem. Often males and females, by age eleven, have developed strong sex-stereotyped attitudes concerning socially appropriate behavior and gender roles in society (Chivers, 1986). Although improvements have been made, many people still attribute cultural differences to gender. Cultural gender differences play an important role in career selection.

***How Does Culture Affect Females in Science?*** There are cultural disincentives for women to pursue careers in science, technology, and mathematics. Proportionally fewer women and minorities have been encouraged to develop a sufficient background for scientific careers, and they are underrepresented in these careers, although more women are employed in science careers today than during the prior decade.

The current problem of gender inequity has arisen from several factors; some still persist despite the enlightened efforts or many to improve conditions and to encourage more females to pursue science. Consider:

- Parents, teachers, school counselors, and peers discourage females from pursuing scientific careers (Elfner, 1988).

*Females deserve equal encouragement and access to science.*

- Most early childhood elementary teachers are women who lack strong background in science; their lack of confidence can reinforce children's beliefs that women are not supposed to like science (Chivers, 1986; Shepardson & Pizzini, 1992).
- A shortage of appropriate female science and engineering role models reinforces the belief that science is a male domain (Jones & Wheatley, 1988; Hammrich, 1997).
- Young males report more positive attitudes toward science and young females less positive attitudes; females report less confidence and more fear of success in careers like engineering; females report that physics courses are too difficult (Jones & Wheatley, 1988; Kahle & Rennie, 1993; Hammrich, 1997).
- Females may not be socialized at home or at school to develop and demonstrate scientific skills and may not be encouraged to develop practical ability,

independence, and self-confidence. Several studies reveal that skills and characteristics associated with scientists are those often attributed to masculine characters: high intellectual ability, persistence at work, extreme independence, and apartness from others. Females may be hesitant to pursue science because they fear that they will be considered unfeminine (Jones & Wheatley, 1988; Shepardson & Pizzini, 1992; Hammrich, 1997). Even the toys typically given to boys require more assembly and manipulation than the toys given to girls.

- When women have problems, they tend to blame themselves for the problems or the inability to solve them, whereas when men have difficulties, they tend to place the blame outside themselves. These differences can tend to develop female feelings of learned helplessness and may cause females to believe that they are not intellectually capable (Jones & Wheatley, 1988).

- Teachers reflect the values and expectations thrust upon them by the dominant society and can unintentionally perpetuate sex stereotypes in science. In addition, sex bias can be observed in the practices of teachers and the assignments of science teachers. Female science teachers usually are assigned to introductory science classes and biology, whereas males more often are high school department chairmen and are assigned to teach such advanced science classes as chemistry and physics (Jones & Wheatley, 1988; Kahle & Rennie, 1993).

*How Do Teachers Contribute to Gender Problems in Science?*   Although the role of teachers perpetuating sex-role stereotypes has not been fully explored, the literature indicates that teachers are not consciously and intentionally sex stereotyping students. Many teachers do try to treat males and females fairly and equally. Often teachers tell us that they want all children to develop to their full potential. But some effects are larger than life. We were all raised in a society in which gender differences are prevalent. Parents, school counselors, other teachers, social workers, books, and television have taught teachers (even you!) that certain behaviors are appropriate for females and others are appropriate for males (Sadker, Sadker, & Thomas, 1981; Shepardson & Pizzini, 1992; Hammrich, 1997; Pollina, 1995; Shakeshaft, 1995). Bias by gender will begin to change only when you are able to recognize the subtle messages that steer males and females toward particular behaviors and career choices.

Considerable evidence indicates that teachers' expectations affect students' performances. Elementary teachers often perceive males to have higher scientific ability than females. This perception usually sends a negative message to females, influences the self-perceptions of females, and determines the tasks and responsibilities that teachers assign to students during scientific activities (Shepardson & Pizzini, 1992). More likely, females are given passive roles to perform during group activities (Baker, 1988; Kahle, 1990; Shakeshaft, 1995), which reinforce teachers' perceptions that females are less interested and less capable in science (Shepardson & Pizzini, 1992). Cooper's model (1979) is based on this evidence and explains how sex differences in achievement may stem from differences in teacher expectations (see Figure 5.1). The model, which consists of the following steps, can be useful for overcoming gender stereotypes:

**Step 1. Form different expectations for students.**

Regardless of gender, hold high but realistic expectations for all students.

**Step 2. Believe that females are as capable in science as males.**

Do not be tempted to assign class roles or jobs based on flawed beliefs that females are better note takers and writers and males are better handlers of equipment.

**Step 3. Encourage females to take the lead in activities, to make lab decisions, to take measurements and handle equipment.**

Do the same for males, but without leading them to believe they are better at it than females.

**Step 4. Strive for equal amounts and types of nurturant contact with females and males.**

Several studies in preschool and elementary classrooms indicate that males often receive more attention from teachers and more feedback about their

**FIGURE 5.1    Overcoming Gender Stereotypes**

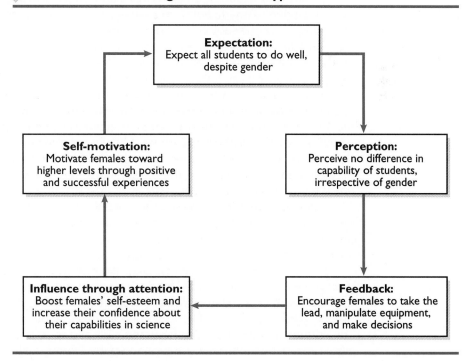

performance (Jones & Wheatley, 1988; Shepardson & Pizzini, 1992). Added attention can bolster student beliefs about the importance of their effort and encourage them to work harder.

**Step 5. Provide opportunities for success.**

As children master classroom tasks, they become more motivated to strive for even higher quality. Females will undertake and excel at physical science study instead of achieving dramatically less than males do by the seventh grade.

***What Can You Do to Overcome Gender Inequality in Science?***    Gender bias can begin at an early age. The younger the child when you begin to address the issue, the better your chances of having an impact. From early childhood, males are often treated as if they are expected to be more independent, creative, and manipulative. These early experiences may affect their development of spatial and verbal abilities (Levin & Ornstein, 1983). Males often have many more opportunities to experience science-oriented activities than females, although females have the interest to become more involved in science, if given the opportunity (Kahle & Lakes, 1983; Kahle & Rennie, 1993; Shakeshaft, 1995). Some things you can do to help promote gender equality in your science class include the following:

*Strengthen your science preparation.* Particularly if you are a female, strive to strengthen your experience with science and project the importance of science to your students. You do not want to suggest that science is not for women. Your attitude toward the subject will have a powerful effect on all the children.

*Strive to become aware of your own subtle biases and different expectations for students.* Examine how you assign classroom tasks and the daily life examples you use of science at work for evidence of subtle gender bias.

*Experiment with single-sex class groups.* Until you develop more skills at creating and maintaining a nonsexist learning environment, females may receive less biased treatment if they are not paired with males for small-group activities. Females in mixed groups have been found to spend more time than males watching and listening, whereas in same-sex groups females spend the same amount of time as males in same-sex groups on hands-on science processes and experimental tasks (Rennie & Parker, 1986; Shepardson & Pizzini, 1992; Rop, 1998).

*Expect the same from females as from males.* Examine your reinforcement for equality, fairness in discipline, and encouraging nonverbal behavior toward females, especially during science class. Ensure that females participate fully in all science activities.

*Be aware of the difficulties some females may experience when using equipment unfamiliar to them.* Logical-mathematical, spatial, and bodily kinesthetic intelligences (Gardner, 1983) are essential in science; however, they are not confined to one gender. Rather, differences in social expectations often lead parents to give different types of toys to boys and girls and encourage different types of social interactions through games and sports. Young males are often encouraged to manipulate objects that are very similar to the tools and equipment of science. Young females may not have been encouraged by their parents to use a variety of tools and could have some initial difficulty with science equipment. A little extra time and encouragement early on will help females build their confidence so they can cope easily (Pollina, 1995) and develop important skills.

*Hands-on learning is a great equalizer.* Science process-oriented learning tasks help females to acquire manipulative experiences that put them on par with males, making access to science learning more equal (Humrich, 1988; Shepardson & Pizzini, 1992).

*Treat science as gender free.* Do not always refer to scientists as males; lift up female scientists as role models.

*Invite female science role models.* Males will be well served too, because they will see new opportunities for females.

*Help female students develop personal characteristics that are associated with success in science.* Encourage them to break away from any submissive behavior patterns and encourage them to become more independent and self-reliant. Also encourage females to explore new topics and materials and to test out their new ideas and interests (Kahle & Rennie, 1993; Shepardson & Pizzini, 1992).

*Screen teaching materials.* Examine all print materials and media for gender bias. Posters, textbooks, filmstrips, and other media should have equal representations of males and females.

Anna Pollina (1995) offers specific actions in Table 5.3 on page 156 to help you bring gender balance to your science lessons.

## Similarities in Learning

Children from other cultures or who are not English speakers benefit from specific management and teaching techniques. The recommendations we have offered reveal some similarities. Indeed, most children can benefit from the suggestions recommended for special groups of learners. Children benefit when they are taught with the learning styles they prefer.

***Multiple Intelligences and Learning Styles.*** Multiple intelligence is a popular psychological and educational concept that embodies an effort to understand how cultures and disciplines shape human potential by studying how individual learners respond to different types of content and solve problems or construct something that is valued (Checkley, 1997). Eight intelligences are recognized: linguistic, logical-mathematics, spatial, bodily kinesthetic, musical, interpersonal, intrapersonal, and naturalist. Each intelligence has a particular representation in the brain and each individual may be particularly good or impaired in one or more of these intelligences (Gardner in Checkley, 1997). Multiple intelligences are focused on content or products of learning (Silver et al., 1997), whereas learning styles focuses upon the processes of learning: the ways learners think and feel as they solve problems, interact and create products that represent learning (Silver et al., 1997).

## ◆ TABLE 5.3    Bringing Gender Balance to Your Science Lessons

Despite change efforts for more than a decade, females are greatly underrepresented in fields such as physical sciences, engineering, and technology. Past efforts that have attempted to increase female involvement in the sciences ranged from awareness programs in elementary schools to direct intervention at the collegiate level. Often the change efforts attempted to "masculinize" the females—to help them participate in the sciences by becoming more aggressive, more analytical, emotionally tougher, and more competitive. These efforts yielded spurious results; decreases in female self-esteem were recorded. Anna Pollina reports ten recent successful and proven strategies, based on research, that celebrate the characteristics that many females bring to science, which are vital to science and science education.

1. *Connect science and technology to the real world.* Connecting any subject to the lives of real people and the good of the world is a powerful hook for females.

2. *Choose metaphors carefully, and have students develop their own.* In the past we have asked females to "tackle" problems, used "batting averages" to illustrate points, and have used the "paths of rockets" to demonstrate principles of physics. Use images of science that are more comfortable for females. This is more than political correctness—it is essential.

3. *Foster an atmosphere of collaboration.* Turn taking in small groups of circled students is not collaboration. Small groups work for females if all group members are taught to listen, be respectful, be noncompetitive, and are held responsible for one another's learning.

4. *Encourage females to act as experts.* Females begin to see themselves as scientists when the group is responsible for verifying its own logic, and when the students are responsible for critiquing their own work as well as the work of their peers.

5. *Give females the opportunity to be in control of technology.* Expect females to share in the uses of technology, to demonstrate its uses to others, to complete basic repairs, and to deal with simple emergencies.

6. *Portray technology as a way to solve problems.* Females most often use technology as a tool rather than as a toy. One way to help them see that technology is relevant to their lives is to emphasize the networking and communications capabilities. Pairing females can help to create a comfortable, supportive way to use the technology.

7. *Capitalize on females' verbal strengths.* Encourage all students to express the logic for their choices and solutions in spoken, written, or picture form. Proofs should be well-constructed, complete arguments.

8. *Experiment with testing and evaluation.* Embedded assessments work well for females. These are alternatives to right/wrong choices and make use of females' abilities to synthesize material, make connections, and use their practical intelligence. Some examples could be working in groups to perform experiments, identify patterns, hypothesize outcomes.

9. *Give frequent feedback, and keep expectations high.* Females may tend to need more encouragement than males in science. You can do this by giving frequent feedback such as homework checks, quizzes, and comments that reinforce the students' beliefs in their control over the material.

10. *Experiment with note-taking techniques.* Females are dutiful learners who can become so absorbed in the task of note taking that they miss opportunities to become involved in important discussions. Try "no-note-taking-allowed" times, distribute written summaries, or have diagrams and figures on file for learners to access when they are needed.

*Source:* A. Pollina, "Gender Balance: Lessons from Girls in Science and Mathematics," *Educational Leadership 53,* 1 (1995): 30–33.

*Children perceive in different ways and prefer various learning environments.*

The concept of learning styles arises from the general acceptance that we all learn in a variety of ways (processes), that those ways can be identified, and that teachers can teach in ways that capitalize on student preferences. If they begin from a position of strength (preferred learning style), learners can be exposed to other ways of learning and expand their repertoires as they overcome weaknesses.

Teaching to accommodate different learning styles helps teachers reach each individual. Students who need special assistance receive instruction through their preferred learning style during the intervention process. Children learn about how they learn and are encouraged to use their strengths. All benefit from the variety of approaches. Teachers also plan instruction carefully to make certain that all children have an opportunity to learn through their own preferred styles.

*Types of Styles.* Learning styles are often classified by function. As learners, we have different modes of perception, we prefer various environments, we are motivated by different things, we express ourselves uniquely, we think differently, and we prefer various levels of mobility as we learn. True individualization is a challenge. At least nine learning styles can be identified by function (Dunn & Dunn, 1975) and are considered widely representative of children's preferences for processing information:

1. *Visual*—prefer to perceive by seeing words, numbers, charts, models, objects, and so on.

2. *Auditory*—prefer to perceive meaning by hearing.
3. *Bodily kinesthetic*—prefer to be involved, hands on.
4. *Individual learners*—prefer to work alone. This type of student may be more confident in his or her own opinion than in the ideas of others.
5. *Group learners*—prefer to learn with at least one other child.
6. *Oral expressive*—can easily tell or explain their ideas and opinions. They may know more than they can reveal on a test.
7. *Written expressive*—write fluent essays or good answers on tests. Their thoughts are organized better on paper than they are presented orally.
8. *Sequential*—have the ability to arrange thoughts and ideas in a linear, organized fashion.
9. *Global*—have the ability to be spontaneous, flexible thinkers. These learners may be quiet and intuitive and order their thoughts randomly, preferring to do things their own way.

All learners do not fit exclusively into one style and outstanding performance using one or more of these styles may indicate a strong, specialized intelligence. Many children may share strong preferences among several styles. All students can be served better when learning opportunities are provided in multisensory, multiexpressive, and multienvironmental modes. The following suggestions can help a wide variety of learners, particularly those who have special needs.

*Establish classroom and study routines.* Many children are unable to organize unaided, and traditional school learning cannot occur until organization is established. You can provide a helpful model for children if you are well organized and consistent in your classroom. Children will then know what to do and how to do it.

*Limit choices.* Democratic learning and cooperative learning encourage choices, but this approach may not help children who get confused easily. Asking "Would you like to . . . " implies choice. As an example, if your intention is to have a child put science equipment back on the storage shelf or follow a specific instruction, it is better for the child if your instructions are explicit and/or provide limited choices.

*Make certain the children are attending to what is going on.* Asking students to repeat instructions or information, requesting a response to a specific question, requiring that a child complete a specific motor task, and maintaining eye contact are some ways to determine the extent to which a child may be attending to what is going on around him or her. Focus on each child often.

*Give clues to help remembering.* Use mnemonic devices, rhymes, auditory associations, linking associations, and visual clues to help the child remember. Help the children construct personal memory devices.

*Sequence instruction carefully.* Concept mapping and task analysis can help you to find the most logical sequence of any task. The four Ws help to begin a task analysis: *what* to teach, *where* to begin, *when* the objective has been met, and *what* to teach next. Figure 5.2 provides a more detailed model for analyzing and determining the sequence for science concepts.

**FIGURE 5.2   Concept Analysis Model for Teaching Children with Special Needs**

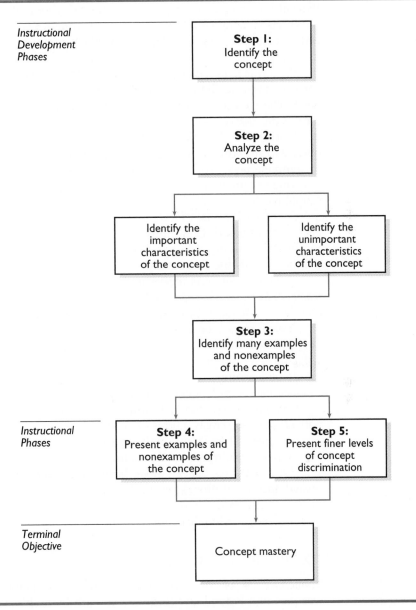

*Instructional Development Phases*

**Step 1:** Identify the concept

**Step 2:** Analyze the concept

Identify the important characteristics of the concept

Identify the unimportant characteristics of the concept

**Step 3:** Identify many examples and nonexamples of the concept

*Instructional Phases*

**Step 4:** Present examples and nonexamples of the concept

**Step 5:** Present finer levels of concept discrimination

*Terminal Objective*

Concept mastery

*Source:* Adapted from "Concept Analysis: A Model for Teaching Basic Science Concepts to Intellectually Handicapped Students" by Jack T. Cole, Margie K. Kitano, and Lewis M. Brown in Marshall E. Corrick, Jr. (Ed.), *Teaching Handicapped Students* (Washington, DC: NEA, 1981), p. 52. Reprinted with permission.

*Separate teaching and testing.* Worksheet assignments may seem to the students more like a test than the type of reinforcement activity you may intend. Provide instructional assistance to encourage learning and to help lower the failure rate. An example at the top of a worksheet or a list of guiding questions can transform the assignment from a test into a learning task. Also provide models, cues, verbal and written prompts, and correct answers as feedback.

*Be specific with criticism and praise.* Tell the child exactly why the response is correct or wrong. Telling the child to try number two again will cause him or her to change an answer, but he or she will not know what to change. When part of the answer is correct, tell the child; also identify what is not correct.

*Provide time clues.* Some children may have difficulty remembering time sequences, estimating time intervals, and determining the amount of time needed to complete tasks. By routinely displaying schedules in prominent places and referring to time in the classroom, you can help students learn to structure their school work.

*Confer with special education teachers, second-language teachers, and gifted and talented coordinators.* Continuity of content and consistency of management and routines help many children. Coordinate your classroom activities with those of other classes the child attends.

*Show empathy, encouragement, sensitivity, and understanding for each child's attempts to learn, to remember, and to conform to your routines.* Point out the child's abilities and respect the child as a human being.

*Provide kinesthetic experiences, practical hands-on learning activities with concrete, relevant materials.* Children who are experience-deficient will benefit, as will children who prefer this type of learning. Hands-on experiences stimulate minds-on learning.

*Identify desired behaviors, set clear expectations, and reduce distractions.*

*Simplify.* Break each task down into its simplest steps; assist the students with step-by-step instructions.

*Give frequent feedback.* Small improvements deserve praise, and precise direction helps children continue to improve.

*Use the preferred learning mode.* If the child has a dominant mode of learning (visual, tactile, auditory), use it. Regard the preference as a strength and try to build success on it. Then use this preference to help build self-esteem on successes before tackling learning weaknesses.

## SCIENCE FOR EXCEPTIONAL CHILDREN

Public Law 94–142 of 1975 (the Education for All Handicapped Children Act) was part of a federal law (Individuals with Disabilities Education Act, IDEA) that helped to ensure a place for students with disabilities in American public schools. This law was amended in 1990 and again in 1997. Now called the Individuals with Disabilities Education Act, IDEA ensures that all children with disabilities have the right to a free, appropriate public education. The law includes specific categories of disability: deafness, hearing impairment, mental retardation, orthopedic impairment, other health impairment, serious emotional disturbance, specific learning disability, speech impairment, and visual impairment.

A "least restrictive environment" is encouraged so that students with disabilities are educated in regular classrooms where appropriate. Placement decisions are based on extensive assessment, parental consent, and decision making among school personnel that must follow due process of law.

The presence of students with disabilities in regular classrooms does not mean that the curriculum must be the same for all children. Federal law states that the schooling of children with disabilities must be differentiated according to their special needs and provided with necessary support. This may require a degree of individualized education not usually found in typical classrooms. The Individualized Education Program (IEP) prescribes goals for the school year based on present performance levels, specific educational services the school must provide, the extent to which the student participates in the regular classroom, and schedules and procedures for evaluation. Indeed, many educators believe the intent of the IEP benefits all children. Table 5.4 on pages 162–164 provides a brief description of adaptations that help students who have special needs.

## Teaching Children Who Have Learning Disabilities

A child with a learning disability has the intellectual potential to succeed in school. But for some reason, the child's academic achievements are significantly below the expected level of performance in a specific subject such as reading or mathematics.

**What Is a Learning Disability?**   A child can be identified as having a learning disability if a school evaluation team finds a severe discrepancy between the child's achievement and intellectual ability in one or more of these areas: oral expression, listening comprehension, written expression, basic reading skill, reading comprehension, and mathematics calculation (Hallahan & Kauffman, 2000). The child may perform at or above the expected level in some school subjects but poorly in others. When this happens it is especially frustrating for the child and makes identification of the disability difficult. The child may develop failure-avoidance techniques that surface as behavior problems to draw attention away from areas of academic failure.

At least 5 percent of school-age children have learning disabilities (Hallahan & Kauffman, 2000). Perhaps 5 to 10 million children today may have some type of learning disability. The numbers have increased over time, in part because of greater sensitivity in assessment and diagnosis, teacher alertness for possible learning disabilities, and increases in poverty. For example, the number of children who live in poverty has increased from 15 to 19 percent since

**TABLE 5.4    Teaching Children Who Have Special Needs**

| Special Need | Environmental Adaptation | Materials Adaptation | Teaching Adaptation | Assessment Adaptation |
|---|---|---|---|---|
| Cultural | Carefully select visuals and non-print materials for cultural inclusion. Represent plural culture. Maintain clear classroom organization. Establish empathic relationships. | Use culturally representative materials. Avoid cultural stereotypes. Use broad themes to include all cultures. | Set explicit expectations, and give explicit instructions. Use divergent questions to encourage pluralism and inclusion. Challenge inaccurate statements. Include careful consideration of issues. Use experience-rich methods. | Provide and accept diverse contexts for assessment activities. |
| Non-English-speaking | Be patient. Use visual aids to help communicate. Provide direct experience. Encourage high levels of activity. | Maintain a conceptual focus. Enrich vocabulary development. | Be verbally clear. Maintain written clarity; use outlines. Emphasize concepts. Link concepts to experiences. Use guest speakers and field trips. Reduce test anxiety. | Encourage the use of pocket translators and dictionaries. Use pictorial assessment devices, puzzles, and performance tasks. |
| Gender | Nurture independence and self-confidence. Use hands-on learning activities. Use female role models in the sciences. | Identify and eliminate gender bias in materials. Use a wide variety of manipulatives. | Experiment with heterogeneous and single-sex grouping. Use cooperative learning techniques. Maintain high but realistic expectations for all. Provide frequent progress feedback. | None |
| Learning style preferences | Include all styles. | Select a balance of visual, auditory, kinesthetic, oral, and written materials. | Provide activities to match preference for individual, group, sequential, visual, verbal, auditory, and global learners. | Assess concepts through verbal, written, kinesthetic, individual, and group opportunities. |

| Special Need | Environmental Adaptation | Materials Adaptation | Teaching Adaptation | Assessment Adaptation |
|---|---|---|---|---|
| Learning disability | Show empathy. Seat away from distractions during introduction and when giving instructions. Focus attention by putting with well-behaved student for activity | Use concrete manipulatives. Screen out irrelevant materials and distractions. | Show clear expectations. Simplify; give cues and specific praise. Use dominant learning mode and multisensory activities. Use concept analysis. | Provide specific criticism and praise. Try oral tests. Modify reading and writing exercises if needed. |
| Intellectual | Limit visual and verbal distractions. | Select appropriate reading level. Use concrete, relevant manipulatives. | Use concept analysis. Simplify. Praise. Use repetition. Maintain eye contact. Engage in physical activity. Give feedback, use cues, cooperative learning. Use examples and nonexamples. Use brief periods of direct instruction. | Verbal tests. Provide assistance with written tests. Provide small-step progress checks. |
| Visual | Provide clear, predictable traffic pathways. Maintain organized, predictable locations for materials and storage. Provide good lighting. Seat student near activity. Sighted student tutor can assist. | Use voice tapes and audiotapes. Print materials should be large, clear, and uncluttered with numerous colors and geometric designs. Adapt materials to special equipment students may have to use. | Emphasize uses of other senses. Taped instructions or science information can be provided. Pair with sighted students. | More verbal assessment. Assist with written assessment. Assist with physical manipulation of objects during performance assessment. |

(*continued*)

**TABLE 5.4** *(continued)*

| Special Need | Environmental Adaptation | Materials Adaptation | Teaching Adaptation | Assessment Adaptation |
|---|---|---|---|---|
| Hearing | Seat so vision is not obstructed. Seat away from distracting background noises. | Modify for making observations through other senses. Use captioned films and videos. Use printed text to accompany audiotapes. Model or illustrate spoken instructions. | Face the child when speaking. Speak distinctly; do not shout. Use written outlines. | Avoid spoken forms of assessment. |
| Orthopedic | Identify and remove physical barriers. Provide adequate space for movement. Seat near exits for safety. Check tables and desks for proper height. | Identify devices that assist handling of objects, such as spring-loaded tongs, accountant's pencil grips, test tube racks. | Encourage physical manipulation of objects. Pair with nonimpaired student peer. Provide student training time with equipment prior to use. | Provide assistance with writing and manipulation of materials. |
| Behavior | Seat away from distractions. Provide well-lighted quiet space for study. | Train in use prior to providing special equipment. | Use brief activities. Give praise and cues. Reinforce desired behaviors. Obtain attention and establish eye contact prior to discussion or giving instructions. | None |
| Gifted | None | Advanced reading materials. Greater application of technology. | Emphasize problem solving. Accelerate pace. Arrange mentorships. Emphasize processes, mathematics, and uses of technology. | Increase expectations for analysis, application, and hypotheses. Use open-ended assessment devices. |

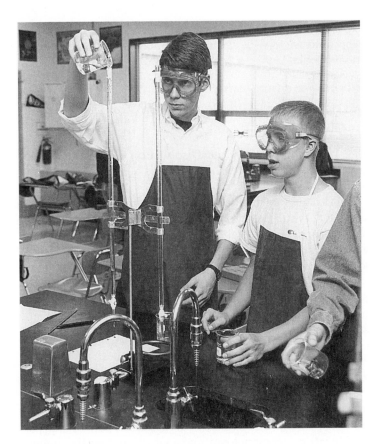

*Exceptional children learn science with the proper type of support and encouragement.*

the 1970s (U.S. Department of Education, 1977; Hallahan & Kauffman, 2000). Nationwide, nearly 30 percent of the students who receive special education services attend regular classrooms (Hallahan & Kauffman, 2000).

Learning disabilities are not diseases. There is no single learning disability. Disabilities include dysgraphia, disorders in written language; dyscalculia, disorders in arithmetic; dyslexia, disorders in receptive and expressive language and reading; and difficulties in perception of spatial relations and organization. Some famous people who have had learning disabilities include Thomas Edison, Albert Einstein, Winston Churchill, Cher, and Tom Cruise.

*How Can You Help a Child with Learning Disabilities?*   Structure is the most important concept when teaching children with learning disabilities. These children have perceptual and cognitive difficulties that may make it impossible for children to mask out unnecessary stimuli such as sights and sounds in the background of the classroom. Ways to promote structure include class and study routines, limited choices, focused attention, memory clues, sequenced instruction, clear distinctions between instruction and testing, specific criticism and praise, time clues, conferences with special education teachers, and empathy and encouragement (Coble, Levey, & Mattheis, 1985).

### Teaching Children Who Have Intellectual Disabilities

Some children in your classes will have intellectual disabilities, also referred to as *mental retardation.*

***Who Are the Children Who Have Intellectual Disabilities?***   There are different categories of mental retardation, and each has a range of different functions the child is expected to achieve.

Children with a mild degree of mental retardation requiring intermittent support may be included in your classroom. *Educable mentally retarded* (EMR) has been a term used to describe this level of intelligence and applies to about 11 percent of special needs children in U.S. public schools (Cheney & Roy, 1999). The American Association of Mental Deficiency describes children who have mental retardation as having subaverage intelligence and being deficient in behavior and responsibility for their age-related cultural group. These limitations affect academic and motor skills. Children with intellectual disabilities are capable of learning some academics, acquiring social skills, and developing occupational skills.

***How Can You Teach Children Who Have Intellectual Disabilities?***   Peer acceptance is very important for the child with an intellectual disability. By acquiring as much information as you can about the child, you can prepare to emphasize strengths while teaching to overcome weaknesses. School support services and special education personnel can make situation-specific suggestions to assist any particular child. However, the recommendations in Table 5.4 can help you enhance the child's academic skills.

Concept analysis is a time-tested strategy that has great potential for teaching science to children who have intellectual or learning disabilities as well as children who are not disabled. See Figure 5.2 for a visual guide to the five distinct steps of concept analysis (Cole, Kitano, & Brown, 1981).

### Step 1. Identify the concept.

Select the main idea to be taught.

### Step 2. Analyze the concept.

Identify the concept's critical attributes (characteristics that make the concept different from others) and its noncritical attributes.

### Step 3. Identify several examples and nonexamples of the concept.

Examples illustrate the critical attributes, and nonexamples do not contain the attributes.

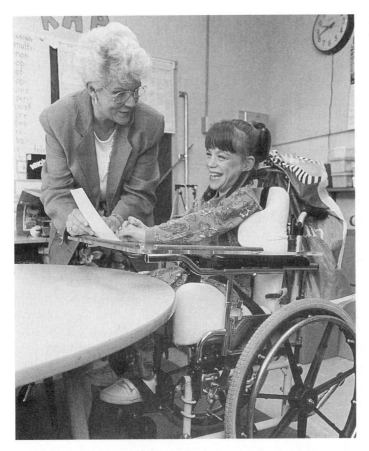

*Help children to overcome barriers to learning science.*

**Step 4. Present the examples and nonexamples of the concept.**

Use a variety of media and hands-on experiences to present the examples of the concept and to expose the children to nonexamples as well. The examples should be used to help children identify other examples that you have not identified for them. Comparisons with the nonexamples help to identify the attributes and nonattributes and help children transfer their learning to other situations.

**Step 5. Present finer levels of discrimination.**

A funnel approach can be used to move the children from making simple discriminations to more difficult comparisons.

### Teaching Children Who Have Physical Disabilities

Physical disabilities include visual, hearing, and orthopedic impairments. Conservative estimates suggest that less than 0.5 percent of school children may have a physical disability and about half of those have multiple disabilities, one-fourth have a chronic health problem and one-fourth have an orthopedic impairment without other serious complications (Hallahan & Kauffman, 2000).

***What Barriers Do Children with Physical Disabilities Face?***   Although few in number, children with physical disabilities carry huge burdens that limit their access to science education. Most of these burdens arise from the barriers the children encounter, such as

- parents and school advisers who limit the children through stereotypes and low expectations,
- classroom structures that limit accessibility and reduce exposure to tactile manipulative experiences that are critical to basic learning in science,
- science programs that have not been modified or adapted to meet the needs of children who have physical impairments,
- teachers who may harbor fearful or negative attitudes or who may treat the children in an overly protective or cautious manner.

***Why Is Science Important for Children Who Are Physically Disabled?***   Science instruction should begin at an early age and continue throughout schooling for children who are physically disabled. As early as 1983 the National Science Board Commission on Precollege Education in Mathematics, Science, and Technology offered three reasons for early and sustained education in science:

**1.** Science emphasizes hands-on experience and exploration of the environment. It can help to fill some experiential gaps that may have evolved because of extensive hospital stays and/or overprotectiveness of schools or parents. Science can help to develop the individual's independence and overall positive self-image.

**2.** Recent scientific and technological advances have provided tools such as computers, talking calculators, control systems, versabraille hook-ups to computers, and special telephone systems. These advances can help to mitigate the limitations imposed by a physical disability and can enable the individuals to become independent, contributing members of society. Science instruction that emphasizes making observations, collecting and organizing information, and making conclusions can help develop the individual's mental and manipulative readiness for using new technology.

**3.** Job opportunities in the future will require greater knowledge and understanding of technological devices. Computers will continue to be an important part of many jobs. Advances in technology have helped children with physical disabilities learn and provide new employment opportunities for them. Children with physical disabilities will need the background, training, and self-confidence to seek these opportunities.

***Visual Impairments.***   Children who are *educationally blind* and *partially sighted* are increasingly benefiting from regular education experiences. The educationally blind cannot read printed materials and must learn from voice, audio tapes, braille reading, and other forms of nonprinted materials. They may have residual vision and should be encouraged to use it as widely as possible. Children who are partially sighted can read printed materials, but that material must be larger than standard school print. Magnifying devices can also be used to enlarge standard print.

Children with severe vision problems are identified at an early age. However, less severe problems often go undetected for years. Regular classroom teachers may be the first to notice sight problems. Some behaviors that may indicate vision loss include squinting at the chalkboard, holding a book closer or farther away than most other children, blinking or otherwise distorting the eyes, holding the head at an odd angle, and unusual sensitivity to light. Refer all children who demonstrate any of these behaviors to the school official who can arrange a vision screening. Parents and children appreciate early notification.

*Teaching Children with Visual Impairments.* An audio-tactile teaching approach helps children who have visual impairments. Verbal lessons can be audiotaped for later playback, written assignments and tests can be tape-recorded, and a personal recorder with headphones can be used by children who are educationally blind without disturbing the rest of the class. (Be certain to provide verbal or tape-recorded feedback about answers too.) Magnified print materials and visual aids with high contrast can help children who are partially sighted.

Science process skills (Chapter 3) can provide helpful tactile experiences for the student with a visual impairment. Tactile experiences are more helpful than passive participation. Ideas include:

- modeling various birds and habitats with clay
- illustrating the carbon cycle of a forest with papier maché
- constructing leaf print books from old newspapers
- designing constellations by constructing paper stars
- illustrating a food chain by using natural objects
- designing cloud formations from cotton balls
- building bridges and other structures using drinking straws
- building a replica of a coral reef
- illustrating an electromagnetic wave by using iron filings and magnets
- constructing replicas of prehistoric tools

Instruction that stimulates the greatest range of senses (multimodal instruction) is vital for children with physical impairments. Commercial materials exist and may be modified to assist the student who is visually impaired. Programs such as the Elementary Science Study and Science: A Process Approach II have been used with over 3 million students. Teacher supplements are available with suggestions for modifications for students with disabilities. Adapting Science Materials for the Blind (ASMB) was developed from two

Science Curriculum Improvement Study units for use with visually impaired children in mainstreamed classrooms. Science Activities for the Visually Impaired (SAVI) have been designed especially for middle-level children.

Pair children with visual disabilities with sighted children. Several researchers have found that this approach enables the child with a visual impairment to achieve on par with their nondisabled peers. The sighted member of a team can translate the class experiences to the child with a visual disability, who can obtain an understanding through other senses. Together both can report the results of an experiment or activity.

*Hearing Impairments.*   *Deaf* and *hard of hearing* are two types of hearing impairments. Regular classroom teachers occasionally work with children who have profound hearing losses, but more often have students with some lesser degree of hearing loss. Common types of hearing impairments concern volume and pitch. Another type is intelligibility—the volume of a sound may be adequate, but it is garbled. Hearing aids, lipreading, expressions, and gestures help the child with a hearing disability succeed in the regular classroom.

Deafness is often identified early in childhood, but mild hearing losses frequently go undetected. The following behaviors may signal a hearing impairment that should be referred to school personnel for screening: odd positioning of the head while listening, inattention during discussions, often asking the speaker to repeat, and asking classmates for instructions.

*Teaching Children Who Have Hearing Impairments.*   Language development is one of the major problems for children who are hearing impaired. Direct experience with objects is essential if children are to develop language sufficiently, and objects from a child's environment enhance learning of scientific concepts. When we provide rich experiences, children who have hearing impairments can improve

> language performance, observing and listening skills, vocabulary, the learning of science concepts and development of cognitive skills through direct experiential experiences in science. In order for this learning to occur, students must have the opportunity of "doing science" by hands-on, inquiry, real-life experiences through direct physical manipulation of objects that focus attention on patterns of interaction in physical and biological systems. The pairing or coupling of handicapped and nonhandicapped children also seems to be an effective means for students to learn science (Brown, 1979, p. 89).

Observations students must make can be adapted. For example, auditory observations may be changed to visual observations, as in the case of the sounds made by different sizes of tuning forks. Have the child transfer the sound wave to water or sand and compare what happens as an alternative to hearing. Other techniques teachers can use are similar to those used for multilingual children, including seating the child near the front of the room so vision is not obstructed, looking directly at the child and obtaining his or her attention before speaking, shaving beards or mustaches so lips are visible for the student's lipreading, speaking loudly and distinctly without shouting, pairing students, and using a written outline for activities that require several steps.

*Orthopedic Impairments.*   Orthopedic impairments are disabilities caused by diseases and deformities of the muscles, joints, and skeletal system. Examples include cerebral palsy, spina bifida, amputations, birth defects, arthritis, and muscular dystrophy. Temporary injuries are not covered by federal law because they can be corrected. A child with an orthopedic impairment may require an appliance such as a wheelchair, walker, crutches, or skeletal braces.

*Teaching Children with Orthopedic Impairments.*   Generally, the way an orthopedically disabled child learns is not affected. Adjustments are more physical than educational. Be aware of and attempt to remove physical and psychological barriers in your classroom. Examine the curriculum materials and activities and modify them to include the child with a disability without sacrificing their purpose or science content. Do not underestimate the capabilities of the child. Become familiar with the function and maintenance of any appliance the child uses.

## *Teaching Learners Who Are Gifted and Talented*

Children who are gifted or talented may comprise 3–5 percent of the U.S. school population (Hallahan & Kauffman, 2000) and are not included in the federal law. However, federal legislation does encourage states to develop programs and to support research for students who are gifted and talented (Hallahan & Kauffman, 2000). Gifted or talented children do have special needs that are not usually served well by the instruction given to most children. Gifted and talented children are included in this chapter because most teachers have children of this type in their classrooms, and authorities have questioned the wisdom of pulling gifted children out of the regular classroom for special instruction.

Some of the problems experienced by children who are gifted and talented parallel disabling conditions described earlier in this chapter. The definition and processes used to identify children who have special gifts involve similar difficulties that exist for children who have mental retardation or learning disorders. Whereas most may feel a moral obligation to help those who have a disadvantage, the child with a special gift may be presumed to find a way to excel on her or his own (Hallahan & Kauffman, 2000).

However, like children who have disadvantages or who are different, children who are gifted and talented also benefit from a balanced view of humanity and become prepared to work and live in the greater society. Children who are gifted should be considered as individuals who have unique needs and abilities, and their education should attend to those specific needs and abilities.

*Who Are Gifted and Talented Learners?*   Children who are gifted and/or talented show promise of making superior progress in school. These children may demonstrate advanced progress in academic achievement in a school subject or exceptional ability and creativity in the arts. Their special intelligence and talents are observed and may be verified by achievement and IQ tests or superior performance in a subject or artistic area. In addition, gifted children may demonstrate other traits such as sensitivity to the needs of other children, a need for independence, a predisposition for expression, a capacity for social leadership, broad interests in different school areas, apparent natural talents in the arts, and such noticeable behaviors as intensity, persistence, self-assured introversion, or detachment from what they believe are mundane topics.

Children who are gifted and talented have a wide range of possible characteristics. This range makes it difficult to generalize about all gifted children. Gifted and talented children can represent a tremendous challenge to the science teacher.

Academically gifted children may appear to become easily bored with instruction offered to the rest of the class. If you have not majored in science, you may have some anxiety about having a scientifically gifted child in your class. Fear not. Feeling unprepared in science should not stop you from teaching gifted children. Perhaps your anxiety will be eased if you can keep the issue in perspective. Remember that you are an adult who teaches children, and the experiences of adulthood provide advantages when working with the student who is gifted. Despite all the knowledge a young gifted learner may have, he or she is still an elementary or middle school student, and the student's social, emotional, physical, psychological, and cognitive development is not complete. As an adult, you still have much to offer. All learners enjoy seeing their teacher get excited about their students' work. Having a gifted child in your science class is reason to rejoice and will give you a wonderful opportunity to become a real facilitator and guide rather than a messenger.

***Teaching Learners Who Are Gifted and Talented***    Children who are gifted in science often are capable of accelerated and more detailed learning. You can enrich their experiences by encouraging them to pursue the subject to a greater depth. You may also accelerate their instruction by drawing on topics from advanced grades or by arranging for the child to work with a mentor (perhaps an older student, another teacher, or a science career professional) on special science topics. It is not uncommon for gifted students to perform two or three years above grade level in the subject or area where they show talent (Hallahan & Kauffman, 2000; Piburn & Enyeart, 1985). Therefore, more flexibility in written assignments and higher expectations for verbal communication are necessary. Try having gifted learners engage in more speculation about scientific events, hypothesize, and develop arguments and counterarguments that pertain to scientific/social issues. Have gifted learners demonstrate the application of science as well as the relationships between science and material learned in other subjects. The following teaching strategies are often appropriate for gifted learners.

*When encouraged and supported, exceptional children can overcome exceptional challenges.*

*Develop open-ended learning activities.* Whereas children who have learning and intellectual disabilities benefit from narrowly focused, sequential activities, children who are gifted should be challenged to develop their intellectual reasoning through open-ended activities that have many possible outcomes. These activities avoid step-by-step recipe procedures and do not have predetermined results. Several of the cooperative inquiry teaching methods of Chapter 1 and the tools of questioning in Chapter 8 are useful when working with gifted learners.

*Use the gifted students as classroom leaders.* These children may become reliable informal teachers of their peers who can greatly enhance the classroom atmosphere. Children who are gifted can also be used as resource persons, researchers, science assistants, and community ambassadors for exciting school programs.

*Use technology, science processes, and mathematics.* Scientific observation can be enhanced through mathematics. Encourage gifted children to use higher

## Teaching Exceptional Students

Who has the wisdom and ability to predict which of our students will succeed and which will not? People who have disabilities are often erroneously thought to be mentally deficient, but the prevailing social attitude has slowly changed. Thanks to federal laws, inclusion, and local school efforts to service better the special needs of children are greater than at any time in the history of schooling. All children are given more encouragement and are provided with more opportunities to achieve their full potential.

After decades of turning away students with disabilities, universities learned to accept them for scientific career training and removed physical and psychological barriers. A three-year survey by the American Association for the Advancement of Science reported a resource group of more than 700 scientists with disabilities. People with disabilities *can* do science. But our schools still must do more. Robert Menchel, a senior physicist for the Xerox Corporation who has been deaf since the age of 7, has visited many schools. He says:

> The lack of development of a basic science curriculum from kindergarten to the twelfth grade is a national disgrace and one that puts the deaf child at a disadvantage in comparison to the nonhandicapped child. Furthermore, these students are still being pushed into stereotyped job roles and dead-end jobs. For the female students it is even worse.

Robert Hoffman, a researcher who has cerebral palsy, speaks about the effects of isolation due to a disability:

> When one is born with a disability severe enough so society shoves him into a special program (which non-handicapped people develop), one becomes separated from "normal" persons. All through his school years, he learns from other disabled students, and the teachers design studies to fit the limitations of his physical handicap.

John Gavin, a research scientist with a physical impairment, cautions those who have no apparent disability:

> One of the least desirable traits of the human condition is our propensity to avoid those among us who are afflicted with overt physical disabilities. While this may be an inherent psychological carryover from those days of survival of the fittest, it is more likely we do

forms of mathematics and statistics as often as possible. Engage them in more precise measures and more extensive uses of science process skills. Technology will challenge gifted students to expand research capabilities as well as quantify and communicate their scientific findings.

*Reinforce and reward superior efforts.* Some school programs for gifted and talented children use pull-out approaches: learners are placed in special programs or given accelerated instruction. Inclusion can also benefit children who are gifted. Adaptations of science content and changes in instruction with more options for the gifted learners can provide suitable instruction in the regular classroom. Science content adaptations could include emphasizing higher levels of thinking, abstraction, and independent thinking. The challenge is fundamentally the same as with any other child: Help the child learn how to learn. Reinforcement and rewards for effort and work well done are usually all that is necessary to help gifted children keep their high level of not wish to have a reminder that we are potentially and continually eligible to join them.

Teachers become the key. A caring teacher with a positive can-do attitude is consistently ranked highly by children with disabilities. Teachers who care seem to expect that their students can learn at a high level. These teachers try to see that all children fulfill the high expectations held for them.

Language development is one of the major problems of children with hearing impairments. Researchers report that direct experience with objects is essential and that utilization of objects from a child's environment enhances his or her learning of concepts.

The most significant changes needed for teaching children who have visual impairments are related to the adaptation of educational materials and equipment to take advantage of each child's residual vision.

Children who are orthopedically disabled are a heterogeneous group, and it is difficult to prescribe general methods and adaptations that will serve *each* child well. However, pairing a child with an orthopedic impairment with a child with no disabilities helps both. The child who is impaired still needs

direct physical experience with the science phenomena to the greatest extent possible. For example,

> a magnet can be taped to the arm or leg. Another student can bring objects in contact with the magnets. The child should be able to feel and see which objects interact with the magnet and which do not. In this way, the child [with a disability] is involved in the decision making and discovery that is the major emphasis of [the] lesson.

Dean Brown's ground-breaking research showed that children with physical disabilities learned to understand science concepts and that they developed higher levels of reasoning skills if given the opportunity. Children with disabilities need direct, experiential, sensory experiences in science. Many researchers have repeatedly expressed the need for doing science through hands-on, inquiry-based, real-life experiences.

*Source:* Adapted from the literature review by Dean R. Brown, "Helping Handicapped Youngsters Learn by 'Doing,'" in Mary Budd Rowe (Ed.), *What Research Says to the Science Teacher,* Washington, DC: National Science Teachers Association (1979), 2: 80–100 and D. P. Hallahan and J. M. Kauffman, *Exceptional Learners,* Boston: Allyn & Bacon, 2000.

motivation for learning. Some suggestions for reinforcing and rewarding superior effort include public recognition for effort, extra credit or waiver of standard assignments, positive teacher comments, extra leadership opportunities and/or classroom responsibilities, and encouraging students to do real research projects.

*Provide extra- or cocurricular learning opportunities.* Your classroom will have limited teaching resources, and your time will also have limits. Out-of-class or out-of-school learning options may also help the gifted student continue to learn science. Use community library resources or make arrangements for the child to do special work at a community college or nearby university. Develop and utilize community resource personnel: Construct a network of science-related resource people and arrange mentor-intern relationships. Start a science club for students with special interests. Begin an after-school science lab— encourage the learners to design and pursue experiments. Student teachers or field experience interns from a nearby university may be able to assist with the science lab instruction and programming.

## HOW CAN PARENTS HELP MEET CHILDREN'S SPECIAL NEEDS?

More parents are realizing the importance of science. Reinforce its importance often with those parents who are already aware of it. For parents who are unaware, share these ideas through school or class newsletters and during conferences with parents. Children will have a much better chance of finding a job if they have a good background in mathematics, science, and computers and their development rate will be lower than those who do not have science and technology skills. As well, "scientific jobs pay wages that are nearly 50 percent higher than nonscientific jobs that require the same number of years of education" (Linn, 1994, p. 1).

Science can help break the cycle of unemployment, underemployment, and poverty in culturally different and special-needs populations. Scientific careers command higher levels of pay, and demands for personnel are increasing.

Science skills develop over time, and development builds on older skills. "If you don't use it, you'll lose it" applies here. The science foundation begun during childhood will increase each individual's potential for later success.

*Science is found in all aspects of life and is important to children's successful futures.*

Also, science depends on mathematics. Students should be encouraged to study mathematics every school year.

All students learn science through hands-on, minds-on experiences. Children should be encouraged to handle physical objects, make measurements and direct comparisons, and ask frequent questions about what they observe and experience.

## How Can Parents Help Their Children Study and Prepare for Science?

Parents are invaluable when it comes to educating children. They are closest to the special needs their children may have and are naturally protective of their children's best interests. Parents can help their children succeed in science by following these suggestions:

*Stimulate interest in and foster feelings for science.* Parents can help their children realize that science can be fun and help them experience success, with its feelings of excitement, discovery, and mastery.

*Include science in the child's everyday experiences.* Children can be asked to count and form sets of utensils at dinner time and can help to measure ingredients. Include them also in repairing broken appliances or building a model airplane.

*Establish a regular study time and provide a designated space for study away from distractions.* Work with the teachers to develop effective ways to communicate with children who have vision and hearing disabilities. Equipment modifications can be developed for children who have physical disabilities, and these can be shared with the school.

*Check with their children every day to make sure homework and special projects are completed.* They should ask to see completed homework and any tests or projects that have been graded or returned.

*Offer to read assignment questions.* Even if the parents do not know the answers, a stronger academic bond will be formed between parent and child. The child will benefit from an interested adult role model, forming the impression that school, homework, and effort are important.

*Ask whether their children have any difficulties with science or mathematics.* Suggest that parents talk with their children at least once per week about this and then follow up by communicating with you if there appear to be problems.

*Use a homework hotline if the school has one.* This may be school based or supported by individual teachers for their classes during designated hours.

## What Are Some Extra Science Activities Parents Can Do to Help Their Children?

Some teachers, even entire schools, arrange home-based science activities to supplement school instruction. Parents become enthusiastic and develop a stronger bond with the school. They often say, "Let's have parent involvement programs more often." "It helps me keep in touch with my child." "The activities didn't take too much time, so it was simple to include them into our busy evening schedule." "I think it's great to get the parents involved. Each activity we did benefited our older child and the younger child who is not even in school!" (Williams-Norton, Reisdorf, & Spees, 1990, pp. 13–15). Meaningful activities can be found for young children in magazines such as *Click* and *Dragonfly* and in Nancy Paula's (1992) *Helping Your Young Child Learn Science,* published by the U.S. Department of Education (stock number 065-000-00520-4).

The rich variety of science teaching resources makes it easy to suggest home study extensions. Giving parents options to choose from helps them overcome limits of time and materials. When selecting options and making suggestions to parents, keep these criteria in mind (Williams-Norton, Reisdorf, & Spees, 1990, p. 14):

*The activities should be at grade level and developmentally appropriate for the child.* Select options with the special needs of the children in mind.

*Activities should require materials that are available at home.* No parent will welcome traveling to gather together materials, and many cannot afford the expense.

*The activities should supplement what is taught in school, not duplicate it.* Do not expect parental teaching to be a substitute for your own responsibility.

*Provide complete and accurate instructions and explicit instructions for safety.* Try the activities yourself before sending them home. Do they work? Are the instructions clear? Are they safe? Can a child do the activity with minimal adult guidance? Revise the instructions as necessary for the children you teach, again being mindful of the special needs of the children.

*Select activities that emphasize simple and accurate concepts.* Cross-check the concepts of the activity with those of your textbook or science program. Are they consistent? Or are there differences in terminology and accuracy of information? If they are different, modify them or select another activity. Choose activities that emphasize a main science idea, and encourage the parents to continue emphasizing this main idea.

*The activities should be fun.* Parents and children will enjoy a special time together when the activity is fun. No one, not even an adult, will do something that is not enjoyable if it can be avoided. Encourage parents to share the joys and mysteries of science with their children. Scientific attitudes and positive values parents give to science at home also will benefit school science.

*Develop the concepts of sink or float and density* by floating common objects such as straws and plastic buttons in plain water and in salt water. Because the density of salt water is greater, objects that sink in plain water often float in salt water. Try adding different amounts of salt to water to explore the effects of salt concentration on density and floating.

*Explore primary and secondary colors.* Following the directions on food coloring packages, prepare different colors and arrange them in glass jars. Dye macaroni or paper to represent the colors of a rainbow. Combine the three primary colors to produce every color.

*Demonstrate magnetism* by having children compare the effects of magnets on different objects in the kitchen. Let the children predict which objects will and will not be attracted to the magnets.

*Use building blocks to develop the concepts of set and order.* Lay a foundation of three blocks; then place two blocks on the next layer and one on the top layer. Ask the children to count the blocks and to estimate how many blocks would be necessary to build towers six and ten blocks high.

## CHAPTER SUMMARY

A single science teaching method by itself is insufficient. Each hands-on science lesson must be accompanied by adaptations to suit the needs of each special student. Nothing is so unequal as equal treatment without exception.

There is no single method or science program that can be used to teach all children fairly and equally all the time. However, one single factor does benefit *all* children: hands-on science—where all children have abundant opportunities to benefit from multisensory stimulation in cooperative settings. This approach has the potential to become the great equalizer. Children who are culturally different may acquire missing experiences through hands-on science. Non-English-speaking children can use

science to learn and develop language skills. Young females can overcome skill deficits, gender stereotypes, and career limitations through hands-on, minds-on science. Exceptional children are given new opportunities because of hands-on science and its ability to include all children in minds-on experiences. Gifted and talented children also benefit as they are introduced to new experiences and are motivated to process those experiences at an advanced intellectual level.

Parents play a vital role with students who have special needs. Teachers should inform parents about the importance of science and offer activities to strengthen the school-home learning connection.

## DISCUSSION QUESTIONS

**1.** Cultural differences can have a positive impact on the social climate of a classroom. What are some ways you can encourage the expression of differences and make a positive impact on all children?

**2.** Take the picture of a scientist you drew in Chapter 3, and draw another one now. How do the pictures compare? What features are similar? How many of these features do you observe: male, middle aged, bald, glasses, facial hair, lab coat with pocket protector, test tubes? How can these features reflect bias, attitudes, stereotypes, and values? Where did the impressions portrayed in the pictures come from? What types of multicultural education concepts are

reflected in the picture? How can social context and media influence impressions? How are the impressions you have of science and scientists likely to influence young children?

**3.** Blindfold yourself or attend a class while wearing earplugs. How is your ability to function impaired? What long-term cumulative effects could result from your temporary disability if it were to become permanent? How could those effects influence your ability to function in a regular classroom?

**4.** Brainstorm ideas suitable for teaching science to gifted students. What differences are found on your list according to grade level? How would you work with a youngster who is gifted and who also has a cultural or language difference and/or a disability?

**5.** Brainstorm ideas related to classroom organization. How can a typical self-contained room be converted to better suit the needs of special students? Look especially for barriers that might limit the inclusion of children who have physical disabilities. What complications might a teacher encounter? What are some ways to overcome these complications?

## BUILD A PORTFOLIO

**1.** Interview a teacher whose students are culturally different from himself or herself. Inquire about how the science program or instruction has been modified to recognize and use cultural differences in a positive way. What effects have the teacher's efforts had on all of the children?

**2.** Peruse several science textbooks from different publishers. Report observations about possible gender bias, omitted discussion of cultural differences, and potential for adaptation for non-English-speaking, disabled, and/or gifted children. What suggestions are provided in the teacher's guide?

**3.** Choose any lesson from a science textbook or hands-on program. Demonstrate how you would adapt it to provide special instruction for female students or children with learning disabilities, intellectual disabilities, impaired vision, hearing loss, or orthopedic impairment.

**4.** Sketch the floor plan of an elementary classroom. Examine the floor plan carefully and make changes to show adaptations that would assist children with orthopedic impairments.

**5.** Use the concept analysis model presented in this chapter (Figure 5.2) to make changes in a science lesson plan. How would you use the model to instruct children who are learning disabled or intellectually disabled? How could the model be used with all children? What are the possible benefits and limits?

**6.** Complete the following survey "How Equitable Is Your Science Program and Your Teaching?" What do you conclude about your willingness or ability to provide equitable science teaching and learning? Refer to the accompanying survey.

## How Equitable Is Your Science Program and Your Teaching?

*Directions:* Answer each question with a yes or a no. If a question does not specifically or completely pertain to you, try to offer a yes or no response based on what you know and think you would do. If possible, respond to each item as a member of a multicultural, gender, and exceptional representative team including parents, learners, administrators and other teachers. If uncertain, try to collect the necessary information in order to substantiate your answers.

### I.   The Science Education Program in General

Does the school's science instruction and curriculum:

_____  1. Use hands-on activities on a regular basis?

_____  2. Include grouping and cooperatively learning activities routinely?

_____  3. Equally emphasize content and the processes of problem solving equally?

_____  4. Encourage learners to talk about their science learning?

_____  5. If a textbook is used, relate the text's information to science in everyday lives of a culturally diverse society?

_____  6. Include information on a regular basis about careers using science?

_____  7. Include role models who represent both genders and persons of different racial, cultural, linguistic, and exceptional (handicapped and gifted) groups for students to interact with on a regular basis?

_____ 8. Provide access for all students to technology and ensure equal experiences with it?

_____ 9. Integrate science content and processes with other core subjects such as language arts, social studies, and mathematics?

_____ 10. Strive to develop and encourage positive attitudes toward science for all teachers, administrators, parents, and students?

_____ 11. Develop partnerships with science and industry that include participants who represent both genders and people of different racial, cultural, linguistic and exceptional (handicapped and gifted) groups?

_____ 12. Assess what students know and can do in science with performance-based criteria that emphasize the open-ended nature of science and the importance of using language for description and questioning?

_____ 13. Ensure that all counselors, teaching staff, and parents are aware of strategies that encourage equitable participation of female, minority and exceptional students in science?

_____ 14. Monitor all teaching materials for their equal representation of both genders and people of different racial, cultural, linguistic, and exceptional groups in the science community?

## II. Science in PreK through Upper Elementary

_____ 15. Provide professional development for all teachers to update and improve their science teaching skills?

_____ 16. Support and train teachers who are uncomfortable teaching science?

_____ 17. Emphasize accountability for teaching science on a regular basis in all classrooms?

_____ 18. Encourage and facilitate out-of-school learning experiences at all levels and for all skills groups?

_____ 19. Monitor extracurricular activities for equitable representation of students of both genders and of different racial, cultural, linguistic, and exceptional groups?

_____ 20. Establish guidelines for science fair projects that deemphasize the "wow" effect of experiments and encourage children to formulate their own questions and explore science in their own natural environments?

_____ 21. Publicly acknowledge strong commitment to science as an integral part of the school curriculum rather than as enrichment or an option?

_____ 22. Provide assistance for teachers in obtaining the necessary materials and equipment for teaching science with an experiential emphasis?

_____ 23. Form partnerships with parents to define their roles in supporting science education for their children?

_____ 24. Deemphasize the textbook approach to science in favor of an experience-based approach?

_____ 25. Do outreach efforts that include parents who are representative of the entire student population on decisions regarding science activities and explorations with children?

**Scoring:** If you have scored as an individual, the credit one point for each of the questions where you responded yes.

20–25 points: Congratulations! Share what you do with other schools and take a look at what is happening at the secondary level in your district.

10–19 points: Good start, keep working at it! You have the elements of a good beginning. Examine your negative responses for any pattern. What is working for the school at this grade level? What is missing? Share the checklist with others and discuss a plan of action for improving.

0–9 points: It's never too late. Examine your positive responses and try to build on your successes. What has made it possible for these to be incorporated in science education in your school? Then examine the questions where you provided a negative response. Try to identify barriers and speculate about potential solutions to help your school to elevate its science program to a more equitable level for all students.

_Source:_ Adapted from the work of Martha A. Adler: How Equitable is Your Science Education Program? The Checklist. Dwight D. Eisenhower Mathematics and Science Education, V4, No. 1, 1994, pp. 6–8.

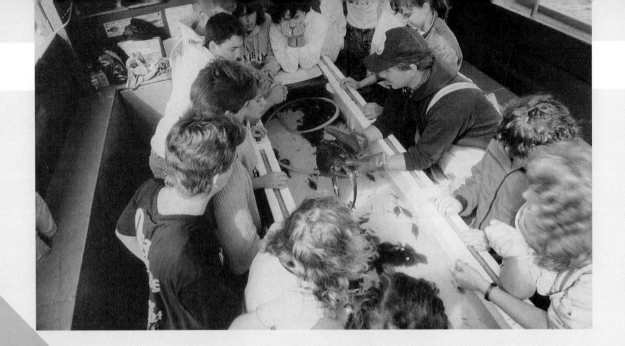

## CHAPTER OUTLINE

# CHAPTER 6

# What Goals Promote Scientific Literacy?

Being an experienced principal did not make this part of his job any easier. Mr. Emerson always felt some personal loss when any one of "his" teachers left for other opportunities. However, the chance to interview new teacher candidates always encouraged him because teachers were becoming more sophisticated, with new inquiry teaching methods and emphasis on activity-based reflective learning. Mr. Emerson had invested much time and energy to help teachers find their school an exciting place. To call their school a zoo was a compliment, not an insult. All of the classrooms and offices had plants and animals, and each hallway pronounced a different science theme. Science was emphasized and was used as a way to integrate social studies, mathematics, reading, and language. Indeed, education was alive in the school and made as real as possible. Pride ran high, and it was important to maintain the proper mix of teachers to support the school's vision. Mr. Emerson was hopeful the next candidate would be a good fit, especially for the science program. Everyone in the school was proud of the progress made toward new science program standards. After a brief guided tour and warm-up session of chatting, the interview began.

"Jennifer, would you please tell me what you think your most important goals should be for science, and how you could meet them."

"Well," replied Jennifer, "as you know I am not a science specialist."

"The position does not call for a specialist, Jennifer. We are proud of our science program and want all teachers to support it. So what do you think you would try to accomplish in science if we hire you?"

Jennifer thought briefly, then responded. "I think a good science program should be more than science. Its focus should be broader than science facts. Don't get me wrong. Facts are important, but they should not drive the entire program. I like to think in terms of what I would like children to be able to understand and be able to do."

"Such as . . . ?"

"I would like children to understand that even *they* are responsible, in some small way, for what happens to our environment. That even *they* should think about it. So I guess that means they should be able to think and solve problems. In addition, they should understand that something like science is both good and can be bad if misused." As she continued, Jennifer spoke with more ease: "I would like the children in my class to be curious, aware, and even skeptical from time to time. I don't want them to depend on me for the answer; I want them to learn how to figure out some things for themselves. I think this is important, especially when they grow up and have to solve their own serious problems. I think that what they do in science should carry over to other subjects. As an example, technology is all around us, and children usually adapt very quickly to new technology with enthusiasm. At the same time, I would like the children to have some awareness of the historical relationship between science and technology and how that history affects our society, especially our daily lives. This might seem to you as if I am talking about teaching college-level courses to children or avoiding science by teaching social studies. That's not what I mean. I would try to put all of this on the children's level, to connect with what they know and have experienced. I would try to make my science teaching practical by connecting the children's experiences with essential science concepts."

"How would you teach, Jennifer, to make your goals happen?" asked Mr. Emerson.

"Obviously the children need to *do* science. I think hands-on science is more than a slogan. I want children to get their minds involved in what they are doing. Conceptual learning should be emphasized over memorizing science facts. Facts are certainly necessary; they help to build a base for understanding the concept of a lesson. But students must have concrete experiences before an abstract concept is introduced. Ideally, the students would be able to construct the concept, with my guidance, by thinking about their own experiences. This means that my teaching would include inquiry teaching, so I would introduce new science words or technical terms only after the students and I have thoroughly experienced the concept. Also, I think it is important to be selective. I would focus on fewer concepts than most textbooks introduce but attempt to go into greater depth and help students apply what they learn to real life. I would try to connect new learning with the students' prior learning. I also think it is important to expose the students to all of the science disciplines, to try for a good balance between earth, life, and physical science."

Mr. Emerson asked, "Would you please describe an example of some topic where you might be able to do these things as you just described?"

"One way is to make the learning real. For example, I would try to help the children develop a knowledge of the working world—how their clothes are constructed, what the differences are among fabrics and comfort, and how those are connected to science and new technologies. A theme that might guide this type of study could be "Form and Function." We would examine the function of particular fabrics and how they vary and how their constructed forms differ, such as differences between polyester and cotton or wool. Studying the source of these materials permits us to integrate earth and life science. The construction and function help us apply physical science concepts. Another example is to examine why it is important to cook certain foods in particular ways and to brush our teeth, and why some plants grow better in certain environments than others. I would want the students to see examples of how science is used by society and the problems as well as the good that causes. I would also like children to understand that science offers important career opportunities, that it is also important to many other careers, and that no one has to become a scientist to benefit from science."

"Jennifer," said Mr. Emerson, "what you have described sounds much like what many educators would call a literacy education, where you would attempt to overcome the unfortunate perceptions of narrow boundaries that many believe exist between the subject areas. Instead you would attempt teach for connections among and between all subjects. Is this what you really mean?"  ◆

## INTRODUCTION

The Third International Mathematics and Science Study (TIMSS) and the National Assessment of Educational Progress (NAEP) have been the object of many popular press articles describing the science achievement of school youth. General reports of elementary children reveal relatively good performance at achieving basic proficiencies in science. However, a decline is apparent as students move into high school and are expected to meet higher goals. The U.S. science curriculum is described as covering too many topics at each grade without sufficient depth; repetition seems to prevail as children advance through school. The science curriculum is believed to be insufficient and teaching methods are criticized for their failure to prepare learners to meet more rigorous proficiencies.

The TIMSS, especially, analyzed the curriculum and methods of instruction in science. Its findings and those of the NAEP suggest that the science that is taught and how it is taught in schools bear responsibility for lower than expected student performances. The implications for science education are that (1) fewer science topics should be covered and learning science content should be deeper and (2) science processes should be emphasized more in order to encourage a greater depth of understanding (Wilson and Blank, 1999). These curricular and instructional recommendations add urgency to the questions raised in our opening scenario, especially since a 1999 study concluded that none of the most widely used middle grades science textbooks is adequate to teach fundamental concepts. Texts were criticized for covering too many topics with too little depth and for including classroom activities that failed to help students relate experiences to the underlying scientific concepts (*Education Week*, 1999).

Mr. Emerson raises fair questions in the opening scenario. Does any one subject in the elementary or middle school curriculum hold dominion over the others, and can it lay claim to being more important than others in the development of literacy? Or, as in Jennifer's description of her preferred goals in science, is it realistic for science to appear broad enough to cover so much? Or, is Jennifer actually describing a way to add depth to fewer science topics? We try to respond to these questions in this chapter by dividing it into three parts:

1. an examination of scientific literacy
2. a review of several recent and influential reform efforts in science education
3. a synthesis of goals from those reform efforts that are designed to promote scientific literacy in elementary and middle schools

## WHAT IS SCIENTIFIC LITERACY?

A literate person has a fundamental command of the essentials: what one needs to know and be able to do in order to function as a contributing member of a society. Not long ago the standard refrain in education was that a literate person commanded the basics of reading, writing, and arithmetic. But this view is too narrow to provide an education that helps our youngsters survive in a complex world with its wonders of technology and sophisticated social, economic, and political problems. Tomorrow's leaders and policy makers must know more, have a different worldview, and possess an impressive array of skills. What does a scientifically literate person know, and what is that person able to do in a modern society?

In this time of change and challenge, many definitions of scientific literacy have been written. We refer to that advocated by the organization that set the national standards in science education, the National Research Council (NRC):

> Scientific literacy means that a person can ask and find or determine answers to questions derived from curiosity about everyday experiences. It means the ability to describe, explain, and predict natural phenomena. It means the ability to read with understanding articles about science in the popular press and engage in social conversation about the validity of the conclusions. Scientific literacy implies that a person can identify scientific issues underlying national and local decisions and express positions that are scientifically and technologically informed. A literate citizen should be able to evaluate the quality of scientific information on the basis of its sources and the methods used to generate it. Scientific literacy also

*Science helps improve our lives.*

implies the capacity to pose and evaluate arguments based on evidence and to apply conclusions from such arguments appropriately. (NRC, 1996, p. 22)

The NRC also reminds us that scientific literacy is not an all-or-nothing happening; a person may be scientifically literate in some fields or topics of study but not in others. Furthermore, scientific literacy is developed over a lifetime. Schooling is important, but literacy continues to develop during the adult years. The development of scientific literacy is influenced, as the details of its description suggest, by the attitudes and values of the individual, as well as the habits of mind and conceptual understandings that the individual uses and knows. Very broadly, then, a scientifically literate person has a capacity to use essential scientific attitudes, processes, and reasoning skills, and science types of information to reach reasoned conclusions and use the ideas of science in meaningful ways. This is representative of an ancient proverb's wisdom: "Teach a person how to fish, feed the person for a lifetime." Various reform efforts in science education pursue lifelong learning through efforts that strive to develop attitudes, skills, and knowledge. In other words, educators are encouraged to believe that if they teach a person how to learn, the person will learn for a lifetime.

Positive scientific attitudes—persistence, curiosity, humility, a healthy dose of skepticism—motivate learners to approach a task or problem with enough interest to find solutions for themselves. There is a relationship between attitudes, interest, achievement, and perception of one's successes, summed up by the saying, "success breeds success." Anyone who has ever persisted with a problem long enough to solve it knows the sweet feeling of achievement and that "can-do" perception that accompanies success. The relationship among these factors appears to be cumulative and conveys the notion that children's achievement increases as they develop more positive attitudes and more interest in science (as well as other subjects). As achievement increases, motivation and desire stimulate the development of new learning skills, and that leads to greater understanding of the information, which is accumulating at a dizzying pace. Therefore, the processes of science are the skills by which observations are acquired and meaning is constructed by the learner. Processes can provide the type and quality of the science experience desired for children where thinking is expanded and improved.

Process skills, as literacy-building tools, have tremendous carry-over value in and out of school (see Chapter 3). They are also vital to adult living. They are the mechanisms by which problems are identified, explored, and solved. Whether the adult mission is to improve or improvise on a recipe; determine the cause of a blown fuse (or tripped circuit breaker); troubleshoot the cause of a car's failure to start; plan the best route to run a new line for an extension telephone; identify evidence and separate it from opinion while listening to a political candidate; or determine how to thread a sewing machine, the processes of science contribute to solving the problem.

Children are naturally interested in science and associated science topics. Surveys done in elementary schools show that children choose science a majority of the time when given lists of school topics from which they can choose. Parents report, too, that their children list science as one of their favored school subjects (Mechling & Oliver, 1983a).

Like you, children cannot escape the importance of science; it affects every aspect of their lives. However, the intent of scientific information is that it be a means, not an end. Science content can help children become responsible consumers and personally learn how to benefit more from learning science. If science content is applied to real circumstances, scientific information and areas of study provide meaningful contexts for developing literacy skills. Recommendations from science organizations, such as the National Science Teachers Association, urge that children have daily opportunities to relate science to their own lives and that science study not be limited to science time. Other organizations, such as the American Association for the Advancement of Science and the National Research Council, urge that science content be used to organize meaningful standards that address the historical, social, technological, and interdisciplinary nature of science. The information, attitudes, and skills of science can be used to enrich other school experiences, and times of reading, art, music, social studies, writing, mathematics, discussion, physical education, and so on, can be used to deepen an understanding of science. Science is central to the education of literate citizens.

# WHAT REFORM EFFORTS HAVE SOUGHT TO PROVIDE GOALS FOR SCIENTIFIC LITERACY?

Science teaching goals may be provided by your state curriculum or by major science improvement efforts, such as those offered by the National Science Foundation (NSF), the American Association for the Advancement of Science (AAAS), the National Science Teachers Association (NSTA), or the National Research Council (NRC). Modern goals respond to urgent needs and are based on the knowledge of what works. We describe four reform efforts important for their contemporary breadth and depth: Project Synthesis of the NSF, the Scope, Sequence, and Coordination Project of the NSTA, Project 2061 of the American Association for the Advance of Science, and the National Science Education Standards of the NRC Committee on Science Education and Assessment.

## Project Synthesis

The NSF supported $2 billion worth of programs and courses developed in mathematics and science during the 1960s and 1970s. Major social and political pressures removed adequate levels of funding for science education during the mid-to-late 1970s, much as pressures to reduce the national deficit caused the Congress to review support for education in the mid-1990s. Teachers and

## EXERCISE 6.1

### What Is the Relationship Between Science and Other School Subjects?

We have listed some common topics in science that you may be asked to teach. Science has considerable potential for integration with other subject or skill areas. How could you help make this integration work for you as you attempt to educate scientif- ically literate learners? List several subjects into which the science topics could be integrated, and exchange your ideas with your classmates to develop a resource file of ideas.

| Science Topic | Related School Subject/Topic/Skill | Science Topic | Related School Subject/Topic/Skill |
|---|---|---|---|
| simple machines | _____ | energy | _____ |
| growth | _____ | plants | _____ |
| nutrition | _____ | animals | _____ |
| weather | _____ | space | _____ |
| electricity | _____ | life cycles | _____ |
| sound | _____ | senses | _____ |
| color | _____ | adaptations | _____ |

citizens concluded that federal funds had been wasted and, in the wake of mixed research reports, that the programs had not accomplished what they were designed to do. It was in this setting that the NSF responded to congressional pressure and awarded contracts in 1976 for several landmark studies of science education (Harms, 1981).

Consensus within and among the Project Synthesis research groups yielded several general conclusions about the status of science education. For the most part, these conclusions are still accurate today and contribute much of the knowledge base that recent reform standards and change-efforts are built upon. These conclusions are

1. Science education at all levels is given a low priority when compared with the importance of language arts, mathematics, and social studies. School systems generally do not support science adequately.
2. Textbooks dominate science teaching and learning and limit what can be accomplished.
3. School science programs generally emphasize preparing students for the next grade level of study or for college.
4. Teachers become the curriculum to the extent that they decide what will be taught or studied. Therefore, individual teachers determine many of the goals of science education. These goals are often incongruent with the national agenda and with what works in elementary science education. (Weiss, 1978; Holdzkom & Lutz, 1984)

These general conclusions led researchers and science educators to proclaim that existing science programs did not serve the majority of children well. In fact, many existing programs served only about one out of every ten pupils well. Their primary goal was to recruit students into science careers. These conclusions helped to set a new goal for science literacy for the 1980s. This goal had four outcomes.

***Outcome I: Science Enhances Each Learner's Personal Development.***   Science education should help learners use science to improve their own lives and to learn how to cope with an increasingly technological world.

This outcome focused on ways to enhance each student's curiosity, honesty, imagination, self-confidence, and ability to be persistent, make decisions, cope with changes, examine values, reason logically, and practice the ethics of science. This outcome reflected the many ways science and technology affect one's life. Included were the attitudes and abilities one needs to become a responsible consumer, to maintain a healthy body, and to use science in making daily decisions and solving daily problems.

***Outcome II: Learners Understand the Interrelationships of Science, Technology, and Society.***   The science curriculum must prepare students to function as informed citizens and to deal responsibly with science-related social and technological issues. Opportunities must be provided for students to develop a greater ability to understand the impact science has on social issues and the way science shapes our expectations about responsible citizenship: personal interaction with the environment, responsible consumerism, respect for environmental order and aesthetics, and so on.

In addition, this outcome taught that technology and science are worthy human endeavors, that there are distinctions between them, and that students must recognize their impact on the future of society.

*Outcome III: Science Develops Each Learner's Academic and Process Skills.* The science curriculum must provide all students opportunities to acquire the academic knowledge and skills they need to solve personal problems and to continue lifelong learning. Therefore, emphasis was given to improving children's thinking skills. The science program attempted to prepare students who were likely to pursue science and science-related careers with the fundamental knowledge and skills necessary to support further education in their career fields.

This outcome concentrated on what children needed to become scientifically literate and urged that the curriculum include the knowledge, concepts, principles, and ideas of science, as well as the attitudes, values, and ethics of science and critical thinking and problem-solving skills.

*Outcome IV: Science Helps to Expand Each Learner's Career Awareness.* Science education must give *all* students an awareness of the nature and scope of the science- and technology-related careers that exist. The science curriculum must provide opportunities for children to develop an awareness of how important science is to different occupations and professions. This outcome helped students realize that science is relevant to all fields of employment. It also included development of positive attitudes toward science-related careers and an awareness that these careers provide occupational opportunities for women, minorities, and persons with disabilities. Some examples include the many careers in research, engineering, laboratory technology, equipment design, and computer programming; they include jobs in which people apply scientific knowledge, in such fields as agriculture, nutrition, medicine, sanitation, conservation, and so on. Students became informed about the contributions people in such careers make to society as well as the specific educational preparation, interests, attitudes, and abilities associated with each career. Students realized that science, mathematics, language arts, and social studies are interrelated, and they understood the interrelationships of science, technology, and society.

## Scope, Sequence, and Coordination of Secondary School Science (SS&C)

The NSTA supports an effort to reform science programs in grades 7 through 12. A brief description is provided here for the middle school teachers who may be affected by such school curricula and for elementary teachers who must strive to prepare learners for the advanced grades. SS&C encourages all learners to study each science discipline every year for six years, from seventh through twelfth grades. This means that science programs that follow SS&C recommendations include the study of biology, chemistry, physics, and earth and space sciences within the parameters of each year's science course. This is a radical change from the layer-cake approach, where students typically study earth science in the ninth grade, biology in the tenth grade, chemistry in the eleventh, and physics in the twelfth grade, although more than half of the secondary school students in the United States do not take a science course beyond the tenth grade.

Curricula based on SS&C spread the study of each science discipline over several years, using inquiry teaching and discovery learning approaches that are consistent with how students learn. Each student learns from each discipline first without complex mathematics, while encountering the major concepts of science in an interdisciplinary fashion without the artificial barriers of the separate disciplines. The curriculum is designed so that teachers can help learners make conceptual connections that span the science disciplines. These connections often are coordinated through science themes, such as changes in biological organisms that are influenced by changes in biochemistry. A theme, such as change, can be used as an organizer for examining differences over geologic time, as well as change within the concepts of cause and effect in

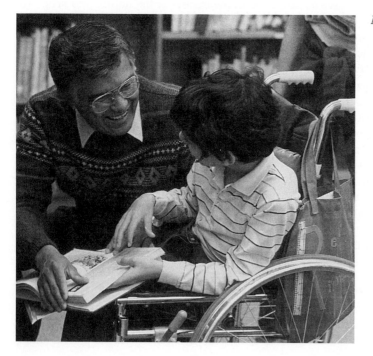

*Modern science includes all children.*

physical sciences. This approach provides a substantial opportunity for students to learn chemistry and physics when more than half of the student population never takes those separate courses. Early evidence from using SS&C in middle schools shows that students seem to be developing an affinity for science rather than a fear of it (Willis, 1995a).

## Project 2061

The AAAS commissioned a comprehensive initiative to improve science education, *Project 2061*—named for the year Halley's Comet will next reappear (Rutherford & Ahlgren, 1990). Project 2061 recommends several principles for effective science instruction. Guided by the National Council on Science and Technology Education, the project relies on scientists, engineers, and mathematicians to provide ideas for the project staff and consultants. Teams of consultants and reviewers consist of scientists, teachers, educators, historians, philosophers, and others who use science and reflect on its place in human affairs. Project 2061 is built upon several important guiding principles. Each principle suggests some elements that should be included in the new goals for science instruction. They address the following ideas:

- What science students should know must be carefully identified.
- Effective science instruction must encourage student diversity and serve the needs and interests of all students with a common core of knowledge and experiences.
- Students should learn science concepts rather than a list of science topics.
- Learning outcomes should be accomplished through appropriate teaching practices that begin with questions and phenomena that interest children and should be directed toward helping them find out how things work.
- The science curriculum should be selective and relevant and should not try to cover the full spectrum of the sciences.
- Science should be integrated with other subjects (such as mathematics and the humanities) when integration will *not* make learning science substantially more difficult.
- Science learning goals should be more generic without reference to a specific science course.
- Students must learn that science is tentative, not absolute, and that it is evidence oriented, speculative, and creative.
- Science curricula should include content that deals with social issues and technology when possible.
- Science taught in school should be based on explicitly stated educational criteria (Rutherford & Ahlgren, 1988, pp. 75–90).

The principles of Project 2061 stimulated efforts to develop science programs that emphasized fewer science concepts but strived to explore concepts in more depth. The boundaries between traditional science subjects and content topics are softened, and stronger conceptual linkages are emphasized; "teaching for connections" captures the intent of the curriculum. In addition, nontraditional topics are included in the curriculum, such as the nature of science and mathematics and important episodes in the history of science and technology.

*Themes* identify some ways of thinking that help make conceptual connections across the fields of science, mathematics and technology. Project 2061 urges that a curriculum be designed and used to help students gradually learn and use the ideas of the themes. Themes help learners construct meaning from their experiences and ideas. Therefore, some teachers and curriculum developers use themes as conceptual organizers to teach and write curriculum. Project 2061 recommends that teachers see that themes arise naturally from the science content that is built into a curriculum rather than impose themes on the content. Some themes that seem to arise naturally from typical science content are systems, models, constancy and change, and scale. Project 2061 claims that these themes "pervade science, mathematics, and technology and appear over and over again, whether we are looking at an ancient civilization, the human body, or a comet. [The ideas connected by themes] transcend disciplinary boundaries and prove fruitful in explanation, in theory, in observation, and in design" (AAAS, 1993, p. 261).

As an example, let us consider the theme of systems. The meaning envisioned for this theme is described and supported by particular outcomes as benchmarks for grades 2, 5, and 8.

> One of the essential components of higher-order thinking is the ability to think about a whole in terms of its parts and, alternatively, about parts in terms of how they relate to one another and to the whole. People are accustomed to speak of political systems, sewage systems, transportation systems, the respiratory system, the solar system, and so on. . . . [M]ost people would probably say that a system is a collection of things and processes (and often people) that interact to perform some function. The scientific idea of a system implies detailed attention to inputs and outputs and to interactions among the system components. If these can be specified quantitatively, a computer simulation of the system might be run to study its theoretical behavior, and so provide a way to define problems and investigate complex phenomena. But a system need not have a "purpose" (e.g., an ecosystem or the solar system) and what a system includes can be imagined in any way that is interesting or useful. (AAAS, 1993, p. 262)

Table 6.1 provides examples of the outcomes recommended by Project 2061 for this theme for grade levels from kindergarten through high school. Curriculum developers and schools use these outcomes to design experiences for students that encourage the long-term development of scientific literacy among learners; teachers use them to keep daily lessons focused on meaningful grade-level outcomes that contribute to long-term literacy.

## National Science Education Standards

The NRC coordinated the development of the national standards for K–12 science education. Diverse working groups from professional organizations, states, and other countries offered ideas that the NRC examined and trans-

## TABLE 6.1  Example Benchmark Outcomes for a Theme of Systems, Project 2061

*Primary grades*

Experiences with a variety of dissectable and rearrangeable objects, such as gear trains and toy vehicles and animals, as well as conventional blocks, dolls, and doll houses in order for children to learn how to predict the effects of removing or changing parts. By the end of the second grade, students should know the following concepts:

- Most things are made of parts.
- Something may not work if some of its parts are missing.
- When parts are put together, they can do things that they could not do by themselves.

*Intermediate grades*

A variety of experiences with mechanical systems that include familiar hardware devices that can be taken apart and reassembled with familiar hand tools. By the end of the fifth grade, students should know the following concepts:

- In something that consists of many parts, the parts usually influence each other.
- Something may not work as well (or at all) if a part of it is missing, broken, worn out, mismatched, or disconnected.

*Middle school*

Analyses of parts, subsystems, and interactions; to move beyond calling everything a system. Students should work cooperatively on projects to design, assemble, and trouble-shoot systems, such as bicycles, clocks, mechanical toys, battery-powered circuits, aquariums, and gardens. By the end of the eighth grade, students should know the following concepts:

- A system can include processes as well as things.
- Thinking about things as systems means looking for how every part is related to others. The output from one part of a system (which can include material, energy, or information) can become the input to other parts. Such feedback can serve to control what goes on in the system as a whole.
- Any system is usually connected to other systems, both internally and externally. Thus, a system may be thought of as containing subsystems and as being a subsystem of a larger system.

*Source:* Adapted from AAAS, *Benchmarks for Scientific Literacy* (New York: Oxford University Press, 1993), pp. 264–265.

formed into draft standards. More than 40,000 copies of the draft were reviewed by individuals and focus groups of teachers, scientists, and businesspeople. The standards are based on goals that strive to prepare students who are able to

- use scientific information and processes appropriately in making personal decisions;
- experience the attitudes and excitement of knowing about and understanding the natural world;
- increase their economic productivity;

- engage intelligently in public discourse and debate about matters of scientific and technological concern (NRC, 1996).

These broad goals may be addressed through school science programs that provide experiences that

- are personally and socially relevant to the child;
- include a wide range of knowledge, methods, and approaches so that students can analyze personal and societal issues critically;
- encourage students to think and act in ways that reflect their understanding of the impact science has on their lives, society, and the world;
- encourage students to appreciate science;
- help student develop an appreciation for the beauty and order of the natural world (NRC, 1996).

The standards are based on a belief that a systemic approach to reform is necessary for meaningful change to occur. Although many of the goals focus on improving student learning, the standards describe important science content to be learned, teaching approaches, professional development needs for teachers, and broad-based assessment techniques that must be used to chart progress. In total, the standards describe the overall science program expectations that educators should strive to achieve. Table 6.2 on pages 198–199 describes briefly the expectations for each standard area. The systemic nature of the National Science Education Standards is shown in Figure 6.1. Note that systemwide reform for scientific literacy requires a coordinated effort across all of the five interrelated standards.

## GOALS PROMOTING SCIENTIFIC LITERACY

The extensive bases of research and recommendations from these significant reform efforts help us to set new goals for effective science instruction. These goals provide a foundation for planning and influence the science improvement initiatives that arise from national organizations, states, and school districts. All of these goals intend to help educators pursue scientific literacy for learners. However, as the National Science Education Standards make clear, focusing only on student improvements and new standards for teachers falls short of repairing the systemic support structures that are necessary for broad and sweeping changes. The necessary systemic changes fall beyond what a single teacher can do. Still, there is reason for hope and perseverance. The goals toward literacy that each teacher can pursue are focused on learners: what we would have all learners know and be able to do in science.

The science content standards make clear the science subject matter expectations we should have for all learners across various levels of schooling. These standards are detailed and help us set clear learning outcomes—the kinds of changes that teachers can pursue in classrooms in the name of scientific literacy. The standards describe conceptual content outcomes that are distributed across the three science domains typically found in elementary and middle school sci-

**FIGURE 6.1   National Science Education Standards for Systemic Reform**

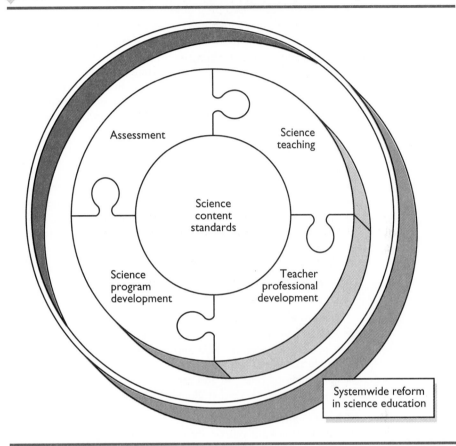

ence programs: physical, life, and earth/space science. (These outcomes are lengthy and are set out in Appendix A.) In brief, the content standards make it possible to identify essential science topics that all children should learn, such as characteristics and life cycles of organisms; properties, position, and motion of objects; and structure and history of the earth and solar system. The science content standards describe a foundation, not a ceiling for learning.

The standards and specific outcomes provide a context for scientific literacy that strives to provide students with powerful ideas that help them understand the natural world. The standards recommend concepts and processes that can be used as integrative mechanisms to unify students' science experiences, first by helping to establish meaning during the early grades, then later to enhance learning in the middle grades by providing students with the big picture that cuts across scientific ideas.

# TABLE 6.2 National Science Education Standards

*Teaching Standards*

Teachers of science must:

- Plan an inquiry-based program for their students.
- Guide and facilitate learning.
- Engage in ongoing assessment of their teaching and of student learning.
- Design and manage learning environments that provide students with the time, space, and resources needed for learning science.
- Develop communities of science learners that reflect the intellectual rigor of scientific inquiry and the attitudes and social values conducive to science learning.
- Actively participate in the ongoing planning and development of the school science program.

*Professional Teacher Development Standards*

The professional development of science teachers:

- Requires learning science content through the perspectives and methods of inquiry.
- Requires integrating knowledge of science, learning, pedagogy, and students and applying that understanding to science teaching.
- Enables teachers to build the knowledge, skills, and attitudes needed to engage in lifelong learning.
- Requires preservice and inservice programs that are coherent and integrated.

*Assessment in Science Education Standards*

Assessments require:

- Designs and procedures that are consistent with the decisions they are to inform.
- Assessment of both student achievement and the opportunity to learn science.
- A good fit between the type and quality of data collected and the consequences of the decisions and actions taken.
- Fair, unbiased practices and uses.
- Sound inferences about student achievement and the opportunity to learn.

*Science Content Standards*

All students in kindergarten through eighth grade should:

- Develop abilities necessary to do and understand scientific inquiry.
- Understand fundamental physical science concepts about properties and changes of materials; position and motion of objects; light, heat, electricity, and magnetism; motions and forces; and transformations of energy.
- Understand fundamental life science concepts about characteristics of organisms; life cycles of organisms; environments; structure and function of living systems; reproduction and heredity; regulation and behavior; populations and ecosystems; and diversity and adaptations of organisms.
- Understand fundamental earth and space science concepts about properties of earth materials; objects in the sky; structure of the earth's system; earth's history; and earth's position and role in the solar system.
- Understand fundamental science and technology concepts, such as distinguishing between natural and human-made objects; abilities of technological design; and the relationship of science and technology.

*Source:* National Research Council, *National Science Education Standards* (Washington, DC: National Academy Press, 1996).

**TABLE 6.2** *(continued)*

*Science Content Standards (continued)*

- Understand fundamental personal and social perspectives in science, such as health; characteristics and changes in populations; types of resources; changes in environments; science and technology in a local context; natural hazards; risks and benefits; and science and technology in society.
- Understand science as a human endeavor; the nature of science and scientific knowledge; and the history of science.
- Construct conceptual connections among science experiences through unifying concepts and processes such as order and organization; evidence, models, and explanation; change, constancy, and measurement; evolution and equilibrium; and form and function.

*Science Education Program Standards*

All science programs in kindergarten through eighth grade should:

- Be consistently articulated within and across all grade levels to encompass clearly stated goals, curriculum framework, teaching practices, assessment policies, support systems, and leadership for supporting and maintaining these elements.
- Contain all of the content standards embedded in a variety of curriculum patterns that are developmentally appropriate, interesting, and relevant to students' lives. Emphasize inquiry as a learning tool, and the curriculum should connect with other school subjects.
- Be coordinated with the mathematics program in order to improve students' understanding of science and mathematics overall.
- Give students access to appropriate and sufficient resources that include time, materials and equipment, space, teachers, and the community.
- Provide all students equitable access to opportunities that help them meet the standards.
- Help schools become communities that encourage, support, and sustain teachers as they implement an effective science program.

*Science Education System Standards*

The overlapping systems that affect science education include professional societies, the government judiciary, and the private sector. These systems must:

- Use a common vision to set policies that influence the practice of science education at the program level, while allowing for adaptations to local circumstances.
- Coordinate policies within and across agencies, institutions, and organizations.
- Provide continuity for reform efforts by sustaining policies over sufficient time.
- Support new policies with adequate resources.
- Provide equitable support for all students.
- Be reviewed frequently for possible unintended effects on the classroom practice of science education.
- Encourage individuals to take responsibility for making changes described by the standards.

*Themes* are recommended tools for teaching and learning that are described by the standards. They help us unify the science concepts and processes by organizing the instruction and providing a context for connection among various student learning experiences. Potential science themes are: order and organization; evidence, models, and explanation; change, constancy, and measurement; evolution and equilibrium; and form and function.

The standards recommend four other content factors that intend to make science appealing and meaningful learning for all students and offer new learning outcomes that add depth and breadth to the subject matter content of science. Figure 6.2 illustrates the relationships and interrelationships of the seven factors that compose the content standards for students.

Several of the content factors cluster conveniently around four new dimensions for science teaching: science as inquiry, science and technology, sci-

**FIGURE 6.2   Relationships and Interrelationships of the National Science Education Content Standards**   An appropriate theme provides an organizing mechanism for designing instruction drawn from the areas of physical, earth/space, and life sciences. Each lesson is shaped by the new dimensions of science education.

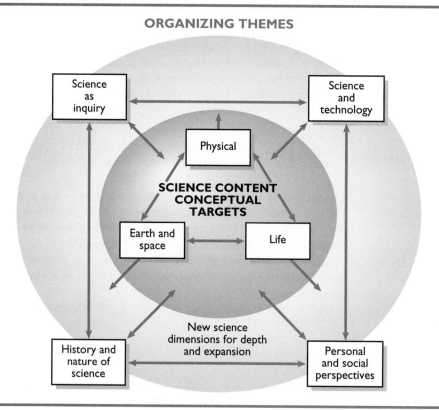

ORGANIZING THEMES

Science as inquiry

Science and technology

Physical

SCIENCE CONTENT CONCEPTUAL TARGETS

Earth and space

Life

New science dimensions for depth and expansion

History and nature of science

Personal and social perspectives

*Science goals focus on the interrelationships of learners, their inquiry processes, society, technology, and the history of science.*

ence in personal and social perspectives, and history and nature of science. These new dimensions should complement all science lessons that have conceptual targets in the physical, life, and earth and space sciences. The functions of these dimensions and the learning outcomes are outlined in Table 6.3 on pages 202–205.

### Science as Inquiry

Inquiry means the use of the processes of science, scientific knowledge, and attitudes to reason and to think critically. As described by the standards, inquiry assists in constructing an understanding of scientific concepts, learning how to learn, becoming an independent and lifelong learner, and further developing the habits of mind associated with science. Learning outcomes for the inquiry dimension require students to be able to understand inquiry and do a variety of types of science activities in order to learn the uses and skills of inquiry and develop a greater capacity to inquire.

*Inquiry* is the process that students should use to learn science. They should be able to ask questions, use their questions to plan and conduct a scientific investigation, use appropriate science tools and scientific techniques, evaluate evidence and use it logically to construct several alternative explanations, and communicate (argue) their conclusions scientifically (NRC, 1996).

## TABLE 6.3   Four New Dimensions of Science Content Standards and Outcomes

*Dimension 1. Science as Inquiry Standard*
The students will

1.1  Develop abilities necessary to do scientific inquiry.

- Ask questions about objects, organisms, and events in their natural environment.
- Plan and conduct simple science investigations.
- Use simple science equipment and other appropriate tools that extend their senses in order to gather, analyze, and interpret data.
- Use data to construct descriptions, explanations, predictions, and models.
- Identify relationships between evidence and explanations.
- Communicate, critique, and analyze the work of other students and recognize and analyze alternative explanations and predictions.

1.2  Understand about scientific inquiry.

- Ask and answer questions and compare answers to what scientists already know about the world.
- Select the kind of investigation that fits the questions they are trying to answer.
- Realize the instruments provide more information than a scientist can obtain only by using his or her senses, and enhance the accuracy of that information.
- Develop explanations that are based on observation, evidence, and scientific concepts.
- Describe investigations in ways that make it possible for others to repeat the same investigation.
- Review and ask questions about the results of others' work and realize that science advances through legitimate skepticism.

*Dimension 2. Science and Technology Standard*
The students will

2.1  Develop an ability to distinguish between natural objects and objects made by humans.

- Realize that some objects occur in nature and that other objects have been designed by people to solve human problems.
- Categorize objects into two groups, natural and designed.

2.2  Develop an ability to understand and produce a technological design.

- Identify an age-appropriate problem for technological design, propose a solution, and design it, perhaps by collaborating with others.
- Evaluate a product or design and communicate the results to others by describing the process of technological design.

2.3  Understand about science and technology.

- Realize that science and technological design often have similarities and differences that make it necessary for scientists and engineers to work together, often in teams with other professionals, in order to solve problems.

**TABLE 6.3** *(continued)*

- Understand that science and technology provide opportunities to women and men of all ages, groups, backgrounds, races, religions, and abilities to do various scientific and technological work and that a person's appearance, gender, race, or national origin should not influence acceptance or rejection of his or her contributions to science or technology.
- Understand that tools help scientists to make better observations, measurements, and equipment for investigations and that science helps drive technology.
- Understand that people have always had questions about the natural world and that scientists have invented tools and techniques to help answer those questions.
- Understand that technological designs have constraints and that the technological solutions may have intended benefits and unintended consequences, some of which may not be predictable.

*Dimension 3. Science in Personal and Social Perspectives Standard*
The students will

3.1  Develop an understanding of personal health.

- Understand that safety and security are basic needs of humans.
- Demonstrate responsibility for their own health through regular exercise routines.
- Understand that good nutrition is essential to health, develop nutritious eating habits, and recognize that nutritional needs vary with age, sex, weight, activity, and body functions.
- Recognize and avoid substances that can damage the human body, including environmental hazards (e.g., lead, radon), and recognize that prescription drugs can be beneficial if taken as directed.
- Recognize the potential for accidents, identify safety hazards, and take precautions for safe living.
- Understand that the sex drive is a natural human instinct; the consequences of new life and disease must be understood.

3.2  Identify characteristics and describe changes in populations.

- Understand that human populations include groups of persons who live in a particular location.
- Understand that density refers to the number of individuals of a population who can live in a particular amount of space.
- Realize that the size of a human and animal population can increase or decrease and that populations will increase unless factors such as disease, insufficient food, or disasters limit it. Overpopulation increases the consumption of resources.

3.3  Identify types of resources.

- Understand resources are materials we get from the living and nonliving environment to meet the needs of a population.

*(continued)*

- Identify examples of resources such as air, water, soil, food, fuel, building materials, and the nonmaterial such as quiet places, beauty, security, and safety.
- Understand that the supply of resources is limited but that recycling and reduced use can extend the length of time that resources are available; over-consumption and overpopulation deplete resources.

3.4  Identify environments and changes.

- Understand that the concept of environment includes the space, conditions, and factors that affect an individual's or an entire population's quality of life and ability to survive.
- Realize that environmental changes can be caused by natural or human causes and that some changes are good, some bad, others neither good nor bad.
- Understand that internal and external changes in the earth's system cause natural hazards and destruction of life.
- Understand that pollution is a change in the environment that can influence health and survival or limit the activities of organisms, including humans; pollution can be caused by natural occurrences and human activity.
- Comprehend that some environmental changes occur slowly and others rapidly and describe examples of each (e.g., weather, climate, erosion, movements of large geologic masses).

3.5  Recognize the benefits and challenges of science and technology.

- Understand that inventions and problem solutions can affect other people in helpful and harmful ways.
- Recognize that science influences society through its knowledge and world-view and that technology influences society through its products and processes.
- Identify risks and analyze the potential benefits and consequences and understand that risks and benefits relate directly to personal and social decisions.
- Describe how science and technology have improved transportation, health, sanitation, and communication and realize that the benefits of science and technology are not always available to all people.
- Understand that science and technology have advanced through the contributions of many different people, different cultures, and at different times throughout history.
- Realize that scientists and engineers have codes of ethics that require humans who are part of their research to be fully informed about the risks and benefits associated with the research.
- Understand that science cannot answer all questions and that technology cannot solve all human problems or meet all human needs.

*Dimension 4. History and Nature of Science Standard*
The students will

4.1  Understand that science is a human endeavor.

- Realize that science and technology have been used for a long time.

**TABLE 6.3** *(continued)*

- Understand that women and men have made important contributions to science and technology throughout history.
- Understand that there is still much to learn about science.
- Understand that doing science requires persons of different abilities and talents.

4.2  Understand the nature of science.

- Realize that scientists use consistent procedures to test explanations and to form ideas.
- Understand that scientists do not always agree, particularly when active research is pursued in new experimental areas, but that science ideas are supported by considerable observation and confirmation, even though the nature of science is tentative.
- Understand that scientists expect their ideas and research to be evaluated by other scientists and that while scientists may disagree over conclusions, they agree that skepticism, questioning, and open communication are essential to progress in science.

4.3  Understand the importance of history to science.

- Realize that studying the lives and times of important scientists provides further understanding about the nature of scientific inquiry and the relationships between science and society.
- Realize that the history of science reveals that the scientists and engineers of high achievement are considered to be among the most valued contributors of any culture.
- Trace the history of science to understand how difficult it was for innovators to break through the dominant scientific preconceptions of their times and to reach conclusions that seem obvious today.

*Source:* Adapted from National Research Council, *National Science Education Standards* (Washington, DC: National Academy Press, 1996), pp. 121–171.

### Science and Technology

Science and technology complement the inquiry standard. This standard places emphasis on helping students develop scientific abilities and science understandings and to understand connections between the natural world and the human-designed world. Decision making is an important student outcome that arises from student activity associated with the process of identifying scientific problems, determining risks and benefits, designing solutions, and evaluating solutions (NRC, 1996).

### Science in Personal and Social Perspectives

Meeting this standard ensures that learners understand that science is a part of personal and social issues. This dimension encourages teachers to help learners

# WHAT RESEARCH SAYS

## What Are Teachers' Attitudes Toward Reform?

To what extent do experienced teachers support and participate in the new spirit of science education reform? Scott Willis (1995) reports the results of a survey of 6,000 teachers from grades 1 through 12 were asked about their preparation, teaching beliefs, and teaching methods. Following are some of the highlights from the report:

- Nearly all teachers believe that hands-on student activities should be part of science education.
- Ninety percent of the elementary and middle school teachers believe that students should receive direct concrete experiences before they are exposed to abstract science concepts and technical terminology.
- Ninety percent of the elementary and middle school teachers believe that students learn best when science is connected to a personal context or to social issues.
- More than 90 percent of the elementary and middle school teachers support some form of cooperative group learning.
- Seventy percent of the elementary and middle school teachers believe it is a good idea to emphasize depth over breadth—covering fewer science concepts but going into greater depth.
- Almost one-third of the grades 1 through 4 teachers disagree with the recommendation to teach science concepts *before* the terminology associated with those concepts.

- Although the reform literature urges less emphasis on science facts, half of the elementary teachers and almost two-thirds of the middle school teachers put heavy emphasis on having their students learn "important terms and facts in science."
- Thirty percent of the teachers of grades 1 through 4 believe that students learn best in groups with peers of similar abilities. Most doubt that heterogeneous grouping is best for all students.
- Seventy-five percent of the elementary and middle school teachers rate their science textbooks as "good" or better, although most reform advocates are critical of these books.
- Elementary teachers are confident in their ability to use recommendations offered by the science reform movements, such as cooperative learning.
- Many elementary teachers do not feel confident in their ability to teach some of the science concepts recommended by the reform movements.

Despite the stresses and anxieties brought by reform, a national poll shows that the longer teachers work with reform standards, the more likely they are to support them, and the more unlikely they are to join a "pushback" movement. (*USA Today*, October 18, 1999).

*Source:* Adapted from S. Willis, "Reinventing Science Education: Reformers Promote Hands-On, Inquiry-Based Learning," ASCD *Curriculum Update* (Summer 1995).

---

achieve outcomes that will help them develop decision-making skills to solve personal and community problems. The standard provides ideas to help expose students to matters of making personal health choices, help students understand changes in populations and the complications of resource usage, and become aware of science and society issues on local, national, and global levels (NRC, 1996).

## History and Nature of Science

Science is ongoing, and the ideas change over time. The history and nature of science standard encourages teachers to provide learning experiences that use the history of science to inform the present, predict likely changes in the future, and appreciate that science is not a static or absolute discipline. This dimension of scientific literacy helps students appreciate the human role in science and how that role has helped shape various cultures (NRC, 1996).

## CHAPTER SUMMARY

Part of the answer to the question, "What are the goals for science teaching?" lies in the belief that science is an essential component of literacy and must achieve its proper place in the school curriculum. If science is regarded as a single subject to be focused upon only in itself, this defeats the conception of the basics that are necessary for an effective education. Science can help learners develop important attitudes that foster desired habits of the mind and positive levels of self-esteem. The attitudes typically arise from successes experienced while developing many skills. In science we call these *process skills* (they were described in Chapter 3). The processes are ways in which important outcomes are achieved, such as increases in language skills, social skills improvements, and advances in reading, in addition to new levels of knowledge. Acquiring knowledge is typically the focus of many subjects. In science, this is one desired outcome. Even so, the knowledge gained in science is viewed as a pathway or route to other destinations. The content of science may be integrated with other subject and skill areas; it fills the many interests of children and can have a tremendous impact on children's lives.

Various reform efforts inform us as we change science programs, adjust expectations for learners, and modify teaching habits. The National Science Education Standards describe seven essential parts that are necessary for systemic reform. As teachers we cannot meet the standards by ourselves, but we can focus on the content standards that fall within our responsibility as teachers. The content standards require further study. Although understanding fundamental science content concepts is important, some may misperceive that the standards are concerned only with the physical, life, and earth/space science concepts and learning activities for children. This is not true; to focus only on those topics shortchanges students, depriving them of additional essential experiences.

The physical, life, and earth/space science content is an important context for developing scientific literacy. The standards require four new dimensions of science learning to ensure that real progress is made toward helping students achieve literacy in science. These new dimensions challenge us to help students understand science as a process of inquiry, understand the interrelationships between science and technology, benefit from science personally and understand the social perspective of science, and understand and appreciate the history and nature of science. Parts of the many outcomes for these new dimensions predictably overlap and complement learning. The challenge will be to find a way to link all of these dimensions of science learning and literacy to the content context.

## DISCUSSION QUESTIONS

**1.** What principles guide your views on teaching and learning? Combine your beliefs into a philosophy statement, and write it down. How does your philosophy compare with the goals and standards of science education given in this chapter? How do your ideas compare with those of others in your class? Which of the reform efforts do you embrace philosophically?

**2.** Survey your state department of education, school district, and science professionals to compile a list of the main goals for elementary or middle school science education. How does this list compare to the recommendations of the National Science Education Standards, Project 2061, Scope, Sequence, and Coordination Project, and Project Synthesis?

## BUILD A PORTFOLIO

**1.** Imagine that you are preparing for an interview with a school principal or a director of personnel. You have heard that this question will be asked: "What are your top four or five goals for teaching science in _____ grade" [your choice of grade level]? How would you answer this question?

**2.** Examine several popular elementary science textbooks or school science programs, or both. How do these materials attempt to meet the new standards and dimensions of scientific literacy?

**3.** How can you act on the science standards by building them into your lessons? Examine how we use the goals in our lesson plans located in the last part of this book. What other suggestions do you have for using the standards?

## PART III

# The Expansion

## Continuing Our Learning, Developing Skills, and Using the Tools of Science

The Explanation phase of our text likely filled in the reasons behind the standards, methods, and priorities of science teaching. The purpose of the Expansion part is to help you deepen your understanding and expand your skills in

- identifying and mapping essential science concepts into a meaningful sequence, planning effective inquiry-based lessons that promote constructivist learning principles, and authentically assessing student learning outcomes;

- understanding and mastering the principles of effective questioning;

- developing a philosophy, knowledge of and skills in safe classroom management and science teaching;

- identifying effective supplements and using science texts and curriculum materials effectively;

- understanding the roles and becoming more skillful in using effective technologies for science teaching.

The details of Chapters 7–11 will help you to construct the following story line.

## Story Line

An effective science teacher must acquire and use fundamental skills in order to plan, implement, sustain, and evaluate the processes of inquiry if students are to construct accurate and meaningful scientific understandings.

## Concepts

*Chapter 7* The concepts of science must be mapped, holistic lessons planned, and learning assessed authentically in order to students to achieve the outcomes of the National Science Education Standards.

*Chapter 8* A teacher who understands the roles of questioning and develops skills in using questions effectively will promote scientific inquiry and authentic learning.

*Chapter 9* Authentic learning carries some risk, and it is the teacher's responsibility to maintain the safety of the children, as well as to create and organize a classroom environment for efficient and effective learning.

*Chapter 10* Many useful texts and teaching materials are available to supplement the science program. Teachers must screen them to ensure that those selected support specific outcomes and the new goals of modern science.

*Chapter 11* Technology, properly selected and used, can increase student interest, enhance the purpose for learning, add meaning to lessons, help to make conceptual connections within and between lessons, accommodate individual student differences, and elevate student attitudes.

## CHAPTER OUTLINE

# How Can You Plan Constructivist Science Lessons and Assess Student Performance?

It was spring, and Jennifer was near the end of her first year of the fourth-grade teaching position that she had won over forty-two applicants. Jennifer was astounded to learn that the competition had been so keen; she could not believe that she was better prepared for the position than the other applicants, especially since some had several years of teaching experience. When she politely inquired during casual conversation midway through her first semester, Jennifer learned that she had impressed Mr. Emerson, the principal, and the teaching staff with her views on teaching and that the science demonstration lesson that she taught was perceived by the staff as being on the cutting edge of the movement stimulated by the National Science Education Standards. Mr. Emerson and her fourth-grade teaching team of three other teachers had high expectations for Jennifer. The fact that she was a first-year teacher did not tempt them to make excuses for her; the school's staff had its focus on providing what was best for the students in order to meet state proficiency test standards.

Jennifer did not disappoint anyone. She proved her value among her teammates, and her humble, self-effacing ways made her a joy to collaborate with. Jennifer read widely, eagerly collected teaching ideas, and was genuinely grateful for suggestions. She was flattered when other teachers indicated interest in her science lessons and how those lessons could interface with some of the topics taught by her teammates who, among themselves, chose to specialize in one subject, which was taught to all fourth-grade students who rotated through the mod. Jennifer thought her teammates were only being kind, but they recognized considerable skill and potential for teacher leadership and recommended that Mr. Emerson appoint her to the Professional Development Council (PDC).

Jennifer accepted her appointment to the school PDC, although she was surprised by the offer, thinking the appointment should be given to someone with more experience. Science was the topic for next year's PDC agenda. The school had a recent curriculum revision that attempted to fulfill the National Science Education Standards. Curriculum decisions for her school district were made by a local control process and site-based management. The state recommended a general curriculum model and materials that schools might use but let the schools determine how best to devise and implement the curriculum. The standards made it difficult to select a single textbook and still be able to prepare students well for the statewide mandatory proficiency test, given to students each year at each grade level. The test was designed to measure progress toward fulfilling the standards. The PDC was concerned with the teachers' needs that were identified on a survey they had taken. The survey spoke of high frustration levels and a desire for extensive inservice in teaching toward the standards.

Coincidentally, the school's student proficiency test scores were received the same day as Jennifer's first meeting with the council. Teacher comparisons were discouraged but were unavoidable. Jennifer's students were the only ones who scored above the norm. Was this a fluke, or did this first-year teacher do something different to encourage higher student performance?

Jennifer felt somewhat defensive at first but soon realized that her colleagues' questions were professional and were asked in the spirit of schoolwide collaboration. Did she feel overwhelmed by the standards? What science concepts did she teach, and how did she decide when and how to teach them? Was there an order that worked best? How did she bring some balance from the science disciplines into her lessons? What did she do with the four new dimensions of science: science as inquiry, science and technology, science in personal and social perspectives, and history and nature of science? How could she possibly fit them into science lessons?

Jennifer described the frustrated feelings she too experienced at first. The standards advocated covering fewer concepts but actually seemed to expect teachers and students to do more in science than had ever before been attempted. Jennifer explained that desperation motivated her to think back to some of her experiences during teacher preparation. She found a way to connect certain experiences and use them as tools for dealing with the expectations that the standards seemed to bring.

Jennifer described a tool called *concept mapping* that helped her to sort and organize the science content concepts into story lines that addressed specific themes. One of the other teachers thought that the concept mapping technique seemed like brainstorming and webbing used in language arts, but Jennifer demonstrated that mapping was much more than that and explained how the techniques helped her to find a focus for the individual lessons. Jennifer designed each of her lessons for a single concept but planned comprehensively to help students construct their understanding of the concept and to connect it with other concepts from other lessons. Over time, students seemed to be able to make many connections among what they learned. Students even learned to make their own concept maps to illustrate their understanding. Jennifer used those maps to conduct formative evaluations of her teaching and her students' learning.

Jennifer also described a *learning cycle model* that she used to foster a culture of inquiry and to plan the sequence of student activities, in order to ensure that the concept was built from direct student activity and then expanded in order to connect with the new content outcomes given by the National Science Education Standards.

She shared some of her lesson plans with the other PDC members. Some members asked her to explain what she meant by *explore, explain, expand,* and *evaluate.* They were curious why Jennifer had students do activities first without explaining the point of the lesson and why she did not always test students at the end of her lessons, although the "evaluate" part of her planning model seemed to indicate that she would assess student learning at the end of each lesson.

Her lesson plans seemed to contain several activities that were related to each other, in a sequence over several days, sometimes requiring that almost a whole day be devoted to science. Of course, these special occasions were supported by Jennifer's teammates and at times they helped her teach science to all of the 100 fourth graders whom they shared. The PDC concluded that the ideas that Jennifer learned and used might help other teachers, and they decided to plan next year's professional development agenda around concept mapping, learning cycle planning, inquiry, teaching techniques, and authentic assessment. Jennifer was consulted often about how to do this and to suggest where the PDC might find assistance.                    ◆

## INTRODUCTION

You say that this scenario is too far-fetched? Rest assured, it is not. We find that many of our new teacher graduates experience situations very much like this one. They have skills that are different—in some ways more sophisticated—than more experienced teacher professionals have and that make them in demand when schools and teachers find themselves facing the challenges afforded by change and meeting the pressures of public accountability. New science standards and rising expectations for students and teachers require new ways of thinking and doing business. One new challenge is to convert typical planning processes into an approach that supports constructivist teaching and inquiry-based learning. In this chapter we

1. explore the use of concept mapping as a planning and assessment tool,
2. investigate a constructivist inquiry-based model for planning lessons that unifies the National Science Education (content) Standards,
3. explore several assessment techniques that are appropriate for inquiry learning.

## CONCEPT MAPPING

"Outcomes are high quality, culminating demonstrations of significant learning in context" (Spady, 1994, p. 18). William Spady reminds us that the operative word is *demonstration*. Outcomes identify in general terms the end product that we expect students to develop or achieve. The National Science Education Standards, and other reform movements (such as Project 2061's Benchmarks), identify the essential contexts and the types of high-quality end products that we should expect from scientifically literate students. Sometimes these end products—outcomes—are described for a particular grade level, but most often they are listed for a cluster of school grades. The grade-level placement, order, fit, and process of the steps required for successful demonstration of these end products are not defined. This planning chore is the duty of the curriculum developers or, more likely, each teacher. Several of the questions asked of Jennifer in our chapter scenario sound anxious and imply the uncertainty that this chore can cause for teachers.

There is a tool that can help teachers and curriculum developers to face the challenge of planning: *concept mapping*. Concept maps are essential tools for planning and teaching, and they can help improve student concept constructions, while helping to avoid misconceptions (Haney, 1998). Concept mapping is a more recent development that is becoming widely used as constructivist learning models become more accepted in science education.

Concept mapping helps students fulfill high-quality and meaningful learning outcomes in science. Maps provide concrete visual aids to help organize information before it is learned. Science textbooks are beginning to use concept maps to introduce chapter materials and are among their end-of-chapter activities. Teachers who have used them have found that they provide a logical basis for deciding what main ideas to include in (or delete from) their lesson plans and science teaching. Concept maps can be developed for an entire course, one or more units, or even a single lesson. We have developed concept maps for each chapter of this book. These maps introduce you to the dominant ideas and illustrate the relationships among the chapter's concepts and are available in the instructor's manual. Please ask your instructor for copies.

A concept map is a tool that illustrates the conceptual connections understood by the map's creator. Each person may construct a different map, depending on how he or she understands the subject of the map. Never try to memorize a concept map. Instead, study it for the conceptual story that it tells, paying attention to the main ideas and the relationships among them.

### Necessary Definitions

Some definitions must be provided before we can proceed. Bear in mind the fundamental purpose of education: to help students find new meaning in what they learn. We refer to this as *meaningful learning*. David Ausubel (1968) contrasts meaningful learning with rote learning, which is the result of many disjointed lessons. Concept maps use three types of knowledge: facts, concepts, and generalizations.

*Meaningful Learning.*   Meaningful learning implies that as a result of instruction, individuals are able to relate new material to previously acquired learning. This means that learners see new knowledge in the light of what they already know and understand; hence they find new meaning. Knowledge continually grows, but in a fashion that encourages connections with what learners already know. If these connections are missing, learners may regard the ideas they are taught as useless abstractions that only need to be memorized for a test.

As an example, learning that electricity flows through a circuit can be meaningful for children if they are able to see (with a teacher's guidance) that this idea applies to their previous understanding about how and where electricity is used (Figure 7.1). Children may have previously believed that electricity comes from the wall where an electric switch or outlet is located. When someone turns the switch on or plugs an appliance into the outlet, the electricity flows to a lamp or an appliance. A teacher would facilitate learning by helping children understand that electricity indeed flows through the switch or comes out of the outlet, but also that there are continuous electric wires between the electric pole outside the house and the switch or outlet inside the house, and between the switch or outlet and the appliance. Unless children are able to see

**FIGURE 7.1   Example Concept Map**

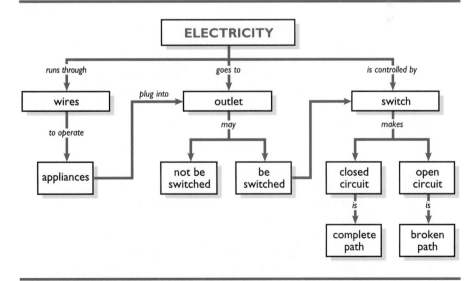

these connections between the existing knowledge and the new, they are likely to regard this generalization about electricity as an abstraction, or something to memorize without exactly knowing its importance.

*Rote Learning.*    Memorization without understanding and without a connection to the previous knowledge is called *rote learning.* Rote learning promotes memorization of facts; meaningful learning promotes conceptual understanding.

*Facts.*    A *fact* is a singular occurrence that happens in the past or present and that has no predictive value for the future. Thus, the information that you are now reading in this book at a specific time of day is a fact, just as a statement about what you ate for lunch or dinner yesterday is a fact. These facts may be completely isolated events that give no indications about your study or eating habits. On the other hand, if you regularly read your science methods book at the same time, or if you consistently eat salad for lunch and chicken or fish for dinner, then these seemingly isolated facts have much in common with your similar actions at other times.

*Concepts.*    Common attributes between facts can be described and named. The name given represents a *concept.* Interestingly, your behavior today or yesterday can be described by a single word or brief phrase. Words such as *preparation* and *follow-up* or a phrase like *nutritious diet* are examples of concepts based on an accumulation of facts. The definitions of these concepts may include descriptions such as "you read your textbook before and after the science methods class," or "you try to eat foods that are low in calories, fat, and cholesterol." A concept covers a broader set of events than a singular occurrence that might happen at random. Therefore, concepts by their nature are abstract. Other examples of concepts are computer, animal, mineral, vegetable, food chain, magnets, solution, conservation, and buoyancy. All require that we know the definition to understand the meaning. In fact, most words in the dictionary represent concepts. All learners, especially young children, need to experience many examples of singular occurrences or facts before they can develop the abstract understanding necessary for conceptualization. But once they learn the concept, they do not need to learn isolated facts that are subsumed in it. They can reconstruct these facts when they need them.

*Generalizations.*    *Generalizations* are broad patterns between two or more concepts that have predictive value. Generalizations are rules or principles that contain more than one concept and that have predictive value. Thus, a statement such as "like poles in magnets repel each other and opposite poles attract" is a generalization, and it can predict what would happen if two magnets were brought next to each other. Learners must know the concepts of *magnets, poles, attraction,* and *repel* before they can fully understand the meaning of the generalization.

## *What Are Concept Maps?*

Concepts are abstract ideas. Concept maps, on the other hand, are concrete graphic illustrations that indicate how a single concept is related to other concepts in the same category (see Figure 7.2). As you begin to learn about concept maps, you may prefer to think of them as sophisticated planning webs that reveal what concepts children must learn and how the concepts must be related. Curricula are primarily designed to teach concepts that students do not already know. Therefore, teaching and learning will be greatly enhanced if we know which concepts should be included and which need to be excluded from instructional programs.

Concept maps show relationships among different smaller and larger concepts. By looking at a concept map and considering the level of the children's abilities and other instructional factors, you can make a decision about the scope of the concepts you need to cover in an instructional program. Joseph Novak states that

> a good curriculum design requires an analysis first of the concepts in a field of knowledge and, second, consideration of some relationships between these concepts that can serve to illustrate which concepts are most general and superordinate and which are more specific and subordinate. (Novak, 1979, p. 86)

A concept map's visual illustration of main ideas is the primary advantage it provides over other ways of planning instruction. A concept map shows

**FIGURE 7.2  Concept Map for Air**

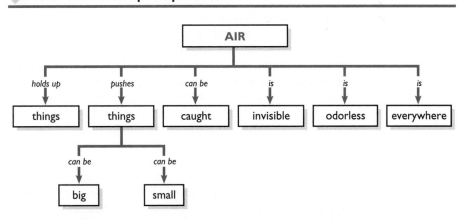

*Source:* This figure represents concepts found in the first-grade text (Addison-Wesley, publisher) described by John R. Staver and Mary Bay in "Analysis of the Conceptual Structure and Reasoning Demands of Elementary Science Texts at the Primary (K–3) Level," *Journal of Research in Science Teaching* 26, no. 4 (1989): 334.

hierarchical relationships: how various subordinate concepts are related to the superordinate concepts. A relationship can descend several levels deep in the hierarchy of concepts. The relationship between superordinate and subordinate concepts is shown in Figure 7.3.

A concept map is different in several ways from the outline or table of contents generally found at the beginning of a book. First, outlines do not show any definite relationships between concepts; they simply show how the material is organized. Concept maps, on the other hand, show a definite relationship between big ideas and small ideas, thus clarifying the difference between details or specifics and the big idea or superordinate concept. This can be helpful when a teacher must decide how much emphasis to give to specific facts as compared to concepts in a lesson.

The second difference is that concept maps provide visual imagery that can help students recall information and see relationships between concepts. Outlines do not provide such imagery. Outlines do serve a useful function: They indicate a sequence of different steps. Concept maps, on the other hand, show hierarchies of ideas that suggest psychologically valid sequences. These hierarchies may not match the linear sequence, or outline, that a teacher has decided to use for a presentation.

Third, concept maps can show interrelationships between ideas, or *crosslinks*. These help to "tie it all together," as students often remark.

### Why Should Concept Maps Be Developed?

Concept maps help teachers understand the various concepts that are embedded in the larger topic they are to teach. This understanding improves teacher planning and instruction (Starr & Krajcik, 1990). Since the science knowledge domain is vast, and most of us have acquired it in pieces at different stages, we are not likely to see the important connections between the separate ideas we teach. As an exercise, mapping provides an opportunity to express our understanding about various concepts and to show relationships with other similar and dissimilar concepts. Ultimately, the larger topic or unit (superordinate concept) is hierarchically arranged. This arrangement shows facts at the bottom and subordinate concepts arranged in relationships with each other in the body of the map (see, for example, the details of Figures 7.1, 7.2, and 7.3). Our experience with hundreds of teachers and students has convinced us that they gain new insight from developing concept maps when they structure what they know around a superordinate concept. This observation is also supported by Novak and Gowin (1986): "Students and teachers often remark that they recognize new relationships among concepts that they did not before" (p. 17). As well, concept maps help learners encode information into meaningful networks that enhance long-term memory (Eggan & Kauchak, 1992) and help reduce students' anxiety while improving achievement and enhancing self-worth (Jegede et al., 1990).

Concept mapping is one of the most crucial steps to take while deciding what to include in a curriculum, unit, or lesson plan. Clear mapping may help

# FIGURE 7.3  Expanded Concept Map of Air

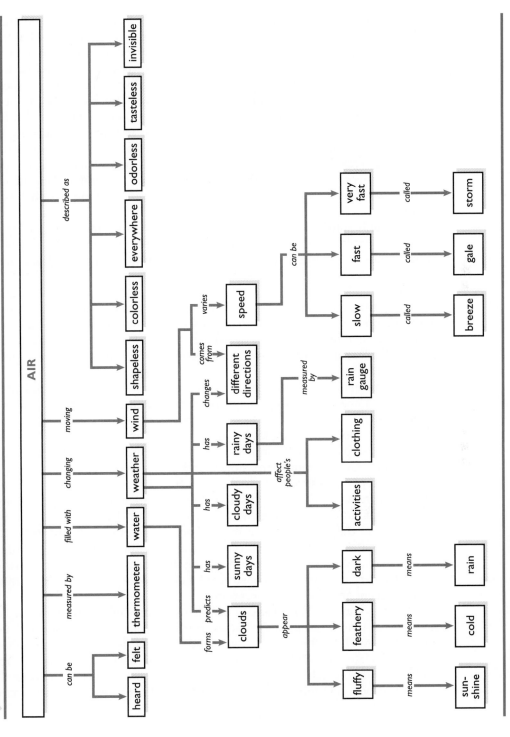

*Source:* The figure shows the relationship of several levels of subordinate concepts as provided by John R. Staver and Mary Bay, in "Analysis of the Conceptual Structure and Reasoning Demands of Elementary Science Texts at the Primary (K–3) Level," *Journal of Research in Science Teaching* 26, no. 4 (1989): 339. The researchers examined the contents of the Merrill first-grade science text.

to avoid student-formed misconceptions (Czerniak & Haney, 1998). Without concept maps, teachers choose to teach what they can remember or what they prefer. The topics they select in this manner may be appropriate at times, especially for teachers who have had previous successful experiences with the material, but this process opens a major psychological flaw in the process of curriculum development and lesson planning. The concepts or topics chosen may be so disconnected from each other that learners are baffled and see no connections. Learners may also fail to receive new meaning because they cannot link the new material with what they have previously learned. As a result, learners may resort to memorizing isolated facts, treating the experiences and ideas with less thought than we prefer. This mental inaction would defeat the modern science goal of developing new habits of the mind.

Although some material must be memorized, sustained memorization has questionable value in science. Taking the time to identify concepts yields clear science topics and helps to determine which topics are worth learning. Mapping concepts suggests specific objectives that teachers must establish for pupils. Concept maps can help you see the logic of the relationships among specific concepts. Once you see this logic, you can decide how much depth or breadth to include in lessons so that students will see the same conceptual relationships. These decisions consist of choosing the proper activities and learning aids, as well as selecting the appropriate type of pupil evaluation.

You can also use concept maps to organize the flow of the classroom lessons. We have used concept maps as advance organizers to focus students' attention and guide them along to seeing a bigger picture and for use as a mental scaffolding for organizing their thoughts and discoveries. You can use concept maps as road maps to indicate the direction in which instruction is to proceed in your classroom—up, down, and across the map. Students can be shown concept maps several times during instruction so that they can see what has been covered and how it fits with the rest. Creative primary teachers have used concept maps as a reading and meta-cognitive tool by posting sight words that represent the science idea of the day on a large bulletin board, then discussing cumulative meanings with children and inviting them to suggest organizational relationships between and among the words. Over time, the class of young learners cooperatively constructed a class concept map that illustrated their emergent and changing conceptions.

Another way you can use concept maps is for student evaluations. For example, display large pieces of newsprint in a conspicuous place and use them daily to show the science ideas students have learned and how these ideas interrelate. This daily effort is an example of formative evaluation. You could ask intermediate and middle school children to develop maps at the end of instruction to reflect what they understand, a process called *summative evaluation*.

## Steps for Developing a Concept Map

A concept map can be developed for the entire course for a year or semester, or for a single unit, or even for a single lesson. Figure 7.4 shows the relationship of concepts in a concept map. The following steps work for all concept maps:

**1.** List on paper all of the concepts (names of topics) that pertain to a general area you will teach. Only the names are needed at this stage. No descriptions are necessary. For example, let us say you have examined your next science chapter or module and have listed the following topics: air, weather, clouds, storms, and effects of weather.

**2.** Note any specific facts (examples) that are either essential for students to learn or that you find especially interesting. The facts and examples you list

**FIGURE 7.4  Concept Map for Concept Maps**

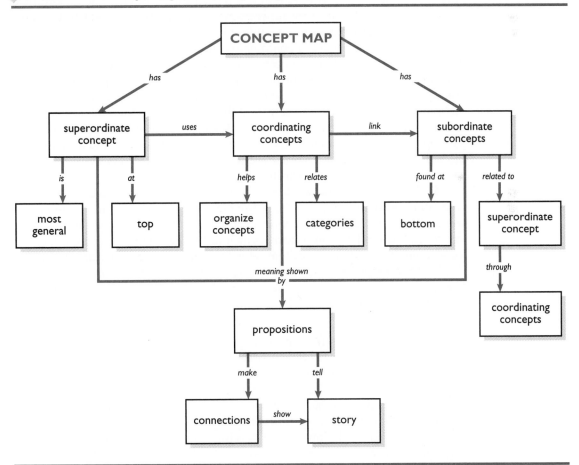

might include air moves, measurements are used to track air movement, moving air causes weather, weather can be helpful or harmful, and weather helps us decide what clothes to wear.

**3.** From the list of concepts, choose what you find as an overarching concept (superordinate), and place it at the top of the paper. (You may want to use a large sheet of newsprint or other suitable drawing paper.) You decide that the overarching concept is *weather*. It seems that all other ideas relate to it. Satisfied, you now line up the other concepts by going to Step 4.

**4.** Arrange the first level of subordinate concepts underneath the superordinate concept. Generally, this stage requires the use of propositions or linking words like *provides, types, contains, can be,* and so on to develop the appropriate connections between subordinate concepts. Refer to the second line of boxes in Figure 7.4. (The first level of subordinate concepts is known by another term, *coordinate concepts,* because they link or coordinate the superordinate concept and the subordinate concepts found lower in the hierarchy. Each coordinate concept is related to the same superordinate concept, but it is distinctly different from other concepts arranged at that level of the hierarchy.)

**5.** After the first level of coordinate concepts has been identified, start arranging other subordinate concepts that are directly related to the level above. Similarly, you can develop further hierarchies by going down several levels. You will find that specific facts will be examples of certain individual subordinate concepts that will most likely be at the bottom of the hierarchy. See, for example, in Figure 7.3 that *clouds* is a subordinate concept connected to coordinate concepts of *water* and *weather,* and the concepts *fluffy, feathery,* and *dark* are connected to *clouds* to show other subordinate concepts in the hierarchy; each concept relates back to the superordinate concept, *air.*

**6.** Draw lines to show relationships among the subordinate, coordinate, and superordinate concepts. The entire hierarchy should resemble a pyramid. Write linking words (propositions) on the lines to show relationships among concepts. These relationships form principles. Refer to Figure 7.4 and notice the connecting lines with propositions—for example, *has, uses,* and *through.*

**7.** After the entire map has been developed, mark or circle certain subordinate concepts that are particularly appealing for your students or are at the appropriate difficulty level. These would generally constitute your course or unit for the given time period.

There are three more important points. First, try to minimize jumping around the entire map; try not to select topics without a strong rationale. The strongest reason for selecting a topic should rest on the knowledge the children acquired earlier. During the appropriate phases of your instruction (called *concept invention* and *expansion,* which are explained later in this chapter), you need to help children link the new concept with previous learning.

Second, balance the number of specific details you teach in terms of how well they contribute to overall conceptual development. Remember, the factual information sits at the bottom of the map, and your purpose is to have children understand what rests at higher levels of the map. Teaching factual information alone does not help children to develop concepts at a higher level unless you make specific attempts to move up the hierarchical ladder.

Third, use Figure 7.5 to self-evaluate your concept map. The criteria of the rubric will help you to move from a novice level of mapmaking toward a level of mastery and integration of conceptual understanding of science into your graphic portrayal of abstract ideas.

## FIGURE 7.5    Holistic Scoring Rubric for Concept Maps

### 4 Integrating
- Map has frequent branching.
- Cross links are frequent and logical.
- Linking words are present and appropriate.
- Concepts are logically presented and show various levels.
- All concepts are included on the map and others are added to support related concepts.
- Examples are abundant and relevant.

### 3 Mastering
- Map has frequent branching.
- Cross links are present and logical.
- Linking words are usually present but not always appropriate.
- Most concepts are logically presented and show various levels.
- Most concepts are included on the map.
- Examples are present and relevant.

### 2 Developing
- Map has some branching.
- Cross links are few and not necessarily logical.
- Linking words are used sparingly and are not always appropriate.
- Concepts are not logically presented and/or lack various levels.
- Several concepts are not included on the map.
- Examples are sparse.

### I Novice
- Map is rather linear.
- Cross links are not evident and/or are not logical.
- Linking words are not evident and/or are inappropriate.
- Concepts are not logically presented and/or lack various levels.
- Large gaps exist in concept representation.
- Examples are not evident or are irrelevant.

*Source:* Haney, J. (1998) Concept mapping in the science classroom: Linking theory to practice. *The Agora,* Vol. VIII, September, p. 6.

# PLANNING CONSTRUCTIVE INQUIRY SCIENCE LESSONS

Reform efforts, such as the National Science Education Standards, direct our attention toward teaching for the goal of scientific literacy. Standards identify numerous outcomes that we attempt to help students achieve. Embedded in the outcomes are dozens of essential science concepts, skills, values, and cross-disciplinary science knowledge that students are expected to demonstrate. Constructivist learning theory cautions us against attempting the futile effort of frontal teaching. How can we address the new expectations held aloft for science teachers and students?

## *Selecting Performance Outcomes and Developing Curriculum*

Concept maps illustrate clusters of concepts that share relationships with other science concepts. These relationships make it possible to identify a unifying theme that can help us construct units of science experiences for learners. The Standards' content outcomes help to provide parameters that are useful for selecting learning outcomes and developing a curriculum that encourages full, active participation and student conceptual constructions. See Appendix A for a list of outcomes for grades K–4 and 5–8. The standards, outcomes, and concept maps are tools for making prudent selections to avoid the "fill-up-the-empty-time" approach. Used appropriately, mapping and planning can help to make wise choices so lessons have clear expectations, abundant opportunities for students to construct understanding through inquiry, and expanded contact with science in many contexts. Some general planning principles can help us help students develop their thinking skills and learn meaningful science:

**1.** *Provide a variety of activities for learning.* Activities that provide children opportunities to experience and manipulate real objects are essential. Emphasize direct physical and mental involvement for children in primary and intermediate grades. All children must be given opportunities to explain what they experience and to communicate to others in written and spoken language. All learning activities should be expanded to address as many of the goal clusters as possible.

**2.** *Introduce concepts and specialized vocabulary after children have gained firsthand experiences with the object or concept.* As a general rule, teachers should talk less and involve students more. One way of doing this is to tell less and ask more. Questions are devices for encouraging children to use their minds. Chapter 8 is devoted to the uses of questions.

**3.** *Interact with children and have them interact with each other.* Questions stimulate interaction, and interaction encourages thinking. Ask children to describe what they have done or observed. Encourage children to ask each other questions about their experiences and to ask *why* questions.

**4.** *Focus learning experiences so that children are encouraged to discover concepts.* Focusing on concepts, the main ideas behind learning, helps children learn connections more easily and removes the learning barrier of disconnected facts.

A unit plan consists of goals, objectives, learning activities, teaching methods, and assessment. Two types of goals are included: global goals or outcomes selected from visionary science groups and national recommendations that guide the elementary science program (such as those provided here and in Chapter 6) and goals set by the teacher or the school that guide the unit itself. Objectives are smaller, specific statements of what students will do. Learning activities consist of descriptions of what teachers and students will do; they are selected to fulfill the objectives. When the learning activities have been completed, the performance objectives will have been met, and when the objectives have been met, the unit goals will have been achieved. In turn, when the unit goals have been achieved, meaningful progress will have been made toward accomplishing the science program goals—the curriculum.

### Developing Objectives

Objectives are more narrowly focused than goals and consist of the many smaller steps you take to accomplish a goal. Objectives are descriptions of what you, the teacher, expect your students to *do.* This last word is important. Objectives make clear the particular expectations teachers have for their students; objectives use key *action words*—verbs—to describe what students will do to satisfy the teacher that they are meeting the goals. Objectives are beneficial because they help sequence instruction properly, suggest appropriate learning activities and resources, and specify the appropriate evaluation procedures.

Different kinds of objectives exist. The type recommended in this chapter may be called a *performance* or an *instructional objective.* Named after its intention, this objective is a statement that describes what students are expected to be able to do. This type of objective has four parts and can be remembered by the letters A, B, C, and D.

**A** is the **audience** (class, group, or child) for whom the objective is intended.

**B** is the **behavior** that a teacher expects from the children.

**C** is the **conditions** that are necessary for the learning to take place (such as the prerequisites, prior activity, arrangements, or support materials that are needed).

**D** is the **degree** or minimum level of student performance that shows that the children have completed the objective satisfactorily.

For example, "Given plastic drinking straws, straight pins, thread, tape, modeling clay, paper clips, and metal washers (*conditions*), each fourth-grade child (*audience*) will build (*behavior*) a structure that is at least 30 centimeters tall, uses at least three triangles, and supports at least ten washers without falling down (*degree*)." (Addresses the National Science Education Standards K–4 unifying concept of "Systems, order, and organization;" the Science as Inquiry Standard; the Physical Science "Properties of objects and materials" outcome; and the Science and Technology "Abilities of technological design" outcome.)

The behavior stated in an objective must follow a precise rule: The behavior must be observable or detectable. Verbs like *appreciate, desire, feel, know, like,* and *understand* are too general to use in an objective, yet these verbs are fine when used in a goal, because a goal *is* more general. Verbs like *build, classify, measure,* and *match* are much more precise, and the teacher can measure or observe accomplishment; there is no need to make assumptions about whether a child has done them. Lists of science process skills are rich sources of verbs for your objectives.

## Planning the Lesson—4Es

Effective science lessons have a central focus and clear expectations for student performance. The *lesson concept*—the main science idea—is the central focus. Lesson objectives help define the expected types and levels of performance, or what and how the students are to demonstrate that they understand the con-

*Effective science lessons stimulate learners' minds, shape attitudes, and provide learning opportunities for physical manipulation of learning materials.*

cept and can apply their understanding to useful matters. Conceptual understanding, to have lasting value, must be applied to the student's world. This application expands the depth of learning and helps fulfill the new dimensions of science outcomes: experiencing science as inquiry, understanding the interrelationships of science and technology, using personal and social perspectives to understand science, and comprehending the nature of science throughout its history.

The planning model presented here uses a conceptual focus, helps learners to construct meaning, encourages students to expand understanding of that fundamental meaning, and evaluates student performance in authentic ways. Called a *learning cycle* (see Figure 7.6), this series of planning and teaching steps helps teachers to encourage learners to construct meaning from direct experiences, then expand that understanding through direct treatment of the new dimensions of science. The lesson planning model in this chapter closely follows the original format of the Science Curriculum Improvement Study (SCIS, see Chapter 10), which is credited with the greatest student achievement gains in major research studies and significant improvements in student science attitudes and inquiry skills, when compared to similar experimental science programs and traditional science curricula (Shymansky et al., 1982; Bredderman, 1982). Our planning model has been modified to stimulate a full range of student inquiry and reflect constructivist learning expectations and to emphasize appropriate student evaluation. This approach is simple and thorough, and has considerable potential to effect improvements in students' learning. The planning model also becomes the teaching method. A detailed description of the teaching method was introduced in Chapter 1. The elements of planning are given here.

**FIGURE 7.6    The Planning and Learning Cycle**

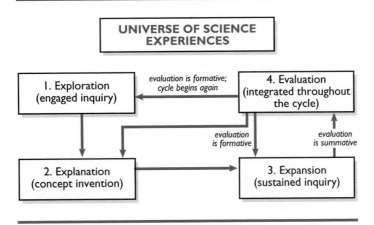

The four phases of the science planning and learning cycle provide most of the structure for planning an effective science lesson. Once you identify the concept that is to be learned, you can structure the learning activity to take advantage of the learning cycle. Then you can add descriptions of the proper ways to evaluate what the children learn.

The *4-E approach* is recommended: exploration, explanation, expansion, and evaluation. The following questions should help you plan for each step of the learning cycle as you write the lesson plan. The parenthetical remarks suggest the aspects of science and teaching strategies that may be used. A sample science learning cycle lesson plan is shown in Exhibit 7.1 on pages 229–232.

### Step 1. Planning for student exploration

Children must have concrete materials and experiences if they are to learn concrete concepts. Abstract concepts are largely inappropriate, even with concrete materials, until around age 15 for most pupils. The learners must become engaged in the context of the inquiry and be stimulated by the teacher and objects in order to undertake free and guided inquiry. Use these guiding questions:

- What do I want the children to learn? (goals, objectives, attitudes, processes, products)
- What concepts will be invented? (science products)
- What activities must the children do to find and to construct the needed data? (processes, information, answers to questions)
- How will I engage the learners in the exploration?
- How will I stimulate the learners to engage in the processes of inquiry?
- What kinds of records should the children keep? (process skills)
- What kinds of instructions and encouragement will the children need? (attitudes)

Teachers need to direct the children's activities and suggest what kinds of records they should keep. *They should not tell or explain the concept.* State the instructions succinctly, even in the form of objectives. Plan this step carefully so that it is student centered and student-activity based.

### Step 2. Planning for explanation

The main purpose of this phase is to reach mental equilibrium through accommodation, as described in the theory of Jean Piaget (see Chapter 4). Equilibrium is reached when a new concept is formed and/or linked to previously understood related concepts. Here students must focus on their primary findings from exploration, and the teacher must help them by introducing proper language or concept labels. This step was originally called *concept invention.* The teacher's task is to lead students through a discussion so that students can discover the concept by inventing it for themselves. The teacher's technique is to question skillfully so that students use the experiences of their explorations to construct scientific meaning. The teacher acts as a facilitator and introduces any

## Simple Circuits (NSES K–4 Physical Science Outcomes)

**Concept statement to be invented**

A *circuit* is a pathway that electricity follows from the power source, through the bulb, and back to the power source.

**Additional concepts that are important for expansion**

Open or closed circuit, series circuit, parallel circuit, switch, filament, insulation, conductor.

**Attitudes to emphasize**

Curiosity, open-mindedness, perseverance, positive approach to failure, co-operation.

**Materials needed**

Dry cells, wires, flashlight bulbs, bulb holders, switches, wire strippers, screwdrivers, scissors, aluminum foil, paper clips, paper fasteners, masking tape, small pieces of cardboard.

**Safety precautions:** Have students use not more than five dry cells in the same circuit to limit shock potential and to preserve light bulbs.

EXPLORATION: What process skills will the students use?

(Observation, predictions, classification)

What will the students do?

Teacher's instructions to students: "Using only the three pieces of equipment given to you, light the bulb. Once you are successful, find three other ways to light the bulb. You can use only the three pieces of equipment you have been given. Carefully draw a picture of each method you use to try to light the bulb. Label your drawings *will light* and *will not light*. Be certain to show exactly where your wire is touching and how your bulb is positioned with the battery."

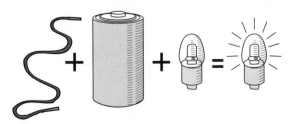

*(continued)*

**EXHIBIT 7.1    A Sample Lesson Plan Based on the Planning and Learning Cycle**

**EXPLANATION:** What is the concept? How will the concept be constructed?

Concept: A *circuit* is a pathway that electricity follows from the power source, through the bulb, and back to the power source.

Have students draw their pictures on the chalkboard. Use your finger to trace the pathway that electricity from the battery flows through when the bulb lights and when it does not light. This path is called a *circuit*. Using the students' own ideas and words, construct an explanation that a *circuit* is a pathway electricity follows from the power source to the bulb and back to the power source. Show the students that contact with the bulb must be made in two specific places. The path must be complete from the battery, through the bulb, and back to the battery for the bulb to light. A key question to ask: "In how many places must metal touch the bulb for it to light?" The answer is "two": the side and bottom conductors of the bulb must be included in the circuit.

**EXPANSION:** What process skills will the students use?

(Making predictions, classifying, controlling variables)

How will the concept be applied and expanded?

Challenge the students to light more than one bulb, combine batteries for more power, and add equipment such as a bulb holder, a switch, and more wires. Ask what happens to other bulbs when one is unscrewed. Make a circuit so all bulbs go out when one is unscrewed: a series circuit. Make a circuit so the other bulbs remain lighted when one bulb is unscrewed: a parallel circuit or a separate series circuit; look carefully. Construct a paper clip switch and demonstrate its function.

*Science in Personal and Social Perspectives*

1. Name some devices you use that require an electrical circuit.
2. What type of circuit is needed?
3. What would your life be like without electricity controlled by circuits?
4. How is electricity "made"? What resources are necessary? How has demand for electricity changed with population growth?

*Science and Technology*

A set of car headlights is one example of a specific circuit used for safety purposes. When one light burns out or is broken, the others remain lighted.

1. What are other examples in which the type of circuit used is important for safety or convenience?

**EXHIBIT 7.1   (continued)**

2. A flashlight uses a simple series circuit and is an example of technology. How has the simple flashlight improved or affected your life? your community? the world?

3. Use the idea of a circuit to make a flashlight out of these materials: cardboard tube, wire, two D-cell batteries, flashlight bulb, paper clip, two paper fasteners, bottle cap, tape.

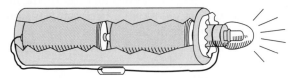

### Science as Inquiry

Plan, conduct, and explain investigations that illustrate: short circuits, open and closed circuits, series and parallel circuits. Identify new concepts in new lessons, such as resistance, cell versus battery, and electromagnetism. Use the concept of open and closed circuit to solve circuit puzzles.

### History and Nature of Science

**1.** Thomas Edison experimented thousands of times before he successfully found a material suitable as a filament that could be used to complete the circuit in a light bulb. How would our world be different today if Edison had never succeeded?

**2.** Who needs to know about circuits? Name careers, and have students identify those careers that they previously did not know about that rely on some knowledge of electrical circuits. Some possibilities include electrician, appliance repair person, architect, city planner, electric power producer, computer engineer, car/truck repair person.

**3.** How have the expectations changed over time for people in these careers?

**EVALUATION:** How will the students show what they have learned?

(The lesson's performance objectives go here.)

1. Given a prediction sheet containing different circuit diagrams, the students will correctly identify all of the circuits as complete or incomplete by marking them *will light* or *will not light*.

2. The students will construct a working switch from cardboard, two paper fasteners, a paper clip, and two wires.

3. The students will construct, demonstrate and describe the operation of a series circuit and a parallel circuit. Each circuit must include at least two bulbs and be controlled by the paper clip switch.

4. Students will accurately draw a diagram and correctly label the parts of the circuit they use to make their flashlights.

*(continued)*

5. Each student must construct a flashlight that functions properly. Students must show the teacher that the switch turns the light on and off.
6. Each student will cooperate with group partners, volunteer to assist those who request help, and demonstrate a positive approach when having difficulty with manipulative tasks.
7. Each student will describe three ways to use circuits and identify at least two different inventions that control the flow of electricity through those circuits.
8. Each student will describe at least three safety precautions that they take to avoid accidents with electricity.
9. Each student will use inquiry skills to solve correctly four circuit puzzles.

**EXHIBIT 7.1**   *(continued)*

special vocabulary that must accompany the concept. Plan this step carefully so that it does not become completely teacher centered; your lectures must be minimal. Use these questions as you plan for this part of your lesson:

• What kinds of information or findings are students expected to provide? (products, process skills)
• How will the students' findings from the exploration phase be reviewed and summarized? (teacher questioning, pupil discussion, graphing, board work)
• How can I use the students' findings and refrain from telling them what they should have found, even if they are incorrect or incomplete? (teacher questioning, guided construction, attitudes)
• What are the proper concept labels or terms that must be attached to the concept? (products)
• What reasons can I give the students if they ask me why the concept is important? (teacher exposition, lesson expansion)

The last question automatically leads to the next phase: Expansion.

### Step 3. Planning for expansion

The purpose of this phase is to sustain the inquiry by helping students organize their thinking and by applying what they have just learned to other ideas or experiences that relate to the lesson's concept and to help the students to expand their ideas. It is very important to use the language of the concept during the expansion-of-the-idea phase. Plan this phase for student involvement. Consider using these questions:

• What previous experiences have the children had that are related to the concept? How can I connect the concept to these experiences? (new activities, questioning)
• What are some examples of how the concept and the activities encourage the students' science inquiry skills? (learning activities, questioning)

*Effective science lessons stimulate unique learner products.*

- What examples can be used to illustrate the interrelationship of science and technology and the contributions of each to society and the quality (or problems) of life? (discussion, readings, uses of multimedia, class projects)
- In what ways has science benefited the students personally? (class projects, reflective questioning)
- What are examples of how science has influenced our society, policies, and laws? (linkages with social studies, current events)
- What have been the dominant ideas of science throughout recorded history, and how have those ideas and the nature of science changed over time? (linkages with social studies, documentaries, class projects, discussion, biographies)
- What new experiences do the children need in order to expand on the concept? (processes, attitudes, activities)
- What is the next concept related to the present one? How can I encourage exploration of the next concept? (products, processes)

### Step 4. Planning for evaluation

The purpose of this phase is to go beyond standard forms of testing. Learning must occur in small increments before larger leaps of insight are possible. Your evaluation of students can be planned in terms of outcomes and pupil performances. Several types of records are necessary to form a holistic evaluation of the students' learning and to encourage conceptual understanding as well as process skill development. Table 7.1 reflects the need for continual evaluation, not just end-of-chapter or end-of-unit testing. Evaluation can occur at any point in the lesson. Consistent evaluation can help to reveal misconceptions before they become deeply rooted. Ask yourself:

- What key questions should I ask to encourage deep exploration? (processes, attitudes)
- What questions can I ask to help students think about their data in an effort to construct realistic concepts? (processes)
- What questions will expand conception and achieve several science goals? (processes, products)
- What behavior (mental, physical, attitudinal) can I expect from the students? (attitudes, processes)
- What hands-on assessments can the students do to demonstrate the basic skills of observation, classification, communication, measurement, prediction, and inference? (processes)
- What assessments can students do to demonstrate the integrated skills of identifying and controlling variables, defining operationally, forming hypotheses, experimenting, interpreting data, and forming models?

**TABLE 7.1    Types of Appropriate Evaluations for the Learning Cycles**

| Phase | Purpose of Evaluation | Type of Evaluation |
|---|---|---|
| Explore | Determine possible misconceptions | Questioning and student answers, pictorial assessment |
|  | Document students' uses of process skills | Process skills checklists |
|  | Encourage exploration | Record observations, make predictions, ask observation questions |
|  | Improve social skills and interactions | Teacher observations, checklists |
| Explain | Clarify concept constructions | Group discussions, data processing, picture drawing, constructing models, reflective questioning |
|  | Document conceptual change | Concept mapping, interviews, pictorial assessment |
| Expand | Document ability to use integrated process skills | Reflective questioning, hands-on assessment |
|  | Determine students' abilities to transfer learning to new situations | Inventions, writing activities, presentations |
|  | Stimulate new interests, make connections to previous learning | Projects and activities that address standards outcomes, portfolios |

- What pictorial assessments can students do to demonstrate how well they can think through problems that require both knowledge and the integration of ideas? (products)
- What reflective question assessments will indicate how well the students recall and use what has been learned? (products)

# HOW CAN YOU EVALUATE STUDENT LEARNING?

Children learn more and better when we focus clearly on the learning outcomes and objectives we want them to achieve, because planning, teaching, and evaluation go hand in hand. Next we explore these connections.

## *Limits and Purposes of Tests*

Typical forms of evaluation, such as standardized tests and teacher-prepared paper-and-pencil multiple choice or true-false tests, have severe limits. True, they are easy to use and grade. However, their formats limit what they can evaluate; their almost exclusive focus on facts inhibits inductive reasoning, development of scientific process skills, and affective factors of learning. Indeed, facts are necessary, and children cannot do much science or effectively reason scientifically without a solid factual base. Children may be able to memorize the facts, however, without having any idea about how to apply them. Being able to identify or describe a scientific procedure or apparatus on paper does not mean a child knows when that procedure is appropriate or how to use the apparatus properly. Consider the following test items, which are similar to those used during a National Assessment of Education Progress (Raizen & Kaser, 1989):

1. [The child is given a picture of four animals; one is a bird and the other three are mammals.] Which one of these animals is not a mammal?
2. Which of the following is used to measure temperature: feet, degrees, centimeters, minutes, calories?
3. Mary and Jane each bought the same kind of rubber ball. Mary said, "My ball bounces better than yours." Jane replied, "I'd like to see you prove that." What should Mary do?
   (a) Drop both balls from the same height and notice which bounces higher.
   (b) Throw both balls against a wall and see how far each ball bounces off the wall.
   (c) Drop the two balls from different heights and notice which bounces higher.
   (d) Throw the balls down against the floor and see how high they bounce.
   (e) Feel the balls to see which is harder.

The first item asks for a factual answer that could be memorized. The second item also requires a factual answer, but a student could answer correctly without ever having had science, since everyday experience could prevail.

Although the third item is more complex, as a teacher you could find it difficult to determine why a pupil gave a wrong answer, since there is no way to evaluate the child's reasoning with this format. Benjamin Bloom sums up the emphasis of traditional testing practices: "Teacher-made [and standardized] tests are largely tests of remembered information. . . . [It] is estimated that over 90 percent of test questions the U.S. public school students are now expected to answer deal with little more than information" (Bloom, 1984, pp. 4–16). Bloom claims that instructional material and classroom teaching rarely rise above the lowest level of his taxonomy for the cognitive domain: the *knowledge level*. In response, science testing is receiving a great deal of attention, and alternative forms of elementary and middle school science assessments are being developed.

## Selecting the Tool for the Task

*Evaluation, testing, assessment, performance assessment,* and *authentic assessment* are terms frequently used by educators interchangeably, but they are not the same. In the Evaluation phase of the learning cycle lesson, we intend for the evaluation to remind us to select the most appropriate and timely tool for determining what students understand and can do so that modifications can be made to instruction or appropriate intervention can be given to correct possible misconceptions among students. Our intention fits Nancy Murphy's (1994) definition of *authentic assessment*: "the determination and documentation of students' current understandings so that teachers might better address students' immediate needs" (p. 14). Therefore, teacher evaluation of student understanding and performance should be ongoing and cumulative (formative), rather than have only a summative function—that is, done only at the end of units or chapters. Periodic, focused assessments become the tools of evaluation.

Anne Grall Reichel (1994) offers several questions for planning appropriate assessment tools and placing those tools within the proper scope of teaching:

- Have I determined the skills I want to assess?
- Have I focused on key conceptual ideas and problem solving?
- Have I established criteria to assess student learning?
- Have I made my expectations clear to my students?
- Have I designed instructional tasks with opportunities to create, perform, or produce an end product?
- Am I beginning to make assessment an integral part of my teaching rather than an end point?
- Have I involved students in the evaluation of their own work (Reichel, 1994, p. 25)?

The learning cycle planning and teaching model described in this chapter requires timely and continual teacher assessment of student understanding and skills. Table 7.1 lists several appropriate assessment types that support the expectations for students during each phase of the learning cycle. Most of the effects offered by these assessment types cluster into three types of teacher-designed assessment devices: pictorial assessment, reflective questioning, and hands-on assessment. These approaches were invented by the Full Option Science System (FOSS) of the Lawrence Hall of Science in Berkeley, California, as special techniques to support constructivist teaching and learning through authentic assessment. We used the original version of FOSS as a model for designing authentic assessments for the lesson that is featured in this chapter.

*Pictorial Assessment.*   Pictorial assessment requires students to complete reasoning tasks that differ from traditional fill-in, multiple-choice, and one-answer tasks. The nature of the analysis depends on the types of pictures (or illustrations) used and the context associated with the pictures. Pictorial assessment encourages students to demonstrate their capability to use science process skills appropriately. Some tasks that students may be asked to do could include estimating, predicting, comparing, classifying, identifying properties, determining sequences of events, and designing an experiment.

Pictorial assessment uses pictures that represent familiar objects and events. The assessment device couples well with learning activities and can be completed concurrently. Students are required to apply what they have learned and to communicate what they understand. Often more than one correct answer or solution is possible an assessment task. Some tasks encourage students to estimate their answers, then do a hands-on task that permits them to check their estimations. Other assessments may ask students to complete a pretest and then use a similar activity as a pictorial assessment post-test, such as those shown in Figure 7.7 on pages 238–239. Figure 7.8 on page 240 is another type of pictorial assessment; both complement the learning cycle plan in Exhibit 7.1.

*Reflective Questioning.*   This type of assessment consists of written tasks that expect students to respond to a wide range of intellectual tasks. Use of basic and integrated science process skills may be necessary. For example, students may have to recall essential information, analyze information that is provided, apply what they have learned to new but related circumstances, and integrate information in order to construct answers to unusual situations. Students will find it necessary to read instructions carefully, then follow the directions. Students may list responses, construct illustrations, select the best response from choices given, defend their choices, or write extensive responses that can be evaluated for language arts concepts and skills, as well as science.

Reflective questioning assessments require students to reflect on the lesson's content and to use their knowledge in a way that is different from the way it was experienced in the lesson. This type of assessment encourages students to use a variety of approaches to solve a problem. Problems often require more

**FIGURE 7.7   Pictorial Assessment of Simple Circuits**

# Pre-test

Will the bulb light or not? Below each picture, make your prediction by writing either "Yes" or "No."

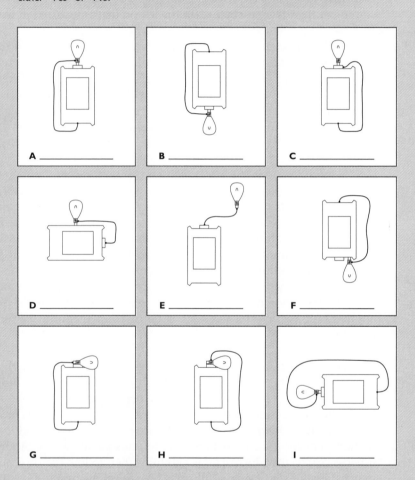

A _____   B _____   C _____

D _____   E _____   F _____

G _____   H _____   I _____

Now, use your materials to try each prediction.
Which of your predictions were correct?
Which picture diagrams do not work? Why do you think they might not work? What do they seem to have in common?
What do the pictures that worked have in common?

# Post-test

Will the bulb light or not? Write "Yes" or "No" on the prediction line under each picture.

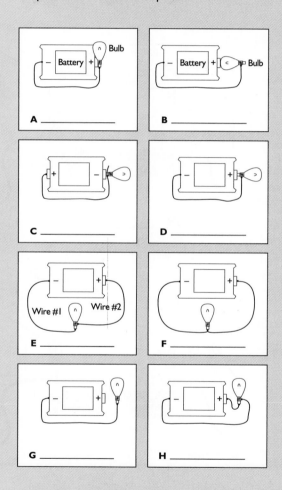

Which picture diagrams will *not* light?
What would you do to each one to make it light?

◆**FIGURE 7.8   Pictorial Assessment**

Please examine the pictures carefully. These objects were used in class and contain some parts that relate to concepts that we studied in earlier classes: *insulation* and *conduction*. Other parts and functions represent concepts that we are now studying.

Use the word list to identify the parts shown by the arrows. Words may be used more than once, or not at all. Write your answers on the blank line by each arrow.

**Word Bank**
open
closed
series
parallel
switch
insulator
conductor
short circuit

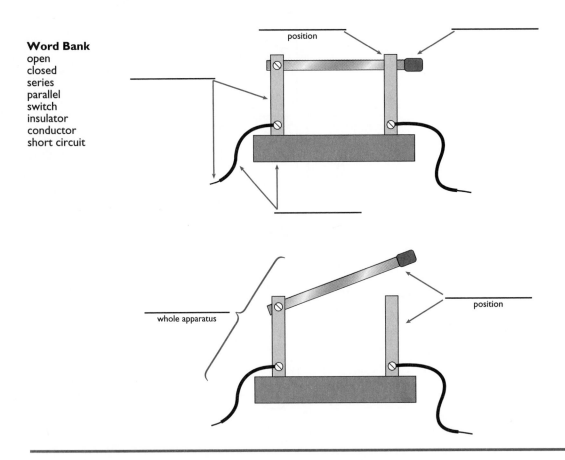

than one step in arriving at a solution, and teachers must be prepared to accept all reasonable and correct answers. We have been delighted to observe students discover creative or unique answers and solutions that we did not have in mind when devising the reflective questioning assessment. Figures 7.9 on page 241 and 7.10 on page 244 illustrate this type of assessment tool; both complement the learning cycle plan in Exhibit 7.1.

FIGURE 7.9    Reflective Questioning Assessment of Simple Circuits

Pictures A, B, C, and D show batteries, bulbs, wires, and sockets. These pictures represent some of the circuits that we constructed in class. Examine each carefully and answer the questions below the pictures.

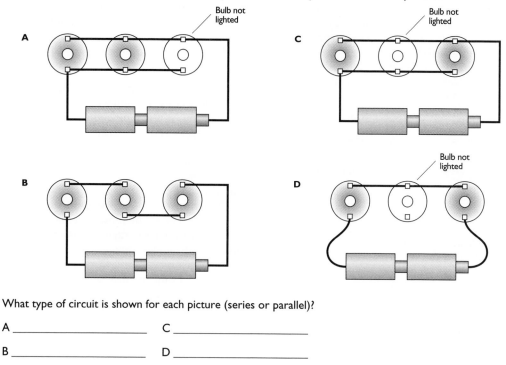

What type of circuit is shown for each picture (series or parallel)?

A _____        C _____

B _____        D _____

Why do you think the bulbs do not light in A, C, and D? There might be many reasons, so please organize your work and explain completely.

What would you do to make the unlit bulbs light in circuits A and C? Please describe all possibilities you can think of.

Go back to circuit D and trace a pathway to show how you would rewire it to make the bulb light. You may remove some wires or add extra wires if you need them.

*Hands-on Assessment.*    Hands-on assessment requires what the term implies: Students must manipulate materials from the lesson in order to complete tasks that enable them to demonstrate what they understand. Hands-on assessment permits a teacher to observe how well a student can perform. (*Performance assessment* is another name for this tool.) Students

## WHAT RESEARCH SAYS

### Assessment: What to Emphasize?

Recent research and publication of the National Science Education Standards (National Research Council, 1996) illustrate the need for envisioning systemic changes in the activities and methods used to assess science learning. For example, the assessment standards of the National Science Education Standards (p. 100) urge teachers to place

| Less Emphasis on | More Emphasis on |
| --- | --- |
| • Assessing what is easily measured | • Assessing what is most highly valued |
| • Assessing discrete knowledge | • Assessing rich, well-structured knowledge |
| • Assessing scientific knowledge | • Assessing scientific understanding and reasoning |
| • Assessing to learn what students do not know | • Assessing to learn what students do understand |
| • Assessing only achievement | • Assessing achievement and opportunity to learn |
| • End of term assessments by teachers | • Students engaged in ongoing assessment of their work and that of others |
| • Development of external assessments by measurement experts alone | • Teachers involved in the development of external assessments |

However, systemic change occurs slowly and it is understood that the point of measure remains the individual classroom and that teachers may be persuaded to use published tests. The following questions are recommended by the National Center for Improving Science Education and teachers are encouraged to ask these questions when evaluating the quality of a test:

1. Are there problems that require students to think about and analyze situations?
2. Are the levels of thinking and analysis developmentally appropriate for the children?
3. Does the test feature sets of problems that call for more than one step in arriving at a solution?
4. Are problems with more than one correct solution included?
5. Are there opportunities for students to use their own data and create their own problems?
6. Are the students encouraged to use a variety of approaches to solve a problem?
7. Are there assessment exercises that encourage students to estimate their answers and check their results?
8. Is the science information that is given in the story problem and elicited in the answer accurate?
9. Is there an opportunity for assessing skills (both in the use of science tools and in science thinking) through some exercises that call for hands-on activities?
10. Are there exercises included in the overall assessment strategy that need to be carried out over time?
11. Are there problems with purposely missing or mistaken information that ask students to find errors or critique the way the problem is set up?

must use their knowledge and skill in a practical way to solve a problem. Students often must use integrated process skills to identify variables, design investigations, gather information, and demonstrate outcomes of their investigations.

12. Are there opportunities for students to make up their own questions, problems, or designs?

*Source:* Adapted from Senta A. Raizen and Joyce S. Kaser, "Assessing Science Learning in Elementary School: Why, What, and How?" *Phi Delta Kappan* (May 1989): 721.

Slowly, individual teachers' perceptions of assessment have been shifting toward a view where instruction and assessment happen simultaneously. Typical reactions from teachers change from disappointment in how students score on a test toward surprise and elation at how much students know (Kamen, 1996).

Factor in early childhood science, which has been traditionally beyond the scope of written tests and standardized performance measures, and consensus grows for developing authentic, performance-based assessment techniques. As inquiry-based, activity science spreads in use, teachers observe that the opportunities for assessment are embedded in the instruction and students' performances are natural outcomes observed by an inquiring teacher. Bergman (1993) offers the following guidelines for assessing the performance of young children:

1. *Observe.* Children must explore materials before given specific instructions or procedures. Teachers must observe and record changes in what children do as children explore initially and have opportunities for expanding their inquiries later. Do the children perform more complex mental operations? What kind of sorting criteria are evident? Are the children demonstrating more diversity, creativity, and originality? What connections are made between children's free exploration and the teacher's intentions?

2. *Assess in a context.* Use a context as close as possible to the learning activity without merely repeating the learning activity. Avoid the conflict of new, unrelated objects.

3. *Use questions to probe and discover children's understanding.* Listen closely to explanations, which provide valuable insight into the children's thinking, reveal potential misconceptions, and celebrate understanding. Listen also to children's questions; they are windows into their understanding, thinking, and perceptions that often reveal more than any pretest. Open-ended questions provide children opportunities to speak freely without prompting memorization. Withhold your judgment on answers to encourage honest and complete responses.

4. *Record activity and observations over time.* Date entries and look for patterns or trends. How do each child's questions and the nature of investigations change over the school year?

5. *Use children's products.* Young children are naturally drawn to making things. How well do they follow directions? Examine drawings and constructed structures to gain insight into each child's understandings, which are not easily or reliably revealed on written tests.

*Source:* Adapted from Abby Barry Bergman, Performance assessment for early childhood: What could be more natural? *Science and Children* (February, 1993): 20–22.

Hands-on assessment gives a teacher opportunities to determine how well students use science tools and science thinking. This type of performance assessment directly pursues the "science as inquiry" and the "nature of science" dimensions of the National Science Education Standards.

**◆ FIGURE 7.10   Reflective Questioning Assessment of Safety, Circuits, and Electrical Uses**

Imagine that a storm has passed, it is nighttime, and you are walking down the street with a flashlight. The street lights are not working and many houses are dark, but you do notice light coming from some houses. You see a loose electrical wire with one end on the ground and the other end attached to a utility pole. What are three safe things you might do?

1. _____

2. _____

3. _____

What are three electrical devices that you use regularly? List them below and identify the types of circuits that they have (series, parallel, or both). Also for each, list inventions that control the flow of electricity to or within the device. You must identify at least two different inventions overall.

| Electrical devices | Type of circuit used | Invention that controls |
|---|---|---|
| _____ | _____ | _____ |
| _____ | _____ | _____ |
| _____ | _____ | _____ |

Imagine that our community has a power failure for one week. Life must go on, including school! What things would change in your daily routine in which you usually use electricity, but now cannot? Describe your day without electricity, beginning with your morning wake-up and preparation for school, time spent getting to and from school, and your evening until you go to sleep.

_____

_____

_____

_____

Students are encouraged to create their own problems and use their own data in identifying solutions. They are required to think about and analyze science in a practical context; the context can be the physical, life, and earth/space science content standards. Hands-on assessment is easily expanded through the complementary technique of reflective questioning. Fig-

## FIGURE 7.11   Hands-On Assessment: Electricity Mystery Boxes

Find out what is in the six mystery boxes A, B, C, D, E, and F. They have five different things inside, shown below. Two of the boxes will have the same thing. All of the others will have something different inside.

Two batteries:

A wire:

A bulb:

A battery and a bulb:

Nothing at all :

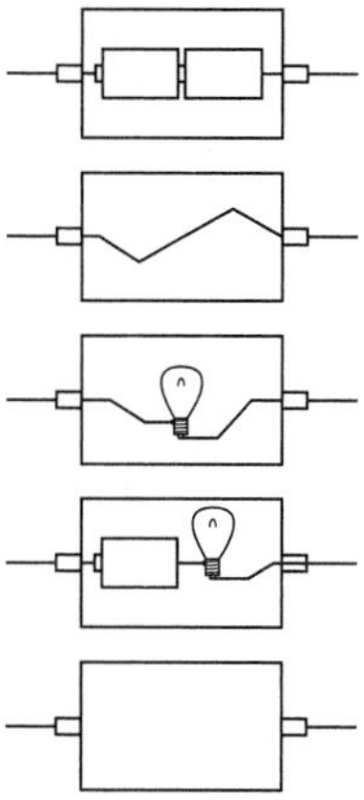

You can use your bulbs, batteries, and wires any way you like. Connect them in a circuit to help you figure out what is inside.

When you find out what is in a box, fill in the spaces on the following pages.

Box A:  Has_____inside.

Draw a picture of the circuit that told you what was inside Box A.

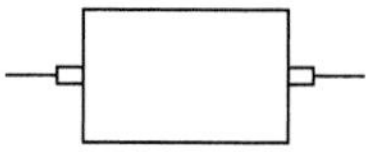

How could you tell from your circuit what was inside Box A?

Do the same for Boxes B, C, D, E, and F.

*Source:* R. J. Shavelson and G. P. Baxter, "What We've Learned about Assessing Hands-on Science," *Educational Leadership* (May 1992): 20–25. Reprinted by permission of the Association for Supervision and Curriculum Development. Copyright © 1992 by ASCD. All rights reserved.

ures 7.11, 7.12 on page 246, and 7.13 on page 247 illustrate the tools of hands-on assessment and complement the learning cycle plan in Exhibit 7.1.

*Teacher Records and Observations.*   Tangible records can reveal a lot about what students know and can and cannot do. Useful records can include the successes and difficulties a child has with homework assignments and notations about the quality of a completed science project, written report, class notes, activity data sheets, and so on. Your teacher records are important because they can reveal the interplay among memorizing, understanding, and using scientific concepts. Emphasis on practical application encourages hands-on, minds-on interaction and helps to address the various dimensions of the science program. Figure 7.14 on page 248 shows a record-keeping system a teacher might use to complement the sample lesson plan on basic electricity. This type of record keeping is useful because it helps to focus a teacher's observations of

◤**FIGURE 7.12   Hands-On Assessment: Electric Circuit Boards**

Below are the pictures of four circuit boards you will find in your science center.  Design a simple circuit tester from a battery, bulb, socket, and wires.  Test the four boards to determine which points (A, B, C, and so on) are wired into the same circuit.  Draw lines on the circuit picture showing where you believe the wires make a connection between the points.  Show your teacher your work, and then open the circuit folder and check the results.  Were you correct?

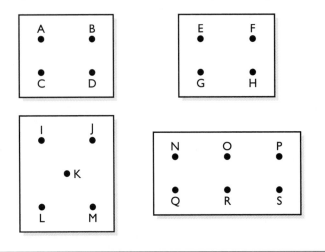

a child on the concepts and processes to be learned. Figure 7.15 on page 248 shows a generic form suitable for an entire class. It may be used as a checklist to keep track of who has and has not demonstrated mastery of the concepts or preferred science skills. This format can be used to record student progress on the pictorial, reflective questioning, and hands-on assessment techniques.

*Rubrics.*   Not all student performances can be classified with simple systems, numbers, or letter grades. The sheer volume of a teacher's work load can limit the types of written or verbal comments offered to students. Therefore, many teachers use rubrics to assess the quality of student work. *Rubrics* are devices, such as checklists, scales, or descriptions, that identify the criteria used to evaluate a student's work. Paul Smith (1995), a middle school science teacher, recommends using rubrics that have been created by the students for students, with teacher guidance. Since students are part of the design process, they clearly understand the expectations and use this understanding to improve their work. The creation of the rubrics also affords additional teaching opportunities.

> **FIGURE 7.13    Hands-On Assessment: Help MacGyver!**

---

MacGyver is in a jam! Lost in a cave, he is using a small candle that is about to burn out. What he really needs is a flashlight—one that can withstand the drafty and damp cave—to help him find his way out. All he has is:

2 size "D" dry cells
1 small 3-volt bulb
1 thin piece of insulated wire. 30 centimeters long (about 12 inches)
1 metal paper clip
2 metal paper fasteners
1 cardboard tube, 15 centimeters long (about 6 inches)
1 roll of masking tape
1 plastic bottle cap
1 small knife

1. Use the materials to sketch a picture of how these things could be assembled to make a temporary flashlight. Make certain you draw your circuit carefully. (Draw your picture here.)

2. Now help MacGyver. Follow your plan. Did the light work? Keep trying! Now show MacGyver his new light and explain to him how it works.

---

For written work, Smith (1995) asks students to consider two questions: "What information should go into the written response?" and "How should the information be presented?" He uses a peer and parental review system that encourages students to prepare and improve written drafts. Parents and caregivers appreciate the rubrics because they help them to improve guidance

## FIGURE 7.14 Student Progress Report

**Student's Name:** Raul
**Lesson or Unit:** Basic Electricity

| *Concept Number* | *Description of Activity or Skill* | *Teacher Rating Low 12345 High* | *Teacher Comments* |
|---|---|---|---|
| 1 | Open circuit using one bulb, wire, and dry cell | 5 | Was the first to do it in group |
| 2 | Closed circuit using same materials | 3 | Had difficulty, needed my help |
| 3 | Closed circuit with bulb socket | 4 | Easily done after I helped with clips |
| 4 | Series circuit, 2 or more bulbs | 5 | Done independently |
| 5 | Parallel circuit | 2 | Having difficulty, made 2 series circuits |
| 6 | Short circuit | 4 | |
| 7 | Use a knife switch | 5 | Easily done |
| 8 | Make a paper clip switch | 5 | Concept easily shown |
| 9 | Construct a flashlight | 4 | No circuit trouble, difficulty with bulb connections only |

## FIGURE 7.15 Class Record-Keeping System

**Unit:** Basic Electricity

Objective, Concept, Skill, or Activity Number

| *Children's Names* | *1* | *2* | *3* | *4* | *5* | *6* | *7* | *8* | *9* | *10* | *11* | *Comments* |
|---|---|---|---|---|---|---|---|---|---|---|---|---|
| Emerson | | | | | | | | | | | | |
| Frankie | | | | | | | | | | | | |
| Jaclyn | | | | | | | | | | | | |
| Jana | | | | | | | | | | | | |
| Jay | | | | | | | | | | | | |
| Julie | | | | | | | | | | | | |
| Joy | | | | | | | | | | | | |
| Marilyn | | | | | | | | | | | | |

*Note:* This format is easily managed by a spreadsheet program available for all popular microcomputers, if a value number is assigned to each object. Some teachers prefer a coding system that shows progress, such as: + for entirely correct, *n* for partially correct, *u* for mostly incorrect, or – for entirely incorrect.

offered while helping with homework. Smith claims that students are able to make better sense of what they learn and that student satisfaction is very high with his participatory approach.

Rubrics can help a teacher encourage students to give better responses to reflective questioning assessments. The rubric shown in Figure 7.16 has been

**FIGURE 7.16  Reflective Questioning Assessment Rubric**

This is a scoring rubric for a learning-cycle lesson on simple circuits. A score of three indicates what the class believes all students should be able to do. A score of four indicates that the students exceeded expectations.

Content scale

| 0 | 1 | 2 | 3 | 4 |
|---|---|---|---|---|
| • No work completed | • Few concepts<br><br>• Models not used in explanation<br><br>• Some awareness of safety<br><br>• Some awareness of technology uses | • Some concepts explained<br><br>• Three common safety examples<br><br>• Three common technology examples | • Uses circuit model to explain differences<br><br>• Identifies differences in series, parallel, open, closed circuits<br><br>• Uses concepts from previous lessons, e.g., conductor, insulator, etc. | • Uses additional concepts to explain differences, e.g., switch, resistance, energy flow<br><br>• Unusual safety and/or technology examples |

Style scale

| 0 | 1 | 2 | 3 | 4 |
|---|---|---|---|---|
| • No work completed | • Poor organization<br><br>• Many misspellings<br><br>• Punctuation missing or inappropriate | • Clear organization<br><br>• Very few misspellings | • Appropriate punctuation | • Extremely clear, concise writing |

First reviewer's name: _____

Score for content: _____          Score for style: _____

Comments:


Second reviewer's name: _____

Score for content: _____          Score for style: _____

Comments:

generalized for use with reflective questioning assessments. It illustrates Smith's recommendations. Figure 7.17 provides a general rubric that you may use for a variety of science tasks.

*Systematic Observation.*    The types of records shown in Figures 7.18 and 7.19 require systematic teacher observation. Systematic observation is another source of information that is helpful to meaningful evaluation. Teachers always make observations, but systematic observation goes beyond being aware that Emily is interested in birds, Joel asks questions all the time, and David creates messes. Systematic observation is illustrated in this example:

> A teacher divides the class into working groups to figure out a way to test the strength of different brands of paper towels. As the children work on the problem, the teacher walks about the room, listens carefully to the questions the children ask each other, and observes how they approach the task. The teacher notes who does nothing, who appears to have difficulty, who has trouble measuring, who asks the most interesting questions, and who offers the most interesting ideas.

Systematic observation is guided by a structure; the teacher's observations are focused on specific tasks. These tasks include trying to determine how well the children demonstrate their understanding of the science ideas, how well the children use the science process skills, and what types of scientific attitudes the children demonstrate. Figure 7.18 illustrates an observation

### FIGURE 7.17   General Scoring Rubric

This scoring rubric may be used for a variety of science activities or to offer guidance for developing expectations for activity-specific rubrics. The number in parentheses could be correlated with a scoring scale.

**Poor** (0):  The student did not do the task, did not complete the assignment, or did not show comprehension of the activity.

**Inadequate** (1):  The product or performance does not satisfy a significant number of the criteria, does not accomplish what was asked,  contains errors,  or is of poor quality.

**Fair** (2):  The performance or product meets most of the criteria and does not contain gross errors or fundamental omissions.

**Good** (3):  The performance or product completely meets the expectations described by the criteria.

**Outstanding** (4):  All of the criteria are met,  and the performance or product exceeds the expectations for the task; additional effort or outstanding features are shown.

*Source:* Adapted from S. Price and G. E. Hein, "Scoring active assessments," *Science and Children* (October 1994): 26–29.

## FIGURE 7.18   Recording Science Process Skills

**Directions:** Circle the number that best represents the skill level you have observed.
Number 1 means *having difficulty,* 2 means *fair,* 3 means *good,* 4 means *outstanding.*

| Name | Observation | Classification | Communication | Measurement | Prediction |
|------|-------------|----------------|---------------|-------------|------------|
| Sam | 1 2 3 4 | 1 2 3 4 | 1 2 3 4 | 1 2 3 4 | 1 2 3 4 |
| Wanda | 1 2 3 4 | 1 2 3 4 | 1 2 3 4 | 1 2 3 4 | 1 2 3 4 |
| Herman | 1 2 3 4 | 1 2 3 4 | 1 2 3 4 | 1 2 3 4 | 1 2 3 4 |
| Kara | 1 2 3 4 | 1 2 3 4 | 1 2 3 4 | 1 2 3 4 | 1 2 3 4 |

*Note:* The process skills can be changed and the form expanded to address better the science skills
your lessons emphasize.

form for science skills. Table 7.2 on pages 252–254 defines the attributes of
the skills.

Science learning improves when student attitudes are positive (Yager &
Penick, 1987). There are dramatic differences between traditional science classrooms and exemplary ones in which teaching and assessment involve all aspects of science. Positive attitudes about science greatly influence students'
achievement levels and process skills, as is shown by research on exemplary
science classrooms (Yager & Penick, 1987). These results are now prompting

## FIGURE 7.19   Evaluating and Recording Science Attitudes

Check those attitudes or record the number of times each student demonstrates the desired
scientific attitudes during the observation period.

| Name | Is curious | Cooperates | Persists | Is open-minded | Safely uses materials |
|------|-----------|-----------|----------|----------------|----------------------|
| Celeste | ✓✓✓ | ✓✓ | ✓ | ✓ | ✓ |
| Jen | ✓ | ✓✓✓✓✓ | ✓ | ✓✓✓✓ | ✓✓✓ |
| Tikara | ✓✓✓✓ | ✓✓✓ | ✓✓✓✓✓ | ✓✓ | ✓✓✓ |
| Jon | ✓ | ✓✓✓ | ✓✓ | ✓✓ | ✓✓ |
| Sara | ✓✓ | ✓✓ | ✓✓✓ | ✓✓✓✓ | ✓✓✓✓ |

**TABLE 7.2    Definitions and Indicators of Basic and Integrated Process Skills**

*Basic Processes*

**Observation:** involves active engagement with the manipulation of objects and the use of the senses, directly or indirectly, with simple or complex instruments. This process

- describes objects' attributes,
- describes changes in terms of actions,
- describes changes with accuracy in terms of patterns and relationships.

**Classification:** systematically imposing order to data based on observational relationships. This process

- creates groups by using a single attribute and expresses linear relationships,
- creates groups and subgroups using one attribute to express symmetrical relationships,
- creates groups using several attributes together to express symmetrical relationships among different groups.

**Communication:** exchanging information through a variety of media. This process involves

- expressing opinions;
- explaining using sense data (touch, taste, hearing, sight, and smell);
- explaining causal relationships.

**Measurement:** describing an event by using instruments to quantify observations. This process

- uses nonstandard instruments, such as paper clips, hands, and feet;
- uses standard instruments, such as rulers, balance scales, and graduated cylinders;
- uses standard instruments with precision, such as measuring within tenths or hundredths when using the metric system.

**Prediction:** stating future cause-and-effect relationships through manipulation of objects. Accuracy of prediction is based on information gathered through observations. This process includes

- guesses from minimal supportive evidence,
- guesses based on limited observable facts,
- guesses based on an accurate understanding of cause-and-effect relationships.

**Questioning:** raising uncertainty. This process

- focuses on the attributes of objects,
- focuses on relationships and patterns within an experiment,
- focuses on events and patterns abstracted from an experiment.

## TABLE 7.2 *(continued)*

**Using numbers:** expressing ideas, observations, and relationships in figures rather than words. This process

- uses numbers to express ideas without relating them,
- uses numbers to express relationships,
- uses numbers to express relationships in precise terms.

*Integrated Processes*

**Interpreting data:** finding patterns or meaning not immediately apparent among sets of data that lead to the construction of inferences, predictions, and hypotheses. This process

- identifies a single pattern among objects within an experiment,
- uses accuracy to identify a single pattern among objects within an experiment,
- uses accuracy to identify multiple patterns among objects.

**Controlling variables:** identifying and selecting factors from variables that are to be held constant and those that are to be manipulated in order to carry out a proposed investigation. This process involves managing

- one manipulative variable without holding others constant,
- several manipulative variables and holds at least one variable constant,
- several manipulative and constant variables at the same time.

**Designing experiments:** planning data-gathering operations to determine results. This process involves

- collecting data through trial-and-error processes;
- testing questions and hypothesizing with an attempt to identify and control variables;
- using organized, sequential plans to test hypotheses and interpret results in measurable terms.

**Inferring:** providing explanations, reasons, or causes for events based on limited facts. Inferences are of questionable validity because they rely heavily on personal judgment. This process

- explains by making guesses,
- explains using observable data,
- explains using quantifiable observable data.

**Defining operationally:** describing what works. This process

- explains how to measure variables in an experiment,
- states relationships between observed actions to explain phenomena,
- explains relationships by generalizing to other events not observed.

*(continued)*

**◆ TABLE 7.2** *(continued)*

**Hypothesizing:** tentatively accepting an explanation as a basis for further investigation. Constructing generalizations that include all objects or events of the same class. The hypothesis must be tested if credibility is to be established. This process involves making

- statements based on opinions,
- statement based on simple sensory observations without explanations,
- statements used to create concepts through explanations.

**Formulating models:** describing or constructing physical, verbal, or mathematical explanations of systems and phenomena that cannot be observed directly. Models may be used in predicting outcomes and planned investigations. This process

- creates one-dimensional explanations,
- creates multidimensional models,
- creates scalar multidimensional explanations.

*Source:* G. W. Foster & W. A. Heiting, "Embedded Assessment," *Science and Children* 32, 2 (1994): 30–33. Reprinted with permission from NSTA Publications, copyright 1994 from *Science and Children*, National Science Teachers Association, 1840 Wilson Boulevard, Arlington, VA 22201-3000.

teachers to question the traditional view that attitudes are inconsequential. Figure 7.19 shows one way you can evaluate and record the levels of your students' science attitudes.

Social skills are important to science learning. Karen Ostlund (1992) tells us that we are not born with a set of instinctive behaviors that help us to interact well in social settings. Social skills are learned. If we expect students to work together in cooperative science activity groups or on science projects in smaller teams, then we must assess the extent to which the learners develop those skills. Table 7.3 lists important social skills that students can learn if we encourage them. Systematic record-keeping formats (similar to those shown in Figures 7.18 and 7.19) can help us to monitor the status of students' social skills.

According to Ostlund (1992), science social skills group into three types:

1. *Cluster skills*—behaviors that involve a student's ability to move into a science learning group quickly and quietly and to get the task started.
2. *Camaraderie skills*—which help all learners feel better about themselves and about each other as they work together. These skills help build a sense of cohesiveness and encourage stable operation of the science group.
3. *Task skills*—pertaining to management chores and ranging from the skills that are necessary for mastering a task to those that use critical thinking to construct a deeper level of understanding.

**TABLE 7.3   Science Social Skills**

Science social skills can be observed and recorded by a teacher, or used as a part of a student self-evaluation. As an example, for student self-evaluation you could ask students to rate how often or how well they do the following.

*Cluster skills: How often do you*

- move into groups quietly?
- stay with your group?
- use a quiet voice to speak within your group?
- call the people in your group by their names?
- look at the person in your group who is talking?
- keep your hands and feet to yourself?
- share materials with your group mates?
- wait and take your turn?
- share your ideas?

*Camaraderie skills: How often do you*

- avoid saying "put-downs"?
- encourage others in your group to participate?
- give each person in your group a compliment?
- show your support to others with words or actions?
- describe how you feel when it is appropriate?
- try humor or enthusiasm to help energize your group?
- criticize the idea, not the person?
- allow each person in the group to talk before you talk again?

*Task skills: How often do you*

- ask questions of your group members about the task?
- ask for help from group members?
- ask group members to explain what you do not understand?
- offer to explain things to another group member?
- check for understanding with group members?
- state the purpose of the task and make certain others understand it?
- watch time and let others know when time is short?
- offer ideas about how best to do the task?
- value other group members' contributions?
- summarize the material to help others in your group?
- develop ways to help the group remember important details?
- encourage other group members to share their thinking?
- ask others to plan out loud how they would solve a problem?
- compare viewpoints when there is a disagreement and try to reach agreement?
- combine parts of different persons ideas into a single point of view?
- ask others to explain their reasons?
- help other group members reach a conclusion?
- check your group's work against the instructions?

*Source:* Adapted from K. L. Ostlund, "Sizing Up Social Skills," *Science Scope* (March 1992): 31–33.

*Student Self-Assessments.*    Student self-assessments are an important part of the authenticity found in constructivist science teaching. Self-assessments can range from the informal collections of reflective tape-recorded (for nonreaders) or written journal notes, to more formal efforts, such as those revealed through self-evaluation ratings. A student portfolio is a common technique that is used to organize and present the self-assessment.

A *portfolio* is a selection of student work that is collected over a period of time (Hein & Price, 1994). A portfolio's purpose is often to tell a story about the student's science activities. The contents of a portfolio may be focused on illustrating a student's abilities to solve problems, show thinking and understanding, illustrate content and capability of written communication, and reveal science connections that a student is able to make across many lessons and the views that students have of themselves in science (Glencoe, 1994).

Teachers decide in various ways who has the responsibility for selecting the work and the criteria it is to fulfill. At times, students may make the selection "according to criteria established collaboratively between themselves and their teacher. Criteria might be the 'piece that was hardest for me to do,' 'my best piece of work,' 'the project I learned most from doing,' 'a piece that shows important science learning' " (Hein & Price, 1994, p. 48).

Whatever the work selected, the process of reflection assists the selection and presentation process. Students must reflect and show the depth of their reflection when they explain why they made their selections. Explanations may be verbal or written and may be encouraged through teacher and student interviews.

A student *journal* is a type of self-assessment. A journal can assist the reflective process when students are encouraged to record what they have done and what they have learned. A journal may provide a written summary that is helpful for planning and constructing a portfolio. The following examples are appropriate for a portfolio:

- written report of a project or investigation
- responses to open-ended questions
- examples of problems that have been formed or solved
- journal excerpts
- science art
- individual student's contribution to a group report or project
- photographs or drawings of science models
- teacher check-sheets and recorded observations of student performance
- uses of science tools, equipment, and suitable technologies to solve problems or to complete an activity

- examples of how science is important to the student
- descriptions of safe science practices learned and applied in another setting, such as at home
- linkages of science history and how views have changed as a result of study
- examples of how science is used in the community and careers that use the science topics that have been studied

Portions of a portfolio may be evaluated by the teacher individually or collectively within the portfolio package. Items in the portfolio should invite student self-evaluation. Figure 7.20 on page 258 provides a format that invites students and teachers to have input into the evaluation in an open-ended way. Figures 7.21 on page 259 and 7.22 on page 260 illustrate more specific student self-evaluation approaches that may be used to inform teachers and caregivers about how students perceive their own learning.

## CHAPTER SUMMARY

The National Science Education Standards ushered a new era of exciting learning opportunities for students and new instructional challenges for teachers. Constructivist teaching and inquiry-based learning requires careful planning that places conceptual focus, acts of created understanding, essential experiences, and authentic assessment in a carefully balanced dynamic system. In this chapter we have built upon the learning cycle described in Chapter 1 by illustrating a planning model that will help you meet the new challenges.

Concept mapping is a tool that helps teachers identify essential concepts and the relationships among concepts. The tool is helpful for making fundamental planning decisions in order to fulfill the outcomes of the content stan-

dards. Concept mapping is also a useful evaluation tool.

The 4-E learning cycle provides a dynamic planning system that balances student-centered exploration with teacher-guided conceptual construction. Expansion nurtures understanding as the new dimensions of science learning are fulfilled. Evaluation is continual and is fit to the task. Tools for authentic assessment include pictorial analysis, hands-on performance tasks, reflective questioning, and systematic observation. Many illustrations show various types of teacher records and student products, including portfolios, that verify the types and levels of understanding. These techniques are pragmatically illustrated by supporting a central lesson throughout the chapter.

## DISCUSSION QUESTIONS

**1.** Contemporary movements in education usually embrace the preference for students to demonstrate learning outcomes. Performance or behavioral objectives may be used for this purpose. What advantages or disadvantages do you see with this type of objective?

**FIGURE 7.20  Portfolio Evaluation Form**

---

**Portfolio Topic** _____

Student: _____

Teacher: _____

Date: _____

1. Concepts, procedures, process skills explored: _____

   _____

   _____

2. Areas of growth in understanding: _____

   _____

   _____

3. Unfinished work or work needing revision: _____

   _____

   _____

4. Assessment of the following areas:

   (a) Problem-solving work: _____

   _____

   _____

   (b) Reasoning and critical thinking: _____

   _____

   _____

   (c) Use of language: _____

   _____

   _____

   (d) Other: _____

   _____

   _____

---

*Source:* Glencoe Science Professional Series, *Alternative Assessment in the Science Classroom,* (1994). (ERIC Document Reproduction Service No. ED 370 778), p. 37.

**FIGURE 7.21** **Student Self-Evaluation Checklist**

## Student Self-Evaluation Checklist

Name: _____

Date: _____

**Did the circuit problems**

Finished some ·····························································································  Finished them all

**Worked with the materials**

Messy ·····························································································  Always careful

**Recorded and described in my journal**

Wrote a little ·····························································································  Wrote a lot

**Practiced important safety rules**

Some of the time ·····························································································  All of the time

**Discussed ideas and results with the class**

Some of the time ·····························································································  All of the time

**Worked well with classmates**

Some of the time ·····························································································  All of the time

**Used time well**

Wasted time ·····························································································  Worked hard

**Learned from the lesson**

Learned a little ·····························································································  Learned a lot

Things I liked or did well: _____

_____

Things I did not like: _____

_____

*Source:* Adapted from G. E. Hein and S. Price, *Active Assessment for Active Science: A Guide for Elementary School Teachers* (Portsmouth, NH: Heinemann, 1994).

**FIGURE 7.22   Student Self-Evaluation Rating Scale**

---

**Self-Evaluation Rating Scale**

Name: _____

Date: _____

**Directions:**   Rate yourself.  On a scale of one (low) to ten (high), how well did you do each of the following activities?

**Making a switch**
Didn't understand what to do                                                              Made a great one

| 1 | 2 | 3 | 4 | 5 | 6 | 7 | 8 | 9 | 10 |

**Making circuits**
Had trouble                                                                                      Easy to do

| 1 | 2 | 3 | 4 | 5 | 6 | 7 | 8 | 9 | 10 |

**Solving circuit puzzles**
Had trouble                                                                                      Easy to solve

| 1 | 2 | 3 | 4 | 5 | 6 | 7 | 8 | 9 | 10 |

**Electricity mystery boxes**
Did some                                                                                          Did all

| 1 | 2 | 3 | 4 | 5 | 6 | 7 | 8 | 9 | 10 |

**Making the flashlight**
Could have tried harder                                                                    Did my best

| 1 | 2 | 3 | 4 | 5 | 6 | 7 | 8 | 9 | 10 |

**Overall feeling about the electricity lessons**
Liked them a little                                                                           Liked them a lot

| 1 | 2 | 3 | 4 | 5 | 6 | 7 | 8 | 9 | 10 |

Things I liked or did well: _____

_____

Things I did not like: _____

_____

---

*Source:* Adapted from G. E. Hein and S. Price, *Active Assessment for Active Science: A Guide for Elementary School Teachers* (Portsmouth, NH: Heinemann, 1994).

## BUILD A PORTFOLIO

**1.** Examine a textbook or science module and teacher's manual for any grade level you choose. Construct a concept map for the material you select. State your opinion about how the printed materials' organization helps make connections between associated concepts.

**2.** Prepare several plans for science teaching. First map the concepts you wish to teach, and then use the learning cycle planning format demonstrated in this chapter. What new dimensions of science education are you able to address?

**3.** Prepare a lesson plan using the 4-E approach. How many learning activities do you have, and where do they fit into the cycle? What science dimensions do you pursue? How do you evaluate student's learning?

**4.** Construct appropriate ways to evaluate the children's science knowledge, skills, and attitudes for your plans in projects 3 and 4.

**5.** Prepare the rubrics you will need for project 4.

**6.** How could you use rubrics to help you evaluate a student's portfolio?

## CHAPTER OUTLINE

# How Can You Use Questions to Promote Science Inquiry?

Mrs. Barcikowski extended warm greetings to each as the children came running into the lab. A table in the middle of the room was piled with rocks of many different types, colors, shapes, and sizes. Each child was encouraged to pick up several samples and look at them carefully. The children rubbed the samples, held them up to the light, and used magnifying glasses to make closer inspections. The room was buzzing with activity, including the predictable horseplay of a few, and the buzz was punctuated with the exclamations of scientific discoveries. All the while, Mrs. B expressed her interest by asking many different questions that helped the children sharpen their observations.

Then she had the children gather around her on the piece of old carpet. When all were seated, Mrs. B began making conversation with such casual questions as, "How many of you have a hobby? How 'bout your parents or brothers or sisters? What are some of your hobbies?"

After a moment of listening and encouraging, Mrs. B said, "It seems that many of you collect different things for a hobby. Right?" Smiles and nodding heads gave her an entry. "I do too. In fact one of my favorite things to do on vacation is to look for unusual rocks to add to the collection I've been sharing with you today. Would you like to see one of my favorites?" Holding up a smoothly polished quarter-sized sample for all to see and passing around others for them to hold, Mrs. B said, "We've been studying the concept of properties for many of our lessons. Let's use properties to help us study rocks. What kinds of properties do you observe in this rock?" The children's observations were accepted with encouragement and occasional praise. Another key question Mrs. B asked was, "What other rocks from our pile seem like this one?" After noticing variety in the color, size, and shape of the other samples, a child pointed out that some of them were more different than alike. "True," Mrs. B confirmed. "I guess we need to focus a bit. What property appears to be the same in each of the samples?"

"Crystals?" offered a child.

"That's right! This type of rock is known especially for its crystals. What kind of rock do you think this is?" Mrs. B reminded the children to refer back to their observations while they tossed ideas around among themselves. She watched them closely and then invited Elizabeth, who seemed unsure, to venture a guess.

"Well, it looks kinda milky so I guess it's called . . . a 'milk rock?' " asked Elizabeth as she groped for an answer. The other children laughed, but Mrs. B reminded them to be polite; then she smiled as she saw how a connection could be made.

"I know you go to the grocery with your parents. What sizes of containers does milk come in?"

Elizabeth thought to herself: gallon? half gallon? Somehow those didn't seem right. Then an idea came to her. "A quart rock?" Elizabeth hesitantly asked.

"Good try. Almost, Elizabeth, just one more letter," encouraged Mrs. B as she wrote the word quart on the lap chalk board and held it up for all to see. "Let's add a zzz sound to this and see what we have. Q-u-a-r-t-z. What does that spell, Elizabeth?"

"Quartz!" exclaimed Elizabeth, with emphasis on the z.

"Now everyone," encouraged Mrs. B.

For the next several seconds, the class spelled and pronounced the new word like cheerleaders. Then Mrs. B referred them back to the samples and continued her questions, always waiting patiently, encouraging, and building on the children's ideas. She paused periodically to add a point or two of her own. By the lesson's end the children had learned that quartz is a common mineral found in rocks and comes in many different colors. When polished smooth, quartz may be used in jewelry as a semiprecious stone, and quartz crystals are used to manufacture prisms, lenses, watches, computer chips, and other electronic gadgets. They even learned that the scientific name is silicon dioxide, $SiO_2$.                                                      ◆

## INTRODUCTION

Questions are tools for planning, teaching, thinking, and learning. What do you know about classroom uses of questions and your own questioning skills? It is typical for teachers to use questions intuitively or even out of habit. Some may even achieve satisfactory results. Yet considerable research suggests that many teachers do not realize that modest improvements in their questions can result in substantial gains for their students. In science, the students' questions play an important role in the nature of their inquiry and in their learning; they need to be encouraged. The National Science Education Standards' Teaching Standard B (NRC, 1996, p. 32) prompts teachers to guide and facilitate learning by

- focusing and supporting inquiries while interacting with students;
- orchestrating discourse among students about scientific ideas;
- challenging students to accept and share responsibility for their own learning;
- recognizing and responding to student diversity and encouraging all students to participate fully in science learning;
- encouraging and modeling skills of scientific inquiry, as well as the curiousness, openness to new ideas and data, and skepticism that characterize science.

Productive questions take students forward in their thinking, and they enable a teacher to construct a mental framework for helping students to construct their own understandings.

The mission of this chapter is to

1. raise questions about questions and report the effects that questions have on students' achievement, attitudes, and thinking skills;
2. explore the different types and uses of questions;
3. investigate how questions can be used;
4. offer some suggestions you can use to monitor and improve your own questions;
5. provide a rationale for using students' questions as an important part of your teaching.

## QUESTIONS ON QUESTIONS

What is a question? We use questions often, but do you know much about their proper uses and effects? This part of the chapter raises seven important questions about questions. Try answering them from what you already know. Then read on to check your answers (see Figure 8.1 on page 266). How well informed are you about this most potent teaching tool?

- What kinds of questions do teachers ask, and what kinds of answers do they require?
- Why do teachers use questions?
- How do questions affect students?
- How are teacher questions and student answers related?
- How do teachers use questions to involve all students?
- What is wait-time, and why is it important?
- What types of questions are used most in elementary science books and tests?

### *What Kinds of Questions Do Teachers Ask and What Kinds of Answers Do They Require?*

Research verifies that elementary teachers use questions more than any other teaching tool. For example, one study reports that third-grade teachers asked

## FIGURE 8.1   What Is a Question?

A question is an interrogative sentence that asks for a response. A question is expressed in simple, clear, straight-forward language that students can understand. A good question stimulates thinking, and should be adapted to the age, abilities, and interests of the students.

A good question is one that is appropriate and is used for a specific purpose. Questions are used:

- to find out what is not known or to find out whether someone knows
- to motivate
- to provide drill and practice
- to help students organize thinking
- to develop an ability to think
- to interpret meaning
- to emphasize a point
- to show relationships

- to establish cause and effect
- to discover interests
- to help develop appreciation
- to provide review
- to reveal thinking processes
- to diagnose learning difficulties
- to evaluate
- to give practice
- to permit expression

**Four types of questions:**
1. Memory questions establish or review the facts.
2. Convergent questions have one correct answer and require reasoning.
3. Divergent questions have several answers and help to promote possibility thinking and creativity.
4. Evaluative questions promote decision making and defensible judgments.

**How do you use questions?**

**How do you use children's questions?**

reading groups a question every 43 seconds (Gambrell, 1983), while another study found that teachers ask as many as 300 to 400 questions each day; the average is 348 (Levin & Long, 1981). Most agree that the number of teacher questions depends on the nature of the activity. Even so, teachers ask between 30 and 120 questions per hour (Graessser & Person, 1994). Most of these questions seem to be asked in a rapid-fire question-answer pattern. The pattern and extent of question use appears to have changed little for more than fifty years, with teachers asking about 93 percent of all questions and giving children little time to respond or opportunity to ask their own questions (Martin, Wood, & Stevens, 1988). The questions' effectiveness is limited by this type of use.

Abundant use of questions would suggest considerable room for variety, but, in fact, the questions teachers usually ask require factual answers and low levels of thinking. Knowledge and comprehension levels make up at least 70 percent of the questions, while questions that require application, analysis, synthesis, or evaluation thinking are used much less often (Martin, Wood, & Stevens, 1988). Many teachers request factual information, and in the context of the National Science Education Standards appear to be poor role models for productive questions that stimulate inquiry (Graesser & Person, 1994).

## Why Do Teachers Use Questions?

According to Mary Budd Rowe (1973), a science educator, teachers use questions for three main purposes:

1. To evaluate or to find out what the pupils already know.
2. To control the functions of the classroom: inquisition used as a classroom management strategy or to reduce off-task behavior.
3. To instruct children by suggesting resources and procedures, focusing observation, pointing out differences and discrepancies, and so on.

Questions have other uses as the stock in trade of teachers, and the potential far exceeds the three fundamental uses Rowe details. (See Table 8.1.)

### TABLE 8.1    How Can Teachers Use Questions?

- To arouse students' interest and motivate participation
- To determine students' prior knowledge before a lesson begins
- To determine students' thoughts and other information essential to a problem before it is explored
- To guide students' thinking toward higher levels
- To discipline disruptive students by asking them to explain their behavior
- To provide listening cues for students with difficulties and to focus inattentive students' attention
- To diagnose students' strengths and weaknesses
- To help students develop concepts or see relationships between objects or phenomena
- To review or summarize lessons
- To informally check students' comprehension
- To evaluate planned learning outcomes, such as performance objectives

What other uses can you add to this list?

## How Do Questions Affect Students?

The questions teachers choose and use can influence students in three areas: attitudes, thinking, and achievement.

### How Do Questions Influence Students' Attitudes?

Attitudes influence how students participate, think, and achieve. Students with positive attitudes tend to look more favorably on a subject, teacher, or method of teaching. Students with negative attitudes often link them to a subject, school experience, or teacher and tend to resist and perform poorly. From his research, William Wilen (1986) concludes that teachers' uses of questions play an important part in shaping children's attitudes, thinking, and achievement. "Students must develop positive attitudes toward higher-level questioning if instructional approaches such as inquiry are to be effective," Wilen (1986, p. 21) writes.

### How Do Questions Influence Students' Thinking?

Nearly 40 years ago, Hilda Taba (Taba, Levine, & Elsey, 1964) discovered that the questions teachers used influenced the students' levels of thinking. Teachers expected students to think at a certain level (according to Bloom's taxonomy of the cognitive domain), composed and used questions for the expected level, and then received responses from students that matched their expectations. Teachers can and do control the thought levels of students (Arnold, Atwood, & Rogers, 1973). In fact, Gallagher and Aschner (1963) reported that a mere 5 percent increase in diver-

*Appropriate questions can improve children's attitudes, thinking, and achievement.*

gent questioning can encourage up to a 40 percent increase in divergent responses from students. Divergent thinking is important for problem-solving tasks and for learning that requires creativity. Also, high-level questions help students to evaluate information better and improve their understanding of lower-level facts (Hunkins, 1970).

How pupils think must match the requirements of teachers' methods if students are to become confident learners. The questions learners ask are indicators of the thinking they are doing and of the impact of your questions. Dorothy Alfke gives us this recommendation to help children improve their thinking through questioning:

> Inquiry learning must involve questions **asked by, meaningful to, and potentially productive for** the learners. . . . Young people must ask the kinds of questions which lead them back to doing something with the materials in order to derive answers. They need to ask the kinds of questions they can get answers to. . . . [If] learning how to learn, inquiry learning, and conceptual learning are high in your value system, develop the skill of asking operational questions in your classes. Listen to the kinds of questions your children are asking as they interact with new observations of science phenomena. Listen also to the questions you, as a teacher, are asking your students, because your questions have a heavy influence on the kinds of question patterns your students are developing. (Alfke, 1974, pp. 18–19)

Even young children can learn to change their thinking behavior. For example, second-grade nonnative speakers of English learn to modify their own thinking and question-asking strategies when they are exposed to proper questioning and reinforcement (Zimmerman & Pike, 1972). Iva Brown (1986) sums up best the importance of questioning on pupil thinking:

> The key to successful classroom experiences with hands-on science activities is clearly the use of questioning in the instructional process. Without well-thought-out questions in the lesson, manipulative activities may soon deteriorate into rather meaningless messing around. (p. 152)

Questions can make the difference between learning from *meaningful* manipulation of materials and *meaningless* messing around. This belief is based on a process-product model of classroom learning, in which specific teaching behaviors provide useful pupil learning experiences. The product of this process is pupil achievement. This model suggests that "increases in the quantity and quality of pupil behaviors should result in concomitant increases in pupil achievement" (Tobin & Capie, 1982, p. 3). The assumed increases are attributed to the quality of verbal interaction. For example, teachers and students are reported to talk about 71 percent of the time in activity-based classrooms, compared to 80 percent of the time spent talking in nonactivity-based classrooms. In average activity-based elementary science classrooms, 29 percent of the questions are at a high level, while only 13 percent of teachers' questions are high level in average nonactivity-based classrooms (Bredderman, 1982).

***How Do Questions Influence Students' Achievement?***   Do the changes in verbal interaction make a difference? Apparently, yes. The studies here are limited, but the results show that a teacher's questions can produce pupil achievement superior to levels attributed to written questions found in textbooks and on worksheets (Rothkopf, 1972; Hargie, 1978). Some earlier studies appear to conflict with this conclusion (Rosenshine, 1976, 1979). However, more recent studies suggest that key ingredients of effective verbal interaction may have been missing in the earlier research. For example, Kenneth Tobin (1984) describes increased achievement for middle school students in science when teachers redirected questions, used probing strategies, and used wait-time to increase student discourse and reaction. Higher-level questions seem to stimulate greater science achievement when combined with a longer wait-time (Riley, 1986).

## How Are Teacher Questions and Student Answers Related?

Raising the level of questions is all well and good, but it makes a difference only if students actually think and respond on the same level as that required by the questions used. Is this what happens?

Greater use of higher-level questions may be a significant difference between hands-on science learning and traditional teaching, according to Ted Bredderman (1984). He reports a direct relationship between the level of questioning and the level of response in elementary science lessons. Bredderman observed specially trained teachers (such as reading teachers trained in the SCIS program, see Chapter 10) raising the level of questioning in reading lessons. His research suggests that questioning levels "can be raised through activity-based science training, which could have the effect of raising the cognitive level of classroom discourse and could result in increased achievement" (Bredderman, 1984, pp. 289–303). Other researchers found that higher-level questions had a positive influence on the language development of young children and on skills such as analytical thinking (Kroot, 1976; Koran & Koran, 1973). What is the general conclusion? There is a positive relationship between higher-level questions and higher-level student answers (Barnes, 1978). We recommend using more advanced questions to obtain more thoughtful answers from children.

## How Do Teachers Use Questions to Involve All Students?

Exemplary teachers treat different pupils equitably and are capable of adapting instruction according to student needs, including the levels of questions they use. How equitable is the questioning treatment that is found in typical elementary classrooms?

Studies done in urban classrooms show that teachers call on students whom they perceive as high achievers more frequently than on students they perceive as low achievers. Also, teachers are less likely to react to the responses received from low achievers: 3 percent fail to react to high achievers and 18 percent fail to provide feedback to low achievers. When high achievers hesitate to answer, they are given more time to think. Low achievers receive less and often no time, perhaps out of regard for the students' feelings. High achievers also receive more opportunities to exchange ideas with teachers at higher thought levels. Similar data show questioning differences between Caucasian and African American students, with African American males most deprived of opportunity (Los Angeles Unified School District [LAUSD], 1977).

What is the relationship between where a student sits in a classroom and the number of opportunities the student receives to answer questions? In a study of first-, sixth-, and eleventh-grade classrooms with traditional seating arrangements of rows facing the teacher's desk, the students most likely to be asked questions were seated in a T shape, with the top of the T across the front of the room and the stem of the T down the middle (see Figure 8.2). Certainly the shape was not always perfect, yet there were distinct areas in the back of the classrooms along the sides where students were seldom involved in questioning and instructive verbal interaction (LAUSD, 1977). Who sits in these areas most often? Who needs more opportunities, feedback, and encouragement? Answer: lower-achieving students.

## What Is Wait-Time and Why Is It Important?

Pause for a few seconds and think about what happens when you are the student and a teacher asks you a question. Unless you have memorized the answer, you must decode the meaning of the question (no small task if it is unclear

**FIGURE 8.2 Where a Child Sits Can Make a Difference**

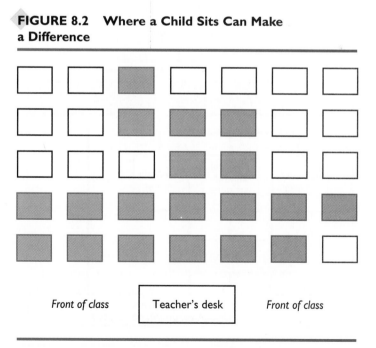

or if multiple questions are used); think, "What do I know?" about the question's possible answer; ask, "How can I say the answer without sounding foolish?"; actually form the answer; and then give the response to the teacher. All of these steps take time, as suggested by Figure 8.3.

Wait-time is defined in different ways, but usually two types of wait-time are recognized. *Wait-time 1* refers to the length of time a teacher waits for a student to respond. *Wait-time 2* is the length of time a teacher waits after a student has responded before the teacher reacts to what was said.

**FIGURE 8.3   Questioning Map: Students Need Time to Think**   What happens after a learner asks a question?

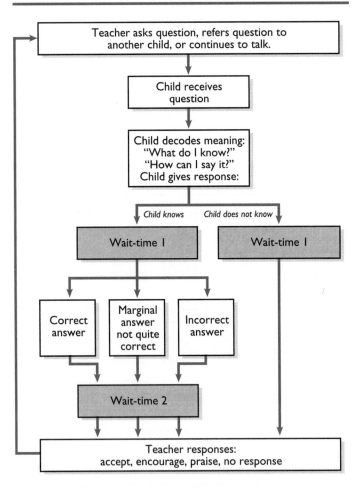

How long do teachers typically wait? Rowe (1974) first researched this topic and reported an average for wait-time 1 of about one second. Wait-time 2 was equally short, with teachers often only parroting the students' answers or providing very low-value feedback, such as, "Okay," "Uh-huh," or "Good." Many teachers wait about 1 second for students to respond without any adjustment for the difficulty of the question and then almost immediately react to what the students have said without giving the response much thought. "Evidently students are expected to respond as quickly to comprehension questions as they are to knowledge-level questions," and teachers believe they can accurately predict what students will say (Riley, 1986). Under what conditions do you think wait-times of 1 second or less *are* appropriate?

There is a growing list of advantages we can expect from increasing the length of wait-times. Kenneth Tobin (1984) reports increases in the length of student responses, increases in student achievement, and changes in teacher discourse. Teachers tend to "probe and obtain further student input rather than mimicking pupil responses" (p. 779). Yet there is a possible threshold effect; a certain optimal length of wait-time exists depending on the type of question, advises Joseph Riley II (1986). Tobin and Capie (1982) recommend an overall wait-time of about 3 seconds with an approximate mix of 50 percent lower-level questions and 50 percent higher-level questions to produce optimal pupil responses. They advise us to establish the facts first in order to give the students something worthwhile to think about before building on the base of knowledge by using higher-level questions. Tobin (1984) even suggests that an effective strategy is to ask the question, wait, call on a student to answer, wait, then redirect the question or react accordingly (see Figure 8.4 on page 274).

Some teachers encourage cooperative types of learning by using the think-pair-share approach. A teacher asks the question and waits; students think about possible answers for 10 to 20 seconds; students then pair up and compare answers. A student pair is then asked to share its answer with the class.

Students might find the waiting time awkward at first and misinterpret your intentions. We have had considerable success with learners by telling them about wait-time and why we are going to use it, then cueing them to think before responding. Try waiting at least 3 seconds before you respond, and you may discover the benefits reported by Rowe (1970):

- Student responses can become 400 to 800 percent longer.
- The number of appropriate but unsolicited student responses increases.
- Failure of students to respond decreases.
- Pupils' confidence levels increase.
- Students ask more questions.
- Low achievers may contribute up to 37 percent more.
- Speculative and predictive thinking can increase as much as 700 percent.
- Students respond and react more to each other.
- Discipline problems decrease.

**FIGURE 8.4   A Whole Class Questioning Strategy**   There are times when questions should be used with the whole class. This questioning strategy can maximize student involvement.

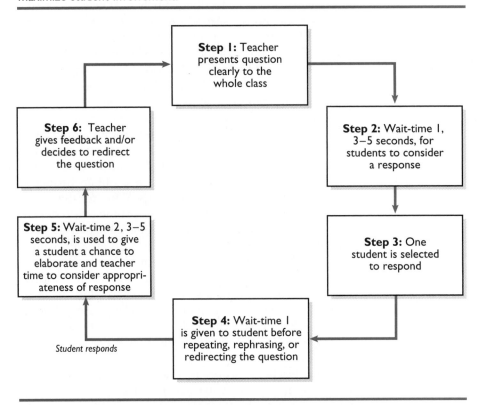

*Source:* This strategy is based on the research of Kenneth Tobin (1984) as reported in "Effects of Extended Wait-Time on Discourse Characteristics and Achievement in Middle School Grades," *Journal of Research in Science Teaching,* vol. 21, no. 8, pp. 779-791.

## What Types of Questions Are Used Most in Elementary Science Books and Tests?

Textbooks have a profound impact on curriculum, teachers, and instruction because student texts and teacher guides often determine the level of questions used. Questions, as we have learned, influence the extent of thinking and learning that takes place. Low-level questions have been consistently used in textbooks for several school subjects, but high-level questions have seldom been found. For example, of more than 61,000 questions from history textbooks, teacher guides, and student workbooks, more than 95 percent were devoted to recalling facts (Bennett, 1986). Another researcher found that only 9 out of 144 lesson plans in the teacher guides from the basal readers of four major publishers contained questions distributed over Bloom's various cognitive levels (Habecker, 1976). Overall, series of elementary science textbooks are no better, but recent improvements are encouraging as publishers enact the science standards. Excellent resource experiment books are also available; they pose questions based on the science processes (see Exercise 8.1).

These findings also raise concern for tests and the printed materials they represent. What types of test items are provided? Tests supplied by text publishers appear to be devoted to low levels of thought as well. Gregory Risner (1987) studied the cognitive levels of questions demonstrated by test items that accompanied fifth-grade science textbooks. Rated on Bloom's taxonomy, Risner found about 95 percent of the test questions devoted to knowledge or comprehension, about 5 percent used for application, and 0.2 percent used for evaluation; analysis and synthesis questions were neglected completely. All types of questions are important, but consistent overuse of any one type can limit learning. You must be able to identify questions necessary for stimulating desired levels of thought and then build those questions into your teaching.

## EXERCISE 8.1

### Science Process Questions*

The questions below are representative of those found in books for children. Use these science processes to label the questions: observing, communicating, hypothesizing/experimenting, measuring, comparing/contrasting, and generalizing/predicting.

| Process | Question |
| --- | --- |
| _____ | 1. Which plants seem to be sturdier: ones left in sun or ones left in shade? |
| _____ | 2. Most rain in clouds comes from the ocean; why doesn't it rain over the ocean and nowhere else? |
| _____ | 3. Which plant do you think will grow better? |
| _____ | 4. Do the creatures react to such things as light or shadows or an object in their path? |
| _____ | 5. What was the temperature? |
| _____ | 6. Which length works best? |
| _____ | 7. What can you move with the air you blow through a straw? |
| _____ | 8. Which seeds stick to your clothes as you walk through a weedy field? |
| _____ | 9. What happens to the number of breathing movements as the temperature drops? |
| _____ | 10. How long does the solution bubble? |

*For a complete discussion, see Sandra Styer, "Books That Ask the Right Questions," _Science and Children_ (March 1984): 40–42, or W. Harlen, _Teaching and Learning Primary Science_ London: Paul Chapman Publishing, (1993), pp. 83–86.

## WHAT RESEARCH SAYS

### Using Questions in Science Classrooms

One function of teaching science is to help learners develop higher levels of thinking. To do this you must facilitate better communication with and among your students. One way to encourage communication is by asking questions. "Teacher questions can serve a variety of purposes," such as

- Managing the classroom ("How many of you have finished the activity?")
- Reinforcing a fact or concept ("What name is given to the process plants use to make food?")
- Stimulating thinking ("What do you think would happen if . . .?")
- Arousing interest ("Have you ever seen such a sight?")
- Helping students develop a particular mind-set ("A steel bar does not float on water; I wonder why a steel ship floats?")

Science teachers are concerned about helping students to become critical thinkers, problem solvers, and scientifically literate citizens. If we want students to function as independent thinkers, we need to provide opportunities in science classes that allow for greater student involvement and initiative and less teacher domination of the learning process. This means a shift in teacher role from that of information giver to that of a facilitator and guide of the inquiry are learning process.

Few children are able to construct their own understanding from an activity without teacher guid-

ance. Productive questions help teachers to build a bridge between learning activities and student thinking. According to Mary Lee Martens (1999, p. 26), productive questions help learners

- Focus their attention on significant details (What have you noticed about . . . ? How does it feel/smell/sound?)
- Become more precise while making observations (How many . . . ? How often . . . ? Where exactly . . . ?)
- Analyze and classify (How do they go together? How do these compare?)
- Explore the properties of unfamiliar materials, living or nonliving, and of small events taking place or to make predictions about phenomena (What about . . . ? What happens if . . . ?)
- Plan and implement solutions to problems (What is a way to . . . ? How could you figure out how to . . . ?)
- Think about experiences and construct ideas that make sense to them (Why do you think . . . ? What is your reason for . . . ?)

Central to this shift in teacher role are the types of questions that teachers ask. Questions that require students to observe characteristics, recall data or facts have a different impact on pupils than questions that encourage pupils to process and interpret data in a variety of ways.

The differential effects of various types of teacher questions seem obvious, but what goes on in class-

## WHAT ARE THE DIFFERENT TYPES OF QUESTIONS?

Many innovative scientists would never have made their most important discoveries had they been unable to think divergently in their pursuit of the new. Through thinking nontraditionally and divergently, scientists like Copernicus, Galileo, Pasteur, and Salk discovered solutions, formulated theories, and made discoveries that revolutionized the modern world. The need for divergent thinking did not die with their achievements (Pucket-Cliatt & Show, 1985, pp. 14–16).

rooms? In one review of observational studies of teacher questioning, spanning 1963–1983, it was reported that the central focus of all teacher questioning activity appeared to be the textbook. Teachers appeared to consider their job to be [seeing] that students have studied the text. Similar findings have been reported from observational studies of teachers' questioning styles in science classrooms. Science teachers appear to function primarily at the recall level in the questions they ask, whether the science lessons are being taught to elementary students or secondary school pupils.

Why doesn't questioning behavior match educational objectives? One hypothesis is that teachers are not aware of the customary questioning patterns. One way to test this hypothesis is to use a question analysis system.

You can do several things if you want to improve your questioning behavior by using a wider variety of questions. First,

> locate a question category system [you] can use comfortably and then apply it, during lesson planning and in post-lesson analysis. Because of the variety of things that go on during a lesson, a post-lesson analysis is best accomplished by tape-recording the lesson or at least those parts of the lesson containing the most teacher questions.

Are the kinds of questions you ask different? What kinds of teacher-student interaction patterns seem to exist? Are some patterns of interaction more effective than others? Compare your written and oral questions. Do they accomplish what you intend? If you use a variety of oral questions to promote different levels of thinking, quiz and test questions should do the same. Students quickly figure out what you value and then strive for it.

George Maxim (1997, p. 42) offers practical suggestions for helping young children improve their thinking through productive questioning:

- Use age-appropriate questions to stimulate children to think about concrete objects in order to form simple abstractions.
- Use questions to help children interpret the sensory information they received by manipulating objects and encourage them to exchange points of view with adults and peers.
- Encourage children who are entering the period of concrete operations (7–11 years) to uncover reflective abstractions by challenging them to answer "Why?" questions.

*Source:* Unless otherwise cited, excerpted from Patricia Blosser, "Using Questions in Science Classrooms," in Doran, R. (ed.), *Research Matters . . . to the Science Teacher,* vol. 2 (1985) (ERIC document no. 273490).

These scientists learned to think divergently—broadly, creatively, and deeply about many possibilities. They learned how to ask the right questions at the right time. "Wrong questions tend to begin with such innocent interrogatives as why, how, or what" (Elstgeest, 1985, p. 37). Jos Elstgeest (1985) provides an excellent example in this brief story:

> I once witnessed a marvelous science lesson virtually go to ruins. It was a class of young secondary school girls who, for the first time, were let free to handle batteries, bulbs, and wires. They were busy incessantly, and there were cries of surprise

*Questions can encourage children to develop science process skills.*

and delight. Arguments were settled by "You see?" and problems were solved with "Let's try!" Hardly a thinkable combination of batteries, bulbs, and wires was left untried. Then in the midst of the hubbub, the teacher clapped her hands and, chalk poised at the blackboard, announced: "Now, girls, let us summarize what we have learned today. Emmy, what is a battery?" "Joyce, what is a positive terminal?" "Lucy, what is the correct way to close a circuit?" And the "correct" diagram was deftly sketched and labeled, the "correct" symbols were added, and the "correct" definitions were scribbled down. And Emmy, Joyce, and Lucy and the others deflated audibly into silence and submission, obediently copying the diagram and the summary. What they had done seemed of no importance. The questions were in no way related to their work. The rich experience with the batteries and other equipment, which would have given them plenty to talk and think about and to question, was in no way used to bring order and system into the information they actually did gather. (pp. 36–37)

Elstgeest defines *good questions* as those taking a first step toward an answer, like a problem that actually has a solution. The good question stimulates, invites the child to take a closer look, or leads to where the answer can be found. The good question refers to the child's experience, real objects, or events under study. The good question invites children to show rather than say an answer.

Good questions may be modeled after the science process skills in which learners are asked to take a closer look and describe what they find. Try matching the questions and skills in Exercise 8.1.

There are several additional ways to classify questions. When presenting information from the research on questions, we have often referred to Bloom's taxonomy of the cognitive domain. It is possible to write questions for each level of the taxonomy. See Figure 8.5 for examples.

- *Knowledge-level* questions request the memorized facts.
- *Comprehension-level* questions stimulate responses of memorized information in the students' own words.

**FIGURE 8.5    Bloom's Taxonomy of Cognitive Domain**

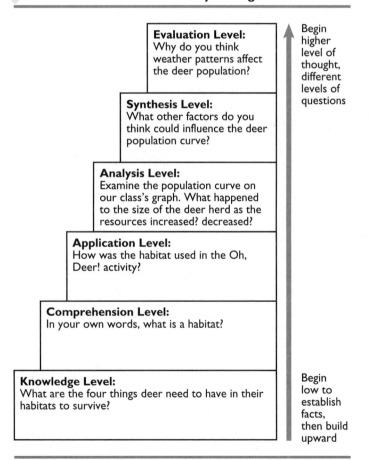

*Source:* B. S. Bloom, *Taxonomy of Educational Objectives, the Classification of Educational Goals, Handbook I: Cognitive Domain* (New York: Longman, 1956).

- *Application-level* questions cause students to use information while thinking about how to put what they have learned to use in a new context.
- *Analysis-level* questions require that students break down what they know into smaller parts to look for differences, patterns, and so on.
- *Synthesis-level* questions stimulate children to consider variety, new ideas, or original possibilities.
- *Evaluation-level* questions require children to make choices and provide reasons.

The taxonomy suggests that learners cannot make a learned judgment until they know the facts, understand the facts, can apply the facts, can dissect the facts, and can reorganize the facts so that new perspectives are revealed (Bloom & Krathwohl, 1965; Morgan & Saxton, 1991).

Educators often disagree about the level at which a question is written. This can make Bloom's taxonomy difficult to use, but it is worth learning. Spreading your questions across the taxonomy's range can make you a more effective teacher.

Gallagher and Aschner (1963) offer a simple and useful method for classifying questions. This method has four types of questions that address all of Bloom's levels and incorporate the science processes. The simplicity of this method makes it useful for all subject areas. Table 8.2 provides a level-of-thinking context, and Figure 8.6 provides examples of the following kinds of questions:

- *Cognitive memory questions* require students to recall facts, formulas, procedures, and other essential information. This is similar to Bloom's knowledge and comprehension levels and helps students establish the facts before moving toward higher levels. Memory questions also assist observations and communication. *Example:* "Do you see the bubbles rising from the liquid? What is the common name for acetic acid?"

---

**TABLE 8.2   Levels of Thinking Questions Require**

| Question Type | Level | Type of Thinking Expected |
| --- | --- | --- |
| Closed questions | Low | Cognitive memory operations; convergent operations |
| Open questions | High | Divergent thinking operations; evaluative thinking operations |

*Source:* A comparison of Gallagher and Aschner's questions as adapted from P. Blosser, *How to Ask the Right Questions* (Washington, DC: National Science Teachers Association, 1991), p. 4.

## ◆ FIGURE 8.6　Composing the Correct Level of Questioning: Higher Levels of Thought

| QUESTION CATEGORY | | | SAMPLE QUESTION PHASES |
|---|---|---|---|
| Evaluative Thinking | **Bloom's Evaluation Level:**<br>• Make choices<br>• Form values<br>• Overlap critiques, judgments, defenses | **How and Why Reasonings:**<br>• Choose, appraise, select, evaluate, judge, assess, defend, justify<br>• Form conclusions and generalizations | • *What do you favor...?*<br>• *What is your feeling about...?*<br>• *What is your reason for...?* |
| Divergent Thinking | **Bloom's Synthesis Level:**<br>• Develop own ideas and information<br>• Integrate own ideas<br>• Plan, construct, or reconstruct | **Open-ended Questions for Problem Posing and Action:**<br>• Infer, predict, design, invent<br>• Hypothesize and experiment<br>• Communicate ideas | • *What do you think...?*<br>• *What could you do...?*<br>• *How could you design...?*<br>• *What do you think will happen if...?* |
| Convergent Thinking | **Bloom's Application and Analysis Level:**<br>• Uses of logic<br>• Deductive and inductive reasoning<br>• Construct or reconstruct | **Closed Questions to:**<br>• Focus attention, guide, encourage measurement and counting, make comparisons, take action<br>• Use logic, state relationships<br>• Apply solutions<br>• Solve problems<br>• Hypothesize and experiment<br>• Communicate ideas | • *If "A", then what will happen to "B"...?*<br>• *Which are facts, opinions and inferences...?*<br>• *What is the author's purpose...?*<br>• *What is the relationship of "x" to "y"...?* |
| Cognitive Memory | **Bloom's Knowledge and Comprehension Level:**<br>• Rote memorization<br>• Selective recall of facts, formulas, instructions, rules, or procedures<br>• Recognition | **Managerial and Rhetorical Questions:**<br>• Simple attention focusing, yes-no responses<br>**Information:**<br>• Repeat, name, describe, identify, observe, simple explanation, compare | • *What is the definition of...?*<br>• *What are the three steps in...?*<br>• *Who discovered...?*<br>• *In your own words, what is the meaning of...?* |
| Intended mental activity → | | | ← Key function or science processes |

- *Convergent thinking questions* cause students to apply and analyze information. To do this successfully, children must have a command of cognitive memory types of information. Convergent questions assist in problem solving and are useful for the basic science processes: measuring, communicating, comparing, and contrasting. *Example:* "What kind of chart, graph, or drawing would be the best way to show our class's results?"

- *Divergent thinking questions* stimulate children to think independently. Students are given little teacher structure or prior information; they are encouraged to do possibility thinking by combining original and known ideas into new ideas or explanations. Questions of this type require synthesis thinking and promote creative problem solving and the integrated science processes (hypothesizing and experimenting). *Example:* "Why do you think these seedlings are taller than those?"

- *Evaluative thinking questions* cause students to choose, judge, value, criticize, defend, or justify. Often the simple question "Why?" or "How?" propels thinking to this level after students are asked simple choice or yes-no types of questions. Processes stimulated by evaluation questions include making predictions, reaching conclusions, and forming generalizations. *Example:* "What things make a difference to how fast the seeds began to grow?"

Science for many children, unfortunately, may be an exercise in closed thinking, in which memory and convergent questions are emphasized. Children are prodded to seek the so-called right answer or verify the correct results. Teachers should use both open and closed types of questions. *Open questions* are those that encourage divergent and evaluative thinking processes. Because they are traditional and expedient, *closed questions* have been used most often by teachers. Yet there is a danger associated with overuse of closed questions. "Convergent questions sacrifice the potential for many students to be rewarded for good answers, since their focus is a search for one right or best answer" (Schlichter, 1983, p. 10). Because science is a creative process, much more divergent thinking must be encouraged. Try your hand at classifying convergent and divergent questions in Exercise 8.2, and experiment with both while you teach. Be advised that there are risks for teachers who use divergent or open-ended questions:

> The risks for the teachers who practice divergent question-asking should not be underestimated: an open-ended question can alter the day's schedule, spark discussion on topics the teacher may not be prepared for, and shift the teacher's role from guardian of known answers to stimulator of productive (and often surprising) thinking. But they are risks well worth taking. (Schlichter, 1983, p. 10)

There are risks associated with using *any* type of question. What can you do to limit the risks? How can you learn to use questions more effectively?

## WHAT ARE THE KEYS TO EFFECTIVE QUESTIONING?

*Plan specific questions.* Take the time to write specific questions before you teach. List six to eight key questions that cover the levels of thinking you wish to promote, and then use the questions as a guide for what you teach. The questions should help establish the knowledge base of information and then help build

## EXERCISE 8.2

### Identifying Convergent and Divergent Questions

Convergent questions mean to elicit the single best answer, while divergent questions encourage a wide range of answers without concern for a single correct answer. Use the letters C and D to classify the following questions:

_____ 1. What kinds of food make your mouth water?

_____ 2. What name do we call the spit in your mouth?

_____ 3. What is another name for your esophagus?

_____ 4. How many intestines does your body have?

_____ 5. How many weights do you think you can add to your structure before it falls down?

_____ 6. Are you kept warm by radiation, conduction, convection, or all three?

_____ 7. Why does sound travel faster through solids and liquids than it does through air?

_____ 8. What kinds of uses does a balloon have?

_____ 9. How does electricity work?

_____ 10. How do you use electricity?

Check your answers with those at the end of the chapter. How well do we agree? What makes it difficult for you to classify questions?

toward higher levels. Avoid yes-no questions unless that is your specific purpose; instead, focus the questions on the lesson topic by building toward the objectives. Open-ended questions can stimulate exploration, and convergent questions can focus concept invention. Both, along with evaluation questions, can contribute to expansion of the lesson's main idea. Pay attention to the types of questions used in children's books; then select books and materials with many different types, and supplement them with your own questions for special purposes.

*Ask your questions as simply, concisely, and directly as possible.* Make your purpose clear, and use single questions. Build upon previous questions once they have been answered, and avoid multiple, piggy-backed questions. These confuse students and indicate that the question is not well defined in the teacher's mind.

*Ask your question before selecting who should answer.* This helps keep all learners listening and thinking. Pause briefly after asking the question so everyone can think about it. Then select an individual to respond. Give both high and low achievers a chance to answer, and try to provide equal and genuine feedback. Involve as many different types of students as possible, volunteers and non-volunteers. A total class shouting out answers could create discipline problems. Limit rapid-fire, drill-and-practice questions to times when specific facts need to be gathered or reviewed. Avoid parroting the students' answers, but do try to use the students' ideas as much as possible.

*Practice using wait-time.* Wait-time 1 is often 1 second or less. Practice waiting at least 3 seconds for students to respond to most questions, especially if students are exploring or trying to expand on the lesson's main idea. Wait-time gives the children opportunities to think, create, and demonstrate more fully what they understand. Higher-level questions may require a wait-time longer than 3 seconds.

Wait-time 2 may need to be longer than wait-time 1. Rowe (1974) believes this wait-time is more important, especially when the occasion calls for critical or creative thinking. Quality and quantity of student responses increase, low achievers respond more, and the teacher has more time to think carefully about the questioning sequence.

*Listen carefully to your students' responses.* Encourage students nonverbally and verbally without overkilling with praise. Make any praise or encouraging remarks genuine. Check to make certain the children's responses match the level intended by your questions, and prompt them if the level is not appropriate. Do not always stop with the right answer. Probing benefits students who are partially correct and helps them construct a more acceptable answer. As a general rule, do not move on to another student before giving the first student a chance to form a better answer. This is a great opportunity to gather clues about students' misconceptions, incomplete information, or limited experiences. A brief questioning sequence may be all that is needed to overcome important learning problems.

*Try using more questions to produce conceptual conflict.* Piaget's research (Wadsworth, 1996) suggests that learners should be in a state of mental disequilibrium to help them adapt or add new mental constructions to their thinking:

*What do you think will happen if* we add more weight to the boat?

*If* we add a drop of soap *then* what could happen to the surface tension?

*How would you* design a test to determine the effects of fertilizer on plant growth?

*What evidence do you have to support* your identification of the limiting factors?

*What other ways are possible to* explain the effects of sunlight on plant growth?

*How can you explain* to the others what you did and what you discovered?

*What do you think causes* newsprint to look larger when viewed through a water droplet?

*Talk less and ask more, but make your questions count.* Ask, don't tell. Use questions to guide and invite your students to tell you. Work with students by exchanging ideas instead of conducting an inquisition. Try to make discussions more conversational by asking students to share thoughts and react to each other.

*Try to use questions that yield more complete and more complex responses.* Given consistently adequate wait-time, students should give longer and more thoughtful answers. The effectiveness of any specific question you use is never any greater than the answer you are willing to accept. Establish a base of information first; then build on it by asking questions that require more complex answers. Ask students who give short, incomplete answers to contribute more.

*Listen carefully, ask concise, direct questions, practice wait time, and match the level of the questions to the level of the child.*

*Ask different types of questions to encourage all children.* Some learners seem unprepared for or incapable of answering high-level questions. If this is the case, try beginning your questions at a low level before attempting a higher level; build upward. Recalling information with frequent low-level questions for review, recitation, and drill helps children experience success, develop confidence, and establish a reliable foundation to build higher thinking upon. But do not let your questioning stagnate. Begin with closed questions to establish a firm footing, and then move on to more open-ended questions. Use divergent and evaluative questions less often initially, and increase their use over time if your students have difficulty responding as you desire.

Learners who have already had more successful and satisfying school experiences are eager and appear more capable of responding to higher levels of questions sooner. Reflective discussions that mix convergent, divergent, and evaluative questions can form a strategy for critical and original thinking. Yet despite the type of student, several studies show that lower-level questions promote greater achievement gains for all primary children when learning basic skills.

Several learning theorists and researchers remind us about differences in how primary and upper elementary children think. Each group processes information differently because of differences in mental development. Yet appropriate experiences can help mental development reach its full potential in each group. Questions related to the processes of science provide the momentum for this development.

For younger children in primary grades (ages 5 to 10), use questions to stimulate:

- observation of basic properties. *Example:* "What do you see happening to the Silly Putty?"

- classification based on similarities and differences. *Example:* "Which of these animals is an insect?"
- communication to show thoughts and increase the value of the experience as well as to develop cooperation and interpersonal relations. *Example:* "What are you observing? How do you feel about what you see?"
- measurement, using numbers and time. *Example:* "What is the final temperature? How much time did it take to reach that temperature?"
- prediction to form guesses based on what is known. *Example:* "What do you think will happen to the brightness of the bulb if we use a longer wire?"

For older children in upper elementary and middle grades (ages beyond 11), use questions that will help them to:

- identify variables. *Example:* "What variables did we keep the same?"
- control variables. *Example:* "What variables seemed to affect the size of your soap bubbles?"
- form operational definitions based on verified information. *Example:* "From what we did in this experiment, how should we define 'force?' "
- form and test hypotheses to reach conclusions. *Example:* "Why did the electrical resistance increase in this experiment?"
- interpret data from experiments. *Example:* "What do the green and pink color changes of the purple cabbage juice indicate?"
- form models to explain occurrences or represent theories. *Example:* "What kind of relationship between the species is suggested by their population graphs over the same length of time?"

*Determine whether the children are providing answers equal to the level of your questions.* To do this you will need to monitor your questions and your students' responses.

*Realize when* not *to ask a question.* According to Morgan and Saxton (1991), times when it may not be appropriate to ask questions include

- when students have insufficient knowledge and experiences from which to draw an answer (this is a good time to encourage children to ask *their* questions);
- when children are making progress on their own and your question would be an intrusion that impedes productive work;
- when students seem to be despondent or having personal problems. Instead of asking a question to which a student may feel obliged to respond, try making an observation such as "Tina, you seem quiet today" and then become an active listener if Tina chooses to do the talking.

## HOW CAN YOU IMPROVE YOUR QUESTIONING?

You can improve your questioning with training and practice. One way to improve is to videotape or tape-record a lesson in which you use questions, play back the recording, identify the questions, and analyze them. Observation instruments or checklists such as those in Table 8.3 can be used. A more informative approach is to structure your observation and analysis around your questions. For example,

- What kinds of questions best stimulated learners to engage in the inquiry?
- What questions best nurtured development of process skills?
- How did you use questions to help learners construct conceptual understanding?
- What types of questions sustained or expanded the inquiry?
- How often did you use cognitive memory questions?
- How does this amount compare to your uses of convergent, divergent, and evaluative questions?
- How are your questions phrased? Do you avoid yes-no questions as much as possible?

### TABLE 8.3    Effective Questioning Checklist

Do you

____ 1. use broad or narrow questions to accomplish your objectives?
____ 2. avoid yes-no questions unless that is your intention?
____ 3. avoid repeating student answers and avoid sounding like a parrot?
____ 4. encourage students to ask questions?
____ 5. expand on students' ideas?
____ 6. stop the discussion after receiving the right answer?
____ 7. use wait-time of at least 3 seconds?
____ 8. avoid asking multiple or piggy-backed questions?
____ 9. avoid answering your own questions?
____ 10. ask students to clarify, summarize, and review material?
____ 11. avoid repeating your questions?
____ 12. rephrase misunderstood or unclear questions?
____ 13. call on volunteers and nonvolunteers?
____ 14. ask questions at different levels?
____ 15. talk less and ask more?
____ 16. use good grammar on a level understood by the children?
____ 17. encourage student-to-student discussion?
____ 18. use questions to punish or embarrass students?

*Source:* Adapted from Iva D. Brown, "Topic 4: Teacher Questioning Techniques," *Staff Development Project—Science Grades K–6* (Jackson, MS: Mississippi Association for Teacher Education, 1986) (ERIC Document no. ED 285726), p. 159.

- How do you know your questions are on the appropriate level for your students?
- What evidence did you find indicating that you adjust questions to the language and ability levels of the students?
- Are your questions distributed among all learners regardless of ability, gender, socioeconomic status, and where they are seated?
- How often do you call on nonvolunteers? How do you decide which nonvolunteer to call upon?
- How often do you use probing to encourage students to complete responses, clarify, expand, or support a decision?
- How long do you wait? How do you use wait-time? What benefits do you receive from using wait-time? How does your use of wait-time 1 compare with wait-time 2?
- How well do the written questions on your plan match the verbal questions you use in class? Do your test questions represent the same levels as questions used in class?
- How often do children ask questions? What types of questions do they ask? Under what circumstances do they ask questions?

## WHY USE STUDENTS' QUESTIONS?

The children's questions worry me. I can deal with the child who just wants attention, but because I've had no science background I take other questions at face value and get bothered when I don't know the answer. I don't mind saying I don't know, though I don't want to do it too often. I've tried the let's-find-out-together approach, but it's not easy and can be very frustrating. (Jelly, 1985, p. 54)

### Why Bother with Students' Questions?

"Can one black hole swallow another?"
"Why do fireflies light up?"
"How does a steel ship float when it weighs so much?"
"Why are soda cans shaped like a cylinder and not a rectangle?" (Perlman & Pericak-Spector, 1992, pp. 36–37)

Children's questions give precious insight into their world and illustrate topics of interest. Their questions can surprise teachers who might underestimate the ability of particular children and may suggest that certain learners have more ability than is evident from their reading and written work. The questions students ask also give a guide to what they know and do not know, and when they want to know it. These questions give clues about what science content is understood and the level of concept development—if we are willing to listen closely. Questions could also indicate an anxious child, or simply reveal a habit formed by one who has been reinforced to ask questions (Biddulph, Symington, & Osborn, 1986).

*Children's questions can be used to develop interesting problems for science inquiry and to encourage the useful habit of reflection.*

Questions help students focus and gain knowledge that interests them. Incessant "Why?" questions can be a method of gaining attention, but unlike the two-year-old, the school age child who asks, "Why?" reveals an area where understanding is lacking and is desired. Questions help young children resolve unexpected outcomes or work through problem situations; they can also be a way of confirming a belief. Children's questions also help them learn more quickly. "When they are following their own noses, learning what they are curious about, children go faster, cover more territory than we would ever think of trying to mark out for them, or make them cover" (Holt, 1971, p. 152).

Encouraging students to ask questions develops a useful habit: reflection. Habits take time to form, and question asking is a habit that can enrich a school's curriculum. Time spent in contemplation helps form this habit. Asking oneself questions and hazarding guesses about their answers stimulate creative thinking, provide a means for solving critical problems, and can help a child learn "to find interest and enjoyment in situations that others would see as dull or boring" (Biddulph, Symington, & Osborn, 1986, p. 78).

*How Can You Stimulate Students' Questions?*

Four factors stimulate children to ask questions. If you want children to ask more questions, you should provide adequate stimulation, model appropriate question asking, develop a classroom atmosphere that values questions, and include question asking in your evaluations of children.

*Stimulation.*   Direct contact with materials is a first step. What kinds of materials stimulate curiosity in children and provide them opportunities to explore? The best indicator is the materials children bring in spontaneously. The sharing has a built-in curiosity factor and requires little effort to conduct discussion; simply invite them to share and ask questions. The mind will be on what the hands are doing.

*Modeling.*   Teacher question asking is modeling. Learners must be shown how to ask good, productive questions. Showing genuine enthusiasm and consideration for what interests others can show children how to do the same. Consider some of the following ways to bring this modeling into the routine of your classroom (Jelly, 1985).

*Share collections and develop classroom displays,* much as Mrs. B did in our opening scenario. Link these activities to regular classwork and organize them around key chapter questions. Use one of the question classification systems described earlier in this chapter to help you ask questions at many different levels. Invite children to share their own collections and create class displays while building questions into the discussion the children share with classmates.

*Establish a problem corner in your classroom or use a "Question of the Week"* approach to stimulate children's thought and questions. These approaches can be part of regular class activity or used for enrichment. Catherine Valentino's (1985) Question of the Week materials could be a good place to start until you acquire enough ideas of your own. Consider one of her examples, "I Lava Volcano," a photo of an erupting volcano, which asks these questions: "Do volcanic eruptions serve any useful purpose? Over millions of years, what changes would occur on the earth if all volcanic activity suddenly stopped?" Valentino's full-color weekly posters and questions stimulate curiosity and inquiry.

Prepare lists of questions to investigate with popular children's books. Encourage students to add their own questions to the list.

Use questions to organize any teacher-made activity cards that learners may use independently. Encourage children to think of their work as an investigative mission and to see themselves as clue seekers.

Try a KWHL chart. Marletta Iwasyk (1997) describes the importance of modeling curiosity and productive questioning at the beginning of discussions by focusing basic questions on the topic of study and recording the children's answers to four basic questions (Figure 8.7).

For primary grade learners Neil Dixon (1996) offers the "Planning House" as a concrete metaphor for stimulating children to inquire and to record questions systematically. The roof of the house represents the outcome of the inquiry, which results from the planned steps taken, whereas the lower levels of the house show how children began the inquiry and then worked their way up toward the outcome question (Figure 8.8 on page 292).

**FIGURE 8.7    A KWHL Chart**

| K | W | H | L |
|---|---|---|---|
| What do I **Know** about _____? | What do I **Want** to know about _____? | **How** can I find out about _____? | What did I **Learn** about _____? |
| List all ideas in order to document prior knowledge, preconceptions, and possible misconceptions. | List the students' questions here. Their questions give opportunity for engagement and may reveal your oversights. | List all possible sources and resources, e.g., books, Internet, people to ask, etc. | Completed after the inquiry, facts and discoveries listed here may differ from those listed for "**K**." |

John Langrehr (1993) recommends two additional tools that teachers can use to model effective questioning and help learners improve their thinking and question-asking skills. Figure 8.9 on page 293 provides sixteen question starters that should help any student to design focused, thoughtful questions. Consider the topic of insects. Using the question starters shown in the matrix, students should be able to expand their inquiry by asking questions such as: *What is* an insect? *How is* an insect different from a spider? *What can* insects do that humans cannot? *Where would* you expect to find insects? *Why might* insects be better able to survive a forest fire than mammals? and so on.

Langrehr also recommends that we show students how to use a *connection map* (Figure 8.10 on page 293) in order to improve their questioning and construction of mental connections among and between the various ideas that may be illustrated by the map. Less able thinkers tend to think more generally, while more capable thinkers tend to think more abstractly. As a tool, the connection map encourages each student to record several key words in boxes that surround a central idea. Encourage students to write connecting words between the boxes that form simple sentences that make sense. This student-designed map can help you peer inside the thinking of the student. Simple questions such as "Why?" or "How?" can encourage students to construct more thought-provoking questions that stimulate productive experimentation.

*Classroom Atmosphere.*    Suchman (1971) believes students inquire only when they feel free to share their ideas without fear of being censored, criticized, or ridiculed. Successful teachers listen to children and do not belittle their curious questions. Establish an atmosphere that fosters curiosity by praising those who

◀ **FIGURE 8.8   The Planning House**

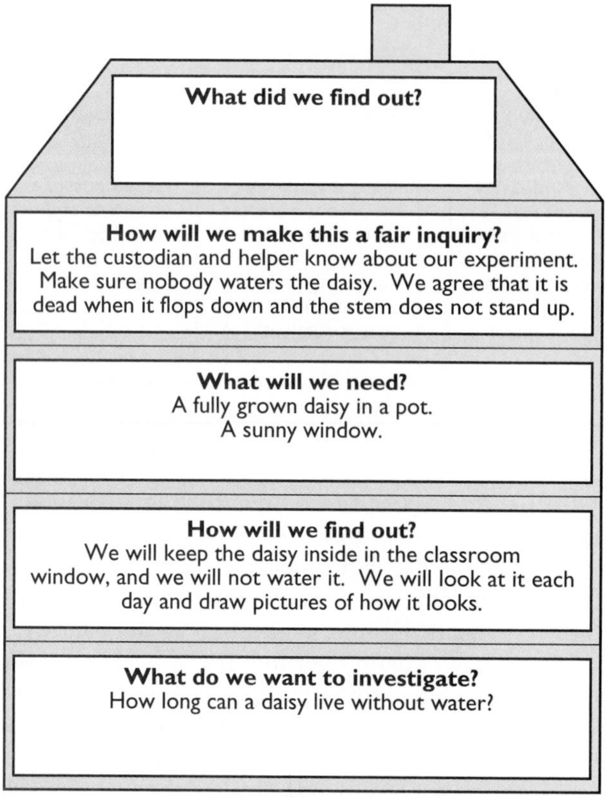

**What did we find out?**

**How will we make this a fair inquiry?**
Let the custodian and helper know about our experiment.
Make sure nobody waters the daisy.  We agree that it is
dead when it flops down and the stem does not stand up.

**What will we need?**
A fully grown daisy in a pot.
A sunny window.

**How will we find out?**
We will keep the daisy inside in the classroom
window, and we will not water it.  We will look at it each
day and draw pictures of how it looks.

**What do we want to investigate?**
How long can a daisy live without water?

invent good questions; reinforce their reflective habits. You can provide opportunities for questions by

- using class time regularly for sharing ideas and asking questions as learners talk about something that interests them,
- having children supply questions of the week and rewarding them for improvements in their question asking,
- helping children write lists (or record lists for nonreaders) of questions they have about something they have studied. These questions can be excellent means for review, for showing further interest, and for providing an informal evaluation of how clearly you have taught a topic.

*Question Asking and Evaluation.*   Have students form questions as another way of evaluating their learning. This factor can stimulate habits of question

◥**FIGURE 8.9  Question-Formation Matrix**

|  | Object/Event | Situation | Reason | Means |
|---|---|---|---|---|
| Present | What is ...? | Where is ...? | Why is ...? | How is ...? |
| Possibility | What can ...? | Where can ...? | Why can ...? | How can ...? |
| Probability | What would ...? | Where would ...? | Why would ...? | How would ...? |
| Imagination | What might ...? | Where might ...? | Why might ...? | How might ...? |

*Source:* S. Langrehr, "Getting Thinking into Science Questions," *Australian Science Teachers Journal* 39 (4), (1993): 36.

◥**FIGURE 8.10   Question Connection Map**

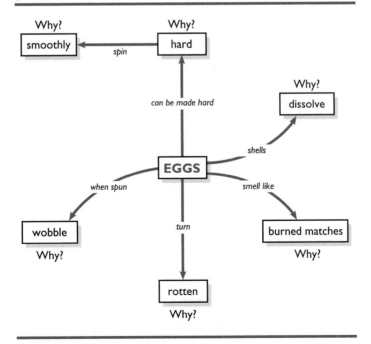

*Source:* Adapted from J. Langrehr, "Getting Thinking into Science Questions," *Australian Science Teachers Journal* 39 (4), (1993): 36.

asking and is different than if you, as teacher, ask questions children must answer. Include a picture or description of a situation in a test occasionally, and call for children to write productive questions about it. In another approach, the students list questions they believe are important for a more complete understanding of the material they have just studied. Lists of their questions can be evaluated for the number and the quality of the questions; quality should refer to the relevance of the question to the topic as well as the thought required to answer it.

## How Can You Use Students' Questions Productively?

When children ask, focus your listening on the ideas represented by their questions. You will need to help them clarify their questions until they learn to ask better ones by themselves. Sheila Jelly (1985) offers a strategy you can use to turn children's questions into productive learning opportunities. Figure 8.11 is based on Jelly's recommendations.

**FIGURE 8.11   How Should You Respond to Children's Questions?**

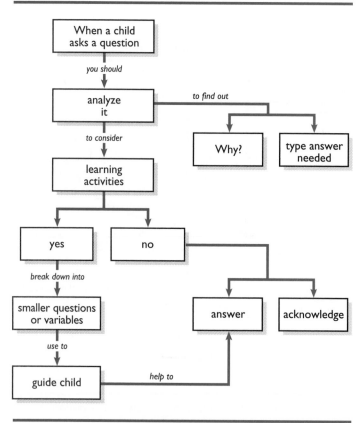

## CHAPTER SUMMARY

If there is a universal teaching tool, the question is it. Questions provide unique opportunities for teachers and students to become involved in productive dialogue; questions invite both teachers and learners to think and respond in many different ways.

We know that the potential of questioning is underused and that many teacher questions are closed and stimulate low-level thinking. Questions may be misused if the wrong types of questions are used before children are capable or ready to respond at the level demanded. Know when not to question. Productive questions stimulate productive thinking and curiosity. Effective questions contribute to students' improved attitudes, expanded capability for thinking, and increased achievement.

As teachers, we need to afford all learners equal opportunities to learn through our questioning techniques. Old habits may have to be changed. We must strive to give children adequate time to think by expanding wait-time; screen textbooks, tests, and other print materi-

als for evidence of good questions; and help children develop the habit of inquiring and reflecting by encouraging them to ask their own questions.

All questions are not equal; they come in such different types as Bloom's taxonomy, open and closed, science processes, memory, and evaluation. Questions should be selected or composed for specific purposes.

You can question well by using the keys for good questioning described in this chapter. Periodically analyze how you use questions and form a plan for self-improvement. Check your skills against your plan and revise as necessary.

Students' questions provide benefits for teachers, children, and the science program. Teachers can encourage learners' questions if they use materials and activities that simulate questions, model good questioning skills, provide a supportive classroom atmosphere, and include children's question asking in evaluation techniques.

## DISCUSSION QUESTIONS

**1.** Based on your school experiences, what differences have you noticed about how your teachers used questions? How do your elementary, secondary, and college teachers compare on using questions?

**2.** What types of questions do your teachers usually ask? How well do the questions match with the teachers' intentions? Justify your answer.

**3.** How do the elementary teachers you have observed use questions to begin a lesson? to focus children's observations? to lead children toward conclusions? to bring closure to a lesson?

**4.** What priority do you believe teachers should give to children's questions? What strategy should they use?

**5.** How important is it for teachers to monitor their own uses of questions?

**6.** Observe a science lesson. Record the number and types of questions asked by the teacher, and try to measure the average wait-time. How do your observations correspond to the average uses of questions and wait-time described in this chapter?

## BUILD A PORTFOLIO

**1.** How well do you use questions? What evidence do you have to support your answer? What

do you think you can do to improve your questioning skills? Audio- or videotape yourself using questions when you practice teaching. Use the recommendations of this chapter to focus an evaluation of your questioning skills, and begin by comparing the numbers of closed and open questions you use.

**2.** Using any of the methods for classifying questions described in this chapter, write and label samples of two questions for each level. Work within class groups to evaluate the quality of the questions. How well do you avoid yes-no questions, require more than rote memory, and avoid unproductive questions?

**3.** Use several of the questions you have written to speculate about pupil replies and appropriate teacher responses. List the questions and the replies for the pupil and teacher.

**4.** Tape-record a class session in which children ask questions. Transcribe these questions, and describe how you could respond to them if you were the teacher. How does your response method compare with Sheila Jelly's suggestion?

## ANSWERS TO EXERCISE 8.1

1. Observing
2. Hypothesizing/experimenting
3. Generalizing/predicting
4. Observing
5. Communicating
6. Measuring
7. Hypothesizing/experimenting
8. Comparing/contrasting
9. Generalizing/predicting
10. Measuring

*Questions come from the following sources:*

1. Seymour, S. (1978). *Exploring fields and lots: Easy science projects.* Champaign, IL: Garrard Publishing.
2. Bendick, J. (1971). *How to make a cloud.* New York: Parents' Magazine Press.
3. Seymour, S. (1970). *Science in a vacant lot.* New York: Viking Press.
4. Zubrowski, B. (1979). *Bubbles: A children's museum activity book.* Boston: Little, Brown.
5. Seymour, S. (1978). *Exploring fields and lots: Easy science projects.* Champaign, IL: Gerrard Publishing.
6. Renner, A. G. (1979). *Experimental fun with the yo-yo and other scientific projects.* New York: Dodd, Mead.
7. Milgrem, H. (1976). *Adventures with a straw: First experiments.* New York: E. P. Dutton.
8. Selsam, M. E. (1957). *Play with seeds.* New York: William Morrow.
9. Seymour, S. (1969). *Discovering what frogs do.* New York: McGraw-Hill.
10. Zubrowski, B. (1981). *Messing around with baking chemistry: A Children's Museum activity book.* Boston: Little, Brown.

## ANSWERS TO EXERCISE 8.2

1. Divergent, because *how* many different kinds of food make *your* mouth water?
2. Convergent, saliva.
3. Convergent, gullet.
4. Convergent, small and large intestines.
5. Divergent, because this question asks for a prediction that depends on several factors that stimulate many different answers.
6. Convergent, because you are asked to select an answer from those given.

7. Convergent, because a specific concept is used to answer the question.

8. Divergent, because who knows the answer to this one? Only your imagination limits the possibilities.

9. Convergent, because descriptions about electron flow rely on a specific concept.

10. Divergent. Think about it: How many *different* ways do you use or depend on electricity?

## CHAPTER OUTLINE

# How Can You Create a Safe, Efficient, Inquiry-Based Science Classroom?

Nine-year-old Celeste sat reading her current issue of *3-2-1 Contact Magazine*. She was intrigued by an article about volcanoes. At the end of the article was an activity on making a volcano. She read over the list of materials she needed. "Let's see," she said half out loud, "the water I can get from the sink; in the bottom cupboard I can find the large baking pan; in the upper cabinet there's the white vinegar, red food coloring, baking soda, and dishwashing liquid; in the first drawer on the right I should find the glue, masking tape, and scissors; and in the drawer on the left I can find the tin foil and teaspoons." Celeste collected the materials from their storage areas and found the clay flower pot and the potting soil stored with the garden supplies. She checked over the materials list once again. "I think I have just about everything I need to make my own volcano," she announced to Sarah, who was passing by.

Ten-year-old Sarah looked over Celeste's shoulder at the magazine, then took a quick inventory of the materials Celeste had collected. "You forgot an empty tuna can," Sarah proclaimed. Celeste looked pensive for a moment and then shouted, "I know. I can go to the recycling bin, I'll probably find just what I need in there!"

In a few moments Celeste was back with an empty tuna can. The two girls arranged the materials according to the directions in the magazine. They dumped the baking soda down the vent of their newly formed volcano. They mixed the vinegar, dishwashing liquid, water, and food coloring together. They were just about to pour the vinegar mixture into the vent when they were startled by a command from an adult: "STOP! What do you think will happen to you if you continue to look down that vent as you pour in the liquid? How are you going to protect your eyes and your clothing? And do you think it's a good idea to do that on the carpet?"

A surprised look came over their faces. "Oh, I'm sorry! I forgot about that," exclaimed Celeste. "I guess I was so excited after reading this article, I really wanted to try it out as quickly as possible. Come on, Sarah. Let's move this off the carpet and then go get our goggles and put some old sweatshirts on before we make our volcano erupt."

Twanna returned from the supply table of the second-grade classroom with her hands full of materials. "Did you get the paper, iron filings, hand lens, and magnets?" asked José.

"Yes I did," responded Twanna. "Let's get going."

"First, we need to be sure that we have plenty of room to perform this activity," stated José, who was the manager and recorder for the science activity. "Are you sure that you have all the materials now, Twanna?"

Twanna, the materials manager for the activity, ran off to get a box. In a few minutes she returned from the supply table with a shoebox with one end cut out of it.

"Now," stated José, "lay the shoebox flat on the table and place the white paper over it. While I am doing that, Twanna, you need to pour some iron filings onto the second sheet of paper and examine them with your hand lens."

José went about his work while Twanna poured the filings from the glass jar onto the paper. "Wow!" she squealed. "Look at these things! They look like baby fish hooks and spears. Why are they so jagged?"

"Maybe they were simply made using a file on an old piece of pipe," said José. "My father makes them all the time when he puts new pipes in people's houses."

"Okay," said Twanna. "Are you ready for the filings now?"

"Si," replied José. "Put them on the paper covering the shoebox now."

Twanna poured half her filings onto the paper and leaned forward to watch José, who picked up the large bar magnet and reached under the paper with it. "Watch to see what happens to the iron filings as I move the magnet around under the paper," he stated.

Both students were peering at the shoebox from opposite sides, their eyes on the same level as the filings. Just as José touched the lower right edge of the paper with the magnet, Twanna sneezed. Several of the iron filings sprayed into José's face, with a few of them entering his right eye. "Oowww!" shrieked José as he twirled from his chair, eyes buried in his hands. "Help me, please!!!"

How could this accident have been prevented? Were there any oversights that you noticed?

The Roosevelt sixth-grade class finally arrived at its destination, the old Wilson farm. As the bus rolled to a stop, Mr. J arose and addressed the class: "Please remember our purpose here today. We are visitors to these animals' homes, so do not disturb them or the plants. In science we observe, measure, and record; we don't destroy or disrupt. Let's review our lesson plans for today's environmental science."

Following a five-minute clarification of the outcomes and precautions for the activity, Mr. J answered student questions. "Now for our safety guidelines," he stated. "Are there any questions concerning the safety items on your activity page such as equipment operation, accident procedures, and the buddy system? Remember to stay with your buddy and never allow yourself to be separated from myself, Mr. P, Mrs. M, or Ms. O by more than 50 meters in this pasture area. If you need help in an emergency, please use your whistles. We adults were here earlier this morning checking out the area and found no hazards to worry about during this mapping exercise. But please be careful, just in case."

Mark and Alicia filed off the bus, confident of their purpose.

"Let's see," said Alicia. "We need to proceed 50 meters to the northeast to pick up our first marker, then 60 meters to the east for our second one. Do you have the map, compass, and whistle ready, Mark?"

"Yes, I do," replied Mark. "Put on your helmet."

As the students proceeded about 20 meters into the trees, they noticed that the terrain became more rugged and difficult to negotiate.

"See these little lines, Alicia?" remarked Mark, looking at the map. "They are the little hills we are walking over now. Another 30 meters and we should spot the first marker."

Just as they came over the next hillock, they both spotted a green plastic lid, partially hidden in the leaves.

"What is that?" asked Mark.

"I don't know. Let's check it out," replied Alicia.

As they cautiously lifted the lid, it broke into several pieces. Revealed before them was a deep hole about 1 meter in diameter. It did not appear to have a bottom, although there was water down about 2 meters.

"Let's explore it," suggested Alicia.

"No way! Let's get help!" replied Mark.

"Don't be silly," said Alicia. "We can check it out, finish our assignment and return before anyone knows. It could be our secret."

"What if that water is over your head?" persisted Mark. "How long could you stay afloat? I say we get help before some animal or another person falls into it."

"I guess you are right," agreed Alicia. "Use that whistle!"

What was the difference between the safety emphasis in this scenario and those in the first two? Could you credit the judgment simply to the older age of the students? ◆

# INTRODUCTION

The first scenario could have taken place in any activity-based science class where the teacher gives the students time to engage in different kinds of inquiry at a science learning center. The girls were able to create the volcano immediately to satisfy their natural curiosity because they knew where the materials were stored and could easily obtain them. The person who reminded them of basic safety rules, however, was not their teacher. It was their mother.

The sisters know where everything is kept in their home. When they want materials for a project, such as building a volcano, they know where to get them. This same familiarity with materials storage that children feel in their homes, including what things they are allowed to touch and those they are to avoid, should occur in the classroom. Teaching children safe science practices and instilling in them a basic safety philosophy, as emphasized in the third scenario, are important for a safe and efficient activity-based science classroom.

This chapter uses two organizing questions: *What are the foreseeable hazards associated with valued educational activities?* and *What materials are necessary for the activities?* The chapter helps you construct answers for these questions by

1. encouraging you to develop a philosophy of safe science teaching;
2. helping you understand your legal responsibilities;
3. helping you understand when and how to use safety equipment;
4. encouraging you to perform safety assessments of your classroom, lab, field site, or working space;
5. examining the tasks necessary for safe and efficient storage of equipment and materials;
6. suggesting methods for distributing, maintaining, and inventorying science materials.

# DOCUMENTED NEED FOR SCIENCE SAFETY

The *National Science Education Standards* (NSES) (National Research Council, 1996) states that students at the K–4, 5–8, and 9–12 levels should know and be able to "utilize safety procedures during scientific investigations." Within Teaching Standard D of the NSES, it is stated

> Teachers of science design and manage learning environments that provide students with the time, space, and resources needed for learning science. In doing this, teachers ensure a safe working environment.
>
> Safety is a fundamental concern in all experimental science. Teachers of science must know and apply the necessary safety regulations in the storage, use, and care of the materials used by students. They adhere to safety rules and guidelines that are established by national organizations such as the American Chemical Society [ACS] and the Occupational Safety and Health Administration [OSHA], as well as by local and state regulatory agencies. They work with the school and district to ensure implementation and use of safety guidelines for which they are

responsible, such as the presence of safety equipment and appropriate class size. Teachers also teach students how to engage safely in investigations inside and outside the classroom.

These Standards provide a blueprint for improving the teaching and learning for *all* students premised on an inquiry-based, student-centered curriculum. They also demand a greater understanding of applicable laws, codes, and professional standards for ensuring safety for students. To probe these Standards in greater detail, you may wish to review the complete document on line at *http://www.nap.edu/readingroom/books/nses*.

Reasonable and prudent judgment would dictate that informed science education professionals would follow appropriate laws, codes, and the guidelines of their profession, especially those involving the safety of minors in their charge. How many science educators, however, know the applicable tort legislation that applies to their teaching; the applicable OSHA regulations concerning Bloodborne Pathogens, Lab Standard–Chemical Hygiene Plans, or the Right-to-Know (U.S. Dept. of Labor, 1990); what safety equipment is essential according to fire or electrical codes; or what is appropriate student enrollment limits in labs according to the science teaching profession?

A 1997 study by Gerlovich raised serious doubts, however, concerning teacher understanding of these vital safety issues. Table 9.1 on page 304 provides an overview of that information. A quick review of the participant background section of the table indicates that the teachers surveyed are experienced science educators, averaging fifteen years of teaching.

The table is divided into the following sections:

- Understanding of the National Science Education Standards
- Understanding of Legal Management Issues
- Understanding of Safety Facilities, Equipment, Practices
- Understanding of Chemical Management Issues

To date, 1230 science educators from 11 states have participated in this ongoing study. Within each of the major sections in the table there are entries containing fractions. The numerator indicates the number of respondents who know this information. The denominator reflects the total number of respondents (1230).

The professionals surveyed have a very poor understanding of vital safety information. The implications are especially far reaching when considered within the context of the inquiry-based curriculum sought in the National Science Education Standards.

Within the section titled Understanding of the National Science Education Standards, only one-third of the respondents knew that OSHA set the safety standards for science settings, while less than 1 in 15 knew the appropriate class size for the Standards-based curriculum.

Within the Understanding of Legal Management Issues section, it is especially disturbing that less than 6 percent knew the Due Care duties teachers

◆ **TABLE 9.1**  **Science Teacher Understanding of Science Safety Issues**

| National Safety Study Teacher Understanding of Critical Issues | | | | | |
|---|---|---|---|---|---|

*Participant Background*

| K–6 Teacher | 7–12 Teacher | Supervisors | Professors | Other | Total Participants |
|---|---|---|---|---|---|
| 94 | 971 | 140 | 8 | 17 | 1230 |

Average Years Experience—15 years

*Understanding of the National Science Education Standards*

| Environment | OSHA | Class Size |
|---|---|---|
| 34/1230 | 407/1230 | 22/1230 |

*Understanding of Legal Management Issues*

| Tort Law | Sovereign Immunity | Save Harmless | Negligence | Due Care |
|---|---|---|---|---|
| 598/1230 | 157/1230 | 85/1230 | 137/1230 | 67/1230 |

*Understanding of Safety Facilities, Equipment, Practices*

| Lab Size | Class/Lab Size | Counter Space | Number Exits | Fume Hood | GFI |
|---|---|---|---|---|---|
| 65/1230 | 211/1230 | 139/1230 | 867/1230 | 250/1230 | 258/1230 |
| Fire Extinguisher | Safety Goggles | Fire Blanket | Placement | Enrollment | Eye Rinse Time |
| 147/1230 | 57/1230 | 281/1230 | 113/1230 | 260/1230 | 238/1230 |

*Understanding of Chemical Management Issues*

| Storage | Right-to-Know | Lab Standard | NFPA | 5.MSDS |
|---|---|---|---|---|
| 351/1230 | 81/1230 | 92/1230 | 134/1230 | 301/1230 |

*Source:* J. A. Gerlovich, "Safety Standards: An Examination of What Teachers Know and Should Know about Science Safety," *The Science Teacher,* 64 (3), (1997): 46–49.

must satisfy to prevent allegations of personal negligence as the result of a student personal injury.

Within the Understanding of Safety Facilities, Equipment, Practices section, respondents knew the number of exits necessary for a science room; however, they did not know appropriate class size recommended by NSTA. Especially disconcerting is the lack of knowledge surrounding appropriate safety equipment (GFI, fire extinguisher, goggles, fire blanket), and the placement of such items as mandated by local, state, and OSHA codes.

Within the Understanding of Chemical Management Issues section, there is a serious lack of understanding relative to chemical storage, Material Safety Data Sheets (MSDS), National Fire Protection Association (NFPA) codes, and such legislation as the Right-to-Know and Lab Standard.

Many of the issues delineated in this study are discussed, in some detail, later in this chapter.

Another study by Gerlovich, Wilson, and Parsa (1998) suggests that ignorance of safety information may be related to increasing numbers of science accidents, lawsuits, and related costs. In a pre/post assessment of teachers participating in a safety inservice program conducted by the study's authors, the participants' knowledge of safety items was very poor prior to the inservice. After participation the participants' knowledge in each of the areas identified in Table 9.1 increased substantially. In particular the area of safety management showed near-perfect understanding after the inservice.

Table 9.2 is derived from the same study by Gerlovich, Wilson, and Parsa. It shows a significant increase in the number of instances of bodily injury claims and the number of lawsuits against Iowa schools between 1990 and 1996. There was also a corresponding increase in the cost of claims for that same period. These data were filtered to reflect only claims involving science teaching settings. Are these accidents due to poor understanding of safety information and procedures?

Table 9.3 on page 306 provides an analysis of the types of accidents taking place in these Iowa settings. It is helpful for teachers to know that just over 50 percent of all science-related injuries involved chemicals. Teachers should be extra cautious when using chemicals with students. They should review the various legal standards regarding lab safety, chemicals in the workplace, and personal protective equipment requirements for which science teachers and their districts are liable. Teachers need to be knowledgeable about the chemical

**TABLE 9.2  Bodily Injury Claims/Lawsuits, Iowa School Science Settings, 1990–1996**

| Time Frame | 1990–1993 | 1993–1996 |
|---|---|---|
| *Bodily Injury Claims* | | |
| Number of Claims | 674 | 1,002 |
| Cost | $1,678,075 | $2,300,172 |
| *Lawsuits* | | |
| Number of Suits | 96 | 245 |
| Cost | $566,305 | $1,238,662 |

*Source:* J. A. Gerlovich, E. Wilson, & R. Parsa, "Safety Issues and Iowa Science Teachers," *The Journal of the Iowa Academy of Science* 105, 4(1998): 152–157.

**TABLE 9.3   Science Injury Types Reported in Iowa Schools: 1990–1996**

| Percentage of Injuries | Associated Cause | Comments |
|---|---|---|
| 55% | Chemicals | 45% chemical burns 40% eye injuries (splash/explosion) 15% inhalation |
| 20% | Cuts | Glassware, scalpels, needles, animal bites |
| 10% | Burns (nonchemical) | Bunsen burners, glassware |
| 10% | Slips and Falls | Running, horseplay, falls from chairs or stools |
| 5% | Eye Injuries | Observing eclipses |

*Source:* J. A. Gerlovich, E. Wilson, & R. Parsa, "Safety Issues and Iowa Science Teachers," *The Journal of the Iowa Academy of Science* 105 4(1998): 152–157.

they use with students. Material Safety Data Sheets (MSDS) can be invaluable in assessing chemical hazards. The use of common household materials can also lessen such hazards.

The next category in Table 9.3 indicates that about 20 percent of the accidents involved "cuts." Although most of the cuts were minor injuries, a greater concern is the legal standard that now defines blood as a "hazardous material," with specific procedures to be followed to avoid exposure to various blood-borne pathogens. Approximately equal percentages of the science-related accidents involve various types of burns and slips and falls, whereas only 5 percent involved eye injuries.

From studies such as these, it is apparent that inservice teacher understanding of critical science safety information is seriously lacking. One of the goals of this chapter is to ensure that preservice teachers have a working knowledge of science safety before they enter the profession. In addition, it is hoped that science teaching professionals will cultivate an ongoing need for safety vigilance throughout their careers.

## WHY ALL THE CONCERN OVER SAFETY?

Children are natural scientists because they are curious about everything in their physical world. Given the opportunity, they will investigate events and objects of all types and see beauty and intrigue in events that adults accept as mundane. Sometimes it is difficult for children to separate danger from fascination. The teacher's responsibility is to balance these two factors, with information from publishers, science experts, peers, and consideration of their own teaching environment (student abilities and maturities, equipment available) in order to ensure that science learning is effective yet safe.

Natural events provide effective learning opportunities for elementary students. Ice storms, tornadoes, thunderstorms, floods, the first snowfall, a gentle rain, and the changes of the seasons are all natural phenomena about which elementary students are curious. When these events happen around them, students become even more curious about their cause and thus receptive to learning what causes the events.

In order to keep students safe while attempting to construct an understanding of science concepts through hands-on science activities, the teacher must have a simple yet effective safety philosophy that guides the students. It is important to identify appropriate grade-level concepts and worthwhile explorations in order to enact an effective safety philosophy. Once those are clearly identified then the teacher must ask, "What are the foreseeable hazards associated with valued educational activities?" Ask yourself, "Would a respected peer use the same materials or activity I have selected? What adjustments might another teacher make to fit the needs of students according to their emotional, social, and academic abilities? What group size or class setting would a reasonable teacher use to make the activity effective and safe?"

You must think about any foreseeable hazards your students may encounter as they participate in your activities. Be sensitive to such issues as chemical problems about which you may have insufficient knowledge, fire hazards, potential eye injuries from sharp objects or flying projectiles, and overcrowding. If the foreseeable hazards exceed the educational value of the knowledge or experience students could gain from their direct participation in them, you have some choices to make:

1. Provide additional safety parameters, such as safety goggles, fire blankets, eyewashes, and additional supervision.
2. Limit the activity to a teacher demonstration, in which you are the only one who manipulates the equipment, and students become active observers. (In many instances this is the most logical and educationally responsible choice.)
3. Eliminate the activity entirely from the curriculum. Unless you have recently performed a detailed assessment of the entire science curriculum across grades, you might be surprised at how many duplicate activities of little value exist in science classes that may be taught primarily because of tradition (Gerlovich & Hartman, 1990).

## WHAT ARE YOUR LEGAL RESPONSIBILITIES?

Although this section focuses on tort law as it relates to science teaching, the principles and philosophy apply to all school subjects. There are several legal concepts you must be familiar with in order to understand your legal responsibilities.

## Tort

A *tort* is a wrong, or injury, that someone has committed against someone else. The injured party generally wants restitution for the injury or damages. The resolution of such conflicts between litigants (*plaintiffs* being those who bring the claim and *defendants* being those against whom the claim has been filed) generally occurs in a court, involving lawyers, a judge, possibly jurors, and witnesses, and is referred to as a *lawsuit*.

## Reasonable and Prudent Judgment

The U.S. legal system does not require educators to be superhuman in the performance of their duties. It is expected only that they be *reasonable and prudent* in their judgment when performing their duties with students. Educators need only do what reasonable persons with comparable training and experience would do in similar situations. They must ask themselves if whether their peers would endorse the activities being performed with students. Proceed with confidence only if these questions are answered affirmatively. If not, add more safety features, limit the activity to a teacher demonstration, or eliminate it entirely. As science teachers, we must attempt to anticipate reasonable hazards, eliminate them, or be confidently prepared to address them.

## Foreseeability

If you discover something amiss in your teaching environment, you should request corrections, preferably in writing, as soon as possible (see Figure 9.1). Essential items such as fire extinguishers, fire blankets, eyewashes, or safety goggles need to be obtained or repaired immediately; less important items, like nonskid floor wax, could be discussed with administrators for future correction. All known hazards and appropriate emergency measures should be explained to students as well.

The foreseeable hazards of all activities, as well as appropriate emergency reactions, should be completely explained to students *prior* to an activity. Field trip sites should be reviewed very carefully by the teacher before students arrive. Ask the owner or proprietor of the field site about any known hazards

*Prudent judgment and proper supervision fulfill most legal responsibilities.*

**FIGURE 9.1    Request for Correction of Safety Concern**

Date filed with administrator: _____

Secretary's initials: _____

**Request for Correction of Safety Concern**

Date: _____                    Room: _____

The following is a safety concern in the science area:

_____        _____
(Teacher name)                              (Signature)

CC:  Teacher, Dept. Chair

*Source:* J. Gerlovich & K. Hartman, *The Total Science Safety System: Elementary Edition,* computer software (Waukee, IA: JaKel, Inc., 1998).

or potential hazards to students. Any sensitivities to foods the class might be working with should be ascertained before the activity begins. Any phobias should be known before students are placed in potentially frightening situations. The teacher *must* know about any medical problems that students may have—for example, medication schedules, allergies, fears, and anxieties. Before ever involving students in activities, ask yourself, "What could go wrong with this activity, and am I prepared to address the problem?" If you can answer the questions affirmatively, proceed with confidence.

## Negligence

Before you can be held accountable for personal injury accidents, it must be proven that you were negligent. *Negligence* has been defined as "conduct that falls below a standard established by law or profession to protect others from harm" (School Code of Iowa, 1988). It is sometimes described as failure to exercise due care.

## Due Care

*Due care* may be defined as your duty to protect your students (School Code of Iowa, 1988). For younger or disabled students, the degree of care provided must be increased. You must remember that you are the authority in the classroom. You, or an equally qualified adult substitute, must be with students at all times, especially when the potential for injury exists. During science activities, when materials and chemicals are being manipulated, your presence is essential. If you need to leave the room during such activities, you must make certain that an equally qualified person assumes this responsibility. Due care is often summarized in three teacher duties: instruction, supervision, and maintenance (School Code of Iowa, 1988).

*Instruction.*    You must ensure that the instruction is appropriate for the physical and mental development levels of your students. Since textbooks form the

*Determine the educational value of an activity before doing it.*

basis of many science programs, you would be wise to ensure that safety is an integral and conspicuous component. Strive to select textbooks that parallel your safe science teaching philosophy.

All activities in which students are involved should be weighed for their educational value versus the hazards involved in having students perform them. If the foreseeable dangers outweigh the educational value of the activity, it must be limited to teacher demonstration, have more safety features added, or be eliminated from the science experience (Gerlovich & Hartman, 1992). As a service to teachers, newsletters are supplied by safety-conscious scientific supply companies. Many such equipment supplier newsletters include safety columns and hints, as well as more effective safety equipment ideas for young students.

*Rules* should be clearly written and explained to students. Copies of the most important rules should be posted conspicuously throughout the room. Serious consideration should be given to developing and implementing a *student safety contract* (see Figure 9.2) for students in the upper grades (4–6). The contract should identify all foreseeable hazards and appropriate actions to be taken, describe the location and proper use of safety equipment items, and explain essential rules. At this level, students should sign a contract that indicates their understanding. It is best to explain and have students initial only a couple of items each day. Teachers should collect these forms between each event and retain them for dissemination at the next safety discussion session. Teachers may wish to administer safety tests to determine the degree of student understanding.

Discipline during science activities should be fair, consistent, and firmly enforced. Safety is so important that no one should be exempt. The only exceptions should be based on a student's obvious physical or mental limitations.

**FIGURE 9.2   Student Safety Contract**

---

**Student Safety Contract**

My teacher told me, _____ , about these
                              (student name)
safety items in my science class.

1. Safety rules                                        _____

2. How to find and use these:

   (a)  Fire extinguisher                              _____

   (b)  Fire blanket                                   _____

   (c)  Goggles                                        _____

   (d)  Eyewash                                        _____

   (e)  Drench shower                                  _____

   (f)  Safety can                                     _____

   (g)  Heat sources (bunsen burner,
        alcohol lamp, microwave oven, etc.)            _____

   (h)  Electrical equipment                           _____

   (i)  Telephone or intercom                          _____

3. What to do during:

   (a)  Fire                                           _____

   (b)  Chemical splash to the body                    _____

   (c)  Eye emergency                                  _____

   (d)  Chemical spill                                 _____

   (e)  Electrical emergency                           _____

Date: _____          Teacher: _____

---

*Source:* J. Gerlovich & K. Hartman, *The Total Science Safety System: Elementary Edition,* computer software (Waukee, IA: JaKel, Inc., 1998).

Students will support teachers in their activities a great deal more if they feel that everyone is treated fairly. You may also wish to involve students in the safe science and discipline rules for the class.

You are a role model. You set the safety expectations for your class by example. Students cannot be expected to take safety seriously if you do not observe all guidelines. Be especially careful to wear safety equipment items (goggles) and observe all safety rules. Explain all safety considerations and have all safety equipment items available before beginning any activity. Safety should be something that students expect you to enforce.

Consider simulating foreseeable emergencies—for example, a student who receives a chemical splash on his clothing, face, or eyes; a classroom or clothing fire caused by science items; finding another adult to give emergency assistance; evacuating the room—and proper safety responses as part of your daily teaching. Following instruction, you might evaluate students on their proper and expeditious performances. Accent the positive; emphasize what you want students to *do.* Be careful to protect students from any hazards during the simulations.

Should an accident or incident occur, collect as much information as possible from witnesses (student and staff). An accident or incident report (see Figure 9.3 on page 312) can help focus the report should legal repercussions arise from the incident. These accounts are powerful, firsthand evidence of what actions were taken and the teacher's commitment to safety. Some states set limits on the length of time after an incident occurs wherein legal action can be taken. When this statute of limitations for legal actions passes for the incident, dispose of the materials. These reports can also be very effective learning tools when used with other classes.

◆**FIGURE 9.3    Teacher Accident/Incident Report**

1.  Staff member completing the report: _____

2.  Date of accident/incident: _____

3.  Time of the accident/incident: _____

4.  Location of the accident/incident:


5.  Staff/student(s) involved in the accident/incident:

    (a)  Staff (report attached)                    (b)  Student (report attached)

        _____                        _____

        _____                        _____

        _____                        _____

        _____                        _____

6.  Teacher description of the accident/incident:


7.  Immediate action taken to deal with the emergency:


8.  Corrective action taked to avoid a repeat of the accident/incident in the future:




_____               _____
      (Date report completed)                     (Signature of person completing report)

*Source:* J. Gerlovich & K. Hartman, *The Total Science Safety System: Elementary Edition,* computer software (Waukee, IA: JaKel, Inc., 1998).


*Supervision.*    The duty of supervision, as part of due care, can be a significant challenge. Teachers should always be in the classroom when scientific equipment or chemicals are accessible to students. The only exceptions to this rule are times of extreme emergencies or when the supervision has been delegated to another equally qualified person. Overcrowding, class size, and field trips are matters that require specific supervisory attention.

*Adult volunteers enhance due care through supervision on field trips.*

There is increasing evidence that *overcrowding* is the root cause of accidents in science settings. Supervision should increase when the danger level of the activity increases, the number of students with disabilities in the class increases, and the learning environment differs from the conventional classroom setting. Teachers must be aware of overcrowding and initiate corrections as soon as possible. The Texas Education Agency recommends at least 30 square feet of floor space for each student (including storage and teacher preparation area) in elementary school science classes.

The National Science Teachers Association (and numerous other professional science teaching organizations) recommends that the teacher-to-student ratio never exceed 1:24 during science labs and activities (National Science Teachers Association, 1983). The classroom teaching environment has a significant influence on the safety that can be provided to students. In its 1989 safety guide, the Texas Education Agency recommended two types of floor plans for teaching elementary school science that may provide a model for the nation. Emphasis was placed on safety equipment, a maximum of twenty-four students during science activities, and extensive open space leading to at least two exits. There is adequate room for students to move about without bumping into each other or equipment. Students can also be readily supervised by the teacher from any point in the room. There must be no blind spots.

For field trips, you should obtain parent or guardian release forms or waivers for all students and apprise the administration of the event (Figure 9.4 on page 314). The activity should be an integral part of the course. Teachers should use only school-sanctioned and insured vehicles. Supervision should generally be increased to one teacher or other qualified adult to ten students. It is imperative that teachers and other assisting adults preview the field site for hazards *before* students are involved. Students should be apprised of any known hazards and appropriate reactions in an emergency, such as described in this chapter's third scenario. Be careful to consider poisonous plants and plants with thorns or other irritating parts, and check for poisonous or biting animals. On the school grounds, look for broken glass, holes, drug paraphernalia, and other unexpected items.

Implement the buddy system on field trips, pairing students and holding them responsible for each other (Rakow, 1989). Buddies can apprise adults of

◆**FIGURE 9.4   Safety Considerations for Field Trips**

1. The teacher has visited the field trip site prior to involving students there.   _____
2. The activity is a well-planned part of the science course.   _____
3. The activity is appropriate for the mental and physical age of the students taking the trip.
4. Transportation is via school or school-sanctioned vehicles only.   _____
5. Clear, appropriate rules of behavior are established, and the students understand them.   _____
6. All field trip dangers are pointed out to students in advance and again when students arrive at the site.   _____
7. Students are dressed according to the demands of the environment and weather.   _____
8. Supervision is increased according to the novelty and danger inherent in the field trip environment.   _____
9. Equipment is in a proper state of repair.   _____
10. Equipment is designed for the mental and physical ages of the students using it.   _____
11. Students know how to use the equipment properly.   _____
12. If students are to be separated from the teacher at any time, prearranged meetings are planned.   _____
13. The buddy system of pairing students in teams is used to help ensure safety and mutual responsibility.   _____
14. The teacher is aware of any student medical needs (allergies, medication schedules, phobias).   _____
15. Signed parent or guardian permission forms have been received and processed.   _____
16. For extended-length field trips, appropriate medical and liability insurance policies have been obtained.   _____
17. First-aid kits appropriate for the environment are available.   _____
18. All safety procedures have been demonstrated and are understood by students.   _____
19. The teacher has talked with the landowner or proprietor concerning hazards and special points of interest before involving students at the site.   _____

*Source:* J. Gerlovich & K. Hartman, *The Total Science Safety System: Elementary Edition,* computer software (Waukee, IA: JaKel, Inc., 1998).

any problem. Of course, very young students (grades K–3) should not be separated from adult supervision at any time. The teacher should arrange for upper elementary students to meet at prearranged times and these times should be adhered to explicitly. Increase the adult supervision for young learners.

*Maintenance.*   Maintaining the educational environment is the third teacher duty. It is imperative that you attempt to foresee hazards and expedite their correction. You are not expected to be superhuman in your identification or make the repairs yourself. However, a logical, regular review of the teaching envi-

*What must a teacher do to ensure safe field trips?*

ronment is a reasonable expectation. The information available in the safety equipment and safety assessment sections of this chapter can help you with maintenance. For additional information concerning legal concept and case studies, visit the American Association of Law Librarians Web site at *http://www.aallnet.org/aallnet.web.html*.

### Federal and State Legislation

A vital state law or statute about which you should instruct students relates to eye protective equipment (safety goggles) (School Code of Iowa, 1988). You must insist that appropriate eyewear approved by the American National Standards Institute (ANSI) (School Code of Iowa, 1988) is provided to all students whenever the potential for eye injury exists. These federal equipment criteria were established to ensure minimum quality standards. You must insist that such eyewear meets ANSI standards and that you and your students wear them.

Compliance with these federal equipment standards is ensured when you see "Z87" printed on the goggle. The faceplate will not shatter, splinter, or fall backward into the face of the wearer if hit by a 1-inch ball bearing dropped from 50 inches, or by a quarter-inch ball bearing traveling at 150 feet per second. In addition, the frame will not burn. The teacher is responsible for insisting that the purchasing agent order only goggles that conform to these standards. Goggles that do not meet ANSI Z87 standards, that do not fit the students, or that have scratched faceplates, missing vent plugs, or damaged rubber moldings or headbands should not be used.

Require students to wear the goggles whenever there is the slightest chance that someone could sustain an eye injury in your classroom. Remember that injuries can happen even when students are walking about the room while others are performing science activities. Think also about injuries that could happen with such simple chemicals as salt or vinegar or with flying objects like rubber bands or balloons. Attempt to foresee such problems and act accordingly.

Most state statutes require that goggles be cleaned before students wear them. Such equipment should be stored in a relatively dust-free environment such as a box or a cabinet. (Secure a copy of your state's eye protective equipment legislation

*Safety goggles*

from the state department of education or school administration, and check for specific details.) Remember, in many states this is the law.

In addition to the eye protective equipment (goggle) legislation for your respective state, you need to investigate and, likely, comply with appropriate federal and/or state OSHA standards that directly impact on all school science instruction, such as Bloodborne Pathogens, Right-to-Know legislation, and Lab Standard–Chemical Hygiene Plan. Each of these are described briefly below, however, for additional information concerning your state, check the OSHA website at *http://www.osha.gov* or contact your state department of education for questions.

***Bloodborne Pathogens.***   On December 6, 1991, OSHA issued its final Bloodborne Pathogens Standard. It mandates engineering controls, work practices, and personal protective equipment that, in conjunction with employee training, are designed to reduce job-related risk for all employees exposed to blood. Employers must establish a written exposure control plan that identifies workers with occupational exposure to blood and other potentially infectious material and specify means to protect and educate these employees. Other requirements include hepatitis B vaccinations and applicable medical follow-up and counseling following personal exposure. The standard became effective May 30, 1992. Under 29 Code of Federal Regulations (CFR), Part 1910.1030, Subpart Z, the Department of Labor, OSHA released the 1992 Bloodborne Pathogens "Standard Summary Applicable to Schools."

> The intent of this standard summary is to offer schools an overview of the OSHA standard to eliminate or minimize occupational exposure to Hepatitis B virus (HBV), which causes hepatitis B, a serious liver disease; Human Immunodeficiency Virus (HIV), which causes Acquired Immunodeficiency Syndrome (AIDS) and other bloodborne pathogens. Based on a review of the information in the rulemaking record, OSHA has made a determination that employees face a significant health risk as the result of occupational exposure to blood and other potentially infectious materials because they may contain pathogens. OSHA further concludes that this exposure can be minimized or eliminated using a combination of engineering and work practice controls, personal protective clothing and equipment, training, medical surveillance, Hepatitis B vaccination, signs and labels and other provisions. This summary includes scope and application, definitions, exposure control, methods of compliance, Hepatitis B vaccination and post-exposure evaluation and follow-up, communication of hazards to employees, recordkeeping, and effective dates.

***Right-to-Know.***   The Occupational Safety and Health Administration (OSHA) Hazard Communication Standard, or Right-To-Know (RTK) Legislation, pertaining to hazardous chemicals in the workplace was originally drafted as Final Rule in 1983 and became effective November 25, 1985. The standard can be found in Title 29 of the Code of Federal Regulations in Subpart 2 of Part 1910 (*Federal Register*, November 25, 1989 and August 24, 1987). Many OSHA regulations have compliances based on national consensus standards from such organizations as the American National Standards Institute (ANSI), National Fire Protection Association (NFPA), and the Department of Transportation (DOT).

All privately financed educational institutions are covered by the federal standard as well as the Right-to-Know laws in force in their respective states. Publicly funded schools must comply with their respective state government statutes. All RTK legislation is designed to help employees recognize and eliminate the dangers associated with hazardous materials in their workplace.

The legislation requires that a *written program* be developed and that all affected employees know its contents. The details of such legislation will vary from state to state. Check with your Department of Education, federal (Chemical Emergency Procedures and Right-to-Know questions 1-800-424-9346) or state OSHA office, or Department of Labor. The program need not be detailed; however, it must include the following items:

1. Written hazard assessment procedures
2. Material safety data sheets (MSDSs) for all hazardous chemicals
3. Labels and warnings
4. Employee training

*Laboratory Standard—Chemical Hygiene Plan.*   As of January 31, 1991, laboratories engaged in activities that are encompassed within the definition of "laboratory use" must have in place a written Chemical Hygiene Plan (CHP) outlining how the facility will comply. This is according to OSHA Occupational Exposures to Hazardous Chemicals in Laboratories Chemical Hygiene Plan, (29 CFR, 1910.1450). This OSHA standard applies to all employers engaged in the laboratory use of chemicals. "Laboratory use" means

> chemicals are manipulated on a laboratory scale where the chemicals are handled in containers designed to be safely and easily manipulated by one person; multiple chemical procedures are used; procedures are not of a production process; protective laboratory equipment and practices are in common use to minimize employee exposure.

The plan requires that employers, *including schools,* develop a comprehensive plan for identifying and dealing with chemical hazards. The plan must include all employees who could be exposed to these chemicals and it must be updated annually.

## SAFETY EQUIPMENT

Certain safety equipment items are essential when teaching science activities. You should be confident that such items are immediately accessible when needed, that you and students can operate them, and that the items are appropriate for your students. Students should also be taught proper operation and location of all safety equipment items they might need to use, including fire extinguishers, fire blankets, eyewashes, safety goggles, and a telephone or intercom, if available. You might need duplicate safety items in more than one location in the room. Every student should have a set of goggles during science activities when eye protection is needed.

### Electrical Equipment

Whenever possible, hot plates with on-off indicator lights should replace open flames. This simple change could eliminate many fire situations from science rooms. You should not have to use extension cords for hot plates, since the room should have sufficient electrical outlets. Extension cords on the floor create tripping hazards unless they are in cord protectors. Do not allow cords to be draped across desks or other work areas in order to prevent students from inadvertently upsetting apparatus. Electrical outlet caps should be in place when the outlets are not in use. In primary grades, outlets should be covered at all times so students cannot stick metal items in the plug holes, which could cause electrocution or burns.

*Alcohol lamp*

### Heating Equipment

If open flames are periodically necessary, be certain that emergency fire equipment is functioning properly and is immediately available. If alcohol lamps, sterno cans, or candles must be used, place them in pie pans filled with damp sand. Should a spill occur, the pie pan will prevent flaming liquids from spreading to clothing, tables, and other items. Alcohol looks like water; be sure to keep it off items where it might be treated like water. If you put alcohol in lamps, add a small amount of table salt so that the flame burns a bright orange color. Large quantities (½ liter or more) of alcohol or other flammable liquids should never be brought into the room, and students should never have access to quantities of these liquids.

*Safety can*

### Flammable Liquid Storage

If you are storing flammable liquids, such as alcohol, do so only in small quantities in the manufacturer's original container or in an approved safety can. A safety can is made of heavy-gauge steel or polyethylene. It has a spring-loaded lid to prevent spilling and to vent during vapor expansion caused by a heat source. It also has a flame arrester or heat sump in the throat of the spout to help prevent explosions.

### Loose Clothing and Long Hair

Loose clothing (especially sweaters) and long hair should be restricted when students are working with open flames. This seems obvious, yet clothing and hair commonly cause accidents. Be careful to pull long hair back so that it does not hang down over the flame, and restrict loose clothing by pushing up sleeves and securing them with pins or elastic (nonrestricting rubber bands) to keep clothing from falling into open flames.

### Fire Blankets

Fire blankets should be of the proper type and size and in the proper location.

They should not be so large that students could not use them in an emergency. Check to be certain that they are placed in conspicuous locations and easily retrievable by all students and staff, including those with disabilities. Unless otherwise recommended by your fire marshal, these blankets should be made of wool. Fire blanket display and storage containers should be carefully checked for proper function. Be sure to eliminate containers with rusted hinges and latches, blankets still stored in plastic wrappers, and blankets made with asbestos fiber. Six-foot vertical standing fire blanket tubes should be avoided since they can result in facial burns. Do not attempt to extinguish torso fires by wrapping a student in the fire blanket. Because of the chimney effect, heat is pushed across the student's face, causing facial burns. The stop-drop-and-roll procedure endorsed by fire departments appears to be most effective at extinguishing body fires and presents the fewest drawbacks.

*Fire blanket*

### Fire Extinguishers

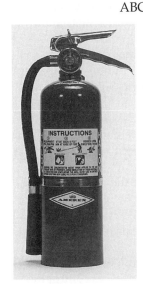

ABC triclass fire extinguishers are usually preferred by fire departments because they can extinguish most foreseeable fires, such as fires from paper products, electrical items, and grease, that are likely to happen in elementary science. In settings where microcomputers are used regularly, it might be wise to investigate halon extinguisher types. These have been used in aviation for years because their fire-extinguishing chemicals do not foul contacts as dry chemical types will in delicate electronic navigation, communications equipment, and computers. Halon has also been preferred over carbon dioxide for extinguishing fires within electronic equipment, such as computers, because they do not cause the cold thermal shock to sensitive electronic microcircuits. Teachers should confirm such suggestions with their local or state fire marshal. The major disadvantage to halon is its harmful effect on the earth's ozone layer. Since such small quantities of this ingredient are in the halon and such emergency tools are used so infrequently, we believe that the benefits outweigh the drawbacks.

It is a good idea to have fire department personnel come into your classroom to demonstrate appropriate fire procedures and equipment to students. You should be confident and comfortable in using fire equipment items. You should also establish the habit of checking the pressure

*Fire extinguisher*

valve on fire extinguishers in or near your room to ensure that they are still adequately pressurized. It would also be wise for students to heft extinguishers, unfold and use a fire blanket, and rehearse foreseeable emergencies involving fire.

### Eyewash and Shower

It is recommended that 15 minutes (2.5 gallons per minute) of aerated, tempered (60–90 degrees Fahrenheit), running water be deliverable from an eyewash to flush the eyes of a person who has suffered a chemical splash. At the elementary and middle school level, eye irritants could include salt, vinegar, sand, alcohol, and other chemicals. You should explore the installation of the fountain fixture type eyewash station (Sargent-Welch Scientific Company). It is not expensive ($60–70) and is easy to install by screwing it into an existing gooseneck faucet. The fixture allows the plumbing to be used as both an eyewash and a faucet simply by pushing a diverter valve. Should traffic patterns or room designs change, fountain fixtures can be moved to other faucets easily. On a temporary basis, you can stretch a piece of surgical tubing over a gooseneck faucet in order to deliver aerated, cool, running water to the eyes of a chemical splash victim. In the event of chemical spills on other and/or larger parts of the body, drench showers are recommended. Again, it is critical that such equipment be easily accessible to all staff and students. Be certain that the hot water faucet handle has been removed from any sink eyewash to prevent accidental burns that could be caused by hot water.

Eyewash station

Bottled water stations are not recommended because they can become contaminated, and they cannot deliver 15 minutes of aerated running water. They should be used only when there is no alternative, such as in field settings, and where you maintain strict control of them.

Critical safety equipment such as fire blankets, fire extinguishers, eyewashes, and drench showers should be located within thirty steps or 15 seconds of any location in the science room. These vital equipment items should be checked for proper operation every three to six months.

Teachers who work with chemicals must understand the properties, hazards, and appropriate emergency procedures to follow in the event of an accident. Material Safety Data Sheets (MSDS) and the Merck Index (Budavari et al., 1989) provide such comprehensive information from chemical manufacturers. They identify the material, listing hazardous ingredients, physical and chemical characteristics, fire and explosion hazards, reactivity with other substances, health hazards, precautions for safe handling and use, as well as control measures. You can secure additional information concerning science equipment and material and MSDS's directly from manufacturers or suppliers such as VWR Sargent Welch. Check for them on their Web site at *http://www.sargentwelch.com*.

We also recommend that you secure a copy of *School Science Laboratories: A Guide to Some Hazardous Chemicals* (1984) or *The Total Science Safety System* (Gerlovich & Hartman, 1992). Both encompass chemical management systems. Check the Additional Readings section of this chapter for addresses.

## PERFORMING SAFETY ASSESSMENTS

You must be prepared to assess the safety situation within your teaching environment (classroom or field trips) regularly and accurately. The best way to accomplish this task is to develop and use safety software checklists regularly. The Total Science Safety System–Elementary (Gerlovich & Hartman, 1990) is available in Macintosh and IBM formats. This software will help you develop a customized assessment system that fits your academic and facility needs. In addition, you can create complete and easily accessible records that can be updated regularly and printed as needed. These records could provide a defense in the case of an unforeseeable accident or injury lawsuit.

Elementary and middle school science safety checklists should include but not be limited to the components outlined in Figure 9.5 on page 322. The assessments should be performed every semester in order to ensure that safety items are identified and corrected in a timely fashion.

Any safety problems should be corrected as soon as practical. This is best accomplished by informing the administration of the problem in writing. State the facts of the problem without explanation. Request an answer within ten days.

The Total Science Safety System (Gerlovich & Hartman, 1992) provides checklists concerning life, earth, and physical science activities and procedures, and forms such as a student safety contract, an accident/incident report, and request for safety correction.

## WHAT MATERIALS ARE NECESSARY FOR THE ACTIVITIES?

As the foreseeable hazards are addressed, you should determine materials that are needed for the activity. Identify readily available items, and determine where any additional items can be obtained. A good suggestion is to divide the remaining items into categories: items to be purchased through a scientific supplier, items that can be purchased locally through a discount or hardware store, and items that can be made for little or no cost from recycled materials.

A Science Activity Planner form (Figure 9.6 on page 323) will facilitate your ordering needs. Fill out this sheet at least six weeks before you teach the lesson to allow time for vendor shipping and/or the steps your order must go through for approval of purchase and appropriation of funds in your school district. Figure 9.7 on page 323 provides an example of how this form can be used.

◄ **FIGURE 9.5   Science Safety Checklist**

This listing is only representative of teachers' safety duties.  Check off these items you are well informed about or prepared for and ask your instructor for more information about the remaining items.

| Item | Well Prepared or Informed | Item | Well Prepared or Informed |
|------|---------------------------|------|---------------------------|
| Teachers understand their teaching duties of | | Teachers ensure that all safety equipment is functioning and available | _____ |
| Instruction | _____ | Teachers ensure that all science equipment is of the right size and is appropriate for their students | _____ |
| Supervision | _____ | | |
| Maintenance of the environment, equipment | _____ | Teachers ensure that students know how to use safety and other science equipment items | _____ |
| Teachers attempt to foresee hazards and correct them | _____ | Teachers ensure that the following fire safety equipment is available whenever they are using open flames: | |
| Teachers' activities are consistent with those recommended by their textbooks, professional organizations, state agencies, federal standards | _____ | Fire blanket | _____ |
| | | Fire extinguisher | _____ |
| Teachers use student safety contracts with upper elementary students | _____ | Fire alarm | _____ |
| Teachers use only ANSI Z87 approved safety goggles | _____ | Teachers ensure that loose clothing and long hair are confined when students are using open flames | _____ |
| Teachers insist that students wear safety goggles whenever the potential for an eye injury exists | _____ | Teachers ensure that an eyewash is available and functioning whenever the potential for an eye injury existis | _____ |
| Teachers ensure that classes are not overcrowded (fewer than twenty-four students per teacher) | _____ | Teachers use only chemicals for which they have MSDS sheets that they have reviewed for hazards. | _____ |
| Teachers ensure that field trips are not overcrowded (fewer than ten students per adult) | _____ | Teachers ensure that extension cords are used only when absolutely necessary, and then only grounded types | _____ |
| Teachers review the field trip site before taking students | _____ | Teachers ensure that all electrical outlets are capped when not in use | _____ |
| Teachers use the buddy system on field trips | _____ | | |

*Source:* J. Gerlovich & K. Hartman, *The Total Science Safety System: Elementary Edition,* computer software (Waukee, IA: JaKel, Inc., 1998).

### *Items Purchased Through a Scientific Supplier*

Microscopes, slides, cover slips, thermometers, magnets, and electrical bulbs are the typical kinds of materials supplied by many reputable science equipment vendors. Science teachers in your school may already have suppliers they regularly deal with. Talk with fellow teachers about companies they have used in the past. If you are uncertain, request supply catalogs from companies.

Do not be quick to order from the vendor. Be a wise shopper, and compare prices and quality. Ask questions of others who may have previously ordered

**FIGURE 9.6    Form for Science Activity Planner**

Concept to be taught: _____

_____

Material needs: _____

_____

Items available through school inventory: _____

_____

Items available at no cost/recycle: _____

_____

**Scientific supplier** (indicate vendor name, catalogue number, description, number needed, cost per unit, total cost):

**Local store** (indicate store name and exact cost):

**FIGURE 9.7    Science Activity Planner Example**

**Concept to be taught:** The circular path electrons follow is called a *circuit*.

**Material needs:** *For each student:* Battery, flashlight bulb, insulated copper wire, switch, bulb socket, cardboard tube (toilet paper tube), paper clip, two brass fasteners, plastic cap from a gallon milk container or a 35mm film can.

**Items available through:**

| | |
|---|---|
| **School inventory** | Bulbs, switches, wire |
| **No cost/recycle** | Cardboard tubes, milk caps, film canister caps |
| **Scientific supplier** | Delta Supply, Nashua, New Hampshire |
| | 57–020–9769, Bucket of batteries, 30, $29.95, $29.95 |
| | 57–020–5644, Bulb sockets, 30, $4.85/pkg. of 6, $24.25 |
| **Local store** | John's Dollar Store on Main Street |
| | 1 box of paper clips, 79¢ |
| | 2 boxes of brass fasteners, $1.45 |

*A variety of materials is necessary for effective science instruction.*

materials from a particular vendor. "How good is their service? Are they willing to meet needs quickly or slow in processing orders? What type of return policy do they have? Are they willing to take a purchase order or do they need to be paid up front?" A complete listing of science vendors, updated yearly, is available from the National Science Teachers Association.

Does your current textbook publisher supply prepackaged kits that go along with their activities? If so, will it be necessary to replenish materials in those kits? Is there a specific supplier you should order those kits from? If your answers to these questions are yes, then determine which items need to be replaced and if it is possible to replace only the used items or necessary to order a new kit. You may often come across prepackaged general science kits, such as one that supplies all materials you will need to do a unit on electricity. Under both circumstances, you must determine your needs. Will you use all of the materials provided in the kit? Will it be less expensive to order the items individually?

Carefully examine the supply catalogs. You may spot items that could enhance a lesson—an item you did not even think of in your original list of materials. Perhaps you found the item in two different catalogs, each at a different price. As you gain experience in ordering, you will find that companies differ in prices on equivalent items. If you are placing a big order with one company, it is usually more economical to purchase the higher-priced item from it along with the rest of your order. The money you may save on the price of the item with a different vendor could be spent on shipping charges.

The task of ordering supplies with school money may appear overwhelming. But if you follow a few easy steps, the work is painless. First, plan ahead. Avoid waiting until the last minute to order supplies. Often district paperwork or supply availability may delay shipment. Live plant or animal specimens can be ordered several months in advance with an indication of when you want them shipped. Once you have determined what items you will need and from which suppliers, you probably will have to obtain a purchase order. Check with the principal or school district treasurer about the proper procedure. Most often this involves filling out the purchase order completely. *Completely* means not only names of items but catalog numbers, quantities, prices, shipping charges, complete name, address, and phone and/or fax number of vendor. Remember that you need only one purchase order per vendor. Once it is completed, you will need to obtain the authorized signatures before you can mail it. If the purchase order form has duplicates, mail the original to the vendor. If it is a single copy, make a copy for the administration and one for yourself.

If you phone in the order, be sure to provide the vendor with all information included on the purchase order, especially the purchase order number. After the initial order is placed, it is customary to write on the purchase order

*Local restaurants, grocery stores, or discount stores are usually willing to donate items such as paper cups, containers, or straws to meet your science activity needs.*

the date and time the order was phoned in. You may be required to send the vendor a copy of that purchase order. If so, make sure to write on the purchase order, "This is a copy of a phone order."

### Items Purchased Locally

Consumable items—paper cups, bags, straws—are some of the common items purchased from local vendors. If you teach in a community that is very supportive of its local schools, you may be able to get donations of consumable items from local restaurants, grocery stores, or discount stores. Even the local lumber yard may be willing to supply a class with yard or meter sticks or scrap lumber.

Discount stores that specialize in overruns are an excellent source for science supplies. As you walk up and down the aisles, scan the shelves thinking about science concepts you could teach with various items. You may be surprised at what you come up with. Simple toys like yo-yos, ball and jacks, paddle balls, and rubber balls can be used to teach a variety of scientific concepts. Paper clips, masking tape, batteries, or wire can start you on the way to a terrific electricity unit. Inexpensive bubble gums or chocolate chip cookies can lead to exciting lessons that focus on the scientific method. Never underestimate the science possibilities in a discount store.

Local stores may already have agreements with your school district, such as charge accounts or cash credit accounts. Check with the school district treasurer. You may be able to charge the items at those stores. Other stores may take purchase orders. Occasionally you may have to provide your own money. If this is the case, find out the procedure for reimbursement in your school. Does the principal have a fund from which you can immediately be reimbursed upon turning in your receipt? Is a receipt necessary? Do you need a petty cash voucher from the school before you make a purchase? What kind of information does the vendor need to supply on that voucher? Do you need to supply the vendor with a tax-exempt number from the school so that you are not charged sales tax? Ask all of these questions *before* you go out and spend your own money. You do not want to find out after the fact that since you did not complete the proper paper trail, you will not be reimbursed.

### Items Made from Recycled Materials

You've been caught again rummaging through the bin at the local recycling center. Embarrassed? There is no need to be when it's done in the name of science! What was it this time? Looking for cans to paint black for a unit on heat? Was it a plastic soda bottle to make another Cartesian diver? Do you need various size jars for a sound unit? Whatever the science topic, usually one or two items can be found in a recycling bin. Of course, you can avoid those embarrassing moments by encouraging your students to bring in materials they ordinarily throw away. Setting up a recycling area in your classroom will provide a quick source for those necessary items and teach students the importance of recycling.

In the scenario at the beginning of this chapter, Celeste needed a tuna can so she went to the area in her home where recyclables were stored; thus she did not have to hold off creating the volcano for lack of a tuna can. Cans are not the only useful recyclable item. Styrofoam plates from prepackaged meats are useful in many activities. They make great placemats for messy activities that involve liquids. Styrofoam egg cartons can be turned into charcoal crystal gardens in no time, or they can be used to stack small items like rock collections. Toilet paper and paper towel tubes can be used in making flashlights, and aluminum pie plates are useful for heating water. Plastic containers with lids, such as the ones that food comes in at the grocery store, can be used for storage. Your imagination is your only limit when it comes to deciding what to do with recycled materials.

### Live Items

**Plants.**  Plants should be kept in areas where they can thrive, be readily viewed, and be protected. Be careful to study only plants about which you are knowledgeable. Do not use plants that present hazards from oils (poison ivy, poison oak, poison sumac, poinsettia, and other local plants) or hazards from saps (oleander, stinging nettle, and other local plants). In addition, no plants that are poisonous if eaten should be accessible to students, including those shown in Table 9.4.

**Animals.**  Whenever animals are to be used in science activities with students, it is imperative that care be exercised to protect both the animals and the

**TABLE 9.4    Plants That Are Harmful If Eaten**

| | | | |
|---|---|---|---|
| Some fungi (many mushrooms) | English ivy | Lily-of-the-Valley | Rhubarb |
| Aconite | False Hellebore | Mayapple | Scotch Broom |
| Azalea | Four-O'clock | Milkweed | Skunk Cabbage |
| Buckeye | Foxglove | Mistletoe | Sumac |
| Belladonna | Herbane | Morning Glory | Sweet Pea |
| Bloodroot | Holly | Mountain Laurel | Tansy |
| Buttercup | Hyacinth | Nightshade | Tomato |
| Caladium | Hydrangea | Oleander | Virginia Creeper |
| Castor Bean | Indian Tobacco | Philodendron | Wild Tobacco |
| China Berry | Iris | Poinsettia | Wild Tomato |
| Croton | Jack-in-the-Pulpit | Poison Oak | Wisteria |
| Daffodil (bulb) | Japanese Yew | Pokeweed | Yellow Jasmine |
| Dieffenbachia | Jimson Weed | Potato (sprouts) | |
| Elderberry | Jonquil (bulb) | Privet | |
| | Lantana | Rhododendron | |

*Source:* J. Gerlovich, & K. Hartman, *The Total Science Safety System: Elementary Edition,* computer software (Waukee, IA: JaKel, Inc., 1998).

students. It is obvious that animals stimulate learning in many life science and biology classes. They can, however, present some unique hazards to students. Teachers should anticipate such hazards as much as possible so that neither students or animals are injured. Be careful, for instance, not to allow animals to be handled when they are eating.

Do not allow dead animals in the room, as the exact cause of death may not be determinable. Many warm blooded animals carry and transmit diseases to humans through ticks, mites, and fleas. Be certain that adequately sized and clean cages are provided to all animals. Cages should be kept locked and in safe, comfortable settings. Since most supply houses are required to quarantine animals and check them for disease before sale, it would be wise to obtain study animals only from these dealers. If any are purchased locally, check for general health of all animals before purchase.

Heavy gloves should be used for the handling of animals that might bite.

Students should wash their hands immediately and thoroughly when finished working with animals; this will help prevent students from inadvertently transmitting germs. If an animal dies unexpectedly, have it examined by a local veterinarian. This is cheap insurance in helping prevent disease complications.

Guidelines on the use of live animals in the classroom are available from the National Association of Biology Teachers (NABT). They are well developed and provide the teacher with more depth of understanding in deciding what animals to bring into their classroom and under what conditions. The guidelines can be found on the NABT Web site at *http://www.nabt.org*. For additional information concerning the responsible use of animals in the classroom, you may want to check the National Science Teachers Association Handbook (NSTA, 1996) or their Web site at *http://www.nsta.org/handbook/animals.html*.

### Safety/First Aid Kits

For most elementary programs, a common *Science Safety Kit* should be compiled that addresses all common, foreseeable emergencies. It can then be moved from room to room, within the building, and be used wherever hands-on, inquiry-based science activities are being undertaken by the students. The kit outlined in Figure 9.8 represents the basic necessities.

## STORAGE

### Central or Classroom Storage Access

The biggest task is over—or so you think. The materials have been ordered and are beginning to arrive. So where do they go? Does your school have a central storage area for science materials? Are the materials you ordered solely for your classroom use, or will you be sharing them with other teachers? Who will be allowed access to the materials? Do you have space in your classroom to store materials? Before you begin stocking your classroom shelves, find the answers to these questions.

### ◆FIGURE 9.8    Science Safety/First-Aid Kit

1. ANSI Z87–approved eye protective equipment (24 sets = 1 per student)
2. Alcohol pads, or other appropriate sterilizing agent, for cleaning eye protective equipment
3. Fountain fixture or other appropriate eye-rinse station
4. An approved ABC tri-class fire extinguisher
5. An approved fire-retardant wool fire blanket
6. Surgical mask for addressing bodily fluid splashes
7. Rubber gloves for addressing bodily fluid splashes
8. Red biohazard bag for disposing of materials soiled with bodily fluids
9. Ground fault interrupter (GFI) on electrical outlets near faucets
10. Electrical outlet caps—for use when outlets are not being used
11. Surgical bandages, surgical gauze, hypoallergenic tape
12. Electrical circuit analyzer to check for safe, functioning electrical outlets
13. Emergency response telephone numbers (poison control center, hospital, fire department, front office, nurse, etc.)
14. Sealable plastic bags for disposal of materials
15. Paper towels and kitty litter for absorbing spills
16. Lysol and/or bleach/water solution (10 percent bleach/90 percent water) for sterilizing hard surfaces
17. NFPA chemicals hazard labels
18. MSDS's for hazardous chemicals
19. Safety signs identifying strategic safety equipment

*Source:* J. Gerlovich & K. Hartman, *The Total Science Safety System: Elementary Edition,* computer software (Waukee, IA: JaKel, Inc., 1998).

*Central Storage Area.*    Some schools designate one room or area in the school to keep all science materials. If this is the case at your school, find out who is responsible for maintaining that area. Careful inventory should be maintained of the items stored there. It is best if one person is responsible for keeping the inventory current. Teachers who borrow materials should be held responsible for their return. One person should have the authority to request the return of borrowed materials after a reasonable time period. Sign-out sheets (see Figure 9.9 on page 330) should be completed by any staff member who uses materials from the central storage.

The teachers should determine who will have access to the central storage area:

- Will only science teachers be allowed to use it?
- Will other teachers have access?
- Will students be allowed to borrow items from central storage?
- Who will be responsible for disseminating the materials? Will it be done on an honor system?

**◀FIGURE 9.9   Science Equipment Checkout Form**

---

**Science Equipment Checkout form**

Name: _____

Grade and/or subject area: _____

Room number: _____

Date of checkout:                    Expected date of return:

_____             _____

Items borrowed:

_____

_____

_____

Signature: _____

---

These questions may appear trivial, but once you count on items for a particular activity only to find that someone has borrowed them without signing them out, you will not be too happy. Often it becomes a wild-goose chase to find out who used the materials last. If the search comes up short, you may end up omitting a valuable lesson for lack of supplies. Some ground rules can avoid any unnecessary searches or hard feelings.

*Classroom Storage.*   If you store materials in your classroom, plan where the materials will be located. The first consideration is who will have access to those materials. Will the students be allowed access to everything, or will safety reasons prohibit total access? Where can you store materials that you consider dangerous to students? Ideally any hazardous materials should be stored in locked cabinets.

Think about the storage of live specimens. If plants are brought into the classroom, is an area available near windows to facilitate plant growth? Is shelf space available near a window, or will you have to appropriate a table or bookshelf to set up near a window? Can artificial lights be used on the plant? If window space is minimal, where will this designated artificial light be? Should the students have access to these plants? Do they present any potential harm to the students if ingested?

If you know that students will need access to certain materials, arrange materials so that they are on shelves or in cabinets within easy reach. If there are certain materials, such as chemicals or cleaners, that need to be out of the stu-

*Proper materials storage makes preparation and replacement easier.*

dents' reach, a locked cabinet or cupboard is a necessity. Plans should be made to make shelves or cabinets if these do not exist in your classroom. Rather than looking at your classroom negatively and simply deciding that there is no place to put anything, think creatively. Could an unused corner make an ideal storage area? Could you get a local business to donate some unused bookshelves or storage cabinets? Could the school's maintenance personnel make some shorter shelf units for student access? Try to have these problems solved before the materials arrive.

Not all items will be stored. For instance, if you have a learning center that constantly requires the use of a balance, leave the balance out. Other activity areas may be set up where materials are always left out. The students should know that they are free to move items from one center to another. For example, going back to the first scenario, if Celeste and Sarah were working on their volcano at school in the science activity center and realized that they needed red food coloring, which was always out at the food center, they could go over and get the food coloring without having to ask for permission to move it from one center to the next.

Freedom to move materials creates a learning environment that is adaptable to the students' needs. To avoid creating an inventory nightmare, establish some simple task assignments. Most children like to be useful and help the teacher. In the primary grades, the teacher can create a poster for each center with a picture of the necessary items. Older students can have a written supply list for each center. Students can be assigned to the different centers on a rotating basis and be responsible for making sure that at the end of the school day the items for their assigned center are in place. When consumable items are needed, the students should write them on a master list for the teacher, indicating which items are needed at each learning center. The teacher can then use this list to obtain the materials, then give the items to the student responsible for that center to put in their proper place. Gentle reminders to students about returning items to the place where they found them will facilitate the task of taking inventory.

### Storing and Dispensing Materials

No matter where materials are stored, you will need to decide how to store them. Will they be arranged according to units, such as electricity, weather, and simple machines, or will the items be stored separately? Once you make this decision, choose from among numerous ways to arrange the items, from shelves to shoeboxes to plastic storage bins. Table 9.5 identifies the advantages and disadvantages of several storage possibilities.

Whether items are kept in a central storage area (see Figure 9.10 on page 334) or in the classroom, you still need to think about how the students will collect them for a particular activity. When items are stored in a central location, you may want to collect the materials at least a day ahead of time to make sure everything needed for a given activity is still available. Decide how many of what item you will need. Once the items are in the classroom, appoint students to arrange the materials for the various working groups.

In a safe and efficient activity-based science classroom, the teacher does not have to do all of the advance work for a particular science activity. The teacher can appoint responsible students to collect the science materials. A simple way to disseminate the materials is to have a materials list posted for the activity, assign particular students to gather materials, and provide those students with buckets or plastic bins to put the collected materials in for that activity. Each materials manager for the day should be responsible for collecting the correct number of items for his or her group to do the activity and be responsible for counting the materials at the end of the lesson, collecting them in the bucket, and returning them to their proper place.

The teacher could appoint one or two students to count the items in the buckets, making sure everything is returned after use. The teacher can put the used materials back in their proper storage areas in the classroom or assign students to help with that task. If the materials go back to a central storage area,

**TABLE 9.5   Materials Storage**

| Materials Stored | Advantages | Disadvantages |
| --- | --- | --- |
| As units | All material together<br>Can present lesson at any time without rummaging through shelves for necessary materials | Question of who is responsible for replacing consumable items<br>Scarce resources cause unit to be picked apart and used for other activities |
| Individually | Ideal storage in schools where resources are scarce<br>Works well when materials are centrally stored, easier to collect | Time needed to pull several items together for each teaching unit<br>Additional storage space necessary to store individual items in classroom |
| On shelves | Items can be shelved alphabetically for quick and easy retrieval<br>Efficient method for storing glassware and large items | Difficult to determine where one letter ends and the next begins<br>Difficult to store items in multiple quantities<br>With multiple users, need to rearrange shelves frequently |
| In plastic bags | Sealable bags are ideal for small items<br>Can be labeled with permanent markers<br>Available in a variety of sizes to accommodate various sized materials | If seal not made, items fall out and get lost<br>With extended use, labeling wears off<br>Tear with frequent use |
| In shoeboxes or cardboard boxes | Inexpensive way to store multiple items like thermometers, magnets, and marbles<br>Easily labeled and can be covered with an adhesive plastic for prolonged use<br>An ideal size for storing on shelves | Since opaque, necessary to open to determine contents<br>Even covered, eventually wear out |
| In plastic storage bins | Available in a variety of shapes and sizes<br>Clear so items stored are visible<br>Can be labeled with permanent markers<br>Many guaranteed to last at least five years | Better-made containers are costly<br>Lids crack on less expensive containers if heavy things are stacked on top |
| Using color coding | Ideal for identifying hazardous materials by using orange safety stickers<br>Identify quickly consumed items with one color, facilitates reordering needs | Advantages lost if all teachers do not understand or remember color codes<br>If color code key not posted, difficult to locate material |

**FIGURE 9.10    Central Storage Area Design**

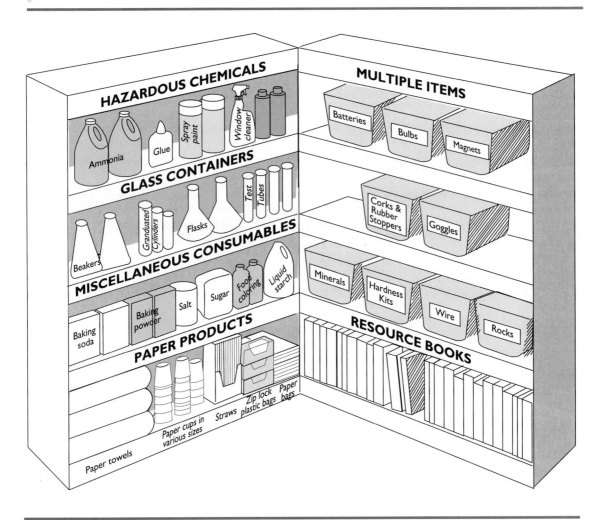

the teacher should make sure they are returned to their proper place as soon as possible. Other teachers may be counting on the use of those materials.

Keep safety concerns in mind when returning used materials. Were hazardous materials used during the activity? (Any material labeled toxic, ignitable, corrosive, or reactive should be considered hazardous.) Many common household items used at the elementary level in science activities could fall into these categories—such items as bleach or ammonia, carpet shampoos, window cleaner, paints, and glues. Does your school have an appropriate system to handle disposal of these wastes? Which materials could be recycled? What procedures should be followed to dispose of used materials? Remember that hazardous waste improperly handled can pollute drinking supplies, poison humans, or contaminate soil and air. The teacher should be responsible for disposing of used hazardous materials. If you are uncertain about disposing of a particular item, check with the local fire marshal or local office of the Environmental Protection Agency. These agencies will be able to instruct you on proper disposal. Many local fire departments are equipped to handle low-level toxic waste. All high schools should have a plan in place for handling waste from the chemistry classes. Check to see if your district has one. If it does not, work with local agencies to develop a safe and reliable disposal system.

# ROOM ARRANGEMENT

Carefully planned lessons and ample supplies are not enough to carry off a successful inquiry-based science activity. The physical arrangement of the classroom is an important consideration. Barriers such as classroom size, traffic patterns, blind spots, poles, and walls will require a teacher to be creative about utilizing the available space.

Before you begin moving furniture around, draw a scale floor plan of your classroom (see Figure 9.11 on page 336). Ask yourself the following questions when deciding how to arrange the classroom:

- What is the best way to utilize the space I have available?
- What kinds of activities will my students be involved in?
- What kinds of materials will be used?
- What type of furniture do I have in my classroom?
- Will I need any additional furniture, or should I eliminate some of the furniture that is already in there?
- What kind of flooring does the classroom have? Is it appropriate for the activities my students will be engaged in?
- Where are the entrances and exits in this classroom?
- Where are the electrical outlets?
- What kind of traffic patterns do I wish to develop?
- What are the potential hazards with the arrangement I have in mind?

The suggestions that follow are designed to help you arrange your classroom to maximize your students' science experiences while allowing you to maintain flexibility to accommodate the teaching of other subject areas.

## Large-Group Science Activities

Flat surfaces offer the best means of engaging in science activities when working with an entire class. If you are in a classroom with tilted desk tops, you will need to be creative; child-sized tables are one alternative. Another is to designate space on the floor for children to participate in science activities.

◆ **FIGURE 9.11   Classroom Floor Plan**

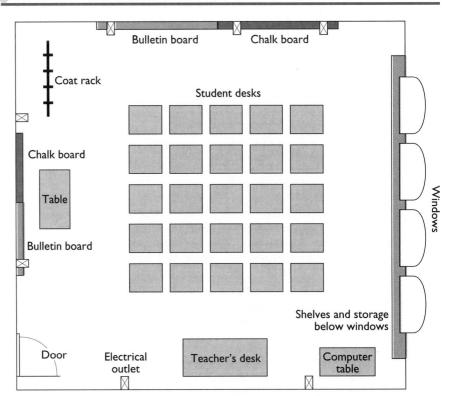

Divide the class into small working groups of three or four students each. Current recommendations are that elementary school classrooms should provide at least 30 square feet of space for each student and have no more than twenty-four students for labs and activities. Although elementary science classes are not laboratory based, if all students are to have sufficient feedback and guidance in science projects, twenty-four students is a manageable number. While the physical constraints of your classroom may not allow you this much area or your class size puts you beyond the twenty-four-student limit, whenever possible optimum space should be allocated and ideal class size should be maintained.

Whether the students are working at small tables, several flat-topped desks pushed together to make a larger working area, or on the floor, consider the type of flooring in the classroom. A nonslip tile floor is best but not a necessity. Carefully taping down an inexpensive vinyl floor remnant in the designated science area will save a carpet from messy spills and facilitate clean-up.

Create an area where you can collect materials for science activities before the class uses them. This place should also function as an area where science

## WHAT RESEARCH SAYS

### Class Size and Science Achievement

First, small classes are supported in primary grades. Kindergarten, first, second, and third grade classes should be as small as economically feasible. If cost were not an issue, the limiting factor to reducing class size . . . seems to be the social value of cooperation among very young children.

Second, . . . it seems evident that these changes should be accompanied by research-based changes in teaching methods that take advantage of these changes. One prominent study concludes that reducing class size and proportionally increasing educational expenses by as much as 50 percent might be necessary to increase the student's achievement by a mere 10 percentile points. It may be that reducing class size in itself is not an efficient use of public funds.

Third, the research on teaching and learning (rather than the research on achievement) supports the idea that very large class sizes cannot provide students with reasonable instructional and motivational systems. Safety problems also increase with class size. Small groups make it easier for teachers to monitor problem solving, attempt to improve understanding, and create an atmosphere of scientific inquiry. These factors are among the many that are not measured by most achievement tests.

Fourth, teachers must couple their arguments for smaller classes with requests for other improvements that would help their students achieve. . . . Most science classrooms . . . lack adequate supplies and equipment. . . . Such tools, along with reasonable inservice, might make science truly exciting and academically productive.

. . . Teachers need small classes [to] conduct hands-on laboratory activities and intense follow-up discussions. . . . In large classes, it is unlikely they can prepare and inspire students for tomorrow's world of science.

*Source:* W. Holliday, "Should We Reduce Class Size?" *Science Teacher* (January 1992): 14–17.

demonstrations occur. Preferably, this area should be close to the science storage area if supplies are stored within the classroom. Storage space for student projects should also be planned near this area. If possible, choose an area near the sink.

The physical arrangement of the desks and tables should be dictated by the type of activity going on in the classroom on any particular day. If space and furniture availability permit, a permanent science area can be maintained within the classroom. If space is a problem, desks and tables can be moved into configurations like those shown in Figure 9.12 on page 338, which will facilitate learning in an activity-based science classroom. Whenever possible, this area should be near windows to allow the use of natural light. Space should be arranged to eliminate traffic congestion and to provide a clear path to all classroom exits.

### Science Learning Centers

When working with the entire class for science lessons, a teacher committed to learning cycle–constructivist approaches will find that science learning centers satisfactorily accommodate additional expansion activities for each lesson. You can design the learning center so that it focuses on a particular concept brought

**FIGURE 9.12    Arranging an Activity-Based Classroom**

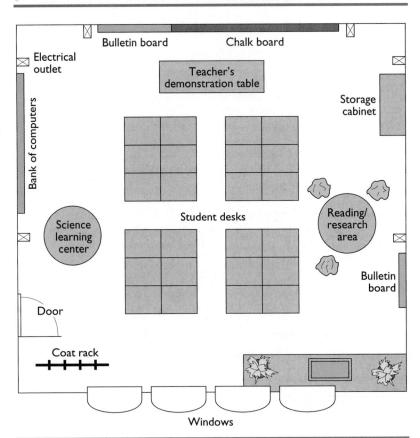

out in a class lesson and provides additional experiences for the students, who will come to a greater understanding of the concept. The center should not simply be a place where the brighter students or those who finished their assignments first get to go. All students should be encouraged to use the learning center at their convenience, to engage in activities that provide additional experiences with a particular science concept. Once all of the students have had sufficient time to use that expansion activity, change the activity at the center to address a new concept you are teaching.

Another approach to science learning centers is to design them so that students gain greater experience in the processes of science. When you present science lessons to a large group of students, the chances that each student has adequate time to make observations, predictions, measurements, and so on are slim if a more-skilled peer blurts out the answer first. The learning center can be designed so each child has a chance to work in the area, gaining experience in solving problems, measuring, predicting, using scientific instruments, and so on. You can change the learning center weekly, with different process skills as the focus (see Figure 9.13 on page 340).

A science learning center can also be designed as a *discovery area*—a place where children create inventions from a variety of provided materials. They can be considered challenge areas, where the teacher creates a problem for the week, and using the materials provided, the students work to solve the problem. Science learning centers can be the place where students can play teacher-prepared or commercially prepared science games.

Whatever you decide the focus of your science learning center should be, a few simple rules must be upheld to ensure its success. The guidelines for a science learning center are set out in Table 9.6 on page 341.

Figures 9.14 and 9.15 on pages 341–342 provide examples of some typical science learning centers. Centers should be found in an area of the classroom where they are least likely to interfere with normal classroom operations. The information provided on classroom safety should guide you in the placement of the science learning center.

A pegboard or a felt board can be designed so that it will stand on its own atop a table or desk and can easily be stored when necessary. Pockets made from cloth or heavy cardboard serve as areas to hold activity cards, instructions, or small materials needed for the activity. Any material sturdy enough to withstand student wear, without being so heavy that it topples over, will serve as the backdrop for your science learning center. Appropriate pictures or diagrams should be displayed on this board. If the activity requires a more formal means of record keeping, place record sheets or assessment sheets in a pocket on the board. Figure 9.16 on page 343 provides an example of a typical science learning center backdrop.

## Bulletin Boards and Other Displays

An activity-based science classroom should include a science bulletin board and a science display area. Lettering used for the bulletin board should be no smaller than 4 inches high. Plan the topic to be addressed, and focus on one concept. Don't use too many words. Try to find visuals that will enhance the students' understanding of the concept, but avoid using too much material. If display colors, sizes, and shapes change too frequently, the intended message may get lost.

Science displays should be designed to appeal to the students' natural curiosity. They can be theme oriented and designed by the teacher or a collection of unrelated items provided by the students. For a theme highlighting mammals, the display table could contain pelts of various mammals for the students to touch and to compare and antlers or horns for the students to determine the animal it came from and its age. There may be footprints of various mammals with a challenge to the students to determine which animal left the print. Books or picture of various mammals would be left at the table.

◆ **FIGURE 9.13    Process-Oriented Science Learning Center Lesson**

**1.  Obtain light bulb record books**

*Process Skill:* Recording data

Each student will receive a light bulb record book. The outer covers are made from yellow cardboard. Several sheets of white paper for students to record their data are stapled between the covers.

**2.  Page 1 of record book**

*Process Skill:* Observing

On the table is a box with a bulb sticking out of the top. A switch protrudes from one side. A card near the box states:

> Make as many observations as possible. Write the word OBSERVA-TIONS on the top of page 1 in the light bulb record book. Record your observation on that page.

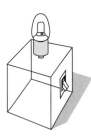

**3.  Record Book**

*Process Skill:* Predicting

A card that is numbered with a 3 and has a drawing of the box with the bulb will be at the center with the following directions:

> Label the next blank page in your record book PREDICTIONS. Predict what is inside the box causing the bulb to light. List and/or draw your predictions on that page.

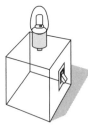

**4.  Record book, battery, bulb, wire**

*Process Skill:* Manipulating materials

Card numbered 4 near a battery, bulb, and wire, asks the students to do the following:

> Label the next blank page of your record book MANIPU-LATING MATERIALS. Take the battery, bulb, and wire from the table. Using only those three pieces of material, get the bulb to light. Record in the record book drawings of ways you manipulated the materi-als—whether the bulb lit or not.

**5.  Record book, battery, bulb, wire, bulb holder, switch**

*Process Skill:* Manipulating materials

At the next station the above materials will be laying near card number 5. The students will be asked to do the fol-lowing:

> Label the next blank page of your record book MANIPULAT-ING MATERIALS. Take the battery, bulb, wire, bulb holder, and switch from the table. Get the bulb to light as you did at station 4. This time wire it so that the switch will turn the bulb on and off. Record in the record book drawings of ways you manipulated the materials—whether the bulb lit or not.

**6.  Record book, box, battery, bulb, bulb holder, wire, switch**

*Process Skill:* Interpreting data, inferring, formulating models

The above materials will be found at station 6. The students will be asked to do the following:

> Label the next blank page of your record book INTERPRETING DATA, INFERRING, FORMULATING MODELS. Using the materials given and your results from activi-ties 4 and 5, try to create a box like the one you observed at sta-tion 2 and 3. When finished go back to your prediction page in the record book. Was your prediction correct?

### TABLE 9.6  Science Learning Center Guidelines

1. The purpose and objectives for the activity are made clear; the students understand what they are supposed to do at each center. The activity is designed so that it enhances the students' understanding of a concept rather than serving to frustrate and confuse.

2. *All* students have an opportunity to work at the center before the activity is changed.

3. Activities at the center do not interfere with other lessons going on in the classroom. Activities that require darkness, loud noises, or excessive amounts of physical activity are not appropriate for a learning center. The center is in an area where the teacher can readily observe the children in action.

4. At least one 2-feet-by-4-feet table or work area of equivalent size is dedicated to this center. If the activity requires additional space, adequate floor space will be allocated. If audiovisual materials are to be used, electrical outlets are close by.

5. Consumable materials at the centers are replenished frequently.

6. When water is required for an activity, the center is located close to a water source. If this is not possible, care is taken so that children running to sinks or water fountains are not interfering with students engaged in other classroom tasks.

### FIGURE 9.14  Science Learning Center

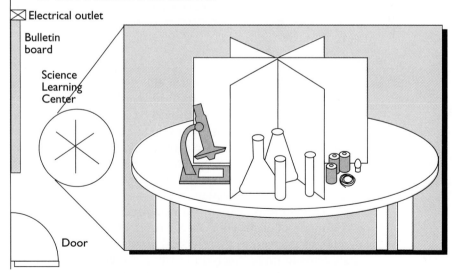

• Outlets should be available when needed

• Bulletin board contains pertinent science information

• Center is located near door to gain access to water from fountain in hall since no water is available in this classroom

**FIGURE 9.15    Science Learning Center**

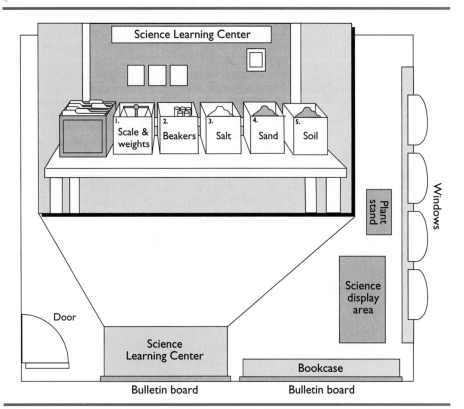

In a hodge-podge approach, the display area may be a catch-all for the various science-related items children come across that they would like to share. Items on the display table should be ones the students are allowed to touch: household items, like an old radio or clock that can be taken apart to examine the inner works, for example, or unusual rocks or plant parts that may serve to pique a student's curiosity. An item that requires special care, like a geode or a parent's rock collection, that a student brings in may be better suited for teacher-supervised display.

Large-group instruction or small science learning centers? No matter what the mode of instruction is, science learning will be facilitated when careful thought is given to the physical arrangement of the classroom. Allowing the students to travel freely to learning centers implies that certain behaviors are expected of the students. Using instruction time to teach cooperative roles will faciliate class exploration.

**FIGURE 9.16   Science Learning Center Backdrop**

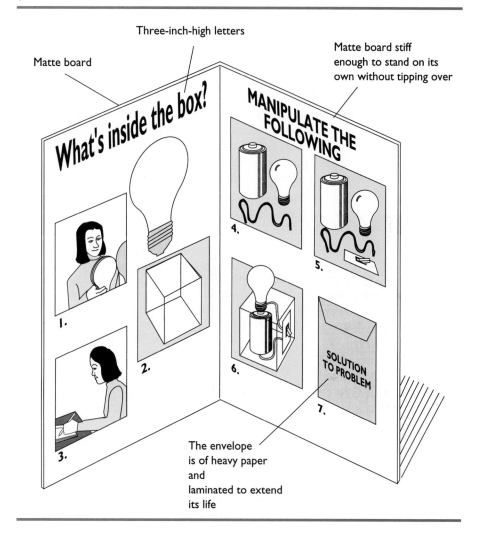

CHAPTER SUMMARY

By asking, "What are the foreseeable hazards associated with valued educational activities?" and "What materials are necessary for the activities?" teachers can be successful in creating an efficient, safe environment for activity-based science. Once the concepts to be taught are clearly identified and grade-level-appropriate activities are chosen, decisions about materials needed to teach those concepts, storage of the materials, and safe practices while handling them must be decided upon. Generally storage decisions depend on school building space restrictions and the safety philosophy embraced by the teaching faculty.

Teachers must attempt to foresee problems posed by activities and address them; teach appropriately for the emotional, physical, and intellectual levels of their students; and provide adequate supervision applicable for the environment and the degree of hazards anticipated, in addition to ensuring that the environment and equipment items are properly maintained. Teachers who are sure that they have addressed all of these concerns can proceed with confidence. If they cannot, adjustments should be made—adding more safety features, limiting the activity to a teacher demonstration only, or eliminating the activity.

The physical arrangement of the classroom directly affects the success of the activity-oriented science lesson. When physical barriers impede the completion of an activity, the students can become frustrated. If materials are not readily available to bring a child from a state of disequilibrium to equilibrium, a teachable moment may be lost. A flexible learning environment, carefully planned and designed to promote student exploration, will greatly facilitate science learning.

## DISCUSSION QUESTIONS

**1.** You are planning a field trip with your first-grade class to the local prairie ecosystem (or other special local ecosystem) to study plants. All parent and guardian release forms have been returned with the exception of one. Would you allow the student to attend the activity anyway? Give three reasons for your answer.

**2.** A student in your third-grade class asks you if he can bring his pet northern banded water snake to class to show during your reptile unit. What would be your response? What information would you want to support your decision? Where would you secure such information?

**3.** You are preparing to do a simple chemistry experiment with your sixth-grade class. A student says that she has new safety glasses provided by her optometrist and would rather wear them than your safety goggles. What would be your response? Why?

**4.** Ask representatives from the local fire department to visit your classroom and demonstrate the proper procedure for dealing with a personal-clothing fire and the proper use of fire extinguishers. If possible, ask that the fire personnel set small demonstration fires outside in containers and show how the various extinguisher types put out paper, electrical, and grease fires.

**5.** Visit an elementary school that has a central storage area for science materials. Does this area appear well maintained? Is someone responsible for checking materials in and out? Who keeps inventory of supplies? How well managed do you think the storage area is? What recommendations would you make for it?

**6.** During a unit on insect behavior, several children bring to school both live and dead insects. What should be done with the dead insects? the live ones? Should the students be encouraged to bring insects into the classroom? Why or why not? What do you believe your responsibility is to the insects and to the students' attitudes toward insects?

## BUILD A PORTFOLIO

**1.** Develop a written plan for conducting a safety assessment of a school science classroom in your area. Include all necessary forms and checklists, as well as a time line for its completion.

**2.** Select an elementary school in your area, and develop a written checklist for performing a safety assessment of its grounds. Be sure to address items that are indigenous to your area, including hazardous plants and animals, automobile traffic, difficult-to-supervise areas, natural hazards (streams, lakes, and so on), and human problems (construction areas, glass).

**3.** Interview an elementary science teacher responsible for ordering science equipment. Find answers to the following questions:

- What vendors does he or she use to purchase science equipment and why?
- How good is the service provided by that vendor?
- How quick is the vendor to process orders?
- What type of return policy does the vendor have?
- Does the vendor take purchase orders or require payment up-front?
- What procedures does the school follow in placing and paying for orders?
- If you had to set up an ordering system, would you recommend the one used by the teacher you interviewed? If not, how would you design it differently?
- What safety features are followed for classroom storage of materials?

**4.** Identify a grade level range (PreK–2; 3–4; 5–6; 7–8) you feel comfortable teaching. Design a science learning center for that grade level range around a particular theme such as outer space or the rainforest. Draw a diagram of what it will look like. What kinds of items, activities, and experiments would you place there? What safety precautions should you consider? What if your class contained students with special needs such as hearing impairment or wheelchairs? How would you design this learning space?

## CHAPTER OUTLINE

# CHAPTER 10

# Science Materials, Programs, and Resources: What Are the Best Practices?

Marjorie Becker had divided the science methods class into research teams. Their purpose was to pick a science topic and locate all the materials available on that topic in the lab, library, and college curriculum collection. The team members were to examine and compare the materials, classify them by intended purposes, and then use their findings to speculate about what makes an effective science lesson. They were told to be prepared to generalize beyond single lessons because the class would attempt to identify the characteristics of an effective science program. The groans that were prompted by the need to include text and nontext publications of the last thirty years subsided when Professor Becker demonstrated the speed and ease of *Science Helper,* the CD-ROM system containing hundreds of government-sponsored lessons from experimental science programs.

Professor Becker reconvened the class and asked the groups to report. She listed the features the students found most often among the materials: objectives, suggested teaching methods, materials needed, background information, illustrations, assessment devices, and ideas for extending the activities. Some older materials and many newer lessons contained references to themes, conceptual frameworks, skills to be developed, ideal group sizes, key vocabulary, lesson rationales, competencies, and subjects with which the lessons could be integrated. When she asked for the groups' ideas about effective programs, she received such replies as: "They emphasize subject matter most and produce higher test scores," "Effective programs are those that children like," and "You can tell the program is effective if more children take science in high school and if more want to enter scientific careers." These replies fell short of Dr. Becker's hopes, so she guided the class into a discussion of the assignment, pressed them to give specific examples of what they found, and repeated the assignment's central question: What makes an effective science program?

The students' thinking expanded a bit with the observation that some materials prepared in the past decade have features that resemble those of the experimental programs of the 1960s but that the newer science textbooks seem to contain several features not found in science textbooks of the earlier era. Still, Professor Becker sensed frustration. Her suspicion was confirmed when one brave soul, Donald, asked, "I don't understand why you had us look at out-of-date materials. Why did you have us do this assignment? Don't the developers and publishers agree on what's best, and shouldn't we always just try to use the most recent materials?"   ◆

## INTRODUCTION

We are likely to repeat mistakes of the past if we are ignorant of history. In fact, the National Science Education Standards' history of science content standard encourages a historical development perspective of science. Looking back, we see considerable similarity among the recommendations that arose from several science education reports during the mid-1940s, again during the late 1950s and early 1960s, and still again during the late 1980s and mid-1990s. Calls for more intellectual rigor, increased standards, elevated expectations, improved student discipline, increased classroom time on task, improved test scores, and enhanced teacher subject expertise often make up the substance of these reports, but different approaches were used in attempts to fulfill the recommendations. Indeed, devoting more time to intellectual subject matter in science is a common and worthwhile goal, but when it is the only expectation, it falls short of fulfilling the larger goal of more effective science programs. The key to effective science instruction is selecting and using hands-on activities effectively with the proper mix of science content and processes.

Calls or mandates for improved pupil achievement and recommendations for producing these improvements may be naively based on uninformed right-wrong perspectives resting on faulty assumptions about what should be taught and learned and about how youngsters learn and should be taught. But what role are you expected to play? You will be involved, at some point in your career, with science program development. More immediately, your concern is probably for selecting the best materials available to plan and teach effective lessons. Can you afford to ignore the lessons of the past? This chapter provides a foundation that can help define what is best and help you form a rationale for what you choose to do.

This chapter

1. describes dominant beliefs about science education in the past;
2. describes several model elementary science programs that have been influential in shaping modern elementary science curricula and research on effective teaching practices;
3. reviews the effects these model programs had on children's science achievement, skills, and attitudes;
4. exposes false assumptions about learning and teaching science and reveals assumptions that shape new science curricula;
5. offers recommendations for an effective elementary science program;
6. explores supplemental resources.

## DOMINANT BELIEFS IN SCIENCE EDUCATION

*Quality* and *excellence* are two widely held goals for education in general. The elementary science program must have high quality and demonstrate excellence in its curriculum and teaching. Critics and supporters agree on these goals, but they by no means agree on the direction the program ought to take, the science subject matter that is most worth knowing, or the conditions that best foster that knowing (Hurd, 1986). As an example, consider these conflicting beliefs about science education:

• Science is structured and consists of a body of well-known facts, concepts, principles, and theories that are useful to and should be learned by all.
• Science is a way of doing and constructing meaning from what is done.
• Science is important for its own sake; everyone needs to learn about science.
• Everyone is affected by science; therefore, everyone needs to learn science.
• To be most useful, science must be relevant; therefore it must be taught so that it can be understood and useful to those who learn it.

Which of these beliefs appear compatible to you, and which appear to conflict? Why is it that experts' beliefs openly conflict? Let us take a brief look back in time to understand the importance of the issues surrounding these beliefs as well as how they affect the answer to the main question that guides this chapter: What are the characteristics of science materials and programs?

## CHANGES OVER TIME: LEGACY OF THE PAST

*Biology, Chemistry, Physics,* and *Earth Science* are common school science curriculum labels. Even within general science and elementary science courses these labels persist as topics or units of study. They arose from their parent scientific research disciplines, which were popular during the 1800s. However, since about 1900 these disciplines of study have not accurately represented the important areas of science. Thousands of diverse scientific journals now report

*Past programs prepared children to become scientists.*

experimental findings from a countless number of new fields of science and technology. Distinctions among the different fields of science are now made more by the type of problem being researched than by the discipline being served. Today there is simply too much—too many facts of science to be learned in a school science program. The amount of scientific information continues to double about every five years. So what should be taught? At times this question has been answered with an issues-and-problems approach.

A specific problem in science education has always been to resolve the issue of how the schools could best prepare "citizens to live in a culture most often described in terms of achievements in science and technology" (Hurd, 1986, p. 355). In the 1930s and 1940s, elementary schools tried to resolve this issue by teaching in a "prescribed authoritative manner almost exclusively through single-author textbooks" (Sabar, 1979, pp. 257–269). Basically, science was a reading program that covered a large body of information and used the subtle but powerful force of conformity and consensus to control the direction of American society and to aid citizens as they tried to adjust to society's new directions. The important facts, concepts, and theories of science that were taught were based on the consensus of specialists. Specialists told previous generations of teachers what was important to know and teach.

Teacher emphasis on pupil conformity and learning science by reading is still highly visible today. Another emphasis from the past that is still widely supported is the cry to get back to basics, with emphasis on reading, writing, and arithmetic. This chant began after World War II for the same reasons that it can be heard today: the perceived overall low quality of high school graduates as shown by their falling achievement scores and poor job skills and the need for citizens to keep pace with scientific and technological breakthroughs of other advanced countries (Sabar, 1979, p. 258). Ironically, this last need makes the study of science a basic need for all, a basic literacy subject in the school curriculum, as described in Chapter 6.

## MAJOR ELEMENTARY SCIENCE PROGRAM MODELS: LOOKING BACK FOR THE SOURCE OF WISDOM

Efforts began earlier, but it was the launching of the Soviet satellite *Sputnik* in 1957 that caused the most serious attempts at science curriculum reform. During the twenty-five years after *Sputnik,* $2 billion was spent to support mathematics and science education in elementary and secondary schools. The main goal then, as many believe it should be now, was to prepare future scientists and engineers, mostly out of a concern for national defense. As important as this goal is, we now know that defense issues rise and fall in urgency and that "this is a goal that is appropriate for only 3 percent of high school graduates, and a goal where we have traditionally spent 95 percent of our time, efforts, resources and attention" (Yager, 1984, p. 196).

### The Alphabet Soup

The decade after *Sputnik* is known for its alphabet soup elementary science programs (see Table 10.1). Three programs developed during that decade are worth mentioning now because of their goals, their effects on children's learning, and the eventually improved quality of modern textbooks and other curriculum materials. Several of the assumptions the programs were based on have been supported over time by a growing body of research, while other assumptions have fallen from favor. The programs we refer to here are known as SAPA, SCIS, and ESS.

Science—A Process Approach (SAPA), Science Curriculum Improvement Study (SCIS), and the Elementary Science Study (ESS) were regarded as innovative programs in their day. Designed and field-tested during the 1960s and then revised during the 1970s, these experimental programs had several features in common:

- They were developed by teams of scientists, psychologists, educators, and professional curriculum specialists rather than written by single authors or single expert specialists.

### TABLE 10.1 Examples of Alphabet Soup Elementary Science Programs

**SAPA** (Science—A Process Approach), American Association for the Advancement of Science Commission on Science Education, 1963
**COPES** (Conceptually Oriented Program in Elementary Science), 1967
**ESSP** (Elementary School Science Project), University of California, Berkeley, 1962
**E-SSP** (Elementary-School Science Project), University of Illinois, 1963
**ESSP** (Elementary School Science Project), Utah State University, 1964
**ESS** (Elementary Science Study), 1964
**IDP** (Inquiry Development Program), 1962
**MinneMAST** (Minnesota Mathematics and Science Teaching Project), 1966
**SSCP** (School Science Curriculum Project), 1964
**SCIS** (Science Curriculum Improvement Study), 1961
**SQAIESS** (Study of a Quantitative Approach in Elementary School Science), 1964
**USMES** (Unified Sciences and Mathematics for Elementary Schools), 1973
**WIMSA** (The Webster Institute for Mathematics, Science and the Arts), 1965

*Source:* Information excerpted from Paul DeHart Hurd (ed.), *New Directions in Elementary Science Teaching* (Belmont, CA: Wadsworth Publishing, 1968). Note that dates given are approximate beginning dates for each program.

- Federal funds were widely available for development, research, field testing, dissemination, and teacher inservice training.
- Each project was developed from particular assumptions about learning drawn from prominent theories and used to form a specific framework for each project. Behavioral and cognitive-development psychology had major influences.
- Each project was developed from what were assumed to be the ways children learned best. Specific teaching approaches were emphasized and were used to help children learn the ways and knowledge of science and to develop the attitudes of scientists.
- Active pupil learning was assumed to be very important. Each project provided hands-on learning experiences for all children because it was assumed that manipulatives help children learn best.
- The projects did not provide a standard textbook for each child. In fact, a workbook for recording observations was as close as some children came to anything that resembled a textbook.
- There was no attempt to teach all that should be known about science. Specific science processes or content areas were selected for each project, thus narrowing the field of topics to a specialized few.
- Attention was given to the basic ideas of science, the concepts and theories, with the intention of increasing the number of citizens who would seek careers in science and engineering.
- The programs were conveniently packaged. Equipment was included with curriculum materials. This made the programs easier to use and reduced teacher preparation time by eliminating the need to gather diverse equipment.
- Mathematical skills were emphasized. The programs were more quantitative than qualitative. Emphasis was placed on student observation, careful measurement, and the use of appropriate calculations to form ideas or reach conclusions.
- Science was taught as a subject by itself and was not associated with social studies, health, or reading. At times, science was treated as a pure subject that was believed to have inherent value for all children.
- The teacher's role changed. Teachers used such less direct methods of teaching as inquiry and functioned as questioners and guides for students. They avoided lecturing or more didactic forms of direct instruction. The teacher was *not* to be an expert who spoke what children should memorize.

SAPA, SCIS, and ESS are landmark elementary science programs, still available today. As shown in Figure 10.1, they differ essentially on two factors: the amount of structure or flexibility each contains in its design for classroom use and the emphasis each gives to science content, attitudes, or thinking processes. Let us explore each program briefly to understand better the legacy that has brought positive influences to the options available in elementary science education today.

**FIGURE 10.1   Structure and Emphasis Comparisons of Landmark Elementary Science Programs**

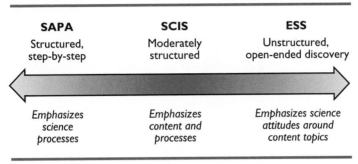

*Note:* Each program is available from Delta Education, P.O. Box 3000, Nashua, NH 03061-3000. Phone: 1-800-442-5444.

## Science—A Process Approach (SAPA)

### SAPA's Prime Assumptions.

> Children need to learn how to *do* science, and this means acquiring the skills essential to learning and understanding science information. These knowledge-acquiring skills are called cognitive [thinking] skills or process skills and are similar to the procedures used by scientists to acquire new knowledge. Process skills may be compared to the program [of] a computer. Computers are incapable of handling information without a program to provide directions; the human mind does not cope effectively with incoming information in the absence of learning strategies (a program). (Hurd, 1968, pp. 11–12)

The American Association for the Advancement of Science's Commission on Science Education assumed that a sequential program was necessary for developing a child's intellect. In 1963, a team of scientists, psychologists, elementary teachers, and curriculum specialists developed plans and materials for trial versions of what became Science—A Process Approach. The program is based on two assumptions: first, that prepared materials must consider the intellectual development of the child, and second, that a total program must use a sequential approach for the long-range development of the child's intellectual skills. The first assumption worked well. Materials that were developed on the child's ability level were appropriate. Incremental advances in the complexity of the materials seemed to help children develop intellectually. However, the long-term sequential approach proved too rigid to use without difficulty in schools where children attend school irregularly or transfer in mid-year.

*Description of SAPA.*   SAPA is the most structured of the three programs we explore here. Its structure arises from behavioral psychology. The underlying psychological assumptions were that any skill can be broken down into smaller

*Effective programs promote scientific inquiry.*

steps and that children need to learn lower-level skills before they can learn more advanced skills. Predictably, the original version of SAPA developed into a set of skills to be mastered through a complex, highly structured hierarchy (see Figure 10.2 on pages 356–357) and step-by-step teaching.

Skill development takes precedence over science subject matter in SAPA. Even after revision and the development of SAPA II, the content of science is important only as it serves as a vehicle for developing thinking processes. The complex task of inquiry, therefore, is broken into a series of smaller, easier-to-acquire skills. All skill development is expected to arise from a child's direct experiences performing prescribed learning tasks, usually with concrete manipulable objects. Hands-on learning involves children in doing science the way many scientists say they do it themselves—carefully planned step-by-step procedures.

SAPA science process skills are divided into two types: *basic* and *integrated* skills. In the primary grades (K–3) children develop these basic process skills: observing, using space/time relationships, classifying, using numbers, measuring, communicating, predicting, and inferring. In the intermediate grades (4–6) children use the basic process skills as a foundation for developing more complex skills: controlling variables, interpreting data, formulating hypotheses, defining operationally, and experimenting.

The knowledge explosion in the sciences helps SAPA justify its approach; it is a unique program that emphasizes science skills over content. Creators of SAPA believe that it is impossible for individuals, including scientists, to keep up to date in all the sciences and that it is also unrealistic to expect children to learn everything about science. SAPA's intention is to equip each child with the thinking skills that can be used to solve problems they find in the future.

SAPA is a complete K–6 program. The learning activities in the revised SAPA II are packaged in a series of 105 ungraded learning modules, with approximately 15 modules per traditional grade level. Each module is devoted to a specific skill. SAPA II arose in 1975 from extensive field testing, program evaluation, and materials revisions, and it is an improvement over the original design. Clusters of modules help teachers overcome the rigid sequence of skills used in the original flowchart approach (Figure 10.2). SAPA II strives to reflect important changes in science education, is more flexible than the original design, reflects a greater emphasis on environmental topics, and attempts more pupil individualization. Students have no books, yet copy masters are available; modular teacher guides are used in place of a teacher's textbook guide.

Each learning module has the same features and structure (Figure 10.3 on pages 358–359). The cover of each module presents the specific process skill that is emphasized within. The module title identifies the science content selected, and behavioral objectives specify what each child should be able to do at the end of the module. The sequence chart inside the cover shows the relationship and fit of the module's objectives with those of related modules (refer to Figure 10.2). A complete rationale justifies the purpose and describes the benefits of the module's activities for children and their intellectual development. The instructional procedure gives an overall introduction and describes each specific learning activity. Materials needed are listed with each activity, and modules contain about three to six activities. Each module contains a section, generalizing the experience, for extension of the learning activities. Evaluation is emphasized strongly in SAPA. An appraisal section describes class performance options for evaluation, and the competency measure section fully describes evaluation tasks that can be used with individual children. Specific questions and suggested answers are given. Competency measure tasks are keyed to the specific module objectives.

*SAPA Program Effects.* Did SAPA make a difference? James Shymansky et al. (1982) and Ted Bredderman (1982) say yes. Shymansky et al. specifically report that students learning science in the SAPA program outperformed children who learned from traditional science programs by seven statistically significant percentile points on measures of achievement. (Traditional programs were defined as those whose development followed pre-1955 models, emphasized the information of science, and used laboratory activities to verify or to supplement lessons.) This difference may not seem great, but take a closer look. Let us suppose that two classes of elementary students take the same standardized achievement test in science and all differences are controlled except the program that they learn science from. One class learns from the traditional textbook approach that is designed to teach science facts through reading and memorization; the other class learns from a program—SAPA—that does not stress facts or science information but instead focuses on doing science and developing thinking skills. The result? Let us say that the average student score from the traditional science program class is at the fiftieth percentile on a test designed to

**FIGURE 10.2   SAPA Then and Now**

# Using Space/Time Relationships

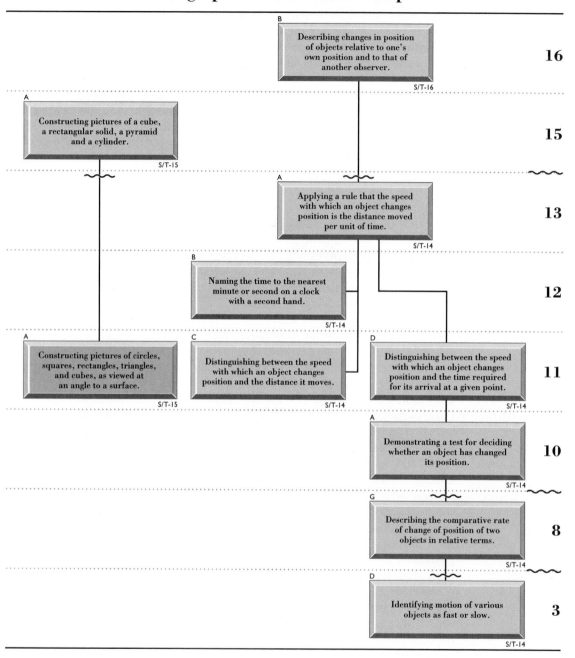

*Source:* Delta Education, Inc., P.O. Box 3000, Nashua, NH 03061-3000. Reprinted by permission of copyright holder.

# Science... A Process Approach
## Planning Chart

| IX | X | XI | XII |
|---|---|---|---|

**Module 32**
Classifying/d
*Terrarium*

Separating living organisms into categories. Constructing a simple classification system and demonstrating its use. Placing new organisms in the appropriate categories of an established classification system.

PREMOD: 16

**Module 39**
Measuring/g
*Solids, Liquids, and Gases*

Measuring the volume of liquids using metric units. Naming a substance as being a solid, a liquid, or a gas. Describing a substance as a solid, a liquid, or a gas by using various physical characteristics, such as shape and appearance.

PREMODS: 17, 23, 32

**Module 42**
Classifying/e
*Sorting Mixtures*

Demonstrating a specified method for classifying the components of a mixture by size. Ordering the components of a mixture by size. Ordering the components of a mixture by volume or weight.

PREMODS: 26, 39

**Module 41**
Measuring/h
*Temperature and Thermometers*

Demonstrating how to use a thermometer to measure the temperature of a gas or liquid, and naming temperature in degrees Celsius. Using a thermometer to measure temperature change, and naming initial and final temperatures in degrees Celsius.

PREMODS: 21, 27, 30

**Module 31**
Communicating/d
*Life Cycles*

Describing an animal according to several of its characteristics. Describing the changing characteristics of a young animal as it grows from one stage to another.

PREMOD: 16, 28

**Module 36**
Observing/l
*Animal Responses*

Describing the kinds of locomotion characteristic of animals having various shapes and appendages. Identifying an animal's response to an identified stimulus.

PREMOD: 31

**Module 43**
Communicating/e
*A Plant Part That Grows*

Distinguishing between a developing new plant and the original plant it is growing from. Describing vegetative growth qualitatively. Describing the techniques used to produce growth from plant parts other than seeds.

PREMOD: 36

**Module 33**
Inferring/a
*What is inside?*

Distinguishing between statements that are observations and those that are explanations of observations, and identifying the explanations as inferences. Constructing inferences in terms of likelihood rather than certainty.

PREMOD: 18

**Module 40**
Inferring/b
*How certain can you be? Shake and Peek*

Describing new observations that are needed to test an inference. Identifying observations that support an inference. Distinguishing between an inference that accounts for all of the observations and one that does not.

PREMODS: 29, 33

**Module 35**
Using Space/Time/f
*Symmetry*

Identifying objects that have line or plane symmetry. Demonstrating that some objects can be folded or cut in one or more ways to produce matching halves. Identifying and describing bilateral symmetry.

PREMOD: 12

**Module 45**
Using Space/Time/g
*Lines, Curves, and Surfaces*

Identifying, naming, and constructing straight and curved paths on plane and curved surfaces. Determining whether a surface is a plane surface. Identifying linear and circular motion.

PREMODS: 27, 35

## Determining Sequences Within the Program

One convenient order for using the modules is the *numerical sequence* with which they are coded. If that order is followed, children will have the opportunity to develop skills in a sequence in which success is highly probable. Frequently it is necessary or desirable to alter the sequence when several teachers share materials, weather conditions interfere, or other scheduling problems arise. It is not necessary to use the modules in numerical sequence so long as the children have mastered the prerequisites before a module is begun.

FIGURE 10.3   Excerpts from a SAPA II Module

MODULE

# 44

# SCIENCE...

Predicting/b

*Surveying Opinion*

## Sequence

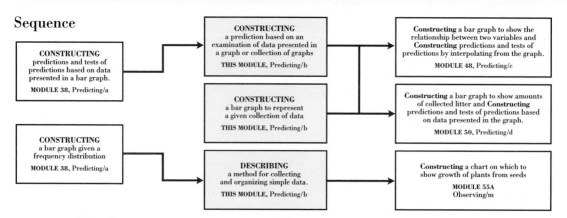

CONSTRUCTING
predictions and tests of
predictions based on data
presented in a bar graph.
MODULE 38, Predicting/a

CONSTRUCTING
a prediction based on an
examination of data presented in
a graph or collection of graphs
THIS MODULE, Predicting/b

Constructing a bar graph to show the
relationship between two variables and
Constructing predictions and tests of
predictions by interpolating from the graph.
MODULE 48, Predicting/c

CONSTRUCTING
a bar graph to represent
a given collection of data
THIS MODULE, Predicting/b

Constructing a bar graph to show amounts
of collected litter and Constructing
predictions and tests of predictions based
on data presented in the graph.
MODULE 50, Predicting/d

CONSTRUCTING
a bar graph given a
frequency distribution
MODULE 38, Predicting/a

DESCRIBING
a method for collecting
and organizing simple data.
THIS MODULE, Predicting/b

Constructing a chart on which to
show growth of plants from seeds
MODULE 55A
Observing/m

### Rationale

It is essential that contributing evidence upon which a prediction is based be collected, organized, and recorded in a clear and usable way. The activities in this module provide children with experience in making predictions based on data recorded in a survey of children in the school, thus using the children's natural interest in collecting, interviewing, and surveying.

You must be sure to point out carefully the limitations on the dependability of predictions based on an opinion survey. Emphasize that accurate predictions are difficult in the early phases of the survey, and are impossible if they are based on only small bits of information. As more data are added, trends or patterns are often noticeable. These trends can be used to make more reliable predictions...

Because favorite kinds of snacks are the subject matter of this module, the results of the surveys are unpredictable and may vary considerably with locale, time of year, the children's previous experience, and other factors. Remember that although the children will be very much interested in the results of the survey, these results are merely a means to an end. The objective is to provide experience in making predictions based on available evidence...

In *Activity 3*, the children survey other groups in the school. Take advantage of the excitement that such surveys create and the opportunity they provide for improvement of communication skills, but be sure to plan the surveying procedures carefully with the other teachers involved...

**Vocabulary:** predict, prediction, survey, opinion, tally, poll, polling

### Instructional Procedure

Ask the children what the word *predict* means to them. They may have several suggestions. For example, they may recall that when they studied *Shadows, Using Space/Time Relationships e, Module 29*, they were asked to predict the two-dimensional shapes of the shadows of a three-dimensional object...

The children should also recall the predictions they made from the bar graphs they constructed in *Using Graphs, Predicting a, Module 38*.

Perhaps some child will mention that the weather man predicts the weather. Another may recall a time of national elections when there were predictions about which candidate would win. Remind them that predicting is telling what you think is going to happen based on experience.

If possible, bring periodical or newspaper examples of polls that have been taken. A copy of a survey made within the school would be useful too. Discuss the value of surveys. Use questions as these: What is an opinion? What is a survey? How is the information obtained when we survey opinion? Suggest that the class make its own survey...

**Materials:** Surveys, several examples from periodicals or newspapers.

### Activity 1

Give each child a piece of paper and a pencil. With no preliminary discussion ask the children to write down the names of three of their favorite kinds of snacks. Be sure that they do this independently. Then collect their papers.

Tell the children that you have just taken a *poll* of their favorite snacks. Ask which snack the children think was named the most times. After several children have expressed their ideas, ask why they think a particular snack was the most popular. Suggest that their ideas are largely guesses because, at this point, they have little or no evidence to use as a basis for making predictions...

**Materials:** Writing paper, 1 sheet for each child, Pencils, 1 for each child

*Source:* Delta Education, Inc., P.O. Box 3000, Nashua, NH 03061-3000. Reprinted by permission of copyright holder.

# A Process Approach II

**Objectives** At the end of this module the child should be able to:

1. **Describe** a method for collecting and organizing simple data.
2. **Construct** a bar graph to represent a given collection of data.
3. **Construct** a prediction based on an examination for the data presented in a graph or collection of graphs.

### Activity 2

Ask the children for their ideas about organizing the data so that each child can have a copy of the results. There should be a number of suggestions. Try to accept one of them.

If the children do not suggest a feasible plan, use the following procedure. Give each child one paper marked during the previous activity, a clean sheet of paper, and a pencil. Call on the children to read from their marked papers. When a snack is first mentioned, tell everyone to write it down and put a tally mark next to it; each time it is mentioned again, have everyone put another mark next to the snack. Several children will probably have listed specific candy bars, flavors of ice cream, and so forth. Have the children tally all such listings under general headings, such as "candy" and "ice cream." Some children may list two items such as "cookies and milk." In this case put one tally next to "cookies" and another next to "milk..."

For the purpose of discussion, ask the children to imagine that milk was named more often than any other kind of snack, and that it was listed 20 times. Also ask them to imagine that candy was named 6 times and ice cream was mentioned 4 times. Figure 1 shows how these data may be graphed...

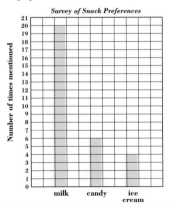

*Survey of Snack Preferences*

### Generalizing Experience

Some children may be much more interested in this series of activities than are others. You should provide opportunities for the most interested children to continue with the surveys and to report the tallies to the others in the room...

Ask the children to make additional surveys about snack preferences. For example, have them ask a teenager, their mother or father, or some other friend to list three favorite kinds of snacks. You will get greater cooperation from the parents if you send a note with the child describing the project and the importance of the information. The children should get data from the same number of adults as there are members in their room. Tell the children that they should make their predictions beforehand and discuss the reasons for them. Then have them make the tabulation and discuss the results. If you find that more practice in graphing is desirable, you could have the children graph these data before they discuss the results...

### Appraisal

Divide the children into two groups, each containing about the same number of boys and girls. Ask everyone to write on a piece of paper the names of their three favorite flavors of ice cream. Have the children in one group tabulate their own data, and ask the other group to do the same. Be sure the groups do not overhear each other's results...

### Competency Measure

**Task 1** (Objective 1): Say to the child, *In planning for the school picnic, the P.T.A. members want to get an idea of how many hamburgers, hot dogs, and cold-meat sandwiches to make. Tell me how they could get the information they need.* The child should describe a method of surveying some of the children in the school.

**Task 2** (Objective 2): Say, *A poll in Miss Brown's room of 30 children gave the following data abut preferences: hamburgers, 15 children; hot dogs, 10 children; cold-meat sandwiches, 5 children.* Give the child the data on a piece of paper or write the information on the chalkboard. Then give him a piece of graph paper and say, *Make a graph showing the number of times each kind of food was chosen.* The child should include the following entries on the graph: a proper title that identifies the subject of the graph, a scale of numerals on the vertical number line, the name of the teacher whose children were surveyed—perhaps included in the title, the proper labeling of the horizontal base line and vertical number line, bars drawn to the correct height to show the number of choices. If the child makes any errors in constructing the graph, correct them before continuing.

**Task 3** (Objective 3): Ask the child, *Could you use your graph to predict exactly how many times hamburgers would be chosen by the children in another room?* The child should indicate that an exact prediction probably cannot be made.

**Task 4** (Objective 3): Show the child the two picture cards of graphs—one showing a graph that represents the choices made by the children in Mr. Smith's room, the other showing a graph that represents the choices made by the children in Miss Jones' room. Read the labels below the horizontal base line of each graph. Say, *Look at the three graphs—the one you made and the two I have just given you. Make a prediction about which kind of food the children in Mrs. White's class will select most often.* The child should say, "Hamburgers."

**Task 5** (Objective 3): Ask, *Why did you make that selection?* The child should identify a pattern that supports his or her answer.

measure knowledge of science facts. Then by comparison, the average student in the SAPA class achieves at the fifty-seventh percentile on the same test—a distinct and significant achievement gain. The SAPA students knew more facts.

SAPA has several other factors going for it even more important than the performance of the average children from our example. In each case, these findings arose from research and careful study the findings are real, not imagined. SAPA students scored fifteen percentile points higher than non-SAPA students on measures of attitude toward science. On tests of process skills, SAPA students scored thirty-six percentile points higher than children from traditional programs. In such other areas as related study skills (reading and mathematics), creativity, and Piagetian tasks, SAPA children scored higher by 4, 7, and 12 percentile points, respectively. Many of the assumptions that undergird SAPA appear to produce differences, just as its developers envisioned.

## Science Curriculum Improvement Study (SCIS)

### SCIS's Prime Assumptions.

> In a world where there is so much to learn and know, concepts provide an intellectual economy in helping to organize large amounts of information. [T]his is the way concepts serve scientists and it is also the way concepts can improve children's learning. There is too much to be known, even by children, to expect it can be learned by rote and as isolated facts. But a large amount of information can be organized into a few concepts. Systems of related concepts can then be built to form principles or rules whereby children are able to interpret and explain new observations and experiences. . . . One advantage of having children form concepts is that new information can be more easily related to that already known. The result is the likelihood that both the new information and related concept will have greater meaning, and understanding will be increased. If on the other hand, new information cannot be brought into an organized form, there is a likelihood that the new information will confuse rather than aid understanding. . . . [E]ach new relevant observation acquires meaning because it becomes associated with many previous experiences. (Hurd, 1968, pp. 9–10)

The Science Curriculum Improvement Study (SCIS) was developed to help elementary school children form a broad conceptual framework for understanding science. Teams of scientists, educators, and psychologists began work in 1961 to produce the first of what eventually became three SCIS versions: SCIS and SCIIS were developed by the same team and SCIS II by another. The most recent version is called SCIS3+. SCIS materials are available through Delta Education of Nashua, NH; *http://www.delta-ed.com.* The related versions are described here and are generically called SCIS.

The conceptual curriculum is organized around the structure of science as scientists see it. Specific concepts are chosen for their wide application and potential usefulness in each child's future. The unique challenge of SCIS is to provide a program that will help children explore science, guide children's thinking, and help children to form concepts and link them together within SCIS's conceptual structure.

*Description of SCIS.* SCIS is a sequential program that emphasizes both process and content, making SCIS rather middle of the road according to Figure 10.1. The instruction is less structured than in SAPA. Specific teaching approaches complement the program's intention: to reach pupils at their current level of development as they form the intended science concepts.

The original version of SCIS introduced concepts that were new to elementary science. These concepts were linked together to form such units of study as properties, relativity, systems, interactions, variation and measurement, and ecosystems. Understanding these concepts yielded the primary goal of SCIS: scientific literacy. The program is divided into two parts: a physical/earth science sequence and a life/environmental science sequence. Each grade level's program contains concepts and essential processes prerequisite for study at the next grade level (see Figure 10.4).

The SCIS concepts represent different levels of abstraction. For example, the first level pertains to matter, living things, variation, and conservation of matter. The second level includes concepts of interaction, causal relations, relativity, and geometric relations. The third level concepts pertain to energy, equilibrium, steady state, and the behavior, reproduction, and speciation of living things. The levels continue through to level six, dealing with concepts more appropriate for students at higher elementary grades. These concepts are somewhat complex when compared to simpler collections of facts; therefore, in SCIS instruction receives special attention.

SCIS gives children direct, concrete experiences. The teacher's role is to help children acquire and use their observations to form the broad conceptual

## FIGURE 10.4 SCIS Structure and Sequence of Units

| K | Beginnings | |
|---|---|---|
| | **PHYSICAL EARTH SCIENCE SEQUENCE** | **LIFE ENVIRONMENTAL SCIENCE SEQUENCE** |
| 1 | Material Objects | Organisms |
| 2 | Interaction and Systems | Life Cycles |
| 3 | Subsystems and Variables | Populations |
| 4 | Relative Position and Motion | Environments |
| 5 | Energy Sources | Communities |
| 6 | Scientific Theories | Ecosystems |

*Source:* Delta Education, Inc., P.O. Box 3000, Nashua, NH 03061-3000. Reprinted by permission of copyright holder.

ideas of science—to guide, not to tell. The instructional method has three distinct phases and is known as the *learning cycle* (Karplus, 1964):

- Phase 1, *exploration* in an activity-oriented setting, permits the children to explore the learning materials or phenomena.
- Phase 2, *invention,* does not leave children to their own devices but guides them toward the concepts by gathering their observations and using them to invent ideas that help the children organize and understand their experiences.
- Phase 3, *application,* helps the children discover relationships and broaden their experiences by giving them opportunities to use the newly formed concepts in new contexts.

Although most of the attention is given to academic skills through concept formation, SCIS also gives attention to student attitudes and thinking skills. The skills developed in the program are similar to those developed in SAPA: Students carefully observe, record their observations, make comparisons, recognize similarities, use measurements, and develop vocabulary as they discuss their experiences and form meaningful concepts.

Each grade level of SCIS is packaged conveniently, and most grades have two modular kits: one for physical/earth science and one for life/environmental science. Each kit contains all the equipment and materials needed for teaching the specific unit and accommodates classes of up to thirty-two children. Materials are carefully selected to provide the specific experiences each child needs to form the selected concepts; some materials are consumable and need regular replacement. Print materials include wall charts, game boards, card decks, and visual transparencies. Student manuals (record books) are provided for each grade level except kindergarten. Children use the manuals to record their observations and complete investigations that help to evaluate their progress. An evaluation packet provided for each unit helps the teacher determine each child's concept formation, skill, and attitude development. Living materials are needed for approximately half of the school year; these materials are provided for a fee at the time specified by the teacher. Extending Your Experiences (EYE) cards for concept expansion, review, remediation, and special projects can be used with individual children, small groups, or an entire class.

The teacher's guide is exceptionally well organized. Guides contain a concise lesson plan, the synopsis, lists of materials, background information, tips for advance preparation, specific teaching suggestions, helpful illustrations, descriptions of optional activities, and descriptions of ways to do concept and process evaluation. All of these materials are packaged with a complete kit for every unit.

Each unit of the new SCIS3+ materials includes correlation of all activities to the National Science Education Standards, Benchmarks for Science Literacy Project 2061, age-appropriate related literature, and related software titles.

***SCIS Program Effects.***   What kinds of effects did SCIS have on children? Again, we can look to James Shymansky and his fellow researchers (1982) for some answers. In achievement tests, students in SCIS programs scored 34 percentile points above children from traditional science programs. Of the three programs we describe in this chapter, SCIS had the greatest effect on pupil achievement, outdistancing SAPA and ESS by 30 and 27 percentile points, respectively.

Concurrently, SCIS produced gains of 21 percentile points in science process skills and 34 percentile points in children's creativity when compared to traditional programs. Smaller improvements were measured in pupil attitudes, related study skills such as reading and mathematics, and Piagetian tasks. An unexpected benefit of SCIS is reported by Renner and Marek (1988). The first-grade unit, material objects, was compared to a commercial first-grade reading readiness program. Children in the experimental group studied material objects without reading readiness, and children in the control group studied traditional reading readiness materials without material objects. Both groups were equivalent and were pretested with the Metropolitan Reading Readiness Test and then posttested six weeks later. The SCIS experimental group outscored the control group in all areas—word meaning, listening, matching, alphabet, numbers, and total score—except copying (Renner & Marek 1988, pp. 193–196). Apparently the thinking skill development in the SCIS program was much more potent than direct reading readiness instruction. The assumptions that SCIS developers made about children's learning appear to be valid, given the extent of gains in achievement, process skills, and other important aspects of learning.

## The Elementary Science Study (ESS)

### ESS's Prime Assumptions.

> The central question is whether whatever a child learns is more meaningful and is retained longer if he works his own way through a topic [discovery] or if it is taught him by assertion. Proponents of the discovery approach cite the following values in its favor: (1) Children are motivated by the satisfaction they receive from finding out things for themselves, and satisfaction is recognized as an important attitude in stimulating learning; (2) since children are more personally involved with information and ideas in a discovery approach, deeper understanding of subject matter results and forgetting is reduced; (3) discovery procedures help children develop strategies of inquiry, or process skills . . . ; and (4) transfer of learning is improved.
>
> [Discovery in ESS means that] children explore freely with the materials of a topic until they begin to ask questions of their own. These questions form the basis for further investigation. Teacher direction is at a minimum and the pupils are permitted to pursue their own lines of inquiry in a capitalization on the natural curiosity and ability of children to profit from self-directed experiences. Given this freedom, each child can delve into features of a problem that are interesting and important to him. Discovery learning in this approach is seen as increasing motivation and improving the intuitive meaning of observations. (Hurd, 1968, pp. 18–19)

The developers of ESS believed that the elementary school should provide children with abundant time to explore and to examine relationships between humans and the physical and living world. Terms like *free discovery* and *guided discovery* arose from the teaching methods used with ESS. David Hawkins, developer of ESS, used the term *messing about* to describe the class time students should spend in unguided exploration activities—the initial learning phase of ESS. Developers believed that learning must provide children with interesting and enriching experiences and that abundant, varied activities must be available. A number of psychologists supported the ESS goals by stressing the importance of free, unstructured periods of exploration during the initial phases of learning. Also, psychologists affirmed that children learn at different rates, have different interests, and learn different things from the same learning activity. These views support the notion that learning must be individualized—a feature of ESS.

*Description of ESS.*   The main goal of ESS for teachers is to provide students with a wide variety of learning materials, which are packaged into unit booklets. Some topics stress experiences with skills fundamental to learning, such as weighing, graphing, and using instruments, while other topics emphasize science concepts. All have been field-tested and revised during development so that they continue to motivate children and foster positive attitudes toward science.

ESS originally contained fifty-six different units with a suggested range of grade levels. Now about thirty-eight different units are in print (see Figure 10.5 on pages 366–368 for some examples). Each unit takes several weeks to complete and contains material useful for a K–9 science program. Although no pre-packaged course of study exists, the units can be easily adapted to fit most existing curricula. Each unit stretches across a range of grade levels and can be used in any sequence, unlike SAPA and SCIS. Each unit strives to develop science concepts and thinking skills simultaneously. The rationale is that children acquire mental strategies for organizing their observations as they form science concepts based on those same experiences. This belief is consistent with Piagetian developmental psychology and the learning theory of Jerome Bruner (1962).

The questions children ask are highly valued in ESS. In fact, this is the main intent of the ESS materials: that children will raise all kinds of questions about their experiences and try ways to work with the materials that have not been pre-planned by the teacher. As a consequence, teachers have to expect that children will talk with other children as they compare observations and form explanations about what they experience.

ESS has a flexible structure and emphasizes attitudes as the discovery method is used by children to learn science content. The kits consist of low-cost materials and provide the kinds of direct experiences favored by program developers. As the units vary, so do the kits. Some kits are meant for entire classes of thirty students, but most are for smaller numbers: groups of about six, or individual students for certain activities (see Figure 10.5). Each kit and teacher's guide can be purchased separately, giving more freedom and flexibility when selecting curriculum materials for the science program than either SAPA or SCIS. Some ESS units may be used by purchasing only the teacher's guide without the expense of a commercial kit.

A teacher's guide accompanies the pupil kit. The guide contains background information and teaching tips that are suggestions rather than specific directions. Notes on classroom management share examples of the kinds of questions that teachers could ask children and examples of the kinds of answers children may give or the types of questions children may ask. Other suggestions help the teacher become a guide or adviser of inquiry rather than a provider of information. This teacher role ensures that the responsibility for learning is shifted to the child, as each is stimulated to devise her or his own way of acquiring and making meaning out of information from the exploration (see Figure 10.6 on pages 370–371).

ESS has no student textbooks. Worksheets, pictures, and supplementary brief booklets, called readers, accompany some of the units, while brief film loops provide learning experiences not easily acquired otherwise. There is considerable variation among the many ESS units, but this variation serves a fundamental purpose: to promote unguided exploration that motivates children to pursue topics of interest. ESS assumes that this kind of experience will help each child develop useful learning skills and that knowledge gained from this approach is meaningful and long lasting.

*ESS Program Effects.*   ESS strives to help children learn science and thinking skills through positive attitudes. Does this work? Again we can refer to the report of James Shymansky and his fellow researchers (1982) (see Table 10.2). Yes, to an extent ESS is successful. Achievement gains were less than with SCIS and SAPA, yet children who learned science by ESS did outperform their age-mates in traditional science programs by an average of 4 percentile points. Attitude improvements were impressive: average ESS scores were 20 percentile points above the averages of children from traditional programs, by far the largest advance of the three programs we compare in this chapter. Substantial increases in creativity and process skill development were shown by 26 and 18 percentile point gains, while completion of Piagetian tasks was 2 percentile points above those of traditional programs. Achievement gains were not as great as the theoretical assumptions of

**TABLE 10.2   Performance Improvement for Students in Classrooms Using ESS, SCIS, or SAPA as Compared to Students in Traditional Classrooms**

|  | Percentage Points Gained | | |
| --- | --- | --- | --- |
| Performance Area | ESS | SCIS | SAPA |
| Achievement | 4 | 34 | 7 |
| Attitudes | 20 | 3 | 15 |
| Process skills | 18 | 21 | 36 |
| Related skills | * | 8 | 4 |
| Creativity | 26 | 34 | 7 |
| Piagetian tasks | 2 | 5 | 12 |

*No studies reported

Source: James A. Shymansky, William C. Kyle, Jr., and Jennifer M. Alport, "How Effective Were the Hands-On Science Programs of Yesterday?" *Science and Children* (November–December 1982): 15.

FIGURE 10.5   ESS Scope and Sequence Chart

# Elementary Science Study Scope (ESS)

| UNIT | K | 1 | 2 | 3 | 4 | 5 | 6 | 7 | 8 | 9 |
|------|---|---|---|---|---|---|---|---|---|---|

**1 Growing Seeds** — Children learn what seeds are, how seeds grow and change, and how seeds differ from other small objects. Activities, including observing and recording growth, may be done as a class or in small groups.

**2 Match and Measure** — This practical unit is an introduction to measurement. Children determine length, area, and volume with a variety of tools and materials.

**3 Mobiles** — Construction of mobiles introduces students to principles of balancing, develops a feel for symmetry of shape and motion, and shows effect of weight on a balanced system.

**4 Primary Balancing** — After the initial challenge of balancing the beam, children learn the importance of weight and its position on the beam in relation to the fulcrum point. Further explorations reveal that weight is not a function of volume. Other activities include sorting, counting, and balancing odd-shaped boards on a half-ball fulcrum.

**5 Pattern Blocks** — With 250 blocks in six colors and shapes, children progress from casual play to creating elaborate mosaic designs, they also use mirrors to create new patterns. Math content includes measurement, symmetry, counting, shape, and proportion.

**6 Geo Blocks** — With the set of 330 unpainted, hardwood blocks the children move from free play activity to concepts of size, shape, one-to-one correspondence, and conservation of volume.

**7 Eggs and Tadpoles** — Observation of the changes from egg to tadpole to frog gives students direct experience with the concept of a life cycle.

**8 Tangrams** — Children assemble the 7 piece puzzle into various configurations, including the basic 4-inch square. They soon discover basic geometric relationships between the pieces and through visual experience learn to deal with problems analytically.

**9 Attributes Games and Problems** — Manipulation of the blocks, cubes, and people pieces provides experience in classification, class and relationship, and logical thinking processes.

**10 Spinning Tables** — Children explore the effects of circular motion by making designs and observing liquids and solid objects placed on revolving discs. Predictions and error stimulate discussion and further experimentation.

*Source:* Delta Education, Inc., P.O. Box 3000, Nashua, NH 03061-3000. Reprinted by permission of copyright holder.

# Scope and Sequence Chart

| UNIT | K | 1 | 2 | 3 | 4 | 5 | 6 | 7 | 8 | 9 |
|------|---|---|---|---|---|---|---|---|---|---|

**11 Brine Shrimp**

This durable organism provides children with concrete evidence of a life cycle and effects of environmental conditions on living things.

**12 Printing**

Through the handling of individual letters and formulation of words in the type holders, children learn the basics of printing. They also develop an appreciation of the printed word as a means of communication.

**13 Structures**

Students build structures with materials chosen to create structural problems. They learn to deal with properties such as size, strength of materials, and design configuration.

**14 Sink or Float**

Students discover that buoyancy of an object is a property of both the object and the liquid. Investigations involve different materials and shapes placed in liquids of varying densities.

**15 Clay Boats**

Children discover how to make clay float, and develop predicting, weighing, and measuring skills while learning about volume displacement and buoyancy.

**16 Drops, Streams & Containers**

Children observe characteristics of common liquids when these liquids are poured into one another or dropped on different surfaces. New ways to transfer liquids are developed.

**17 Mystery Powders**

Through use of scientific method, students progress from identification of harmless, common white powders to more advanced analysis of properties.

**18 Ice Cubes**

Activities with ice introduce the students to the effects that heat, insulation, shape, and conductivity have on melting rates. Thermometers are used to measure freezing and melting points.

**19 Rocks and Charts**

Children discover the many individual characteristics of a mineral which make it different from others. Rock sorting and chart making develop useful classification skills.

| Physical Science | Life Science | General Skills | Earth Science | Math |
|---|---|---|---|---|

367

**FIGURE 10.5** *(continued)*

**GROWING SEEDS: Exploration of Simple Plants** ▶

Students determine which samples are seeds. This is accomplished through external and internal observation, and planning. Growth rate is recorded on graphs.
*Grades K–3 (6–8 week program)*

◀ **BALLOONS AND GASES: Introduction to Common Gases**

An introduction to common gases. The generation of common gases allows students to discover some properties of gases and to differentiate between one gas and another. Students work with simple acids, bases, and bromothymol blue, or color indicator. "Mystery" gases are introduced by the teacher and the students attempt to identify them using their previous experiences.
*Grades 5–8 (1–22 class sessions)*

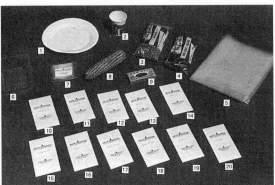

◀ **EGGS & TADPOLES: Observing a Frog's Life Cycle**

Students observe a frog develop from egg through various tadpole states and, with great care, even to a young frog. The students will answer many of their questions through observation and group discussions.
*Grades K–6 (3 week to 6 month program)*

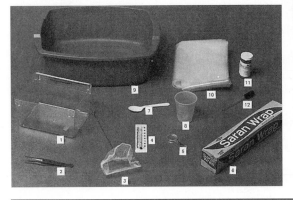

ESS might suggest, yet these assumptions were not completely wrong given the other substantial gains children made from the ESS program.

SAPA, SCIS, and ESS have shown some superior characteristics and effects when compared with traditional science programs. Yet each program is based on a different design and a different teaching approach, and for different reasons. Developers of the programs made different assumptions but shared some in common as well. What are the characteristics of effective science teaching that should be included in a science program?

## WHAT WORKS?

Take a look in a large number of elementary classrooms where science is taught and what do you see? Perhaps you observe what Donald Wright reports: "Fifty to 80 percent of all science classes use a single text or multiple texts as *the* basis for instruction. . . . For students, knowing is more a function of reading, digesting, and regurgitating information from the textbook or lab manual than it is of analyzing, synthesizing, and evaluating" (Wright, 1980, p. 144).

Furthermore, you may have an impression that a direct, authoritative, prescriptive approach with the same pace for everyone and where the 3 Rs are emphasized is actually the best way to teach science. As added support for this view you could refer to the fact that the three NSF-sponsored programs we have just mentioned have never been used by more than 30 percent of the school districts in the United States; also, only 7 percent of K–6 teachers have ever attended an NSF-sponsored meeting (Weiss, 1978). Certainly if the government spent millions to develop these programs, they would be used if they actually worked, right? Wrong.

What the three programs we compare all have in common is a hands-on curriculum and teaching approach. Despite what is widely believed and practiced, the hands-on, minds-on learning approach is superior to the traditional approach. James Shymansky and his colleagues (1982) tell us that synthesis of the abundant research shows conclusively that children in a hands-on science program achieve more, like science more, and improve their problem-solving

*Hands-on, minds-on learning makes the difference.*

FIGURE 10.6 Excerpts from an ESS Teacher's Guide

# Part 1: Simple Circuits

## Beginning Circuits

### Before Starting to Teach

Materials you will need:
2  8-inch pieces of #20 bare copper wire
2  8-inch pieces of #22 plastic-covered copper wire
3  #48 (PB) bulbs
3  D batteries
1  wire stripper

The following suggestions will guide your initial exploration. If you take enough time to try your own ideas as well, you will be ready for the variety of ideas your students are sure to propose.

Try to light one of the bulbs, using a piece of bare wire and a battery. Some people have taken 20 minutes to light the bulb the first time, so do not worry if yours does not light right away. See how many different ways you can devise to make the bulb light. It is helpful to make sketches of your various attempts, including those that do not work.

Using the plastic-covered wire, light a bulb. You will have to remove the covering from the ends. The wire stripper is designed to remove the plastic cover without cutting the wire. You can adjust the knob so that the wire opening will cut only the plastic.

**Stripper**

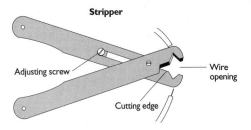

Place the wire in the opening and close the handles; then pull the stripper toward the end of the wire, so that it strips off a piece of the covering.

Now try some connections using a battery, a bulb, and two wires. You may find some surprises. For example, you know that the bulb in A below will light, but what will happen when you add another wire, as in B or C?

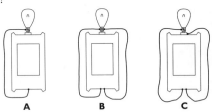

A    B    C

### In the Classroom

Materials you will need for each child:
1  8-inch piece of #22 plastic-covered copper wire
1  #48 (PB) bulb
1  D battery

For each group:
1  wire stripper

To have available:
extra supplies of the above materials

It is suggested that the students work in groups of two to four. Although they don't need to share equipment for the initial activity, they will soon need to do so.

Each student should have a box or paper bag in which to keep his materials at the end of each class period. It has worked well for children to keep the materials originally passed out to them for the duration of the unit. They use these materials, as well as others to be distributed later, continually. Whether or not the children take equipment home to work with is up to you.

#### LEAD-OFF QUESTION
*Can you make the bulb light with one battery and one wire?*

Some children will take 20 minutes to light the bulb, while others will take only five. Once one child in a class manages to make the bulb light, his method catches on quickly. Probably only five or six will light the bulb on their own. The rest will follow a neighbor's lead.

As the bulbs are lighted, assure the children that there are different ways to light bulbs, and have them look for more. Invite them up to the chalkboard to draw the various ways they have tried. Ways in which the bulb does not light are just as important and should be drawn on the board, too.

It is extremely important to give children this time for free investigation with the equipment, so that they can pursue whatever questions occur to them. Their questions at this early stage will provide good leads for later work. After doing these first experiments, some children may bring household bulbs into the class. One such class connected seven batteries to a 50-watt bulb and still saw no light. Then a girl felt that the bulb was warm; they added another battery or two and were rewarded by a slight glow. One battery was removed, and the bulb dimmed. The class then went on to compare the number of batteries required to light bulbs of various sizes.

#### FOLLOW-UP QUESTION
*How many different ways can you light the bulb?*

#### ACTIVITIES CHILDREN MAY TRY
• Using two or more batteries, light the PB.
• Find out how many bulbs can be lit with one battery.
• Find out how brightly a bulb will shine when three, four, or eight batteries are used.
• Find out how many batteries it takes to burn out a bulb.
• Use plastic-covered wire, light a PB.
• Use more wire to see if a PB will still light.

*Source:* Delta Education, Inc., P.O. Box 3000, Nashua, NH 03061-3000. Reprinted by permission of copyright holder.

- Find out which will wear out first, if contact between a battery and a PB is maintained for a long time. How long does it take?
- Attach a wire from one end of the battery to the other. See how the battery feels after five minutes in this situation and after an hour.
- See if the battery will light a bulb after an hour.

*Note:* When investigating the different ways that will light the bulb, children often discuss the question, "Does turning the battery around make another way?" The fact that a battery works both ways is an exciting discovery to many.

## POSSIBLE DISCUSSION QUESTIONS

After three or four sessions with these materials, the children will be ready to come together as a class to share their experiences. One way to begin such a discussion is to draw some circuits on the board and ask if the class can predict whether the bulbs in the arrangements will light. Below are examples of some circuits you may want to discuss.

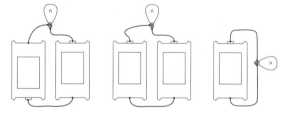

*Will these bulbs light? Why?*

Let the children discuss all their ideas. Have them try out each new circuit with the equipment to verify their predictions. Perhaps some students will want to make generalizations about the features of those circuits in which the bulb lights and those in which the bulb does not light.

*What did you find out in the last few lessons?*

You'll find that many children will have forgotten some of their work because they did not keep a record of it. They should now see the need for simple notes and diagrams.

*How many ways did you find to make the bulb light?*
*Does the bulb have to be touching the battery?*
*Does the wire have to be wrapped around the bulb?*
*What special places must be touched on the bulb for it to light?*
*Can you make a "rule" about lighting the bulb?"*

Be prepared for a variety. Give each child who has something to say a chance to be heard.

### Teaching Background
Since this is the initial section of the unit, it has been designed to open the way to many later areas of investigation. The general background presented here is, therefore, intended to suggest ways in which you can help children both to go further and to understand where they are going.

A bulb can be lit essentially in four ways, using one wire and one battery. (Actually, turning the wire around could be considered to be creating new ways, too.)

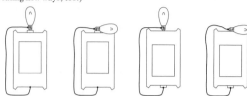

In each case, the bulb lights with the same brightness. Asking a child about the brightness of different arrangements helps him to see that brightness is a way to tell something about a circuit.

Since the battery lights the bulb with equal brightness, regardless of which way it is facing in the circuit, children may wonder why some batteries are marked with a "+" (positive) and a "–" (negative) at the top and the flat end respectively. If the bulb can't tell one end from the other, why do we bother about designating the poles positive and negative? This question will be answered when the children start working with more than one battery. At that time, the students will see that with two or more batteries in a circuit, the direction of each is important.

The "flow" of electricity usually comes up sooner or later. Does the electricity "flow" in circuits from the positive to the negative end of the battery or vice versa? This is a very difficult question to answer experimentally. It is further complicated by the fact that when different materials are used in circuits, different things happen. Students who are quick to explain simple circuits in terms of a particular direction of flow might profit from a question such as: "Are you sure? What difference would you notice if the flow were actually the reverse?" Since the students have noticed that the bulb works equally well on both ends of the battery, they should begin to realize that the particular direction of electricity flow doesn't matter in this situation.

When students start lighting more than one bulb with one battery, or one bulb with more than one battery, a great many possibilities for further investigation emerge.

The changes in brightness of the bulb can be accounted for, if you recognize that the bulb is acting like a meter, giving a measure of how much or how little of "something" is in the wire. If children can group the results of their experiments in such a way that they see relationships between, and common elements in, activities that dim and activities that brighten a bulb, they are on the way to understanding what is happening.

### Predicting Sheet 1
Prediction Sheet 1 illustrates twelve situations closely related to many of the activities your children may have investigated in the first section.

After a child has thought about each circuit and marked the sheet accordingly, discuss some of his predictions with him. What reasons are given for a particular answer? When a child predicts incorrectly or cannot describe a convincing basis for his prediction, recommend that he test his prediction by making the circuit. He may then be able to give a clearer explanation for some results.

skills more than children who learn from traditional textbook-based programs. The hands help the minds grow by constructing meaning. These conclusions endured resynthesis even though original statistics have been revised to yield results of greater precision (Shymansky, et al., 1990).

Ted Bredderman (1982) adds support to this view. Bredderman's research is provided as a part of *Project Synthesis,* a massive research effort funded by the National Science Foundation to determine the effects of past experimental programs so that present and future science education goals could be revised. Bredderman's research collected the results from sixty studies that involved 13,000 students in 1,000 elementary classrooms over fifteen years. He analyzed the results of these studies carefully through meta-analysis procedures to sort out conflicting findings reported in the literature. His conclusion clearly shows what works:

> With the use of activity-based science programs, teachers can expect substantially improved performance in science process and creativity; modestly increased performance on tests of perception, logic, language development, science content, and math; modestly improved attitudes toward science and science class; and pronounced benefits for disadvantaged students. (Bredderman, 1982, pp. 39–41)

Hands-on, minds-on learning makes the difference. Exploring, investigating, and discovering are essential to meaningful learning and effective science teaching. When children solve problems and make discoveries, they are learning how to learn and constructing meaning for themselves. Jerome Bruner (1961) points out the benefits for children as they make discoveries through active learning:

- Children's intellectual potency is increased; their powers of thinking improve.
- Children's rewards for learning shift from those that come from the teacher or someone else to those that are found inside themselves from the satisfaction they feel.
- Children learn the procedures and important steps for making discoveries and find ways to transfer these to other learning opportunities.
- What children learn takes on more meaning, and they remember it longer.

While all three programs surveyed here report successes, they also have limitations. From the research that has been synthesized, it seems prudent to mix emphases on science content and process skills for the most potent teaching and learning combination. Yet researchers like Ted Bredderman and James Shymansky and his colleagues warn against abandoning the traditional textbook-based programs in complete favor of SAPA, SCIS, ESS, or the like. Instead, they recommend incorporating the useful methods and materials into existing science programs as a step toward improvement.

What are we to do? First, realize that some of the effective science programs remain. Several schools still use SAPA, SCIS, and ESS. Parts of these can be added to existing school programs to provide children with more hands-on learning opportunities. Next, be aware that there have been substantial improvements in recent editions of textbooks and that new generations of curriculum supplements have been developed. These supplements may be available through your university or state department of education. Both of these types of resources have capitalized on several features that made the alphabet soup programs successful. For example, we find more frequent use of student learning activities with a focus on specific conceptual outcomes, better organization of teaching materials, and convenient packaging of curriculum materials; we can attribute these improvements to the effects of the hands-on, minds-on programs.

Programs like ESS, SAPA, and SCIS definitely filled a void that existed when elementary science textbooks were nothing more than a lesson in reading. Without national science standards, many science textbooks tried to cover everything with very little depth. The alphabet soup science programs proved that hands-on and minds-on could go hand-in-hand.

It would seem that the lessons learned would follow up the grades from the primary and intermediate science textbooks into the middle schools texts. In a recent study by the American Association for the Advancement of Science (AAAS) this did not prove to be the case. The AAAS Project 2061 Middle Grades Science Textbooks Evaluation completed in 1999 found that out of nine middle school science textbooks none were ranked satisfactory on a number of rating criteria. The study identified key ideas from the National Science Education Standards in the earth, life and physical sciences and from *Benchmarks for Science Literacy* from AAAS. The study identified categories on which to judge the science content within those key areas. It looked at how well the textbook (1) provided a sense of purpose and conveyed that in a clear manner; (2) took into account student ideas by addressing commonly held beliefs about the key idea; (3) engaged the students with relevant phenomena; (4) developed and used scientific ideas; (5) promoted student thinking about phenomena, experiences, and ideas; (6) assessed student progress; and (7) enhanced the learning environment. The textbooks studied were all found unsatisfactory. In most cases they covered too many topics, providing very little depth in any of them. The only middle school material deemed satisfactory in this study was actually a supplement titled *Matter and Molecules,* created at Michigan State University in 1988. A detailed look at the books involved in the study and the results can be found through the American Association for the Advancement of Science Web site at *http://www.project2061.org.*

A study of this nature indicates that there is still much confusion as to what science and how much of it should be taught at the K–8 level. As evidenced by this study, the National Research Council's National Science Education Standards and the American Association for the Advancement of Science's Project 2061 are slowly becoming the standard to guide textbook construction. Many state science curricula are using these as their guide. We now know that if the elementary science program is to serve *all* children well, specific assumptions must

## Emphasis on Excellence

The National Science Education Standards provide criteria for excellence in developing K–8 science programs and improving science teaching, learning, and assessment. The standards for excellence are grounded in five assumptions:

- The vision of science education described by the Standards requires changes throughout the entire system.
- What students learn is greatly influenced by how they are taught.

- The actions of teachers are deeply influenced by their perceptions of science as an enterprise and as a subject to be taught and learned.
- Student understanding is actively constructed through individual and social processes.
- Actions of teachers are deeply influenced by their understanding of and relationships with students (National Research Council, 1996, p. 28).

Achieving these standards for excellence requires several changes throughout the system of science education. Therefore, the excellent science program must encompass the following changes in emphases (National Research Council, 1996, p. 224):

| *Less Emphasis On* | *More Emphasis On* |
| --- | --- |
| • Developing science programs at different grade levels independently of one another | • Coordinating the development of the K–12 science program across grade levels |
| • Using assessments unrelated to curriculum and teaching | • Aligning curriculum, teaching, and assessment |
| • Maintaining current resource allocations for books | • Allocating resources necessary for hands-on inquiry teaching aligned with the Standards |
| • Textbook- and lecture-driven curriculum | • Curriculum that supports the Standards and includes a variety of components, such as laboratories emphasizing inquiry and field trips |
| • Broad coverage of unconnected factual information | • Curriculum that includes natural phenomena and science-related social issues that students encounter in everyday life |
| • Treating science as a subject isolated from other school subjects | • Connecting science to other school subjects, such as mathematics and social studies |
| • Science learning opportunities that favor one group of students | • Providing challenging opportunities for all students to learn science |
| • Limiting hiring decisions to the administration | • Involving successful teachers of science in the hiring process |
| • Maintaining the isolation of teachers | • Treating teachers as professionals whose work requires opportunities for continual learning and networking |
| • Supporting competition | • Promoting collegiality among teachers as a team to improve the school |
| • Teachers as followers | • Teachers as decision makers |

guide program development and science teaching. Science must be taught so that children construct meaning from direct science experiences and expand their problem-solving and thinking skills. Furthermore, the subject matter must provide opportunities for children to develop personally; to learn about the many interrelationships among science, technology, and our society; to grow intellectually through inquiry; and to be exposed to the history and nature of science.

Each science program can evolve from its present condition to a level where relevant learning opportunities are provided for all children. The following list of assumptions and supported research is associated with effective science programs. The list is gleaned from research supported by the National Science Foundation and the National Science Teachers Association's recommendations for exemplary elementary science programs. These assumptions reveal some of the impact of historically significant science programs and predict the future trends science programs will face. We suggest that you keep these assumptions handy and let them help you plan more effective science instruction as well as advise your school principal or curriculum committee.

## Supported Assumptions About Effective Elementary Science Programs

**1.** National Science Foundation experimental elementary science programs and sponsored new approaches to teacher preparation have been successful, even though a low percentage of schools (30 percent) have used the programs and an even smaller percentage of teachers (7 percent) have received direct training.

**2.** Effective elementary science programs keep pace with changes in science, society, knowledge, and trends in schooling.

**3.** Most current elementary school science programs do not serve all children well. Effective programs have meaning for diverse audiences.

**4.** Effective science programs strive to promote children's personal development; to help children explore the interrelationships among science, technology, and society; to continue academic preparation through inquiry; and to build awareness of the history and nature of science.

**5.** Effective programs have no single author but are developed by teams with teacher involvement. Extensive classroom testing and program revision are necessary and must be done frequently.

**6.** Students learn successfully in different ways; multiple views on learning add diversity and help to balance the effective science program.

**7.** Programs that emphasize conceptual learning appear to be most effective overall and produce the greatest and most enduring gains in achievement when conception is a learner's construct.

**8.** Multiple teaching methods are useful, and hands-on learning opportunities are necessary for all children. Overall, inquiry methods and learning cycles are useful methods for helping children learn science concepts.

**9.** What is taught—the substance of science—must be useful and relevant for each child. Publications such as the National Science Education Standards help guide content selection.

**10.** Packaging the program is helpful and reduces teachers' preparation time. New generation science curriculum supplements have several common features that add impact to the materials. They identify relevant themes, define purposes or objectives, give background information, list materials needed, state procedures for teaching, identify essential vocabulary, offer ideas for evaluation or lesson expansion, and so on.

**11.** The history and nature of science makes it possible to integrate topics into other subject lessons. Science's diversity enriches other parts of the school curriculum and adds to its power as a literacy subject.

**12.** A less direct, teacher-as-guide instructional role is effective because students are encouraged to assume greater responsibility for their own learning.

**13.** Conceptual learning takes time and should not be rushed; effectiveness rather than time efficiency should be the driving force of the curriculum.

**14.** Learners in constructivist science programs achieve more, like science more, and improve their problem-solving skills more than children who learn from traditional textbook-based programs. Innovative newer generations of science textbooks incorporate many of the features of the effective experimental programs.

**15.** Effective science programs promote children's intellectual development by improving their thinking through inquiry and problem-solving processes.

**16.** Materials and learning activities must match the child's level of development to have the greatest impact.

**17.** Students receive intrinsic rewards from the personal discoveries they make through firsthand learning experiences with manipulatives.

**18.** The science students learn from effective programs helps them transfer their learning to other circumstances better, get more meaning, and remember what they learn longer.

### Scenario

Once the students in Professor Becker's class realized the importance of looking at some of the older science programs they soon discovered that most of the new materials were developed by lessons learned in the older materials. Some of the student teams were surprised to learn that the school they were doing their science field study in was using *Science A Process Approach*. One team in particular was working with Mr. Blevin's fifth grade class as they went through the *Animal Responses Module 36*. The student team of Kara, Cade, and Rosita were looking for ways to extend the lesson beyond what was provided through the SAPA module.

"I wish I knew more about animals and how they respond to stimuli in the environment. I don't remember learning much about animal behavior in my undergraduate work," admitted Rosita.

Kara agreed "I can't remember much either, but I think I saw an article about this very topic in one of those *Science Scope* journals Mr. Blevin had in the back of his room. I'll check it out later this afternoon."

Cade jumped in with, "I saw a television program just last week about a local naturalist that does all sorts of programs with elementary students out at the nature center. I wonder if she'd come to the school to talk to the students. I'd like to see the nature center anyway, so I'll go over and talk to her."

Rosita responded with, "While you're doing that I'm going to go through that resource Professor Becker shared with us last week, Project Wild. I'll bet there's an activity in there we can use to expand Mr. Blevin's students understanding of animal responses to environmental changes."

Within two days Kara, Cade, and Rosita had found an activity out of a supplemental resource, had background information from an NSTA middle school teacher journal, and found a human resource to come into the school to provide additional insights to the topic at hand.

During their next science method's class the student team shared with Professor Becker the excitement they felt once they completed teaching the planned expansion activities with Mr. Blevin's class. "I couldn't believe how much work we put into that unit. The neat thing was that once we started looking, the amount of print and human resources on our topic was unbelievable," stated Cade.

Kara added, "The students came alive when the local naturalist walked in with the red-tailed hawk and the fox snake."

Rosita summed it up with, "Considering the reaction of the students, I could not imagine just using the science textbook. So many things exist to make the science concepts come alive, judging by the look on the students faces and the way they could explain the concepts studied, spending the extra time to bring in additional resources was well worth it!"

## THE NEXT GENERATION OF SCIENCE PROGRAMS

Lessons from the past have helped to improve the wonderful new resources available to teachers. This exciting era of curriculum and program development has helped to renew interest in science. Science programs are attempting to keep pace with changes in the fields of science and technology and to investigate the impact of each on our society through the eyes and experiences of children.

The new generation of science programs strives to serve the needs and interests of all learners, not an intellectual elite. New programs often emphasize conceptual development through constructivist techniques, use multiple teaching methods to fill multiple student interests, and incorporate multiple views on human diversity. Many programs promote such additional science outcomes as students skilled at science inquiry and problem solving; investigations of interrelationships among and between science, technology, and society; awareness of the history and tentative nature of science; and an expanded awareness of career opportunities in science.

The direct and sustained involvement of classroom teachers is one of the greatest factors shaping new science programs. Attempts are made to match the students' levels of development to appropriate learning experiences and help strengthen the conceptual constructions of learners by connecting learning experiences and central concepts to science themes. Table 10.3 on page 378

**TABLE 10.3   Common Science Themes**

| Earth Systems | Benchmarks | California Framework | Biological Sciences Curriculum Study (BSCS) | National Assessment of Educational Progress (NAEP) | National Science Education Standards (NSES) | Project Learning Tree (PLT) |
|---|---|---|---|---|---|---|
| | | | | | Order and organization | |
| Aesthetics | Constancy | Stability | Cause and effect | | Constancy | |
| Interaction | Patterns of change | Patterns of change | Change and conservation | Patterns of change | Measurement and change | Patterns of change |
| | | Energy | Energy and matter | | | |
| | Scale | Scale and structure | Time and scale | | | Structure and scale |
| Evolution | Evolution | Evolution | Evolution and equilibrium | | Evolution and equilibrium | |
| Scale & Systems | Systems | Systems and interactions | Systems and interactions | Systems | | Systems |
| Nature of Science | | | Probability and prediction | | | |
| | | | Structure and function | | Form and function | |
| Careers | | | | | | |
| | | | Diversity and variation | | | Diversity |
| | Models | | Models and theories | Models | Models | |
| Human impact | | | | | | Inter-relationships |

illustrates the thematic similarities and differences among several new science programs. Continual classroom testing of materials and lessons and frequent revision through formative evaluation assist these programs through rapid

*New science programs provide a variety of experiences to help children understand their complex worlds.*

stages of evolution. Hence, conceptual flaws are reduced, and supported assumptions about learning are expanded.

Although there are numerous small-scale efforts to produce the next generation of science programs, space permits us to share only a sample of the larger efforts that have endured rigorous evaluation and received national (often international) attention.

***AIMS.*** *Activities to Integrate Mathematics and Science* publishes elementary and middle school curriculum materials that integrate mathematics and science for grades K–9. These materials are provided in easy-to-use teacher manuals that have been produced and classroom tested by teachers. Workshops and seminars are available through the AIMS organization, P.O. Box 8120, Fresno, CA 93747, *http://www.aimsedu.org*. Titles include *Floaters and Sinkers, Jawbreakers and Heart Thumpers, Glide into Winter with Math and Science, Pieces and Patterns*, and *The Sky's the Limit!* Some are available in Spanish.

***Delta Science Modules.*** This series of forty paperback modules ranges from *Air* to *Observing an Aquarium* to *You and Your Body*. Lessons are suitable for intermediate and middle school grades, provide easy-to-follow instructions that help teachers guide students through constructivist learning opportunities, and offer reasonably authentic assessment devices. Modules may be purchased separately or as a set. Kits of hands-on materials are available at additional cost. Available from Delta Education, P.O. Box 3000, Nashua, NH 03061-3000, *http://www.delta-ed.com*, 800-258-1302.

***Earth Systems Education.*** This middle school science resource guide is a joint product of the Ohio State University and the University of Northern Colorado. Through a K–12 scope and sequence, teachers are urged to use the classroom-tested materials to develop among learners the values of aesthetics and stewardship through practical local learning experiences that help students to explore state, national, and global earth issues within the context of various science disciplines. Six principles unify the learning experiences. Contact the Earth Systems Education Program at the Ohio State University, (614) 292-9826. School of Natural Resources, OSU, 221 Coffey Road, Columbus, OH 43210, *http://www2.ag.ohio-state.edu/~earthsys/index.html*.

*ECO-NET.*   Downloadable resource files, e-mail, and conferencing support are available through this Internet access resource. The resources cover an array of environmental issues and provide real-time support. A computer and modem are necessary, and a monthly fee plus connect time charges apply. Contact the Institute for Global Communications, 18 DeBoom Street, San Francisco, CA, 94107.

*FOSS.*   *Full Option Science System,* of the Lawrence Hall of Science in Berkeley, California 94720, is distributed by the Encyclopaedia Britannica Educational Corporation. For grades K through 6, student equipment kits and print materials are accompanied by some of the most innovative assessment alternatives we have seen. Children do science, construct concepts, and perform direct evaluation exercises in the areas of life, physical, and earth science and scientific reasoning and technology. A correlation to NSES can be found on the FOSS Web site, *http://www.lhs.berkeley.edu/Foss/Foss.html.*

*GEMS.*   *Great Exploration in Math and Science* is designed for students in grades K through 12. Science and mathematics are integrated in twenty-four different teacher activity publications and student project booklets. Available through the Lawrence Hall of Science in Berkeley, California 94720, topics include *Animals in Action, Bubble-ology, Buzzing a Hive, Crime Lab Chemistry, Fingerprinting, Mapping Fish Habitats, Oobleck,* and *Vitamin C Testing.* The GEMS Web site is *http://www.lhs.berkeley.edu/GEMS/.*

***Insights: An Inquiry-Based Elementary School Science Curriculum.***   This K–6 curriculum is designed to develop children's understanding of key science concepts while improving the student's abilities to think creatively and critically; encouraging problem solving through experiences in the natural environment; fostering the development of positive attitudes about science; bridging science concepts to current social and environmental events; and integrating science with the mathematics and language arts curriculum. What is unique about this curriculum is that it was designed to specifically address the needs of an urban student. It was developed by a coalition of Education Development Center science curriculum specialists and teams of elementary teachers from urban centers such as Baltimore, Boston, Cleveland, Los Angeles, New York, Montgomery County (Maryland), and San Francisco. A detailed description of the curriculum can be found at *http://www.edc.org/ CSE/imd/insights3.html.* The curricular materials can be ordered through Kendall/ Hunt at *http://www.kendallhunt.com* or call 800-542-6657, ext. 1042.

*Kids-Net.*   *National Geographic Kids Network* of Education Services, Dept. 5389, Washington, D.C. 20036 involves children in a nationwide computer network; learners collect data in their home environments and send the information to the national server. Sharing information helps children to make comparisons and discover concepts about water quality and rain, for example, on a national and global scale. Learners are linked with practicing scientists. The Web site for this is *http://www.nationalgeographic.com/kids/index.html.*

***PEACHES.*** The Peaches Program is another science program developed through the Lawrence Hall of Science at the University of California at Berkeley. This program is designed for children ages 4–6, grades PreK–1. Numerous science and mathematics activities and projects as well as professional development opportunities for the early childhood educator are all a part of the Peaches program. Details on this program can be found at *http://www.lhs.berkeley.edu/PEACHES/*

***Projects WILD and Aquatic.*** Two different versions of a great idea, these projects emphasize wildlife and aquatic life, respectively. Interdisciplinary and for grades K–12, the materials accommodate major school subjects and skills areas by involving children in direct and simulated wildlife experiences. The purpose is to increase awareness first, then to build toward making personal decisions and taking responsible human actions. The teacher-designed materials make it easy to bring outdoor wildlife concepts into the classroom. Students love the outdoor action sections. The activity guides are available only through training sessions. Information can be obtained by contacting Project WILD, 5430 Grosvenor Lane, Bethesda, MD 20814, *http://www.projectwild.org*.

***Project Learning Tree.*** This new generation of a classic is designed to help learners better understand the forest community and its relationship to the day-to-day lives of people and animals. Each lesson is classroom-tested, linked to a specific science theme, and supported by conceptual story lines. Themes include diversity, interrelationships, systems, structure and scale, and patterns of change. The materials are available by attending special workshops. Contact the American Forest Foundation, 1111 19th Street, N.W., Suite 780, Washington, D.C. 20036, *http://www.plt.org*.

***Project WET (Water Education for Teachers).*** This program helps teachers explore water issues with learners. One hundred multidisciplinary activities support this resource, which are also supported by such supplements as special topic modules, models, children's literature books, and living history materials. Write to Project WET, 201 Culbertson Hall, Montana State University, Bozeman, MT 59717.

***SEPUP.*** *Science Education for Public Understanding Program* is developed and provided by the Lawrence Hall of Science in Berkeley, California 94720-5200. The materials are arranged in modules. The original program, CEPUP, emphasized chemical education; new modules address physical, earth, and life sciences as well as science processes. SEPUP emphasizes an integrated approach to teaching issues-oriented science. SEPUP kits are designed for children in grades 6 through 8 and address topics like pollution, household chemicals, waste, and chemicals in foods. Yearlong SEPUP courses for grades 7 through 10 strive to make science concepts relevant to the real world. Chem-2 for grades 4–6, *http://www.kks.berkeley.edu/sepupl*.

***TOPS Learning Systems.*** The Task Oriented Physical Science (TOPS) materials center on physical science concepts. The over forty modules are designed for students in grades 3–10. Each module comes with reproducible masters that include detailed instructions for hands-on, concept based activities around a given theme. A complete listing of the TOPS modules can be found at *http://www.topscience.org* or by contacting TOPS Learning Systems, 10970 Mulino Road, Canby, OR 97013.

*Windows on Science.*   This K–6 program is described as a multisensory learning model that combines images and activities to make science come alive for the learner. It contains eleven volumes organized around primary science, earth science, life science, and physical science. Teacher guides with reproducible masters are included with each volume. Students are encouraged to design experiments, create models and apply their understanding in a real life context. What makes this year long program unique is the videodisc that comes with each volume. This videodisc provides numerous visual clips to reinforce the science concepts. Detailed information including ordering information is provided on the Optical Data Corporation Web site at *http://opticaldata.com/catalog/wos/wosmain.html.*

## SUPPLEMENTAL RESOURCES

*Resources* are things that can be turned to for support or help. We encourage you to be resourceful—to be readily able to act effectively—as you arrange science experiences for your students. A teacher who uses the textbook as the entire teaching guide limits the variety and quality of instruction. Adding community resources increases learning opportunities, allows experiences that address the goals of a comprehensive science education program, provides the link between the students' present and future experiences, and makes the teaching process personal for both students and the teacher. Including additional resources requires time and planning, but teachers discover through experience that the addition of information and hands-on activities goes beyond the walls of the classroom and the world of academia and often creates the most memorable learning experiences of all. For example, the Thomas Jefferson Magnet School in Euclid, Ohio, uses animals in its curriculum. Each room has permanent animal residents: chinchillas, hamsters, a pot-belly pig, iguanas, finches, a turtle, a python, a snake, a parakeet, a parrot, and a rabbit. An English springer spaniel resides in the office and greets all arriving guests. This novel use of resources within the classroom provides an exciting learning experience.

You may never fully know the effect any learning activity has on your students, but many class reunions are spent discussing the memorable events of the school years. You should hope that the experiences you provide students are ones they will remember and value. The classroom may be the typical location for learning, but the walls may be extended to the community where students will spend their lives.

The link between the community and the classroom is not a new concept. John Dewey (1916) made the following statement, still appropriate, in his *Democracy and Education* more than seventy years ago:

*Community resources stimulate children's interests in science and its practical value.*

The development within the young of the attitudes and dispositions necessary to the continuous and progressive life of society cannot take place by direct conveyance of beliefs, emotions, and knowledge. It takes place through the intermediary of the environment, the environment consists of the sum total of conditions which are concerned with the execution of the activity characteristic of the living being. The social environment consists of all activities of fellow beings that are bound up in carrying on the activities of any of its members. It is truly educative in its effect, in its efforts, in the degree in which an individual appropriates the purpose which actuates it, becomes familiar with its methods and subject matters, acquires needed skills, and is saturated with its emotional spirit. (quoted in Decker, 1981, p. 39)

The need for relevance in education is paramount as the country finds its educational system questioned in relation to a new technological and global society. This society's ability to respond to profound and rapid changes is dependent on an adequate and educated human resource base. Therefore, our mission as educators is to prepare an educated and scientifically literate citizenry capable of responding to technological advances. The characteristics of the future workforce likely will mirror these changing demographics, with more minorities and women prepared to enter employment than at the present. Programs within schools must respond to these changes, promote a comprehensive understanding of the role of science in human affairs, and stress the importance of a scientifically literate workforce.

Areas of emphasis within the classroom should attempt to

- encourage student interest in science by broadening K–12 initiatives that emphasize the interrelatedness of science and society;
- strengthen the curricula so that they better address societal and ethical concerns, internationalize course content, and focus on communication and analytical skills;
- utilize innovative instructional delivery systems that reach wider audiences more economically with more effective learning experiences;
- promote education that relates to emerging technologies and careers and includes the development and dissemination of career information and networking with science professionals and stressing scientific literacy in grades K–12.

Gladys Dillion (1977), inservice director of the Flint (Michigan) Community Schools, contends that using community resources has the following effects:

- Gives learning in school closer relations with actual life situations, needs, and problems.
- Develops interest in school work that impels (rather than compels) children to come to school.
- Clarifies teaching and learning by making use of concrete, firsthand illustrations and demonstrations.
- Provides experience in planning, problem solving, and critical thinking.
- Develops skills of observing, asking questions, searching for information, and seeking relationships.
- Places knowledge and skill in the context of functional learning: learning to use by doing.
- Brings related content areas and skills together and uses them to meet problems and situations.
- Provides common learning and common adjustment to problems and differences in needs, abilities, and interests.
- Emphasizes achieving good human relations and practicing them.
- Increases opportunities for understanding and practicing the responsibilities of community citizenship.

School communities can become laboratories that assist with effective and relevant teaching. Our community resources can also help us to involve parents. Safran (1974) gives examples that directly relate to teachers. Community involvement

- enables teachers to draw on supplemental and often unique adult resources,
- provides teachers with additional information about the children they teach,
- encourages teachers to recognize other perceptions of what they do,
- permits teachers to understand more about the community their school serves,
- makes possible political alliances between teachers as workers and parents as consumers to contend with school bureaucracies.

## WHAT RESOURCES ARE AVAILABLE?

### Human Resources

A readily available and often overlooked resource is your colleagues. Using colleagues as resource persons for instructional guidance and assistance enables us to broaden educational activities and to foster cooperation.

Your colleagues—other classroom teachers, the principal, the school nurse, the resource teacher, the librarian—are all potential sources of assistance. The experienced teacher who is willing to share activities, materials, and support is a natural aide. Teachers in another school or grade level may be able to suggest teaching activities and loan equipment or share materials. Upper-grade-level students are also sources of help because they may be available to provide a demonstration or to serve as a teaching assistant or tutor.

Community volunteers can provide enriching services. Communities may contain engineers, professors, sewage treatment personnel, medical professionals, computer specialists, and mechanics who are interested in education. In addition, parents may offer suggestions. Corporations and institutions may have an educational officer who can assist by providing names of employees who are willing to volunteer their time and talent to assist within the schools. Consider contacting retirement groups, chambers of commerce, local women's clubs, local, state, or national agencies, or even the Yellow Pages. Their members are experienced and may have time to volunteer.

A volunteer can enable you to devote more time to planning, diagnosing the individual needs of students, and prescribing learning activities for these needs. Volunteers may offer other benefits. They extend the number of people available to help the teacher and often bring skills that professional educators do not have, so the educational process maximizes opportunities for all students. Perhaps most important are the positive effects that volunteering can have on the volunteers themselves, and the public relations value is certainly important (Hager-Shoeny & Galbreath, 1982).

Table 10.4 on page 386 lists vocations that volunteers might have. Look to individuals such as these to help with your school program.

Not all volunteers feel confident to make a presentation to a classroom on their particular area of interest. They may prefer instead to be involved in one or more of the following ways:

- demonstrating scientific concepts,
- serving as a mentor,
- tutoring,
- providing science fair project assistance,
- providing career choice assistance,
- reviewing school safety equipment,
- assisting in science competition instruction,
- demonstrating societal and technological applications of content,
- furnishing specialized equipment,
- assisting in speakers' bureaus,
- spearheading public awareness campaigns,
- encouraging projects for girls and minorities,
- arranging field trips,
- maintaining equipment,
- assisting with special demonstrations.

The tips in Table 10.5 on page 387 may help volunteers feel comfortable in their roles. Volunteers may not always be aware of the relevance of their knowledge and skills to elementary students; explain the benefits the students will receive from his or her assistance. The following advice was adapted from list of suggestions for volunteers prepared by the Lane County Juvenile Department in Eugene, Oregon (Hager-Schoeny & Galbreath, 1982):

- Invite volunteers to serve as partners.
- Clearly define the differences in the tasks and roles of employees and volunteers.

**TABLE 10.4   Science Classroom Volunteers**

| Area of Science | Volunteer |
| --- | --- |
| Animals | Zoologist, entomologist, microbiologist, zookeeper, veterinarian, beekeeper, marine biologist, paleontologist, cytologist, animal trainer, physician, forest ranger, physiologist, chemist, ecologist, neurobiologist, wildlife manager, farmer, rancher, geneticist, anatomist, mammalogist, limnologist, nurse, dietitian, x-ray technician, pharmacologist, forensic specialist, pharmacist |
| Plants | Botanist, paleobotanist, agronomist, horticulturist, farmer, forest manager, chemist, ecologist, geneticist, paleontologist, nutritionist, landscape architect, soil pathologist, soil scientist conservation officer, park ranger, agricultural extension agent |
| Weather | Meteorologist, ecologist, agronomist, TV weather forecaster, airport flight controller, geologist, oceanographer, climatologist, fisherman, boat captain, farmer, pilot, environmentalist, soil and water conservation agent |
| Physical and chemical properties | Chemist, biochemist, pharmacologist, architect, inventor, mechanic, carpenter, molecular biologist, physicist, ecologist, musical instrument maker, musician, toxicologist, metallurgist, geologist, photographer, builder, police lab forensic criminologist, materials scientist, technician, water company technician, engineers: chemical, textile, industrial, cosmetics developer, gemologist, acoustical engineer, optical engineer, mechanical engineer, civil engineer, building inspector, potter, nuclear engineer, agricultural engineer, ceramic engineer |
| Electricity | Physicist, geologist, computer hardware/software designer, electrician, radar technician, amateur radio operator, designer, industrial engineer, electrical engineer, telephone system technician, thermal engineer, mechanical engineer, electronic engineer, electrical inspector, inventor, radio/TV engineer |
| Earth and space science | Astronomer, geologist, paleontologist, pilot, astronaut, geographer, cartographer, ecologist, physicist, biologist, chemist, surveyor, geotechnical tester, aerial photographer, volcanologist, seismologist, oceanographer, soil scientist, aeronautical engineer, aviation engineer, construction engineer, civil engineer |
| Behavioral and social science | Animal psychologist, clinical psychologist, marketing professional, business manager, psychiatrist, sociologist, anthropologist, city planner, applied economist, school psychologist, historian, archaeologist, geographer, pollster, market research analyst, demographer, statistician |

*Source:* North Carolina Museum of Life and Science, *Science in the Classroom,* as cited by Triangle Coalition for Science and Technology Education, *A Guide for Planning a Volunteer Program for Science, Mathematics, and Technology Education* (College Park, MD: Triangle Coalition, 1992), p. 59.

- Screen volunteers and accept only the ones who can contribute. Check references and interview each candidate as you would a prospective employee.
- Require a specific commitment of time and resources from volunteers.
- Provide an orientation program to acquaint volunteers with their functions.
- Provide supervision.

**TABLE 10.5   Tips for Teachers Working with Volunteers**

1. Take time to talk with the volunteer outside the classroom, explaining class procedures, schedules, expectations, and objectives.
2. Prepare the volunteer with specifics about the assignment, where materials can be found, and what the learning objectives are.
3. Make the volunteer comfortable by explaining the obvious support facilities: where to place personal items, find a rest room, and get a cup of coffee.
4. Keep channels of communication open with the volunteer. Exchange a home number if appropriate and convenient. Plan and follow the schedule developed for the volunteer. Inform the volunteer of a schedule change as soon as possible. Keep in mind that volunteers have additional responsibilities and cannot be expected to wait for an assignment or materials preparation and that their responsibilities may prevent them from fulfilling their commitment. You will need to be understanding if this occurs.
5. Keep a special folder for regular volunteers with current assignments.
6. Inform volunteers about the students' level of ability, special problems, and students who need assistance.
7. Encourage your volunteer to sign in and to wear a name tag. Other faculty members and administrators will want to acknowledge a volunteer in the building.
8. Let every volunteer know how much you and the class appreciate the help. A thank-you note goes a long way toward making the experience a rewarding one for a volunteer.
9. Evaluate the volunteer encounter. Consider the specific request, the background of the volunteer, and the constraints of the situation.

*Source:* Project Technology Engineering Applications of Mathematics and Science, Yakima Valley/Tri-Cities MESA, *Tips for Teachers Working with Volunteers,* as cited by Triangle Coalition for Science and Technology Education, *A Guide for Planning a Volunteer Program for Science, Mathematics, and Technology Education* (College Park, MD: Triangle Coalition, 1992), p. 54.

- Make assignments based on the volunteer's skills, knowledge, interests, capacity to learn, time available, and resources.

## *Print Resources*

Professional organizations can provide a richly varied form of support. The leading national organization in K–college science education is the National Science Teachers Association (NSTA). With headquarters in Washington, D.C., it provides services to nearly 50,000 members in the United States and Canada. NSTA activities include professional conventions, publications and journals, and science education position statements.

NSTA holds three regional conventions each fall and an annual national convention in early spring. NSTA's national conferences reach more than 18,000 science educators, perhaps the largest gathering of science educators in the world. The organization also produces for its members, journals appropriate for

*Give volunteers tips that will help them be successful with your students.*

different grade levels: *Science and Children* for the elementary grades, *Science Scope* for the middle school grades, and *The Science Teacher* for the high school level. The NSTA also produces for its members a newspaper, *NSTA Reports!* published six times a year. This paper is a source of news and information about science content, state association activities, and updates on teaching materials and programs. As a member of NSTA you may also purchase special NSTA publications on topics like women in science and science safety. The NSTA Web site at *http://www.nsta.org* provides a complete list of these special publications. Two other useful NSTA resources, both magazines, are available through subscription: *Quantum: The Magazine of Math and Science* and *Dragonfly: The Magazine for Young Investigators.*

Membership applications, samples of publications, copies of the policy position statements, and an annual catalog of resources and materials can be obtained through the NSTA national headquarters located at 1840 Wilson Boulevard, Arlington, VA 22201-3000, (703) 243-7100. All materials and orders can be purchased via the Internet at the NSTA Web site, *http://www.nsta.org.*

NSTA has chapters and affiliated groups in most states. The activities of the state organizations, which vary by state, are an excellent resource. Membership costs are usually very low, and state groups provide a mechanism for building professional contacts and learning from colleagues.

In addition to professional organizations, state and federal agencies provide educational services. County agricultural extension services give information on soils, insects, and related information. These services are directly connected with universities and will be of assistance in locating additional information. The U.S. Department of Agriculture has many initiatives directed at improving K–12 science education through both nontraditional areas such as 4-H and traditional resource curriculum offerings. State land management or natural resources departments usually have education directors who provide assistance and training to teachers and recommend such classroom volunteers as geologists, conservationists, and agronomists. To contact personnel in these agencies, consult the telephone book for your county seat or state capital.

The National Aeronautics and Space Administration (NASA) has an extensive educational infrastructure throughout the country, with regional centers offering educational resources that include lesson plans and extensive slide, photo, and video libraries. Teacher workshops are provided through the agency. In recent years NASA has become a valuable electronic resource in a variety of ways: (1) the Internet—the NASA Web site is an invaluable source of information for science resources related to space and space flight. The URL is *http://www.nasa.gov.* (2) video—NASA CONNECT provides scheduled programs delivered via local cable and the Internet. These 30-minute programs geared toward grades 3–8 are designed to explore a specific research topic and depict the collaborative nature of NASA research, which involves creativity, critical thinking, and problem-solving skills. Teacher supplements and student activities aligned with the video are available at *http://edu.larc.nasa.gov/connect/.* (3) interactive video—Scientists at many of the NASA centers are taking advantage of interactive video links to provide live sessions to students on various science topics. Schools with interactive video capabilities can visit the NASA Web site to find out which NASA centers are involved with interactive video programming and to schedule a virtual visit.

State departments of education are also a source for information or print resources. States organize their agencies differently, but most have at least one science consultant. Many states are organized around regional centers that provide inservice, equipment, and assistance to classroom teachers. Write to your state science consultant for specific information.

## *Microcomputer Applications*

Modern technology can strengthen the understanding of concepts if we recognize the experiences the students bring to us and use the technology to clarify any misconceptions and stimulate proper concept formation (Nickerson, 1995). Simply sitting students in front of a computer will not bring about conceptual understanding. Choosing software that promotes active mental processing and student discoveries is vital and must ensure for students a state of mindfulness while they interact with the technology and motivate and engage the students to enable them to form appropriate conceptualizations. Computer software, however, is no substitute for active teaching and learning.

*It is important to select software that promotes thinking.*

## CHAPTER SUMMARY

This chapter explores many assumptions that are made while forming an answer to the principal guiding question: What are the characteristics of effective elementary science instruction? A broad view is taken by examining assumptions that undergird landmark experimental programs tested extensively in elementary schools. The characteristics of these effective older programs provide a foundation for learning and practicing techniques of effective instruction.

The historical sense of this foundation can help you separate the gimmicks from genuine improvements. At times the assumptions are explicit; at other times we find subtle hidden assumptions that tend to reveal themselves as we probe into past events and future recommendations for science education.

The primary concept of this chapter is that effective elementary science programs are built on dominant beliefs that arise from the past and effectiveness research. Assumptions change as some fall from favor or are proven wrong; new ones are added to reflect changes in the knowledge base and different priorities. Assumptions help guide changes in science programming and affect your teaching by stimulating changes in science materials as well as by setting new expectations and identifying future trends.

## DISCUSSION QUESTIONS

**1.** What do you think an effective elementary science program should contain? How would you defend your position to a teacher or school administrator who holds an opposing view?

**2.** Examine copies of several different science textbooks for the same grade level. What evidence do you find that shows inclusion of the criteria for effective programs?

**3.** Which would you believe, the research findings and criteria for effective programs such as those from sources cited in this chapter, the opinions of several teachers, or a report made by a presidential advisory committee? Why?

**4.** Examine a school's course of study or curriculum guide for elementary or middle school science. Identify the assumptions about effective science programs and compare them to those stated at the end of this chapter. Report your comparison.

**5.** Examine samples of SAPA, SCIS, and ESS materials and compare them with current elementary science textbooks and supplementary curriculum materials such as Project WILD, Project Learning Tree, FOSS, SEPUP, AIMS, and others. How do the older experimental elementary science programs compare with the newer generation of textbooks and teaching materials? What features are similar? Why?

**6.** Brainstorm resources not mentioned in this chapter that are useful in elementary science instruction. How can you enhance your instructional methods by including resources in your teaching plans?

**7.** Brainstorm ideas related to the development of a school resource file and ways to ensure it is useful and current.

**8.** Identify three resources that are especially useful in the instruction of students with special needs. Share these resources with teachers, and ask them for a critique of the materials.

**9.** Research the purposes, fee structure, and service of the National Science Teachers Association, and identify publications that will be useful as you plan science lessons. Locate membership information, meeting schedules, and publications from your state or local science education organization.

# BUILD A PORTFOLIO

**1.** Refer to the assumptions about elementary school science summarized at the end of this chapter. How could you use these assumptions to form a philosophy of science teaching? What is your philosophy?

**2.** Use the assumptions about elementary science programs to develop a survey, and then use the survey to interview several elementary teachers, principals, scientists, parents, and so on. What do you conclude about the accuracy of different people's assumptions?

**3.** Compose a list of supplemental resource curricula that you would like to include in your lesson plans on three different topics. Compare your list with that of two or more classmates; combine the three lists to keep for future reference.

**4.** Locate three hands-on resources not mentioned in this chapter that have the potential to be used within an elementary classroom for science instruction. Define the planned use, and identify specific goals and objectives that would be met by the use of these resources.

**5.** Identify one resource each that will enhance a lesson in environmental education, electricity, digestion, or plate tectonics, and show how the resources correlate with your goals and outcomes.

**6.** Identify an activity from one resource curriculum that will enhance a lesson by providing experiences that will increase your students' skills in observing, questioning, classifying, measuring, and using numbers.

## CHAPTER OUTLINE

# How Can You Use Educational Technology to Enrich Your Classroom?

Scenario 1 Elementary Students with Access to a Wide Variety
of Educational Technologies

A small group of Ms. Ramirez's fifth-grade students were sprawled on the floor, pouring over several pages of data they had just pulled off the Internet from a centralized database on stream quality. Another group was off in the corner near the sink, doing a separation test from a soil sample they took from the bottom of their local stream. A third group was at the computer entering new data and changing that into colored bar graphs, while a fourth group was transferring digital images of the stream in question from the digital camera to the computer. After 40 minutes had passed Ms. Ramirez pulled the group together.

"Okay students, I'd like to spend a few moments having each team give me a status report. Kevin, how far along is your team on their stream study project?"

"We just need to check one more source on the Internet to verify these figures and we'll be ready to put our electronic presentation together. We'd like to go to Mr. Hill's room after school some day this week so he can help us edit our video and digitize it to put into our presentation. Could you find out from him which night he can work with us?"

"I'm happy to hear how much progress your team has made during the past two weeks. I'll check with Mr. Hill to determine when he's available to work with you. Are there any other groups that need to work with Mr. Hill?"

"Oh, Ms. Ramirez," said Carla "our team also needs to edit its video. We still need to scan in some still images we took with Sam's camera and add those to our presentation. Our group worked on graphing the data we collected and made graphs that compared our data to data we pulled from that national database you identified for us on the Internet. We're starting to see some interesting comparisons."

"That's great, Carla. What about your group, Ronaldo? How much work does your team have left to complete?"

"We'll probably need a few more days before all of our work is ready to share with everyone. Our team just scheduled a videoconference with an aquatic biologist from the university. We're going to use the desktop conferencing equipment in the library tomorrow afternoon and link to the scientist right at his desk. Mrs. Harp from the library set that up for us and taught us how to make the video phone call at 2 P.M. tomorrow. We're still figuring out how to videotape that session. Charles and Kathy talked to Mr. Hill about that at lunch today. He said he'd have to think about it, but that he'd try to find a way to capture some of that conference on video for us. We'd like to use that in our presentation."

"So, let me see, Kevin, Carla, Ronaldo, ah, Sally, you've been awfully quiet, what's your group been up to?"

"Well, Ms. Ramirez, our group's been as busy as the others. We're just struggling with one problem. We have some data that seems like it's wrong. We're not sure if it was the pH meter that didn't work right, if the meter wasn't hooked to the computer and calibrated right to give us an accurate reading, or if those of us that read the meter messed up. Do you think if we went out today and got another pH reading that we could just plug that number into our data, or would we have to collect all the other data we're using to make our conclusions as well."

"Well, you've raised an interesting problem, Sally. I'd like to pose that to the entire class. What do you think about this team's problem? To help them come up with a solution I'd like all of you to think about that article we pulled off of the Internet last week. Remember the one about the scientists at three different labs, assuming they were doing exactly the same thing with rats in their study and still got different results. What kind of conclusions would they draw from their data if one of the scientists decided to just change one number because it didn't look right. Especially if they didn't inform the others."

A lively discussion ensued in this technology-rich fifth-grade classroom. The debate ranged from e-mailing several scientists to get their ideas, doing an Internet search on the use of accurate data, to having the students demonstrate to the class exactly how they used the pH meter complete with the computer hookup, just in case they did it right and their original data were correct.

## Scenario 2  Elementary Students with Access to a Few Educational Technologies

"Mrs. King, are we meeting with your class this afternoon?" shouted three kindergarten students across Marshfield Elementary School's playground to the sixth-grade teacher.

"Of course! If you're ready to share your experiences my students are ready to listen," replied Mrs. King.

As Kathy King walked back into her sixth-grade classroom a smile came over her face. All of the planning she did this past summer with the kindergarten teacher, Tom Denton, was paying off. Even after fifteen years of teaching in elementary schools, Kathy King was still excited when she discovered new ways to get students interested in science. This year she collaborated with Tom to help the children in the primary grades move beyond thinking science was just "playing with stuff" to giving them opportunities to explain their understanding of the "science" behind the "play." For her sixth-grade students it was an opportunity for them to review the science they learned over their years of elementary school before taking the statewide proficiency test at the end of sixth grade.

Kathy and Tom developed kinderpals, where her sixth-grade students were paired with kindergarten students in an effort to have a "real audience" for the sixth-grade students to share their understanding of the science they learned throughout their years at Marshfield Elementary. The project also gave the kindergarten students an opportunity to share their understanding of what they were learning through their science activities even before they had developed the ability to write down their understandings. The sixth-grade students would "capture" the thoughts of the kindergarten students through what looked like "play and conversation" to the kindergarten students. Prior to their weekly visits to Mr. Denton's class, Mrs. King's class would do the activity Mr. Denton was going to do with his class. Mrs. King would explore with her students the science behind the activity and assign them some additional reading on the given concept or concepts as a refresher for them on previously learned materials.

The plan called for starting with the kindergarten and sixth-grade students this year and expanding it up and down the grade levels over subsequent years. As constructivist educators both Tom and Kathy believed in the value of building on their student's experiences, yet they struggled with getting those experiences into proper conceptual formation. Using even the lowest of education technologies that were available to them in their school—cassette recorders, some old donated computers, and two newer computers with Internet access in the library—proved to be a real asset to their data-collection needs.

Kathy's thoughts were interrupted by her own students' animated conversations as she entered her classroom. Ron was engaged in a heated debate with Sarah and Carmen. "But Jimmy really did get the idea of surface tension after we talked about all the things he did with bubbles," stated Ron.

"I thought you were just supposed to tape the two of you having a conversation about what he just did with the bubbles" Sarah said.

"I did do that, but while I was typing up some of his ideas so I could practice my keyboarding skills, something I heard Jimmy say on the tape had me puzzled. The next time we went to Mr. Denton's room I asked Mr. Denton if Jimmy and I could 'play' over at the water table. I started asking Jimmy some questions about the bubbles he made last week and then I asked him if we could try to make bubbles with just plain water. After stirring up water in a cup, we started playing around to see how many things we could put in a cup of water without it overflowing. I remembered the activity we did in our own class with paperclips in a cup to explore surface tension, so I started telling Jimmy about it. All I know is that when I then took a bowl and shook pepper on the top of the water Jimmy told me it must be surface tension that kept the pepper on top. You should have heard him scream when I put a drop of soap into the bowl and all the pepper fell to the bottom!"

Kathy King could not help jumping in with the comment, "What do you plan on doing the next time you go down to Mr. Denton's class with your *kinderpal* Jimmy? Have you thought about going to the library with him and jointly generating a picture of Jimmy's experiences using the KidPix Software?"

"I didn't think of that, but what a great way to help Jimmy remember what surface tension is!"

At that suggestion other students jumped into the conversation, some wanting to use the Internet connection in the library with their kindergarten charges to find out more information on various topics they were exploring in their class, others wanting to jointly create e-mail letters to community partners with their *kinderpals* that question the partners on how they use some of the "science" the kindergarten students were learning in their jobs. The ringing of the bell interrupted the enthusiastic sixth graders as they headed over to Mr. Denton's kindergarten class to make good on their plans. ◆

## INTRODUCTION

The students in Ms. Ramirez's class from the first scenario are not as unique as some may think. Technology initiatives throughout the United States have spent millions of dollars to get educational technology into the K–12 schools, right down to the classroom level. The students at Marshfield Elementary in the second scenario are not as fortunate. However, as evidenced by the *kinderpal* plan of Mrs. King and Mr. Denton, even low-end technology can still offer useful tools for data collection and analysis. Whether you are an advocate of the technology being as accessible as the classroom or moving the students down the hall to the lab, there's no doubt about it, the tools available for the twenty-first-century classroom will dramatically change the way classrooms function. The artifacts we collect of student work are no longer reliant on paper, pencil, and chalk. The artifacts created in today's classroom provide the students with multiple opportunities to construct knowledge and to demonstrate what they know.

Those resistant to applying educational technology at the elementary level should reflect on the nature of technology itself and how those applications have benefited society. As an example, for one of this book's authors growing up in the city produced an idealized view of farm life. The "country kids" were envied, thinking it would be like *Rebecca of Sunny Brook Farm* every day, getting up when the rooster crowed to feed the chickens, check under their nests for eggs, and bring them back in a tidy basket, smiling and humming a happy tune.

*Older learners can become technology mentors for younger children.*

Many years later good friendships were formed with those "country kids." They laughed at the author's romantic view of farm life. The horror stories they shared about the backbreaking labor were nothing to be dreamt of longingly. On the bright side they talked of how advances in technology actually saved them hours of hard labor. Now chickens are raised in tight quarters in which all food and water is carefully measured. Eggs automatically drop down onto conveyor belts that move them along for easy collection. Egg production is not the only technological advancement on the farm. Baling hay, planting and picking crops, as well as grain storage have changed dramatically with advances in technology.

The lumber industry is another area in which childhood myths were dispelled with the advances of technology. Images of the burly lumberjack were transformed after a visit to some lumber sites in northern Oregon. That burly lumberjack was really teams of average-size humans (females included) using various machines to fell, strip, and drag the pines up the steep hills. Once at the lumber mill, machines using laser scanners and a computer program determined exactly how many and what kind of boards would be cut from each log. Within a matter of minutes that log became several strips of lumber of varying widths and thickness.

While in schools we tend to think of technology in terms of computers, just about any artifact of our modern world is really technology. The preceding examples demonstrate the real-world applications of technology. The opening scenarios share some uses of educational technology in the elementary school. This chapter is designed to help you think about how to use education technology in the classroom and apply it in a real-world context, much as the students in Ms. Ramirez's, Mr. Denton's and Mrs. King's classes did. It answers the question of *why* one would use educational technology and *how* one could apply it in the context of science teaching. This chapter does this by examining the National Educational Technology Standards, the varying skill levels for the teacher and student in using Educational Technology, and by providing examples of how to apply the National Educational Technology Standards to science lessons designed to meet the National Science Education Standards.

## WHY USE EDUCATIONAL TECHNOLOGY?

Chances are that in a school rich in educational technology a teacher like Ms. Ramirez is given more opportunities to enhance her technology skills so that she incorporates more of the available technology into her student's classroom experiences. However, as Mrs. King and Mr. Denton demonstrated, even in a setting in which access to educational technology is difficult, the choice of applying educational technology in the learning environment is often driven by the task at hand, not the available technology.

Educational technology can be seamlessly incorporated into a classroom whether you are a teacher more comfortable using classroom content strictly prescribed by the school curriculum or you are in a school environment in which creating content based on statewide learning outcomes is encouraged. Even though you may be an expert at using one computer application, you may be at a novice level on another. Teachers must overcome the notion that they must be experts at all educational technology before their students are given a chance to use it. As Ediger's (1994) studies on *Technology in the Elementary Classroom* have revealed, applying technology in the classroom does several things to student learning: (1) it increases interest even in rote tasks; (2) it provides purpose for learning; (3) it can attach meaning to an ongoing lesson; (4) it provides opportunities to perceive knowledge as being related, not isolated bits; (5) it allows for individual student differences; and (6) it can impact student attitudes toward learning.

*Computers help young children to expand uses of their senses.*

## National Technology Standards

The artifacts of student learning—anything created by our students as evidence of their understanding of a given concept—can be created in a variety of formats as teachers provide opportunities for the students to use the educational technologies in the creation of such artifacts. As shared in the opening scenario, using instructional software on computers is not the only use of this valuable educational technology tool. The International Society for Technology in Education has established National Educational Technology Standards for Students in grades K–12. These six standards are general enough that students can move from exhibiting novice level understanding to practicing the skills on a regular basis and eventually exhibiting mastery with increased experience. Table 11.1 lists the *Technology Foundation Standards for All Students.*

Applying these skills within the context of a science lesson can strengthen the understanding of the science concepts if we recognize and value the experiences students bring with them and then use the technology to clarify any misconceptions and stimulate proper concept formation (Nickerson, 1995). Conceptual understanding will come about when student interaction between

**TABLE 11.1    Technology Foundation Standards for All Students (June 1998)**

1. Basic operations and concepts
   - Students demonstrate a sound understanding of the nature and operation of technology systems
   - Students are proficient in the use of technology
2. Social, ethical, and human issues
   - Students understand the ethical, cultural, and societal issues related to technology.
   - Students practice responsible use of technology systems, information, and software.
   - Students develop positive attitudes toward technology uses that support lifelong learning, collaboration, personal pursuits, and productivity.
3. Technology productivity tools
   - Students use technology tools to enhance learning, increase productivity, and promote creativity.
   - Students use productivity tools to collaborate in constructing technology-enhanced models, preparing publications, and producing other creative works.

4. Technology communications tools
   - Students use telecommunications to collaborate, publish, and interact with peers, experts, and other audiences.
   - Students use a variety of media and formats to communicate information and ideas effectively to multiple audiences.
5. Technology research tools
   - Students use technology to locate, evaluate, and collect information from a variety of sources.
   - Students use technology tools to process data and report results.
   - Students evaluate and select new information resources and technological innovations based on the appropriateness to specific tasks.
6. Technology problem-solving and decision-making tools.
   - Students use technology resources for solving problems and making informed decisions.
   - Students employ technology in the development of strategies for solving problems in the real world.

*Source:* International Society for Technology in Education (ISTE), NETS Project, *http://cnets.iste.org/sfors.htm.*

*Technology helps learners to collaborate, publish, and interact with peers, experts and other audiences.*

the educational technology and the science content is purposeful. Choosing software that promotes active mental processing and student discoveries is vital and must ensure for students a state of mindfulness while they interact with the technology and motivate and engage the students to enable them to form appropriate conceptualizations. Computer software, be it instructional software such as the multitude of titles created to address a specific science topic or application software designed to create a document or draw a picture, is no substitute for active teaching and learning. It can however, become an essential part of that teaching and learning, a means for creating student artifacts of the concepts studied.

## Levels of Use

Utilizing a computer in a science classroom seems like a contradiction of constructivist science teaching. However, as modeled in the opening scenarios, when appropriately used as a learning tool, computers can help learners to construct an understanding of complex concepts. At the most basic or novice level, software applications can be used to observe scientific phenomena directly. The software can provide a concrete example of an object, provide facts, or recall basic information. Novice users of educational technology can easily use drill-and-practice software. As Berger's (1994) study notes, rarely is there mindfulness associated with this type of computer-assisted instruction.

A novice in applying the ISTE technology standards would be capable of using software applications that supply scientific information. Information provided in CD-ROM encyclopedias and atlases or software applications that evaluate student performance, keep records, or guide students to resources rarely require anything more than novice-level skills to use them successfully.

As students are given more opportunities to apply the technology in their regular classroom activities, through practice they become more proficient in various computer tools and advance to another technology level. Many of the productivity tools that assist in the creation of multimedia productions require students to have more than a simple working knowledge of the software application. Software simulations typically require more than beginner-level skills as well. Although computer simulations are no replacement for actual experimentation, simulations do "provide a valuable conceptual tool which should be augmented with actual experiments in the classroom," according to McKinney (1997).

Simulation software applications may be a pictorial, verbal, numerical, or graphical representations of reality. Simulations that integrate all four forms of representation appear to offer the best opportunity to stimulate conceptual change. *The Voyages of Mimi I and II* (Bank Street College of Education, 1994, 1995) are popular programs that effectively integrate all four representations. This interactive program, designed primarily for middle school students, makes use of video, print, and computer software to engage students in an interdisciplinary unit centered on the real adventures of the explorer ship *Mimi.*

Computer-based laboratories, which effectively integrate numerical and graphical data as quickly as a probe attached to the computer can record it, often require technology skills beyond the novice level. Using sensors and timing devices attached to a computer, students can do such things as monitor heart rate, detect strength and direction of external forces, determine the strength of magnetic fields, record temperature, record pH of liquids, measure amplitudes of audio sources, sense and record humidity changes, imitate the spectral response of the human eye, sense and record changes in pressure, and use an ultrasonic motion detector to measure distance, velocity, and acceleration (Arbor Scientific, 1996).

Not all simulations require advanced technology skills. Software such as *Amazon Trail II* (MECC, 1999) for students from fourth grade up can participate in a virtual journey to the Amazonian rainforest in South America. Many dialogue guides with both text and audio conversations support the interaction along the journey. Other simulations that are attribute mapped do not allow for student-created models of unidentified phenomena (Snir, Smith, & Grosslight, 1995). Some software designed to simulate frog dissection falls into this category, whereby the given attributes are already defined by the software with little room for manipulation of variables. This type of computer simulation may be an insufficient substitute for a certain level of dissection.

Students proficient in all six categories of the National Educational Technology Standards are at a level of technological literacy in which they can use software applications that simulate experiments in which variables may be manipulated and extended beyond ordinary phenomena. At this level, computer models can be created that lead to explorations of unidentified phenomena. This metaconceptual level is one in which a student uses models to explain reality, reflects on those models, and then suggests the manipulation of variables that project far beyond what can be created in the laboratory. This type of software is *structure mapped.* This means that a code is built into the software that allows it to search for laws that govern the behavior of objects (Snir, Smith, & Grosslight, 1995). One such computer application is *Sir Isaac Newton's Games* (Schwartz, 1985, 1995). This software has the capability of removing the abstraction of friction so that a student can perceive the motion of an object in a friction-free environment. Removing friction helps a student to arrive at a more complete understanding of Newton's laws of motion, phenomena that cannot be accurately observed or understood in the friction-filled environment of a typical school laboratory.

Microworlds are computer-based laboratory experiences that simulate real-world phenomena. Students can explore undefined phenomena when given proper guidance and intervention by the teacher. Students can be given "what-if" predictive situations in order to evaluate and reflect on scientific theories, pose problems that can be solved only through computer-enhanced simulations, and construct the meaning of concepts based on computer-simulated evidence. An inquiring science educator can bring the use of computers to their highest level of application by using microworld environments to give students opportunities to explore and discover scientific theories by using problem-solving strategies to ask, "What is the real problem?" "How do we know it's a problem?" "How can we go about solving the problem?" Microworlds truly embody the spirit of constructivism in its application.

## The Networked Classroom—Removing the Walls

Although they are numbered, the National Educational Technology Standards are not linear. One does not have to know all of the basic operations of a computer before beginning to use it as a communication tool. Novice users of technology are capable of using the computer as a communication tool long before they have mastered the use of productivity tools. In fact using a wide area network (WAN) enables us to expand the boundaries of the classroom walls and to create a virtual classroom with schools across the globe.

For teachers a network provides increased opportunities to collaborate with other educators over matters of daily instruction or educational reform. Teachers have greater access to additional information, knowledge, and points of view by eliminating barriers of time and place. Networked teachers may discuss issues and access varied resources, including other teachers and resource agencies. A network encourages the development of professional skills: deliberation, collegial consensus building, and development and sharing of ideas related to the profession of teaching.

Future teachers may find that skills in using networked resources such as the World Wide Web (WWW) can provide them with opportunities to link with practicing teachers through sites such as the *Global Learning Co-op* and the *GLOBE Project.* The WWW can provide teachers access to standards for science instruction for every state—often an understanding of local standards is expected during job interviews. It can also expose them to teacher grant award competitions and competitions for elementary students, and it can introduce them to various science education associations (O'Brien and Lewis, 1999).

Various national databases exist to support science teaching. Some national services include the National Science Teachers Association (NSTA), the National Consortium for Environmental Education and Training (NCEET), the National Aeronautics and Space Administration (NASA), and the National Park Service. These sources provide Web sites filled with lessons, resources, and knowledge of various science topics. The Eisenhower National Clearinghouse (ENC) for Mathematics and Science Education is a national database. Like the other sites it provides lessons and lists of resources as well as identifying which print, video, or computer software is available for the teaching of science and mathematics. One added benefit to this site is its extensive software reviews, done using an evaluation protocol that goes beyond the publisher's description of the software or computer operating requirements. It was created in conjunction with the state of Ohio's agency responsible for providing Educational Technology funding to all Ohio K–12 schools, Ohio SchoolNet. The protocol used focuses on interactivity, student engagement, technical characteristics, skills development, and the correlation of the instructional software to state and national standards for Science, Mathematics, Social Studies, and Language Arts. All reviews are posted on the ENC Web site at *http://www.enc.org* and the Ohio SchoolNet Web site at *http://www.ohioschoolnet.k12.oh.us.*

Teachers should critically review any electronically accessed lesson, no matter which Web site is accessed to acquire the science resources. Just because a source is "published" on the Internet does not necessarily mean it is a worthwhile task. Table 11.2 suggests evaluation criteria for judging the worthiness of

**TABLE 11.2   Is This a Worthy Task?**

Is the task based on sound and significant content?

- Identify the concepts and/or skills.
- Is the content accurate?

Is the task based on knowledge of students' understandings, interests, experiences, and the range of ways that diverse students learn?

- Identify why the task might appeal to your students.

Are all safety measures properly addressed and followed in any lessons provided? If not, can appropriate safety measures be easily applied to the given task? If you answer no to this second question, do *not* use this lesson.

| In your opinion to what extent would the task: | a lot | | | | not at all |
|---|---|---|---|---|---|
| • engage students' intellect? | 4 | 3 | 2 | 1 | 0 |
| • actively involve students? | 4 | 3 | 2 | 1 | 0 |
| • develop students' understandings and skills? | 4 | 3 | 2 | 1 | 0 |
| • stimulate students to make connections to other disciplines? | 4 | 3 | 2 | 1 | 0 |
| • stimulate students to make connections to the real world? | 4 | 3 | 2 | 1 | 0 |
| • call for problem formation, problem solving, and reasoning? | 4 | 3 | 2 | 1 | 0 |
| • promote communication/interaction among students? | 4 | 3 | 2 | 1 | 0 |

*Technology helps learners to explore and understand social, ethical, and human issues.*

electronically accessed lessons. Please use this table to help you sort and separate the safest and most promising resources.

For students, networked learning environments provide real-world applications of science concepts. Collecting data that will be shared in a nationwide database such as the *Everglades Information Network and Digital Library* or the *GLOBE Project* or the *National Pill Bug Project* encourage students to be more careful in applying proper scientific procedures when they collect their data on a local level to be shared nationally.

*Parks as Classrooms*, an interactive computer-based project funded primarily by the National Park Service, is designed to promote greater understanding and appreciation of the natural and cultural heritage of the United States and to develop sustainable partnerships among parks, schools, and communities. Through this network, data are collected to monitor air, water, and land resources on parklands. This interactive project can simulate landform changes and cycles in populations within the parks (Corporation for Public Broadcasting, 1995).

The National Geographic Society offers *Kids Network,* a combination of software designed to meet curricular needs, telecommunications access to classrooms around the world, teacher guides and lesson plans, hot-line support, and access to unit scientists (National Geographic Society, 1995). There are various problem-based links to join. The introductory link introduces students to scientific research methods; another deals with what is in water; others allow students to explore phenomena such as solar energy, food, acid rain, trash, and weather.

Although national projects can be accessed and joined, having access to a wide area network within the classroom can encourage students and teachers to start their own science research projects and to invite schools throughout the nation to join the research effort. Collaborative projects can be designed to explore bodies of water, landfills, groundwater movement, seasonal changes per latitude, or any local problem or issue that may have global impact. The impact of projects like these is best stated by one teacher who responded to the question, "What are your most compelling reasons for integrating educational technology into the curriculum?" as posed by Randy Knuth of the Internet in September 1995:

> I think we should go beyond integration into the classroom and create a new context for learning that maximizes the learning potential of technology and telecommunications. From my perspective . . . the reason is relevancy. We can extend learning beyond the walls of the classroom . . . to do real stuff with real

people for compelling reasons . . . with real results that have real significance. Students are not dumb . . . they know when it matters and when it is simply an exercise. . . . Connect them to their communities through technology! And give them economic viability! (Knuth, 1995).

Using educational technology as a communication tool goes beyond transporting graphics and text. Depending on the connectivity, students can participate in networks that transport voice, video, and data. Schools throughout the nation are linking together to share in scientific explorations with full motion video and voice interface. From the primary level through college, students are linking with content providers to enrich and enhance the lessons studied within the classroom. Zoos, museums, and cultural institutions are revamping the way they present their content to take advantage of the visual medium offered through interactive video networks. Linkages like these promote greater student interaction and discussion of concepts. Providing students with as many opportunities as possible to articulate their understanding of concepts will promote greater conceptual construction and retention. Advancing technologies offer students opportunities on an ever-increasing basis.

## HOW CAN EDUCATIONAL TECHNOLOGY BE APPLIED IN THE CONTEXT OF SCIENCE TEACHING?

The National Science Education Content Standards provide a list of concept statements for the three science divisions, Physical, Life, and Earth and Space Sciences. One would never think of having students simply memorize the concept statements. In fact the Science Standards provides many suggestions for effective science teaching, all strongly encouraging active student exploration to construct an understanding of the science concepts. The lessons provided in the back of this textbook serve as examples of how the standards can be explored through student-centered inquiry activities within a learning cycle format.

Just as the National Science Education Standards make recommendations for how a science concept may be best learned, so too does the International Society for Technology in Education strongly suggest that the teaching of the National Educational Technology Standards should not take place void of context. Tables 11.3–11.6 on pages 406–419 create a profile of these standards within the context of a science lesson. The National Science Education Content Standards for a grade-level range are found across the top of each table along with the title of a lesson that is included in the back of this textbook. The tables are intended to demonstrate how you could apply the National Educational Technology Standards for a given grade range to a given science lesson to create experiences for the students to develop their technology skills as they are learning a particular science concept.

The lessons found in Part IV of this book can be accomplished without the use of educational technology. However, as you read through the tables and recall Ediger's six findings on what educational technology can do to enhance learning, you will discover that by applying a few of these suggestions to the lessons provided, educational technology can truly enrich the learning experience.

**TABLE 11.3A   Grades K–2 National Educational Technology Standards (NETS) as applied in the context of lessons using the National Science Education Standards (NSES):  Physical Science Content Standards for grades K–4**

| *NSES:*<br>*Content Standards*<br>*for K–4* | | *Physical Science Standards* | |
|---|---|---|---|
| NETS for<br>Grades K–2 | Properties of Objects<br>& Materials | Position & Motion<br>of Objects | Light, Heat, Electricity<br>& Magnetism |
| *Lesson Name* | Physical Properties of Matter | Sound versus Noise | Heat Energy |
| *Basic Operations* | Students make use of software like *Sammy's Science House* to introduce observing, classifying, and comparing skills. | During the School and Magazine Sound Search the students use audio recorders to record and play back the sounds they hear. | Students use the computer to write three tips for crayon storage. They will print out and save their tips on a disk. |
| *Social, Ethical &*<br>*Human Issues* | Demonstrate responsible use of software by storing it properly and working cooperatively at the computer workstation. | Students work in cooperative teams to input noise observations into database. | Students look out for themselves and peers to warn when too close to hot plate or touching hot wax. |
| *Productivity Tools* | Students use a preformatted database to record and save egg observations. | Students use a preformatted database to record and save noise classifications. | Students take a series of digital photos as the birthday candle is burning. They download with teacher's help. Have students tell a story of how heat energy changed the candles in each photo. |
| *Communication*<br>*Tools* | Students make use of e-mail to send a survey to e-mail-pals on which brand of chocolate chip cookie is "best." | Adults work with student(s) to find an Internet site for an airline. Obtain e-mail contact to find out how that airline deals with "noise" problems for employees working on the runway. | Students make use of interactive video links such as a live link to a company that makes aluminum soda pop cans and ask their workers as they watch them work how heat energy is used in production. |
| *Research Tools* | Students make use of encyclopedias on CD-ROM to find the physical characteristics of an object not readily available in the classroom. | Teacher can download various audio files from the Internet and have students teams play them on the computer, then classify sounds. | Adults work with students to find an Internet site for a crayon manufacturer. Look at Web site to determine how heat energy is used in making crayons. |
| *Problem-Solving*<br>*and Decision-*<br>*Making Tools* | Students use a digital camera to take a picture of an object they found around the school. Each student's picture can be downloaded and printed by the teacher. The students will then be asked to group them by similar physical properties. | As an assessment the students can use headsets to listen to various audio CD's while on the computer. They will enter the correct sound classification into a preformatted database. | Students use information learned from exploring the crayon manufacturer's Web site and/or through the live link with the can company to write a home plan for safe candle storage and use. |

**TABLE 11.3B    Grades K–2 National Educational Technology Standards (NETS) as applied in the context of lessons using the National Science Education Standards (NSES): Life Science Content Standards for grades K–4**

| *NSES:* Content Standards for K–4 | *Life Science Standards* | | |
|---|---|---|---|
| NETS for Grades K–2 | Characteristics of Organisms | Life Cycles of Organisms | Organisms & Environments |
| *Lesson Name* | Plant Parts and Needs | Bird Life | Colors of Wildlife |
| *Basic Operations* | Students use a laserdisc such as *The Wonderful World of Plants*, part of the series "Science Alive Interactive Multimedia," for up-close views of plants and their parts. | Introduce and/or reinforce the concept through use of software titles such as *Animals and How They Grow* and *Birds and How They Grow*. | Students use software such as *Multimedia Animals Encyclopedia* to find examples of colorful animals. |
| *Social, Ethical & Human Issues* | Students demonstrate respect and care for their environment as they work together collecting plant samples. | Students show respect and care for classroom animals as they observe their life cycle during the year. | Students work cooperatively as they search the Internet for Web sites that provide examples of colorful animals. |
| *Productivity Tools* | Students use a draw/paint program to create pictures of plants collected or bean sprouts in expansion activity and label plant parts on drawings. | Students enter into a preformatted database the weight and length of the virtual bird the teacher has created for each student team on a daily basis. | Students create a slide show using software such as *Microsoft PowerPoint* that uses a picture and text on each page to tell a story about animals and their use of coloration. |
| *Communication Tools* | Contact local universities, flower shops, state naturalists, and the like to ask permission for students to e-mail questions on how their profession makes use of plants. Be sure responses are age appropriate. | Students use an interactive video link to teleconference with a local zoo to find out about the life cycle of an animal of the class's choice or the most recently born animal at the zoo. | Students use an interactive video link to teleconference with a local zoo or wildlife refuge to observe animals in their natural habitat and discuss their use of camouflage. |
| *Research Tools* | Students go to the American Horticultural Society's Web site (AHS): *http://www.ahs.org* or the AHS Kid Links: *http://www.ahs.org/nonmembers/hotlinks.htm* to get information on plant care. | Students use a CD-ROM encyclopedia like *Encarta* to find information on how an assigned animal grows. | Students go to Web sites of companies that make clothing used for hunting. Look at on-line catalogs and speculate as to what kind of habitat a hunter wearing that clothing would hunt at. |
| *Problem-Solving and Decision-Making Tools* | Using a teacher-created spreadsheet with pictures and names of plant parts such as a beet or spinach across the top and student names on the side, the student will enter in whether the part is a stem, root, or leaf. | Students use a digital camera to take pictures of the classroom animal as it grows. They download pictures to the computer and label the different stages of growth and present the life-cycle story to a public audience. | Taking data from a teacher-created database, students use the computer graphing software to make a graph of animals that have one, two, or more colors. |

**TABLE 11.3C   Grades K–2 National Educational Technology Standards (NETS) as applied in the context of lessons using the National Science Education Standards (NSES): Earth and Space Science Content Standards for grades K–4**

| NSES: Content Standards for K–4 | Earth and Space Science Standards | |
|---|---|---|
| NETS for Grades K–2 | Properties of Earth Materials | Objects in the Sky |
| *Lesson Name* | Earth Layers | Solar System and the Universe |
| *Basic Operations* | A piece of software that will give the students some good photos of the Earth is *Our Earth.* | Introduce and/or reinforce the concept through use of software titles such as *Exploring the Solar System and Beyond* and *The Magic School Bus Explores the Solar System.* |
| *Social, Ethical & Human Issues* | Share time with other student teams fairly on the computer and in dividing up clay for class activities. | Students willingly share information found through books or computer software with others studying similar planets. |
| *Productivity Tools* | Students enter into a prepared map of the world on the computer the names of the continents and oceans. | Students create an electronic postcard by drawing with a draw/paint program the planet and providing text to tell about the planet the student is visiting. |
| *Communication Tools* | Adults assist in finding Web sites on earthquakes. See whether there is an area to e-mail questions to earthquake survivors. May need to edit responses for age-appropriate content. | Have students e-mail their planet postcards to one another or to key pals in other classrooms. |
| *Research Tools* | Students explore Web sites on earthquakes that show how crustal plates move and find places where earthquakes occur on Earth and create a list of those countries. | Students work with an adult to go to a Web site like NASA's to find one interesting piece of information on the planet assigned that they want to share on their postcard. |
| *Problem-Solving and Decision-Making Tools* | Students enter into a prepared map of the world on the computer the names of the countries where the crust is moving. Label these "potential earthquake sites." | Students use the information learned by reading other student's postcards to explain why they couldn't go on a regular airplane to any other planet but Earth. |

**TABLE 11.4A**  Grades 3–4 National Educational Technology Standards (NETS) as applied in the context of lessons using the National Science Education Standards (NSES): Physical Science Content Standards for grades K–4

| NSES: Content Standards for K–4 | Physical Science Standards | | |
|---|---|---|---|
| NETS for Grades 3–4 | Properties of Objects & Materials | Position & Motion of Objects | Light, Heat, Electricity & Magnetism |
| *Lesson Name* | Characteristics of Matter | Loudness and Pitch | Simple Circuits |
| *Basic Operations* | Simulation software like *Mystery Matter* can take the students through some problem-solving experiences to test for an unknown. | In the series *Thinkin' Things Collection I*– there is an activity called Oranga Banga in which students become familiar with the sounds of a variety of instruments. | A great complement to this lesson is the software *Gizmos & Gadgets*. It introduces various physical science concepts, including electricity through simulations and problem-solving experiences. |
| *Social, Ethical & Human Issues* | Students will work collaboratively in testing for the unknown and in using any lesson materials. | Students will show respect to others as they create sounds during the lesson activities and in controlling the volume of sound coming from the computer. | Student-led discussion around things found in the classroom that use electricity and what could happen if students don't use them appropriately. Students collaborate on safety policy. |
| *Productivity Tools* | Students work with teacher to identify fields for a database designed to collect observations about unknowns. They enter observations into database. They create a database of white powders complete with name and description and use the database to find matches to the unknowns. | Students create a slide presentation with recorded audio to demonstrate how the length of a vibrating object determines pitch. | Students use a draw/paint program to show the difference between a series and a parallel circuit. |
| *Communication Tools* | Students compose an e-mail message to send to another student in the class. They include sentences where they talk about at least three elements using their chemical symbol. Have the other student send back a reply identifying the element by name. | Many record labels have Web sites with e-mail links to musicians. Students choose a musician to e-mail questions to about how loudness or pitch problems impact the quality of their recordings. | Students take a virtual fieldtrip to Edison's boyhood home and various laboratories via the Internet to learn about Edison's experiences in finding the right filament for the light bulb. URL is *http://www.thomasedison.com/* |
| *Research Tools* | Using CD-ROMs, Internet, or local library systems, students find various images of the periodic table of elements. Why do some have more elements on them than others? | Have students pick one musical instrument and listen to various audio recordings of songs that use that instrument. How does loudness and pitch differ with each song? | Students pick one of Edison's inventions that makes use of a circuit and use the Internet to identify the invention and to research information on that invention. |
| *Problem-Solving and Decision-Making Tools* | Students develop a strategy for determining whether an object is a solid, liquid, or gas. A chart-making program or a draw/paint program or digital images could help in explaining this strategy. | Students use a variety of resources to find information on materials that can be vibrated to produce sound. Use this information to create a "homemade" musical instrument. Share a song on the instrument with the class. | Students look around the school or home for examples of poor electrical safety practices. They use a digital camera or a regular camera to capture the examples, then download or scan in the images. They write a safety story explaining what's wrong and how to correct it. |

**TABLE 11.4B** **Grades 3–4 National Educational Technology Standards (NETS) as applied in the context of lessons using the National Science Education Standards (NSES): Life Science Content Standards for grades K–4**

| NSES: Content Standards for K–4 | Life Science Standards | | |
|---|---|---|---|
| NETS for Grades 3–4 | Characteristics of Organisms | Life Cycles of Organisms | Organisms and Environments |
| *Lesson Name* | Skeleton | "A Bug's Life?" | Wildlife and Domesticated Animals |
| *Basic Operations* | *The Magic School Bus Explores the Human Body* and *The Human Body* are two software programs that could be used to enhance concepts introduced in this lesson. | *Bug Adventure* and *Wolves* from the series "Explore-A-Science Plus; Explore-A-Story Plus" are software titles providing experiences that could be used as the introduction to this lesson. | *Multimedia Animals Encyclopedia, The San Diego Zoo—The Animals!* and *Animals in Our World* are resource CDs that can provide pictures for the activities instead of magazines. |
| *Social, Ethical & Human Issues* | Students work cooperatively at workstations and demonstrate care in using and storing computer software. | Students should be sure that all members of their collaborative team have an equal opportunity to manipulate the materials used in the lesson, including software explorations. | Students should be taught that responsible use of electronic resources includes giving the resource credit for the pictures they use, just as they would when using a print resource. |
| *Productivity Tools* | Use word processing or draw/paint software for the students to write poems, with pictures if desired, about bones. Get ideas from poems such as those of Shel Silverstein. | Students use graphing software to create a pie chart of number of bugs found in different stages of their life cycle, i.e., number found as larva, number found as pupa, number found as adult. | Send the class outside around the school or take them on a walking field trip to the neighborhood around the school. Using the digital camera have students take pictures of animals they see. Come back to class, download, and categorize as to domestic or wild. |
| *Communication Tools* | Students create faxpals with doctors at a local hospital. Fax student-created "bone poems" and ask doctors to respond via fax with "bone poems" of their own. Use these poems to check for student understanding of concept. | Students create a database of bug Web sites. They identify things like URL, who created it, which show best pictures of all stages of the bug's life cycle, which show pictures of the most ugly bug, etc. | Students contact veterinarians, wildlife biologists, and/or zoo keepers via e-mail to ask them how they determine whether an animal is wild or domestic and whether it is okay to make a wild animal domestic. |
| *Research Tools* | Students use the Internet to find nutrition Web sites that share information on how to keep bones strong. Share information found in student-created multimedia presentations | Using library and CD-ROM encyclopedia resources, students draw and/or write a story about the life cycle of an assigned animal. | Using electronic resources such as *Multimedia Animals Encyclopedia* and *The San Diego Zoo—The Animals!*, students pull a picture of one animal and add text to the image explaining why it is domestic or wild. |
| *Problem-Solving and Decision-Making Tools* | When given images of numerous animals students should determine whether the animal has a skeleton. If in doubt they should use resources like digital encyclopedias or laserdiscs to find out more information about the animal in question. | Using a teacher-created Web-based worksheet, the students should pull down from a series of photos of various stages in the life cycle of an animal images of the animal in the correct order from birth to death. | Students visit a local veterinarian to find out the special needs of trying to make a wild animal domestic. Then they write a story for the local paper or create a flyer explaining why children shouldn't bring wild animals home and try to raise them. |

**TABLE 11.4C    Grades 3–4 National Educational Technology Standards (NETS) as applied in the context of lessons using the National Science Education Standards (NSES): Earth and Space Science Content Standards for grades K–4**

| *NSES:* *Content Standards* *for K–4* | *Earth and Space Science Standards* | |
|---|---|---|
| NETS for Grades 3–4 | Properties of Earth Materials | Objects in the Sky |
| *Lesson Name* | Fossils | Radiant Energy |
| *Basic Operations* | *Fossils* software or a Web site such as that for Chicago's Field Museum of Natural History at *http://www.fmnh.org* provides experiences for concept development. | The National Geographic Society's *Solar Energy Kit* includes software for exploring the sun and radiant energy. |
| *Social, Ethical & Human Issues* | Students go only to Internet site identified by the classroom teacher and ask permission to move to linked Web sites before leaving assigned site. | Students show respect for one another during class activities by making sure other students are not harmed by inappropriate use of objects heated through radiant energy or by focusing the magnifying glass on one another while out in the sun. |
| *Productivity Tools* | With adult assistance students browse the Internet for other sites that share information about fossils. They create bookmarks of their favorite Web sites for this type of information. | Students use a variety of productivity tools such as word processing, graphs, tables, digital images, or video clips to prepare a presentation on how to protect people from the damaging effects of the sun. |
| *Communication Tools* | Students engage in an interactive video-conference with a museum or historical society to find out more about fossils and what they tell us and how they are different from artifacts. | Students e-mail meteorologists with questions about the strength of the sun's rays. Do they think our summers are getting warmer? If so, what do they think is causing it? What can we do about it? |
| *Research Tools* | Using the information collected through the interactive video conference, students write a story of how a leaf can end up becoming a fossil. | Students create an electronic survey titled "Fact or Fiction" with statements about how children can protect themselves against the damaging rays of the sun. They send it out to e-mail pals from another classroom, then analyze and report on survey results. |
| *Problem-Solving and Decision-Making Tools* | Take a field trip to a local quarry or bring in rock samples from a local quarry and have students examine them for evidence of fossils. Ask them to make predictions as to whether they are plant or animal species. Visit museum Web site to compare local findings to those shown at the museum. | Students use a world map to mark places that receive more of the sun's energy than others do, and determine the type of clothing people living there would wear. They go to Web sites that describe life in those countries and explain why some countries may actually wear clothes different from what they predicted and why. |

**TABLE 11.5A Grades 5–6 National Educational Technology Standards (NETS) as applied in the context of lessons using the National Science Education Standards (NSES): Physical Science Content Standards for grades 5–8**

| *NSES:* *Content Standards* *for 5–8* | *Physical Science Standards* | | |
|---|---|---|---|
| NETS for Grades 5–6 | Properties & Changes of Properties in Matter | Motions & Forces | Transformations of Energy |
| *Lesson Name* | Sound Production | Simple Machines–The Lever | Mirrors and Reflection |
| *Basic Operations* | This software can be used by students to expand their understanding of sound production through whale sounds collected during the Second Voyage of Mimi in the software, *Scuba Science Module.* | Students can pull from experiences with the software *Gizmos & Gadgets* and *Miner's Cave* to build on classroom experiences with simple machines, in particular their experiences with the lever. | Use of software like *Sound and Light* by Prentice Hall can give students opportunities to experience other examples of reflection not created through classroom activities. |
| *Social, Ethical & Human Issues* | E-mail students that rely on "feeling" the vibrations created to produce sound—students that may attend schools for hearing impaired students. Collect their thoughts on the importance of vibrations to "feel" sound. | Students use the Internet to investigate uses of the lever and other simple machines as found in various machines. They create a diagram that classifies the various machines by use and engage in a debate on the need for the various machines. | Students use the Internet to research information on the Hubble telescope and/or other reflecting telescopes. How do students know the information they collected is accurate and reliable? Can what they read about the telescope influence future federal funding for the Hubble telescope? |
| *Productivity Tools* | Create slides, including audio clips of various objects that create a sound by vibrating a string. | Using graphing software, students generate a pie chart showing the percentage of simple machines found within a given machine. | Students compose, edit, and publish a paper on the importance of space telescopes to life on earth. |
| *Communication Tools* | Students participate in an online forum such as the Physics Link—A Guide to Physics on the Web to "ask the experts" at *http://www.physlink.com/.* | Students go to a Web site such as "Work is Simple with Simple Machines" at *http://www.ed.uri. edu:80/SMART96/ELE MSC/ SMARTmachines/machine.html* to participate in one of the online activities and provide feedback or ask questions to site authors via e-mail. | Students can get ideas for additional activities about the Hubble Space Telescope from the "Amazing Space: Education Online from the Hubble Space Telescope" at *http://oposite. stsci.edu/amazing-space.html.* Or engage in activities and online exchanges through the "Explorations in Education from the Space Telescope Science Institute" at *http://www.stsci.edu/exined/.* |
| *Research Tools* | Students can use a Web site such as the Physics Link—A Guide to Physics at *http//www.physlink. com/* to research sound and/or other properties of matter. | Use an instructional software resource such as "The Ways Things Work" for additional information on simple machines and their many uses. | Have students work with a group to explore three Web sites related to transformations of energy such as that explored in the activity "Mirrors and Reflection," then develop criteria for evaluating the information supplied by the site. |
| *Problem-Solving and Decision-Making Tools* | In this activity students see how one form of energy changes to another, causing vibrations to produce sound. Can sound travel through other forms of matter besides air? Students should devise a strategy to demonstrate their response. | Have the students using a spreadsheet or database, categorize the following items as a first-, second-, or third-class lever: hammer, nutcracker, seesaw, wheelbarrow, bottle opener, and fishing rod. Where are the fulcrum, effort, and load on each item? | Ask students what advantage a concave mirror may have over a convex mirror. In what objects would its use be an advantage? Use some of the resources above to help answer these questions. |

**TABLE 11.5B   Grades 5–6 National Educational Technology Standards (NETS) as applied in the context of lessons using the National Science Education Standards (NSES):  Life Science Content Standards for grades 5–8**

| NSES: Content Standards for 5–8 | Life Science Standards | | |
|---|---|---|---|
| NETS for Grades 5–6 | Structure & Function | Reproduction & Heredity | Regulation & Behavior |
| *Lesson Name* | Temperature Receptors on Skin | Sex-linked Genes | Crickets: Basic Needs of an Organism |
| *Basic Operations* | The *Human Biology & Health* laserdisc shares additional information on skin receptors beyond classroom activities in this lesson. | The *Genetics & Heredity* software and/or software like this can provide experiences in examining sex-linked traits like those studied in the activity. Can use as an introduction to the lesson or to reinforce concepts learned in the lesson. | *Davidson's ZooKeeper* provides students with problem-solving activities on the environmental needs of animals. Use to extend the experiences with crickets in this activity to other animals. |
| *Social, Ethical & Human Issues* | Have students use the Internet to determine ways in which people keep cool during the summer without the aid of fans or air conditioning? Can any of those ideas work where they live? | Ask students how advancements in technology have changed the way society views genetic evidence in criminal cases? | Students determine the role society has played on changing the habitat of certain animals. How does human behavior impact animal's behavior? Students e-mail state wildlife biologists to find out what their state is doing to preserve local animal habitats. |
| *Productivity Tools* | Create an image of the human body. Use during the expansion activity as a data sheet to record where receptors are on the various spots of the body. | Students create a database to record the various combinations of "straw" genes and the traits they could possibly pass down to the next generation. | Students create a slide presentation of the behaviors unique to a given animal. They add video and/or pictures from the Internet in the presentation. |
| *Communication Tools* | The University of Washington sponsored Web site "Neuroscience for Kids" at *http://faculty.washington.edu/chudler/neurok.html* provides information on the central nervous system. Additional information on skin receptors and an opportunity to contact scientists with questions about the skin and the nervous system can be found at a link with this site at *http://faculty.washington.edu/chudler/receptor.html* | By using the search engine Yahoo genetics page at *http://dir.yahoo.com/Science/Biology/Genetics/* numerous Web sites that deal with genetics—many with online discussions and/or chats about a particular heredity issue—can be found. | Students participate in an online project such as the Annenberg/CPB Math and Science Project—The Journey North at *http://www.learner.org/jnorth/* for online interactive projects that deal with animal migration. They find other sites that deal with other behaviors unique to a given animal. |
| *Research Tools* | Students use the Web site listed above or perform a search to find a Web site related to the central nervous system. Through their research they either describe the structure of the central nervous system and/or explain two other functions for the central nervous system | Students conduct a keyword search using a search engine such as Yahoo.com or Altavista.com to find three Web sites related to the study of heredity. They work in teams to create a list of sex-linked traits not discussed in class. | Students choose a behavior such as migration or hibernation. They research via the Web, a resource CD-ROM, or laserdisc for examples in which animals exhibit that behavior and offer possible explanations as to what benefit that behavior offers the animal. |
| *Problem-Solving and Decision-Making Tools* | Students choose the appropriate resource, either print, electronic, or Web-based to explain how Gregor Meissner in 1853 discovered the *Meissner's corpuscle.* | One trait studied in this heredity activity on sex-linked genes was baldness. There are a lot of products that claim to reduce hair loss. Knowing what they know about sex-linked genes, do students think that these products will work for everyone? Have them use the various resources mentioned above to write a position statement on the use of such products. | What can humans learn by studying animal behavior? Students identify an animal behavior that has changed the way humans interact with that animal. They use resources such as those listed above to help identify the impact understanding those behaviors have had. |

*(continued)*

**TABLE 11.5B** *(continued)*

| NSES: Content Standards for 5–8 | Life Science Standards | |
|---|---|---|
| **NETS for Grades 5–6** | **Populations & Ecosystems** | **Diversity & Adaptations** |
| *Lesson Name* | Owl Pellets | Animal Adaptations |
| *Basic Operations* | *Ecosystems; Island Survivors, a Computer Simulation in Ecology* provides the students with experiences on ecosystems that can then be built on by doing the Owl Pellets activity. | *Adaptations for Survival in the Sea* and *A Field Trip into the Sea* provide examples of animal adaptations that can extend the understanding acquired in this activity. |
| *Social, Ethical & Human Issues* | Students collect data that shows the changes in a given animal's population over the last ten years. They predict how changes in human population have impacted changes in that animal's population. | Competition for resources over time will lead to adaptations to ensure the animal's survival. Ask students to choose one resource they use most often in their lives (e.g. water, certain foods) and perform an e-mail survey to determine how other people would live if that resource were taken away. How would they adapt? |
| *Productivity Tools* | Students create a spreadsheet for a given animal and record the population of the animal over a ten-year period. In the spreadsheet students calculate change in population over time. | Using various resources, students create a booklet on animal adaptations. |
| *Communication Tools* | Students participate in a threaded discussion about a particular animal and the factors that impact its population. One such site is the Ornithology home page at *http://www.rgs.edu.sg/virtual/bio/flylab/Ornithology. html.* It contains information on bird populations and factors that influence this. | Students participate in an online forum such as the "Great Outdoors Recreation Pages Forum" at *http:// www.gorp.com/gorp/interact/default.htm* for discussions on conservation issues related to plant and animal diversity. From this forum they go to the linked Web site *http://www.gorp.com/gorp/publishers/falcon/wild.azr.htm* to explore the diversity of plant and animal species in Arizona. |
| *Research Tools* | How are human populations counted? Students work in groups to visit the Web site of their state and at least two neighboring states. What is the population of those states? How are those populations determined? Students share those results in a graphic display. | Students identify a particular plant and/or animal and conduct a Web search to identify the adaptations for survival of that particular organism. They identify a particular biome and explore the diverse animal and/or plant populations found within. They create a slide presentation with pictures and text of the diverse organisms. |
| *Problem-Solving and Decision-Making Tools* | Students choose an issue such as deer population and create a map of their state showing the deer population by county. They use resources such as the state department of natural resources Web site to complete the map or e-mail local wildlife officials for this information. Do they think these counts are accurate? How would they conduct a deer population count? Why do they think it is important to have an accurate count? | Students choose one animal and use the resources identified above to determine the needs of that animal, including its habitat. They pick a different habitat. Could the animal they chose adapt quickly enough to survive in the new habitat? Why or why not? |

**TABLE 11.5C** Grades 5–6 National Educational Technology Standards (NETS) as applied in the context of lessons using the National Science Education Standards (NSES): Earth and Space Science Content Standards for grades 5–8

| *NSES: Content Standards for 5–8* | *Earth and Space Science Standards* | | |
|---|---|---|---|
| NETS for Grades 5–6 | Structure of the Earth System | Earth's History | Earth in the Solar System |
| *Lesson Name* | Weathering | Crustal Plate Movement | Constellations |
| *Basic Operations* | *Dynamic Earth* laserdisc by Prentice Hall provides additional experiences with weathering beyond those offered in this activity. | *A Teacher's Guide to the Geology of Hawaii, Volcanoes National Park http://volcano.und.nodak.edu/vwdocs/ vwlessons/atg.html* is a great resource site to send students to download and save materials related to class activities. | *Lost in the Universe* by Houston Space Museum or *Where in Space is Carmen Sandiego* by Broderbund can provide 3-D views of constellations not captured in print materials. |
| *Social, Ethical & Human Issues* | Students conduct a Web search of Internet sites that provide information on various obelisks or monuments that are subjected to weathering, such as those found in Egypt or the Washington Monument in D.C. How have human actions contributed to the rapid weathering of these objects? | Students generate a map of the world, plotting the spots throughout the world where most volcanic activity occurs. E-mail students from schools found in those regions. Discuss how volcanic or earthquake activity impacts their daily lives. Generate a list of ways the students can ease the burden of those affected by the disaster and follow through on those plans. | Discuss what early civilizations believed about constellations. Students search the Internet for Web sites dedicated to constellations and the study of stars. How can one separate fact from fiction when it comes to theories about how stars have formed? |
| *Productivity Tools* | Students use a digital camera on the *Weathering Field Trip* to collect examples of weathering. They put these into a booklet and provide text to explain possible causes of weathering. | Create a linear series of slides or cards demonstrating the evolution of a volcano. Provide appropriate text to explain the diagrams. | Students create a "then and now" chart for some constellations to compare the differences in beliefs about their formation. |
| *Communication Tools* | The Web site *http://www.aerospace. nasa.gov/edu/educator.htm* sponsored by NASA has links to weathering-related activities and scientists to e-mail for questions. | Students participate in an online chat with others in their grade level from countries and/or states affected by earthquake or volcano activity. They can discuss how their school or city prepares for such disasters. | Students explore the NASA Web site, in particular the "kids" pages for interesting information and activities with stars or the solar system. The direct URL is *http://www.nasa.gov/ kids_stars.html.* Students participate in an online chat with a NASA "Space Scientist" by going directly to *http://quest.arc.nasa.gov/sso/index.html.* |
| *Research Tools* | Students choose at least five rocks and five minerals. Using a variety of electronic resources such as the Internet, CD-ROM, and laserdisc, they create a chart displaying good/bad uses of that rock or mineral. Keep in mind how weathering can impact some of those on the chart. | Students use a variety of resources to identify sites of volcano and earthquake activity around the globe. They prepare a display of their findings and are prepared to offer up a possible explanation on why the sites are found at the places they've identified. | Students research the NASA Web site or similar Web sites to create a presentation on two constellations, one found in the northern hemisphere and one found in the southern hemisphere. They explain why they can't see both of them in the nighttime sky from their house. |
| *Problem-Solving and Decision-Making Tools* | Students work with a group of classmates to create a checklist on "signs of weathering." Visit the various monuments and/or statues found in their town or local town. Using their checklist they look for signs of weathering. As a class determine a course of action for preserving those they find in greatest danger of falling apart due to the impact of weathering. Make this a class or schoolwide project to follow through on the plan. | Using the resources shared above and others they may find through an Internet search, students design a model of a structure that they believe will hold up best when crustal plates move. They create that model and test their ideas. | Why would anyone want to name stars or groups of stars? What value does it serve the majority of us that never move beyond the earth's surface? |

# TABLE 11.6A Grades 7–8 National Educational Technology Standards (NETS) as applied in the context of lessons using the National Science Education Standards (NSES): Physical Science Content Standards for grades 5–8

| NSES: Content Standards for 5–8 | Physical Science Standards | | |
|---|---|---|---|
| NETS for Grades 7–8 | Properties & Changes of Properties in Matter | Motions & Forces | Transformations of Energy |
| *Lesson Name* | Using the Scientific Method to Solve Problems | Toys in Space | The Slinky Potential |
| *Basic Operations* | Students can explore matter and the changes in properties of matter while at the same time learning about using the scientific method to solve problems through use of a CD-ROM called *Chemistry Set* or in using *General Science Labs with Computers: General Science Experiments using the Science Workshop Program and Interfaces from PASCO Scientific.* | After exploring the various *toys* in this lesson the students can view the video *Astrosmiles* from NASA to determine the accuracy of their predictions. Using the laserdisc *Motion, Force & Energy* by Prentice Hall will also enhance their understanding of motion and forces. | Software such as *Interactive Physics Simulations* by Addison-Wesley can provide the students with additional experiences on energy transformation that are difficult to reproduce in the classroom. |
| *Social, Ethical & Human Issues* | Have the students choose a topic that interests them. Search the Internet for information on that topic. Ask them to apply the skills they learned in *Using the Scientific Method to Solve Problems* to determine the validity of the information they found via the Internet on their chosen topic. | Ask the students to find evidence via the Internet to support their position on the following statement: "I (believe/do not believe) that studying how objects behave in space can help us use them more efficiently on Earth." | How do automobile air bags demonstrate the transformation of energy? What dilemma has air bag technology presented to society? Initiate an electronic chat with students from other schools on this topic. |
| *Productivity Tools* | By using a pH meter to determine the acidity/alkalinity of the unknown solutions, students can narrow down their choices in identifying the unknowns. | Assign each student group one of Newton's laws of motion. Ask the students to use a multimedia software application to draw a model of their assigned law when applied to an object. | Have the students work collaboratively to produce a multimedia presentation demonstrating the conversion of kinetic energy to potential in various sports and/or games. |
| *Communication Tools* | Have the students work in teams to create videotape that demonstrates how to apply the scientific method in solving a problem. Have them create the problem scenario and then go about solving it. Invite their parents in for a public viewing. | Ask the students to use word processing software to write a fictitious story about how the behavior of either an astronaut or a mouse changed after several days of living in space in the absence of gravity. | Have the students create a public service announcement about the importance of leaving space between cars while driving in traffic. Include information such as the distance needed to stop a moving car at a given speed. |
| *Research Tools* | Have the students use a variety of electronic resources, whether it is software such as an Encyclopedia on a CD-ROM or a Web site for an Encyclopedia resource, to find everyday examples of a solution, mixture, suspension, and a colloid. | The students can access Web sites with experts in science areas to ask additional questions about the behavior of objects in the absence of gravity and the practical applications of such knowledge—in addition to the NASA site another interactive expert site is *Ask an Expert Page*—to get information about science, math, and other subjects at *http://njnie.dl.stevenstech.edu/curriculum/aska.html.* | Assign student teams to do research on different amusement park rides. Search the Internet for descriptions of different rides. Create a database of ride names; include the heights of the roller coasters and the circumference of rides that move in a circle. |
| *Problem-Solving and Decision-Making Tools* | Create a computer-generated table listing characteristics of the unknown substances against characteristics of known substances. Use the table to narrow down the identification of the unknowns. | Provide the students with a set of data demonstrating Newton's laws of motion. Ask the students to select and use the appropriate technology resources to help them determine which laws are demonstrated. | Using the database the students created above, identify whether the ride possesses rotational or translational kinetic energy or both. |

**TABLE 11.6B**  Grades 7–8 National Educational Technology Standards (NETS) as applied in the context of lessons using the National Science Education Standards (NSES): Life Science Content Standards for grades 5–8

| NSES: Content Standards for 5–8 | Life Science Standards | | |
|---|---|---|---|
| NETS for Grades 7–8 | Structure & Function | Reproduction & Heredity | Regulation & Behavior |
| *Lesson Name* | Building Microscope Skills | Passing of Traits | Osmosis and Capillary Action |
| *Basic Operations* | The CD *Microscope Nature Explorer* can be used to enhance the classroom experience on microscope use or can be used to introduce the microscope before the lesson begins. | The organism that easily illustrates genetic traits is the fruit fly. Time, funding, and/or suitable lab space may limit your ability to use the fruit fly to demonstrate genetic traits. The software *Macfly* provides numerous simulations of fly genetic experiments. | A laserdisc such as *Cells: Building Blocks of Life* by Prentice Hall can be used to explore osmosis in greater detail. |
| *Social, Ethical & Human Issues* | Ask the students to respond to this question: "If you were to purchase a microscope over the Internet what precautions should you take before buying?" | Have the students create and give a survey on opinions about using technology to alter traits inherited by human offspring. | The students will demonstrate their knowledge of citing resources found on a Web site during the expansion phase of this lesson as they trace the history of when flowers were artificially colored. |
| *Productivity Tools* | If the technology is available, have the students connect the microscope to the computer monitor and bring an object in focus. | The students can use digital cameras to take photos of family members that all exhibit a similar inherited trait. | Work with the students to create and edit videotape of a carnation as it draws up colored water so that the change can be shown within 5 minutes of time. |
| *Communication Tools* | Ask the students to prepare a brochure using a software application like *PageMaker* to explain proper care and use of a microscope. | The students can put the digital pictures of an inherited family trait into a *PowerPoint* presentation to demonstrate their understanding of inherited traits. | Working in small groups the students can use the technology to assess the impact of drought on the plants in a given area. As they report on their assessment include possible strategies to minimize water loss for the plants. |
| *Research Tools* | Students can conduct research on various types of microscopes and prepare a brochure describing the different types and explaining when to use each type. | Assign each student group to use the Internet to research the inherited traits carried through the generations of a famous family. | Students can make use of a Web site such as the Virtual Cell Web site [*http://ampere.scale. uiuc.edu/~m-lexa/cell/cell.html*] to look closely at plant cells or the Cells Alive Web site [*http://www.cellsalive.com*], which provides videos of cell activity. |
| *Problem-Solving and Decision-Making Tools* | Have the students create a table to go along with the first activity to identify the crystal properties for the slides they prepared. | Provide students with datasets of human traits. Have them determine whether they were inherited due to an environmental factor. | Project a series of digital photos of carnations in various stages of being colored through capillary action and osmosis. Ask the students to explain how the phenomenon occurred. |

*(continued)*

**417**

## ▶ TABLE 11.6B   (continued)

| *NSES:*<br>*Content Standards*<br>*for 5–8* | *Life Science Standards* | |
|---|---|---|
| **NETS for<br>Grades 7–8** | **Populations & Ecosystems** | **Diversity & Adaptations** |
| *Lesson Name* | Plant Photosynthesis | Starch Exploration |
| *Basic Operations* | The laserdisc *Life Science, Level III from the series: Newton's Apple Multimedia Collection* provides the students with additional activities with photosynthesis, such as measuring oxygen production in green plants. | The *Science 2000, Science 1. Grade 7* software is centered on four key questions. The activities that could build on the overarching concept of diversity and adaptations address the question, "How can we evaluate and improve the health of our lake?" by exploring the need for diverse yet compatible organisms within a lake. |
| *Social, Ethical &<br>Human Issues* | Work with the class to create a form that helps your students critically review a Web site. Assign student teams to go to different Web sites about Rainforests and using the class review form, evaluate the information included in that Web site. | The students should cite sources they use to help them defend one side of this statement: "The United States should/should not send starch-containing foods to underdeveloped countries." |
| *Productivity Tools* | Students create a database of organisms that are considered producers. How do they differ from consumers or decomposers? | The students should use a microscope attached to a monitor to examine various starch grains. They should be responsible for the proper care and use of this technology. |
| *Communication<br>Tools* | Students participate in an online chat with a university botanist. Determine which area of plant study is his or her specialty. Ask whether the plants studied contain chlorophyll or a different type of pigment. If so ask the botanist to explain the difference and what role that pigment may play in photosynthesis. | Have the students prepare and participate in mock interviews for a job in a frozen food factory. Videotape the mock interviews. During the interview the interviewer or interviewee must share some knowledge about starch grains. Have the class prepare a rubric for evaluating each group's understanding of the concepts studied and use the rubric while viewing the taped interviews. |
| *Research Tools* | Have students prepare a report from the chat session in which they interviewed a botanist. Share all information that related to plant photosynthesis. | Have the students work in teams to use a variety of research tools to determine the conditions necessary to grow starch-containing foods. |
| *Problem-Solving and<br>Decision-Making<br>Tools* | Provide the students with a problem about a science exploration and require them to plan the experiment to solve the problem, clearly identifying the variable that should be manipulated and the variable that should be controlled. | After they research the conditions necessary for growing starch-containing foods, have the students use a map of the world and mark the areas on the map where ideal growing conditions exist for starch-containing foods. |

**TABLE 11.6C   Grades 5–6 National Educational Technology Standards (NETS) as applied in the context of lessons using the National Science Education Standards (NSES): Earth and Space Science Content Standards for grades 5–8**

| NSES: Content Standards for 5–8 | Earth and Space Science Standards | | |
|---|---|---|---|
| NETS for Grades 7–8 | Structure of the Earth System | Earth's History | Earth in the Solar System |
| *Lesson Name* | Cooling Crystals | Aging Man/Aging Earth | The Expanding Universe |
| *Basic Operations* | Web site *Geologylink* [*http://www. geologylink.com*] provides information on geologic events happening throughout the globe. | The Web site *A Science Odyssey, Then and Now* [*http://www.pbs.org/wgbh/ aso/thenandnow/earth.html*] provides valuable information on the structure of the Earth over time and the various living organisms that existed during the many changes the planet went through. | A resource such as the CD-ROM *The Great Solar System* provides insight into the planets and their positions within our solar system. |
| *Social, Ethical & Human Issues* | Some people claim that crystals found in rocks have certain powers to impact human lives. Working together with the class, examine some Web sites that explore these beliefs. Help the students create some critical questions that can help them examine the information presented for validity and reliability. | How has technology changed the age of the Earth? Working in teams, have the students identify at least three things we once held as fact about the history of the planet Earth but were changed with the discovery of new evidence revealed through the application of technology. | Explore the idea that modern technology can fix the problem of pollution on earth. Can space stations help resolve this problem or that of overpopulation in certain areas of the planet Earth? |
| *Productivity Tools* | Student groups could plan and produce a multimedia presentation on crystals found in various igneous rocks. | Students can use a draw/paint software application to create a timeline depicting the various types of human beings found on the planet over time. | Assign a different planet to each student group. Have them prepare a multimedia presentation that describes three unique features of their planet and two features that classify it as a planet. |
| *Communication Tools* | Have student groups research a career provided by the teacher that applies knowledge of crystal formation to that career, e.g. geologist, geophysicist, volcanologist, jeweler, sculptor, or geographer. Ask the groups to create a flier that would encourage the reader to enter that career. | Assign e-mail pals among your students. Require them to e-mail a description of one type of early organism found through fossil evidence on the Earth to their e-mail pal. Remind them not to give a name to that organism. The recipient should e-mail back the name of the organism they believe it is based on the description provided. | Have the students use desktop publishing software to prepare a press announcement about a planet that will be visible in the nighttime sky. Encourage them to be descriptive yet factual so they convince the readers to go out to view the site. |
| *Research Tools* | Student teams can investigate how the prices of precious jewels are affected by crystal formation. Search the Web for the current value of at least two precious gems. | Physicist Steven Hawking has developed new theories about the origin of the universe. Working in teams have the students use various resources, i.e. Internet, CD-ROM, books, to find information on Steven Hawking and his theories. Have each team report its findings by identifying which source it came from. Ask the teams to evaluate which resource gave more detailed information, which was easier to understand, and which provided more pictures or drawings to help them understand the theory. | The students should demonstrate the ability to use a search engine while looking for information on their assigned planet for their multimedia presentation. |
| *Problem-Solving and Decision-Making Tools* | Have students create a database of various igneous rocks and classify them by crystal size; or use a prepared decision table that describes the crystals by size and shape. Use it to determine the type of rock from a given sample of rocks. | Ask the students to identify evidence of sea floor spreading while they are looking at a map of the ocean floor. | Have students create a table comparing life on Earth to life in a space station. Ask them to use this chart to make a decision about why they would or would not chose to live in a space station. |

## CHAPTER SUMMARY

Some time in the future, you and your students may pick up a newspaper and read a headline like "Genetic Engineering Unravels the Aging Process" or "Ozone Hole Increases." The stories following these headlines will be important to both you and your students. They will deal with important quality-of-life issues that you, as citizens, may need to form an opinion about or make a decision concerning your future. Being able to understand the consequences of your choices is important to you and to your students.

As a teacher, you will need to ask yourself whether you have done your best to provide your students with the skills they need to make these future decisions. Emphasis on student inquiry through questioning, research, issue resolution, and higher order thinking skills must be constantly practiced as much as consistent use of educational technology to create the artifacts that demonstrate the students' ability to perform such skills.

Scientific and technological knowledge are changing so rapidly that it is becoming more difficult to prepare students for this complicated task. Textbooks cannot keep pace with the new discoveries in science; however, as a classroom teacher you can supplement your textbook and your program with experiences and opportunities that are not available through print materials.

Stimulate learning by serving as the bridge between the resources that are relevant and available to you and the students in your classroom. Appropriate applications of educational technology can extend the learning environment beyond the confines of the classroom. Only your imagination and energy limit your uses of educational technology, which can provide inquiry-based learning opportunities that stimulate your students and provide an atmosphere for scientific discovery.

## DISCUSSION QUESTIONS

**1.** Review the National Educational Technology Standards provided in Table 11.1. Visit the International Society for Technology in Education Web site at *http://cnets.iste.org* to review the specific performance indicators for each standard at a given grade range. Do you think these are realistic expectations for all students? Why or why not?

**2.** Defend the notion that the National Educational Technology Standards provided in Table 11.1 are not linear. Do you believe it is possible for your students to be more proficient in some technologies than you are? Would they intimidate you? Explain your feelings. Identify one educational technology tool you'd like to become more proficient at and establish a plan for reaching proficiency.

**3.** Discuss what criteria you may use to choose instructional science software. Is it enough to make your instructional software purchasing decisions based on the vendor's description? What criteria will you use to make your decision?

**4.** What are three advantages of accessing information for a given science lesson from the Internet? What are three advantages of having your students access information from the Internet? What criteria do you believe are important to determine the worthiness of a given Web site?

## BUILD A PORTFOLIO

**1.** According to the Technology Related Assistance Act of 1988, assistive technology includes "any item, piece of equipment, or product, whether acquired commercially, off the shelf, modified, or customized, that is used to increase, maintain, or improve the functional capabilities of individuals with disabilities" (P.L. 101-407 from McLane, 1998). Identify some assistive technologies that are especially useful in the instruction of students with special needs when using educational technology in your science class. You may find these at the following special education Internet Web sites: *http://www.cec.sped.org* and *http://www.edc.org/FSC/ASSIST/*. Choose one type of special need such as hearing impairment or blindness. Use one of the lessons provided in Table 11.3a to identify which assistive technologies you will need to apply in order to accomplish the activities listed for each of the National Educational Technology Standards.

**2.** Access the National Science Teacher's Association (NSTA) Web site at *http://www.nsta.org*. Research the purposes, fee structure, and service of the association. Identify the NSTA publications that will be useful as you plan science lessons. Locate membership information, meeting schedules, and publications from your state or local science education organization. Add this information to your Science Portfolio.

**3.** Choose a lesson identified in Tables 11.3–11.6. Using the Internet, identify three Web sites that provide content information about the concept identified in the lesson; identify three Web sites that provide additional student activities re-

lated to the concept identified in the lesson. Make sure the URL is accurately recorded. Use Table 11.1, "Is This a Worthy Task?" to judge the value of each identified Web site.

**4.** Select a content area and grade-level range from the National Science Education Standards. Choose a science concept and identify at least three instructional science software applications that will promote greater concept attainment. Identify whether the software is considered drill and practice, a tutorial, a simulation, or a microworld application. Write a summary of what the software was designed to do and your views of how valuable you believe the software will be for students in the grade level you chose.

**5.** Find a Web site that serves as a national database for a given science issue. Incorporate the use of that database into a science lesson that addresses one of the National Science Education Standards.

**6.** Identify a science concept for a particular grade level from the National Science Education Standards provided in Appendix A. Create a learning-cycle lesson plan for a given concept. Include activities that require the students to practice each of the six National Educational Technology Standards for Students.

# Lessons, Activities and Teaching Materials to Meet the Goals of Elementary and Middle School Science

The next three sections contain examples of commercial and public domain supplementary materials as they are *modified* to meet the content standards for elementary and middle school science. Section I is devoted to life science lessons, Section II includes physical science lessons, and Section III contains earth and space science lessons. Our intention is to show the techniques for modification, planning, and methods of teaching. Part IV is a resource for ideas and an exemplar of modification techniques.

More than 150 life, physical, and earth science activities are found within 60 lessons designed to fit the 4–E science learning cycle format suggested in the text. A clearly written concept statement can be found at the beginning of each lesson. Any concepts that may be important to the lesson expansion are also identified in the beginning of the lesson.

The student outcomes or objectives are included in the evaluation phase of each lesson. Those of you who expect to see objectives or learner outcomes listed first in an activity are encouraged to look carefully at the evaluation phase of each lesson before starting the exploration phase.

Grade levels are suggested in the beginning of each lesson. Each teacher best knows his or her students' limitations. If, upon reading the lesson, you find the activities too difficult or too easy for your students, then by all means find a lesson more suitable for your students' ability levels.

You will not find a time limit on the lessons. Lessons using a science learning cycle format may take one class period or several class meetings. One lesson may represent a unit or just one piece of that unit. The length of time for each lesson will depend on the ability level of your students and the amount of detail for each activity. Generally, the lessons are organized so that the exploration and expansion phases take one or two class meetings, and the explanation phase one class meeting. Questions designed to meet the goals of science in personal and social perspectives, science and technology, science as inquiry, and the history and the nature of science from the National Science Education Standards may be asked at any time during the lesson. Just because they are listed after the expansion phase does not mean they have to wait until after expansion to be asked. The evaluation phase may also be given in parts, during or after the exploration phase, as part of the explanation phase, and during or after the expansion phase.

These lessons are designed to give your students a chance to explore a science concept thoroughly. Collect materials and try each activity before you present it to your students to make sure everything works according to the plan, to make you aware of any potential problem areas, to ensure that you have foreseen all safety requirements, and to give you an opportunity to correct problems before you are with the students.

Make sure that each student is aware of any safety precautions before engaging in the science activity. If certain skills are required before the students can engage in an activity, then spend the time teaching those skills before starting the new activity. Advance work will ensure the success of a lesson presented in a science learning cycle.

# Life Science Lessons

| Lesson Name | Life Science Content Standards | Grade Level | Activities |
|---|---|---|---|
| **Plants** | | | |
| Plant Parts and Needs | Characteristics of Organisms | K–4 | Plant Dig • Eggshell Planters • Food Storage |
| Osmosis and Capillary Action | Regulation and Behavior | 5–8 | Colored Carnations • Three-Way Split |
| Plant Photosynthesis | Population and Ecosystems | 5–8 | Radish Growth: Light versus Dark in a Bag • Radish Growth: Light versus Dark in Soil |
| Starch Exploration | Diversity and Adaptations | 5–8 | Microscopic Starch • Beans and Starch Grains |
| **Animals** | | | |
| Colors of Wildlife | Organisms and Environments | K–4 | Animal Similarities and Differences • Create a Rainbow Animal |
| Bird Life | Life Cycles of Organisms | K–2 | What Comes First—the Bird or the Egg? • The Developing Chick |
| Wildlife and Domesticated Animals | Organisms and Environments | K–4 | Animal Needs • Domestic versus Wild Charades |
| A Bug's Life? | Life Cycles of Organisms | 3–4 | Ordering Life Cycle Stages • Growing Mealworms |
| Crickets: Basic Needs of an Organism | Regulation and Behavior | 5–8 | Cricket Needs • Cricket Behavior |
| Animal Adaptations | Diversity and Adaptation | 5–8 | Mitten and Tweezer Beaks • Fish Adaptations |
| Owl Pellets | Populations and Ecosystems | 5–8 | Owl Pellet Dissection • Owl Research or Field Trip |
| **Environment** | | | |
| Humans and Trash | Organisms and Environment | K–4 | Trash and Animals • Classroom Landfill and Recycling |
| Useful Waste | Populations and Ecosystems | 5–8 | Rating Garbage • Litter-Eating Critter • Making Paper |
| Litter in Our Waterways | Populations and Ecosystems | 5–8 | Sink-or-Float Litter • Plastic Food |
| **Human** | | | |
| Sense of Taste | Characteristics of Organisms | K–4 | Buds and Tasters • Supertasters |
| Skeleton | Characteristics of Organisms | 1–4 | Bones Assembly Line • Newsprint Bone Bodies |
| Temperature Receptors on Skin | Structure and Function | 5–8 | Soaking Hands • Hot/Cold Receptor Mapping |
| Building Microscope Skills | Structure and Function | 5–8 | Microscope Use and Crystal Comparisons • Charcoal Crystals |
| Sex-Linked Genes | Reproduction and Heredity | 5–6 | Family Traits • Sex-Linked Traits |
| Passing of Traits | Reproduction and Heredity | 7–8 | What Traits Do You Share? • Inherited or Environmentally Altered? |

## Plant Parts and Needs

**GRADE**
K–4
**DISCIPLINE**
Life
Science

### Concept to be invented
Main idea—The basic parts of a plant are roots, stems, and leaves.

### Concepts that are important to expansion
Soil or some nutrient containing medium, air, water, and light is necessary for plant growth.

### Materials needed
*For exploration:*

| | |
|---|---|
| large paper or large plastic bags | resource books on plants |
| spoons for digging, or a spade or shovel | poster paint |
| | art paper |
| white paper | crayons |
| | markers |

*For expansion:*

| | |
|---|---|
| eggshells (halves or larger) | water |
| potting soil | sunlight or artificial light |
| mung beans | colored markers |

➡ **Safety precautions:** Always have the proper adult:student ratio when taking the students away from the school campus. Make sure that the students are buddied up and that they are able to cross streets safely and know enough not to talk to strangers while walking to the dig site or while on the site.

Make sure all students can identify any poisonous plants at the dig site, such as poison ivy or poison oak. If large amounts of poisonous plants are in the area, it may be better to choose a different site.

Demonstrate to the students a safe method for digging up the plants and make sure they practice what was demonstrated. Remind the students never to put anything in their mouths unless the teacher gives prior approval. Do not eat the plants!

## 1. EXPLORATION: Which process skills will be used?

Observing, identifying, comparing

### What will the students do?

*Plant Dig*

Take the students on a walking field trip to an area near the school where plants can be dug up without harming the environment. Identify the plants the students may dig up, and then allow them time to dig, making sure they get most of the root systems. Instruct the students to put their plants in bags and bring them back to school. Once back in class, ask the students to choose one of their plants and spread it out on a piece of white paper. Ask them to use the materials provided to draw pictures of their plants.

## 2. EXPLANATION/CONCEPT INVENTION: What is the main idea? How will the main idea be constructed?

*Concept:* The basic parts of a plant are roots, stems, and leaves.

Once the students have drawn their pictures, provide them with resource books that identify other plants. Ask the students the following questions: How are these plants different from the plant in front of you? How are they the same? What do all of our plants have in common? Continue with this line of questioning until the students understand that the basic parts of a plant are roots, stems, and leaves. Ask the students to return to the drawings they created of their plants. Ask them to label the roots, stems, and leaves in their drawings. At this time the teacher may provide the students with the common names for their plants, or ask the students if they already know what they dug up, or ask them to look through the resource books to identify their plants.

## 3. EXPANSION OF THE IDEA: Which process skills will be used?

Observing, gathering data, recording data, interpreting data, manipulating materials

How will the idea be expanded?

*Eggshell Planters*  Help the students collect eggshells (halves or larger). Ask the students to draw two eyes and a nose on their eggshells with colored markers. Provide potting soil so that the students can fill the shells with soil and sprinkle mung beans on top. Have them put a little more soil on top of the seeds. Sprinkle a small amount of water on the soil. Place the filled shells near the window. Challenge the students to observe the shells each day. When they discover bean sprouts appearing, have them draw a smile on the shell to complete the face.

Once the beans are well grown, ask the students to pull one of the sprouts out. Can you identify its root, stem, and leaves? Ask the students to describe what they did to help the plant grow from the bean seed to the sprout. What things were necessary for plant growth? Make a list on the board. Review with them why the items they identified are necessary for plant growth. Discuss the fact that leaves are necessary to plants because they are the place in the plant where food is created. The water and minerals are taken from the soil through the roots and brought up to the leaves. Gases from the air enter the plant through the leaf, and with the help of sunlight the leaves make food for the plant.

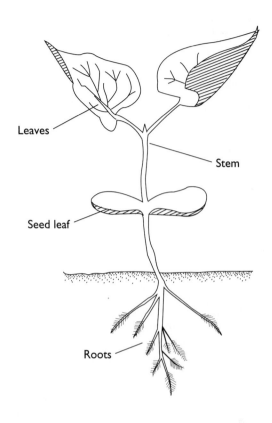

## Additional ideas for expansion

*Food Storage*    The teacher can share with the students ways in which plants store food and what humans do with this knowledge. For instance, when food is stored, such as in nuts and seeds, the leaves drop off because they are no longer needed. Also, food is stored in various parts of plants. Provide the students with actual fruits, vegetables, and seeds (or pictures of them) to classify. Make a bulletin board of drawings done by students of roots, stems, leaves, flowers, fruits, and seeds eaten by humans. Hang the pictures near the appropriate term. Some possibilities are roots (beets, carrots, radishes, sweet potatoes), stems (asparagus, celery, green onions), underground stems (onions, potatoes), leaves (lettuce, spinach, cabbage), flowers (artichokes, broccoli, cauliflower), fruits (apples, pears, tomatoes, peaches, plums, apricots), seeds (nuts, peas, beans).

### Science in Personal and Social Perspectives

- What would your life be like without plants? Why do you need to take care of plants?
- How might taking care of plants help you to develop responsibility?

- Ask the students if any of their parents or grandparents have a garden or grow plants indoors. Discuss the special care these plants need. Discuss how large fields of plants can be watered.

### Science and Technology

- Why do plants sometimes need to be fertilized?
- Do all plants have to be in soil in order to grow? Hydroponic farming does not use soil. Can you think of what it uses instead of soil to grow plants?

### Science as Inquiry

- Why do you need to know what plants need to grow?
- Why is research done on growing plants?
- What must we do to keep the plants healthy?
- During what part of a plant's life cycle can it grow without sunlight? Why?

### History and Nature of Science

- Discuss with the students jobs or professions that involve caring for plants, such as gardening, working as a forest ranger, selling vegetables in a grocery store, or working in a nursery or flower shop.
- Growing and caring for plants takes a lot of work; some of the people who do this are agronomists, horticulturists, florists, botanists, and nutritionists.
- Ask the students to have their parents help them discover what Luther Burbank and Gregor Mendel did to help us understand plant growth better.

**4. EVALUATION:** How will the students show what they have learned?

Upon completing the activities the students will be able to:

- identify the root, stem, and leaf on a complete plant;
- name the four things most plants need to live;
- when given potting soil, sunflower seeds, water, and a cup, demonstrate the steps necessary to grow and care for a plant;
- when given a beet, spinach, and a piece of asparagus, identify which is a root, which a stem, and which a leaf.

## Osmosis and Capillary Action

**GRADE**
**5–8**
**DISCIPLINE**
**Life**
**Science**

**Concept to be invented**
Main idea—Fluid is drawn up the stem of a plant by osmosis and capillary action.

**Concepts that are important to expansion**
Fiber membranes run throughout a flower from the roots to the petals.

### Materials needed

*For exploration (per student group):*

two to three white, long-stem carnations

food coloring

two clear cups or glass beakers

water

knife or sharp blade

➥ **Safety precautions:** Take care not to drop glass or beakers, thus increasing the likelihood of cuts. Use caution if using the knife or sharp blade.

## 1. EXPLORATION: Which process skills will be used?

Observing, predicting, reasoning, inferring, recording data

### What will the students do?

*Colored Carnations*

Separate the class into groups of four to six students. Give each group two carnations and two beakers or clear cups. Fill the cups or beakers with water. Dissolve one color of food coloring in one cup and a different color in the other. Dark colors like red or blue work well. Take one of the carnations and cut a fresh end on the stem (this may be done by the teacher with students in each group assisting). After this cut, split the stem in half, starting a cut with the knife and further splitting it along the fibers without breaking them. Place each half of the stem in each beaker and observe the white flower. Record your observations over 3-minute time periods for a total of 30 minutes.

## 2. EXPLANATION/CONCEPT INVENTION: What is the main idea? How will the main idea be constructed?

*Concept:* Fluid is drawn up the stem of a plant by osmosis and capillary action.

Ask the students questions such as the following to help invent this concept: What did you observe during the first 3 minutes of this experiment? How long did it take before you observed any changes in your flower? What were these changes? Why do you think they happened?

The stems of green plants support the plants and hold up the leaves and flowers. Some plants, like this carnation, have thin, green stems. Other plants, such as trees, have thick wooden stems. The trunk of an oak tree is its stem. It holds heavy branches and thousands of leaves. Water and food move up and down the plant through the stem. Water moves through special tubes in the stem. The water goes from the roots to the leaves and other parts of the plant. Other tubes carry food from the leaves to the roots and other plant parts. The colored water in our experiment is drawn up the stem of the carnation by osmosis and capillary action. The water molecules diffuse through the fiber

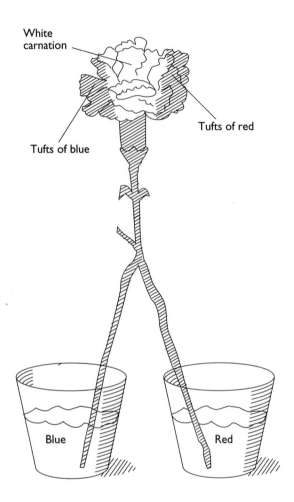

membranes from a lesser to a larger concentration of plant sap (osmosis). The fibers are so tiny that the adhesive force of the water molecules to the fiber walls becomes very great. This capillary force in combination with the osmotic pressure sucks the water up the flower.

## 3. EXPANSION OF THE IDEA: Which process skills will be used?

Communicating, problem solving, experimenting, recording data

### How will the idea be expanded?

*Three-Way Split*   When the stem is split three ways, it is very likely that the flower will be three colored. Ask the students to design an experiment to demonstrate this. This will show that the fibers must somehow run all the way from the stem to the petals of the flower. Encourage the students to experiment with how many ways they can get the stem to split to create as multicolored a flower as possible.

Ask the students to think about the following: What would happen if the stem were cut irregularly, such as diagonally? What if a cut was made that was jagged and cut across the fibers? How many other types of plants can be used to demonstrate this same phenomenon? Demonstrate this.

### Science in Personal and Social Perspectives

- If you wanted to give someone a bouquet of carnations to celebrate the Fourth of July and could find only white ones, what can you do to those to get red and blue ones too? Do you think the same thing is done by florists?
- If you were to receive a bouquet of flowers and you wanted them to stay fresh for a long time, what should you do for them, and why?

### Science and Technology

- How has knowledge of capillary action been used to create more efficient car engines?
- Artificial hearts and other organs are continuously being developed. How will osmosis and capillary action of blood affect the function of these artificial organs?

### Science as Inquiry

- What force is pulling the colored solution up the stem of the carnation in this activity?
- What if the flower were placed in *clear* water? Would the liquid still be drawn up the stem? How could you tell?
- Could a plant live without a stem? Why or why not?

### History and Nature of Science

- Can you name some people who work with plants?
- Why do you think it might be important for a farmer to understand plant growth? a florist? a grocer?
- Would you like to work in any of these occupations? Why or why not?
- How did the tradition of giving flowers on special occasions get started? Can you trace the history of this tradition? Can you trace the history of when flowers were artificially colored?

## 4. EVALUATION: How will the students show what they have learned?

Upon completing the activities the students will be able to:

- explain the purpose of splitting the stem in two during this lesson;
- demonstrate their knowledge of capillary action by explaining the process using a piece of celery, food coloring, a beaker, and water;
- observe several plants in various stages of watering (underwatered, overwatered, just right) and explain why the plant looks as it does.

## Plant Photosynthesis

LIFE SCIENCE

GRADE
5–8
DISCIPLINE
Life
Science

**Concept to be invented**
Main idea—Plants are capable of making their own food by a process called *photosynthesis.*

**Concepts that are important to expansion**
Seeds, moisture, chlorophyll, designing investigations

**Materials needed**
*For each student group:*

radish seeds
two Ziploc bags (large storage size)
two paper towels

one piece of aluminum foil
paper towels
metric ruler

➡ **Safety precautions:** Do not put anything in your mouth. Avoid eating leaves or seeds of plants. Do not play with plastic bags; keep them away from your face.

1. EXPLORATION: Which process skills will be used?

Predicting, observing, inferring, controlling variables, experimenting, reducing experimental error, analyzing

What will the students do?

*Radish Growth: Light versus Dark in a Bag*

Provide each group of students with some radish seeds, two Ziploc bags, two paper towels, and one piece of aluminum foil. Challenge the students to design a way in which they could use these materials to compare the growth of radish seeds. Explain to them that the variable to be manipulated in this experiment is light. All other factors must remain constant. The students must write up the method they plan to use; do not be concerned if the students change too many variables. This will be a valuable lesson to them, as they will soon discover by their experimental results. Once they have designed and written up their experimental methods, including predictions of potential outcomes, give them time to act on their design. Check their uncovered bags each day. When leaves begin to grow in the uncovered bag, uncover the covered bag and compare the two environments.

2. EXPLANATION/CONCEPT INVENTION: What is the main idea? How will the main idea be constructed?

*Concept:* Photosynthesis is a process in which chlorophyll-bearing plant cells, using light energy, produce carbohydrates and oxygen from carbon dioxide and

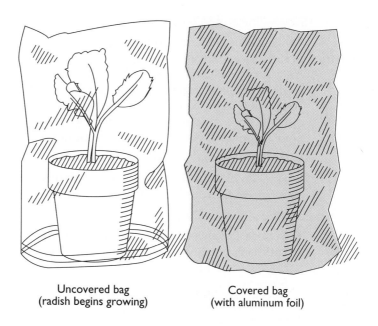

Uncovered bag
(radish begins growing)

Covered bag
(with aluminum foil)

water. Simply put, it is a way in which green plants use the sun's energy to make their own food.

Have the students share the data they collected. Where did you place your bags in the room? Were they both put in the same place? Why is it important to make sure the bags were in the same area? What about the number of seeds you used? Was that kept constant? Is it important to keep the number of seeds the same? Why or why not? What happened inside both of your bags? Was it as you predicted? If so, can you explain why? If not, why not? Did the seeds sprout leaves in both the covered and uncovered environments? What color were they? Which environment appears more successful? Where did the green leaves come from? What gives your skin color? (Pigment.) Do plants have pigment? Does anyone know the name of the pigment that gives plants their green color? (Chlorophyll.) Do you think, based on your experimental results, you can determine what the chlorophyll does for the plant? (It makes food for the plant.) What do we call the process whereby the chlorophyll makes use of light energy to make food for the plant? (Photosynthesis.)

## 3. EXPANSION OF THE IDEA: Which process skills will be used?

Experimenting, hypothesizing, predicting, observing, analyzing, controlling variables, inferring, recording data

How will the idea be expanded?

*Radish Growth:*
*Light versus Dark*
*in Soil*

Challenge the students to design another experiment, this time planting the seeds in soil instead of bags. Once again make light the manipulated variable. Predict the outcome, plan and record the methods, and act on your design. Once the seeds in the light begin to sprout, compare these results to the bag experiment. Were your predictions accurate? Why do you think you obtained the results you did? Did photosynthesis occur in the covered pot? the uncovered pot? Why? Continue to grow the plants and measure and record the results for one month.

### Science in Personal and Social Perspectives

- How do plants help people survive on this planet?
- What would your life be like without plants?

### Science and Technology

- Because they need land to live and grow things on, some people in Brazil are cutting down the tropical rain forests. Should this concern you? Do you think there is a technological solution to the problem of vanishing rainforests? Share your ideas.
- Of what advantage has hydroponic farming been to the people of the world?

### Science as Inquiry

- New concepts for further inquiry include growth rates, leaf shapes, deciduous versus coniferous, and so on.
- Can photosynthesis occur if a plant does not contain chlorophyll?
- Does photosynthesis take place in plants that grow on the ocean floor?

### History and Nature of Science

- What impact has the farming industry had on our daily lives? on the lives of people throughout the world today and in the past 100 years?
- Who was Gregor Mendel (1822–1884)? How did his knowledge of photosynthesis open up an entirely new field of genetics?
- Can just anyone become a landscape architect? What kind of background knowledge does a person in this field need?

## 4. EVALUATION: How will the students show what they have learned?

Upon completing the activities the students will be able to:

- when provided with two of the same plant, one grown in a shady environment and the other in a sunny one, identify which was grown where;
- observe plants growing around the classroom and accurately predict what will happen to the leaves if a small piece of paper is clipped over part of a leaf for one week;
- read a problem about a science exploration and accurately determine which variable should be manipulated and which should be controlled.

LIFE SCIENCE

## Starch Exploration

GRADE
5–8
DISCIPLINE
Life
Science

**Concept to be invented**
Main idea—Starches have a structure that is unique for each type of vegetable.

**Concepts that are important to expansion**
Starch grain, hilum, slide preparation, microscope use

**Materials needed**
*For each student group:*

microscope
five slides
one scalpel
cover slips
tapioca

rice that was soaked in water for at
        least 4 hours
kidney beans
corn kernels
potatoes

➡ **Safety precautions:** Although the starches are edible, the students should be discouraged from tasting them. Caution should be used around electrical outlets for the electric microscopes. The bulb for the microscope will get hot. Students should be reminded of safety techniques when using the scalpel.

1. EXPLORATION: Which process skills will be used?

   Observing, predicting, comparing, manipulating materials, recording data

   What will the students do?

*Microscopic Starch* The students will prepare slides of each of the given vegetables by using the scalpel to gently scrape a newly cut surface of the vegetable. A very small speck of each should be placed on each slide with a drop of water. A cover slip should be applied. The students should make predictions before observing the different starch grains. Will all of them look alike, since they are all starches? What do you think? Record this prediction. The students should observe each prepared slide under the microscope and draw their observations of the starch from each vegetable.

2. EXPLANATION/CONCEPT INVENTION: What is the main idea? How will the main idea be constructed?

   *Concept:* Starches have a structure that is unique for each type of vegetable.

   Key questions to ask the students to help them come to these conclusions are: What did you observe as you looked at the potato grains? How were they

LIFE SCIENCE

different from the corn or rice? What did the bean and tapioca starch look like? Ask the students to compare their drawings to actual pictures of the various grains. Were you able to observe the detail these pictures show? Can you differentiate between parts of the grain?

## Additional information to help develop the concept

The students should find countless oval, ellipsoidal, or even triangular shaped, almost transparent bodies that look like miniature oyster shells when they observe the potato starch grains. Since the grains are not flat, it may help if the students slowly rotate the fine adjustment on the microscope back and forth to get all the parts in focus. Usually on the narrower end the students will find a tiny dark spot that is not in the center of the grain. This is called the *hilum*, the oldest part of the starch grain, around which the remainder of the shell has grown layer by layer until fully formed. If you focus up and down at this point, you will find concentric lines or rings called *striations*, which indicate the layers where the grain has grown larger and larger.

Corn starch is different from potato. The grains may have an irregular globular shape or a very distinct polygonal shape. The shape will vary depending on the part of the kernel the students take their samples from—the horny or the floury portion. Corn starch has a central hilum that is usually a point but sometimes shows two, three, or four radiating clefts.

Rice starch grains are very small and many sided. They may be square, triangular, or pentagonal in shape. The hilum is not distinct, but in some grains a central portion appears brighter. This difference may be due to the drying of the grain. Ovoid or spherical shapes are usually due to a number of grains being compacted together.

Bean starch grains are usually ellipsoidal or kidney shaped. They have an irregular branching cleft running out from the center that appears black because of enclosed air.

Tapioca grains are usually circular or loaf shaped, depending on whether they sit on their flat surfaces or on their sides. The hilum is centrally located, usually coming to a point or small cleft. When students view the flattened surface, the hilum may appear triangular.

Corn starch          Rice starch          Bean starch          Tapioca starch

## 3. EXPANSION OF THE IDEA: Which process skills will be used?

Observing, predicting, comparing, manipulating materials, recording data, hypothesizing

### How will the idea be expanded?

*Beans and Starch Grains*

- The students may brainstorm a list of other starch-containing foods. Obtain these foods, prepare slides, and check students' predictions by looking for evidence of starch grains. Are they similar to any of the grains previously identified? Are they different? What kind of starch do you think this food contains?
- The students may obtain several different kinds of beans. Pose a question: Will all beans contain the same kind of starch grains, no matter the type of bean? Allow the students to design an experiment to answer that question.

### *Science in Personal and Social Perspectives*

- Do you think the differences in the starch grain will affect your ability to digest that starch? Why or why not?
- Are there any other kinds of plants that contain starch grains that humans do not eat? What are these? Why do you think we do not eat them?
- Why are starches important in a person's diet?

### *Science and Technology*

- Why does the United States send starchy foods to underdeveloped countries? What kinds of conditions are necessary to grow starch-containing foods? Can modern technology do anything to help these underdeveloped nations to grow starches on their own?
- What kinds of products have modern industries created that make use of starches? How have these helped modern society? How have these hindered modern society?

### *Science as Inquiry*

- Are all starch grains, no matter the plant they come from, the same? Will starch grains from many different varieties of potatoes look the same? Why or why not?
- What is the name of the oldest part of the starch grain? Does finding this structure under the microscope help in identifying the type of plant the starch grain came from?
- The process skills the students had to engage in to do these activities (predicting, manipulating materials, forming hypotheses, solving problems, recording data, making careful observations) enhance their overall academic growth.

### *History and Nature of Science*

- Why do you think a person responsible for creating frozen dinners should understand that different vegetables have different starch structures?

- What kinds of jobs entail making careful observations and accurately recording what was observed?
- Do you think an insurance adjuster could benefit by learning the skills you utilized while participating in this lesson?

**4. EVALUATION:** How will the students show what they have learned?

Upon completing these activities the students will be able to:

- prepare a slide of starch grains;
- accurately draw starch grains observed under a microscope;
- identify with 80 percent accuracy the various starch grains and their sources;
- explain in writing or verbally why certain starches can be digested by humans while other starches cannot.

## Colors of Wildlife

**GRADE**
K–4
**DISCIPLINE**
Life
Science

**Concept to be invented**
Main idea—Wildlife occurs in a wide variety of colors.

**Concepts that are important to expansion**
Camouflage allows an organism to blend in or hide in its environment.

**Materials needed**
*For the entire class:*
Magazines that have a wide variety of animal pictures, such as *National Geographic, Ranger Rick, National and International Wildlife, Audubon.* Try to have magazines that can be cut up.

Construction paper, crayons or markers, scissors, glue, felt, cotton balls, natural materials from outdoors (acorns, leaves, grass); an appropriate story book with a wide variety of different-colored animals in it will also help introduce the topic. A book such as Richard Buckley and Eric Carle's *The Greedy Python* (New York: Scholastic Books, 1992) is a good selection.

➡ **Safety precautions:** Do not poke each other with the scissors; use them only while seated.

**1. EXPLORATION:** Which process skills will be used?

Observing, comparing, generalizing

What will the students do?

*Animal
Similarities
and Differences*

Introduce the lesson by reading the students a book like *The Greedy Python.* Encourage the students to make note of the color of the python and of all the other animals it comes across. You will return to the ideas provided by the story later.

After the story and brief discussion about it, provide each student group with several wildlife magazines to look at. Ask the students to find pictures of animals, make observations about the animals, and compare the animals to one another. Create two lists on the board. Title one list *similarities,* the other *differences.* Ask the students to share their observations about the animals they found by providing information about the similarities and differences of the animals. Ask the students to each cut out three different animals.

## 2. EXPLANATION/CONCEPT INVENTION: What is the main idea? How will the main idea be constructed?

*Concept:* Wildlife occurs in a wide variety of colors.

Refer back to the story you read. For instance, if *The Greedy Python* was used, you might ask the following questions to help invent the concept: What animals did you see in the book? What colors were they? Why do you think the python was so successful in eating all the animals? Could a green python hide easily in a jungle?

Hold up a variety of different-colored pieces of construction paper. Ask the students to identify the colors. Then ask the students to raise their hands if they cut out animals that match the color of the paper you are holding. Assist them in concluding that animals appear in a variety of colors.

Let the students help in gluing the animals on to the construction paper that matches the animal's color. Hang these animal pages around the room. Ask the student farthest from each picture if it is difficult to identify the animal on the page, that is, a red animal on a red piece of paper. Ask why he or she thinks it is difficult. How would this coloration help it survive in the wild? Draw the students to the conclusion that camouflage allows an organism to blend in or hide in its environment.

## 3. EXPANSION OF THE IDEA: Which process skills will be used?

Observing, manipulating materials, generalizing, comparing, communicating

How will the idea be expanded?

*Create a Rainbow Animal*

Use the materials from the material list to have the students create their own animal. The animals may be real, or they can make them up. Encourage the generalization that wild animals appear in a wide variety of colors and that the animals' colors and markings help them survive. Encourage the students to look for rainbow animals—those that have three or more distinct colors on their bodies. Ask the students to share their creations with one another. Get them to communicate to one another how their animal can hide in its environment.

### Science in Personal and Social Perspectives

- Where would you find _____? (Insert an animal name.)
- Do you think it is as important for a pet to blend in with its surroundings as it is for wild animals? Why or why not?

- Do we need to protect the environment where some animals live? Why?
- What are some things society can do to protect animal environments?

*Science and Technology*

- Hunters used to wear only clothing that blended into the environment when they hunted. Today we see hunters wearing bright orange vests and bright orange hats. Why do you think the design of their clothing changed?

*Science as Inquiry*

- Where could you learn more about a particular animal?
- What are some ways that color helps animals survive?
- Besides color, what other kinds of things can animals use for camouflage?

*History and Nature of Science*

- Can you think of any jobs in which people work with or study animals?
- Can you think of any jobs in which people work with aquatic animals?
- Can you think of any animals that work? (Police dogs, seeing-eye dogs, sled dogs, horses, pigeons, animals that help on a farm.) How are these animals trained?

**4. EVALUATION:** How will the students show what they have learned?

Upon completing the activities the students will be able to:

- construct an animal using a variety of colors when given materials;
- explain how a cartoon animal relates to a real animal;
- make a graph of animals that have one, two, or more colors.

## Bird Life

GRADE
K–2
DISCIPLINE
Life
Science

**Concept to be invented**
Animals have a life cycle that includes being born, developing into an adult, reproducing, and eventually dying.

**Concepts that are important to expansion**
The details of a life cycle are different for different animals.

**Materials needed**
*For exploration:*

reproducible pictures of birds at various stages of their life cycle, that is, egg, 1–2 days old, two weeks old, month old, adult. Enough copies to supply student groups of 4–5 students per group with a set.

computer software such as *Birds and How They Grow* or a video that shows birds as they develop in the nest
poster paper
crayons or markers
glue

*For expansion:*

access to an incubator with developing chicken or duck eggs and
 the ability to make daily
 observations

journal or computer-generated log
 to record observations

➥ **Safety precautions:** Stress the importance of respecting the developing bird and not banging on the sides of the incubator or creating excessive noise while making observations.

1. EXPLORATION: Which process skills will be used?

Observing, comparing, predicting

What will students do?

*What Comes
First—the Bird
or the Egg?*

Provide each student group with a stack of bird development pages. Have the students work in teams to color the various pictures of the bird in different stages of its life cycle. After they complete that task, ask them to lay out each of the pictures in front of the team. Ask them to describe what is different in each picture. If the students are capable of writing, ask them to record these differ- ences on the poster paper under a heading titled "Differences." Ask them to then describe anything the pictures may have in common. Record those on the poster paper under the heading "Same." Then ask the students to decide as a group what picture comes first, then second, then third, and so on. Ask the stu- dents to arrange them in order on a sheet of poster paper.

2. EXPLANATION/CONCEPT INVENTION: What is the main idea? How will the main idea be constructed?

*Concept:* Animals have a life cycle that includes being born, developing into an adult, reproducing, and eventually dying.

Ask the student teams to share items from their list labeled "Differences." Did each of the student teams come up with similar lists? Ask them to explain any observations that did not show up on all of the student team "Differ- ences" lists.

Then ask the student teams to share items from their list labeled "Same." Did each of the student teams come up with similar lists? Ask them to explain any observations that did not show up on all of the student team "Same" lists.

Hang up the team posters with the ordered pictures in the front of the room. Ask the students to look at the posters and check for similar or different orders. Have them share their observations. Ask them to predict why some teams pasted the pictures in one order and other teams in another if differences exist among the posters.

Some sample questions to ask the students as they make their observa- tions are:

- How are the birds in the various pictures similar? How are they different?
- Why do you think this team put the picture of the egg first? Or the picture of the adult bird, or the small bird?
- Which picture represents the bird before it is born?
- Which picture shows the bird just after it is born?
- Which picture shows the bird as an adult?

After the students respond to your questions, explain to them that these pictures represent various stages in the bird's life. Ask them to think about their own life. Do they remember seeing pictures of themselves as a baby? Have they changed since they were babies? Just as they have changed, the pictures that they placed in order show how the bird will change as it gets older. You can use one of the posters to add labels to the pictures such as: egg, one day old, two weeks old, one month old, and adult. Give the student teams an opportunity to rearrange their posters in the order from egg to adult if theirs was out of order.

Explain to the students that what they have done is placed in order the *life cycle* of the bird. Lead them to conclude that animals have a life cycle that includes being born, developing into an adult, reproducing, and eventually dying.

## 3. EXPANSION OF THE IDEA: Which process skills will be used?

Observing, predicting, recording data, drawing conclusions

### How will the idea be expanded?

*The Developing Chick (or Duck)*

This expansion activity can take place in your classroom if you have access to the materials and space permits, or if your school has one central area for containing live animals that is more conducive to this type of activity. Do not do this activity if you do not feel comfortable growing live chicks or ducks or if your building does not have the facilities to accommodate growing birds. You may want to do this activity in conjunction with a teacher from a higher grade level, where older students could be responsible for making sure the needs of the birds are met as they hatch.

Another possibility is finding a Web site that has a live camera trained on an incubator with developing chicks or ducks. Several schools throughout the United States have made this service available. Search the Internet for such a site. This activity is often done during the spring of the year.

Still another possibility is for the teacher to create a "virtual bird" via a computer-generated draw package. "Grow" the bird over a period of days. Provide the students with its weight and height to enter into a database. Ask them to make predictions about changes in the bird's height and weight, amount of feather cover, beak size, and so forth over time.

Once you have established a source for observations, have your students engage in the following activity:

- Visit the incubator site the day the eggs are placed in the incubator. Have them record their observations in a journal. Start with "day 1" and continue beyond hatching. If space and time permit, allow the students to make observations throughout the rest of the year.
- Assign student teams different times during the day to go to the incubator to record their observations on a daily basis. Remind them to not tap on the incubator or to disturb the eggs in any way.

Throughout the time that the students are making their observations, bring the students together as a class on a weekly basis to discuss what they have observed. Have them make predictions about what they could expect to see happen next. If all of the eggs do not hatch, be prepared to discuss why. Offer possible reasons such as improper development, lack of essential needs such as heat to foster egg development, or even the possibility that the egg was not fertilized. If some of the chicks die, be prepared to have a conversation about this as a natural part of a life cycle. You will have to judge if all of your students at this grade level are prepared for this.

Another possible activity to expand on the concept of animals having a life cycle that includes being born, developing into an adult, reproducing, and eventually dying—without going through the expense and time needed to hatch live chicks or ducks—is to show a variety of videotapes that take students through the life cycle of different animals. Conversations about the videotape should lead students to conclude that the details of a life cycle are different for different animals.

### Science in Personal and Social Perspectives

- Could someone have expected you to stay the same as when you were born? Why is this a silly idea?
- If you live in a tiny house or apartment and you have an opportunity to get a puppy, would you choose one who had a mother that was a large dog? What do you know about the life cycle of a dog that might lead you to believe this is not a good idea?

### Science and Technology

- How can an incubator help us hatch an egg if a mother bird is not around?
- If you don't see an animal in every stage of its life cycle, how do you know it went through different stages? What evidence do we use to prove that it did? Think about the evidence we used in our class activities to answer this question.

### Science as Inquiry

- The observations and predictions the students make about the developing bird and conclusions that they draw provide them with early science inquiry skills. Gathering and organizing data extend their inquiry skills.

*History and Nature of Science*

- What do you think your doctor needs to know about the human life cycle to help you as you grow? Invite a pediatrician into your class to share ideas with your students.
- Visit a pet store. Have the students prepare questions to ask the shopkeepers about what they know about the life cycles of the different pets in their store and how that information helps them keep their pets healthy.

**4. EVALUATION:** How will the students show what they have learned?

Upon completing the activities the students will be able to:

- describe what a life cycle is and use it in the context of the life of a bird and the life of a human;
- order pictures in the proper sequence for the life cycle of an animal other than a bird or human;
- label the stages of growth of a given animal from birth to adult.

## Wildlife and Domesticated Animals

**GRADE**
**K–4**
**DISCIPLINE**
**Life**
**Science**

**Concept to be invented**
Main idea—Wildlife includes animals that are not tamed or domesticated.

**Concepts that are important to expansion**
Endangered animals, extinct, threatened, safe

**Materials needed**
*For exploration:*
Pictures of both wild and domesticated animals, attribute blocks.

➡ **Safety precautions:** Do not throw attribute blocks; use care when acting out animals in expansion activity so as to not hit any other student.

**1. EXPLORATION:** Which process skills will be used?

Observing, hypothesizing, inferring, categorizing, recording data

What will the students do?

*Animal Needs*   Using attribute blocks, ask the students to place these blocks into two different groups. This activity will ensure that the students understand the concept of grouping. Next, ask the students to look around the room at the pictures hanging up. What do you observe in the pictures? (Animals.) Divide the class into groups of four to six. Provide them with pictures of both wild and domesticated animals (at least as many pictures as there are students in a group). Each student in the group will pick up an animal and record characteristics of the animal that make it different from any other. Some prompting questions could be: Where do they live? How do they get their food? Are they dependent on humans for their survival? Once each child in the group has listed the characteristics of the animal he or she chose, ask the students to decide how they could put their animals into two different groups. Once they make that decision, then divide the animals.

## 2. EXPLANATION/CONCEPT INVENTION: What is the main idea? How will the main idea be constructed?

*Concept:* Wildlife includes animals that are not tamed or domesticated.

Ask the students questions such as the following to help invent this concept: How did your group decide to divide your animals? What characteristics of your animals led you to this decision? How do the animals in one of your groups get their food? How do the animals in your other group get their food? Do either of your groupings separate the animals into whether they rely on humans for their survival?

Animals that do not rely on humans for survival and that are neither tame or owned are called *wild. Domesticated* animals rely on humans for their survival.

## 3. EXPANSION OF THE IDEA: Which process skills will be used?

Observing, classifying, analyzing, inferring, communicating

How will the idea be expanded?

*Domestic versus Wild Charades*

Ask the students to choose an animal, and without telling anyone else in the class, write down the name of that animal. The students may choose one from a picture in the room or think of one on their own. Divide the class in half, and collect their

| Wild | Domestic |
|---|---|

listed animals in two groups. Explain to the students how the game of charades is played. Have students from one half of the class pick from a pile of animals that came from the other half of the room, and vice versa. Ask the students to look at the name of the animal on the card, and without saying what is written on the card, act out the behaviors of that animal for the students on your side of the room to guess. Write the words *domestic* and *wild* on the board. Once the students guess which animal was acted out, ask the student who just acted out the animal to decide whether that animal should be listed as domestic or wild. Make sure all of the students agree on the listing before acting out the next animal.

### Science in Personal and Social Perspectives

- Name some domesticated animals that we could find in your neighborhood. What would the neighborhood be like if these animals were wild?
- What do you think life would be like if any of the wild animals we acted out no longer existed, that is, they became extinct?
- What do you think would happen if you tried to tame a wild animal?
- Why is a wildlife preserve important to our society?
- Can the study of wildlife give us any ideas about how people behave?

### Science and Technology

- Propose a method to change an animal from wild to domestic.

### Science as Inquiry

- What important facts must we remember when dealing with wildlife?
- What things are important to remember when taking care of pets?
- What is the difference between a wild and a domesticated animal?

### History and Nature of Science

- What type of job requires knowledge of wildlife or requires someone to work with wild animals?
- Interview a zookeeper. What special skills does someone in this line of work need?
- What kind of jobs would have to be created if wildlife started taking over our community?
- Choose a domesticated animal. Search throughout history to determine when it first became domesticated and why.

**4. EVALUATION:** How will the students show what they have learned?

Upon completing the activities the students will be able to:

- give two examples of a wild animal;
- give two examples of a domestic animal;
- list the characteristics of a wild and a domestic animal;
- draw a picture of an animal and identify it as wild or domestic by drawing an appropriate habitat for it.

## A Bug's Life?

**GRADE
3–4
DISCIPLINE
Life
Science**

### Concept to be invented
Animals have a life cycle that includes being born, developing into an adult, reproducing, and eventually dying. The details of a life cycle are different for different animals.

### Concepts that are important to expansion
Plants and animals closely resemble their parents.

### Materials needed
*For exploration:*

a set of reproducible images of a black beetle's life cycle from egg, larva (the mealworm), pupa, and adult (the black beetle)

a set of reproducible images of a butterfly's life cycle from egg,

larva (the caterpillar), pupa, and adult (the butterfly)

a set of reproducible images of a dog's life cycle from birth to adult

*For expansion:*

mealworms to raise as part of the expansion activity; these are available at a pet shop or bait store

materials to raise the mealworm in, such as a large container with a lid and food like bran, flour, dried bread, cracker crumbs and

oatmeal; a slice of apple or carrot will be needed to provide humidity

journal or computer-generated logs to record observations and other data student teams identify as important to collect

➥ **Safety precautions:** Care should be used in handling the mealworms. Avoid placing hands in your mouth after working with the insect. Wash hands immediately after handling any insects.

## 1. EXPLORATION: Which process skills will be used?

Observing, comparing, drawing conclusions, recording data, making hypotheses

### What will students do?

*Ordering Life
Cycle Stages*

Have the students work in teams of two or three. First give the student teams the pictures that represent the life cycle of a black beetle. Do not give them in order from birth to adult. Just ask the student teams to arrange them in that order, if indeed they think they all belong together. Time how long it takes them to put these in order. Stop this activity once each team has recorded how long it took them to come to an agreement as to the proper placement.

Then without explanation ask the students to set those pictures aside. Now provide them with the pictures that represent the life cycle of the butterfly. Once again, do not give them to the students in any kind of order. Again ask the student teams to arrange them in order from birth to adult, if indeed they think all of the pictures belong together. Again time how long it takes for the student teams to put these in order from birth to adult.

Do this same activity a third time, making use of the pictures that represent the life cycle of a dog.

Which took the longest, arranging the life cycle of the black beetle, the butterfly, or the dog? Ask the students to discuss within their groups possible reasons for the time differences.

## 2. EXPLANATION/CONCEPT INVENTION: What is the main idea? How will the main idea be constructed?

*Concept:* Animals have a life cycle that includes being born, developing into an adult, reproducing, and eventually dying. The details of a life cycle are different for different animals

Ask the students as a class to share their reasons for why it may have taken them longer to order one animal's life cycle than another. Ask questions such as:

- Did each of these animals start its life cycle in a similar form?
- At what stage or stages of the life cycle do these animals look different?
- Why was it easier to arrange the life cycle of one animal than another?

The students will be sharing responses such as the animals they are more familiar with are easier to arrange in order from birth to adult. Animals that have basically the same form from birth to adult are easier to arrange. After the students discuss their observations you should lead them to conclude that animals have a life cycle that includes being born, developing into an adult, reproducing, and eventually dying. The details of a life cycle are different for different animals.

## 3. EXPANSION OF THE IDEA: Which process skills will be used?

Observing, predicting, recording data, drawing conclusions

How will the idea be expanded?

*Growing Mealworms*

Provide each student team with the materials you assembled for the expansion phase of this activity. Give the students ample time to make observations of the mealworm. Ask them to recall the exploration activity and to predict what the mealworm will look like as it becomes an adult. Once their observations of the mealworm are complete, guide them in constructing a growth chamber for their mealworms. This is done by placing in a large container with a lid (like a 2-lb coffee can or a plastic shoe storage container with lid) the food mixture of bran, flour, dried bread, cracker crumbs, and oatmeal. By placing an apple slice or carrot, humidity will be added to the environment. Place several mealworms into the container and store in a warm area (between 75° and 80° F). Have students record the number of mealworms placed into the container. Light is not needed for growth, so a warm, dark cabinet or storage area in the classroom will be an ideal growth area. Students should check the container every few days, adding more food and apple or carrot.

Ask the students to collect changes in the mealworm over time. Have any begun to change body form? What do they now look like? How many mealworms are now in the container? Are there other stages in the black beetle's life cycle present? Count and record how many of each.

Since a mealworm will stay in the larval stage for about six months, chances are that the container may eventually contain a form of the black beetle in each stage of its life cycle. It will depend upon the ages of the mealworms when obtained from the supplier. Ideally you'd like to find that within the growth chambers there are black beetles as larvae, pupae, and adults within a few weeks.

Ask the students to explain why their mealworm counts changed. What happened to those mealworms? Do all of the adults look alike? Could you tell one adult from another? Is that an easy thing to do? Ask the students to find within their growth chamber an example of the black beetle in each stage of the beetle's life cycle. Help them to conclude that each larval mealworm ended up looking like its parent, and that each generation of black beetles that follow will look just like their parents in the adult stage of their life cycle.

### Science in Personal and Social Perspectives

- How does having an understanding of the life cycle of an insect help protect your home from being overrun with insects?
- What "bug" problems do you commonly face? During what stage of the bug's life cycle does that "bug" "bug" you?

### Science and Technology

- What kinds of things have cities done to control insect populations like flies or mosquitoes? At what stage of their life cycle are they easier to control?
- Do you think it is a good idea to use chemicals to control insect populations? Why or why not? What kind of an impact will continued use of chemicals have on future insect populations?

### Science as Inquiry

- Design an experiment to determine at which stage in an insect's life cycle they feed and at which stage they reproduce. Use the mealworms and black beetles to carry out your planned experiments. Be sure to apply proper scientific methods such as controlling variables, making consistent observations, and accurately recording data for later analysis.

*History and Nature of Science*

- In the late 19th century growers in California brought the ladybug over from Australia to help battle tiny insects that threatened orange groves. The ladybugs fed on the smaller insects to control their population. Today there are several beneficial insects used by gardeners. These include ladybugs, mealworms, parasitic nematodes, parasitic wasps, praying mantises, green lacewings, and predatory mites. Identify at what stage of the insect's life cycle they are most beneficial. Using an electronic resource such as a Web site or CD-ROM, find pictures of these insects in the most beneficial stage of their life cycle and prepare a multimedia presentation that describes how they benefit gardeners.

4. EVALUATION: How will the students show what they have learned?

Upon completing the activities the students will be able to:

- describe the life cycle stages of an insect and explain how these differ from the life cycle stages of a mammal;
- accurately predict what the offspring will look like when given a picture of an early stage in the life cycle of a given organism (Do the things you learned about animals and their life cycles hold true for plants? Why or why not?);
- design an experiment to show how plants go through a life cycle and demonstrate that each new plant will look like its parent.

## Crickets: Basic Needs of an Organism

GRADE
5–8
DISCIPLINE
Life
Science

**Concept to be invented**

Main idea—All organisms, no matter the size, have a basic need for food, water, shelter, and space in a suitable arrangement.

**Concepts that are important to expansion**

Living organisms respond to stimuli from their environment. Animals in captivity must be able to adapt to their environment in order to survive.

**Materials needed**

*For each group of students:*

one terrarium

one plastic pint container with
   screen top

one hand lens

one piece of black construction paper

seeds (six each of clover, grass,
   wheat, radish, and bean)

*For the entire class:*
Eric Carle's *The Very Quiet Cricket* (New York: Philomel Books, 1990); four plastic bags, each containing eighteen crickets; felt pen, paper clips, tape or staples, chart paper.

➡ **Safety precautions:** Remind the students to wash their hands after handling the crickets. Do not eat the seeds or put them in your mouth. Do not poke each other with the staples or paper clips.

1. EXPLORATION: Which process skills will be used?

Observing, recording data, experimenting, drawing conclusions

What will the students do?

*Cricket Needs*    Begin the lesson by doing something that students of this age level would never expect. Read very animatedly *The Very Quiet Cricket*, by Eric Carle. Although not age appropriate, the story is very effective in getting students to think about the task to come. Divide the class into research groups of four. Allow library time for the students to find answers to the following questions: What is necessary for the survival of a cricket? Are their needs similar to human needs? What requirements do they have for food, water, and shelter? Can many crickets live in a small space? How many can live comfortably together?

2. EXPLANATION/CONCEPT INVENTION: What is the main idea? How will the main idea be constructed?

*Concept:* All organisms, no matter the size, have a basic need for food, water, shelter, and space in a suitable arrangement.

Ask the various student groups to report on the results of their inquiries. Through their reporting, continue to question them to clarify the results of their research efforts. Help the students to draw the conclusion that all organisms, no matter the size, have a basic need for food, water, shelter, and space in a suitable arrangement.

3. EXPANSION OF THE IDEA: Which process skills will be used?

Observing, communicating, problem solving, formulating models, classifying, questioning, hypothesizing

How will the idea be expanded?

*Cricket Behavior*    Set up a terrarium with a few crickets living in it. Encourage the students to make observations about the crickets in the terrarium as they are collecting their data. Assign each of the different research groups from the exploration phase of this lesson one of the following tasks so that they will understand the behavior of a cricket:

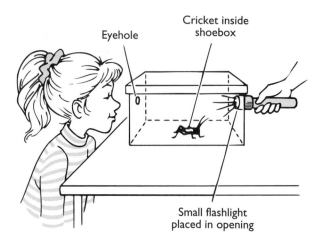

Eyehole

Cricket inside
shoebox

Small flashlight
placed in opening

- Take a cricket from the terrarium. Place it on a smooth surface and then on a rough surface. Watch the cricket for 3 to 5 minutes on each surface. Record your observations. Which surface causes the greater obstacle to movement? Why do you think this is so? Try manipulating the environment in other ways: hot versus cold surface or light versus dark conditions. Return the cricket to the terrarium.
- Obtain a shoebox. Cut a hole on one side about the size of a small flashlight. Cut a hole on the other side just big enough for your eye to peep inside. Take a cricket from the terrarium. Place the cricket in the dark end of the shoebox (opposite end from the flashlight hole) and put on the lid. Cover the flashlight hole with your hand in an effort to make the box as dark as possible inside. Watch the cricket's behavior for 5 minutes. Record your observations. Now place a small flashlight in the hole and turn it on. Observe the cricket for another 5 minutes. Record your observations. Were there any differences in the cricket's behavior when the light was on versus when it was off? If so, why do you think this occurred? Return the cricket to the terrarium.
- Take a cricket from the terrarium and place it in a shoebox. As a group, decide on three different kinds of food you think a cricket might like to eat. Place the three types in front of the cricket. Make sure you keep accurate records about the amount of food placed in the box. It may be important to weigh each food choice. Put the lid back on the box. Place the box in a dark, quiet place in the classroom. Ask the group members to make predictions about which food type they think the cricket will choose. Make and record observations every 30 minutes for one school day. Did the cricket choose the food you predicted? Why or why not? Do you think more than one cricket should be used in this experiment? Why or why not? Return the cricket to the terrarium.

Ask each of the different research groups to report on their findings. Encourage all the students to communicate to one another exactly what they did, why they did it, and what they discovered as a result. Help them in their discussion to come to the following conclusions: Living organisms respond to stimuli from their environment. Animals in captivity must be able to adapt to their environment in order to survive.

### Science in Personal and Social Perspectives

- What legends exist about crickets? How and why have these been handed down through generations?
- What could you do for an animal if it has lost its mother? How could you help it survive without removing it from its environment?
- Why would it be important for you to know how to care for an animal in a situation like that?

### Science and Technology

- Do you think fluctuations in cricket populations could tell us something about what people are doing to their environment? How would you design an experiment to determine what humans are doing to their environment?
- Do you think it is important that humans understand something about other animals no matter what their size? Why or why not?

### Science as Inquiry

- Why does a terrarium need to have soil in it?
- Can a cricket drink water out of a bowl? Why does a cricket rub its wings?
- What are the basic needs of a cricket?

### History and Nature of Science

- What kinds of occupations deal with a variety of animal species? (Game wardens, zookeepers, wildlife officers.)
- What would it be like if there was no one who understood the basic needs of certain animals? Was there ever a time in history when our lack of understanding affected the life of an animal? Provide an example.
- What does an entomologist do?

## 4. EVALUATION: How will the students show what they have learned?

Upon completing the activities the students will be able to:

- design and build their own terrarium for a cricket, making sure that it is designed to meet all of the cricket's basic needs;
- pick one animal and determine its basic needs for food, shelter, water, and space;
- pick a domesticated animal such as a chicken, dog, or hamster and describe the adaptations necessary for that animal to survive in the wild;
- participate in a discussion of how humans would have to adapt in order to survive in the wild.

# Animal Adaptations

### Concepts to be invented
Main idea—The shape of a bird's beak determines the type of food it will eat. This is one form of an adaptation.

### Concepts that are important to expansion
Many animals have developed specialized adaptations in order to survive in their environments. Fish utilize adaptive coloration, body shape, and mouth placement to help them survive in different aquatic environments.

### Materials needed
*For exploration:*
Enough tweezers and mittens so that each student in the class has one or the other of these. Numerous pipe cleaners, paper wads, and strips of construction paper to serve as "food" for the birds. Place pictures of various kinds of birds with different feeding habits all around the classroom.

*For expansion:*
Pictures of various kinds of fish placed around the room. The fish should demonstrate such differences in coloration as light-colored belly, dark upper side, mottling, vertical stripes, or horizontal stripes. Differences in body shape could be flat bellied, torpedo shaped, horizontal disc, vertical disc, or hump-backed. The mouth shapes may be an elongated upper jaw, duckbill jaws, an elongated lower jaw, an extremely large jaw, or a sucker-shaped jaw. A fish tank with fish that live at different levels of the tank would also serve to emphasize the secondary concept. Art materials like crayons, markers, scissors, scrap material, construction paper, chalk, old buttons, yarn, pieces of felt, and so on are also needed.

➡ **Safety precautions:** Remind the students to walk, not run, while participating in the bird-feeding activity. Use caution with scissors in the expansion activity.

1. EXPLORATION: Which process skills will be used?

> Observing, inferring, experimenting, analyzing

What will the students do?

*Mitten and Tweezer Beaks*

Distribute the pipe cleaners, paper wads, and paper strips throughout the room. Place some on the floor and some of them in harder-to-get-to places. Each student will choose the type of "beak" (mitten or tweezers) that he or she wants to use. The students will explore a bird's eating habit by trying to pick up the different types of food using the beak they chose.

2. EXPLANATION/CONCEPT INVENTION: What is the main idea? How will the main idea be constructed?

> *Concept:* The shape of a bird's beak determines the type of food it will eat. This is one form of adaptation.
>
> Ask the students questions such as the following to help invent this concept: Why was it easier for _____ (student's name) to pick up the paper strips than _____ (a different student's name)? Do you see any pictures of birds in this room with a beak that would work like the tweezers? Can you think of any others? What do you think they use these beaks for? What types of food can a bird with a beak like a pair of mittens eat? Birds have a variety of adaptations that help them survive in their environment. Their beaks are one such adaptation.

3. EXPANSION OF THE IDEA: Which process skills will be used?

> Hypothesizing, observing, questioning, classifying, analyzing, inferring, manipulating materials, communicating

How will the idea be expanded?

*Fish Adaptations*    The students will look at pictures of different types of fish and try to categorize them in three different ways: coloration, mouth shape, and body shape. A discussion should ensue on how these three classifications are important adaptations to ensure the fish's survival in its environment. After the discussion, the teacher should assign each student or group of students a particular combination of adaptations from each of the three groups, such as mottled coloration, torpedo body shape, and sucker-shaped jaw. Ask the students to use the art materials provided to create fish with those three types of adaptations. Ask them to create environments in which fish with those adaptations could survive. Have the students share their creations.

*Science in Personal and Social Perspectives*

- What are some ways in which people have adapted to their environment?
- What are some ways in which we share our environment with the birds? fish?
- What has society done to improve the lives of animals in their habitat?

*Science and Technology*

- If you were to make a hummingbird feeder, would it be useful to know the type of beak this bird has, and why?
- What are some disadvantages of taking an animal out of its natural habitat?
- Could an animal adapt quickly enough to survive in a new environment? Why or why not?
- Choose an animal. Outline all of the problems that would need to be overcome for that animal to survive in a different habitat.

*Science as Inquiry*

- Can an animal's inability to adapt to rapid changes in its environment lead to its extinction? What other events may lead to the extinction of an animal?
- Is there any one species of bird that has a beak that allows it to winter in an area with a relatively cold climate? What advantage does this beak shape have over any other?
- If you were to buy a fish from a pet store and wanted one that would clean the food off the gravel in the bottom of your fish tank, what kind of a mouth shape would it have?

*History and Nature of Science*

- How important is it for a zookeeper to understand the special feeding adaptations many animals have developed? Why?
- If you were working at a nature center and were responsible for creating an aquarium that made use of fish found at a local lake, what would you need to know about the local fish to make your display enjoyable for center visitors?

**4. EVALUATION:** How will the students show what they have learned?

Upon completing the activities the students will be able to:

- identify bird beak adaptations and explain how these contribute to the survival of the bird;
- design an ideal habitat for an animal of their choice, emphasizing that animal's special adaptations for survival in its environment;
- explain why several species of fish can live together in one lake without competing with one another for food.

## Owl Pellets

**GRADE 5–8**
**DISCIPLINE Life Science**

**Concept to be invented**
Main idea—Owl pellets contain undigested parts of animals eaten by the owl, such as hair and bones.

**Concepts that are important to expansion**
Digestion, eating habits

**Materials needed**
*For each student group:*
One owl pellet, which may be obtained through a local division of your state's department of natural resources or wildlife. Sterilized pellets can be ordered through a supplier. One dissecting kit, glue, handouts of the skeleton of a vole, mouse, or rat.

➡ **Safety precautions:** Remind the students to use caution when handling the sharp dissecting tools.

**1. EXPLORATION:** Which process skills will be used?

Observing, predicting, inferring, hypothesizing

What will the students do?

*Owl Pellet Dissection*

Provide each pair of students with an owl pellet and a dissecting kit. Ask the students what they think the pellet is. How was it created? What do you think you will find in here as you carefully pick the matted hair away from the owl pellets? After student predictions are shared, instruct the students to keep everything they find as they pick away carefully at the pellets. Try to reconstruct a skeleton of a rodent, using the picture as a guide.

**2. EXPLANATION/CONCEPT INVENTION:** *What is the main idea? How will the main idea be constructed?*

*Concept:* Owl pellets contain the undigested parts of animals eaten by the owl, such as hair and bones.

Ask the students questions such as the following to help invent this concept: What kind of rodent do you think your owl ate? Did you find the remains of more than one kind of rodent? What do these findings tell you about the type of food an owl eats? What is an owl capable of digesting?

**3. EXPANSION OF THE IDEA:** *Which process skills will be used?*

Observing, communicating, problem solving, formulating models, recording data

*How will the idea be expanded?*

*Owl Research or Field Trip*
- Take the students on a field trip to an area where owls are known to nest. Look carefully on the ground around the area. What do you expect to find to indicate to you that owls may be in the area? How are pellets different from owl scats?
- Invite a wildlife specialist to bring an owl to visit your classroom to discuss its characteristics and habitat. Ask your class to prepare in advance sound questions to ask the visitor about the owl.
- Assign each student team to write a report about a different species of owl. This report should include such things as where it is found and its life span, habitat, and food preferences.

*Science in Personal and Social Perspectives*
- What might happen to owls if humans disrupt their habitats?
- What are some ways that owls are adapted to their environment?
- How are we adapted to our environment?
- What has technology done to improve the lives of animals in their habitats? What could society do?

*Science and Technology*
- What are some disadvantages of taking an animal out of its natural habitat and placing it in another environment?
- If you came across some bones of an animal, how could you go about identifying which animal they came from?

*Science as Inquiry*
- What special needs does an owl have in order to survive in any habitat?
- Why were the bones and hair of the rodents not digested by the owls?

*History and Nature of Science*
- What kinds of professions are dedicated to ensuring animal safety? What kinds of careers endanger animals?

**Vole Skelton**

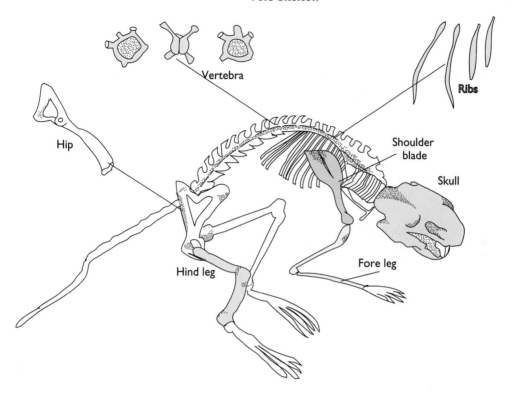

**Other Animal Skulls Found in Pellets**

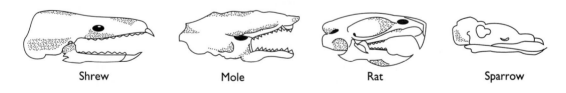

Shrew          Mole          Rat          Sparrow

- In this activity you found the bones of a rodent and reconstructed them to determine which rodent it was. Do any other careers expect you to take evidence and reconstruct it to find answers? Which ones?

**4. EVALUATION:** How will the students show what they have learned?

Upon completing the activities the students will be able to:

- construct a food chain, placing the owl at the highest level;

- dissect an owl pellet and use the bones found to reconstruct the skeleton of a rodent;
- speculate on how information provided through owl pellet dissection can assist people in raising the survival rate of many owl species.

## Humans and Trash

**GRADE**
**K–4**
**DISCIPLINE**
**Life**
**Science**

**Concept to be invented**
Main idea—Human-made trash affects all living matter.

**Concepts that are important to expansion**
Recycling can decrease the amount of waste created by humans.

**Materials needed**
*For exploration:*
Selected (clean) trash, drawing paper, crayons, glue, stapler. Enough of these materials should be collected so that each child in the class can actively participate in the lesson. One large box filled with a piece of trash for each child, five or six medium-sized boxes that can be labeled for glass, paper, plastic, aluminum, tin, and so on.

**Safety precautions:** Remind the students to use caution when handling trash. Do not put fingers in mouth. Wash hands thoroughly after handling trash.

1.  **EXPLORATION:** Which process skills will be used?

    Questioning, inferring, predicting, hypothesizing, communicating, manipulating materials.

    What will the students do?

*Trash and Animals*    Before doing this lesson with the class, collect enough trash so that each child in the class may have several pieces to choose from. Be sure that any trash chosen is free of rough edges, broken glass, or sharp points so that the children will not be harmed during the lesson. Wash out any plastic bags and cans used as trash.

Ask each student to think of an animal and draw a picture of it.

Supply the students with a large selection of trash. Ask the students to choose one piece that particularly intrigues them. Ask the students to draw a picture of how that piece of trash would hurt their animal if the animal came across that piece of trash while outside. Ask the students to attach the piece of litter to their picture. Each student should be allowed to share the picture with the class, explaining how their animal was harmed by the piece of trash they chose. Encourage the students to act out how the animal moved both before and after the trash affected them.

## 2. EXPLANATION/CONCEPT INVENTION: *What is the main idea? How will the main idea be constructed?*

*Concept:* Human-made trash affects all living matter.

Ask the students questions such as the following to help invent this concept: What's wrong with leaving our garbage just anywhere? How do you think trash can hurt animals besides the ways each of you just shared? The teacher can give such examples as: How many of you have been fishing? What happens when your line gets stuck? Just as it tangles up in the weeds, if you simply cut the line and leave it in the water, it can get tangled on ducks' necks, legs, and beaks. It can keep them from walking, flying, and swimming. Sometimes it may become wrapped around their beak, and they starve to death.

Hold up a ring from a six-pack of cans. Could this hurt an animal? How? Explain how fish or birds can get tangled up in it. Check the local wildlife office for pictures of tragedies like these. Show the students how to break up the plastic rings before they place them in the garbage. Explain to them that even though they put them in the garbage, eventually that garbage bag will break down and that plastic ring will be left to cause possible harm to some animal. If they cut it up before placing it in the trash, there is less of a chance of it harming an animal.

In what ways do people get rid of their trash? Do you think the way in which we get rid of our trash harms animals? What do you think we can do to get rid of litter? (Pick up litter alongside the road, reduce our use of materials in excessive packaging, recycle, and so on.)

## 3. EXPANSION OF THE IDEA: *Which process skills will be used?*

Observing, communicating, problem solving, formulating models, classifying, questioning, hypothesizing

*How will the idea be expanded?*

*Classroom Landfill and Recycling*    Refer back to the explanation phase of this lesson. Remind the students of the conversation they had in which you asked about the ways people get rid of their trash. Perhaps some students mentioned that their garbage is hauled away by a service. Ask them to think about where that trash goes after hauling. Introduce the term *landfill* (the place where trash gets hauled to be buried in the ground) if they are not already familiar with it. Ask them to suggest alternatives to taking trash to a landfill. As they make suggestions, list them on the board.

After the students have created a list, show them a large box in the front of the room labeled *landfill*. (Note: The teacher should have filled this box with a

LIFE SCIENCE

piece of trash for every child in the class.) Have each child pick out one item. Ask them if they think it can be recycled. If so, they should place it in the appropriately labeled medium-sized box. Sum up this activity by getting the children to surmise that recycling can decrease the amount of waste created by people.

*Science in Personal and Social Perspectives*

- What can you do to help eliminate excessive trash?
- Do you know what to do with recyclable materials where you live? If not, why not ask your parents to help you work on recycling some of your trash?
- What are some ways businesses can cut down on their trash?
- How can companies that make different products help the environment?
- Do you think businesses have a responsibility to reduce the amount of trash they create?

*Science and Technology*

- Do you think twice about buying a toy that is not only boxed but then wrapped in paper and then in plastic? Do you think the practice of excessive packaging affects our environment?
- Create a map of what happens to a toy's packaging from the time the toy is packaged until the packaging no longer exists.

*Science as Inquiry*

- What kinds of household items can be recycled?
- How does trash harm animals?
- How does trash harm plants?
- It has sometimes been said that one person's trash is another person's treasure. After doing these activities, how true do you think that statement is?

*History and Nature of Science*

- Who is responsible for making sure that animals are not harmed by human trash?
- Who is responsible for making sure that plants are not harmed by human trash?
- Do you think you could make a career out of collecting recycled trash? Can people make money from recycling?

4. EVALUATION: How will the students show what they have learned?

Upon completing the activities the students will be able to:

- separate recyclables into appropriate groups;
- state three ways in which trash harms animals;
- draw pictures of our environment before trash was recycled and after it was recycled. The students will be able to explain the difference between the two drawings.

# Useful Waste

GRADE
5–8
DISCIPLINE
Life
Science

**Concept to be invented**
Main idea—A great majority of human-made waste can be recycled or reused.

**Concepts that are important to expansion**
Recycle, reuse, water, litter, useful and nonreusable waste, landfill, hazardous waste

**Materials needed**
*For exploration:*

| | | |
|---|---|---|
| aluminum can | bug-spray can | bottle cap |
| glass bottle | orange peel | blender |
| newspaper | art supplies (crayons, | water |
| plastic soda bottle | markers, scissors, | old piece of screen |
| tin can | construction paper, | rolling pin |
| cigarette butt | glue, scrap paper) | |
| rope | | |

➡ **Safety precautions:** Be careful of the sharp edges and glass. Exercise care when carrying and using the scissors and blender.

1. EXPLORATION: Which process skills will be used?

Observing, questioning, hypothesizing, predicting, reasoning, recording data

What will the students do?

*Rating Garbage*    Separate the class into groups of four to six students. Give each group the materials listed above (except for the art supplies) concealed in a brown grocery bag. Ask the students to remove the items from the bag, make observations, and rate or arrange the items in order from the most usable to the least usable. The students' reasoning behind their rating scheme should be recorded.

2. EXPLANATION/CONCEPT INVENTION: What is the main idea? How will the main idea be constructed?

*Concept:* A great majority of human-made waste can be recycled or reused.

Ask the students questions such as the following to help invent this concept: What did you find in your bags? How did you rank these items from most usable to least usable? Why did you put _____ (name item) as the most usable? Why did you put _____ (name item) as the least usable? Refuse is often

regarded as useless waste and ends up in landfills and pollutes our environment. Although not all human-made materials can be recycled, they can be reused in a number of ways not originally intended. Why is it important for us to recycle and reuse? What is the difference between recycling and reusing? What can you do to see that materials such as those found in your bags are recycled or, if possible, reused?

### 3. EXPANSION OF THE IDEA: Which process skills will be used?

Communicating, problem solving, interpreting data, classifying, making assumptions, drawing conclusions, manipulating materials

How will the idea be expanded?

*Litter-Eating Critter*

Ask the groups of students to decide what kind of litter-eating creature they could create using the materials found in their grocery bags and the art supplies you make available. After they create plans for their creatures, allow them sufficient time to make and explain to the class just how their litter-eating creatures function.

Hold up the bug-spray can in order to introduce hazardous wastes that are found in the home. Ask the students if they can think of any household items that cannot be disposed of in a regular fashion. Some examples of items that are dangerous and need to be disposed of properly are paint thinners, paints, and motor oils. Ask the students if they are aware why these items cannot be dumped in regular landfills. Explain in detail the impact these items have on the environment.

*Making Paper*    Encourage the students to learn how to recycle paper by doing the following activity with them: Collect different types of paper scraps, and using a blender, cut the paper into very small pieces. Mix the fine paper to a pulp mixture with water. Pour out of the blender and roll flat. This can be done on an old piece of screen using a rolling pin. Place an old towel over the pulp as you roll it flat to help squeeze out some of the excess water. Allow the new piece of paper to dry before use.

### Science in Personal and Social Perspectives

- Do you think you have a responsibility to future generations to reduce the amount of waste you create? Why or why not? Do you think your parents and grandparents thought about the amount of waste they generated in the past and how it affects the quality of your life?
- How can reducing, reusing, and recycling our resources ensure that future generations will have a lifestyle comparable to or better than ours?

### Science and Technology

- How does a landfill function? Who is responsible for selecting a site for the landfill? How long can we continue dumping our waste into the same landfill?
- What technological advances have decreased the amount of waste we put into our landfills? What technological advances have added to the problem of overflowing landfills?
- What things can you do to reduce litter in your home? What plans do you have for reducing, reusing, and recycling waste materials you generate?

### Science as Inquiry

- How can a product be recycled or reused?
- Can all waste products be recycled? If not, is there anything else that can be done with that waste product first before you throw it away?
- Should cost factors prohibit you from recycling waste products? Why or why not?

### History and Nature of Science

- How many different jobs are involved in the recycling of any product?
- Aside from using natural resources, what other sources can manufacturers go to in order to obtain materials to create their products?

## 4. EVALUATION: How will the students show what they have learned?

Upon completing the activities the students will be able to:

- differentiate between litter and waste in terms of definitions and usefulness;
- rank a pile of materials according to which are the most to least recyclable and which are the most to least reusable;
- identify and collect from home one clean waste item, one clean recyclable item, and one clean reusable item;
- start a recycling project for the entire school.

## Litter in Our Waterways

GRADE
5–8
DISCIPLINE
Life
Science

**Concept to be invented**
Main idea—Irresponsible actions by people are causing the earth's waterways to become littered. This upsets the ecological balance of the water.

**Concepts that are important to expansion**
Beaches, floating, lakes, litter, oceans, recycling, rivers

**Materials needed**
*For exploration:*

aquarium
plastic six-pack holder
empty tin can
empty plastic 2-liter soda bottle
metal bottle cap

water to fill aquarium three-fourths
  full
empty aluminum soda can
empty glass soda bottle
metal can opener

➡ **Safety precautions:** Be careful of the sharp edges and glass. Keep hands away from the aquarium.

1. EXPLORATION: Which process skills will be used?

   Observing, questioning, hypothesizing, predicting, experimenting, recording data

   What will the students do?

*Sink-or-Float Litter*

- Display the seven litter items specified in the materials list above. Ask the students to predict which items will sink when placed in the water. Record their predictions. Allow student volunteers to place each item in the water (one at a time) and observe what happens. Record the results and compare with the initial predictions made by the students.
- Ask the students if they think any of the items that floated could sink eventually. After soliciting several answers, point out that some empty containers may fill with water and sink. The time they take to sink may vary based on certain conditions, such as rough water or human manipulation.
- Ask the students to generate a list of litter they think may be underwater in lakes and rivers. Ask the students how they think it got there.

2. EXPLANATION/CONCEPT INVENTION: What is the main idea? How will the main idea be constructed?

   *Concept:* Irresponsible actions by people are causing the earth's waterways to become littered. This upsets the ecological balance of the water.

   Ask the students questions such as the following to help invent this concept: What types of litter sank to the bottom of the aquarium? What types of litter

floated on top? Do you think that those that floated may eventually sink? How do you think litter such as this could end up in a lake or river? What do you think happens to the litter after it sinks? How do you think this affects water life, such as aquatic plants and animals? What do you think will happen to an aquatic animal if it eats a piece of litter such as a plastic bag?

Litter that floats is easily mistaken for food by many aquatic animals. It is not uncommon for sea turtles to mistake plastic bags for jellyfish and eat them. When this happens, the sea turtle thinks it is full because the plastic bag is stuck in its stomach. It eventually starves to death. Ducks and some fish get their beaks or bodies tangled in six-pack rings. This prevents them from eating, and they starve to death. Litter that sinks is not always considered a nuisance. Some sunken ships become places for coral reefs to grow upon.

## 3. EXPANSION OF THE IDEA: Which process skills will be used?

Communicating, problem solving, interpreting data, classifying, making assumptions, drawing conclusions

How will the idea be expanded?

*Plastic Food*   Ask the students to collect and save every piece of plastic waste used in their homes for one week, clean the waste, and bring it to school. Divide the class into groups of four to six. Ask them to pool their plastic collection. Ask the students to classify the waste according to how an aquatic animal might look at

LIFE SCIENCE

that plastic as a source of food. The categories might be definitely, somewhat likely, unlikely. List some animals that would go for the "food" in each of the categories. Share these divisions with the class. Once they have discussed their divisions, ask the students to divide the plastic waste according to whether an animal could get tangled up in it. Again, discuss the classification scheme the students developed and why. Ask the students as a summary activity to state one positive thing they could do to prevent further pollution of a waterway.

### Science in Personal and Social Perspectives

- Does litter affect your everyday life? If so, how?
- What could you do to cut down on litter?
- Why should someone who lives far from a major waterway be concerned with litter in our waters?
- Do you and your family recycle? If so, what and how?
- Who in our community should be responsible for cleaning up our waters?
- What are some projects in your neighborhood that deal with litter control?
- What are some different litter control agencies operating in your community?

### Science and Technology

- Contact a local hospital. Determine how its medical waste is disposed of. Do you think its disposal methods will keep that waste out of our waterways? Why or why not?

### Science as Inquiry

- Are pollutants that float in a waterway just as dangerous as pollutants that sink? Why or why not?
- Are people in danger if they play on beaches near polluted water? Why or why not?
- Can a sunken ship ever be beneficial to aquatic organisms?

### History and Nature of Science

- Are there any special precautions one must take if his or her job is to clean up a waterway?
- How could an oceanographer use his or her knowledge of ocean currents to help the Coast Guard to identify businesses or cruise ship lines that pollute the waterways?
- Do health care workers have a responsibility to the rest of us to know exactly where their garbage will be disposed? How can they prevent it from ending up in the nation's waterways?

**4. EVALUATION:** How will the students show what they have learned?

Upon completing the activities the students will be able to:

- explain how plastic bags could cause the death of a sea turtle;
- give an example of a piece of plastic litter that can be harmful to aquatic life and propose a solution about how this product could be eliminated from the environment without harming wildlife;

- write a letter of concern to a product manufacturer that they believe uses excessive amounts of plastic packaging on its products.

## Sense of Taste

**GRADE**
K–4
**DISCIPLINE**
Life
Science

### Concept to be invented
Main idea—A person can taste sweet, sour, salty, and bitter on every single area of the tongue that has taste buds.

### Concepts that are important to expansion
People with more taste buds taste things more strongly than those with fewer taste buds.

### Materials needed
*For each pair of students:*

| | | |
|---|---|---|
| lemon juice | four paper cups | blue food coloring |
| cocoa powder | wax paper | 10 cotton-tipped swabs |
| brown sugar | magnifying glass | hole puncher |
| salt | | |

*Preparation:*
For each pair of students, label four cups A, B, C, and D. Fill three of the paper cups with water. Dissolve in cup A the salt, cup B the cocoa, and brown sugar in cup C (corn syrup may be used instead of brown sugar). Pour some lemon juice in cup D. Create an outline of a tongue on a sheet of paper, and duplicate it for each pair of students.

**Safety precautions:** Before distributing the cotton-tipped swabs, remind the students that they are to be used carefully and cautiously to avoid eye injury. Also, to avoid contamination of the unknowns and to inhibit the spread of germs, students should be reminded not to put used cotton-tipped swabs back into the cups after they place them on their tongue.

1. EXPLORATION: Which process skills will be used?

Observing, predicting, experimenting, evaluating, generalizing, inferring, recording data

What will the students do?

*Buds and Tasters*  Ask the students to choose partners or assign partners yourself. Each set of partners should be provided with four paper cups labeled A through D, each filled with a different liquid. Ask the students to make predictions as to what kinds of tastes they think they have and where on the tongue they think they will taste them. Once predictions are recorded, have one student dip a clean cotton swab into the paper cup labeled A, then touch the cotton swab to the tip of his or her partner's tongue. He or she will then touch the back and the sides of the tongue. Record how your partner thought liquid A tasted. Was it as predicted? Mark on the tongue map the places on the tongue where liquid A was tasted. Repeat this procedure for liquids B and C. Do the same for each partner. Remember that a *clean swab* should be used for each cup and by each student.

## 2. EXPLANATION/CONCEPT INVENTION: What is the main idea? How will the main idea be constructed?

*Concept:* A person can taste sweet, sour, salty, and bitter on every area of the tongue that has taste buds.

Ask the students questions such as the following to help invent this concept: How did your partner think each liquid tasted? Did you agree with your partner? Did you find any special places on the tongue where these tastes could be detected?

There is no single area on the tongue where each of these tastes can be detected more so than the other. Your tongue is the organ that gives you your sense of taste. If you observe it closely starting at the tip, you will notice thousands of tiny bumps that make you tongue look rough. The tiny bumps are called *filiform papillae*. They are responsible for grabbing onto your food as you chew. The roundish *buttons* you find interspersed within the filiform papillae are called *fungiform papillae*. Anywhere from five to seven taste buds can be found on each fungiform papilla. The taste buds are made up of a bundle of cells, each containing special sensors or receptors that can pick out the four basic tastes of sweet, sour, bitter, and salty. The *circumvallate papillae*, found on the back of your tongue, are larger than the other papillae. Found within deep furrows of the circumvallate papillae are taste buds that also can detect the four basic tastes.

In order to taste your food, you must chew it. Chewing grinds up your food. It also wets the food by mixing it with saliva, the liquid made by small organs in your mouth. When your food is well mixed with saliva, your taste buds can pick up messages about its flavor. Nerves take these messages to taste centers in each side of your brain. Your brain then decides what you are tasting.

Your senses of taste and smell work closely together. The taste of many foods is really a mixture of taste and smell. Food often seems to have no taste when you have a cold. The cold stops up your nose and dulls your sense of smell. When you cannot smell the food, a part of its taste seem to be missing.

## 3. EXPANSION OF THE IDEA: Which process skills will be used?

Observing, problem solving, recording data, inferring

How will the idea be expanded?

*Supertasters*  Ask the students to go back with their partners to perform the following task:

- Cut a piece of wax paper 1 inch square. Punch a hole using the paper puncher in the middle of the 1-inch-square piece of wax paper.
- Place the piece of wax paper on the tip of your partner's tongue just slightly off center. Be sure the tongue is slightly wet so the paper will stick.
- Using a cotton-tipped swab, dab blue food coloring where the hole is. Be careful not to use too much coloring. For accurate data collection, you want just the dot of tongue exposed to be dyed.
- Use the magnifying glass to count the number of larger, raised dots that did not turn blue. These will be the *fungiform papillae*.
- Take the number of fungiform papillae you discover and multiply by six. This will give you an estimate of the number of taste buds your partner has.
- Repeat this procedure for the other partner.

Were you able to find the same number of fungiform papillae on your partner as your partner found on you? Did everyone have the same number of taste buds?

You will discover that the fewer the raised dots, the less likely the person tasted the four basics tastes all over his or her tongue. Some people are *supertasters* because they have a large number of fungiform papillae, whereas those with just a few are considered *nontasters*.

### Science in Personal and Social Perspectives

- Where on the tongue did your partner taste the sweet liquid and the sour, salty, and bitter? Was it the same place as yours?
- Why do you think many adults tolerate flavorings like hot pepper sauce that a baby cannot?

### Science and Technology

- Do you think that people from countries other than your own have different amounts of taste buds on their tongue? How do you explain that many cultures tolerate food much spicier than typical American fare? Does the number of taste buds have anything to do with it? How might you design an experiment to determine the answers to these questions?

### Science as Inquiry

- How do the filiform papillae differ from the fungiform papillae or the circumvallate papillae?
- What do the fungiform papillae and the circumvallate papillae have in common?
- Where on the tongue can the circumvallate papillae be found?

### History and Nature of Science

- Ask the students to generate a list of spices used in cooking. Assign each student a spice. From which country does it originate? How does it grow? How is it harvested? How important is that spice to the society of the country in which in grows? When was it first used as a spice?

- Do you think someone with permanent damage to his or her nose resulting in the loss of the sense of smell would have a promising career as a professional chef? Why or why not?

**4. EVALUATION:** How will the students show what they have learned?

Upon completing the activities the students will be able to:

- list the four major tastes that can be picked out by receptors on the tongue;
- design a method for separating the class into nontasters, regular tasters, and supertasters;
- describe the role of the filiform papillae, fungiform papillae, and the circumvallate papillae.

## Skeleton

**GRADE**
**1–4**
**DISCIPLINE**
**Life**
**Science**

**Concepts to be invented**
Main idea—The internal support system for muscles in mammals is the bones. All the bones arranged together make up the skeleton.

**Concepts that are important to expansion**
Joints help skeletons move.

**Materials needed**
*For each student:*
One large sheet of newsprint, markers, crayons, several brass paper fasteners, a packet of paper bones that when put together will create a replica of a human skeleton.

➡ **Safety precautions:** Explain to the students how to use the brass fasteners. Remind them that they could hurt themselves if they poke themselves or others with the pointed edge.

**1. EXPLORATION:** Which process skills will be used?

Observing, questioning, manipulating materials, analyzing

What will the students do?

*Bones Assembly Line*
Introduce the lesson by reading two poems from *A Light in the Attic,* by Shel Silverstein. The poems are "Day After Halloween" and "It's Hot!" Begin a discussion with the students about the ideas behind the poems. Ask questions

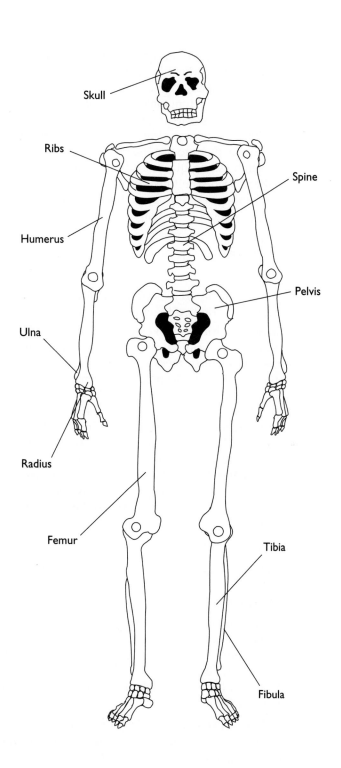

Skull

Ribs

Spine

Humerus

Pelvis

Ulna

Radius

Femur

Tibia

Fibula

such as: What would it be like if we didn't have a skeleton? Why do we need bones in our bodies?

Give each child several brass fasteners and a packet containing paper bones cut into the different major bones of the body using the figure on pages 475–476. Ask the students to empty the packets and to manipulate the materials in any way they wish in an effort to determine what they can create with all the bones. Encourage them to use the brass fasteners to assemble the bones. Walk around the room asking questions like: What do you think all of these different parts make up? Do you think you know where all the parts go? What could the brass fasteners represent in a real body that helps us to move? How do the bones in our body connect for real?

## 2. EXPLANATION/CONCEPT INVENTION: What is the main idea? How will the main idea be constructed?

*Concept:* The internal support system for muscles in mammals is the bones. All the bones arranged together make up the skeleton.

Using a picture of a skeleton and a life-size skeleton, ask the children if they know the nonscientific names of the bones. Write these on the board. If students offer the scientific names, list those as well; compare them to the common name. Show a picture of the muscle system of the human body. Explain to the students how the bones help give the muscles support.

Walk around the classroom very stiffly. Encourage some or all of the students to do the same. Really play it up. Tell them they cannot bend their elbows or knees. You used brass fasteners to connect the bones in your skeleton. Do you think those are used in our bodies? Of course not; what do we have? (Joints.)

Ask the children to demonstrate what would happen to them right now (as they are standing) if they did not have bones in their body. The students should drop to the floor. Summarize that the skeleton supports our muscles.

## 3. EXPANSION OF THE IDEA: Which process skills will be used?

Observing, classifying, recording, manipulating materials

How will the idea be expanded?

*Newsprint Bone Bodies*

Pair up the students and provide each child with a large sheet of newsprint and a pencil. Ask the students to spread the paper out on the floor. The paired children should take turns. One child should lie flat on the paper with his or her face down. The other child should outline the body. Let each child switch roles. After they have created their outlines, have each child fill in the outline with the bones of the body.

### Science in Personal and Social Perspectives

- Do you think it is good to know what is inside our body? Why?
- How do joints help us move?

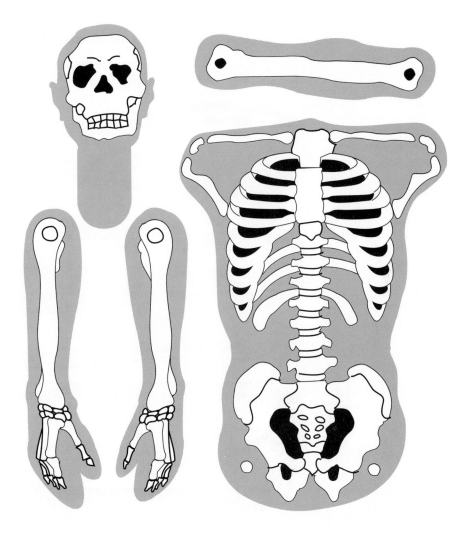

- Could you do the same activities you do on a daily basis if you didn't have a skeleton?

*Science and Technology*

- What do you think scientists do with bones found in nature?
- Do you think bones found by scientists tell them anything about the organism and the environment it lived in?
- How do you think we see our bones inside our body? What is that picture called?

*Science as Inquiry*

- How do bones connect together?
- Why do you think it is good to understand how our bodies move?
- Why do you think we have two bones in our forearms and lower legs?

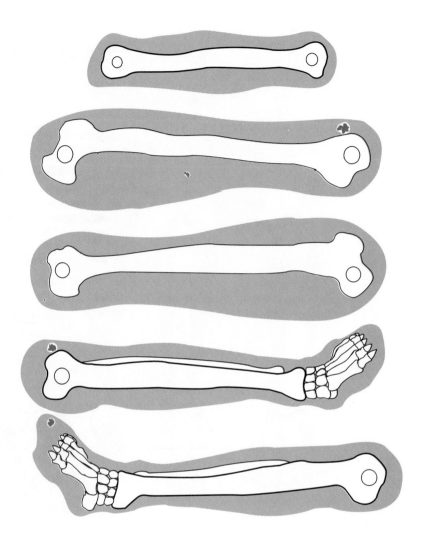

### History and Nature of Science

- What is the name of the person who shows you pictures of your bones inside you?
- If you had some back problems and you wanted your spine readjusted, what type of professional would you go to?
- What would you call a person who went to different locations to dig up buried bones and artifacts?
- What does a doctor do if you have a broken bone? How do you think the first doctors figured out how to mend broken bones?

**4. EVALUATION:** How will the students show what they have learned?

Upon completing the activities the students will be able to:

- assemble a paper skeleton;
- identify at least five bones in the body with common names;
- understand why we need joints in our bodies and explain what they do;
- play Hokey-Pokey Skeleton; that is, do the Hokey-Pokey, but use the common names of bones rather than body parts.

## Temperature Receptors on Skin

**GRADE
5–8
DISCIPLINE
Life
Science**

### Concept to be invented
Main idea—Our bodies have separate spots, called receptors, for feeling temperatures that are hotter or colder than body temperatures.

### Concepts that are important to expansion
Water can feel hot and cold to our bodies at the same time.

### Materials needed
*For each student group:*

| | |
|---|---|
| a source of hot and cold water | two fine-tipped pens, each a different |
| three bowls | color |
| six nails | paper towels |

 **Safety precautions:** Do not poke each other with the nails. Use care around the water: If it is knocked over, be sure to clean it up immediately. Make sure hot water is not so hot that it will scald.

**1. EXPLORATION:** Which process skills will be used?

Observing, questioning, designing an experiment, recording data, predicting, generalizing

What will the students do?

*Soaking Hands*    Divide the students into cooperative working groups of four. Ask the materials manager to obtain three small bowls. Fill one with hot water, one with cold water, and the third with warm water. The groups' mission is to find out how hands feel when placed in water of different temperatures. Encourage the groups to design an experiment to solve this problem. Ask them to record their data. Their experimental designs may look something like this: Each student in the group will take turns placing one hand in hot water and the other in cold. Hands should be left for several minutes in the water. Remove hands from those bowls and immediately immerse them in the warm water. Students should be able to describe what happens next. There may be some variations to this plan. Teachers may find that some groups first put both hands in cold and then in hot. They all should be able to help invent the concept, no matter the experimental design.

## 2. EXPLANATION/CONCEPT INVENTION: What is the main idea? How will the main idea be constructed?

*Concept:* Our bodies have separate spots, called *receptors,* for feeling temperatures that are hotter or colder than body temperatures.

To help invent this concept, ask each of the student groups to report on the experiment they designed. What did you do? What results did you get? Did the water feel hot and cold at the same time? How can that be? Does it have to do with the temperature of the water your hand was in first or just the temperature of your hand? The students should be able to conclude that it has to do with the temperature of the water their hand was in first. On their skin are receptors that sense temperatures different from normal body temperature.

## 3. EXPANSION OF THE IDEA: Which process skills will be used?

Observing, classifying, recording, predicting

How will the idea be expanded?

*Hot/Cold Receptor Mapping*   Ask each student to use one of the pens provided to the groups to draw a square on the back of his or her hand. Place one nail in the bowl of cold water and another in the bowl of hot water. Ask the group members to pair up. Ask one student from each pair to take the nail from the cold water and touch the tip of the nail to any spot in the square of his or her partner's hand. If it feels cold, mark that spot with the pen (marking all the cold ones in the same color). Now switch so that each partner has cold receptors marked. Other student pairs in each cooperative group can be doing the same thing with the hot water and a nail. Be sure to use a different color pen for hot spots. Now exchange bowls and make marks for the opposite water type. Are you surprised at where you find the hot and cold receptors?

### Science in Personal and Social Perspectives

- People say that to test bathwater you should use your elbow, or to test a baby's bottle you should use your wrist. Why do you think they chose those particular body parts?
- Which would you test your bathwater with, your hand or your toes? Why?

### Science and Technology

- On a hot summer day it is nice to enter an air-conditioned building. After you've been in the building for an hour, you begin to think the air-conditioning has been shut off. Why do you think you feel this way?
- How has technology allowed us to exist comfortably in the winter and the summer? Can you design a way to keep cool during hot weather without using an air-conditioner or fan?

### Science as Inquiry

- Could you find a way to pick up a snowball and not feel the cold?
- Which part of your hand is most sensitive to hot things?
- What is a receptor?

### History and Nature of Science

- Why do people who work in meat lockers wear gloves?
- Do you think it is important for someone involved in child care to make sure that his or her heat receptors are not damaged? Why or why not?
- In 1853 Georg Meissner described a corpuscle that became known as *Meissner's corpuscle*. What is this, and what did Meissner do to discover it?

**4. EVALUATION:** How will the students show what they have learned?

Upon completing the activities the students will be able to:

- identify the different hot and cold receptors on each hand;
- explain how water can feel hot and cold at the same time;

- identify the child with the cold hands when looking at a picture of children involved in building a snow fort (the one without gloves);
- view a picture of working firefighters with and without fire coats and identify which ones will feel hot. Why is this not the same as pictures of children in the winter with and without coats?

## Building Microscope Skills

GRADE
5–8
DISCIPLINE
Life
Science

**Concept to be invented**
Main idea—A microscope is used to identify objects not visible to the naked eye.

**Concepts that are important to expansion**
Identifying a compound by its characteristic crystal shape, slide preparation

**Materials needed**
*For exploration:*

| | | |
|---|---|---|
| noniodized salt | water | microscope |
| iodized salt | eye droppers | scale |
| sugar | cups | graduated cylinder |
| alum | slides | pictures of crystals |
| borax | slide covers | |

*For expansion:*

| | |
|---|---|
| water | laundry bluing |
| noniodized salt | household ammonia |

**Safety precautions:** Avoid placing hands near eyes or mouth while working with materials to prepare slides. When using an electric microscope, be sure to use proper safety measures near electrical outlets. The microscope lamp may be hot to touch. Apply the usual safety standards when working with such chemicals as bluing and ammonia.

1. EXPLORATION: Which process skills will be used?

Observing, classifying, recording data, diagramming, comparing, manipulating instruments

What will the students do?

*Microscope Use and Crystal Comparisons*

Measure out 5 grams of each solid. Dissolve each in a separate cup containing 25 ml of water. Be sure to label the cup with the name of the material dissolved in the water. As the solution is forming, label a slide for each solute. Place a drop of each solution on its assigned slide. Allow the water to evaporate. Carefully place the cover slip over the remaining crystals on the slide. Focus each slide under the microscope and record your observations for each at low power. Focus under a higher power and again record observations.

## 2. EXPLANATION/CONCEPT INVENTION: What is the main idea? How will the main idea be constructed?

*Concept:* A microscope is used to identify objects not visible to the naked eye.

Key questions to ask students to help them come to this conclusion are: What shapes did you observe on the slide? How does it compare to a drawing of the crystal shape? Can you share a diagram of those shapes with the class? How are these shapes similar? How are they different? How did the microscope help you to observe the crystal?

## 3. EXPANSION OF THE IDEA: Which process skills will be used?

Graphing, classifying, experimenting

How will the idea be expanded?

*Charcoal Crystals*
- Use the results of the previous crystal comparison activity to graph the crystal shapes versus the number of substances that have that particular shape.
- The students should be encouraged to brainstorm a list of other possible substances that contain crystals. Observe these under the microscope.
- The students will grow a crystal garden in a Styrofoam egg carton by first placing pieces of charcoal into the egg sockets. In a separate container, mix the following substances:

6 tablespoons of water      6 tablespoons of laundry bluing
6 tablespoons of noniodized salt      2 teaspoons of household ammonia

Once this solution is prepared, the students should carefully pour it over the pieces of charcoal in the egg container. The students can then place these in an area in the classroom where they will not be hit or bumped. The crystals will grow for several days. If the students want colored crystals, they may place a few drops of food coloring on the charcoal after the solution is poured on them. The students may wish to make each egg socket a different color. Once the crystals have grown, the students may safely carry them home in their egg cartons. If the crystals do get bumped in transit, sometimes they can be revived by putting a little water on them.

### Science in Personal and Social Perspectives

- While rummaging through your kitchen for a salt shaker, you come across a container you think will work. After placing the salt into the container, you find that no salt comes out of the holes when you shake the container. Why

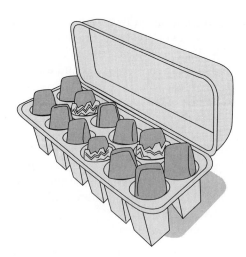

do you think this happened? Will the size of the salt crystals determine the size of the holes that should be on top of a shaker?

- Do you think there are any other areas of your life where the skills you learned in this lesson can be applied? If so, where?
- How do you think your increased knowledge of crystal shapes will help you become a better consumer? Would you buy ice cream that contained frost crystals? Why or why not?

*Science and Technology*

- Knowing that salt or sugar can be placed in solution allowed past generations to preserve foods more easily, thus ensuring their survival. How have our present-day technologies expanded on these early ideas?
- Think about the frozen food industry. How does it make use of their knowledge of crystal formation?

*Science as Inquiry*

- What scientific concepts did you discover while participating in these activities?
- What problem-solving techniques did you employ?
- What procedures were used with the microscope?

*History and Nature of Science*

- How important is it for a gemologist to understand the differences between crystal shapes? Why?
- In addition to knowledge about crystals, what other kinds of skills would a geologist need? a gemologist? a hospital laboratory technician?
- Anton van Leeuwenhoek is credited with creating one of the earliest microscopes. What kind of discoveries was he able to make with his primitive microscope?

**4. EVALUATION:** How will the students show what they have learned?

Upon completing these activities the students will be able to:

- demonstrate proper slide preparation techniques,
- prepare a slide of a crystal and focus it under a microscope,
- identify on a diagram the basic crystal shapes,
- state why different compounds may have different crystal shapes.

## Sex-Linked Genes

**GRADE**
**5–6**
**DISCIPLINE**
**Life**
**Science**

**Concept to be invented**
Traits are passed from parent to offspring.

**Concepts that are important to expansion**
Sex linked traits are carried through sex chromosomes. Heredity information is contained in genes, located in the chromosomes of each cell.

**Materials needed**
*For exploration:*

pictures of several generations of a family where the resemblance over the generations is easy to see, and pictures of family members where the relationship is not so obvious

or arrange to have a family come into your class or have a video of a family showing multiple generations

or have students bring in family pictures of themselves and a sibling or adult family member, or bring in a picture of a family

poster paper or chalkboard to collect class observations

*For expansion:*

50 drinking straws (this is for a class of 25 @ 2 per student)

0.5-cm × 2-cm strips of light and dark blue construction paper (37 total)

0.5-cm × 2-cm strips of light and dark green construction paper (37 total)

0.5-cm × 2-cm strips of light and dark red construction paper (13 total)

➡ **Safety precautions:** None needed

**1. EXPLORATION:** Which process skills will be used?

Observing, comparing, recording data, making hypotheses

What will students do?

*Family Traits*  If you have enough pictures of various families throughout the generations, the students can work in groups of 4–6; if you have a small number of pictures or videotape of a family, then work together as a class. Either way, ask the students to look at the family members closely for similarities. If the students are having trouble or looking confused, encourage them to look for similar traits like hair or eye color, freckles, skin coloration, heights, etc. Ask students to record the things they find that the family members have in common. Tell them to be prepared to share their observations and to draw some conclusions about their observations and those of the class.

## 2. EXPLANATION/CONCEPT INVENTION: What is the main idea? How will the main idea be constructed?

*Concept:* Traits are passed from parent to offspring.

If the students worked as separate teams, ask the student teams to share with the class the pictures they used to make their observations. If they made their observations from videotape, this will not be necessary. As the students share their observations, record commonly recurring ideas for all to see. For example, if one group talks about all family members having green eyes and another group talks about all family members having brown eyes, then record "eye color" for all to see. Continue with the sharing until all students or student groups have had an opportunity to share their observations and until you have a list of observations that includes a variety of traits, i.e., skin, eye, and hair color; body shape and height.

Ask the students leading questions to invent the concept of a trait, such as: Did all the siblings in the picture have the same color of eyes? Or hair? Did you see much resemblance between the mother and her daughter? Or between the parent and the child?

The list of observations that you made are of characteristics we get passed on to us from our parents. Those characteristics are called traits. These traits are given direction by genes that are carried on our chromosomes. We inherit or receive the genes from one or both of our parents. For instance, some of you may have found that a child looked just like one of the parents in the pictures. Others of you may have found that the child looked like a combination of both parents. Thus, traits are passed from parent to offspring. What a person looks like on the outside is called the person's *phenotype*. The inherited traits that make a person look like that (what's in the inside) is called the person's *genotype*.

## 3. EXPANSION OF THE IDEA: Which process skills will be used?

Observing, predicting, recording data, drawing conclusions

### Preactivity Preparation

Before the activity the teacher should cut the straws into 10- and 7-cm lengths. These will be representing X and Y chromosomes respectively. To demonstrate the naturally occurring distribution you will need three times as many 10-cm lengths (X chromosomes) as 7-cm lengths (Y chromosomes). For a class of 25 students you need 37 long and 13 shorter-length straws. To the long straws, tape a strip of light- or dark-blue paper near one end; then tape a strip of light- or dark-green paper a few centimeters below the blue paper. (See diagram.) Tape a red strip to the short straw at the same distance from one end as you taped the blue strip to the long straws. (See diagram.)

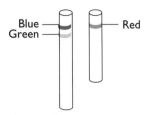

Prepare the rest of the straws in the same manner, alternating the light- and dark-colored bands.

Use the following key: Long straws = X chromosomes; short straws = Y chromosomes; blue strips = color blindness gene (dark blue, the trait is not present; light blue, the trait is present); green strips = baldness gene (dark green, the trait is not present; light green, the trait is present); red strips = hairy ears gene (dark red, the trait is not present; light red, the trait is present).

## How will the idea be expanded?

*Sex-Linked Traits*
Give two straws to each student so that they receive either two long or a long and a short straw. They can not receive two short straws as you are modeling how sex chromosomes are inherited. Remind them of the earlier exploration activity. Explain to them that each straw represents one of the sex chromosomes they inherited from their parents; a long straw represents an X chromosome and a short straws represents a Y chromosome. Two X chromosomes (long straws) means you will be female; an X and Y chromosome (1 short, 1 long straw) means you will be male.

Share the key to the colored bands. Have the students determine their gender and what traits they will inherit. Ask them to identify their phenotype (what they will look like on the outside) and their genotype (what traits their genes carry). For example, if they have one long straw (representing an X chromosome) and one short straw (representing a Y chromosome) they have a male phenotype and XY genotype. If the long straw has a dark blue band and a light green band and the short straw has a dark red band, then the phenotype is a colorblind male. In another example, if a student has two long straws with a dark blue band on one straw and a light blue band on the other and a light green band on both straws, then the phenotype is a colorblind female with an XX genotype.

Have the students trade a straw with another student (just don't end up with two short straws). Again have them identify the phenotype and genotype. Ask them what conclusions they can draw about the three traits—color blindness, baldness, and hairy ears. Use your questioning skills to get them to reflect on the observations they shared about the phenotypes and genotypes.

The students should be led to conclude that color blindness, specifically affecting green color vision, and baldness (premature baldness at the crown of the head) are recessive traits that are only carried by the X chromosome. The gene for hairy ears is a recessive trait carried on the Y chromosome; thus, girls don't get hairy ears. If the recessive gene for hairy ears is present, it is with increasing age that it is expressed more prominently in men carrying this trait. These traits are sex linked. Thus the concept developed is that sex-linked traits are carried through sex chromosomes, and heredity information is contained in genes, located in the chromosomes of each cell.

### Science in Personal and Social Perspectives

- Have you ever known a family where each of the siblings look almost exactly alike or where the child looked as if she were cloned from one of the parents? Can you now explain how this is possible?
- Do you think personality traits can be inherited as well? Explain your answer.

### Science and Technology

- Understanding how traits are inherited has led many couples to seek genetic counseling before having children. What do you think one could learn from genetic counseling?
- There are many products on the market designed to prevent hair loss. Do you think these are useful to someone who has inherited the sex-linked gene for baldness? Why or why not?

### Science as Inquiry

- What is the difference between someone's genotype and phenotype? How can these be determined?
- If you had a grandfather on your mother's side who was bald, will you be bald when you get older? What would your genotype have to be to show up bald if you were a female?

### History and Nature of Science

- Gregor Mendel is known as the "father of genetics." What observations did Mendel make that led to this branch of science? Describe his experiments.
- Genetic engineering is one of the fastest-growing career fields. Research the skills needed to be a genetic engineer and what industries would require the services of someone trained as a genetic engineer.

**4. EVALUATION:** How will the students show what they have learned?

Upon completing the activities the students will be able to:

- describe a trait and explain what it means to inherit that trait;
- when given a particular phenotype, predict the possible genotype for the given traits;
- look at the phenotypes of a given couple and predict the phenotypes of their male and female offspring;
- research information on sex-linked genes and identify other phenotypes that result because of a sex-linked gene other than those discovered in the expansion activity.

## Passing of Traits

**GRADE**
**7–8**
**DISCIPLINE**
Life
Science

### Concept to be invented

Traits are passed from parent to offspring.

### Concepts that are important to expansion

The characteristics of an organism can be described in terms of a combination of traits. Some traits are inherited and others result from interactions with the environment.

### Materials needed

digital cameras to loan students to take home to take pictures of family members that possess similar traits

or—students should bring in family pictures of themselves and a sibling or adult family member, or

bring in a picture of a family where similar traits are obvious

poster paper

index cards (each student should have as many index cards as there are students in the class)

➡ **Safety precautions:** None needed.

---

1.  EXPLORATION: Which process skills will be used?

Observing, comparing, recording data, making hypotheses

What will students do?

*What Traits Do You Share?*

Have students use digital cameras to take close-up pictures of one another. Then allow them to take the cameras home to take a picture of a family member or members with whom they share similar traits. The students should return the cameras to the class, download, and print the pictures they took. If a digital camera is not available, they should bring in a recent photo of themselves and pictures of family members (this can be an aunt, uncle, grandmother, etc. Be sure you are sensitive to the feelings of adopted students or students in step or foster families).

Ask the students to tape or glue the photos on the poster paper. Below the photos create a list of physical traits that the people in the photos share. Display the photo posters around the room.

Provide each student with a stack of index cards. Have students use one card for each poster they observe. On the card they will write the name of the student who prepared the poster, and then list some observable traits of that student as shown by the poster. Once students have listed the traits, instruct them to leave the index cards on the appropriate students' desks. In the end each student should have a stack of index cards with descriptions of traits that other students observed in his or her poster.

## 2. EXPLANATION/CONCEPT INVENTION: *What is the main idea? How will the main idea be constructed?*

*Concept:* Traits are passed from parent to offspring.

Using your questioning skills, encourage students to reflect on the observations their peers made about their poster. Ask questions such as:

- Were the observations your peers made about inherited traits similar to the ones you observed?
- Were you surprised that your peers noticed a trait that you did not see at first? What were some of those?

The students should be making suggestions about traits such as: the shape of the lips, nose, chin, cheekbones, eyebrows, eyes, coloring of hair and skin, height, dimples, freckles, and smile.

Encourage them to conclude that some traits are easily observable and that they are passed from parent to offspring.

## 3. EXPANSION OF THE IDEA: *Which process skills will be used?*

Observing, predicting, recording data, drawing conclusions

*How will the idea be expanded?*

*Inherited or Environmentally Altered?*

Have the students reuse the index cards by passing them back to the student who filled them out. Ask the students to move around the room again, looking at each student's poster. This time ask them to list on the reverse side of the appropriate card any personality traits that they may know about that student. Once completed, have the cards returned to the students to whom they apply. Ask each student to take a new index card and to complete a "personality trait" list for him- or herself as well. Not all students will feel comfortable sharing the results of this activity aloud; instead, ask them to create a data chart that lists the type of personality trait in one column and the number of times someone in the class identified that trait for them in the other. Without naming the personality trait (to eliminate student embarrassment) or by using yourself as an example, ask the students to think about the top three personality traits on their list. Ask them to determine where they think they got that trait from. Is their someone in their family who exhibits the same trait? Does more than one person in their family exhibit that same personality trait? Do you exhibit traits that are a combination of traits from your parents? The characteristics of an organism can be described in terms of a combination of traits.

Ask the students to think about these questions: Do you think this trait is inherited or was it learned by living in the family environment? How far back can you trace this personality trait in your family? To your grandparents? Your great-grandparents? Your great-great-grandparents?

Personality traits may be inherited just like a laugh or the sound of one's voice. However, some personality traits can be acquired through years of living in a certain environment. The same can happen to physical characteristics. Certain traits are inherited, but changes in the gene environment can occur during cell reproduction to alter the phenotype expressed. Thus some traits are inherited and others result from interactions with the environment.

### Science in Personal and Social Perspectives

- What would be the advantage of thoroughly reviewing the observable traits found within your family tree? Would it be as easy to trace personality traits?
- What observable traits do you have that you think you inherited from your male parent? From your female parent? What observable traits do you have that you believe are a combination of both parents?

### Science and Technology

- How have some couples turned to technology to alter the outcome of some observable traits in their offspring?
- Can genetic engineering change the personality traits of an offspring?

### Science as Inquiry

- Choose a famous family such as that of a president, a king or queen, or a known actor. Research the family lineage to identify any inherited traits carried through the generations.
- If you were born with red hair and each of your siblings had brown hair, but you knew of a deceased great uncle with red hair on your father's side of the family, explain how that red-hair gene showed up as your phenotype.

### History and Nature of Science

- Gregor Mendel is known as the "father of genetics" due to his extensive experiments with pea plants. What other organisms have scientists turned to as a means of adding to the ever-increasing body of knowledge in the field of genetics? Share at least two organisms and the work done with those to explain a genetics concept.
- How would one use the concept that some traits are inherited and others result from interactions with the environment to explain why some people have the ability to play a musical instrument and other people in the same family don't have that ability?

## 4. EVALUATION: How will the students show what they have learned?

Upon completing the activities the students will be able to:

- describe a trait and explain what it means to inherit that trait;
- determine how a particular trait such as curly black hair can be found on a child from a family with siblings all having straight black hair and parents with straight black hair;
- explain why when identical twins are raised apart they could exhibit identical personality traits.

# Physical Science Lessons

| Lesson Name | Physical Science Content Standards | Grade Level | Activities |
|---|---|---|---|
| ***Waves: Sound and Light*** | | | |
| Sound versus Noise | Position and Motion of Objects | K–4 | School Sound Search • Magazine Sound Search |
| Sounds Are Different | Position and Motion of Objects | 2–4 | Megaphones and Vibrating Straws • Bell Ringers |
| Vibrations Causing Sound | Position and Motion of Objects | 2–4 | Sound Makers • Waxed Paper Kazoo |
| Loudness and Pitch | Position and Motion of Objects | 2–4 | Soda Bottle Orchestra • Cigar Box Strings • Fish Line Harps • Home-made Music |
| Sound Movement as Waves | Position and Motion of Objects | 2–4 | Vibrating Fork • Striking Rod • Clapping Blocks • Sound Producers? • Tapping Tank • Paper Cup Telephone |
| Sound Waves | Position and Motion of Objects | 2–4 | Soup Can Reflectors • Slinky Waves • Sound Waves and the Ear |
| Sound Production | Properties of Matter | 5–8 | Noise and Sound Identification • Sound Movement • Sound Game: "What Is Sound?" |
| ***Matter*** | | | |
| Characteristics of Matter | Properties of Matter | 3–4 | Plastic Bag Chemistry • Marble Matter |
| Physical Properties of Matter | Properties of Objects and Materials | K–4 | Egg-citing Observations • Chocolate Chip Exploration |
| Changing Matter | Properties of Matter | 5–8 | Physical and Chemical Paper Change • Polymer-Rubber Balls |
| Identification of an Unknown | Properties of Matter | 5–8 | Physical Properties of an Unknown • Chemical Properties of an Unknown |
| Using the Scientific Method to Solve Problems | Properties of Matter | 5–8 | Exploring with Efferdent Tablets • Exploring with Cornstarch |
| Heat Energy | Light, Heat, Electricity, and Magnetism | 1–4 | Liquid Birthday • Liquids to Solids |
| ***Physics*** | | | |
| Structure Strength | Motion and Forces | 5–8 | Simple Construction • Triangle Construction |
| Mirrors and Reflection | Transformations of Energy | 5–8 | Mirrors and Reflectors • What's a Mirror? |
| The Slinky Potential | Transformations of Energy | 7–8 | Energy Conversions with a Slinky • Energy Transfer—Having a Ball! |
| Toys in Space | Motion and Forces | 5–8 | Toy Behavior in Zero Gravity • Toys and Newton |
| Simple Machines: The Lever | Motion and Forces | 5–8 | Lever Creations • Spoons and Nuts • Lever Scavenger Hunt |

## Sound Versus Noise

GRADE
K–4
DISCIPLINE
Physical
Science

**Concept to be invented**

Main idea—Sound can be considered useful or simply noise.

**Concepts that are important to expansion**

Sound can be pleasant or unpleasant.

**Materials needed**

whistle

magazines for cutting up

tape recorder (if possible, one per group)

one blank audiotape per group

➡ **Safety precautions:** The students should be reminded of the importance of walking, not running, as they move through the school to find a place to listen to different sounds. They should use care when carrying pencils or pens to record their observations. Exercise caution when using the scissors in the expansion activity.

**Discrepant event**

While the students are working quietly at their desks, make sure no students are looking, and then take out a whistle and blow it loudly. Ask the children what they first thought when they heard the whistle. Record some of their thoughts on the board.

1. EXPLORATION: Which process skills will be used?

Observing, classifying, predicting, describing, recording data, communicating

What will the students do?

*School Sound Search*

Divide the class into four groups. Send each group to different parts of the school building, such as the janitors' workroom, the playground, the gym or music room, their own classroom. Ask them to go to these areas quietly. Have them sit quietly in their areas for 3 minutes. Create a list of all of the sounds they hear in those areas. Return to the classroom. Instruct the students to work with the people in their group to decide if there is any way they could group the sounds. When all of the groups have analyzed their lists, share the categories of sounds with the rest of the class. Ask the students if any of the groups came up with categories their group never thought of.

2. EXPLANATION/CONCEPT INVENTION: What is the main idea? How will the main idea be constructed?

*Concept:* Sound can be considered useful or simply noise.

Place on the board in separate columns the terms *useful, noise, pleasant,* and *unpleasant.* Ask the students if any of these terms fit the feelings they had when you blew the whistle unexpectedly. Do any of these terms fit the categories you placed your sounds under? If so, which of your sounds would go under the different headings? Encourage members of the group to write their sounds under the appropriate headings. Do all sounds fall *only* into one classification? Fire alarms, whistles—where do they fall? Sounds can be useful or noise depending on circumstances. Sound can be harmful. We need ear protection from some sounds.

## 3. EXPANSION OF THE IDEA: Which process skills will be used?

Observing, classifying, communicating, inferring, manipulating materials, interpreting data

### How will the idea be expanded?

*Magazine Sound Search*

The children will work in groups, looking through magazines, cutting out possible sources of sound. Each group will create an audiotape, mimicking the sounds that the different items they collected make. Each group will place its pictures on a poster, then play its tape to the other groups. The members of the other groups will guess which item the sound goes with, and then determine if it is useful or noise, pleasant or unpleasant, or any combination of these. They must be able to explain why they would classify the item that way.

### Science in Personal and Social Perspectives

- When listening to a radio with headphones on, is it wise to have the volume so loud that those around you can hear it?
- If you were asked to create a sound that would serve as a warning for some devastating disaster like a tornado, what would this sound be like? How would you categorize it? How unique would it have to be?

### Science and Technology

- Why was it necessary for the Occupational Safety and Health Administration (OSHA) to set standards for an acceptable noise level in work areas?
- Personal computers have changed our lives in many ways. While they have been a help, they have also created problems. How have they contributed to the problem of noise pollution, and what has the computer industry done to eliminate some of this noise?
- Many airports near major cities were built in areas long considered migratory routes for some animals, mating habitats for others. The constant roar of jet engines affects the behavior of these animals. What have people done to eliminate some noise hazards brought upon these creatures? What must we continue to do?

### Science as Inquiry

- How would you classify the sound best suited for quiet study time?
- Can sounds be classified into more than one category?

PHYSICAL SCIENCE

*History and Nature of Science*
- Which type of work do you think would be most affected by noise pollution? least affected? Which type of work would you choose? Why?
- Do you think it is important for a music critic to distinguish between a useful sound or noise, a pleasant or unpleasant sound?

**4. EVALUATION:** How will the students show what they have learned?

Upon completing the activities the students will be able to:

- listen to an audiotape of various sounds and classify them according to useful/noise and pleasant/unpleasant;
- take one of the assigned categories—useful/pleasant; useful/unpleasant; noise/pleasant; noise/unpleasant—and over a week find some music that they think fits into their assigned category and explain why they believe it does. They are encouraged to get their families involved in their search. If they cannot find some music that fits their category, they can create their own sound.

## Sounds Are Different

GRADE
2–4
DISCIPLINE
Physical
Science

**Concept to be invented**
Main idea—Sounds vary in loudness and pitch.

**Concepts that are important to expansion**
Loudness is determined by the strength of the vibration. Pitch is determined by the length of the vibrating object. Magnification of sound is achieved by megaphones and speakers.

**Materials needed**
several large and small bells
pieces of at least 8-inch × 8-inch
   square paper

tape
paper straws
scissors

**Safety precautions:** Be careful when using the scissors. Remember basic scissors safety. Be careful when placing the straws into your mouth. During the expansion activity, do not ring a bell in anyone's ear.

**Discrepant event**
Find a time when the students are working quietly in their seats. Take a large and a small bell and ring them at the same time. Ask the students: "Did I get your attention? Did you hear just one noise or two? Did one sound softer than the other? higher than the other?"

1. **EXPLORATION:** Which process skills will be used?

Observing, communicating, inferring, predicting

What will the students do?

*Megaphones and Vibrating Straws*

Ask half the students to shout "hello" to you from their seats. Now ask them to cup their hands around their mouths and shout "hello" again. Ask those who did not yell if they noticed a difference in the sound produced. Now let the other half try it. Give the children pieces of paper and have them roll them into cones. Tape the sides together to maintain the cone shapes. Use the scissors to cut away about 1 inch of the pointed end of each cone. Once again have half the class shout "hello," and then shout again, holding the cut ends of the cones by their mouths. Once again ask the listeners if they noticed a difference in the sound produced each time. Allow the other half to test their cones too.

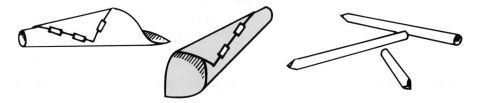

   Give the students one straw each. Ask them to cut a little piece off both sides of one end so that what remains looks like an inverted V. Ask them to predict what will happen when they blow into the cut end of the straw. What do they need to do to get the cut V-shaped pieces to vibrate? As they hold the straws in their mouths, they should continue to blow into the straws and start cutting off pieces at the ends of the straws. What is happening to the sound as the straw gets shorter?

2. **EXPLANATION/CONCEPT INVENTION:** What is the main idea? How will the main idea be constructed?

*Concept:* Sounds vary in loudness and pitch.

When did the "hellos" sound the loudest? When you used nothing, your hand, or your school-made megaphone? What does a megaphone do? It magnifies sound. It increases the strength of the vibration, thus making the sound louder. What happened to the sound produced by the straw as you cut it? Was the loudness of the sound the same? What property of sound changed? The pitch got higher. *Pitch* is determined by the length of the vibrating object.

3. **EXPANSION OF THE IDEA:** Which process skills will be used?

Predicting, designing an experiment, communicating, controlling variables, experimenting, observing, recording data, hypothesizing, inferring

How will the idea be expanded?

*Bell Ringers*    Divide the students into groups. Give each group at least four different-sized bells. Before ringing each bell, ask the students to create a prediction sheet identifying the loudness and pitch of the bell. Have each group design a way that will most fairly and accurately ring the bells. Emphasize the importance of keeping all other variables constant when comparing the four bells, such as having the same person ring the bells for each trial, or having each person in the group ring each bell to see if the person doing the ringing affects the loudness or pitch. After filling out their prediction sheet and designing a way to ring the bells without letting their predictions prejudice them, they should ring the bells. Record your results. Did your results match your predictions? Is there any way you can alter the bell to magnify the sound coming from it?

### Science in Personal and Social Perspectives

- What harm can the earphones on headsets have on your eardrums? What does the magnification of sound do to your eardrums?
- Would the magnification of sound be useful at a baseball or football game? Why or why not? Would everyone at these games appreciate sound being magnified?

### Science and Technology

- How has knowledge of loudness, pitch, and magnification led to the creation of devices that are important for crowd control? for large group communication? for the production of music?
- Why do you think a baseball stadium needs to be designed differently from a concert hall? In which would you want the sound to be louder? to be magnified?

### Science as Inquiry

- How could you control the loudness of the sound created by a piano?
- How could you change the pitch of a guitar?

### History and Nature of Science

- In what careers would you need to understand that loud sounds could set objects vibrating, which could cause structures to collapse? (Safety engineers, contractors, civil engineers, hotel/motel managers, high-rise office building workers.)
- How can a cheerleader save his or her voice by knowing about sound, loudness, pitch, and magnification?

## 4. EVALUATION: How will the students show what they have learned?

Upon completing the activities the students will be able to:

- infer, when given a set of pictures (large bell, small bell, siren, whistle), which would create a loud or soft sound;

- infer, when given another set of pictures (long and short guitar strings, large bell, small bell, man's voice, child's voice), which would create a high or low sound;
- give at least three ways in which one could magnify one's voice.

## Vibrations Causing Sound

**GRADE**
**2–4**
**DISCIPLINE**
**Physical**
**Science**

**Concept to be invented**
Main idea—Vibrations are caused by the movement of air molecules due to a disturbance.

**Concepts that are important to expansion**
There are many ways to produce sounds. You may not be able to see all vibrations.

**Materials needed**
*For exploration:*
prerecorded tape of classroom sounds, tape player, string, wire, meter stick, drum and beans, tuning forks and rubber mallet, pans of water, kitchen fork

*For expansion:*
combs and waxed paper squares

➡ **Safety precautions:** Remind students of the importance of using the rubber bands as instructed. Any other use may result in injury to eyes or faces. Exercise caution when carrying the kitchen forks during the exploration activity.

**Discrepant event**
Ask the students to listen carefully as you play the tape recording of classroom sounds. Try to guess what these familiar sounds are. Can you give any descriptive terms to remember them by?

1. EXPLORATION: Which process skills will be used?

Observing, communicating, recording data, experimenting, predicting, inferring

What will the students do?

*Sound Makers*
- Have the students place their hands on their throats and make sounds. Record what it feels like.
- In groups, ask the students to stretch and pluck rubber bands and strings. Record their observations.
- Have the students place the handle end of a kitchen fork between their teeth. Quickly flick the other end of the fork. What do their teeth feel like?
- In groups, ask the students to tap pans of water and observe.

PHYSICAL SCIENCE

- In groups, have the students tap tuning forks with rubber mallets and observe. Ask them to predict what will happen if they strike a tuning fork and quickly thrust it into a pan of water. Have them check their predictions.

## 2. EXPLANATION/CONCEPT INVENTION: What is the main idea? How will the main idea be constructed?

*Concept:* Vibrations are caused by the movement of air molecules due to a disturbance.

What did it feel like when you placed your hands on your throat and made sounds? Did your hands begin to tingle? What happened to the rubber bands when you stretched them out and plucked them? How did your teeth feel when you flicked the kitchen fork? What path did the water create when the pan was gently tapped? Did the tuning fork tickle your hand when you struck it with the rubber mallet? What happened when you thrust the tuning fork into the water? Was it as you predicted? Elicit the idea that sound is produced by movement. If no one says "vibrate," introduce this term now.

## 3. EXPANSION: Which process skills will be used?

Inferring, experimenting, hypothesizing, communicating

How will the idea be expanded?

*Waxed Paper Kazoo*

Have each student make a comb-and-waxed-paper kazoo by folding a piece of waxed paper over the teeth of a comb. Instruct the children to place their lips on the wax paper and to hum a tune. How is the sound being produced? What is vibrating?

### Science in Personal and Social Perspectives

- How is sound made? Can you avoid sound?
- Do sounds affect the way you feel and act?

PHYSICAL SCIENCE

- Would you want to attend a concert or go to a movie where the sound kept echoing off the walls? Why or why not?

*Science and Technology*

- The quality of speakers and sound systems relies heavily on sound vibrations; how has modern technology eliminated a lot of excess vibrations?
- How important a role does the design of a room play in carrying sound vibrations?
- How did an understanding of sound vibrations help in the creation of the microphone, the phonograph, the telephone, underwater depth sounding, and ultrasound? How have these inventions changed the world?

*Science as Inquiry*

- Knowing that sound is produced by a vibrating object, do you think you can make a bell ring under water? Try it.
- Some birds, like loons, can dive under water for their food and stay down for an extended period of time. Do you think they call to one another while they are under the water? Can they hear each other? What could you do to determine whether your answer is correct?

*History and Nature of Science*

- Who was John William Strutt, also known as Baron Rayleigh? What role did he play in helping us understand how sound behaves? (For second grade, the teacher could give a brief biography of Baron Rayleigh. He was born in England in 1842. While many people before him expressed opinions about the nature of sound—Pythagoras, Galileo, Mersenne, Chladni ("the founder of modern acoustics"), Colladon and Sturm, and von Helmholtz—Baron Rayleigh was the first to put it all together in a book titled *Theory of Sound*, which he published in 1877. A second edition was published in 1894. In 1904 Rayleigh won the Nobel Prize for physics, mainly for his work that led to the discovery of argon and other inert gases. Baron Rayleigh died in 1919.)
- Sound production is important in entertainment. Develop a list of entertainment careers that utilize sound.

**4. EVALUATION:** How will the students show what they have learned?

Upon completing the activities the students will be able to:

- predict from a given set of objects which will vibrate and produce sound (Nerf ball, drum, taut rubber band, loose rubber band, ruler, feather);
- spend one week in which they will be expected to test various wall surfaces to determine which ones allow for maximum and for minimum sound vibrations. They will share their findings with the class and, based on these findings, accurately predict which type of wall surface would be best for a movie theater or a concert hall.

## Loudness and Pitch

**GRADE
2–4
DISCIPLINE
Physical
Science**

**Concept to be invented**
Main idea—Sounds vary in loudness and pitch.

**Concepts that are important to expansion**
Size and strength of vibration will affect loudness and pitch.

**Materials needed**

| | |
|---|---|
| drinking glasses | wooden board with eye hooks and fish line |
| large nail | oatmeal boxes |
| empty soda bottles | wood blocks |
| water | pan lids |
| cigar box | guitar or piano |
| rubber bands | |

 **Safety precautions:** Care should be taken when handling any of the glass containers used in many of the activities. Protect eyes against flying rubber bands—wear goggles!

**Discrepant event**
Ask the students to predict what will happen to the sound as you tap an empty glass with a nail and gradually add water as you tap. Once all predictions are given, begin to tap the glass and fill it as you do so. Did the sound behave as you predicted? What happened to the sound as more water filled the glass? Do you have any ideas why this happened?

**1. EXPLORATION:** Which process skills will be used?

Observing, manipulating materials, predicting, communicating, recording data, inferring, hypothesizing

Soda bottles filled with water at varying levels

Glasses filled with varying levels of water

PHYSICAL SCIENCE

### What will the students do?

Divide the class into four groups. Have each group rotate through the following activities:

*Soda Bottle Orchestra*

Soda bottles, glasses, water, nails: Set up a center with glasses and bottles filled with water at varying levels. Have children explore sound variation with water levels in both glasses and bottles. Ask them to record their observations, taking special note of the relationship between the sound produced and the amount of water in the different containers.

*Cigar Box Strings*

Rubber bands of varying widths and lengths, open cigar box: Stretch the different-sized rubber bands over the open cigar box. Pluck the rubber bands. What kinds of sounds do they make? Record the sounds made by the different-sized rubber bands.

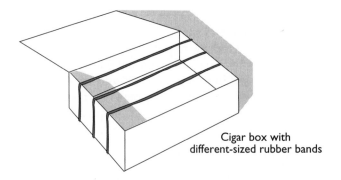

Cigar box with
different-sized rubber bands

*Fish Line Harps*    Make a fish line harp by cutting at least eight different lengths of fish line. String each line through two eye hooks that are screwed into a foot-long piece of board (a 1 × 8 will do) the same distance apart as the string length. (The teacher can make this harp ahead of time.) Pluck the strings. What do you observe about the relationship between the string length and the sound produced? Is there a relationship between the sound produced and the tightness of the string?

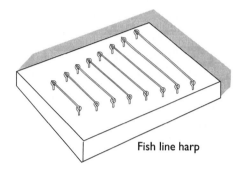

Fish line harp

Strum a guitar, or play a piano in which the guts are exposed. If you are using a guitar, what relationship do you observe between the size of the guitar string and the sound it produces? For the piano, what relationship do you observe between the size of the piano string and the sound it produces?

**PHYSICAL SCIENCE**

**2. EXPLANATION/CONCEPT INVENTION:** What is the main idea? How will the main idea be constructed?

*Concept:* Sounds vary in loudness and pitch.

What did you observe when you tapped the various glasses and bottles? What happened to the sound if you used a lot of force to strike the nail to the container? In which containers were the sounds higher?

How were you able to make the rubber band sound loud when plucked? What types of sounds were produced with very skinny, tightly stretched rubber bands? very fat, loosely stretched ones?

When you played the harp, which length string gave you the highest sound? the lowest? Did you try loosening the strings? What happened to the sounds when the strings were loose?

When you played the guitar or piano, what did you do to create a very loud sound? How were you able to get a very high sound? a low sound?

Summarize all the answers by reinforcing the following: Loudness is determined by the strength of vibration. Pitch is determined by the length of the vibrating object.

**3. EXPANSION OF THE IDEA:** Which process skills will be used?

Predicting, communicating, experimenting, interpreting data

How will the idea be expanded?

*Homemade Music*   Based on your conclusions from the previous activities, choose a song familiar to everyone in your group and try to play that simple melody on the glasses, the bottles, or any of the other instruments. Each group will take a turn performing for the other groups.

### Science in Personal and Social Perspectives

- The ability to produce music enriches the lives of children and can lead to a lifetime skill. The ability to control sound enhances self-concept.
- How could you use sound to help you determine how much soda you have left in a can? or how much milk is left in a carton? or how much laundry detergent is left in its container? or if a new bottle of perfume or aftershave is totally full?

### Science and Technology

- Many video games use sound to heighten the suspense and action of the play. Do you think these games would be as popular if all sound were eliminated?
- What effect does the loudness and pitch of music have on moviegoers? Would scary movies be as effective without the sound effects?
- How has the computer industry made use of the loudness and pitch of sounds in personal computers?

### Science as Inquiry

- What properties affect the pitch of a sound? the loudness of a sound? Can you create an instrument with high pitch and soft sound? with low pitch and loud sound?

### History and Nature of Science

- Children enjoy music for listening and movement and may look to a future as an entertainer. Ask the students to trace the history of an instrument. Who designed it? How does it produce sound?
- Where do you think someone with a background in music production, sound engineering, or the creation of musical instruments could use his or her talents?

**4. EVALUATION:** How will the students show what they have learned?

Upon completing these activities the students will be able to:

- predict whether a high or low pitch will be produced by looking at pictures of various-sized strings or columns of water;
- predict loudness and softness of sound when given pictures of thick or thin strings of the same length;

- create a high-pitched sound when given a straw;
- create a low pitch with a soda bottle.

## Sound Movement as Waves

### Concepts to be invented
Main idea—Sounds move in the form of waves through air, water, wood, and other solids.

### Concepts that are important to expansion
Sound waves must strike your eardrum for you to hear sound; sound waves weaken with distance.

### Materials needed
*Set up the following as activity centers:*
(1) fork and string chime, (2) metal rod, (3) meter stick, wood blocks, (4) pieces of cloth, cotton balls, feathers, cork, Nerf ball, (5) 10-gallon fish tank filled with water
*Per student pair:*
two paper cups and two paper clips per student; string for telephone; tin can and fish line telephone for comparison with paper cup telephone

 **Safety precautions**: Care should be taken when handling the kitchen fork and tuning forks; keep them away from your own eyes and those of your friends. Be careful where you place your fingers as you bang the two wood blocks together; avoid crushing them between the blocks.

### Discrepant event
Ask the students to listen as they tap the sides of their desks. Now ask them to lay their ears on their desk tops while tapping the sides of the desks with the same force as before. Have them describe the sounds they hear. Are there any differences? Why?

## 1. EXPLORATION: Which process skills will be used?

Observing, recording data, predicting, inferring, describing, communicating, measuring, defining operationally

### What will the students do?

Divide the class into five groups. Have each group record its observations while rotating throughout the following activity centers.

*Vibrating Fork*   Tie about a 12-inch length of string to the handle end of a fork. Allow it to bang on the side of a desk or a wall as you set it in swinging motion. Write a description of the sound it creates. Can you manipulate the string or fork in any way to change the pitch or loudness of the sound? Can you feel the vibrating fork through the string?

*Striking Rod*    Hold the metal rod and strike it against a wall, a book, a desk, a variety of surfaces. Is sound produced? Which striking surface will make the rod sound the loudest? the softest? Why do you think this is so?

*Clapping Blocks*    Take turns with members of your group clapping the two wood blocks together. Use the meter stick to measure at what distance the clapping blocks sound the loudest. How far can you move away from the clapping blocks and still hear them?

*Sound Producers?*    Using the cloth, cotton, feathers, cork, and Nerf ball, try to produce a sound. Is it possible to create a sound if you simply drop the items on your desk? What if you strike them with your hand? Are these items capable of producing sound? Why or why not?

*Tapping Tank*    Place your ear to one end of the filled fish tank. Have another student gently tap the glass on the other side of the tank. Can you hear this sound? Did the sound travel through the glass or through the water? This time place your ear so that it is directly above the tank. Have a friend gently drop a quarter into the fish tank when you are not looking. Could you hear when the quarter hit the bottom of the tank?

## 2. EXPLANATION/CONCEPT INVENTION: What is the main idea? How will the main idea be constructed?

*Concept:* Sounds move in the form of waves through air, water, wood, and other solids.

Were you able to make the fork sing? How did you do this? Did the hand that was holding the string feel anything as the fork sang? What about the metal rod? How did you get it to sound the loudest? Could you see the rod moving as it made sound? What about the wood blocks? Were they very loud? How did your hands feel as you banged the blocks together? What about the cloth, cotton, feathers, cork, and Nerf ball? Were you able to get them to make a sound when they were dropped? Why or why not? Do these items behave like the fork, metal rod, or wood blocks? What can those items do that the cloth items cannot? (Help students realize that objects that vibrate will set the air in motion to create a sound.) Could you hear sound through the water? When was it the easiest to detect? Why is it important that your ear be facing the source of the sound? Sound waves must strike your eardrum for you to hear sound.

Based on your observations from these five activities and when we put our ears to our desks and tapped, can you tell me through which media sound waves will travel? Sounds move in waves through air, water, wood, and other solids.

## 3. EXPANSION OF THE IDEA: Which process skills will be used?

Communicating, experimenting, interpreting data, reducing experimental error

### How will the idea be expanded?

*Paper Cup*
*Telephone*

Provide each student with two paper cups and any length of string (minimum 2 feet). Instruct the students to poke a small hole in the end of their paper cups and thread the string through them. Tie the end of the string to a paper clip to prevent the string from slipping out of the cup. Ask the students to work in pairs trying out their paper cup telephones. Experiment with loose string versus tight string, long versus short string. Compare results. Touch the string as they talk to dampen the sound. Ask each pair to try using the tin can–fish line telephone. Is there any difference between this phone and the one you made? Which telephone sets up more vibrations? What can you say about how sound travels?

### Science in Personal and Social Perspectives

- Where in your house would be the best place to set your stereo speakers: on a metal table or a cloth-covered bench? or would neither of these be good? Can you suggest a good place?
- Why do you think most homes have doorbells? How are these better than just yelling for our friends?
- Do you think it is fair for people who are fishing to use a fish echo-locator to determine where the fish are before they begin fishing?
- Do you think it is ethical for someone to use knowledge of sound to eavesdrop on other people for such purposes as collecting military intelligence, listening in on criminals, or listening to other people's conversations?

PHYSICAL SCIENCE

*Science and Technology*

- What materials would you use and how would you go about building a soundproof room? Can you create a plan that would be easy to follow that takes all variables into account in building this room? Work with your parents to create a working model of your design.

*Science as Inquiry*

- A knowledge of the conductivity of sound helps develop further concepts of controlling sound loudness, quality, and usefulness.
- Do you think you could design a tin-can phone that lets three or more people use it at once? Try it. Draw a diagram of your design.

*History and Nature of Science*

- How have marine biologists used their knowledge of sound to study the humpbacked whale? Why should we be concerned with the singing behavior of the humpbacked whale?
- Why would a pilot be concerned with how sound travels? If you were the pilot of the Concorde, would you have a problem trying to get permission to land your plane in Columbus, Ohio? Why?
- How did Alexander Graham Bell apply his understanding of sound? Identify one of his inventions and describe how it works.

**4. EVALUATION:** How will the students show what they have learned?

Upon completing the activities the students will be able to:

- rank-order a given set of materials from good to poor conductors of sound: air, wood, metal rod, cotton string, wire, water, cotton balls;
- take an object that is capable of creating sound when struck and alter it so that when it is struck, the loudness of the sound is decreased.

## Sound Waves

**GRADE**
**2–4**
**DISCIPLINE**
**Physical Science**

**Concepts to be invented**
Main idea—Sound travels in waves. Waves consist of areas of compression and rarefaction. Waves move through the air.

**Concepts that are important to expansion**
Sound waves cause vibrations as they hit the eardrum, causing us to hear sounds.

**Materials needed**
*For each group of students:*
soup can open at both ends                                    Slinkies

balloon                                                a model of the ear (one for the
rubber band                                               whole class)
small rectangular piece of mirror                      a labeled diagram of the ear
flashlight

➡ **Safety precautions:** Be sure that all rough edges are filed off soup cans before
providing them to student groups. Make sure there are no sharp edges on the
mirrors; file if necessary. Encourage the students to use caution near edges of
mirror and soup can.

### Discrepant event
Stretch a piece of the balloon over one end of the soup can. Secure it tightly with
the rubber band. Glue a small piece of mirror on the balloon membrane, slightly
off center. Shine a flashlight onto the mirror so that its reflection shows up on
the chalkboard. Ask the students to observe the mirror's reflection on the board.
Ask one student to come up and speak into the open end of the can. What happens to the mirror's reflection on the chalkboard when someone speaks into the
can?

1. EXPLORATION: Which process skills will be used?

Observing, experimenting, predicting, hypothesizing, inferring

What will the students do?

*Soup Can*
*Reflectors*

Divide the students into groups depending on class size. Have one soup can reflector for each group. Provide each group with a flashlight. Ask the students
to predict and then record what happens to the soup can reflectors as they vary
the loudness of the sound. What do you think is causing the mirror's reflection
to move? Think of this as you begin to play with a Slinky. Stretch and shake the
Slinky, and record what the Slinky looks like as you do this. A diagram may be
useful at this point. Try to label where the Slinky looks mashed together and
where it looks thin on your diagram.

## 2. EXPLANATION/CONCEPT INVENTION: *What is the main idea? How will the main idea be constructed?*

*Concept:* Sound travels in waves. Waves consist of areas of compression and rarefaction. Waves move through the air.

What do you think caused the mirror to move? Can you actually see the balloon moving as someone speaks into the open end of the can? Speaking into the can set the balloon membrane vibrating. Can you feel the vibration of the balloon if you lightly touch it as someone speaks into the open end? What type of pattern does the moving mirror make on the board? How is this pattern similar to the movement of the Slinky?

What would be a good name to describe the path sound travels in? (Waves.) Ask for a volunteer to share his or her drawing of Slinky movement with the class. Reproduce this drawing for all to see. As you moved the Slinky, were you able to detect areas where the Slinky was mashed together? Were you able to detect areas where it was more spread out? These Slinky movements are similar to sound waves. Areas where sound waves are mashed together are called *compression*; areas that are spread out are called *rarefaction*.

## 3. EXPANSION OF THE IDEA: *Which process skills will be used?*

Observing, manipulating materials, inferring, predicting, communicating

*How will the idea be expanded?*

*Slinky Waves*

Ask the students to take turns laying their heads on their desks while another student stretches the Slinky out on top of the desk and releases it rapidly, or have another student hold a ruler over the edge of the desk and strike it quickly. Ask the student with his or her head on the desk what this felt like. What did your ear detect?

*Sound Waves and the Ear*

Provide the students with diagrams of the inner ear. Ask them to label what they believe is the path that sound takes as it reaches our ears. Use the ear model to trace this path for the students. Allow them to check their labeled predictions with the model you are tracing. Remind them that sound waves vary in strength. As the sound waves hit the eardrum, they cause it to vibrate in rhythm with them, causing sound messages to the brain. The human ear can interpret sound waves with frequencies ranging between 16 and nearly 20,000 vibrations per second. Those vibrations above 20,000 are termed *ultrasonic*.

*Science in Personal and Social Perspectives*

- Why is it important that you never put anything in your ear smaller than your elbow? What kind of ear-cleaning products do you think are the safest to use?
- Have you ever tried to talk to your friends while you are under water swimming? Is it easy to understand someone talking under water? Why or why not?

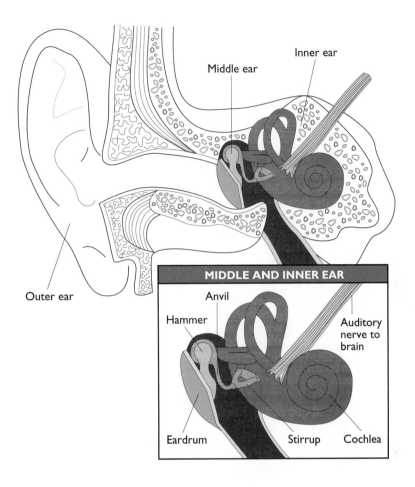

MIDDLE AND INNER EAR

• Interview people in different lines of work who use earplugs, such as factory workers, road construction crews, or building contractors. What types of earplugs do they use? How well do they think their earplugs work?
• Is it a good idea to wear headphones while riding your bicycle? Why or why not?

*Science and Technology*

• How effective are earplugs in preventing potentially damaging sounds from reaching your eardrum?
• Write to the manufacturers of the various earplugs. What materials do they use to make their earplugs? Is any one material better than another? What is the most widely used brand of earplugs? (A teacher can assign this question as homework or as another expansion activity for the class to investigate.)

PHYSICAL SCIENCE

*Science as Inquiry*

- At a track meet, why do you think you see the spark and smoke from the starter's gun before you hear the sound made by the gun? Can you explain this phenomenon in terms of sound waves?
- If someone in the room was speaking to you and you could detect only faint, muffled sounds, what might be the probable cause for your loss of hearing? How is sound supposed to travel from your ear canal to your brain?

*History and Nature of Science*

- What do you think would happen to you if you had a job working at an airport loading cargo onto planes and you did not wear protective headphones?
- Would a piano tuner need to be aware of compression and rarefaction of sound waves? How could he or she apply this knowledge in his or her work?
- Interview a local audiologist. What does his or her job entail? What kind of knowledge is needed to perform the job? Ask if he or she could share with you any cases where a person's job affected his or her hearing. Share the interview with the class.

**4. EVALUATION:** How will the students show what they have learned?

Upon completing the activities the students will be able to:

- identify areas of rarefaction and compression on a diagram of sound waves;
- trace the path of the sound waves from their source through the ear when given a worksheet with a diagram of the ear. The students should be able to label the ear canal, eardrum, bones of the middle ear, and nerve to the brain.

## Sound Production

**GRADE
5–8
DISCIPLINE
Physical
Science**

**Concept to be invented**
Main idea—Sounds are produced by vibrations.

**Concepts that are important to expansion**
A vibrating object has an energy source. Moving energy is referred to as *kinetic*. Vibrations that cause sound can be produced by hitting, plucking, stroking, or blowing an object.

**Materials needed**
*For each student group:*

| | |
|---|---|
| pencil | one balloon |
| paper | small piece of mirror |
| percussion instruments | one flashlight |
| one soup can with both ends cut out | chalkboard |

➡ **Safety precautions:** Remind the students to exercise caution when making sounds with the instruments. They should be reminded not to hold them up to a friend's or their own ear when the sound is loud or piercing. During the expansion activity they must use care when handling the mirrors, and watch for sharp edges on the cans as well.

1. EXPLORATION: Which process skills will be used?

> Observing, recording data, predicting, hypothesizing, experimenting

What will the students do?

*Noise and Sound Identification*

> *Activity 1.* Ask the students to close their eyes, sit perfectly still, and not speak. Tell them to listen carefully to all the noises they can hear, even the slightest sounds that they normally ignore. After a few minutes ask them to open their eyes and write descriptions of every noise they heard and, if possible, identify what they believe is the source of those sounds. Students should describe noises in terms ordinarily used for sounds, such as high, low, loud, soft, hissing, rumbling, piercing, musical.
>
> *Activity 2.* Tell the students that they are going to play a listening game. Ask the students to close their eyes while the teacher makes a sound and then try to guess what the sound was. The first one to guess what the sound was will make the next sound. Make sure everyone gets a turn.
>
> *Activity 3.* Present various percussion instruments to the class, such as drums of various sizes, cymbals, pots, pot lids, and xylophones (toy ones will work as well). Ask the students to guess how you can get each one to produce a sound. Ask the students to predict what causes each one to make a sound. Allow the students to experiment with the various instruments, asking them to take note of how sound is produced on each instrument. Ask the students to describe what it feels like. After students have done this, have them strike the instrument again and then hold it tightly. Ask them if the sound stopped. Why did it stop?

2. EXPLANATION/CONCEPT INVENTION: What is the main idea? How will the main idea be constructed?

> *Concept:* Sounds are produced by vibrations.
>
> *Activity 1.* Ask the students to go back to the first list they made. Make two columns on the board, one labeled *descriptive words* and the other *sound sources*. Ask the students to help fill in the chart from the lists they created. The class will be referring back to this list after they discuss the other two activities.
>
> *Activity 2.* Ask each student: What type of sound did you make for everyone to guess? How was the sound made? What energy source did you use to make it? Add these sounds to the list on the board already; include a third column, *how made*, to the chart.

*Activity 3.* When you hit your instrument, what did you set up? How did you get the sound to stop on your percussion instrument? Go over the list on the board and stress that sound is a type of energy. To make sound, one form of energy is changed to another form of energy. Energy causes movement. Sounds can be produced by hitting, plucking, stroking, and blowing. All of these actions use energy to create vibrations. Vibrations are the source of sound.

### 3. EXPANSION OF THE IDEA: Which process skills will be used?

Experimenting, predicting, inferring

How will the idea be expanded?

*Sound Movement*   Divide the class into groups. Have each group stretch a piece cut from a balloon over one end of a soup can, using a rubber band to hold it tightly in place. Glue a small piece of mirror slightly off center. Darken the classroom, and hold the can at an angle to the blackboard. Using a flashlight, shine the beam so that it strikes the mirror and reflects on the board. Ask the group to predict what will happen to the mirror's reflection on the board as someone speaks into the open end of the can. Ask someone in the group to talk into the open end of the can. Ask the other members of the group to take note of what happens to the mirror's reflection as the person speaks into the can. Do your observations match your predictions? What do you think causes the changes in the reflection? What source of energy causes the balloon to vibrate?

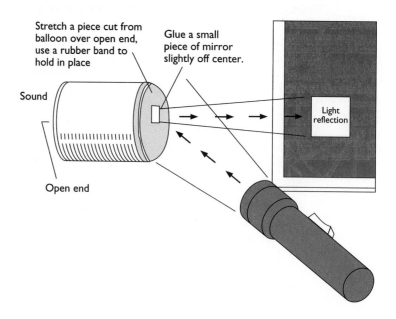

Stretch a piece cut from balloon over open end, use a rubber band to hold in place

Glue a small piece of mirror slightly off center.

Sound

Light reflection

Open end

*Sound Game:*
*"What Is Sound?"*

## Home assignment

This assignment may be done alone or with other family members.

1. Go home and sit down in your bedroom or the room of your choice, close your eyes, and be very quiet for 3 minutes. Listen carefully. Do you hear anything? Write down the sounds you hear and describe them.
2. If you have heard new sounds, what are they, and why do you think you haven't heard them before?
3. How did the quiet make you feel? (To show how the quiet made you feel, you may write a descriptive paragraph, write a poem, or draw a picture.)

## "How well can you match sounds?"

Students will construct a game for younger students. After the students have made the game, they will take it to a primary class and supervise the younger students playing it.

## Materials needed

At least twelve 6-ounce unmarked metal cans, small objects (materials used in cans to make noises could include dried rice, beans, peas, marbles, BBs, gravel, sand, bits of Styrofoam, puffed rice, or any other small objects found around the house), tape.

*Preparation:*

Place small objects in a pair of cans and then seal the cans with tape. Be sure children cannot see in the cans and that the cans are prepared in pairs with approximately the same amount of material in each set of cans.

*Procedure:*

1. Shake the cans and listen to the noise they make.
2. Can you hear the different sounds they make?
3. Do any of the cans make the same sound?
4. If you find cans that sound alike, put them next to each other.
5. Have a friend listen to the cans and see if he or she agrees.
6. You may want to make more cans with different sounds to see how well your friends can tell the difference.

## *Science in Personal and Social Perspectives*

- What would your life be like without sound?
- What are some sounds that you hear around you and how are they made?
- How have people made use of their knowledge that a vibrating body will produce a sound? What types of signals have we created because of this? (Fire alarms, smoke detectors, burglar alarms, fog horns.)
- When you wake up in the middle of the night and hear creaking bed springs or creaking stairs, knowing what you now know about sound, how could you explain away any fears that you might have?

*Science and Technology*

- How do vibrating strings allow us to create a violin, a guitar, or a bass fiddle? Why is it that some of the sounds created by these instruments sound soothing to some, while others may think of them as simply obnoxious noise?
- How do we record and transmit the sounds we make or the sounds that are made around us? Choose something that records sound or something that sound is recorded on. Draw a diagram explaining how it works.

*Science as Inquiry*

- Explain how it is possible to create a percussion instrument. Make one and describe how it works. Use terms like *vibration* and *energy* in your explanation.
- Why do you think you enjoy certain types of music? Survey people of different ages as to their choices in music. Create a pie chart or bar graph to describe your results. Would you have predicted these results?

*History and Nature of Science*

- Why do you think it is important that a car mechanic is able to distinguish one sound from another? How does his or her job depend on recognizing engine sounds?
- Do you think Beethoven was able to continue his musical career after he became deaf? Do you think it is possible for deaf people to "feel" sounds?
- What other occupations can you think of in which reliance on sound is essential?

**4. EVALUATION:** How will the students show what they have learned?

Upon completing these activities the students will be able to:

- describe sources of sound, explaining how a vibration is set up and the energy source for that vibration;
- report on their home assignment "What Is Sound?" and share with the class their poems, paragraphs, or drawings about the sounds they observed;
- work successfully with the younger students when they play the "What Is Sound?" game they made, helping the younger students invent the concept of vibration.

## Characteristics of Matter

GRADE
3–4
DISCIPLINE
Physical
Science

**Concept to be invented**

Main idea—Anything that occupies space and has mass is called *matter*. Matter can be found in a solid, liquid, or gaseous state.

**Concepts that are important to expansion**

Physical versus chemical change, solutions versus mixtures, chemical symbols, chemical formulas, matter can be neither created nor destroyed

**Materials needed**

*For exploration (per student group):*

two Ziploc plastic bags (label one A and the other B); 1 teaspoon sodium bicarbonate (place in bag A and seal closed); 1 teaspoon calcium chloride, sold as ice melter during winter months (place in bag B and seal closed); magnifying glass; small medicine cups with 10 ml of water in each; 5–10 drops of bromothymol blue (number of drops may vary due to the alkalinity of local water supplies; when it is placed in the water, make sure the water stays blue); wood splint; matches

*For expansion:*

three clear cups or plastic beakers, marbles, sand, water, graduated cylinder, and weighing scale

**Safety precautions:** Remind students that safety goggles must be worn at all times. Since this is a guided discovery lesson, they are to listen to the teacher at all times before they begin to manipulate the materials—this is for their safety! Tell students not to taste anything during these activities.

Advanced organizer used to set the stage for this guided discovery activity: Which process skills will be used?

Observing, analyzing, inferring, hypothesizing

What will the teacher and students do?

The teacher should enter the classroom with a lit candle. Ask the class the following: Why does it burn? What helps it burn? How can I make it go out? Act on student suggestions. Why does the candle go out when I place it under a glass? What is it lacking? Could I try to grow plants under glass? Could animals, like a hamster, live under this glass? Why or why not? Through questioning, the teacher should bring out the idea that a way to test for the presence of oxygen in a gas would be to see if a flame stays lit in the gas. If the flame goes out, that would tell us that a gas like carbon dioxide may be present. (If the students are not already aware of fire safety skills, please review them at this time.)

1. EXPLORATION: Which process skills will be used?

Manipulating materials, collecting and recording data, communicating, observing, hypothesizing, predicting, inferring

What will the students do?

*Plastic Bag Chemistry*

Make and record their observations of two unknown white powders found in bags A and B. Use the magnifying glass to make careful observations of the two unknowns. Draw pictures of unknown white powders. (Stress the importance of keeping bags sealed and not tasting the unknown substances. Encourage the students to make observations about the shape of the unknown white powders).

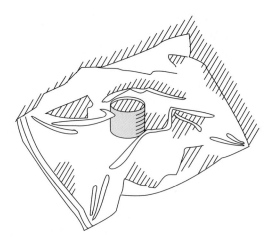

Make observations of the unknown liquid placed before them; record these (work on getting students to realize that the liquid takes the shape of the container).

Introduce the mystery solution and ask students to predict what will happen when the solution is placed in the unknown liquid before them. Have them record the amount of mystery solution that was placed in the unknown liquid and the results of the mixing. (The "mystery solution" is bromothymol blue. Conceal its name on the container and move from group to group asking the students for their predictions of what it is. Then place the 5 to 10 drops of mystery solution in the students' cups.)

Ask the students to open bag A, taking care not to touch or eat the substance, and pour it into bag B. Seal the bag, and record their observations once the two unknown powders are combined together. After they record their observations, ask the students to place the bag on its side and open it. Without mixing the unknown liquid with the unknown powders, place the container with the unknown liquid into the bag and seal it.

Ask the students to design a way in which they can mix the powders with the liquid without actually picking up the bag and shaking it. They should discuss this with the students closest to them. While they design their plan, remind them that they have been provided with a wood splint and some matches (the students should already be aware of appropriate fire safety skills). Ask the students to recall the previous candle demonstration. Do you think a gas will be given off when you mix the unknown powders with the liquid? How will you know? What can you do to determine which gas it is? Encourage the students to incorporate these suggestions into their experimental design.

After sufficient time has been allowed for the students to design their experiment, have them act on their plans. Record their observations. Encourage

them to observe the bags with the magnifying glasses, make some careful observations (not only looking at the bag but also holding it to feel for any changes
in temperature and using the burning wood splint to check for evolution of a
gas—remember we observe with all of our senses), perhaps even drawing what
they see.

## 2. EXPLANATION/CONCEPT INVENTION: What is the main idea? How will the main idea be constructed?

*Concept:* Anything that occupies space and has mass is called *matter.*

By working with the unknown white powders, students can make observations in which they realize that the unknown substances are in a *solid* state of
matter. By observing the unknown *liquid* and the mystery solution, also in a
*liquid* state, they can see they are using another state of matter. Upon mixing
the *solid* with a *liquid,* they can see the bag expanding, thus observing the third
state of matter, a *gas.* Careful use of questions will also get the students to realize that *solids* always retain their shape, no matter the container. *Liquids* take
up the shape of the container, and a *gas* will take up as much space as you
give it.

Ask the students the following questions to help get to the ideas stated
above: You drew pictures of the unknown white powders in bag A and in bag
B. When you mixed them together, did they change their shape? (Work on the
children's understanding of the concept of a solid, which does not change in
shape. Physical change can be observed if they crush the solids; what was created is a *heterogeneous mixture*—a combination of two or more substances each
distinct from the other.) If so, how or why? What shape was the liquid in when
it was inside the cup? What about when you poured it out? Why? What happened to the liquid when the mystery solution was added? Could you tell
where one liquid began and the other ended? (Work on the concept of liquids
taking the shape of their container and only within the limit of the volume that
the sample occupies. Also work on developing the concept of a solution). What
happened when you mixed the solids with the liquids? What did you observe?
(Listing all of their observations will allow you to expand on specific secondary
concepts you want the students to understand, such as physical versus chemical change, heat of reaction, acid formation.) Why did your bag get bigger?
How did you find out what gas evolved? If you used a bigger plastic bag,
would it be blown all the way up, too? Why? (Work on the concept of a gas taking the shape of its container.)

If you are interested, use this activity to introduce the students to chemical
nomenclature. Provide students with the chemical formulas for the unknowns
involved in the activity (older students may help derive these formulas and
help balance the equation).

PHYSICAL SCIENCE

$$CaCl_2 + NaHCO_3 + H_2O + \text{bromothymol blue}$$
$$\rightarrow NaCl(aq) + HCl(aq) + CaCO_3 + H_2O$$
$$CaCO_3 + H_2O \rightarrow H_2CO_3 + CaO$$
$$H_2CO_3 \rightarrow H^+ + HCO^-_3 \rightarrow CO_2(g) + H_2O$$

### 3. EXPANSION OF THE IDEA: Which process skills will be used?

Measuring, predicting, hypothesizing, observing, recording data

How will the idea be expanded?

*Marble Matter*      Provide each student group with three clear cups or plastic beakers, marbles, sand, and some water. Ask the students to weigh a cup, then fill the cup with marbles. Record their weight and number of marbles. Ask them questions such as the following: How many marbles did you put in the cup? Do you think you can put in any more marbles? Did the marbles take the shape of the cup? (Work here to make sure they understand that the marbles did not change their shape.) What was the weight of the cup? What state of matter are the marbles?

Ask the students to weigh another cup. Fill the cup with sand and then weigh it. Have them place a mark on the cup indicating the top of the sand. Use the same line of questioning as for the marbles.

Now ask the students if they think both cups are full. Ask the students if they think they can pour any of the sand into the cup filled with marbles. Solicit

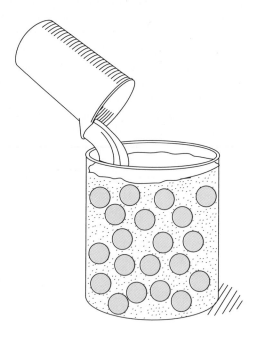

responses. React to responses: I thought you told me the cup with the marbles in it was full; how can you possibly put anything else into this cup?

Have the students pour some sand into the cup of marbles. Mark the new level of sand on the sand cup. What happens? Were you able to add sand into an already-filled cup of marbles? Why? What is the weight of your new mixture? What is the weight of the sand remaining in the cup? Subtract this remaining weight of sand from the original weight of sand. How much sand did you lose? Subtract the original weight of the marbles from the new weight of the marble and sand mixture. Is this amount gained equal to the amount lost from the sand cup? (Reinforce the concept of matter—anything that occupies space and has mass; concept of states of matter—two different solids. Secondary concept—physical change, matter was not created or destroyed, it still has the same weight; nothing was lost, just placed in different containers.)

Weigh a third cup and fill it with water. Weigh this. Ask the students if they think it is possible to put water into an already-filled cup of sand and marbles. Why? Why not? What state of matter is the water? What do you know about liquids? (For older students, instead of weighing the water in a cup, introduce them to a graduated cylinder; have them measure out so many milliliters of water and record the volume of water in milliliters that they pour into the marble-sand cup.)

Was your prediction true? What happened when you tried to add water to the marble-sand cup? Why could the container that was already filled with marbles still hold more sand and water?

Do you think we could have started with the water, then the sand and marbles? Why? What does this tell you about the sizes of molecules of different materials or substances? (The concept of solids versus liquids leads into a discussion of the size of particles. Smaller-size particles can slip between the larger ones. Make an analogy to molecules. Introduction of this new term may lead into a new unit on atoms and molecules.)

### Science in Personal and Social Perspectives

- Which would you rather take a bath in: water mixed with sand or water mixed with bath bubble beads? Why?
- What would happen if you burned a dollar bill? Could you tape it back together and still have a dollar?

### Science and Technology

- How has knowledge of chemical changes allowed the food industry to create cake mixes that can be made in a microwave rather than a regular oven?
- Getting matter to change its shape has allowed us to create many large buildings, like the Sears Tower in Chicago. How is this so?

### Science as Inquiry

- The students engage in manipulative skills during the activities.
- For understanding the concept of physical versus chemical change, ask the students to explain why they can heat snow and get water, or why they can

mix flour, water, baking soda, and sugar together, heat the mixture, and taste not these separate ingredients but a cake.

• Why can't you put a round peg in a square hole?

*History and Nature of Science*

• Using a list of all of the concepts discovered in the activities, ask the students to survey their parents and other adults to see if they make use of any of these concepts in their work. Where do they see them utilized? Are these people in typical scientific careers? Can anyone use these science concepts?

• Early scientists called *alchemists* thought they could turn simple elements into gold. Did everyone believe them at that time? Why or why not? Do you believe them? Why or why not?

**4. EVALUATION:** How will the students show what they have learned?

Upon completing the activities the students will be able to:

• demonstrate a physical change and then a chemical change when given a piece of paper;
• provide examples of solid matter, liquid matter, and gas;
• demonstrate how to capture a gas;
• name five chemical elements;
• name and write the chemical symbols for five elements (intermediate grades). Primary grades should be able to state simple chemical symbols such as hydrogen and oxygen.

## Physical Properties of Matter

**GRADE**
**K–4**
**DISCIPLINE**
**Physical**
**Science**

**Concept to be invented**
Main idea—Physical properties of matter help distinguish one kind of matter from another.

**Concepts important to exploration and expansion**
A cooked egg will spin freely, whereas a raw egg will be difficult to spin. It will have a slight wobble as it spins. The term *best* is arbitrary; members of a group must decide criteria for judging an object the best.

**Materials needed**
*For exploration:*
Hard-boil enough white eggs for half the class. Place randomly in a bowl the cooked eggs and an equal number of raw eggs. Allow each student to pick an egg out of the bowl.

one can of broth or any canned
   liquid
paper towels

one can of dog food
clear container/bowl

*For expansion:*
three or four different brands of chocolate chip cookies, paper towels

*For each student group:*
one ruler
five to ten toothpicks

paper for recording data

➨ **Safety precautions:** Remind students that although you encourage them to make as many observations as possible, they should never taste anything without your permission. Discourage the students from licking the eggshells. Remind them to wash their hands after the exploration activity, especially before they begin the expansion activity.

### 1. EXPLORATION: Which process skills will be used?

Observing, manipulating materials, collecting and recording data, communicating

#### What will the students do?

*Egg-citing Observations*

Enter the classroom carrying the bowl of eggs and acting as if you are greatly troubled. Explain to the students that you boiled some eggs last night for a dinner party and placed them in the refrigerator. When you went into the refrigerator this morning, you found that someone took the cooked eggs and combined them with the raw eggs in this bowl. Now you have to determine which are cooked and which are raw without breaking any of them. Ask the students if they can help you solve your problem.

Ask each student to choose an egg from the bowl. Ask them to make as many observations about their egg as possible. Remind them not to break the egg! Allow sufficient time for the students to collect their data. Encourage them to record their observations. For very young students, ask them to draw their observations. Once they have made their observations, move to the concept invention phase of this lesson.

### 2. EXPLANATION/CONCEPT INVENTION: What is the main idea? How will the main idea be constructed?

*Concept:* Physical properties of matter help distinguish one kind of matter from another.

As the students are making their observations, move among them, encouraging those students who appear to be stumped to think of ways in which observations can be made. Ask questions like: When I make an observation, am I

using only my eyes? What other things can I use to make an observation? Encourage the students to think about ways they can manipulate the egg without dropping or breaking it. Remind the students to record the information they are discovering.

Once the students have made their observations, solicit them from the class. Make a list on the board. Once you have received an observation from each of the students, go back to your original question and ask the students: Now, which of these observations will help me solve my problem? Ask a student to restate the problem (which eggs are raw and which are cooked).

Through the process of elimination, the students will find that some physical properties are more distinguishing than others. For instance, simply observing that the egg is white is not going to help solve the problem, since all of the students have white eggs. However, an observation that "it sounds as if something is moving inside when I shake my egg" or that "my egg will spin or stand on end" are observations that will help solve the problem. Ask the students: Is one distinguishing characteristic enough to decide if an egg is cooked or raw? If some students think so, then ask them to make their prediction about whether their egg is cooked or raw based on that one distinguishing characteristic. Let one student crack an egg only to find that the prediction was incorrect. (Make sure that the student chosen to bring out the idea that one characteristic is not enough has in fact made a wrong decision.)

As you progress through the list of student observations, keep referring back to the original problem. As you narrow down their observations to those that help solve the problem, you may find that the students eventually come to an observation that stumps them: Some eggs spin easily and other sort of wobble but don't spin well. The students aren't sure if it is the raw or cooked eggs that spin easily. At this point the teacher should bring out the cans of broth and dog food. (Two cans of each may be helpful.) Open the can of broth and pour it into a clear container. Ask the students what state of matter the broth is in.

Now ask for a student volunteer to try to spin the unopened can of broth. Ask the student if it is easy or hard to get the can to spin.

Now open a can of dog food. Empty that into a clear container. Ask the students what state of matter the dog food is in. Now ask for a student volunteer to try to spin the unopened can of dog food. Ask the student if it is easy or hard to get the can to spin.

Ask the class to determine if the broth is similar to a raw or cooked egg. What about the dog food? Once they have decided that the raw egg is similar to the broth and the cooked egg is similar to the dog food, ask them to tell you how you can determine if an egg is cooked or raw. Encourage them to list all the criteria that helped them come to their conclusions. The students should conclude that the cooked eggs will spin freely and the raw eggs will wobble like the broth can when spun. Through careful observation you can sense movement in raw eggs when you shake them.

## 3. EXPANSION OF THE IDEA: Which process skills will be used?

Designing an experiment, observing, measuring, predicting, hypothesizing, recording data

How will the idea be expanded?

*Chocolate Chip Exploration*

This expansion activity is more appropriate for students in grades 3–6. For K–2 students, you may want to lead a guided discovery activity using the following ideas:

Remind the students about the concept learned from the exploration activity: Physical properties of matter help distinguish one kind of matter from another. Explain to the students that you would like them to design an experiment using just physical properties to determine which brand of chocolate chip cookies is the best. Allow sufficient class time for groups of students to brainstorm ways in which they could use only physical properties to determine the best brand of chocolate chip cookies. Ask the students to submit a copy of their planned experiment and a materials list to you so that they can perform their experiment in the next class meeting. Suggested materials are included in the materials list at the beginning of the lesson. Be sure to read over the designed experiments to be sure that they are using only physical properties and also that appropriate safety standards are maintained.

On the second day, allow the students to act on appropriately planned lessons. On the third day, ask the different student groups to share the methods they used for determining the *best* cookie and the results of their experiment. Once all of the groups have had a chance to share their results, and especially if the results were different, ask the students if it is necessary to set some criteria for determining which cookie is *best*. The students should conclude that the term *best* is arbitrary—the members of the group must decide criteria for judging an object the *best*.

As a final discussion question, ask the students why you asked them to design their experiment around physical properties. Why could they not taste the cookie to determine the best?

### Science in Personal and Social Perspectives

- If you had to describe your best friend to another student, how would you do that? Would a description such as, "He or she is really nice and cute," be enough? Why or why not?
- If you were talking with a group of people about the best movie you ever saw, do you think everyone in the group would agree with you? Why or why not?

### Science and Technology

- How does the mineral industry determine which mineral is which?
- Why has the auto industry gone from metal bumpers to plastic bumpers? What do properties of matter have to do with this decision?

### Science as Inquiry

- Students engage in manipulative skills during the activities.
- How can you accurately describe an object?
- How can you tell the difference between a raw and cooked egg without cracking the egg open?

### History and Nature of Science

- Pretend you want a new sidewalk in front of your house. You need to hire a cement contractor to do the work. One contractor you interviewed said it didn't matter what kind of material he or she used to pour your sidewalk. Does this person know much about distinguishing physical properties of matter? Would you be willing to hire that contractor? Why or why not?
- Who do you think should be aware of the many different physical properties of matter for their work? What kind of skills are needed for that profession? Have the necessary skills changed in the past twenty years?

**4. EVALUATION:** How will the students show what they have learned?

Upon completing the activities the students will be able to:

- determine, when given an egg, whether it is cooked or raw;
- design an experiment to determine the best brand of paper towels;

*(side margin)* PHYSICAL SCIENCE

- list the physical properties of three or four different things (the teacher can choose any number of items to set before the student: a rock, flower, penny, button, or anything else will work).

## Changing Matter

### Concepts to be invented

Main idea—An alteration of the composition or the properties of matter is called a *chemical change*. An alteration of the shape of matter without a change in its chemical composition is called a *physical change*.

### Concepts that are important to expansion

Small, single units of matter are called *monomers*. A substance that will speed up a chemical reaction without being affected itself is called a *catalyst*. A bond linking the chains of atoms in a polymer is a *cross-linker*. A compound formed by adding many small molecules together in the presence of a catalyst or by the condensation of many smaller molecules through the elimination of water or alcohol is a *polymer*.

### Materials needed

*Per student:*

one piece of scrap paper                         one stirring rod or Popsicle stick
one clear cup                                    one lunch-size Ziploc bag
matches

*For entire class:*

one aluminum pie pan                             borate solution (50 g borax
three large containers of glue (enough             with 100 ml of water)
  to give each student 30 ml)          beaker or graduated cylinder for
food coloring                                      measurements
liquid starch                                    paper towels for cleanup

*The following items are used to introduce the problem:*

Teflon frying pan                                football helmet
compact disc                                     pair of nylons
plastic baby bottle

**Safety precautions and/or procedures:** During the exploration phase, when the paper is burned, the teacher should make sure there is adequate ventilation in the classroom. The teacher should also be sure the matches are kept away from the students and use care when an open flame is present: sleeves must be pushed up, hair pulled back, and eyes protected. During the expansion phase,

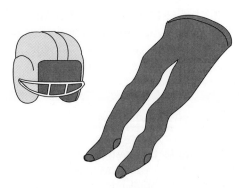

the students should be discouraged from putting their hands in their mouths. Be sure they wash their hands as soon as they are finished with the activity.

1. **EXPLORATION:** Which process skills will be used?

Observing, predicting, inferring

What will the students do?

*Physical and Chemical Paper Change*

*Introduction:* The teacher will allow the children to examine the following items: compact discs, baby bottles, Teflon pan, nylons, and a football helmet. As the students view the items, tell the students that you would like them to think about each item, and that by the time they finish the activities, they should be able to tell you what all the items have in common.

*Student Activity:* Give each student a piece of paper. Ask each of them to make it look different in some way. Then ask each to share what they did to make it look different.

2. **EXPLANATION/CONCEPT INVENTION:** What is the main idea? How will the main idea be constructed?

*Concept:* An alteration of the composition or the properties of matter is called a *chemical change*. An alteration of the shape of matter without changing its chemical composition is called a *physical change*.

Ask such questions as: What did you do to make the paper look different? If they tore it up, ask, "If I taped it back together, would I still have a piece of paper? By changing its shape, did I do anything to change the molecules that came together to make that piece of paper?" Be sure to allow the students to share their comments with one another. Explain that a change in shape with no loss of molecules is called a *physical change*.

If students suggest burning the paper, ask if they think they will still be able to use the paper once you change it by burning it. Then burn it over the

PHYSICAL SCIENCE

aluminum pie pan. Is the paper still in a usable form? Why not? Explain that the paper underwent a *chemical change*. When it burned, carbon atoms were lost.

## 3. EXPANSION OF THE IDEA: Which process skills will be used?

Observing, measuring, recording data, predicting, inferring

How will the idea be expanded?

*Polymer-Rubber Balls*

Do all chemical changes result in the creation of useless matter? Think about that question while you try the following activity. Ask the students to use the graduated cylinders to measure out 30 ml of glue. Pour it into the clear cup. Choose a color from the food coloring and mix it with your glue (use Popsicle sticks for stirring). Do you still have glue in front of you? What kind of change did the glue undergo?

What do you think will happen if you mix the colored glue with the liquid you have in front of you? (The teacher should place in front of half of the class the liquid starch, in front of the other half a borate solution). Please make some predictions, and share them with one another on each side of the room. What do you think will happen when you mix the glue with the unknown liquid in front of you? Make your predictions and record them.

Ask the students to measure out 30 ml of either the starch or the borate solution. Encourage the students to make predictions about how much of the solution they will need to bring about a change in the glue. Since they do not know for certain how much starch or borate solution they will need, encourage the students to add one of these slowly, stirring all the time, until they see a change. Record how much starch or borate solution was necessary to bring about a change in the glue. Record any new observations you may have made about the colored glue.

Did you create anything new, or can you still tell the glue from the starch or borate solution? Can you pick up this new piece of matter? (Encourage the students to do so—the more they manipulate it in their hands, the more the water will come out, and eventually they will have created their own rubber ball.) What do you think you can do with it? What kind of change do you think you created by combining the glue with the starch or the borate solution? Why do you say this?

Go back to the original question: Do all chemical changes result in the creation of useless matter? How many of you think you created a new form of matter that is useful? What did you do differently from your classmates? What do you think you can do with your newly created piece of matter? How useful is it? As a teacher, you may encourage the students from the different sides of the room to compare their newly created rubber balls. Do they bounce the same? Roll the same? Feel the same? Here, two different catalysts were used to create this special kind of chemical change called a *polymerization reaction*. After they

PHYSICAL SCIENCE

PHYSICAL SCIENCE

finish, the students may place their balls in a Ziploc bag, where they will stay fresh for a few weeks.

Do you think that other inventions could have been discovered just by people mixing things together in the lab and making careful observations about how much and of what materials they mixed together?

Teflon, used to coat pans, is one of these accidental chemical combinations that was discovered in a lab when scientists weren't looking for it. Chemists realized that it was possible to get small pieces of matter to link up chemically when a catalyst was used to force the reaction to occur. Sometimes these smaller pieces of matter, called *monomers*, add together in one long chain to create *polymers*. Saran wrap, Lucite, Plexiglas, and Teflon are polymers formed by this additive process. Polymers can also be formed by bringing monomers together, removing water or alcohol through a condensation reaction, and forcing the monomers to link together. This is what happened to form nylon, and this is what happened here to create a new form of matter—rubber balls! In addition to these synthetic polymers, silk, cellulose, and rubber are naturally occurring polymers.

Go back to some of the first items shown to the students: the football helmet, the baby bottle, the CD, the nylons, and the Teflon pan. Encourage the students to think about the activities they just participated in as they try to answer the very first question you asked: What do all of these things have in common?

They were all created by a chemical change in which small pieces of matter, called monomers, were linked together to form polymers. These polymer reactions created new kinds of matter that have proven to be very useful.

### Science in Personal and Social Perspectives

- You're tired of the color of your bedroom, and you want to change the color of your walls. Will your room undergo a physical or chemical change?
- Can you name any products created because of a polymerization reaction that have directly affected your life?
- There is much controversy over the use of Teflon bullets. Police unions bitterly oppose their use. Why do you think this product, formed from a polymerization reaction, is of serious concern to our society?
- Knowledge of chemical changes has led to the invention of many products that have greatly changed society. Can you think of any products that were created as the result of a chemical change?

### Science and Technology

- A technological advancement for many parents is the disposable diaper. Describe the materials used to make a disposable diaper. How has this technological advancement created more problems for society? Suggest possible solutions.

### Science as Inquiry

- Can you demonstrate the difference between a physical and a chemical change?

- Explain how a polymer can be created. How is this a unique type of chemical change?
- Can you name some monomers or polymers that are found in nature? How about some synthetic ones?

*History and Nature of Science*

- Do you think a cement finisher or a beautician needs to understand how a chemical change can occur? Why or why not?
- Are physical or chemical changes common in the type of work your parents do? Identify one of the changes, and explain where it occurs.
- Interview a female over age sixty. Ask her to describe what nylon stockings were like when she was twenty. How and why did they change?

**4. EVALUATION:** How will the students show what they have learned?

Upon completion of the activities the students will be able to:

- appreciate the need to think about a problem first, and then use clear, concise language to communicate the action taken on the problem;
- demonstrate the differences between physical and chemical changes;
- make predictions based on previous experiences;
- utilize the scientific method to solve a newly designed problem;
- explain how certain chemical reactions, such as polymer formation, can result in the creation of useful materials;
- explain what a football helmet, a compact disc, a Teflon pan, a baby bottle, and a pair of nylons have in common.

PHYSICAL SCIENCE

## Identification of an Unknown

GRADE
5–8
DISCIPLINE
Physical
Science

### Concept to be invented
Main idea—Physical properties alone are not always sufficient characteristics to identify an unknown.

### Concepts that are important to expansion
*Indicators* are used to bring about a physical or chemical change in an unknown. Common indicators are iodine, vinegar, and heat.

### Materials needed
*For exploration (for class of 24):*
The following items make up the secret powders: 4 pounds of granulated sugar, two boxes of table salt, 4 pounds of baking soda, 4 pounds of cornstarch, 4 pounds of plaster of Paris.

The following items are necessary for all parts of the lesson: twenty plastic spoons, one box of toothpicks, ten eyedroppers, twenty small cups or containers.

Some optional materials are newspapers, paper towels, broom and dust pan, black construction paper, hand lenses or microscopes.

*For expansion (for class of 24):*
To perform indicator tests the following items are necessary: 1 quart of vinegar, one roll of aluminum foil, 1 ounce of tincture of iodine, crackers, potatoes, one bucket of water or a water source in room, birthday candles (one per student group), small lumps of clay (one per student group), wooden clothespins (one per student group).

➡ **Safety precautions:** Never taste any of the unknown substances unless given teacher permission. Goggles must be worn at all times! Wash hands between testing different unknowns and immediately after the lab is completed. Remove all combustible material from the area of the flame during the heat tests during expansion. Roll up sleeves and tie back hair when using an open flame.

**1. EXPLORATION:** Which process skills will be used?

Observing, manipulating materials, inferring, collecting and recording data, communicating

What will the students do?

*Physical Properties of an Unknown*

Start off the lesson by asking the students the following: Have you ever thought about some of the common substances we use in our homes? For instance, how many of you can name some common white powder substances we may use in our homes? (List these on the board. If the ones used as secret powders are not suggested, make suggestions that will help the students think about those possibilities.) What are they used for? How do we know that what it says on the container is really what is inside? The following activity will provide you with skills to help identify unknown substances.

Provide each student group five small cups numbered 1–5 and containing five different secret powders. The students will also receive five toothpicks to use as stirring sticks, some black construction paper to dump their powders on, and a hand lens. Ask the students to try to determine what the unknowns

are, based on their observations of physical characteristics. The following questions should serve as a guide to encourage the students to focus on physical properties: How are the powders alike? How are they different? Do they feel the same? Does any powder have an odor? Are they the same shade of white? Can you list three properties of each powder? Can you list more than three? Using the hand lens, can you discover anything new about the powders? Are all the powders really powders? Can you describe the particles that make up each powder? Do you think a powder can be identified by the shape of its particles? Describe which properties of the powders seem to be the same and which seem to be different. Which properties are helpful in describing a particular powder?

## 2. EXPLANATION/CONCEPT INVENTION: What is the main idea? How will the main idea be constructed?

*Concept:* Physical properties alone are not always sufficient characteristics to identify an unknown.

Ask the students to share answers to questions asked during the exploration phase. Refer back to the original list of common white powders from home. Ask the students to match up the unknowns to knowns based on physical characteristics they observed. Salt and sugar are made of cube-shaped particles, but salt is much more uniform and less broken. Cornstarch, baking soda, and plaster of Paris are similar in appearance, and it is hard to distinguish one from another simply on the basis of physical characteristics.

## 3. EXPANSION OF THE IDEA: Which process skills will be used?

Designing an experiment, observing, measuring, predicting, hypothesizing, recording data, evaluating, controlling variables, interpreting data, reducing experimental error

How will the idea be expanded?

*Chemical Properties of an Unknown*

*Discussion before the activity:* Ask students if they know why canaries were used in coal mines years ago, or what good it is to know the pH of pool water, or why a gas gauge in a car is useful. Once you obtain answers to these questions, ask what these three questions have in common. Work at getting to the idea that all of these are indicators of some sort: Canaries indicate the quality of the air, pH indicates the acidity or alkalinity of water, and a gas gauge indicates the amount of gas in the car.

Indicators can be used to conduct tests on the secret powders to assist in a more accurate determination of the unknown. These indicators may bring about a physical or chemical change in the secret powder. (Be sure the students already know the difference between a physical change—one in which a change of shape can occur, but the chemical composition of the original material is not altered, such as freezing of water or shredding paper—and a chemical change—a change in the composition of the original material in which molecules are lost and cannot be put back into the material to return it to its original composition, such as burning sugar or mixing vinegar and baking soda.)

During a discussion of the indicators, ask the students the following, to see if they can determine how the indicators can be used in determining the identity of the secret powders: What do you think might happen when water (or iodine, vinegar, or heat added) is mixed with the secret powder? How might you go about doing this without contaminating your secret powder sample? Why is it important to avoid contamination?

*Action:* Observe the reactions of the five secret powders when acted on by the water, iodine, vinegar, and heat. Reaffirm the notion of contamination at this point. Have the students use separate eye droppers for the water, iodine, and vinegar. Be sure they use different toothpicks and clean containers to mix the unknown with the indicator. The students should record their results.

*Water:* What happens to each powder when you put a few drops of water on it? Did each powder mix with the water? Did any of the powders disappear? Did you put the same amount of powder in each cup? Is this important? What will happen if you add twenty drops of water? Fifty? Eighty? Does additional water affect the powders? Did any powders disappear? Where did they go? Did the powder leave the cup?

As students work with the water, they will discover that sugar, baking soda, and salt are soluble in water. By comparing the number of drops needed to dissolve these powders, some students may conclude that sugar is more soluble in water than baking soda and that salt is the least soluble of the three. Both cornstarch and plaster of Paris are insoluble in water. Plaster of Paris will harden if permitted to stand for a short period of time. After hardening, plaster of Paris cannot be changed back into its original state. The concepts of solubility and evaporation, as well as the differences among solution, suspension, and mixture, can be highlighted through this portion of the activity if necessary.

*Iodine:* Place small amounts of secret powders in five separate cups. Add a few drops of iodine. Do all the powders react to iodine in the same way? How can iodine be used to distinguish one powder from another? Take a cracker and a piece of potato; how do these react with the iodine? Was this reaction similar to any of the secret powders' reactions? What do the cracker and potato have in common?

The cup containing cornstarch will show a striking blue-black color when iodine is added. A deep blue or blue-black color on contact with iodine is the standard test for the presence of starch. The starchier the food, the more obvious and deep the blue color will be.

*Vinegar:* Place small amounts of secret powders in five separate cups. Add a few drops of vinegar. What happens when you put a few drops of vinegar on each powder? Did any powder react more than others? Do you think that powders that dissolved in water will also dissolve in vinegar? Which powder do you think will take the least amount of vinegar to dissolve? the most? How can you find out? How can vinegar be used to distinguish baking soda from the other powders? If you place vinegar on an unknown substance and it bubbles, can you be sure that the substance is baking soda? Could it be another substance?

Baking powder fizzes actively when vinegar is added, while other powders fizz only slightly or not at all. Other powders can be tested with vinegar. A solution of powdered milk is curdled by vinegar.

*Heat:* Support a small candle in a lump of clay. This will supply sufficient heat to test the effects of heat on the powders. Fashion the aluminum foil into a small dish to be used to heat the secret powders. Use the clothespin as a handle for your aluminum dish when holding the dish over the flame. Be sure to make a separate dish for each powder.

Remove combustible litter from the area where the candle will be used. Roll up loose sleeves and tie back long hair while working with the burning candle. It is extremely important to use dry powder when performing this activity, to prevent spattering. Never use powders that have been mixed with any liquid. Place a small amount of powder in the dish and heat it.

Did any of the powders change when heated? Was an odor given off during heating? Do all the powders look the same after cooling? Compare them with samples of powders that were not heated. Were any new substances formed by heating?

When heated, baking soda and plaster of Paris seem to remain unchanged, while salt snaps and crackles. Starch turns brown and smells like burned toast. Sugar melts, bubbles, smokes, smells like caramel, turns brown, turns black, and finally hardens. The heat test, then, is a good way to detect sugar, since sugar is the only one of the secret powders to melt and turn shiny black when heated. The same reaction occurs to sugar even when it is mixed with any of the other powders.

After using the indicators, ask the students to share their results to help determine the identity of the unknown powders. Which powder turned black when iodine was added? Can you name the powder or powders that are soluble in water? Which liquid added to which powder caused bubbles? How can a hand lens help you to identify a powder? Is a hand lens helpful in identifying all substances?

### Science in Personal and Social Perspectives

- Why is it important for you to wash your hands before you eat any food?
- Has this activity changed your mind on decisions you make about whether you like a certain food? What about decisions on whether you want a certain person as your friend; do you base that choice on looks alone?

### Science and Technology

- Do you think an automobile manufacturer could be competitive if it based a car's performance ability on results from one test? Why or why not?

Encourage interested students to research the performance tests that cars undergo.

- Which properties of coal or oil make them a useful form of energy for our power plants: physical or chemical?

### Science as Inquiry

- Students engage in manipulative skills during the activities.
- You are given one of five powders. When tested with vinegar, it bubbles. Can you identify the powder? Can you be sure of its identity?
- You are given one of the five powders. It dissolves in water. Can you identify the powder? Are additional tests needed? Can you eliminate any powders?

### History and Nature of Science

- Can you think of any jobs in which avoiding contamination of materials is important?
- What care should be taken when mixing unknown substances with known substances? What good is knowing possible reactions? In what careers might this knowledge be necessary?

*Cornstarch:* The cornstarch can be used to demonstrate how dust explosions occur in coal mines or grain elevators. Cornstarch can also be used to explain how bread becomes toast.

*Baking soda:* The reaction of baking soda and vinegar results in the release of carbon dioxide gas. This gas can be used as a fire extinguisher. Most dry-powder extinguishers utilize baking soda; it can also be used to smother fires.

*Plaster of Paris:* This is nothing more than hydrated calcium sulfate. When mixed into a paste with water, it sets quickly and expands. It is because of this property that it is used as a fine casting material.

*Salt:* Salt can be used to lower the freezing point of water; examples are road salts and salt used in ice cream makers.

*Sugar:* Its numerous uses in foods are obvious, but also our knowledge of the chemical composition of sugar and the food calories it provides have led people to discover sweeteners that work like sugar but with fewer calories.

**4. EVALUATION:** How will the students show what they have learned?

Upon completing the activities the students will be able to:

- when given five unknown powders, demonstrate the steps necessary to identify them by using physical properties;
- demonstrate how water, iodine, vinegar, and heat can be used to identify an unknown powder;
- explain the advantages of an indicator test over reliance on merely physical properties to identify an unknown.

# Using the Scientific Method to Solve Problems

**Concepts to be invented**

Main idea—Problems should be thought out before action is taken to solve them. The *scientific method* is a useful tool in problem solving.

**Concepts that are important to expansion**

Matter can be combined in many ways. It can become a mixture, a solution, a suspension, or a colloid.

**Materials needed**

| | |
|---|---|
| 1-liter 7-Up soft drink | 2 pounds cornstarch |
| 1 liter water | Efferdent tablets or Alka-Seltzer |
| 400 ml alcohol (90 percent |   tablets |
|   or higher concentration) | plastic bins or buckets |
| 1 gallon vinegar | paper towels for cleanup |
| 1 pound flour | balloons |

The teacher may also want to obtain any other clear liquids or unknown white powders the students decide to use in the experiments they design.

 **Safety precautions:** Goggles should be worn by teacher and students during all activities.

**Teacher preparation**

*For clear liquid:* Pour about 400 ml of alcohol as close to 100 percent pure as possible into a container. Typical rubbing alcohol is 70 percent; the water content will cause the Efferdent to dissolve slowly. Therefore, 98 percent rubbing alcohol, also available over the counter, will be more effective.

*For white powder:* Add 1 cup of cornstarch to a large container or plastic bin (old dishwashing containers work well). Slowly add water until a gooey consistency is reached. This material will pour or drip slowly but will not splatter when struck with a quick blow. This is a non-Newtonian fluid. Rather than a solution or mixture, it is called a *colloid:* The starch is suspended in the water.

1. EXPLORATION: Which process skills will be used?

Problem solving, communicating, inferring, designing an experiment, recording data, measuring, observing, defining operationally, synthesizing and analyzing information

What will the students do?

*Exploring with Efferdent Tablets*

Ask the students to imagine traveling through space. All of a sudden the spaceship crash-lands. Tell them, "You have no idea where you landed. You do find several objects on the planet. Your hope is that manipulating these objects will give you some clues about the place where you have landed." Show them a container with a clear liquid in it. This is one of the things found at the landing site. Other items found were several packages of Efferdent tablets, used on earth to clean dentures. Ask them what they think will happen if you drop two tablets into the clear liquid. Encourage a variety of predictions. Now drop the tablets into the liquid. Did you predict accurately? What do you think this liquid could be? In a few moments you will be given a chance to experiment to determine what it is and if there is a way to get the Efferdent to dissolve in it.

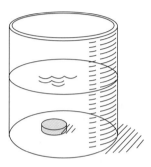

Explain to the students that in addition to the clear liquid and Efferdent tablets, they found some white powder and mixed it with water from their spaceship. Show them the mixture you created. Tell them, "You were trying to figure out what the powder was, especially because it didn't get all gooey like the paste you use at school. Some of you will need to design an experiment to determine what this white powder is."

Now assign the students on one side of the room to solve for one of the unknowns (what the clear liquid is—7-Up or vinegar, for example) and the students on the other side to solve for the other unknown (what the white powder is—flour or baking soda, for example). Encourage use of the scientific method to solve for the unknowns. Use the following guide questions to help plan student experiments: What do you think the problem is? How will you go about solving the problem? What materials do you think you will need? What will you do with those materials to help solve your problem? Do you think it will be important to keep accurate records of the information you collect while doing the experiment you designed?

**2. EXPLANATION/CONCEPT INVENTION:** *What is the main idea? How will the main idea be constructed?*

*Concept:* Problems should be thought out before action is taken to solve them. The *scientific method* is a useful tool in problem solving.

Ask the students to share with you the methods they used to go about solving their problem. Key questions to get them to share are: Do you think it is important to plan before you act? Why? What steps did you use in designing your experiment?

This methodical way of problem solving is called the *scientific method.* The steps to be followed are:

1. State the problem.
2. Generate predictions or hypotheses to help solve the problem.
3. Design an experiment to help solve the problem.
4. Create a list of materials needed to solve the problem.
5. Gather the materials and act on the experimental design.
6. Collect and record the data.
7. Draw conclusions and share them with peers.

## 3. EXPANSION OF THE IDEA: Which process skills will be used?

Problem solving, communicating, inferring, designing an experiment, recording data, measuring, observing, defining operationally, synthesizing and analyzing information

### How will the idea be expanded?

*Exploring with Cornstarch*

Ask the students from the different sides of the room to communicate the results of their experiment to one another. The students on each side will need to communicate clearly to the students on the other side exactly what they did so that the students on the other side can replicate their experiment. Allow the students time to replicate experiments. Now ask them where they think they landed. The students should reason that since they found objects on Earth that behaved in ways they weren't familiar with, perhaps they could still be on Earth.

Once the students from each side of the room have discovered what the unknowns were, the students may want to play with the ooze formed with the cornstarch and water. Demonstrate to the students the balloon method for car-

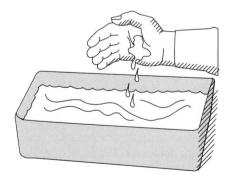

PHYSICAL SCIENCE

rying their ooze in space. Obtain a plastic 1- or 2-liter soda bottle. Remove the cap and cut off the top of the bottle about 2 to 3 inches from the neck. Invert this, place a balloon over the bottle opening, pour the ooze into the funnel, and milk it into the attached balloon. Knot the balloon. Stretch the balloon into various shapes. What happens? Why can you do this?

### Science in Personal and Social Perspectives

- Do you think you can use the scientific method to help you solve personal problems you have?
- How would you go about explaining an important event that happened in your life to a friend? Will the story have the same impact if you leave out important details?
- Do you think it is as important to be able to communicate accurately your feelings about some issue as it is important to be able to give directions for performing a particular task?

### Science and Technology

- How important do you think it is to have motor oil that is the right weight in your car's engine? Can these differences in the oil's weight be affected if dirt particles were dissolved in the oil? Will dirt particles dissolve in the oil, or will they create a colloid?
- Can solutions be created when the materials involved are at temperatures close to freezing? Do you think this knowledge will be important as we try to create space stations hundreds of miles from earth?

### Science as Inquiry

- What are the differences among solutions, mixtures, suspensions, and colloids?
- What steps are involved in the scientific method?

### History and Nature of Science

- If you were an auto mechanic, would knowledge of solutions be beneficial? What kinds of solutions does an auto mechanic work with?
- What other careers rely on knowledge of the differences among solutions, suspensions, colloids, and mixtures? Name three and state why.

**4. EVALUATION:** How will the students show what they have learned?

Upon completing the activities the students will be able to:

- take a given problem and design an experiment to solve it, using the steps in the scientific method;
- demonstrate examples of mixtures, solutions, suspensions, and colloids;
- upon looking at a diagram of a mixture, solution, suspension, or colloid, identify each combination of matter.

## Heat Energy

**Concept to be invented**
Main idea—Adding heat energy to solids causes them to liquefy.

**Concepts that are important to expansion**
Removing heat energy from liquids causes them to solidify.

**Materials needed**

| | |
|---|---|
| hot plate | aluminum foil |
| ten birthday candles | tablespoon |
| saucepan (double boiler) | |

**Safety precautions:** Do not move too close to the hot plate. Do not touch the hot melted wax. Be sure to use a hot plate that has adjustable settings. Melt wax slowly. To avoid fires, melt in a double boiler.

1. **EXPLORATION:** Which process skills will be used?

Classifying, observing, inferring, generalizing, communicating

What will the students do?

*Liquid Birthday*   Allow the students to handle the birthday candles. Ask them to determine whether they are a liquid or a solid. Collect their responses. Once there is consensus as to their solid state, ask for suggestions on how the solid candle could

be turned into a liquid. During this discussion, if no student suggests it, suggest using the hot plate to melt the candles. Place the candles in the double boiler over the hot plate, set at a low setting, and melt them. Ask the students to make observations as heat energy is added to the candles.

## 2. EXPLANATION/CONCEPT INVENTION: What is the main idea? How will the main idea be constructed?

*Concept:* Adding energy to solids causes them to liquefy.

To help the students create this concept, ask the following questions: If you place your hand close to the pan (do not touch it!), does it sense that the pan is hot? What happens to the candles as the heat energy moves from the hot plate to the pan? Can you explain why this is happening? What is a common way in which birthday candles are melted? What other types of things in your home release heat energy? As the hot plate releases heat energy to the saucepan, it is transferred to the candles, causing them to melt. What can you do to change the candles back into solids?

## 3. EXPANSION OF THE IDEA: Which process skills will be used?

Inferring, questioning, observing, communicating

How will the idea be expanded?

*Liquids to Solids*   Ask the students to make predictions about what will happen to the candles once the double boiler is taken off the hot plate. Give each child a piece of aluminum foil and a drop of the liquid wax. Ask the students to make observations of their wax. Divide the class in half. Ask half to determine ways in which they can turn the liquid wax back to a solid in the shortest time possible, the other half to determine ways to keep their drops in the liquid state. In which case do you need to add heat energy? Where is heat energy removed?

*Science in Personal and Social Perspectives*

- Imagine you are riding in a car on a long trip through Florida in July. During the long ride you spend time coloring and drawing pictures. You leave your crayons on the car seat when you stop to eat lunch. What do you think you will find when you return to the car after lunch? Why?
- Where in your home would be a good place to store candles? Why?

*Science and Technology*

- Why do you think it is important to understand why heat energy can melt a solid? Describe how this concept is applied in manufacturing glass objects, such as vases and mirrors.
- The oil used in a car engine is in a liquid state, yet when cool it is very thick. What do you think will happen to it as the car engine continues to run? Will this affect the design of an engine?

*Science as Inquiry*

- What does it take to change a solid object into a liquid state?
- Can objects change their state of matter without gaining or losing heat energy?

*History and Nature of Science*

- Aside from automobile engineers, are there other careers in which people must understand that the addition or subtraction of heat energy will change an object's state of matter?
- How do you think a hairdresser utilizes the concept identified in these activities? If you were having your hair done by a hairdresser, would you feel more comfortable if this person understood something about heat energy?

**4. EVALUATION:** How will the students show what they have learned?

Upon completing the activities the students will be able to:

- demonstrate how heat energy can be added to a rubber band without using fire or a hot plate;
- demonstrate how heat energy can be removed from an ice cube, draw a picture of it, and write three sentences describing how this is done.

## Structure Strength

GRADE
5–8
**DISCIPLINE**
Physical
Science

**Concept to be invented**
Main idea—The strength of a structure depends on the arrangement of the materials used in construction.

**Concepts that are important to expansion**
A variety of materials can be used to create a structure. A triangular arrangement of materials provides a more stable structure than a square.

**Materials needed**

| | | |
|---|---|---|
| straws | toothpicks | toilet paper tubes |
| clay | Popsicle sticks | paper towel tubes |
| glue | string | rolled sheets of newspaper |
| pins | | |

**Safety precautions:** Use care in handling the pins to attach straws together. Do not stand on chairs when building tall structures; ask the teacher for help. Do not throw any of the building materials.

PHYSICAL SCIENCE

1. **EXPLORATION:** Which process skills will be used?

Observing, predicting, manipulating materials, hypothesizing, inferring

What will the students do?

*Simple Construction*

Divide the class into five working groups. Provide one group with straws, another with toothpicks, another with Popsicle sticks, the fourth with toilet paper or paper towel tubes, and the fifth with sheets of newspaper rolled slightly longer than the paper towel tubes but just about the same diameter. Allow each group access to clay, pins, glue, or string to attach the building materials together.

Ask the students to make observations about the materials provided. Ask them to make predictions about how the materials could be used. Encourage the students to think beyond the usual uses for the materials. Allow them to manipulate the materials and to put them together in as many ways as possible. Ask the students to draw pictures of the different creations. Ask them to identify which of their creations remained standing the longest.

2. **EXPLANATION/CONCEPT INVENTION:** What is the main idea? How will the main idea be constructed?

*Concept:* The strength of a structure depends on the arrangement of the materials used in construction. A variety of materials can be used to create a structure.

Key questions to ask to help identify these concepts are:

- What kinds of things did you create with these materials?
- Did anyone create a structure that remained standing?
- What did that structure look like?
- What kinds of materials did you use?
- How long did your structure remain standing?
- Why do you think one structure stood longer than another?
- Do you think you could use the same materials yet make your structure stronger? How do you think you could do that?

3. **EXPANSION OF THE IDEA:** Which process skills will be used?

Observing, predicting, manipulating materials, hypothesizing, inferring

How will the idea be expanded?

*Triangle Construction*

Allow those students who originally created some sort of building to work on making it stronger using the same materials. Encourage students who did not originally create a building to do so, trying to create as strong a structure as possible. Encourage all of the students to share with one another the structures they created. Take the time to point out which structures were sturdier than others and why. Assist the students in realizing that structures in which materials like

PHYSICAL SCIENCE

the straws, toothpicks, popsicle sticks, or paper tubes are arranged in a triangular shape are stronger than those left as squares.

### Science in Personal and Social Perspectives

- Take a field trip with an adult family member to the attic or basement of your house or that of a friend. What kinds of support systems are found in the house? What materials were used? In what arrangements are those support systems placed?
- Think of some common objects found around your house that you typically use once and throw away. Do you think you could use them to create a structure? How long do you think a structure would last if it was built out of the material you have in mind?

### Science and Technology

- Can you name three famous buildings that are known for the uniqueness of their structure?
- Why do you think that certain areas in the United States have strict laws about the types of structures that can be built there?

### Science as Inquiry

- Can you make a house out of a deck of cards? How is it possible? Why is it possible?

- Do you think you can support a 2-pound weight in a structure made out of old newspapers? How will you manipulate the newspapers to make this possible? Try it.

### History and Nature of Science

- Choose one of the following occupations and explain how important knowledge of structural arrangement and strength is to that occupation: mechanical engineer, civil engineer, architect, contractor.
- Do you think a paper carrier or someone working in a fast-food restaurant would use the ideas you discovered through these activities in his or her work? How?

## 4. EVALUATION: How will the students show what they have learned?

Upon completing the activities the students will be able to:

- work in cooperative groups of four and use drinking straws and clay to build a bridge that spans across the classroom. The strength of the structure built will be tested using metal washers.
- view two toothpick structures and determine which of the two has the greater strength and be able to explain why (create them according to the accompanying picture).
- draw a picture of a structure that could survive in an area where strong winds occur often. Write a narrative explaining what the structure is and why it was so designed.

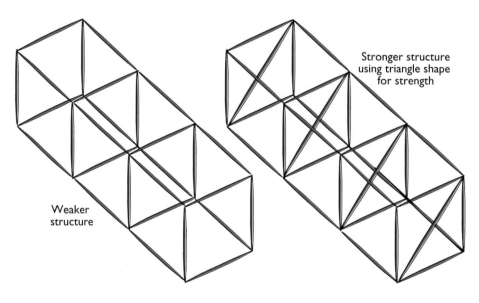

Stronger structure using triangle shape for strength

Weaker structure

# Mirrors and Reflection

GRADE
5–8
DISCIPLINE
Physical
Science

**Concepts to be invented**

Main idea—An object must be shiny, smooth, and reflect light to be called a *mirror*. Light bouncing off a shiny surface is called *reflection*.

**Concepts that are important to expansion**

Mirrors with a bowl-shaped surface are called *concave;* those that are rounded outward are called *convex*.

**Materials needed**

*For each student group:*

| | |
|---|---|
| at least one 2-inch square mirror | black paper |
| one metal spoon | scrap paper |
| aluminum foil | pencils |
| clear plastic | Mylar paper |

➡ **Safety precautions:** Be sure that rough edges on mirrors are filed or taped. Demonstrate to the students the proper handling of mirrors and Mylar paper: hold them by the edges to avoid fingerprints. Stress the importance of sharing.

## 1. EXPLORATION: Which process skills will be used?

Observing, predicting, making assumptions, brainstorming, recording data

### What will the students do?

*Mirrors and Reflectors*

Allow the students to observe various materials and predict if they will be able to see themselves. Ask the students to brainstorm ideas of when and where they have seen mirrorlike materials such as the ones they are working with. Manipulate the materials to see if they can see images of objects in them. Ask the students to describe their observations. Encourage the students to think about the position of that object in the mirrorlike materials versus what it looks like when they look at it directly. Ask the students to predict what their name will look like after they write it on the paper, and look at it in each of the materials. Instruct the students to write their name and view it in the mirror and each of the other materials. Can you see it in all of the objects? Does it look the same as it is written? Why or why not? Can you write it so that you can read it correctly when you look in the mirror?

PHYSICAL SCIENCE

**2. EXPLANATION/CONCEPT INVENTION:** *What is the main idea? How will the main idea be constructed?*

> *Concept:* An object must be shiny, smooth, and reflect light to be called a *mirror*. Light bouncing off a shiny surface is called *reflection*.
>
> Assist the students in creating these concepts by doing the following: Refer back to the list brainstormed during the exploration phase. If terms like *smooth, reflect, light,* and *shiny* are not listed, add them to the list. Ask the students to help explain the meaning of those terms. Can an object be considered a mirror without light? Does the surface of the object need to be shiny? Can surfaces that are rough or bumpy give images as clear as shiny, smooth surfaces?

**3. EXPANSION OF THE IDEA:** *Which process skills will be used?*

> Observing, predicting, manipulating materials, classifying, inferring
>
> *How will the idea be expanded?*

*What's a Mirror?*  Using the same materials from the exploration activity, ask the students to classify them into groups of things that are shiny, things that are smooth, and things that reflect light. Were you able to classify all of the materials? Could some of the materials fall into more than one group? Which materials were shiny and smooth and reflected light? Can you call these objects mirrors?

Can the spoon be considered a mirror? Describe the images seen inside the spoon. Where have you seen mirrors like these before? Have you ever been to a grocery store and seen these kinds of mirrors? What purpose do these mirrors serve? Mirrors with a bowl-shaped surface are called *concave;* those that are rounded outward are called *convex.*

*Science in Personal and Social Perspectives*

- Mirrors are used quite a bit in our everyday lives. When and where have you seen mirrors? What is their purpose?
- How often do you use a mirror? Describe the mirrors that you use.

*Science and Technology*

- How do different people use mirrors? What can be learned by looking in a mirror?
- How do scientists use mirrors? Have you ever used a microscope that uses mirrors? Did you ever see a telescope that makes use of mirrors?
- Can you list at least three machines that make use of mirrors? Draw a working diagram of one of them.

*Science as Inquiry*

- Why is a light source needed in order for an object to be considered a mirror?
- Which type of mirror would you use if you wanted objects to appear larger than they actually are: concave or convex?
- Why do words appear to be written backward when viewed in a mirror?

*History and Nature of Science*

- What careers are linked to the use of mirrors? Do your parents use mirrors in their work?
- Would some careers be more difficult without mirrors? Think of your school bus driver.
- The German chemist Justus von Liebig was instrumental in creating the mirror that we currently use. Trace the history of the mirror, describing the role von Liebig played.

**4. EVALUATION:** How will the students show what they have learned?

Upon completing the activities the students will be able to:

- write their names upside down and backwards on a piece of paper to illustrate their knowledge of what a mirror can do;
- describe the three properties of a mirror or mirrorlike object and use them in sentences;
- classify materials into *shiny, smooth,* and *reflects light* categories.

## The Slinky Potential

GRADE
7–8
DISCIPLINE
Physical
Science

**Concept to be invented:**
Energy is a property of many substances and is associated with mechanical motion. Stored energy is called potential energy. Energy of motion is called kinetic energy.

**Concepts that are important to expansion:**
Energy can be transformed from one form to another. Momentum is described as the mass of an object times the velocity of the object. Momentum is always conserved.

PHYSICAL SCIENCE

**Materials needed:**

*For exploration:*

one Slinky or equivalent-type toy
   per student group
access to a flight of stairs wide
   enough for the Slinky to fit, but

not so wide that the top of the
Slinky ends up falling over itself
onto the same step

*For expansion:*

a golf ball and a Ping-Pong ball
   for class demonstration and/or,
   if time permits, one each per
   student group
access to a hard floor surface for
   dropping the balls, preferably

near a wall where ball heights
   can be marked
tape to mark ball height on wall

➡ **Safety precautions:** Caution students about acceptable behavior while working with the Slinky on the stairs. Ask the students to watch one another as they descend the stairs with the Slinky to avoid falling.

As a precaution students should wear goggles when dropping the golf and Ping-Pong balls, as they cannot control the height and angle of the rebound when the balls are dropped simultaneously.

## 1. EXPLORATION: Which process skills will be used?

Manipulating materials, communicating, observing, inferring

### What will students do?

*Energy Conversions with a Slinky*

Have the students, working in teams, go to designated areas within the school building where they have access to a flight of stairs. Remind them of safety measures while working on the steps. Ask them to predict what will happen to the Slinky when it is placed on the top step of a flight of stairs and they push the top half of the Slinky toward the edge of the step. Ask them to predict how many stairs it will descend before it stops. Do you think it will make it to the bottom of the stairs? Give them an opportunity to have at least three trials with the descending Slinky.

## 2. EXPLANATION/CONCEPT INVENTION: What is the main idea? How will the main idea be constructed?

*Concept:* Energy is a property of many substances and is associated with mechanical motion. Stored energy is called *potential energy.* Energy of motion is called *kinetic energy.*

Ask the students to describe the motion of the Slinky as it descended the steps. Ask them to explain the conditions necessary for a successful journey from the top to the bottom of the steps. What variables must they adjust so the Slinky can move down the entire flight of stairs?

The students should begin to talk of the Slinky uncoiling and coiling as it moved down the steps. Ask them what they think "pulled" the Slinky down. They should be talking about the force of gravity pulling on the end of the Slinky as it moved down the steps.

Explain to them that the Slinky had energy stored in it as it was sitting on the top of the step. This is known as *potential energy.* By pushing the top of the Slinky to get it started down the stairs you imparted some of your own energy to the Slinky. Once gravity takes over, that stored or potential energy is converted to kinetic energy as the coils pull the trailing end of the Slinky down. This energy has now given the trailing end of the Slinky momentum. It is that momentum that causes the end to move up and past the high point of the arc as the Slinky falls over on itself. Gravity then takes over and continues to pull the Slinky down. Again this process is repeated as the Slinky moves down the stairs, transforming gravitational energy and the potential energy of the spring into kinetic energy until it reaches the bottom of the stairs. With this explanation, ask your students at what point in the Slinky's descent does it have its greatest kinetic energy? (When it falls from one step to the next.) At what point is the potential energy the greatest? (When it is poised ready to fall from one step to the next.)

Can you make the Slinky walk back up the steps? Why or why not? (You can't do this because you'd have to create potential energy from nothing. This would be against the law of conservation of energy, which states that energy cannot be created nor destroyed.) In this lesson the students should conclude that energy can be transformed from one form to another. This will be reinforced in the expansion activity.

**PHYSICAL SCIENCE**

## 3. EXPANSION OF THE IDEA: Which process skills will be used?

Observing, predicting, identifying, and controlling variables

How will the idea be expanded?

*Energy Transfer— Having a Ball!*

Hold a Ping-Pong ball and a golf ball up in front of the class. Ask the students to predict how high they think the Ping-Pong ball will bounce if you drop it from chest height onto a hard floor below. Ask them to predict how high they think the golf ball will bounce if you drop it from chest height onto a hard floor below. Collect all predictions—then drop each ball one at a time. Ask some students to mark a spot on the wall behind you with tape at the height of the ascent with the first bounce for each ball. How accurate were their predictions? They should have discovered that when dropped separately from the same height the balls will bounce to approximately the same height.

Now ask the students to predict what will happen when you drop both balls at the same time with the Ping-Pong ball positioned on top of the golf ball. Record these predictions. *Note:* Be sure to practice this before you do it in front of your students so that when the balls are released simultaneously, the Ping-Pong ball will shoot straight up, 10 to 15 feet.

Now drop the balls so that the Ping-Pong ball is positioned over the golf ball. Ask the students again to mark the height of the bounce for each ball. Did the balls respond as predicted? What do you think happened? At what point did the balls have potential energy? When was that converted to kinetic?

Ask the students where the energy came from to cause the Ping-Pong ball to bounce so high? (It came from the golf ball.) What happened to the golf ball if it transferred some of its energy into the Ping-Pong ball? (It bounced lower than it did before.) Repeat this activity or allow the student teams to repeat this activity so they come to understand that particular scientific phenomena become laws when they hold up with repeated testing. In this case they will be justifying the law of conservation of momentum.

In this activity, energy is transferred from the golf ball to the Ping-Pong ball. This demonstrates how momentum is conserved. Momentum is described by the formula $M$ (momentum) = $m$ (mass) × $v$ (velocity). When dropped separately, each ball gained momentum based on the mass of the ball.

A sidebar conversation may need to occur about how friction plays into this experiment. The classroom is not an ideal setting because it can not demonstrate a perfectly elastic collision. There is some loss of kinetic energy with each bounce due to friction. If friction from the air were not present, the ball would bounce at the same height with each bounce.

When the Ping-Pong ball was dropped directly over the golf ball, momentum had to be conserved. In order for that to happen the mass of the golf ball times the velocity of the golf ball had to equal the mass of the Ping-Pong ball times the velocity of the Ping-Pong ball ($m_{gb} \times v_{gb} = m_{ppb} \times v_{ppb}$). Since the golf ball has greater mass than the Ping-Pong ball, to make the equation equal the velocity of the Ping-Pong ball had to increase proportionally. Thus what they observed was the transfer of energy from the golf ball to the Ping-Pong ball to maintain the law of conservation of momentum.

### Science in Personal and Social Perspectives

- How can you apply the concept that energy can be transferred while playing a game of baseball?
- Why is it important to wear a helmet when roller blading or skateboarding? Where is energy transferred from if you are moving along on your skateboard and you hit the pavement and you do not have a helmet on?

### Science and Technology

- What role do air bags in automobiles play if a car stops suddenly? How has the knowledge that energy can be transformed from one form to another been applied in air bag technology?
- Explore the different materials used to make bike safety helmets. Which material absorbs energy transformation more efficiently? What kind of a rating scale do helmet manufacturers use?

*Science as Inquiry*

- Collect balls of various sizes and masses. Predict which ball will allow the Ping-Pong ball to bounce higher when it is used instead of the golf ball in the expansion activity. Support your predictions and justify your outcomes by applying the concept of momentum to the mass and velocity of the balls using the formula $M = m \times v$.

*History and Nature of Science*

- Explore the possible professions that apply the concept of energy transformations to their work end product.
- In recent record the number of accidents on amusement park rides has increased. Using the concepts you learned in these activities, create a job description for a person responsible for inspecting amusement park rides.

**4. EVALUATION:** How will the students show what they have learned?

Upon completing the activities the students will be able to:

- explain the difference between potential and kinetic energy and demonstrate this using a toy such as a Slinky or a top or a Frisbee;
- accurately predict which ball will have greater velocity when dropped simultaneously and vertically in the following order: a basketball under a Ping-Pong ball, a basketball under a volleyball, and a small rubber ball under a Ping-Pong ball;
- create a campaign for increased use of safety helmets while skateboarding, demonstrating the concept that energy can be transformed from one form to another.

## Toys in Space

**GRADE**
**5–8**
**DISCIPLINE**
**Physical**
**Science**

**Concept to be invented**
Main idea—Things that behave one way on earth will behave differently in space due to zero-gravity conditions.

**Concepts that are important to expansion**
An astronaut will experience weightlessness while traveling through space. Toys can be used to explain a variety of scientific principles.

**Materials needed**
*Toys in Space* video (available from NASA, Lewis Research Center, Cleveland, OH) and toys used in the video: wheel-o, yo-yo, paddle ball, ball and jacks, self-propelling car, magnetic marbles, spinning top, Play-Skool Flip Mouse, gyroscope

**PHYSICAL SCIENCE**

➥  **Safety precautions:** Teacher and students should wear goggles to be sure that no eye injuries occur.

1. **EXPLORATION:** Which process skills will be used?

Observing, predicting, manipulating materials, hypothesizing, inferring

What will the students do?

*Toy Behavior in Zero Gravity*

Provide the students with the toys from the materials list. Ask them to play with the toys and make observations about how they function. After adequate time has been spent playing with the toys, ask the students to make predictions as to how they think the toys would function in zero gravity. Encourage the students to make as many predictions as possible.

2. **EXPLANATION/CONCEPT INVENTION:** What is the main idea? How will the main idea be constructed?

*Concept:* Things that behave one way on earth will behave differently in space due to zero gravity conditions.

To assist the students in developing this concept, ask them the following questions: How do the toys work in the classroom? Can you demonstrate them for me? How does gravity behave on earth? What does it do to objects on earth? If there were no gravity on earth, how do you think these toys would behave? Have you ever seen movies of astronauts as they travel in space? How do they look?

3. **EXPANSION OF THE IDEA:** Which process skills will be used?

Observing, predicting, manipulating materials, hypothesizing, inferring

How will the idea be expanded?

*Toys and Newton*

After much student discussion about their predictions, show the NASA videotape *Toys in Space.* Discuss afterward the discrepancies between the students' predictions and what really happened. An astronaut will experience weightlessness while traveling through space.

Toys can be used to explain a variety of scientific principles. If the students really show an interest in the behavior of the toys under zero-gravity conditions, you may want to introduce the students to some of Newton's laws, which govern the behavior of these toys on earth. If you want the students to really understand them, then take care to plan additional activities that engage the students in science processes to enhance their understanding of these laws. The laws are as follows:

1. *Law of inertia:* Every body continues in its state of rest or of uniform motion in a straight line, except insofar as it is compelled by forces to change that state.
2. Force equals mass times acceleration.

3. The force exerted by an object A on another object B is equal in magnitude and opposite in direction to the force exerted by object B on object A.

*Science in Personal and Social Perspectives*

- How do you decide what kinds of toys to play with? Did you ever think that you could use them to help explain science concepts?
- Why do you think you or your friends choose particular toys to play with? Is it important that you play with the same things as your friends? Why or why not?
- Can you choose one of your toys and explain how or why it works? Ask your friends to help you decide which science concept is applied to explain why your toy works.

*Science and Technology*

- Toys are actually like models of particular systems. Why do you think it would be easier to make a toy model of some invention first? What advantage would that give to certain industries?

*Science as Inquiry*

- Is it possible for toys on earth to behave the same way when under zero-gravity conditions? Is it possible for toys in space to behave the same way when on earth?
- Describe two different scientific concepts that can be explained using a bicycle.

*History and Nature of Science*

- Do you think a wheel-o could have been invented if the creator did not understand something about magnetism?
- If you were to become a toy designer, would knowledge of science concepts be useful in your career?

**4. EVALUATION:** How will the students show what they have learned?

Upon completing the activities the students will be able to:

- describe one scientific concept that can be explained with the use of a roller skate;
- create a toy using materials of their choice that can be fun and explain a scientific concept;
- design a toy that can still function in the absence of gravity and write a few sentences to describe it.

# Simple Machines: The Lever

**GRADE**
**5–8**
**DISCIPLINE**
**Physical Science**

## Concept to be invented

Main idea—A lever is a rigid bar that pivots around a point that is used to move an object at a second point by a force applied at a third point. The pivot point is the *fulcrum,* the object moved is the *load,* and the place where the force is applied is the *effort.*

## Concepts that are important to expansion

There are three kinds of levers. A *first-class lever* is a fulcrum between effort and load; the effort moves in the opposite direction of the load, as in a seesaw or a balance. A *second-class lever* is a load between the fulcrum and the effort; effort is applied in the same direction as the load should be moved, as in a wheelbarrow or a bottle opener. A *third-class lever* is an effort between the fulcrum and the load, which magnifies the distance moved by the load but reduces its force, as in a hammer, a catapult, or a fishing rod. Additional terms that may be introduced in this lesson are *resistance, friction, work,* and *machine.*

## Materials needed

*Per student group, for the discrepant event:*

| | |
|---|---|
| sandpaper | cooking oil |
| water | hand lotion |
| marbles or beads | paper towels or wipes |

*For exploration:*

goggles, one long piece of board (18" × ¼" works well), one fulcrum (proportional in size to the long board—for the 18-inch board, triangular pieces cut out of a 2 × 4 work well), any proportionally sized objects to be used as load, such as blocks of wood, small books, metal chunks, or cylinders

*For expansion:*

| | |
|---|---|
| goggles | one rubber band |
| two plastic spoons | peanuts |

➡️ **Safety precautions:** Remind students that safety goggles must be worn at all times. Discourage students from sending the load material flying across the room. Warn them of the potential danger to themselves and other students.

### Discrepant event

*Which process skills will be used?*

Observing, hypothesizing, inferring, drawing conclusions

*What will the teacher and students do?*

Do not show the students what you are giving them. Ask them to put out their hands and place a small amount of one of the following in their hands: sandpaper, nothing, water, hand lotion, cooking oil, two or three marbles or beads. Tell them to be sure not to let anyone else see what they have. Once everyone has received one of the items, then ask the class to rub their hands together (all at the same time) with the objects still in their hands. After the students have had time to do this and to comment on what just happened, then ask questions such as: What did your hands feel like? Who had the hardest time rubbing his or her hands together? the easiest? Why? Did your hands change temperature? What do you think caused your hands to get hot/cold/no change? Why was it easy for some and not for others? What do you think is prohibiting you from sliding or rolling the objects in your hands? (Resistance.) What is this resistance to movement called? (Friction.) What did you need to do to overcome friction? (Exert some energy—effort.) By using effort to move your hands over a distance, you have done work. What do we call an object that will do the work for us? (A machine.)

1. EXPLORATION: *Which process skills will be used?*

Manipulating materials, collecting and recording data, communicating, observing, hypothesizing, predicting, inferring

*What will the students do?*

*Lever Creations*   *Instructions:* Use a long board and a triangular-shaped block in as many combinations as you think possible to move the weighted object (blocks, books, metal pieces). Draw the methods you tried. Discuss possible solutions with your peers. Try to record the results of those as well.

2. EXPLANATION/CONCEPT INVENTION: *What is the main idea? How will the main idea be constructed?*

*Concept:* A lever is a rigid bar that pivots around a point, which is used to move an object at a second point by a force applied at a third point.

Have the students draw the results of their manipulations on the board. With help from the class, identify on their drawings the pivot point, the object being

PHYSICAL SCIENCE

moved, and the place where they had to apply a force to get the object to move. Solicit class ideas as to names for these points. Identify the pivot point as the *fulcrum,* the object moved as the *load,* and the place where force was applied as the *effort.*

Key questions to ask: Did these inventions make it easier for you to do work? What do we call objects that make our work easier? What has the machine we invented allowed us to do? What do you think we call it? Why? Once the concept *lever* has been invented, ask the students if they can see any differences in the placement of the three points on any of their diagrams. If necessary, supply diagrams that show different placements of the points. Key questions: Is there any advantage to changing the position of the three points? What happens to the direction of the effort and load in each of the diagrams? Can you see some practical uses for the different positions of the points? As you go through the different arrangements of the points, identify the three classes of levers: A *first-class lever* is a fulcrum between effort and load; the effort moves in the opposite direction of the load, as in a seesaw or a balance. A *second-class lever* is a load between the fulcrum and the effort; effort is applied in the same direction as the load should be moved, as in a wheelbarrow or a bottle opener. A *third-class lever* is an effort between the fulcrum and the load, which magnifies the distance moved by the load but reduces its force, as in a hammer, a catapult, or a fishing rod.

## 3. EXPANSION OF THE IDEA: Which process skills will be used?

Hypothesizing, inferring, manipulating materials, observing, communicating, collecting and recording data, making assumptions, predicting, formulating models

### How will the idea be expanded?

*Spoons and Nuts*  *Instructions:* Given two plastic spoons, a rubber band, and some peanuts, design and demonstrate a first-, second-, and third-class lever. Share your inventions with the class.

### Home extension: Which process skills will be used?

Inferring, manipulating materials, making assumptions, formulating models, observing, analyzing, classifying

### What will the students do?

*Lever Scavenger Hunt*  Have the students ask an adult to go with them on a lever scavenger hunt. Make a list of all of the places where levers are being used in some form or another. How many of these are combination levers? How many are compound levers of the first, second, or third class? Bring these lists back to school to share with the class.

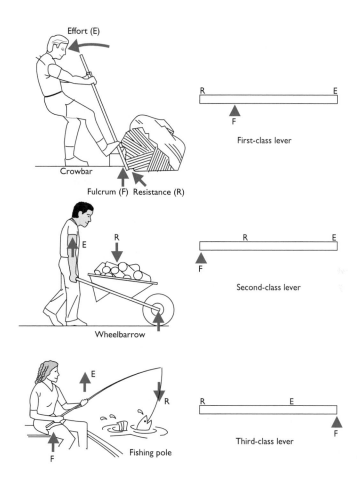

### Science in Personal and Social Perspectives

- Where in your home did you find a lever being used? Did any of these places surprise you? Were any of these uses a case where two of the lever types were used in combination? (Nail clippers, manual typewriter, piano.) Did you find any compound levers? (Scissors, pliers, nutcracker, tweezers.)
- When you need to cut a piece of paper, why is it easier to use scissors instead of a knife? What advantage does using a pair of scissors have over using a knife for cutting?
- Which simple machine makes it possible for people to play a piano?

### Science and Technology

- Why would it be difficult for you to wear your ice skates in the house but not your roller skates? How have industries used this information to overcome friction?

- How do you think the invention of the parking meter has affected your city? How about cities like Chicago or New York?

*Science as Inquiry*

- Students will be able to explain the function of the fulcrum, load, and effort; various combinations of these points can create a first-, second-, or third-class lever. They will be able to explain how machines help us to do work and to overcome friction.
- This activity lays the foundation for new concepts to be identified in new lessons, such as the relationship between effort and work, mechanical advantage, other types of simple machines, and so on.

*History and Nature of Science*

- Archimedes of Syracuse was perhaps the greatest of the Greek mathematicians and scientists. He lived from 287 to 212 B.C. He is credited with inventing the catapult, which the Greeks used during the Second Punic War against the Roman army. It is said that Archimedes was slain during this war while he was studying mathematical figures, which he habitually drew in the dust. What do you think he meant when he said, "Give me a fulcrum on which to rest, and I will move the earth"?
- Who needs to know about levers? Which careers rely on the use and/or knowledge of levers? (Manufacturers of playground equipment, laborers, dock workers, piano makers, typewriter manufacturers, parking meter repair persons.)

**4. EVALUATION:** How will the students show what they have learned?

Upon completing the activities the students will be able to:

- classify the following items as a first-, second-, or third-class lever: hammer, nutcracker, seesaw, wheelbarrow, balance, bottle opener, fishing rod;
- identify the fulcrum, the effort, and the load on each item, when given a hammer, wheelbarrow, and nail extractor;
- predict the direction of the load when effort is applied with each of the following: fishing rod, balance, bottle opener.

# Earth and Space Science Lessons

| Lesson Name | Content Standards | Grade Level | Activities |
|---|---|---|---|
| *Astronomy* | | | |
| The Solar System and the Universe | Objects in the Sky | K–3 | Rhythm Activity • Postcard Writing |
| The Expanding Universe | Earth in the Solar System | 5–8 | Expanding Balloon/Universe • Build a Solar System Salad |
| Constellations | Earth in the Solar System | 5–8 | Connect the Stars • Evening Field Trip • Create a Constellation |
| *Geology* | | | |
| Earth Layers | Properties of Earth Materials | K–4 | Clay Earth Layers • Clay Continents |
| Fossils | Properties of Earth Materials | 2–4 | Fossil Observations • Plaster Molds and Casts |
| Soil Formation | Structure of the Earth System | 5–8 | Soil Separation and Rock Crushing • Soil Components |
| Rock Types | Structure of the Earth System | 5–8 | Rock Categorization • Rock Collection Field Trip |
| Cooling Crystals | Structure of the Earth System | 5–8 | PDB Crystal Formation • Rock Type versus Crystal Formation |
| Weathering | Structure of the Earth System | 5–8 | Freezing Bottle • Weathering Field Trip • Rock Identification • Chemical Weathering • Mechanical Weathering |
| Crustal Plate Movement | Earth's History | 5–8 | Moving Plates • Mapping Volcanoes and Earthquakes • Oatmeal and Cracker Plate Tectonics |
| Aging Human/ Aging Earth | Earth's History | 7–8 | Living Human—Living Earth • The Rock Record |
| *Meteorology* | | | |
| Rain Formation | Objects in the Sky | K–4 | Rain in a Jar • Water Drop Attraction |
| Dew Formation | Objects in the Sky | K–4 | Soda Bottle Condensation • Thermometer Reading and Dew Point |
| Radiant Energy | Objects in the Sky | 2–4 | Temperature and Colored Surfaces • Temperature: Sun versus Shade • Magnifiers: Capture the Sun • Sun Tea |
| Weather Forecasting | Structure of the Earth System | 5–8 | Weather Log Creation • Weather Map Symbols • Weather Data Collection |
| Air Mass Movement | Structure of the Earth System | 5–8 | Coriolis Effect: Globe • Coriolis Effect: Top • Air Movement: Dry Ice • Oil and Water Fronts • Create a Rain Gauge • Air Masses and Parachutes |
| Air Pressure | Structure of the Earth System | 5–8 | Balloon Balance • Paper Blowing • Newspaper Strength |
| Solar Heating | Earth in the Solar System | 5–8 | Temperature versus Surface Color • Optimum Thermometer Placement |
| Air Movement and Surface Temperature | Structure of the Earth System | 5–8 | Convection Current and Surface Temperature in an Observation Box • Paper Bag Balance |
| Uneven Heating of the Earth | Structure of the Earth System | 5–8 | Tower of Water • Aneroid Barometer • Uneven Heating and Air Pressure • Air Pressure versus Water Temperature • Air Temperature versus Movement of Air • Heat Transfer on a Wire • Heat Movement Through Air • Heat Transfer Through Metal • Movement of Smoke over Hot and Cold Surfaces: Clouds • Movement of Smoke over Hot and Cold Surfaces: Wind Patterns |

**EARTH SCIENCE**

## The Solar System and the Universe

GRADE
K–3
DISCIPLINE
Earth
Science

**Concept to be invented**
Main idea—The Earth is part of the solar system.

**Concepts that are important to expansion**
Planets differ from one another.

**Materials needed**
*For exploration:*
books on planets, such as Jeff Davidson, *Voyage to the Planets* (Worthington, OH: Willowisp Press, 1990) and Joanna Cole, *The Magic School Bus Lost in Space* (New York: Scholastic, 1988)
*For expansion:*
Postcard outline, poster paper, paints, and markers

➡ **Safety precautions:** The students should be reminded to sit and listen without poking or hitting one another. During the expansion activity, they should be sure to clean up any paint spills immediately, and they should not put markers or paint brushes in their mouths.

1. **EXPLORATION:** Which process skills will be used?

   Observing, questioning

   What will the students do?

   *Rhythm Activity*
   • You should read such books as *Voyage to the Planets* or *The Magic School Bus Lost in Space* to the students. Ask them recall questions as you are sharing the book with them.
   • Teach the students the following chant, clapping the beat. Allow them to fill in the planet of their choice once they get the rhythm down:

     A–B–CDE, How many planets can there be?
     F–G–HIJ, There are nine we know of today.
     K–L–MNO, To which one would you like to go?
     P–Q–RST, I'd like to visit Mercury.
     U–V–WXY, I've been watching it in the sky.
     Z–Z–ZZZ, Know anyone who'll come with me?

2. **EXPLANATION/CONCEPT INVENTION:** What is the main idea? How will the main idea be constructed?

   *Concept:* The Earth is part of the solar system.

It has been found through observations of the nighttime sky and satellite observations that Earth is just one of nine planets that move around the sun. Each of the planets has unique characteristics because of its distance from the sun. Questions students ask during the reading of the book will also assist in developing the concepts.

## 3. EXPANSION OF THE IDEA: Which process skills will be used?

Inferring, observing, questioning

### How will the idea be expanded?

*Postcard Writing* Once the students know the chant and sing it with all nine planet names, ask them to choose one of the nine as a place they'd like to go on vacation. Break the students into nine planet vacation groups. Ask them to plan a drawing of their planet as close to reality as possible, and then work as a cooperative group to create one drawing of that planet. Draw a sun on your mural paper. Ask the different groups to come up to the mural and place their planet in its appropriate order from the sun.

Give each student a copy of the postcard outline. Ask them to write postcards to family members, describing their trips to the planets they drew. Teach

EARTH SCIENCE

them how to address a postcard. Ask them to design an appropriate stamp for the planet they visited. When all of these are completed, tape the postcards near the planet of origin.

### Questions that help invent additional concepts

- Is the earth all alone in space? (No, there are eight other planets.)
- What else is found in Earth's neighborhood? (Planets, moons, dust, meteors.)
- How do we know there are other planets in our neighborhood? Has anyone ever seen them? (We can see them in the sky; they look like stars. We have satellites that have gone close to them and sent back pictures to Earth.)
- What is unique about your planet? (Answers will vary.)
- How close to the sun is your planet? (Answers will vary.)
- Are all the planets the same size? (No. Go into detail about their planets.)
- Do you think you could live on your vacation planet as easily as you can on Earth? Why or why not?

Students will apply knowledge they learned about their planets to answer these questions.

### Science in Personal and Social Perspectives

- Do you think if Earth were as close to the sun as Mercury you could still live on it? Why or why not?
- If someone told you he or she could take you on a plane ride to the planet Mars, would you believe it? Why or why not?

### Science and Technology

- Do you think a person can invent a way so that it will be possible to live on any of the other planets? How do you think we can do this?

### Science as Inquiry

- Students will be able to name the nine planets, list their order from the sun, and discuss one characteristic of each after completing and participating in the above activities.

### History and Nature of Science

- Do you think that a person responsible for monitoring the air quality of the planet Earth can learn anything from understanding what the atmosphere is like on the planet Jupiter?
- How important is it that space scientists know the positions of the planets before launching satellites or rockets into space? What kinds of skills do space scientists need in order to do their jobs?

**4. EVALUATION:** How will the students show what they have learned?

Upon completing the activities the students will be able to:

- answer the questions included in the expansion phase of this lesson, as well as the new outcomes questions;

- draw lines from the picture of a planet to a group of words that briefly describe the planet. The picture question below is an example of the kind of question that could be made for this assessment:

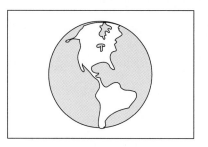

Water and oxygen
present

- create a planet mobile (this can be done as a home extension) out of the following materials: wire coat hanger, paint, tape and/or glue, papier maché or balls of different sizes, string, and cardboard, paper, or newspaper.

## The Expanding Universe

**GRADE
5–8
DISCIPLINE
Earth
Science**

### Concepts to be invented
Main idea—Our universe appears to be expanding. Distances between parts of the universe are vast.

### Concepts that are important to expansion
Planets orbit about the sun. The planets are very small and very far away from the sun.

### Materials needed
*For exploration:*
round balloons (one for each student), wide-tip felt markers (black and red)

*For expansion:*

| | | |
|---|---|---|
| one fresh pea | one dried pea | one small walnut |
| one large walnut | one bean | one smaller bean |
| one 8-inch head of cabbage | one 9-inch head of | one grapefruit |
| one big orange | cabbage | a bicycle |
| the school track | | |

➡ **Safety precautions:** Use extreme caution while blowing up the balloon. Do not allow children to chew on the balloon.

1. **EXPLORATION:** Which process skills will be used?

Observing, predicting, hypothesizing, inferring

EARTH SCIENCE

*What will the students do?*

*Expanding Balloon/Universe*

Instruct each student to

1. inflate a round balloon partially, pinching the neck closed with thumb and forefinger;
2. make specks with a wide-tip felt marker all over the surface of the balloon, noting their positions and letting them dry;
3. blow more air into the balloon and look at it, again noting the position of the specks.

## 2. EXPLANATION/CONCEPT INVENTION: *What is the main idea? How will the main idea be constructed?*

*Concept:* Our universe appears to be expanding. Distances between parts of the universe are vast.

Help the students invent the concept by asking them such questions as:

* What has happened to the distance between the specks? (It has increased, expanded.)
* What do you think will happen to the specks if you continue to add air to the balloon? (They will continue to move away from one another.)
* Imagine that the balloon is space and one of the specks is the neighborhood Earth is found in. Put a red mark on one of the specks to represent Earth's neighborhood. Blow up the balloon some more while watching the red speck. What do you think you could say about space if you were on this red speck? (Earth is very far from other parts of the universe.)

## 3. EXPANSION OF THE IDEA: *Which process skills will be used?*

Observing, communicating, formulating models, recording data

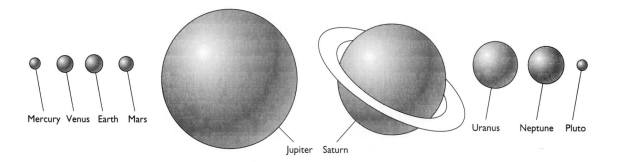

Mercury  Venus  Earth  Mars

Jupiter  Saturn

Uranus  Neptune  Pluto

How will the idea be expanded?

*Build a Solar System Salad*

Have students observe the fixings for a solar system salad (see materials needed). They should decide which of the items correspond to the nine planets and Earth's moon. The students should check with one another to come to some consensus. Then they will discuss decisions with the teacher.

After a discussion on relative sizes, take the salad items out to the school track. While bicycling around the track, drop off the planets to show their relative distance from each other. Allow all the students to participate. Some may be lap counters; others should do the riding. To make it really effective, each student should ride the bicycle. As the children grow tired, the vast distances between the planets will be apparent to them. Each lap represents 211,265 miles in space.

*Mercury:* ⅖ lap

*Venus:* ¾ lap

*Earth:* 1 lap

*Mars:* 1½ laps

*Jupiter:* 5½ laps

*Saturn:* 9½ laps

*Uranus:* 19½ laps

*Neptune:* 30 laps

*Pluto:* 39⅖ laps

**Questions that help invent additional concepts:**

• Which of the salad fixings did you have a hard time assigning a planet to?
• Did you find it necessary to look in some reference books to help you decide which item represents which planet?

*Mercury:* Fresh pea

*Venus:* Walnut

*Earth:* Larger walnut

*Moon:* Dried pea

*Mars:* Bean

*Jupiter:* 9-inch cabbage

*Saturn:* 8-inch cabbage

*Uranus:* Grapefruit

*Neptune:* Big orange

*Pluto:* Small bean

• How did your legs feel after you dropped off the solar system salad fixings?

EARTH SCIENCE

- Imagine you are out in space dropping those items off at the different planets. What would be the total distance you would have traveled? (*Hint:* What is the distance from the sun to Pluto?)
- If the center of the football field represents the sun, what can you say about the planets with respect to the sun? What do the planets do?

### Science in Personal and Social Perspectives

- Do you think it will ever be possible for you to travel to the other planets? Would you like to do this? Why or why not? What do you think you would need to pack for your trip?
- Would you purchase a ticket today to spend some time in a space station? Do you think you will live long enough to use the ticket?

### Science and Technology

- Do you think space stations will solve the problems of pollution and over-population on earth?
- Do you think the vastness of space will allow us to ship our garbage out into space and never be affected by it on earth? How do you think this will be possible?

### Science as Inquiry

- The students will be able to explain the concept of the expanding universe and discuss the implications that has for life as we presently know it on earth.
- Why is it possible to view planets in the nighttime sky? Do all of the planets always maintain the same orbital paths?

### History and Nature of Science

- If it was your job to create a satellite that would move through outer space, sending back to earth information about other planets, what kinds of knowledge do you think you would need to have? What would be the qualifications for your job? Pretend you need to employ someone to fill such a job. Write a job description and give it a title. Does the race or sex of the person applying matter?

## 4. EVALUATION: How will the students show what they have learned?

Upon completing the activities the students will be able to:

- complete the activities above.
- write a few sentences after they participate in the bicycle activity about how they felt when they finished and what they think about the distances between the planets. Ask the students to share their feelings with one another. How tired they became and how much they want to share with others what they did will provide an effective measure of success.
- when provided with ten different kinds of vegetables for a solar salad, use these new items to arrange the members of the solar system. Also ask them

to decide how far they would have to be from one another if 1 inch equals 1 million miles.

## Constellations

GRADE
5–8
DISCIPLINE
Earth
Science

**Concept to be invented**
Main idea—Constellations are groups of stars.

**Concepts that are important to expansion**
Big Dipper, Little Dipper, Polaris or North Star, Cassiopeia, Perseus, and the Pleiades found in Taurus

**Materials needed**
*For exploration:*

| | |
|---|---|
| construction paper | overhead projector |
| one pen or pencil per student | four or five flashlights |

➡ **Safety precautions:** Remind students to be careful not to poke themselves or others with the pen or pencil.

## 1. EXPLORATION: Which process skills will be used?

Observing, predicting, hypothesizing, inferring

### What will the students do?

*Connect the Stars*   The students will view a dot-to-dot pattern presented to them and predict what the pattern will look like once the dots are connected. This pattern is made on the chalkboard by using an overhead projector and black construction paper with holes punched in it for dots as the transparency. Place several different patterns on the overhead. Have the students take turns connecting the dots on the chalkboard.

## 2. EXPLANATION/CONCEPT INVENTION: What is the main idea? How will the main idea be constructed?

*Concept:* Constellations are groups of stars found in the sky. Ask the students questions such as the following to help invent this concept: What do you think these patterns represent? Do you recall seeing these same patterns anywhere? Review each of the patterns again and ask once again if anyone recalls seeing these patterns anywhere.

Patterns represent star constellations. Star constellations are made up of a group of stars and are given a name traditionally based on the pattern they

EARTH SCIENCE

make in the sky. These constellations were named by people in the past and usually have a story or legend attached to them.

Once again, project the patterns up on the board, again connecting the dots. This time go through the names of the constellations presented, and give a brief history of how they got their names. Some easy constellations to showcase are the Big Dipper, the Little Dipper, Cassiopeia, Perseus, and the Pleiades found in Taurus.

Identify the North Star—Polaris—for the students. Explain how all the other constellations in the Northern Hemisphere appear to revolve around this star. Thus, at different times of the year only certain constellations are visible in the nighttime sky in the Northern Hemisphere.

### 3. EXPANSION OF THE IDEA: Which process skills will be used?

Observing, communicating, formulating models, recording data

How will the idea be expanded?

*Evening Field Trip*   • Take the students on an evening field trip to an area where electric lights are minimal. Be sure you pick a clear night. Ask everyone to bring a blanket and lie on the grass. Try to identify as many constellations as possible.

*Create a Constellation*   • Ask the students to create a constellation of their own and name it, much as the ancient Greeks and Indians did as they observed stars in the nighttime sky. Have them write reports about how their constellations got their names. Share the reports orally with the class.

#### Science in Personal and Social Perspectives

• How can star constellations help you if you get lost at night?
• How can you develop watching stars into a hobby?

EARTH SCIENCE

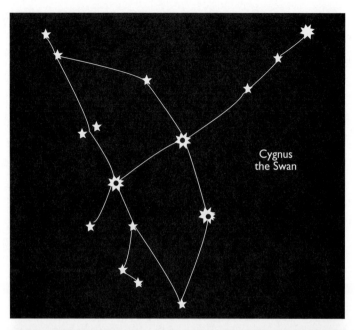

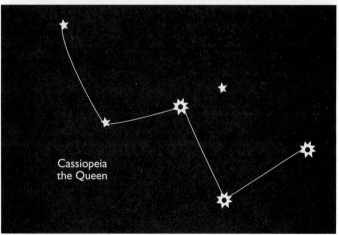

### Science and Technology

- What kind of equipment can you use to improve your view of the stars?
- How has astronomy equipment been perfected since the time of Galileo's first telescope?

### Science as Inquiry

- How can we use our knowledge of constellations to find a particular star in the sky?

- Why do all stars in the Northern Hemisphere appear to revolve around Polaris? Is this our closest star?

*History and Nature of Science*

- How are constellations used by astronomers who study other phenomena in the sky?
- Is there any difference between an astronomer and an astrologer? Do they both use their knowledge of constellations in some form? How?

**4. EVALUATION:** How will the students show what they have learned?

Upon completing the activities the students will be able to:

- identify Polaris, the North Star;
- identify the Big and Little Dippers in the northern sky;
- explain how at least two different constellations got their names;
- identify the star closest to earth.

## Earth Layers

**GRADE
K–4
DISCIPLINE
Earth
Science**

**Concept to be invented**
Main idea—The planet Earth is made up of three layers: the *core, mantle,* and *crust.*

**Concepts that are important to expansion**
Large land masses found on the crust of the earth are called *continents.* Large bodies of water on the crust are called *oceans.*

**Materials needed**
*For exploration (one per student):*
2-inch diameter ball of red, yellow, and gray clay; plastic knife; white construction paper; three crayons of red, yellow, and gray.

*For exploration (for entire class):*
Green and blue clay, green crayon, globe of the earth, tennis ball, soccer ball. Maps of ocean floors are useful but optional.

➡ **Safety precautions:** Remind students to be careful not to poke themselves or others with the plastic knife. Be sure to wash hands after using the clay. Remind them not to eat the clay.

**1. EXPLORATION:** Which process skills will be used?

Observing, manipulating materials, predicting

**EARTH SCIENCE**

What will the students do?

*Clay Earth Layers* Guide the students through this portion of the lesson by first asking them to pick up the red clay and work it into a ball. Ask them to then flatten out the yellow clay and wrap it around the red ball of clay. Finally ask them to flatten out the gray clay and then wrap it around the yellow-covered ball of clay. Ask the students to use their plastic knives carefully to cut the clay ball in half. Ask them to draw on their construction paper what the sliced-open clay ball looks like.

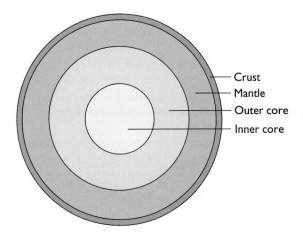

2. EXPLANATION/CONCEPT INVENTION: What is the main idea? How will the main idea be constructed?

*Concept:* The planet Earth is made up of three layers: the *core, mantle,* and *crust.*

Help the students invent the concept by asking them such questions as: What do you think this ball of clay with the different colored layers represents? Accept as many suggestions as possible and provide appropriate responses, all the while steering the students toward thinking about the Earth. If this suggestion is never given, then tell the students you'd like them to think of the clay ball as a representation of Earth and its layers. Since the students are most familiar with things found on the surface of the Earth, ask them to give you suggestions of things they find there. If possible, draw pictures of their suggestions or write the names on the board. Ask if anyone has an idea for another name to call Earth's surface. You may make an analogy to a pie that has a different material on the inside than outside. What do you call the outer covering of the pie? *Crust*—this same name is given to the outer surface of the Earth. Ask the students to label the gray layer on their diagram the *crust.*

Ask the students what they think the yellow layer may be like on the Earth and if they have any ideas as to its name. The yellow clay represents the mantle. This layer of Earth is in a slightly liquid form. It is under enough pressure to heat the rock and melt it. Ask the students to label the yellow layer on their diagram the *mantle.*

Continue with questions to get the children to think about what the very middle of something is usually referred to. Get the students to think about what they call the center of an apple. The *core* is represented by the red ball. Because the core is under such great pressure it is very hot, but also in a solid state. Ask the students to label the red layer on their diagram the *core.*

### 3. EXPANSION OF THE IDEA: Which process skills will be used?

Manipulating materials, observing, hypothesizing, inferring

How will the idea be expanded?

*Clay Continents*   Hold up the tennis ball. Ask the students how they think the tennis ball is like the Earth. Encourage them to use the terms *crust, mantle,* and *core.* Hold up a soccer ball. Ask the students how the soccer ball is like the Earth. Hold up the globe. Tell them that this represents what Earth would look like if they were up in the sky looking down. Ask the students to observe the globe carefully. After they look at the globe, ask the students if they think the soccer ball or the tennis ball is more like Earth's surface. Engage the students in a conversation about how the soccer ball is not one solid piece but many pieces sewn together. The crust of Earth does not look like one solid piece but like many pieces separated by water. The pieces appear to fit together. Ask the students for suggested names for the land masses and the bodies of water. If none are given, tell the students that the land masses are called *continents* and the bodies of water are called *oceans.* If maps of the ocean floor are available, share them with the students. Be sure to point out that the crust still exists below the ocean water.

Provide the students with some green and blue clay. Ask them to put their two halves of clay back together again, gently sealing the gray clay so that they have one ball of clay again. Ask the students to use the green clay to place some land masses or continents on their Earth. Ask them to add blue clay between the continents to represent the oceans. Then ask them to use their green and blue crayons to draw the continents and oceans on their drawings and to label them.

*Science in Personal and Social Perspectives*

- It has been found that the movement of the semiliquid material in the mantle of the Earth causes the crust to move. When the crust moves, earthquakes occur. Have earthquakes ever occurred where you live? What should be done to protect people during earthquakes?
- What continent do you live on?

*Science and Technology*

- How has knowledge about continent movement changed the way we construct buildings?
- Can earthquakes be detected? How?

- Do you think if technology could come up with a way to drain the oceans that would be better for life on Earth? Why or why not?

*Science as Inquiry*

- Which layer of the Earth is very hot yet still in a solid state?
- The land masses on the surface of the Earth appear to fit together, yet many are far apart. Do you think they were once together? If so, why?
- Is there crust under the oceans? How do we know this?

*History and Nature of Science*

- A seismologist would need to understand that the Earth is in layers. Why do you think this is true? What do you think a seismologist does?
- Should oceanographers be concerned about the Earth's layers?
- Many oil companies get their oil out of the North Sea. Do you think these companies used their knowledge of the Earth's layers to find their drilling sites? Why or why not?

**4. EVALUATION:** How will the students show what they have learned?

Upon completing the activities the students will be able to:

- draw a diagram of a cross section of the Earth and label the continents, oceans, crust, mantle, and core;
- identify from a diagram the different layers of the Earth;
- explain how the Earth can be compared to a soccer ball;
- point out continents and oceans on a globe.

## Fossils

**GRADE**
**2–4**
**DISCIPLINE**
**Earth**
**Science**

**Concept to be invented**
Main idea—A record of an ancient animal or plant found in sedimentary rocks is called a fossil.

**Concepts that are important to expansion**
*Fossils* provide clues to ancient environments. Evidence that humans were present during primitive times is called an *artifact*. A hollow space left in sedimentary rock when a plant or animal body decays is called a *mold*. When sediments fill the hollow space and harden, the hardened sediments formed in the shape of the plant or animal are called *casts*.

**Materials needed**
*For exploration:*
A variety of fossil samples for class observations, construction paper, and crayons or markers.

*For expansion:*

seashells (one or two per student)          plaster of Paris
leaves or plants                            water
one aluminum pie tin per student            one plastic spoon per student
petroleum jelly                             paper towels
two paper cups per student                  old newspapers

*Note:* Plastic samples of seashells, readily available through science equipment suppliers, may be preferred over actual seashells. Young children will find these easier to work with.

➡ **Safety precautions:** Students should be reminded not to eat the plaster. Take care to avoid water spills. Should they occur, wipe them up immediately.

## 1. EXPLORATION: Which process skills will be used?

Observing, brainstorming, predicting, hypothesizing, communicating

### What will the students do?

**Fossil Observations**

Pass the fossil samples around to the students without telling them what they are looking at. Ask the students to make careful observations about these unknown objects and to share their observations with the class. Encourage the students to think about what these things could possibly be. Is it a plant or an animal? Is it an image of a plant or an animal, or a piece of the real thing? Do you think it is still on the earth? How do you think this could have been formed? Allow the students sufficient time to brainstorm with one another ideas on their possible origins. Ask the students to draw the unknown object and to color it the way they think it would look if the actual object (plant or animal) were right in front of them. If the students are capable of writing sentences, ask them to write three or four sentences below their pictures describing how they think the image in the rock was formed.

## 2. EXPLANATION/CONCEPT INVENTION: What is the main idea? How will the main idea be constructed?

*Concept:* A record of an ancient animal or plant found in sedimentary rock is called a *fossil.*

Help the students invent the concept by asking them to share with the class the drawings they created. Some questions to ask the students to help invent the concept are:

- Why did you choose those colors for your drawing?
- Depending on the unknown you observed, was it easy or difficult for you to decide what this would look like if it were right in front of you? Why?
- How do you think this was formed?
- Will you please share with us your ideas?

EARTH SCIENCE

Through this line of questioning the process of fossilization can be brought out. When an animal or plant dies, it is covered with mud, rocks, sand, and so on. Pressure is applied over many years, so the layers turn to stone, leaving an imprint of the plant or animal. The records of ancient animals and plants found in sedimentary rocks are called fossils. Additional sourcebooks or films on fossils may be shared with the class at this time. Also share examples of local fossils.

### 3. EXPANSION OF THE IDEA: Which process skills will be used?

Observing, manipulating materials, predicting

How will the idea be expanded?

*Plaster Molds and Casts*

Ask the students to bring in seashells or leaves to use in making an image, or provide these or plastic models for them. Ask the students to use the old newspapers to cover their desk tops. Give each student a pie tin. Provide enough petroleum jelly so that the students can spread a thin-to-medium film over the bottom and sides of the pie tin. Remind them to be sure that the entire inside of the tin is covered with jelly. Once they have chosen the item they want to make an image of, instruct the students to cover the shell or plant with a thin layer of petroleum jelly. Place the shell or plant in the bottom of the pie tin so that the flattest side rests on the bottom of the pan.

In one of the cups for each student, place enough dry plaster of Paris so that when mixed it will be enough to cover the bottom of the pie tin with about 15 mm (½ inch) of plaster. In the second cup place enough water so that each student will have created the proper consistency of plaster once he or she mixes (using the plastic spoon) the dry powder with the water. Once the students have mixed their plaster, instruct them to pour it carefully over the shell or plant into the pie tin. They should allow about 1 hour for the plaster to harden. Remember: As the plaster dries it will become quite warm and then cool. Wait until it has cooled before removing it from the tin.

Once the plaster has hardened, turn the pie tin upside down over the paper-covered desk and tap the tin lightly to remove the plaster cast. The plaster will still be quite wet at this time, so the students need to be reminded to use care as they remove their shells or plants from the plaster. Once the shells or plants are removed, set the plaster casts in a safe place to cure fully (dry out and harden). This should take at least a day. Once the casts are cured, the students will have what is known as a *negative imprint* or *mold* of a plant or animal. If desired, a *positive imprint* or *cast* can now be created by spreading additional petroleum jelly over the surface of the negative imprint and placing it back into a deeper petroleum-jelly-lined pie tin. On top of the first cast pour additional plaster. After it has hardened (about 1 hour) carefully turn the tin upside down and remove the old and new plaster casts. Since the surface of the old cast was thoroughly covered with petroleum jelly, the two casts should readily come apart with a knife blade. The new cast formed from the negative imprint is called a positive imprint. After this has had a chance to harden thoroughly (about

EARTH SCIENCE

**Step 1.** Pour plaster into pie dish.

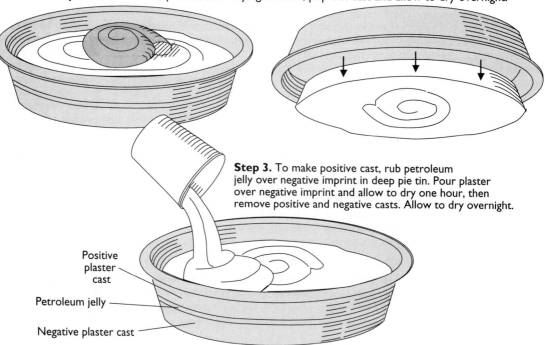

**Step 2.** Push shell into plaster; after drying an hour, pop out cast and allow to dry overnight.

**Step 3.** To make positive cast, rub petroleum jelly over negative imprint in deep pie tin. Pour plaster over negative imprint and allow to dry one hour, then remove positive and negative casts. Allow to dry overnight.

Positive plaster cast

Petroleum jelly

Negative plaster cast

one day), the students may want to paint or color with markers their newly formed fossils.

*Science in Personal and Social Perspectives*

- Why do you want to know about fossils? Has our study of fossils given you any ideas about what life was like in the past?

EARTH SCIENCE

- Do you think you could have lived during the time when dinosaurs roamed the land? Why or why not?

### Science and Technology

- How can fossils tell us what ancient environments were like?
- Evidence left by early people is called an artifact. Some examples are arrowheads, ancient beads, and animal skins used as clothing. Why do you think we don't call them fossils?

### Science as Inquiry

- Why can fossils be found only in sedimentary rocks?
- Can you find fossils where you live? Where do you think you would go to look for fossils?

### History and Nature of Science

- Paleontologists (fossil experts) study and learn from fossils. If you were a paleontologist, what kind of information would you share with others on the imprints you just made?
- How is an archeologist's job different from a paleontologist's? An excellent book for this topic is Gloria and Esther Goldreich, *What Can She Be? A Geologist* (New York: Lothrop, Lee and Shepard, 1976).
- Describe how the Leakeys (Louis, Mary, and son Richard) used fossil evidence to determine the changes in human body form throughout history.

## 4. EVALUATION: How will the students show what they have learned?

Upon completing the activities the students will be able to:

- demonstrate how a fossil can be formed by using sand, water, and a seashell;
- pick out the fossils when given several items to choose from, such as a seashell, a leaf, a sedimentary rock with a shell imprint or leaf imprint on it, a geode, or an igneous rock such as obsidian;
- tell or write in their own words what a fossil is and what information it can provide humans.

## Soil Formation

GRADE
5–8
DISCIPLINE
Earth
Science

**Concept to be invented**
Main idea—Soil is made from finely ground rock and organic material.

**Concepts that are important to expansion**
The rocks and plants found in the local area will determine the kind of soil that is formed. Large amounts of weathered sandstone will create a sandy soil. Slightly smaller particles create a silty soil. Very fine particles will make a clay soil.

EARTH SCIENCE

**Materials needed**

*For exploration:*

soil samples from local area

one piece of white construction
   paper per student

local sedimentary rock samples
   (these are easily broken)

hammer

old newspapers

one magnifying glass per student

one pair of goggles per student

*For expansion:*

sand

organic matter such as leaves or
   grass clippings

soil samples from local area

two small baby food jars with lids
   for each cooperative group

water

➡ **Safety precautions:** Make sure that all students are wearing goggles while smashing rocks with hammers. Wrap the rocks in newspaper and then strike them with a hammer. This will prevent rock pieces from flying everywhere.

   If you choose to take the students outside to collect soil samples, be sure proper safety procedures are followed. Pair up the students and make sure they know the boundaries for soil sample collection.

1. **EXPLORATION:** Which process skills will be used?

   Observing, recording data, classifying

What will the students do?

*Soil Separation and Rock Crushing*  Provide the class with soil samples collected from the local area, or if possible, take the students around the school grounds to collect soil samples. Ask the students to cover their desktops with old newspapers and then place the white construction paper on top of the newspaper. Arrange the students in cooperative groups of three to four to make observations of the soil samples. Use the magnifying glasses to make detailed observations of the individual particles. Encourage students to draw or write a description of their observations.

After the students have made as many observations as possible, ask them to try to separate their soil samples into different parts. How many different ways can you separate the soil samples?

Give each cooperative group a hammer and several pieces of local sedimentary rocks like sandstone or limestone. Remind students to *put on and keep on* their goggles at all times during this section of the activity. Over the newspaper-covered desks, ask the students to wrap the rock samples in newspaper and then pound the rocks with hammers. Do the materials formed look similar to the materials you separated out from the local soil sample?

## 2. EXPLANATION/CONCEPT INVENTION: What is the main idea? How will the main idea be constructed?

*Concept:* Soil is made from finely ground rocks and organic material.

Ask the students to share the results of their observations. What kinds of things did you observe? Were all parts of the soil the same size? How many different ways did you separate your soil samples? Suggestions may include size or color; rocklike or plantlike. What did your rock look like before you crushed it with the hammer? What about afterward? Is there any similarity between the crushed rock and your soil sample? Continue questioning students until they come to the conclusion that soil is made up of small pieces of rock and plant matter.

## 3. EXPANSION OF THE IDEA: Which process skills will be used?

Manipulating materials, observing, inferring, classifying, estimating, predicting

How will the idea be expanded?

*Soil Components*  Provide each cooperative group with two small baby food jars with lids. Ask the students to label one jar *local soil* and the second *homemade soil*. Ask the students to fill the first jar up halfway with one of the local soil samples. Ask the students to place in the second jars some of the crushed rock they just smashed, some sand, and some grass clippings or leaves, so that half of the jar is filled. Into both jars pour enough water to cover all of the solid materials. Place the lids on the jars and shake vigorously. Solicit predictions about what will happen

EARTH SCIENCE

in each jar after it has sat for 1 hour, for 3 hours, and overnight. Ask the students to record their predictions and then place the jars where they will not be disturbed for the times indicated. Ask the students the following questions to help them conclude that the rocks and plants found in the local area will determine the kind of soil formed. Weathered sandstone will create a sandy soil, more finely ground particles will create a silty soil, and very fine particles will create a clay soil. What did the two samples look like after 1 hour? after 3 hours? the next day? If you did not look at jar labels and just at samples, could you tell the difference between the soil in the two jars? How were they similar? different? Look at the settled materials. Can you estimate how much of the sample is sand? silt? clay? How would you classify the soil? What do you think will happen to the grass or leaves if you let the jar sit for one week, one month, or three months? Solicit predictions and then set the jar in a safe place so that students can observe it over a three-month period.

### Science in Personal and Social Perspectives

- What kind of soil is found around your home? Would it be a good soil if you wanted to grow potatoes in your garden?
- Should people be concerned about farmers using excessive amounts of fertilizers in soils? What can be done to prevent excessive use of fertilizers?
- Do you think it is better to have a sandy or a silty soil in your garden? Do you put fertilizers on your soil? If so, why?

### Science and Technology

- As you have discovered, not all soils are alike. Do you think it was important to keep this fact in mind as tractor tires were developed?
- What do you think *no-till* means, and why would farmers be urged to use this method of farming?

### Science as Inquiry

- List at least three components of soil.
- What influence does local bedrock have on the type of soil found in an area?
- Does the rate of weathering and erosion in an area affect the formation of soil?
- Where do you think the minerals found in soils come from?

### History and Nature of Science

- What are the responsibilities of a soil agronomist?
- How important is it for a land developer to understand soil formation?
- What is organic farming? How do these methods of farming differ from other methods?

**4. EVALUATION:** How will the students show what they have learned?

Upon completing the activities the students will be able to:

- take a given soil sample and demonstrate the steps necessary to estimate the amount of sand, silt, and clay in the sample;

- explain how the type of soil found in a local area is dependent on the local bedrock and ground cover;
- write a persuasive argument on why grass is necessary to cover soil or on how soil is different from dirt.

## Rock Types

### Concept to be invented
Main idea—Rocks may be classified into three groups: *igneous, sedimentary,* and *metamorphic.*

### Concepts that are important to expansion
*Igneous* means "fire formed." Cooled magma and lava create igneous rocks such as granite and obsidian. *Sedimentary* rocks are formed in water due to layers of sediments building up from weathered igneous, metamorphic, and other sedimentary rocks, or decaying organic matter; examples are limestone and sandstone. *Metamorphic* rocks are very hard rocks that may be formed from igneous or sedimentary rocks under extreme heat and pressure; marble and gneiss are examples.

### Materials needed
*For exploration (for each cooperative group of students):*
several samples of igneous rocks, sedimentary rocks, metamorphic rocks, one jar, two sheets of construction paper, sand, mud, and pebbles

*For expansion (for each student):*
goggles, hammer and chisel, collection bag, three empty egg cartons, old newspapers, and a marker

➡ **Safety precautions:** Remind students to handle rock samples carefully. No throwing rocks! If you choose to take the students outside to collect rock samples, be sure proper safety procedures are followed. Pair up the students and make sure they know the boundaries for rock sample collection.

**EARTH SCIENCE**

1. **EXPLORATION:** Which process skills will be used?

Observing, classifying, inferring

What will the students do?

*Rock Categorization*

Divide the class into cooperative learning groups of three or four students. Provide each group with sand, numerous rock types, and pebbles. Ask the students to categorize the rocks. What's different about them? How are they alike? After the students have shared the results of their categorizing, ask them to set those samples aside in the categories they identified.

Give each cooperative group a jar and ask them to put rocks, sand, mud, and water into it. Put a lid on the jar and shake it for a few moments. Ask the students to draw a picture of what the jar looks like after the materials have settled.

## 2. EXPLANATION/CONCEPT INVENTION: What is the main idea? How will the main idea be constructed?

*Concept:* Rocks may be classified into three groups: igneous, sedimentary, and metamorphic.

Ask the students to fold a sheet of construction paper into three parts. Now go back to the different piles of rocks the students first categorized. Ask them what kinds of differences they noted. Explain that rocks come in all shapes, colors, and sizes. However, they weren't all made the same way. Use the example of lava from a volcano. What happens to the lava when it dries? It becomes a hard rock called *igneous,* meaning "fire formed." Cooled magma and lava create igneous rocks like granite and obsidian. In the first part of the construction paper, draw or describe how igneous rock is formed. Provide the students with various samples of igneous rocks to observe.

Refer back to the shaken jar. What does it currently look like? Steer the students toward looking at the layers of materials. Did your group classify any of the rock samples based on whether you could see layers? What do you think rocks formed from the buildup of materials in layers are called? *Sedimentary* rocks are formed in water due to layers of sediments building up from weathered igneous, metamorphic, and other sedimentary rocks, or decaying organic matter. Limestone and sandstone are sedimentary. In the second part of the construction paper, draw or describe how sedimentary rocks are formed. Provide the students with various samples of sedimentary rocks to observe.

Ask the students if they think they classified any rocks that have not yet been described. Have the students share those rocks with the rest of the class. Make sure they do not fit under igneous or sedimentary categories. Explain to the students that the igneous or sedimentary rocks can be put under extreme heat and pressure inside the Earth, which changes the look of the rock. These are called *metamorphic* rocks; examples are marble and gneiss. Metamorphic rocks are very hard. In the third part of the construction paper, draw or describe how metamorphic rocks are formed. Provide the students with various samples of metamorphic rocks to observe.

## 3. EXPANSION OF THE IDEA: Which process skills will be used?

Observing, classifying, collecting, comparing, communicating

How will the idea be expanded?

***Rock Collection Field Trip***  This expansion activity may be done as a home extension activity or as a class field trip. Identify a site where students will be permitted to collect rock samples. Either take them as a class or provide instructions to parents to take the students to the collection site. Be sure the students are given instruction on how to use the hammer and chisel to extract rock samples from the bedrock. Encourage the students to break their samples into pieces small enough to fit into the egg carton depressions. Remind the students to think about the different colors and textures that different kinds of rocks have. Classify the collection into igneous, sedimentary, and metamorphic, and designate one egg carton for each rock type. After a sufficient amount of time has passed (one or two months), ask the students to bring their collections to school to share with the class.

### Science in Personal and Social Perspectives

- If you were going to build a home along the ocean, would you want the underlying rock to be igneous, sedimentary, or metamorphic? Why?
- Have you ever washed your hands with a pumice-based soap? Have you ever used a pumice stone to smooth away rough skin? Where do you think this comes from?

### Science and Technology

- Which type of rock is best used for building purposes?
- Would you trust a bridge made of sedimentary rocks? Do you think it would last as long as a bridge made with igneous rocks? What about a bridge made of metamorphic rock?
- Which type of rock would be a wise choice to build a dam with?

### Science as Inquiry

- Where in the world would I easily find an igneous rock? a sedimentary rock? a metamorphic rock?
- Can an igneous rock be formed from a sedimentary one? Can a sedimentary rock be formed from a metamorphic or igneous rock?
- What kind of rock is the local bedrock?

### History and Nature of Science

- Would a civil engineer responsible for placing a bridge across the Mississippi River between Illinois and Missouri need to understand the type of bedrock found in the area before plans for the bridge could be made? Why or why not?
- As a construction worker you decide to build your own home. You want to make it out of stone. Which kind of rock type would you use, and why? Is it important that a construction worker or even a home owner know the differences among igneous, sedimentary, and metamorphic rocks?

## 4. EVALUATION: How will the students show what they have learned?

Upon completing the activities the students will be able to:

- look at six different rocks and identify whether they are igneous, sedimentary, or metamorphic;

EARTH SCIENCE

- identify different areas of the world where the three different rock types can be found;
- reflect, and then write a description of an igneous rock formed when lava cooled outside the Earth.

## Cooling Crystals

GRADE
5–8
DISCIPLINE
Earth
Science

### Concept to be invented
Main idea—The rate at which a crystal cools affects the size of the crystal.

### Concepts that are important to expansion
Crystals can be seen in many rocks.

### Materials needed
*For exploration (for each group):*

| | |
|---|---|
| three glass caster cups | one hand lens per student |
| three small test tubes (10 ml) | grease pencil |
| test tube holder | crushed ice |
| paradichlorobenzine (PDB) flakes (found in supermarkets, hardware stores, pharmacies) | two 500-ml beakers |
| | one 150-ml beaker |
| | tongs |

*For exploration (for entire class):*
hot plates, paper towels

*For expansion:*
samples of the igneous rocks rhyolite, granite, and obsidian; one hand lens per student

➥ **Safety precautions:** Extreme care should be used near the hot plate and in handling the hot water and PDB. Goggles should be worn at all times. Be sure the room is well ventilated when melting the PDB.

1. EXPLORATION: Which process skills will be used?

Observing, predicting, manipulating materials, recording data, drawing conclusions

What will the students do?

*PDB Crystal Formation*

Ask the students to fill one of the 500-ml beakers with 300 ml of water. Place a caster cup in the beaker. Boil the water on the hot plate. Fill the other 500-ml beaker with crushed ice. Place the second caster cup in the beaker. Leave the third caster cup at room temperature.

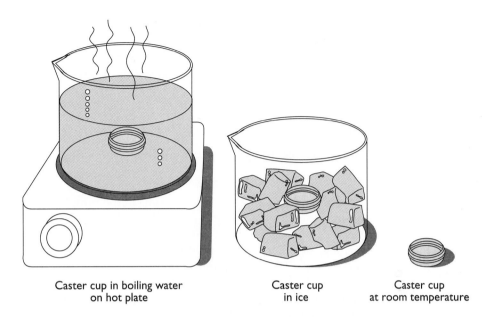

Caster cup in boiling water
on hot plate

Caster cup
in ice

Caster cup
at room temperature

Carefully observe some PDB flakes. Record those observations. Fill each of the three small test tubes with PDB flakes. Half-fill the 150-ml beaker with water. Place the three test tubes in the beaker. Place the beaker with the test tubes on the hot plate. Heat the beaker gently until the PDB melts.

Using the tongs, carefully remove the caster cup from the boiling water. Dry the cup and label it *A*. Using the test tube holder, remove one test tube and pour the PDB into this caster cup. Time how long it takes for the PDB to completely become a solid. Record the time. Record your observations of the PDB flakes for cup A.

Remove the second caster cup from the beaker with ice. Dry the cup quickly and completely. Label it *B*. Pour the second test tube of PDB into this cup. Time how long it takes for the PDB to turn completely solid. Record the time. Record your observations of the PDB flakes for cup B.

Pour the third test tube of PDB into the cup at room temperature. Label it C. Again, time how long it takes for this PDB to solidify completely. Record the time. Record your observations of the PDB flakes for cup C.

## 2. EXPLANATION/CONCEPT INVENTION: What is the main idea? How will the main idea be constructed?

*Concept:* The rate at which a crystal cools affects the size of the crystal.

How does the rate of cooling affect the size of crystals? Record the cooling times for samples A, B, and C on the board. Look at the contents of each caster cup with the magnifying glass. Draw the contents of each caster cup on your paper.

EARTH SCIENCE

When the PDB was placed into the test tubes, there was no difference between tubes. Once it was placed into cups A, B, and C, a change occurred. How are they different? What caused this difference? What conclusions can you draw? The students should conclude that the rate at which a crystal cools affects the size of the crystal formed.

### 3. EXPANSION OF THE IDEA: Which process skills will be used?

Observing, recording data, generalizing, formulating models

#### How will the idea be expanded?

*Rock Type versus Crystal Formation*

Ask the students to observe the crystals in the samples of granite, rhyolite, and obsidian with a magnifying glass. Draw the crystals in each sample on your paper. Compare the crystals in the caster cups to the samples of granite, rhyolite, and obsidian. Which PDB crystals are most similar to the crystals in the rock samples? (Cup A, granite; cup B, obsidian; cup C, rhyolite.)

Granite, rhyolite, and obsidian are igneous rocks essentially made of the same material. Explain why they look different. Where would igneous rocks have a chance to cool slowly? Where would igneous rock cool rapidly? If you saw a rock that contained large interlocking crystals, what would you say about the way it formed? The more slowly a crystal cools, the larger the crystals are. Granite cooled slowly and crystals were able to form. Rhyolite cooled more rapidly than granite, but more slowly than obsidian. Igneous rocks cool slowly deep in the Earth. They cool rapidly on the surface. Large interlocking crystals form slowly inside the Earth.

#### Science in Personal and Social Perspectives

- What kinds of crystals do you eat regularly? (Salt and sugar.)
- How does the size of a crystal determine its quality? Do you think your knowledge of how crystals form will assist you in determining the quality of precious rocks and gems?

#### Science and Technology

- The strength and quality of rocks are important for construction. What is the best type of rock for long-lasting buildings?
- How has the scarcity of quality gems on the market affected your life, your community, or the world?

#### Science as Inquiry

- What kinds of rocks are found in the area where you live? Can you classify them according to their crystal structure?
- Can crystals be found in sedimentary rocks? Why or why not?

#### History and Nature of Science

- What kinds of careers would use information on crystal formation? Some possibilities include geologist, geophysicist, volcanologist, jeweler, sculptor, and geographer.

- Choose one of the career suggestions from the question above and research the skills necessary to enter that career. Provide an oral report to the class.

**4. EVALUATION:** How will the students show what they have learned?

Upon completing the activities the students will be able to:

- identify where a crystal cooled (on the Earth's surface or inside the Earth) and at what rate when given drawings of crystals of different shapes and sizes;
- examine samples of igneous rocks and explain why they have different-sized crystals;
- explain how the prices of precious jewels are affected by crystal formation.

## Weathering

**GRADE**
**5–8**
**DISCIPLINE**
**Earth**
**Science**

**Concept to be invented**
Main idea—*Weathering* is the name given to the various mechanical and chemical processes that break down rock.

**Concepts that are important to expansion**
erosion, soil formation, rock formation—igneous, sedimentary, metamorphic

**Materials needed**
*For discrepant event:*
soda bottle and cap, water, freezer

*For exploration:*
field site to collect data, stereomicroscope, hammer

*For expansion:*
dilute hydrochloric acid (HCl); igneous, sedimentary, and metamorphic rock samples

➡ **Safety precautions:** Review with the students ahead of time the rules that should be followed for everyone's safety during the field trip. Visit the field site before the students do to guard against any possible hazards at the site.

*Freezing Bottle*　　The day before you begin this lesson, take a glass soda bottle and ask a student to fill it with water all the way to the top. Cap the bottle so that no water can escape. Now ask the students what they think will happen to this bottle if you place it in the freezer for a day. Record their predictions on the board, where they will remain untouched until the next day. Twenty-four hours later remove the bottle from the freezer. If the bottle was totally filled before freezing, it should now be cracked, as the ice expanded upon freezing. Ask the students what they observe. Did it behave according to their predictions? Why did this happen? What happens to water when it freezes? Based on your observations, do you think water could do this to other items besides glass? Think about this as we engage in today's activity.

1. **EXPLORATION:** Which process skills will be used?

Observing, hypothesizing, predicting, measuring, using spatial relationships, recording data

What will the students do?

*Weathering Field Trip*

The students will go on a field trip around the school grounds. An old road or empty prairie or field will be an ideal site. Before beginning the trip, the students will be reminded about appropriate care of a collection site. Remind them to take care as they travel through the site and to try not to destroy any animal homes or wildflowers or plant growth. Ask the students to look for rocks that appear to be broken apart. They are to record a description of the area in which they find them, taking care to note the soil conditions (wet, dry, sandy, clayey), an estimate of the original size of the rock, a physical description of the rock (color, shininess, hardness, porosity), and a prediction based on their findings as to what they think caused the rock to break apart. A small sample of the rock should be collected for further study in the classroom. Upon returning to the classroom, the students will make a composite chart of their field observations. Headings for this chart could include *collection site, soil conditions, rock size, physical properties* (color, luster, hardness, pore size), *possible cause for breakage.*

2. **EXPLANATION/CONCEPT INVENTION:** What is the main idea? How will the main idea be constructed?

*Concept: Weathering* is the name given to the various mechanical and chemical processes that break down rock.

Draw the students' attention to the composite chart in the front of the room. In order to guide the students in inventing the concept of *weathering,* ask such questions as: In looking at this chart, are there any we can group together? Do any of them sound as if the different groups of investigators were looking at the same rocks?

Ask the students to bring up the sample rocks whose descriptions sound similar. Do you think these are the same rocks?

Once double sightings have been eliminated, begin to focus on the chart again, this time asking, "Is there any one area where broken rocks were found more often than any other? Or is there any one soil condition where broken rocks are found more often than any other?"

If this is the case, then ask the students if they think this soil condition contributed to the presence of broken rocks. If it is a very wet area, then you can relate this back to the discrepant event—how the freezing and thawing of water will contribute to the cracking of the rocks. If this is a dry area, ask the students if they made note of any vegetation growing in the area. They may have found the broken rocks due to roots growing through the surface of the rock. It may be a very dry area where wind blows through rather rapidly, causing the rocks to break up.

Ask the students if they know of a term to describe the breaking up of rock due to running water, wind, rain, or roots. Introduce the term *weathering* at this point.

What happens to the rock pieces as they are carried by the rain, wind, or running water? What term can we use to describe the carrying away of this weathered material? (Erosion.) Ask the students if they observed the soil where they found the rock. Was it similar in composition to the rock itself? Engage the students in a discussion of how the weathering of rocks assists in soil formation.

## 3. EXPANSION OF THE IDEA: Which process skills will be used?

Observing, classifying, experimenting, predicting, inferring, interpreting data, recording data, communicating

### How will the idea be expanded?

*Rock Identification*

If your students collected rock samples that fell into one type (all igneous, or all sedimentary, or all metamorphic), then in addition to their samples, provide them with rock samples from the missing rock groups. Ask the students to try to group the rock samples according to the characteristics from the composite chart from the first activity. Suggest to them that based on hardness, porosity, and composition, they should be able to group their rock samples into three different groups.

Once they have their samples in three groups, the students can perform the following experiments to determine possible sources of weathering.

*Chemical Weathering*

*Acid Test.* Take one sample from each rock group. Predict what will happen to the rock when you drop three drops of dilute HCl on it. Do you think each rock will react the same way? Which one do you think will weather the most? In nature, what type of weathering could we consider this to be? (This is known as *chemical weathering.*)

*Rust/Oxidation.* Do you notice any color changes in your rock? Are there what appear to be rust spots on the rock? What do you think causes this?

*Mechanical Weathering*

*Water.* Cover the three different rock samples with water and place them in a freezer for a day. Do the rocks crumble easily in your hands? If you strike them with a hammer lightly, do they fall apart? Are the insides still wet? Which rock type was most susceptible to the freezing water? Since the water simply froze and broke the rock apart, this is known as *mechanical weathering.*

*Roots.* In what area did you find this rock? Are there still traces of plant matter on the rock? Did you see any roots pushing up right through the surface of the rock? Do the roots cause chemical or mechanical weathering? Overall, which rocks are most easily weathered and which are most difficult to weather?

EARTH SCIENCE

Can you guess how each of these rock groups was originally formed based on your weathering observations? Lead to a discussion on rock formations: igneous, sedimentary, and metamorphic. Detailed discussions will be provided in a separate lesson for each rock type.

### Science in Personal and Social Perspectives

- Why does one need to use special fishing lures if a river or lake is muddy or murky due to erosion?
- What would you suspect was happening if the water in your favorite fishing stream looked clean, yet the number of fish began to dwindle? You have noticed that some of the rocks along the bank are beginning to crumble and wash downstream. What could you do to verify your suspicions? Whom would you talk to about this problem?

### Science and Technology

- What role does strip-mining of coal or clear-cutting of timber play in allowing the forces of weather to affect erosion?

EARTH SCIENCE

- How has an increased understanding of the forces of weathering and erosion caused us to change our farming practices since the Dust Bowl days of the 1930s?

*Science as Inquiry*

- How does weathering differ from erosion? What factors contribute to soil formation? What processes have occurred to create the different rock types? Can you name the three different rock types?
- In which rock formation would you most likely place a building like the Sears Tower? Why? Which rock type would you be least likely to choose to build a house of? Why?

*History and Nature of Science*

- Why would a civil engineer need to understand the processes of weathering and erosion?
- Do you think a contractor or cement finisher would find knowledge of weathering, erosion, soil and rock types useful in his or her work?
- Research the great pyramids of Egypt. How were they built? What are they made of? When were they built? Would they still exist if they were first built in Chicago?

## 4. EVALUATION: How will the students show what they have learned?

Upon completing the activities the students will be able to:

- draw a diagram showing the relationships among rock types, soil types, weathering, and erosion;
- when given a weathered rock sample and a description of where the sample was found, suggest the most probable source for its weathering;
- list at least four agents of erosion;
- discriminate between constructive and destructive geologic forces.

## Crustal Plate Movement

**GRADE 5–8**
**DISCIPLINE**
**Earth Science**

**EARTH SCIENCE**

**Concept to be invented**
Main idea—The theory of plate tectonics states that the crust of the Earth is not one solid piece but rather several separate plates that are in motion on top of molten material.

**Concepts that are important to expansion**
Continental drift, earthquakes, volcanoes

**Materials needed**
*For exploration (for each group of four to six students):*
four wood blocks                                   plastic shoebox (heavy plastic type,
1 liter of water                                         which will not melt under lightbulb)

a heat lamp or 150–200-watt
    bulb and socket

food coloring
stacks of books to raise box above lamp

*For expansion:*
maps of the world showing the crustal plate boundaries, a list of places famous for volcanic eruptions, a list of sites of recent earthquakes

➥ **Safety precautions:** The students should be reminded to use care with the heat source. Don't place the heat source too close to the plastic box or books. Use care around water and electricity. Wipe up any water spills immediately. Do not touch heat source with wet hands.

## 1. EXPLORATION: Which process skills will be used?

Experimenting, observing, predicting, inferring

### What will the students do?

*Moving Plates*    Each student group should place its plastic box on two stacks of books. The box should be high enough so that a heat source (lamp) will fit beneath. Pour water into the box. Place the four small wood blocks in the box. All the blocks should touch, forming a square. Place the heat source beneath the box directly under the center of the blocks. Turn the light on and place a drop of food coloring in the water where the four blocks meet. Observe the blocks for about 5 to 10 minutes. What happens to each of the four wood blocks? What happens to the food coloring?

## 2. EXPLANATION/CONCEPT INVENTION: What is the main idea? How will the main idea be constructed?

*Concept:* The theory of plate tectonics states that the crust of the Earth is not one solid piece, but rather several separate plates that are in motion on top of molten material.

Ask the students to share their observations on the movement of the four wood blocks and the food coloring. Why do you think this happened? If you were to relate this activity to the Earth's crust, what do you think the blocks represent? (Early land masses that separated millions of years ago.) What would the water represent? (The molten layer of the Earth called the *mantle.*) What happened to the temperature of the water over time? (It warmed up.) What happened to the food coloring? (It slowly moved along the surface as the water continued to warm.) Through questioning along this line, help the students to conclude that the theory of plate tectonics states that the crust of the Earth is not one solid piece but rather several separate plates that are in motion on top of molten material.

## 3. EXPANSION OF THE IDEA: Which process skills will be used?

Observing, predicting, making conclusions

EARTH SCIENCE

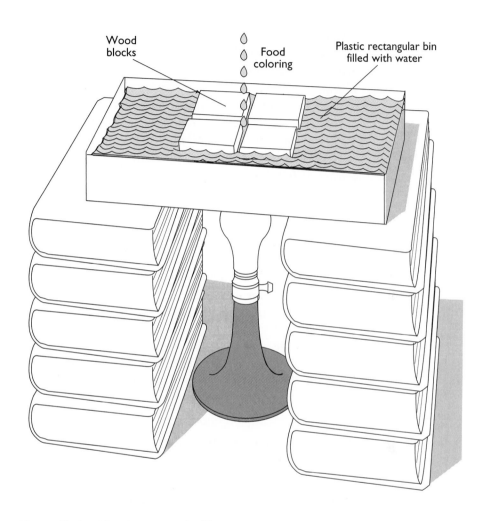

Wood blocks

Food coloring

Plastic rectangular bin filled with water

## How will the idea be expanded?

*Mapping Volcanoes and Earthquakes*

Pair up the students. Provide each pair with a world map indicating the boundaries for the crustal plates. The students should be free to mark on the maps you provide. Provide the students with a recent list of volcanic and earthquake activity. Ask them to plot on the map the places where the most recent earthquakes and volcanoes have occurred. You may give them a list of volcanic and earthquake activity for the past fifty years to plot. Ask the students to share some observations they have made about the relationship between earthquakes and volcanoes from this exercise. The students should conclude that most earthquake and volcanic activity occurs where two or more crustal plates come together.

### Science in Personal and Social Perspectives

• Would you choose to live along a crustal plate boundary? If you did, how might it affect your life?

- Do you think the government should help pay to repair homes for people who chose to build their homes on a known crustal boundary?

*Science and Technology*

- Are you aware of any other theories about formation or movement of the Earth's crust? What part do you think technology has played in theory change and advanced knowledge about different phenomena?
- How do we use our knowledge about movement of the Earth's crust when we construct buildings in areas where crustal plates are known to move?

*Science as Inquiry*

- Is there still movement of the Earth's crust? How do we know?
- A lot of volcanic activity occurs in the Hawaiian Islands. Are they on the edge of a crustal plate? If not, what is causing the volcanic activity? Research the formation of these volcanic islands.
- Explain how a solid crust can move. What does the mantle layer of the Earth have to do with this movement?

*History and Nature of Science*

- Who is Charles Lyell? What career changes led him to many geological discoveries?
- Would a seismologist be concerned with crustal plate movement? Why?
- Why would a civil engineer be concerned with the location of crustal plate boundaries? What does a civil engineer do?

**4. EVALUATION:** How will the students show what they have learned?

*Oatmeal and Cracker Plate Tectonics*

On completing the activities the students will be able to:

- demonstrate the theory of plate tectonics by using a bowl of oatmeal and some soda crackers;
- identify the area known as the Ring of Fire on a world map and explain what it is;
- briefly explain the theory of plate tectonics.

## Aging Human/Aging Earth

**Concept to be invented**
The Earth's processes we see today, including erosion, movement of crustal plates, and changes in atmospheric composition, are similar to those that occurred in the past.

**Concepts that are important to expansion**
Earth history is also influenced by occasional catastrophes such as the impact of an asteroid or comet.

**Materials needed**

*For exploration:*

pictures of the Earth, including
   views from space and close-up
   pictures of various biomes
pictures of the other planets and
   Earth's moon

access to older community members
audio or videotape recorder
journal or notebook to record data

*For expansion:*

geologic maps of your state and the
   region where your school is located. These are maps that show
   the ages of the various rock layers
   identifying the periods and
   epochs, and the depth of each
   layer from the surface.

geologic time scale
access to reference materials
   on the geology of the local
   region, or access to geologists
   who live/work in the region

➡ **Safety precautions:** During the exploration activity the students should work in pairs and never go into an interview without a formal introduction by a trusted adult.

## 1. EXPLORATION: Which process skills will be used?

Observing, inferring, predicting, communicating, comparing and contrasting, formulating hypotheses, using space-time relationships

### What will students do?

*Living Human—
Living Earth*

*Introduction.* The teacher should hang pictures of the Earth around the classroom— scenes from the major biomes such as pictures of forests, mountains, deserts, etc. An old calendar may be a good source for such scenes. Also hang around the classroom pictures of the other planets and the moon. Ask the students to look around the room at all of the pictures. After students have had time to view the pictures, ask them why they think scientists call the Earth a "living planet." Solicit their responses. To get them started, use guiding questions like what do you think is evidence of living things? Do you see any evidence of that in any of the pictures found around the classroom?

Encourage them to think about changes in the surface of the Earth; recall for them events in recent years such as the earthquakes in Turkey, volcanoes in Mexico, and the numerous hurricanes that strike from the Atlantic Ocean. All of these are evidence that the Earth's surface is constantly changing shape, wearing down one area and building up another. The forests and grasslands are evidence that on the planet Earth the sun's energy is being used to grow new life.

Ask them to ponder this question: How is your body like the planet Earth? Solicit student ideas. These may include things like our bodies have mountains and valleys—high and low spots; we are covered with a thin crust—our skin;

EARTH SCIENCE

and we make use of the sun's energy to get food to help us grow as well. Like the Earth, changes have happened to our bodies over time. We've grown since we were babies, we've acquired some cuts and bruises, but even with that our bodies have repaired themselves. This is much like the planet Earth does after a catastrophe like a forest fire or flood.

Conclude with this statement: Just as there are changes in our living bodies over time, so too has the living Earth changed.

*Student Activity.* Assign the students to "interview teams." Explain to them that their task is to identify and interview a person in their community who can share information on changes in the physical environment of the community over time. Stress that the purpose of the interview is to capture stories on changes in the ecology of the region—not social changes. Remind the students of the introductory discussion's conclusion: Just as there are changes in our living bodies over time, so too has the living Earth changed. Ask them to use this conclusion to shape their interview questions. For instance, the students could ask the interviewee to recall something he or she liked to do outdoors when young, like swimming in a certain pond or walking across a frozen creek in the dead of winter. The students could then ask if a young person could still do that today. Is the pond still there? Has the creek been widened or does water still flow there?

Provide the students with audio or videotape recorders for the interviews. Teach them skills in setting up an interview, the proper etiquette in calling the person they want to interview, introducing themselves, showing respect and courtesy to the person speaking, etc. For safety's sake stress to the students the importance of performing the interview as a team. Never go into the person's home without at least another student or a parent present while they conduct the interview. If at all possible, invite the person to the school for the interview.

Ask the students to prepare a multimedia presentation on the ecological changes they discovered through their interviews. Ask them to speculate on causes for the identified changes and to pick at least one change and research the exact reason for that change. For example, if a person said, "As youngsters we used to swim across the Mississippi River," and your students know that this is not possible today because the spot the person talked about is now much wider than it was then, the students should do some research to find out why the river is much wider today. Encourage them to bring in pictures and/or video of the sites in the past and present.

## 2. EXPLANATION/CONCEPT INVENTION: What is the main idea? How will the main idea be constructed?

*Concept:* The Earth's processes we see today, including erosion, movement of crustal plates, and changes in atmospheric composition, are similar to those that occurred in the past.

Hold a public forum for the students to present their findings. Invite the people who were interviewed, parents, and the community to hear the student presentations. A public forum presentation will provide a real-world context for the student work and demonstrate the importance of good communication skills, both spoken and written. As the students share their findings, ask them to classify the causes for the ecological changes as "human-made" or due to "nature." Discuss how both may occur, or how humans may speed up natural causes like erosion. Lead them to conclude that the Earth's processes we see today, including erosion, movement of crustal plates, and changes in atmospheric composition, are similar to those that occurred in the past.

## 3. EXPANSION OF THE IDEA: Which process skills will be used?

Observing, inferring, hypothesizing, interpreting data

### How will the idea be expanded?

*The Rock Record*   Provide the students with a series of maps showing the rock record for your region and for your state. These are typically available through your state's department of natural resources, geology division. The major geologic eras, periods, and epochs should be marked on the maps, as well as the relative thickness of the layers represented. Also provide the students with a geologic calendar, which provides the names and duration for all of the geologic eras, periods, and epochs. If the students have never worked with a geologic calendar, review the components, explaining the differences between eras, periods, and epochs.

Using the maps, ask the students to compare the rock record of the local region to the geologic calendar. Are all of the epochs present in your region? What epoch is missing in your region? How does your region compare with the rest of your state? Are there differences in the thickness of the rock layers? Are the same layers missing throughout the state as are missing in your local region? Ask the students to reflect on their findings from the interview activity. Knowing what and why geologic changes happened in recent times from the interviews with the local people, can you project how some of the rock layers may be absent from the rock record?

Ask the students to determine where in their local rock record did humans first appear on the planet? How far below the surface is that rock layer? When did the dinosaurs first appear on the planet? How far below the surface is that event in your local rock record? What about animals like a horse or a mastodon? When did they first appear on Earth? How far below the surface is that event in your local rock record? Why aren't all of these animals still found on Earth today? Would a process like erosion or even an earthquake wipe out the dinosaurs? What do you think happened in Earth's history to eliminate some animal species? Can we tell this from the rock record?

Use the reference materials on the geology of the local region to provide some answers to these questions. Invite a local geologist or even a paleontologist or a paleobotanist to come in and talk to the class about the local geologic

EARTH SCIENCE

record, explaining the geologic processes that have occurred in their state and region. Conclude this activity by having the students share answers to the questions posed, to restate the primary concept that processes that occurred in the past still occur today, and that the Earth's history is also influenced by occasional catastrophes such as the impact of an asteroid or comet.

### Science in Personal and Social Perspectives

- While we cannot always control the impact that nature has on our local ecology, we can control human impact. Identify one local ecological change caused by humans and propose solutions to minimize such impact in the future.
- The rock layers below the surface were formed by natural processes that occurred, in some cases, hundreds of thousands of years ago. Engage in a debate about the pros and cons of extracting rock below the surface just because we own the land above the surface.

### Science and Technology

- Humans have applied various technologies to extract rock from the Earth. Some mining operations take place at the surface, typically called surface or strip mining. Mining below the ground makes use of a "longwaller." Research these two types of technology, describing how they each work, determining which has the least impact on the local environment, and defending your response.
- To map the ocean floor, sonar is used. What is this device? Can it be used to provide a rock record of the layers of the ocean floor also? If not, how do we determine what the rock record is below the ocean floor?

### Science as Inquiry

- Review the local rock record. What kinds of rock can be found within the first two hundred feet below the surface? Propose a way to verify that the map of the local rock record is correct. Describe in detail what you would need to do to investigate the validity of the map.

### History and Nature of Science

- Would a paleobotanist be a good source of information on changes in our local ecology? Why? What does a paleobotanist do?
- Some scientists believe that by studying the gases that surround a planet like Jupiter today, we can have insight into the ancient atmosphere that surrounded Earth. Why would we want to know more about the Earth's early atmosphere? What can we learn about our own planet from studying the gases that surround other planets?

**4. EVALUATION:** How will the students show what they have learned?

Upon completing the activities the students will be able to:

- discuss the age of the Earth's crust at different locations (i.e. ocean floor, different continents) by describing where it is older than other places, and using that information to explain how the Earth's crust has changed over the last billion years;

- explain why even though the Earth's history is very long and the time of human life on Earth is incredibly short, we have permanently altered our environment. A student will be able to discuss the implications of the environmental crisis as it exists in the context of Earth history;
- when provided with a rock record history of two different areas, explain the differences between the two records;
- explain the difference between a geologic era, period, and epoch.

## Rain Formation

**GRADE**
K–4
**DISCIPLINE**
Earth
Science

**Concept to be invented**
Main idea—Raindrops form as water vapor condenses and falls from the sky.

**Concepts that are important to expansion**
Water cycle, condensation, evaporation, precipitation

**Materials needed**
*For exploration (for each group of four to six children):*
1-quart glass jar with lid, hot-to-boiling water, ice cubes

*For expansion:*
clear plastic lid (coffee can lid), pencil, water, plastic cup, eyedropper, paper towels

➥ **Safety precautions:** The students should be reminded to avoid bumping the tables once the exploration activity is set up. If the hot water spills out, it could hurt the children. If the glass jar breaks, it could cut someone.

1. EXPLORATION: Which process skills will be used?

Observing, predicting, recording data

What will the students do?

*Rain in a Jar*    Set groups of four to six students around a table. In the middle of the table place a 1-quart jar with enough hot-to-nearly-boiling water to cover the bottom of the jar. The teacher should ask the students to make predictions about what will happen when they cover the jar with the lid turned upside down, holding three or four ice cubes. After the students have recorded their predictions and shared them with the class, instruct someone from each group to place the lid carefully over the jar and place the ice cubes on top of the inverted lid. Ask the students to watch the jar for 4 or 5 minutes. What did you observe? Was it as you predicted? Record those observations.

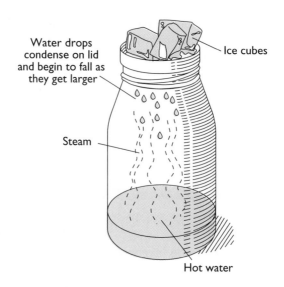

Water drops
condense on lid
and begin to fall as
they get larger

Ice cubes

Steam

Hot water

## 2. EXPLANATION/CONCEPT INVENTION: What is the main idea? How will the main idea be constructed?

*Concept:* Raindrops form as water vapor condenses and falls from the sky.

The students should have observed that water drops collected on the inside of the lid. As time progressed more water drops formed. As the drops became bigger, it got to the point that the lid could no longer hold the drops, and the drops began to fall back into the jar. Ask the students the following questions to help them conclude that raindrops form as water vapor condenses and falls from the sky. What observations did you record? Where do you think the drops of water on the lid came from? (From the *condensation* of water vapor inside the jar. The hot water in the jar *evaporated* and changed into a *gas*—water vapor. When the water vapor hit the cool lid, it *condensed* and changed back to a *liquid.*) What happened to the drops of water as they collected on the lid? (They got bigger as more water vapor *condensed* and collected on the jar lid.) At what point did the water drops start to fall from the jar lid? (As they collected on the lid, they grew bigger and soon pulled together with other drops. Their weight pulled them down.) What do you call water drops that fall from the sky? (Rain.)

## 3. EXPANSION OF THE IDEA: Which process skills will be used?

Observing, inferring, measuring

How will the idea be expanded?

*Water Drop Attraction*

Pair up the students. Provide each pair with a plastic coffee can lid or the like, an eyedropper, a cup of water, and some paper towels. Ask the student pairs to do the following: One student should hold the plastic lid bottom-side-up.

The other student should fill the eyedropper with water and squeeze as many separate drops of water on the lid as possible. The child holding the lid should then quickly turn the lid over. Hold the lid at least 8 to 10 inches over the table-top, directly over some paper towels. Ask the student not holding the lid to use the point of a pencil to move the tiny drops together. What happens when you do this? Ask the students to switch roles, allowing one to hold the lid and flip it and the other to use the eyedropper and pencil. Did the same thing occur?

The water molecules appear to attract one another. As you pull them together it seems as if they readily jump to one another. As they grow bigger, they eventually are overcome by gravity and fall from the lid. Water may fall like this from the sky, not just in the form of rain. The teacher may solicit ideas from the students on other forms in which water falls from the sky (snow, sleet, hail). Explain to the students that all of these are called *precipitation.*

### Science in Personal and Social Perspectives

- Why do you think it rains more in certain places than in others?
- Read the poem "Little Raindrops," by Aunt Effie (Jane Euphemia Browne), to the class. After it is read ask the students if they think they are affected by emotional changes with changes in the weather.

### Science and Technology

- Why do you think meteorologists study rain patterns? Do these patterns affect where people will build cities?
- Why do scientists *seed* rain clouds in dry areas? Do you think farmers in these areas want to be able to make it rain when water is scarce? Why?

### Science as Inquiry

- What do you call it when water turns into water vapor? (Evaporation.)
- When water vapor collects on an object to form water droplets, what is it called? (Condensation.)
- What do you call water that falls from the sky? (Precipitation.)
- What do we call the process by which water evaporates, condenses, and falls from the sky? (The water cycle.)

### History and Nature of Science

- How important do you think it is for a farmer to understand the water cycle?
- If you were a botanist working in the desert, why would you be curious about how a cactus grows?
- When you watch a local weather forecast, does the meteorologist help explain where the next rainfall will come from?

**4. EVALUATION:** How will the students show what they have learned?

Upon completing the activities the students will be able to:

- show how they can make rain when given a jar of hot water, a pie tin, and some ice cubes;

- explain where evaporation, condensation, and precipitation are occurring in the jar demonstration they set up;
- draw a picture of something they think they would not have in their life if it did not rain. Ask them to explain the reasoning behind choosing that object.

## Dew Formation

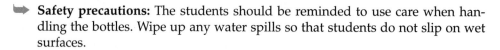

**GRADE**
**K–4**
**DISCIPLINE**
**Earth**
**Science**

### Concept to be invented
Main idea—Cold surfaces collect more water drops than warm surfaces do.

### Concepts that are important to expansion
Dew, frost, temperature measurement with a thermometer, dew point

### Materials needed
*For exploration (for each group of four to six children):*
minute timer or clock with minutes marked off, glass soda bottle, clear container large enough for the bottle to fit in, ice cubes, water, paper towels

*For expansion:*
drinking glass, thermometer, ice cubes, water, paper towels

➡ **Safety precautions:** The students should be reminded to use care when handling the bottles. Wipe up any water spills so that students do not slip on wet surfaces.

1. **EXPLORATION:** Which process skills will be used?

Observing, predicting, measuring, inferring, recording data

What will the students do?

*Soda Bottle Condensation*

Set groups of four to six children around a table. In the middle of the table place a container large enough to hold a soda bottle. In this container place four or five ice cubes and enough water so that once the bottle is placed in the container, it will be covered with cold water up to its neck. Give one child in the group a glass soda bottle. Remind the other students that they each will get a turn. If enough bottles are available, each child may be given one at this time. Ask the children to wrap their hands around the bottle for 2 minutes to try to get it very warm. When the 2 minutes are up, ask the students to exhale inside the bottle. What did you observe? Record those observations.

Then ask the students to make predictions about what will happen after they put the bottle into the container of ice water for 2 minutes, take it out, quickly wipe it off, and again exhale into the bottle. After they have recorded

**EARTH SCIENCE**

their predictions and shared them with the class, the students should take turns putting their bottles into the ice water container, taking them out, wiping off the excess water, and then exhaling inside them. What did you observe? Was it as you predicted? Record those observations.

2. **EXPLANATION/CONCEPT INVENTION:** What is the main idea? How will the main idea be constructed?

*Concept:* Cold surfaces collect more water drops than warm surfaces.

When the students exhaled into their warmed bottles, they may have observed some condensation, but very little. Their warm breath and the warmed bottle did not differ greatly in temperature. Therefore, water vapor did not condense readily. When the students exhaled into the cooled bottles, the difference in temperature between their breath and the bottles was enough to make water drops collect on the cold bottles. The students will be able to conclude that cold surfaces collect more water drops than warm surfaces when you ask them the following questions about what they did. What observations did you record when you exhaled on the warmed bottle? What observations did you record when you exhaled on the cooled bottle? Was there a difference between the two? Why do you think this happened? Do you ever walk through grass on a spring or summer morning? What happens to your shoes on those mornings? (If the students said yes, they may begin to think about getting wet shoes as they walk through the grass. If the students start to respond along these lines, then ask the next set of questions.) Why do you think your shoes got wet? Do you think the grass or the air was warmer? Which was cooler? (The cool grass allowed water vapor to come out of the warm air and condense on the grass.) Do you know what we call the water you find on grass in the morning? (Dew.) When it's a cold morning this dew appears to be frozen. What name do we give it then? (Frost.)

EARTH SCIENCE

## 3. EXPANSION OF THE IDEA: Which process skills will be used?

Observing, measuring, comparing, recording data

How will the idea be expanded?

*Thermometer Reading and Dew Point*

Pair up the students. Give each pair a thermometer. Practice reading the thermometer. Be sure each student knows how this is done. As the students work in pairs, ask them to fill a glass with ice and add enough water to cover the ice. Record the temperature their thermometer is reading. Place the thermometer in the glass. Watch the outside of the glass and record the temperature at which water begins to form on the outside of the glass. Explain to the students that for this particular day, with this particular amount of moisture in the air, the temperature they just recorded would be called the *dew point* for the day. When the air reaches that temperature, then *dew* will begin to form on the grass outside.

### Science in Personal and Social Perspectives

- Other than the noise involved, why do you think it is not a good idea to mow grass very early on a summer morning?
- Explain how your feet could get wet when you run through the grass in the spring.
- Why does frost form on car windows in the winter?

### Science and Technology

- Do you think auto manufacturers are concerned with dew formation when they build new cars? Do you think the auto manufacturers think carefully about the kind of paint they put on new cars because they know dew may form on them? What would happen to a car if dew formed on it day after day and there was no protective paint on it? Would the same thing happen to your bicycle?
- How does a rear window defogger/deicer eliminate frost on the car window?

### Science as Inquiry

- What do you call it when water turns into water vapor? (Evaporation.)
- When water vapor collects on an object to form water droplets, what is it called? (Condensation.)
- When water collects on a cold surface, what may form? (Dew or frost.)
- What is a *dew point?*

### History and Nature of Science

- Why would a landscaper be concerned about dew/frost formation? Have you ever seen plants wrapped in cloth or covered in plastic bags? Why do you think landscapers or home owners do this?
- Do you think a person in the lawn-care business should pay attention to weather forecasts that give the dew point? Do you think it could be used to help the person decide when to start work in the morning?

EARTH SCIENCE

**4. EVALUATION:** How will the students show what they have learned?

Upon completing the activities the students will be able to:

- use a bottle and a bowl of ice water to demonstrate how dew can form;
- demonstrate how to determine dew point using a glass, ice cubes, and a thermometer;
- explain why their shoes get wet when they run through grass on a sunny summer morning.

## Radiant Energy

**GRADE
2–4
DISCIPLINE
Earth
Science**

### Concept to be invented
Main idea—The sun produces energy in the form of heat, referred to as *radiant energy*.

### Concepts that are important to expansion
The sun's heat can be used to perform work.

### Materials needed
*For Activity 1:*
two pie pans, sand, two coins, two black plastic bags

*For Activity 2:*
large glass jar with lid, water, thermometer, graph paper

*For Activity 3:*
magnifying glasses, sheets of paper

*For expansion activity:*
6 tea bags, large jar

➡ **Safety precautions:** Before starting the activities go over the following safety rules:

- The students should call the teacher if the thermometer is dropped and broken. Avoid touching broken glass or the liquid inside the thermometer.
- Activity 3 should be done only by a teacher or other adult.
- Avoid playing with the magnifying glass or placing a hand between the paper and magnifying glass.
- Do not let children stare at or touch the point of light during Activity 3.

**1. EXPLORATION:** Which process skills will be used?

Predicting, observing, hypothesizing, measuring, recording and analyzing data, graphing

What will the students do?

*Temperature and Colored Surfaces*

*Activity 1.* Ask the children to fill the pie pans with sand. Put one pan of sand, one coin, and one garbage bag in direct sunlight. Put the other pan, coin, and bag in shade. Predict what the differences will be between the objects in the sun and those in the shade. After a while have the children feel and compare the objects. How did the objects that were in the sun feel? What about the ones that were in the shade? Why do the things that were in the sun feel warm? Why do they feel cool if they were in the shade?

*Temperature: Sun versus Shade*

*Activity 2.* On the second day, have the students fill two jars with water. Record their starting temperatures. Place one of the jars in the sun and one in the shade. Predict how much temperature change will take place in both as time progresses. Have students record the temperatures of the two jars every half hour for a total of 3 hours. Take a final temperature reading. Graph the results with a bar graph using different colors for the sunny and shady sites.

*Magnifiers: Capture the Sun*

*Activity 3.* (Do this on day 2 while waiting for the results of Activity 2). On a sunny day, hold the magnifying glass over a piece of paper until the light comes to a point. Hold it there for a few seconds. What happens to the paper? What made the hole in the paper? What does this tell you about what the sun does for us? What can the sun do to your skin and eyes?

## 2. EXPLANATION/CONCEPT INVENTION: What is the main idea? How will the main idea be constructed?

*Concept:* The sun produces energy in the form of heat, referred to as *radiant energy.*

What does your graph tell you about a sunny environment versus a shady one? Why do you think there were such temperature differences at the two sites? What does the sun do for the Earth? What do you think might happen if the Earth were closer to the sun? What if the Earth were farther from the sun? What would life be like in either case?

## 3. EXPANSION OF THE IDEA: Which process skills will be used?

Predicting, observing, inferring, hypothesizing

How will the idea be expanded?

*Sun Tea*

Fill a large jar with water and six tea bags. Record its temperature. Predict what will happen to the water after a few hours. (Suggest to the students that they might want to think about more than just a temperature change.) Decide where you would place the jar if you wanted to make tea. Place the jar in that spot. Throughout the day check the jar and record the changes. Ask: "What do you think is happening inside the jar? How did the water change into tea? What part did the sun play in this process? What other ways can the sun's heat be harnessed to help things to work?"

### Science in Personal and Social Perspectives

- Why is the sun important to us?
- What are some of the things we need to be aware of when we are in the sun?

### Science and Technology

- What are some ways in which people use solar energy? (Solar batteries, skylights, heating water to warm rooms, and so on.)
- Are these beneficial? In what ways?
- Why might we need to explore ways to use solar energy in the future?
- Why do clothing manufacturers create lighter-colored clothing for the summer months? Would a manufacturer make more money selling black or white T-shirts in the summer?

### Science as Inquiry

- Why are people more careful about being exposed to the sun during the summer than during the winter?
- New concepts to be identified for invention in new lessons: global warming, the ozone layer, the greenhouse effect.

### History and Nature of Science

- What are some careers in which people can work with solar energy?
- Why would it be important for a botanist, a florist, or a gardener to understand how the sun heats the Earth?

4. EVALUATION: How will the students show what they have learned?

Upon completing the activities the students will be able to:

- while blindfolded, tell which objects were in the sun and which were in shade, and give reasons for the answers;
- create a collage showing the many uses of solar energy;
- draw pictures showing ways they can protect themselves from the damaging effects of the sun.

## Weather Forecasting

**GRADE**
**5–8**
**DISCIPLINE**
**Earth Science**

**Concept to be invented**
Main idea—Weather data can be collected and reported.

**Concepts that are important to expansion**
Controlling variables, use of symbols, cloud types

EARTH SCIENCE

**Materials needed**

*For exploration:*

| | | |
|---|---|---|
| barometer | wind vane | anemometer |
| thermometer | rain gauge | clinometer |
| sling psychrometer | cloud charts | nephoscope |

The students should have had prior experience with this equipment as they were learning about individual weather phenomena such as air pressure, humidity, temperature, air masses, fronts.

*For expansion and evaluation:*

weather instruments listed above; collection of weather maps from newspapers

➡ **Safety precautions:** Use care with weather instruments when collecting data. Outdoors, obey school rules. Avoid talking to strangers, and exercise caution if inclement weather prohibits data collection.

1. **EXPLORATION:** Which process skills will be used?

Brainstorming, observing, formulating models, predicting, measuring, questioning

*Teacher introduction:* How many of you have nicknames? When you write letters or your name in school, do you write your full name or your nickname? Which is easier for you to write?

Try to picture in your mind a McDonald's or a Kentucky Fried Chicken restaurant. Imagine you are in the parking lot, or you are riding down the road and you spot one of these places. What image comes to mind first? How many of you remembered a shape or a symbol for the restaurant first?

Can you think of any other things in your life, like toys, games, or bicycles, where you might remember the symbol for the manufacturer rather than the actual name of the company?

For which stores, restaurants, toys, or games do you find the symbol easiest to remember? How often do you use the item or frequent the store? Do you find that the more you use the item or frequent the store, the easier it is to remember the symbol?

Now imagine you're a meteorologist and you collect weather data every day for years. Just like you and your nickname or McDonald's and their golden arches, would it help the meteorologist to have symbols to record data with instead of words? Why or why not?

What will the students do?

*Weather Log Creation*

Challenge the students to prepare a weather log or a data chart that they will use to collect weather information. Encourage them to keep in mind the previous discussion. Allow the students to break into their own groups. This will help when the students eventually collect weather information on weekends.

Try to give as little input as possible. Give the students time to brainstorm all the factors that may be important to forecast weather. Have the instruments available for them to look over as they try to think of what they need to create a good weather forecast.

Encourage the students to use their designed chart for 1 week. At the start of the next week, ask the student groups to share the information they obtained. As a class, determine the group that was the most accurate in predicting daily weather.

## 2. EXPLANATION/CONCEPT INVENTION: What is the main idea? How will the main idea be constructed?

*Concept:* Weather data can be collected and reported.

Controlling variables is important to making reliable weather observations. Each separate weather measurement is a variable that cannot be controlled. Ask the students the following questions to help them invent the concept:

- Did the weather factors you chose to observe give you enough information to forecast the weather?

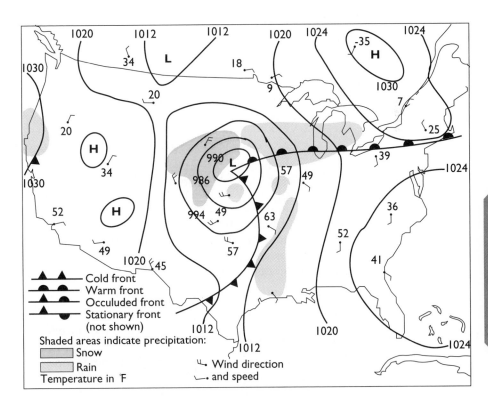

EARTH SCIENCE

- Could you have been more accurate had you collected other types of data?
- Which factors could increase error in your data?
- Did you try to control any human factors that might have made your readings faulty?
- Can you simplify the way in which you recorded your data?

### 3. EXPANSION OF THE IDEA: Which process skills will be used?

Observing, interpreting data, inferring, creating models, making conclusions

How will the idea be expanded?

*Weather Map Symbols*

Symbols can be used to designate some weather observations. Collect a supply of weather maps from as many different newspapers as possible. Once you have a number of maps that vary in sophistication, distribute them to your students and ask if they can interpret them. Create a list on the board of all of the different symbols they observe on the maps. Encourage the students to speculate about what each symbol represents. After exploring the various symbols found on the map, break the class up into six groups. Assign each group one of the following tasks:

1. Draw a station model diagram that shows wind direction and speed, type of high cloud, type of middle cloud, sea-level pressure, pressure change, type of low cloud, dew point, sky cover, present state of weather, air temperature.
2. Create a chart that shows the weather map symbols for highs, lows, fronts, isobars, and air masses.
3. Create a chart titled "Present State of the Weather" that shows and briefly describes the symbols for precipitation.
4. Create a chart titled "Sky Cover" that shows the symbols for the different fractions of cloud coverage.
5. Create a chart titled "Major Cloud Types" that shows the symbols for and names of the major cloud types.
6. Create a chart titled "Wind Scale" that lists the speed and shows the symbols for the wind.

*Weather Data Collection*

As the student groups report on the symbols they discovered to represent the various weather phenomena, ask them to decide how they could use some of this information to make recording weather information easier. How can you use this information to predict weather?

*Science in Personal and Social Perspectives*

- What changes have you experienced in the amount of attention you pay to weather forecasts now that you have had a chance to collect weather information yourself?
- Do you think you can create a family weather station at your house without spending a large amount of money on expensive weather equipment? What types of weather instruments could you create?

EARTH SCIENCE

### Science and Technology

- In the summer of 1990 a sudden flood wiped out the town of Shadyside, Ohio. Could an improved weather radar system have helped to save lives? Could it have prevented the sudden flood?

### Science as Inquiry

- Create graphs for each of the weather factors collected over the one-week time period. Study your graphs. Do you see any great fluctuations in any of the readings over time? If so, with which weather factor?
- Was there ever a dramatic rise or decrease in the barometric pressure?
- Did you examine your graphs to see if any other factor changed dramatically when the barometer did? If you did find some changes, with what other factors?
- What kind of pressure system was over the area when the barometer changed dramatically?
- What conclusions can you draw about the relationships among different weather factors?

### History and Nature of Science

- Survey local radio and television stations. Where do they get their weather forecast information from? Is there a resident meteorologist who prepares the forecast? If so, see if you can interview that person. Prepare some key questions you would like to have answered in the light of the experiences you have just had collecting your own weather data.

## 4. EVALUATION: How will the students show what they have learned?

Upon completing these activities the students will be able to demonstrate the use of symbols for collecting and reporting weather data by completing the following tasks:

- Ask the students to look at the data they collected from the exploration phase of this lesson and consider the following questions: Is there a weather factor you did not consider collecting that you would add now? Would it be important to be consistent in your data collection? In other words, did you consider things like making sure you collect your information at the same time every day, or that at least two people in the group are responsible for reading the instruments to check for accuracy?
- Revise your weather log to include all the factors necessary to make a sound weather forecast. You may ask the teacher for sample weather logs or suggestions on what data to collect. Be sure the variables that can be controlled are controlled!
- Once you have revised your log, show it to the teacher. If it is judged complete, then collect weather data for a month.

Some teachers may have their students so proficient on the various weather instruments that it becomes second nature to them. Collect weather data every day for the entire school year. Your class may want to give a daily weather report to the school on the intercom each day.

## Air Mass Movement

### Concept to be invented
Main idea—When moving air masses of different temperature and different moisture content come in contact, it results in precipitation and other identifiable weather phenomena.

### Concepts that are important to expansion
Fronts, cold and warm

### Materials needed
*For exploration:*

| | | |
|---|---|---|
| globe of the Earth | paper | thermometer |
| medicine dropper | marking pen | hammer |
| colored water | dry ice | matches |
| flat-sided top | container of water | string |

*For expansion:*

| | |
|---|---|
| clear bottle with screw cap | cold water |
| (small juice bottles work well) | red and blue food coloring |
| cooking oil | |

➡ **Safety precautions:** Use extreme caution when handling the dry ice. If the students are immature, the teacher or another adult may need to handle the dry ice for that part of the experiment. Heavy-duty safety gloves should be made available for anyone handling the dry ice. Goggles should be worn. Care should be taken when handling any of the instruments. Exercise care with glass containers.

## 1. EXPLORATION: Which process skills will be used?

Observing, measuring, recording data, formulating models

### What will the students do?

*Coriolis Effect: Globe*

*Station A.* Spin the globe quickly so that it moves in a west-to-east direction. Pretending that you are on the globe at the North Pole, use the medicine dropper to start some colored water rolling in a stream south toward the equator. Carefully record your observations, being sure to include the movement of the water both north and south of the equator.

*Coriolis Effect:*
*Top*

*Station B.* Obtain a small flat-sided top. On a piece of paper draw a circle the size of the top. Push this down over the handle of the top and center it on the top. As you spin the top in a counterclockwise direction (from west to east) with one hand, hold a marker in your other hand and try to draw a straight line on the paper attached to the top. Record what happens when you do this.

*Air Movement:*
*Dry Ice*

*Station C.* Break a piece of dry ice with a hammer and place a few small pieces into a container of water. Be sure to use caution when working with the dry ice (gloves and goggles). Observe the air around the container over a period of time. Measure the temperature of the air mass (1) just above the container, (2) about 1 meter above the container, and (3) near the base of the container. Record these readings.

Light one end of a piece of string and then blow out the flame. The end should begin to smoke. Give the smoking string to the students and have them wave it around the container. Ask them to record their observations of the movement of the smoke.

**2. EXPLANATION/CONCEPT INVENTION:** What is the main idea? How will the main idea be constructed?

*Concept at Stations A and B:* Air masses, low-pressure areas, and fronts move generally from west to east.

- At Station A, in what direction did the stream turn in the Northern Hemisphere? in the Southern Hemisphere?
- What effect do you think the land masses with their mountain ranges will have on the moving air?
- At Station B, what happened when you tried to draw a straight line on the paper from the center to the edge of the top?

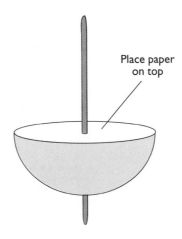

Place paper
on top

- Because of the Earth's rotation, the motion of a body as seen from Earth appears to deflect to the right in the Northern Hemisphere. This fictitious deflecting force is also called the *Coriolis effect.* How do you think the Coriolis effect can help explain the results you obtained when trying to draw a straight line on the paper on the spinning top?

*Concept at Station C:* When moving air masses of different temperature and different moisture content come in contact, it results in precipitation and other identifiable weather phenomena.

- Where was the air mass the highest?
- What happened to the air as it cooled?
- What were your temperature readings around the container? If there were differences, why do you think they occurred?
- What happened when you waved some smoking string in the air around the container? In what direction did the air flow around the container?
- What kind of precipitation do you think could occur if warm air were blown over the cold air flowing from the container?

### 3. EXPANSION OF THE IDEA: Which process skills will be used?

Manipulating materials, formulating models, hypothesizing, inferring

How will the idea be expanded?

*Oil and Water Fronts*

Half-fill a bottle with cooking oil. Add some red food coloring, cap the bottle, and shake well. This will represent a warm air mass. In a separate container, add blue food coloring to cold water. What do you think will happen as you pour the cold water into the bottle of oil? Slowly pour the water into the bottle.

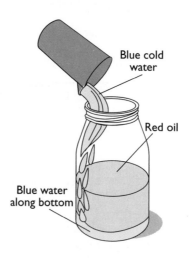

Blue cold
water

Red oil

Blue water
along bottom

The following concepts can be demonstrated with this arrangement of materials:

- Lines of temperature differences between two air masses are called *fronts*.
- A *warm front* is caused by a relatively warm mass of air advancing over a mass of relatively cold air.
- A *cold front* is caused by a mass of relatively cold air displacing relatively warm air.
- Advancing cold fronts lift warm air. Advancing warm fronts result in the warm air being lifted.
- Fronts do not all move at the same speed or in the same direction.
- The amount of moisture in the air controls the kind of weather along the front.

*Questions that help students invent expansion concepts:*

- What happened when you poured the cold water into the oil? Did it behave as you predicted? Which liquid is denser? How do you know?
- Place the screw cap on the bottle. Slowly turn the bottle on its side. How does the heavier liquid move, and what is its final position?
- If a cold air mass moves toward a warm air mass, would the leading edge of the cold air mass be at the ground level or above the ground? Why? (Remember that the blue water represents the cold air mass, and the red oil is the warm air mass.)
- If a warm air mass moves toward a cold air mass, would the leading edge of the warm air mass be at the ground or above the ground? Why?
- How would you describe a stationary front? What factors affect its formation?

*Science in Personal and Social Perspectives*

- If you were planning a picnic for Saturday and you heard on a Thursday weather forecast that a warm front would be moving into the region on Friday evening, would you switch the day of your picnic to Sunday? Why or why not?

*Science and Technology*

- What effect do extremes in precipitation have upon area populations (not just human)?
- How do you think knowledge of such weather phenomena as air masses, fronts, and precipitation have assisted in the invention of the material Goretex, which is now used in running clothes, tents, tarpaulins, and so on? How has this invention allowed us to enjoy our environment more, no matter what the weather conditions?

*Science as Inquiry*

- What kind of pressure system do you think would bring your area a large amount of precipitation? a small amount? Create your own rain gauge to measure precipitation by following the steps below.

*Create a Rain Gauge*

Use the following materials to create your own rain gauge: large straight-sided jar, long narrow jar or large test tube, meter stick, metric ruler, and masking tape. Place a ruler vertically in the large jar and pour in water until it reaches the 10-mm mark on the ruler. Pour this water into the narrow jar, to which you

EARTH SCIENCE

have attached a strip of masking tape. Mark the masking tape at the exact level of the water. This represents 10 mm in the jar. Repeat this procedure for levels of 20 mm, 30 mm, and so on.

Place the large jar outside, away from any obstruction, to collect rain. Why is that important? The top of the jar should be about 30.5 cm above the ground. To read the amount of rain, empty it into the measuring jar at the same time each day. Keep a daily record in a chart form.

Do you think you can determine how much snow you would have had if you had 50 mm of rain collected in your gauge? What about if you have 50 mm of snow? How much rain would that be? The student can do two things here: (1) Obtain a tall, straight-sided container, such as an empty juice can. Carefully fill it with loose snow, but do not pack the snow in the can. Heat the snow until it is completely melted. Use the rain gauge to measure the amount of water. If you know the length of the can, you can compare amount of snow to rain. (2) The student could guesstimate the amount of rain the snow is equal to by knowing that the ratio of snow to rain is usually 10 to 1. A wet, heavy snow may have a ratio as low as 6 to 1, while in dry, fluffy, new-fallen snow, the ratio may be as high as 30 to 1.

### History and Nature of Science

- How is it possible for airplanes to fly in the eye of the storm during a hurricane? What kind of information do pilots need to understand about air masses in order to do this?
- Create a list of all of the types of jobs that can be affected when air masses of different temperatures and moisture contents come in contact. Are any of those jobs in areas in which you would like to work?

## 4. EVALUATION: How will the students show what they have learned?

*Air Masses and Parachutes*

The following parachute activity, as well as the questions covering personal development, science-technology-society, academic growth, and career awareness could be used to assess the students' knowledge of the relationships among air masses, fronts, and precipitation.

### Parachute materials
12-inch square sheet of tissue paper
eight glue-backed hole reinforcers
four strings, 10 inches in length each

washer for weight
paper person (for decorative
   purposes only)

Punch a hole in each corner of the tissue with a pencil point. Place a hole reinforcer on each side of the hole. Tie the four strings to each hole. Tie the loose ends of the strings together around the washer. Be sure the strings end up being of equal length. Decorate with a paper person attached to the washer. You may find that a small hole in the very center of the tissue will help the parachute open more quickly.

Fold up your chute and throw it into the air. Have a partner time from the moment you release it until the moment it begins to descend. Time its descent.

- How does the parachute depend on air pressure?
- What if your parachute came from several hundred meters above the Earth's surface? Would it fall any differently?
- Would the parachute fall differently if a cold front were in the area? What about a warm front?
- What if a warm front were just moving into the area, replacing a cold front. Would it be safe to parachute during that time? Why or why not?

## Air Pressure

GRADE
5–8
DISCIPLINE
Earth
Science

**Concept to be invented**
Main idea—Air has weight.

**Concepts that are important to expansion**
Air can exert pressure. Temperature and air movement are factors that influence air pressure.

**Materials needed**
*For each student group:*

| | | |
|---|---|---|
| modeling clay | three balloons | straw |
| pencil | two books | one index card |
| yardstick | one piece of 8½-inch | one glass of water |
| string | by 11-inch paper | one sandwich bag |

EARTH SCIENCE

*For teacher demonstration:*
one beach ball

*For Science as Inquiry and evaluation:*

two paper lunch bags             one lamp or candle

two balloons and string for       one straw and one Ping-Pong ball
     each student group             per student

➡ **Safety precautions:** The students should take care that when blowing during the activities they don't hyperventilate and get dizzy. Have a paper bag available for any hyperventilating student to breathe into slowly. This will balance the oxygen–carbon dioxide ratio and return the student to normal.

1. **EXPLORATION:** Which process skills will be used?

Observing, predicting, comparing, questioning, describing, manipulating materials, recording data

What will the students do?

*Balloon Balance*    Provide the students with modeling clay, pencil, yardstick, three balloons, and a string. Ask them to manipulate these materials so that they can create a balance such as in the diagram.

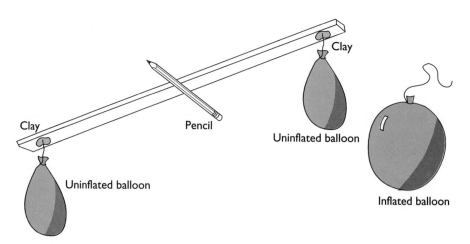

Balloon Balance

     Suspend and balance two uninflated balloons. Ask the students to record their observations. Then ask them to predict what would happen to this balanced system if they were to replace one of the uninflated balloons with an inflated balloon. Record their predictions. Now replace one of the uninflated balloons with an inflated balloon. Record students' observations. Do they match their predictions?

### 2. EXPLANATION/CONCEPT INVENTION: What is the main idea? How will the main idea be constructed?

*Concept:* Air has weight.

What kind of data did you collect? Did you obtain results as you predicted? Hold up an uninflated beach ball. Ask the students to help you weigh it. Now ask one of the students to blow it up. Ask for their predictions as to whether it now weighs the same. How is this demonstration similar to the balance you just created? What happened with your balance when you replaced the uninflated balloon with an inflated balloon? Weigh it. Does it weigh the same? Why? (Air has weight.)

### 3. EXPANSION OF THE IDEA: Which process skills will be used?

Observing, predicting, comparing, manipulating materials, recording data, hypothesizing

How will the idea be expanded?

*Paper Blowing*      Ask the students to place two books (at least a quarter- to a half-inch thick) 3 inches apart on a desk top. Place a sheet of 8½-inch by 11-inch paper across the book lengthwise. Have the students predict if they can blow the paper off the books by blowing into the space between the books. Record your predictions, then try it! Repeat the experiment, this time using a straw placed just under the edge of the paper to blow between the books.

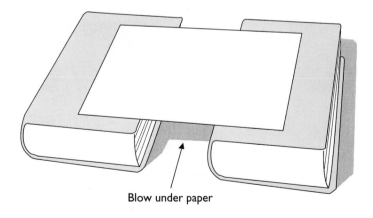

Blow under paper

What happened to the paper when you blew without the straw? with the straw? Were you able to blow the paper off the books either time? Did the

EARTH SCIENCE

paper move at all? If so, how? This activity demonstrates that air has pressure. Air moving fast, such as the air you blew out between the books and underneath the paper, creates a lower pressure than the pressure above the books. Thus you see a slight dip in the paper. When you use a straw to blow through, the straw creates a narrow high-speed path of low pressure between the books. Now the pressure underneath the paper bridge is much lower than the pressure above the paper; thus you observe a big dip in the paper bridge. This dip is caused by the higher air pressure on top of the paper. Thus, air exerts pressure.

*Newspaper Strength*

A good teacher demonstration is to take a yardstick or some other relatively long, thin piece of wood and place it on a table top. Smooth out a large piece of newspaper over the wood. Leave about 6 to 8 inches of wood sticking out one side. Make sure there are no air spaces between the newspaper and the table top. Ask the students if they think you can hit this stick and make the paper go flying. Once you take several predictions, hit the stick. What happened? The stick broke and the paper remained on the table top. Why? Because on every square inch of that paper, air is exerting a pressure of 14.7 pounds per square inch. A full sheet of newspaper is typically 27 inches by 23 inches, or 621 square inches. If there are 14.7 pounds of pressure exerted on every square inch of the newspaper, that means that there is 621 square inches times 14.7 pounds per square inch, or 9128.7 pounds of pressure being exerted by the air on that paper. You would have to hit the stick with a force equal to that amount to get the paper to move!

*Science in Personal and Social Perspectives*

- What does air pressure have to do with a smooth ride on your bike or in a car?
- What happens when your bike gets a flat tire? What does this do to the air pressure in the tire?

*Science and Technology*

- In the second activity you found that faster-moving air causes lower air pressure. How do you think this fact has influenced the design of airplanes?
- Ask a student to demonstrate lift by taping a narrow strip of paper to a pencil. Hold the pencil by your mouth and blow over the strip of paper. What happens to it? How do you think this movement is similar to air blowing over the wing of an airplane?

*Science as Inquiry*

- Does all air have the same weight? Ask the students to replace their uninflated balloons in the balanced system with two paper lunch bags. Get the system to balance. Now place a lit lamp or candle several inches below one of the bags. What happened to that balanced system? Which weighs more: cold or hot air?
- What kind of air pressure do you think would be associated with a cold front? a warm front?

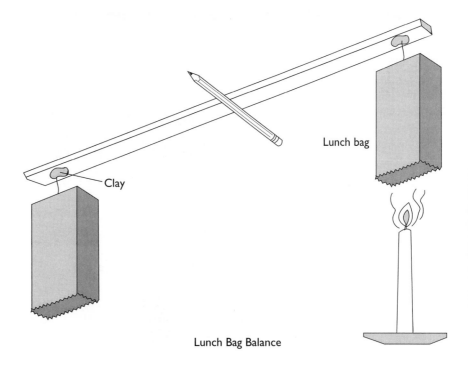

Clay

Lunch bag

Lunch Bag Balance

EARTH SCIENCE

*History and Nature of Science*

- Ask the students to share information with one another on Daniel Bernoulli (1700–1782). He was a Swiss doctor, mathematician, biologist, physiologist, physicist, astronomer, and oceanographer. Can you think of any people today who are as well versed in as many areas as Daniel Bernoulli was? Do you think it is more difficult to be an expert in all of these areas today? Why?
- Invite a pilot to speak to your class. Ask him or her to explain how knowledge of air pressure helps him or her to control an airplane.

**4. EVALUATION:** How will the students show what they have learned?

Upon completing these activities the students will be able to:

- predict and then explain why two balloons suspended on equal-length strings about 3 inches apart come closer together when the students blow between them. They will be able to demonstrate this phenomenon.
- look at a picture of an unbalanced system, in which one balloon is inflated and the other is uninflated, and explain why this system is unbalanced.
- demonstrate that a Ping-Pong ball can hover over the end of a drinking straw. They will also be able to explain why this happens and be able to share and explain this phenomenon to children in a primary grade.

## Solar Heating

**GRADE
5–8
DISCIPLINE
Earth
Science**

**Concept to be invented**
Main idea—The Earth's surfaces are heated unevenly.

**Concepts that are important to expansion**
Uneven heating creates wind and makes the water cycle occur. The sun is the source of energy that determines the weather on Earth.

**Materials needed**
*For exploration (per student group):*

| | |
|---|---|
| three paper cups | three thermometers |
| dark soil | one lamp |
| light sand | satellite photographs |
| water | of the Earth's surface |

*For evaluation:*

| | |
|---|---|
| three metal cans | matte black paint |
| white enamel paint | Styrofoam cups |

*For expansion (per student group):*
One thermometer

➡ **Safety precautions:** The students should be careful when using the lamp and around electricity.

1. **EXPLORATION:** Which process skills will be used?

Observing, predicting, comparing, questioning, describing, manipulating materials, recording data

What will the students do?

*Temperature versus Surface Color* Ask the students to cut the tops off the paper cups so that they are about 4 cm deep. Fill one with dark-colored soil, one with light-colored sand, and the third with water. Instruct the students to place a thermometer into each cup, covering the bulb with about 0.5 cm of soil, sand, or water. Record the temperature of each surface. Place a lit lamp so its bulb is about 15 cm from the tops of the cups. After 5 minutes, record the temperature of each cup. Identify which cup gained heat the fastest, and record this information. Remove the lamp from the cups. Predict which cup you think will lose heat the fastest. Record your prediction. Leave the cups untouched, and after 10 minutes, record the

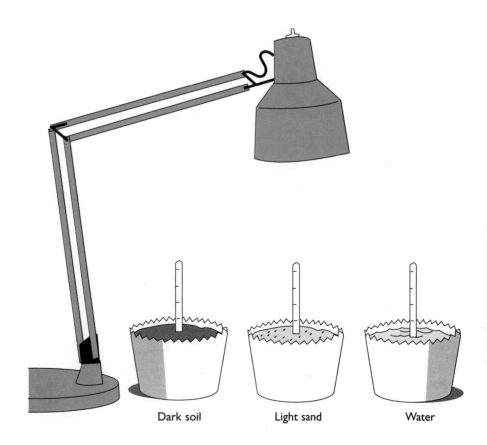

Dark soil        Light sand        Water

EARTH SCIENCE

temperature of each cup. Which lost heat the fastest? Record these data. Did you predict correctly?

## 2. EXPLANATION/CONCEPT INVENTION: What is the main idea? How will the main idea be constructed?

*Concept:* The Earth's surfaces are heated unevenly.

What kinds of data did you collect? Did you obtain results as you predicted? How do you think this activity helps explain the uneven heating of the Earth's surfaces?

Look at satellite pictures of the Earth. Describe the different surfaces. Why do dark-colored surfaces absorb more heat energy from the sun? What do lighter-colored surfaces do that would prevent as much absorption of the sun's energy as dark surfaces? (The lighter surfaces reflect more of the sun's energy, whereas dark land absorbs it. Also, dark land loses its heat faster than water.)

## 3. EXPANSION OF THE IDEA: Which process skills will be used?

Observing, predicting, comparing, manipulating materials, recording data, hypothesizing

How will the idea be expanded?

*Optimum Thermometer Placement*

Ask the students where they think they should place a thermometer to measure the air temperature every day. Ask the students to predict and then record air temperature taken on blacktop, grass, in the shade of a tree, a sandy area, and a gravel area. Take these readings at ground level and at 1 meter from the ground. Does this make a difference? Will the time of day make a difference? Have the students record the temperature at these various sites during different times of the school day. Which gives the most accurate reading for actual air temperature? Once the class decides this, then at that site and time, daily temperature readings can be taken for a weather log for the class. The students can also practice taking temperature readings in degrees Celsius and Fahrenheit.

### Science in Personal and Social Perspectives

- What are ways of staying cool on a hot day or warm on a cold day?
- Why are swimming pools, ponds, lakes, or oceans good places to cool off?
- What kinds of clothes will help keep you cool in summer? What kinds will keep you warm in winter? How and why?

### Science and Technology

- How do we attempt to control the temperature in our homes? What kinds of heating and cooling systems do we utilize?
- What alternative sources of energy, aside from fossil fuels, should we continue to develop? How efficient do you think these are or will be?

EARTH SCIENCE

*Science as Inquiry*

- Aside from unequal heating of the different-colored surfaces of the Earth, temperature is also determined by many other factors. Discuss how the following could affect air temperature: cloud cover, time of day, time of year, wind, latitude, altitude, and oceans or other large bodies of water.
- At what temperature in degrees Celsius does water freeze? boil? At what temperature will water freeze and boil in degrees Fahrenheit?

*History and Nature of Science*

- Who helps supply energy to keep our homes cool in summer and warm in winter? (Coal miner, lumberjack, oil-field worker, power plant operator, heating–ventilation–air conditioning personnel, and so on.) Choose one of these jobs and identify how the workers supply energy. What raw material do they make use of?

**4. EVALUATION:** How will the students show what they have learned?

Upon completing these activities the students will be able to:

- fill three identical-sized cans with tap water. Insert a thermometer through a cover made out of the bottom of a Styrofoam cup. One can should be painted dull black, one left shiny metal, and the last painted shiny white. Ask the students to predict what will happen to the temperature of the water when the cans are placed in direct sunlight or equally distanced from a 150- to 300-watt lightbulb. The students should be able to record the temperature of the water in the cans at 1-minute intervals. They should be able to write a short report of their observations.
- record the temperature of the cans in Celsius and Fahrenheit.
- choose an optimal location outdoors to record daily temperature observations.

## Air Movement and Surface Temperature

**GRADE**
**5–8**
**DISCIPLINE**
**Earth**
**Science**

**EARTH SCIENCE**

### Concept to be invented
Main idea—Air moves downward over cold surfaces and upward over warm surfaces.

### Concepts that are important to expansion
A volume of warm air has less mass than an equal volume of cool air; particles of warm air are farther apart than particles of cool air. Cold air, being heavier than warm air, sinks, pushing warm air upward.

**Materials needed**

*For exploration to make an observation box:*

| | |
|---|---|
| one cardboard box (about 30 cm × 30 cm × 50 cm) | plastic tape |
| | one plastic straw |
| clear plastic food wrap | |

Remove the top of the box. Leave a 3-cm edge for strength. Turn the box over. Cut a window in the new top, leaving half of the top intact. Cut out one side, again leaving a 3-cm edge for strength. Tape clear plastic food wrap to the side and the half window on top. In one end of the box, cut a small hole just large enough to insert a plastic straw. See figure for assistance in construction.

*Additional materials for exploration:*

| | |
|---|---|
| one 35-ml syringe | matches |
| one plastic straw (cut into three even pieces) | ice water |
| | hot water |
| heavy cotton string (three 4-cm pieces) | aluminum pan |
| | metric ruler |
| scissors | |

*For expansion:*

one dowel rod (3 feet long × ¾-inch wide) with hole drilled exactly in center
one dowel rod (1 foot long × ¼-inch wide) to be placed through hole in larger rod
one paper clip used as a sliding clip to balance the rod
two small paper bags of equal size
two thumbtacks of equal size and weight
one 150-watt bulb and socket
extension cord if necessary

➡ **Safety precautions:** Use caution around open flame.

1. **EXPLORATION:** Which process skills will be used?

Observing, experimenting, formulating models, questioning, communicating, inferring

What will the students do?

*Convection Current and Surface Temperature in an Observation Box*

Take a piece of string and fold it in half. Place the folded end into one of the pieces of straw, allowing about 0.5 cm to hang out the end. Be sure it fits snugly in the end. Do this for each piece of straw.

Slip the open end of the prepared straw onto the syringe. Light the string. Collect smoke in the cylinder by slowly pulling out the plunger. Remove the straw and lay it aside where it won't burn anything. You may need more smoke later.

Place a pan of ice water inside the observation box. Be sure the straw is in place through the end of the box, but not hanging over the pan. Let the pan sit for 3 or 4 minutes. After the wait, insert the smoke-filled syringe into the straw of

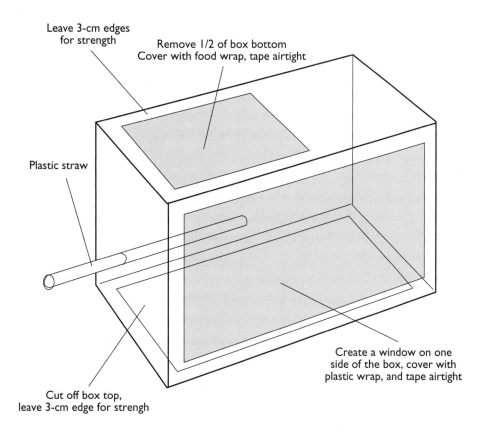

Leave 3-cm edges for strength

Remove 1/2 of box bottom
Cover with food wrap, tape airtight

Plastic straw

Cut off box top,
leave 3-cm edge for strengh

Create a window on one
side of the box, cover with
plastic wrap, and tape airtight

the observation box. Gently force the smoke through the straw into the box. Carefully observe what happens to the smoke as it moves over the pan of ice water.

Complete the procedure using a pan of hot water instead. Once again, make careful observations of the smoke as it moves over the hot water.

2. **EXPLANATION/CONCEPT INVENTION:** *What is the main idea? How will the main idea be constructed?*

> *Concept:* Air moves downward over colder surfaces and upward over warm surfaces.
>
> • What path did the smoke take as it moved over the cold surface? (It spread out slowly over the pan, staying close to the pan's surface.)
> • What path did the smoke take as it moved over the hot surface? (It slowly spread out and upward.)
> • Do you think a force is acting on the smoke as it moves above the warm or cold surfaces? (A force is something that causes a change in shape or a change in motion of a body. It is easy to see the change in shape; this also shows the change in motion.)

EARTH SCIENCE

**3. EXPANSION OF THE IDEA:** Which process skills will be used?

Experimenting, making conclusions, evaluating, generalizing

How will the idea be expanded?

*Paper Bag Balance*   Set up the dowel rod balance as in the figure. Fasten the two paper bags to the balance rod using the thumbtacks. Balance the rod using the sliding paper clip. Hold the rod stationary. Put the lighted bulb just below the open end of the bag on one side. Keep the bulb under the bag for 30 seconds. Then gently let go of the bar. Observe the bag for several minutes.

*Questions that help invent additional concepts:*
- What happened to the bag on the side near the bulb?
- How do you know this?
- Was the temperature of the bag away from the bulb colder or warmer than the bag near the bulb?
- What happened when you gently released the balance?
- From your observations, which has the greater mass? Is it the bag of warm air or the bag of cool air?

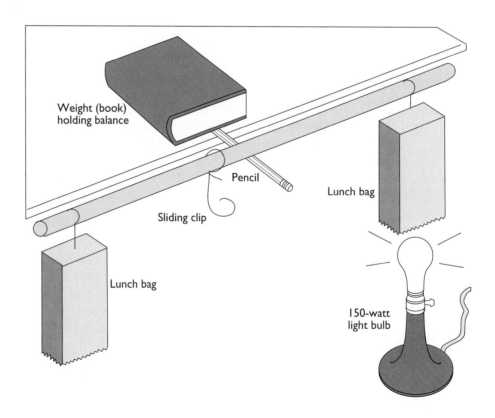

- The bags in this activity have the same volume. Which do you think has more gas particles? Why?
- What do you think this activity demonstrates about what happens to a substance when heated?

Warm air has less mass than an equal amount of cool air: particles of warm air are farther apart than particles of cool air. Cold air, being heavier than warm air, sinks, pushing warm air upward.

### Science in Personal and Social Perspectives

- How would the absence of wind affect your life? Do you think life would be changed in any way if there never was a wind?
- How does the presence of wind affect you personally? How do you think strong winds would affect you if you lived in a coastal city?

### Science and Technology

- How has wind power become a source of energy in some regions of the world? How has this harnessing of the wind changed the lives of people living there?
- How has knowledge of air mass saved lives? In what circumstances?

### Science as Inquiry

- The students will develop process skills needed to identify moving air as wind and to determine that air has mass.
- The students will be able to explain the movement of air over surfaces of varying temperatures and apply this knowledge to explain why wind occurs.

### History and Nature of Science

- How will knowledge of wind behavior assist a pilot in flight? What kind of training must a pilot undergo in order to understand how wind behaves? Can just anyone become a pilot? What skills do you think are necessary to become a successful pilot?
- Read a book on Amelia Earhart. What do you think happened to her when she vanished in her plane over the Pacific Ocean?
- Can you list any other occupations in which knowledge of wind and its behavior is necessary?

## 4. EVALUATION: How will the students show what they have learned?

Upon completing the activities the students will be able to:

- answer all of the questions included in this lesson;
- demonstrate the movement of smoke over cold air and warm air to a group of younger students or parents and be able to explain the concept behind the movement;
- demonstrate that cold air sinks and warm air rises when given a thermometer, a pan of ice water, and a fan.

EARTH SCIENCE

## Uneven Heating of the Earth

**Concept to be invented**
Main idea—Uneven heating of the Earth affects air pressure.

**Concepts that are important to expansion**
Uneven heating of the Earth gives rise to wind patterns that move locally and around the globe.

**Materials needed**
*For exploration:*

| | |
|---|---|
| long clear tube | six rubber bands |
| two rubber stoppers to fit tube (clear caps) | clear tape |
| | one tongue depressor |
| tub of water | one straw |
| two baby food jars (one larger than the other) | scissors or knife |
| | marking pen |
| balloon | |

*For expansion:*

| | |
|---|---|
| two clear-glass drinking cups of the same size | two large can lids |
| | clay |
| water | two tacks |
| food coloring | small lamp with removable shade |
| index card | oven mitt |
| wire | glass beaker |
| candle | |

➥ **Safety precautions:** The students should take care when using any glass containers. Exercise extreme caution when using the hot water to avoid burns. Also, when using the lamp, remember that the bulb can get hot. When using the candle, be watchful of the open flame. Be sure all sleeves are rolled up, all hair is pulled back, and no shirts are dangling into the flame.

1. EXPLORATION: Which process skills will be used?

Observing, measuring, questioning, recording data, predicting, formulating models

What will the students do?

The following two activities could be done ahead of time to introduce the concept of air pressure. Once the students understand this concept, then the third activity can be performed to teach the concept at hand.

*Tower of Water*     Close one end of a long, clear tube with a stopper or cap. Stand this in a tub of water. Fill the tube with water. Seal the top end of the tube with the stopper or cap. Remove the seal at the bottom, keeping the opening of the tube under water. What happens to the water in the tube? Why? What do you think will happen if you remove the stopper from the top of the tube? Try it! Was your prediction correct? Why does all of this happen?

*Aneroid Barometer*  Cut the open end off a balloon. Obtain a large-size baby food jar and extend the balloon over the mouth of the jar. Make sure the balloon is stretched taut. While you hold it, have your partner fasten it in place with a rubber band. Be sure to make a tight seal. Use the second rubber band to make sure the seal is tight. Why do you think a tight seal is important? Draw a sketch of your jar. Show what the balloon seal would look like if the pressure inside the jar were greater than the pressure outside of the jar. Cut one end of the straw at an angle to make it pointed. Gently place a 3-cm strip of tape on the uncut end. Place this on the center of the balloon-covered jar. Be sure it sits securely in the center. Attach a tongue depressor to the smaller jar at the top and the bottom of the jar, using two rubber bands at each location (a total of four). Place the two jars side by side on a level support so that the pointed straw is in front of the tongue depressor. Label the point where it hits 0 to show the starting position.

*Questions for student activities:*

- What do you think will happen to the pointer as the air pressure outside the jar increases?
- What about when the air pressure outside decreases?
- Try increasing the air pressure within the jar by placing your hands over the balloon jar for about 10 minutes. What happens to the pointer?
- Try decreasing the air pressure within the jar by placing the balloon jar in a pan of ice water. What happened to the pointer?

*Uneven Heating*     Make use of the barometers created in the second activity or provide the stu-
*and Air Pressure*   dents with commercially made aneroid barometers. After the students have had a chance to observe how their barometers work, divide the class into three groups. In the very beginning of the school day, instruct one-third of the students to place their barometer in the same safe place in the playground in the sun on the blacktop or gravel; one-third in the same safe place in the playground in the shade on the grass near a tree; one-third in the same area of the classroom. Instruct each group to place a thermometer in their area also. Ask the students to take readings from their barometers and thermometers throughout the course of the school day. Instruct the students to note any changes that occur in the area where they placed the barometer, such as the amount of sunlight, changing shade conditions, or wind picking up or dying down. Remind them about the importance of keeping a careful record of their observations.

EARTH SCIENCE

## 2. EXPLANATION/CONCEPT INVENTION: What is the main idea? How will the main idea be constructed?

*Concept:* Uneven heating of the Earth affects air pressure.

If the students have made careful observations and recorded their data accurately, you should be able to create a class chart of data collected at the three sites. Ask the students from each of the groups to examine their data as a group first. If their data for the different time readings are not all the same, ask them to average the readings for that time period. These averages could be placed on the chart.

Through careful questioning and calling attention to the group data, the children may find that the barometric readings as well as thermometer readings were different at each of the sites. Ask them if they see some sort of relationship between the temperature at the site and what was happening with the barometer. What happened to the barometric reading as your temperature increased? as it decreased? Were the barometer readings any different in the shade than in the sun or the classroom? Why or why not?

The Earth is heated unevenly due to varying types and colors of surfaces found on the Earth. What was the color of the site where you placed your barometer and thermometer? Which color site had the warmest temperatures? the coolest? Were the barometer readings different for these sites? What conclusions can you draw about uneven heating of the Earth and air pressure?

## 3. EXPANSION OF THE IDEA: Which process skills will be used?

Observing, hypothesizing, predicting, communicating

How will the idea be expanded?

*Concept:* Uneven heating of the Earth gives rise to wind patterns that move locally and around the globe.

Set up stations around the classroom so that the children can practice the following:

*Air Pressure versus Water Temperature*
Fill two clear glasses with water. Place an index card on the top of one. Holding the card in place, invert the cup and place it on top of the other cup. Remove the card. Obtain some very hot water. Put food coloring into it. Use this to fill one of the clear glasses from your practice session above. Do the same with cold water and a different color of food coloring. Place a card over one of the cups. Be sure to wear an oven mitt to hold the hot glass. Try inverting the cold over hot and hot over cold. What happens in each set of cups? Why?

*Air Temperature versus Movement of Air*
Draw a spiraling line on an index card. Cut out this snake and tape a thread to the center of it. Blow on the snake from the bottom. What happens to the snake? What do you think will happen if you suspend it above a burning candle? Try it! Why is this snake moving?

*Heat Transfer on a Wire*

Light a candle and allow the melting wax to harden at different spots on a wire. Hold one end of the wire in a candle flame. What do you think will happen to the wax drops on the wire? Does something happen to all of the drops at the same time? How is heat transferred from one end of the wire to the next?

*Heat Movement Through Air*

Remove the shade from a lamp and plug it in. Place your hand carefully near the side of the bulb, keeping the light off. Turn on the lamp. Did you notice a change in the temperature of your hand? Place a cool beaker around the lit bulb. Can you feel the heat from the bulb?

*Heat Transfer Through Metal*

Cover one side of a large tin can lid with candle soot. Fix a tack to the opposite side with candle wax. Fix a tack to the side of a clean tin can lid. Support each lid in a clay mound so the tacks are directly opposite the candle flame, a small but equal distance away. Which tack do you think will fall first and why? Did it occur as you predicted?

As the students rotate through the five stations, set up a sixth demonstration area so that the small groups can observe the teacher perform the following activity.

Make an observation box before beginning the demonstration. The following materials will be needed: one cardboard box (about 30 cm × 30 cm × 50 cm), clear plastic food wrap, plastic tape, one plastic straw.

Remove the top of the box. Leave a 3-cm edge for strength. Turn the box over. Cut a window in the new top, leaving half of the top intact. Cut out one side, again leaving a 3-cm edge for strength. Tape clear plastic food wrap to the side and the half window on top. In one end of the box, cut a small hole just large enough to insert a plastic straw. See figure for assistance in construction.

*Additional materials:*

| | |
|---|---|
| one 35-ml syringe | scissors |
| one plastic straw (cut into three even pieces) | matches |
| | ice water |
| heavy cotton string (three 4-cm pieces) | aluminum pan |
| | metric ruler |

*Movement of Smoke over Hot and Cold Surfaces: Clouds*

*Teacher demonstration:*

1. Take a piece of string and fold it in half. Place the folded end into one of the pieces of straw, allowing about 0.5 cm to hang out the end. Be sure it fits snugly in the end. Do this for each piece of straw.
2. Slip the open end of the prepared straw onto the syringe. Light the string. Collect smoke in the cylinder by slowly drawing out the plunger. Remove the straw and lay it aside where it won't burn anything. You may need more smoke later.
3. Place a pan of ice water inside the observation box. Be sure the straw is in place through the end of the box but not hanging over the pan. Let the pan sit for 3 or 4 minutes. After the wait, insert the smoke-filled syringe into

EARTH SCIENCE

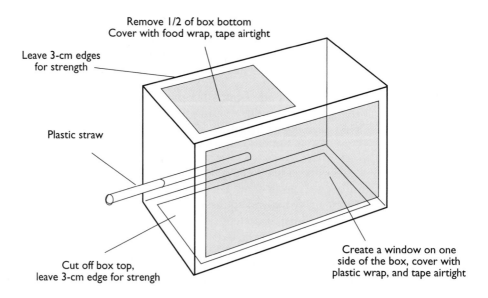

Remove 1/2 of box bottom
Cover with food wrap, tape airtight

Leave 3-cm edges
for strength

Plastic straw

Cut off box top,
leave 3-cm edge for strengh

Create a window on one
side of the box, cover with
plastic wrap, and tape airtight

the straw of the observation box. Gently force the smoke through the straw into the box. Carefully observe what happens to the smoke as it moves over the pan of ice water.

4. Complete the procedure using a pan of hot water instead. Once again ask the students to make careful observations of the smoke as it moves over the hot water.

*Additional activity/demonstration materials needed:*

| | | |
|---|---|---|
| observation/convection box | paper clips | scissors |
| drinking straws | tape | empty soda bottle |
| straight pins | index cards | small fan |
| | clay | |

*Movement of Smoke over Hot and Cold Surfaces: Wind Patterns*

Remove the pan of water used in the activity above and replace it with a candle. Cut a 10-cm hole in the observation box in the lid directly above the candle so that the observation box now looks like the figure below. Light the candle and place it inside the box directly under the hole. Once again inject air through the straw to keep the wick smoking. Observe the behavior of the smoke in the box. Which direction is the smoke in the straw coming from: horizontal or vertical? Place a pan of ice cubes directly below the smoking wick and leave the burning candle in place. What happens to the smoke as it moves over the pan and on toward the candle?

*Concept:* Uneven heating of the earth gives rise to wind patterns that move locally and around the globe. *Convection* is hot air rising above cold. *Conduction* is heat transferred through surface of objects. *Radiation* is heat energy that travels in waves.

EARTH SCIENCE

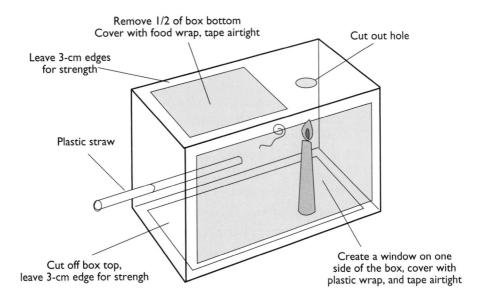

*Questions for student activities:*

- What three types of heating did you experience in the above activities?
- When warm air rises over cold air, what type of current does this represent?
- If you had a choice of the type of heating for your home, would you choose one that made use of conduction, convection currents, or radiation? Which do you think is the most efficient? the least efficient?
- How can a toaster be used to demonstrate the three different types of heating?

*Questions for teacher demonstration:*

- What path did the smoke take as it moved over the cold surface? (It spreads out slowly over the pan, staying close to the pan's surface.)
- What path did the smoke take as it moved over the hot surface? (It slowly spread out and upward.)
- What path did the smoke take as it moved over the ice and on toward the candle? (It stayed close to the pan's surface and then rose up over the candle.)
- Do you think a force is acting on the smoke as it moves above the warm or cold surfaces? (A force is something that causes a change in shape or a change in motion of a body. It is easy to see the change in shape; this also shows the change in motion.)
- What name could you give this change of motion? Why do you think it occurs? (Wind is caused by the uneven heating within the observation box. The teacher should elaborate on this concept of local and global winds.)

EARTH SCIENCE

*Science in Personal and Social Perspectives*

- Do you think you could run a mile in Denver, Colorado, as easily as you could in Chicago, Illinois? Why or why not?
- On a hot summer day, can you feel a difference in your comfort level when you are wearing a dark-colored shirt compared to a light-colored shirt? Why?
- Why do you think you have to bake a boxed cake mix at a different temperature when you are in a place at a high altitude compared to a place closer to sea level?

*Science and Technology*

- What causes winds?
- Why is a desert climate different from a forest climate?

*History and Nature of Science*

- Who was Bernoulli and how did his work explain the concept of air pressure?

**4. EVALUATION:** How will the students show what they have learned?

Upon completing these activities the students will be able to:

- compare cloud patterns of different areas when given satellite photographs;
- look at an aerial map of a coastal state and be able to predict where most of the clouds will form;
- demonstrate the ability to read a barometer;
- explain the difference in barometric readings over land and sea;
- explain why you would expect the air to be warmer in the daytime over land than sea;
- engage in a reflective discussion on the cause of wind and its importance.

EARTH SCIENCE

# Appendix

## National Science Education Standards: Content Standards for K–4 and 5–8

### K–4 Physical Science Standards

**Content Standard B—K–4:**

All students should develop an understanding of:
- Properties of objects and materials
- Position and motion of objects
- Light, heat, electricity, and magnetism

**Properties of objects and materials concepts**
- Objects have many observable properties, including size, weight, shape, color, temperature, and the ability to react with other substances. These properties can be measured using tools such as rulers, balances, and thermometers.
- Objects are made of one or more materials, such as paper, wood, and metal. Objects can be described by the properties of the materials from which they are made, and these properties can be used to separate or sort a group of objects or materials.
- Materials have different states—solid, liquid, and gas. Some common materials such as water can be changed from one state to another by heating or cooling.

**Position and motion of objects concepts**
- The position of an object can be described by locating it relative to another object or the background.
- An object's motion can be described by indicating the change in its position over time.
- The position and motion of objects can be changed by pushing or pulling and the size of the change is related to the strength of the push or pull.
- Vibrating objects produce sound. The pitch of the sound can be varied by changing the rate of vibration.

**Light, heat, electricity, and magnetism concepts**
- Light travels in a straight line unless it strikes an object. Light can be reflected by a mirror, refracted by a lens, or absorbed by the object.
- Heat can be produced in many ways, such as burning, rubbing, and mixing chemicals. The heat can move from one object to another by conduction.
- Electricity in circuits can produce light, heat, sound, and magnetic effects. Electrical circuits require a complete loop through which the electrical current can pass.
- Magnets attract and repel each other and certain kinds of metals.

### K–4 Life Science Standards

**Content Standard C—K–4:**

All students should develop an understanding of:
- The characteristics of organisms
- Life cycles of organisms
- Organisms and environments

**The characteristics of organisms concepts**
- Organisms have basic needs, which for animals are air, water, and food. Plants require air, water, and light. Organisms can only survive in environments in which they can meet their needs. The world has many different environments, and distinct environments support the life of different types of organisms.
- Each plant or animal has different structures which serve different functions in growth, survival, and reproduction. For example, humans have distinct structures of the body for walking, holding, seeing, and talking.

*Source:* NRC. (1996). Science content standards, *National Science Education Standards.* Washington, D.C.: National Academy of Sciences, pp. 123–160.

- The behavior of individual organisms is influenced by internal cues such as hunger and by external cues such as an environmental change. Humans and other organisms have senses that help them detect internal and external cues.

### Life cycles of organisms concepts

- Plants and animals have life cycles that include being born, developing into adults, reproducing, and eventually dying. The details of this life cycle are different for different organisms.
- Plants and animals closely resemble their parents.
- Many characteristics of an organism are inherited from the parents of the organism, but other characteristics result from an individual's interactions with the environment. Inherited characteristics include the color of flowers and the number of limbs of an animal. Other features, such as the ability to play a musical instrument, are learned through interactions with the environment.

### Organisms and their environments concepts

- All animals depend on plants. Some animals eat plants for food. Other animals eat animals that eat the plants.
- An organism's patterns of behavior are related to the nature of that organism's environment, including the kinds and numbers of other organisms present, the availability of food and resources, and the physical characteristics of the environment. When the environment changes, some plants and animals survive and reproduce, and others die or move to new locations.
- All organisms cause changes in the environment where they live. Some of these changes are detrimental to themselves or other organisms, whereas others are beneficial.
- Humans depend on both their natural and their constructed environment. Humans change environments in ways that can either be beneficial or detrimental for other organisms, including the humans themselves.

## K–4 Earth and Space Science Standards

### Content Standard D—K–4:

All students should develop an understanding of:

- Properties of Earth materials
- Objects in the sky

### Properties of Earth materials concepts

- Earth materials are solid rocks and soils, liquid water, and the gases of the atmosphere. These varied materials have different physical and chemical properties. These properties make them useful, for example, as building materials, as sources of fuel, or for growing the plants we use as food. Earth materials provide many of the resources humans use.
- Soils have properties of color and texture, capacity to retain water, and ability to support the growth of many

kinds of plants, including those in our food supply. Other Earth materials are used to construct buildings, make plastics, and provide fuel for generating electricity and operating cars and trucks.
- The surface of the Earth changes. Some changes are due to slow processes, such as erosion and weathering and some changes are due to rapid processes such as landslides, volcanoes, and earthquakes.
- Fossils provide evidence about the plants and animals that lived long ago and nature of the environment at that time.

### Objects in the sky concepts

- The sun, moon, stars, clouds, birds, and airplanes all have properties, locations, and movements that can be described and that may change.
- Objects in the sky have patterns of movement. The sun, for example, appears to move across the sky in the same way every day, but its path changes slowly over the seasons. The moon moves across the sky on a daily basis much like the sun. The shape of the moon seems to change from day to day in a cycle that lasts about a month.
- The sun provides the light and heat necessary to maintain the temperature of the Earth.
- Weather can change from day to day and over the season. Weather can be described by measurable quantities, such as temperature, wind direction and speed, precipitation, and humidity.

## 5–8 Physical Science Standards

### Content Standard B—5–8:

All students should develop an understanding of:

- Properties and changes of properties in matter
- Motions and forces
- Transformations of energy

### Properties and changes of properties in matter concepts

- Substances have characteristic properties such as density, boiling point, and solubility, which are independent of the amount of the sample. A mixture of substances can often be separated into the original substances by using one or more of these characteristic properties.
- Substances react chemically in characteristic ways with other substances to form new substances (compounds) with different characteristic properties. In chemical reactions the total mass is conserved. Substances are often placed in categories or groups if they react in similar ways, for example, metals.
- Chemical elements do not break down by normal laboratory reactions such as heating, electric current, or reaction with acids. There are more than 100 known elements which combine in a multitude of ways to produce com-

pounds, which account for the living and nonliving substances that we encounter.

**Motions and forces concepts**
- The motion of an object can be described by its position, direction of motion, and speed.
- An object that is not being subjected to a force will continue to move at a constant speed and in a straight line.
- If more than one force acts on an object, then the forces can reinforce or cancel one another, depending on their direction and magnitude. Unbalanced forces will cause changes in the speed and/or direction of an object's motion.

**Transformations of energy concepts**
- Energy exists in many forms, including heat, light, chemical, nuclear, mechanical and electrical. Energy can be transformed from one form to another.
- Heat energy moves in predictable ways, flowing from warmer objects to cooler ones until both objects are at the same temperature.
- Light interacts with matter by transmission (including refraction), absorption, or scattering (including reflection).
- In most chemical reactions energy is released or added to the system in the form of heat, light, electrical, or mechanical energy.
- Electrical circuits provide a means of converting electrical energy into heat, light, sound, chemical or other forms of energy.
- The sun is a major source of energy for changes on the Earth's surface.

## 5–8 Life Science Standards

**Content Standard C—5–8:**

All students should develop an understanding of:
- Structure and function in living organisms
- Reproduction and heredity
- Regulation and behavior
- Populations and ecosystems
- Diversity and adaptions of organisms

**Structure and function in living systems concepts**
- Living systems at all levels of organization demonstrate complementary structure and function. Important levels of organization for structure and function include cells, organs, organ systems, whole organisms, and ecosystems.
- All organisms are composed of cells—the fundamental unit of life. Most organisms are single cells; other organisms, including humans, are multicellular.
- Cells carry on the many functions needed to sustain life. They grow and divide, producing more cells.
- Specialized cells perform specialized functions in multicellular organisms. Groups of specialized cells cooperate

to form a tissue, such as a muscle. Different tissues are in turn grouped together to form larger functional units, called organs. Each type of cell, tissue, and organ has a distinct structure and set of functions that serve the organism as a whole. The human organism has systems for digestion, respiration, reproduction, circulation, excretion, movement, control and coordination, and for protection from disease.
- Disease represents a breakdown in structures or functions of an organism. Some diseases are the result of intrinsic failures of the system. Others are the result of infection by other organisms.

**Reproduction and heredity concepts**
- Reproduction is a characteristic of all living systems; since no individual organism lives forever, it is essential to the continuation of species. Some organisms reproduce asexually. Other organisms reproduce sexually.
- In many species, including humans, females produce eggs and males produce sperm. An egg and sperm unite to begin the development of a new individual. This new individual has an equal contribution of information from its mother (via the egg) and its father (via the sperm). Sexually produced offspring are never identical to either of their parents.
- Each organism requires a set of instructions for specifying its traits. Heredity is the passage of these instructions from one generation to another.
- Hereditary information is contained in genes, located in the chromosomes of each cell. Each gene carries a single unit of information, and an inherited trait of an individual can be determined by either one or many genes. A human cell contains many thousands of different genes.
- The characteristics of an organism can be described in terms of a combination of traits. Some traits are inherited and others result from interactions with the environment.

**Regulation and behavior concepts**
- All organisms must be able to obtain and use resources, grow, reproduce, and maintain a relatively stable internal environment while living in a constantly changing external environment.
- Regulation of an organism's internal environment involves sensing external changes in the environment and changing physiological activities to keep within the range required to survive.
- Behavior is one kind of response an organism may make to an internal or environmental stimulus. A behavioral response requires coordination and communication at many levels, including cells, organ systems, and whole organisms. Behavioral response is a set of actions determined in part by heredity and in part from past experience.
- An organism's behavior has evolved through adaptation to its environment. How organisms move, obtain food,

reproduce, and respond to danger, all are based on the organism's evolutionary history.

### Populations and ecosystems concepts
- Populations consist of all individuals of a species that occur together at a given place. All of the populations living together and the physical factors with which they interact compose an ecosystem.
- Populations of organisms can be categorized by the function they serve in an ecosystem. Plants and some microorganisms are producers—they make their own food. All animals, including humans, are consumers, which obtain food by eating other organisms. Decomposers, primarily bacteria and fungi, are consumers that use waste materials and dead organisms for food. Food webs identify the relationships among producers, consumers, and decomposers in an ecosystem.
- For ecosystems, the major source of energy is sunlight. Energy entering ecosystems as sunlight is converted by producers into stored chemical energy through photosynthesis. It then passes from organism to organism in food webs.
- The number of organisms an ecosystem can support depends on the resources available and abiotic factors such as quantity of light and water, range of temperatures, and the soil composition. Given adequate biotic and abiotic resources and no disease or predators, populations, including humans, increase at very rapid (exponential) rates. Limitations of resources and other factors such as predation and climate limit the growth of population in specific niches in the ecosystem.

### Diversity and adaptations of organisms concepts
- There are millions of species of animals, plants, and microorganisms living today that differ from those that lived in the remote past. Each species lives in a specific and fairly uniform environment.
- Although different species look very different, the unity among organisms becomes apparent from an analysis of internal structures, the similarity of their chemical processes, and the evidence of common ancestry.
- Biological evolution accounts for a diversity of species developed through gradual processes over many generations. Species acquire many of their unique characteristics through biological adaptation, which involves the selection of naturally occurring variations in populations. Biological adaptations include changes in structures, behaviors, or physiology that enhance reproductive success in a particular environment.
- Extinction of a species occurs when the environment changes and the adaptive characteristics of a species do not enable it to survive in competition with its neighbors. Fossils indicate that many organisms that lived long ago are now extinct. Extinction of species is com-

mon. Most of the species that have lived on the Earth no longer exist.

## 5–8 Earth and Space Science Standards

### Content Standard D—5–8:

All students should develop an understanding of:
- Structure of the Earth's system
- Earth's history
- Earth in the solar system

### Structure of the Earth system concepts
- The solid Earth is layered with a thin brittle crust, hot convecting mantle, and dense metallic core.
- Crustal plates on the scale of continents and oceans constantly move at rates of centimeters per year in response to movements in the mantle. Major geological events, such as earthquakes, volcanoes, and mountain building, result from these plate motions.
- Land forms are the result of a combination of constructive and destructive forces. Constructive forces include crustal deformation, volcanoes, and deposition of sediment, while destructive forces include weathering and erosion.
- Changes in the solid Earth can be described as the rock cycle. Old rocks weather at the Earth's surface, forming sediments that are buried, then compacted, heated, and often recrystallized into new rock. Eventually, these new rocks may be brought to the surface by the forces that drive plate motions, and the rock cycle continues.
- Soil consists of weathered rocks, decomposed organic material from dead plants, animals, and bacteria. Soils are often found in layers, with each having a different chemical composition and texture.
- Water, which covers the majority of the Earth's surface, circulates through the crust, oceans, and atmosphere in what is known as the water cycle. Water evaporates from the Earth's surface, rises and cools as it moves to higher elevations, condenses as rain or snow, and falls to the surface where it collects in lakes, oceans, soil, and in rocks underground.
- Water is a solvent. As it passes through the water cycle it dissolves minerals and gases and carries them to the oceans.
- The atmosphere is a mixture of oxygen, nitrogen, and trace gases that include water vapor. The atmosphere has different properties at different elevations.
- Clouds, formed by the condensation of water vapor, affect weather and climate. Some do so by reflecting much of the sunlight that reaches Earth from the sun, while others hold heat energy emitted from the Earth's surface.
- Global patterns of atmospheric movement influence local weather. Oceans have a major effect on climate, because water in the oceans holds a large amount of heat.

- Living organisms have played many roles in the Earth system, including affecting the composition of the atmosphere and contributing to the weathering of rocks.

**Earth's history concepts**

- The Earth processes we see today, including erosion, movement of crustal plates, and changes in atmospheric composition, are similar to those that occurred in the past. Earth history is also influenced by occasional catastrophes, such as the impact of an asteroid or comet.
- Fossils provide important evidence of how life and environmental conditions have changed.

**Earth in the solar system concepts**

- The Earth is the third planet from the sun in a system that includes the moon, the sun, eight other planets and their moons, and smaller objects such as asteroids and comets. The sun, an average star, is the central and largest body in the solar system.
- Most objects in the solar system are in regular and predictable motion. These motions explain such phenomena as the day, the year, phase of the moon, and eclipses.
- Gravity is the force that keeps planets in orbit around the sun and governs the rest of the motion in the solar system. Gravity alone holds us to the Earth's surface and explains the phenomena of the tides.
- The sun is the major source of energy for phenomena on the Earth's surface, such as growth of plants, winds, ocean currents, and the water cycle. Seasons result from variations in the amount of the sun's energy hitting the surface, due to the tilt of the Earth's rotation axis.

# References

AAAS (American Association for the Advancement of Science). (1993). *Benchmarks for scientific literacy*. New York: Oxford University Press.

Adeniyi, E. O. (1985). Misconceptions of selected ecological concepts held by some Nigerian students. *Journal of Biological Education, 19* (4), 311–316.

Alfke, D. (1974, April). Asking operational questions. *Science and Children,* pp. 18–19.

Antonouris, G. (1989). Multicultural science. *School Science Review, 70* (252), 97–100.

Appleton, K. (1993). Using theory to guide practice: Teaching science from a constructivist perspective. *School Science and Mathematics, 93* (5), 269–274.

Arbor Scientific Company (ASC). (1996). *Arbor Scientific—innovation in science education*. Ann Arbor, MI: Arbor Scientific.

Arena, P. (1996). The role of relevance in the acquisition of science process skills. *Australian Science Teachers Journal, 42* (4), 34–38.

Arnold, D. S., Atwood, R. K., & Rogers, U. M. (1973). An investigation of the relationships among question level, response level, and lapse time. *School Science and Mathematics, 73,* 591–595.

Ausubel, D. P. (1963). *Psychology of meaningful verbal learning*. New York: Grune and Stratton.

———. (1968). *Educational psychology: A cognitive view*. New York: Holt, Rinehart and Winston.

Baker, D. (1988). *Research matters to the science teacher teaching for gender differences*. National Association of Research in Science Teaching.

Baker, L. (1991). Metacognition, reading, and science education. In C. M. Santa & D. E. Alvermann (Eds.), *Science learning: Processes and applications*. Newark, DE: International Reading Association.

Bank Street College of Education. (1995). *The voyages of Mimi I and II*. Pleasantville, NY: Sunburst Communications.

Barman, C. R. (1996). How do students *really* view science and scientists? *Science and Children, 34* (1), 30–33.

———. (1997). Students' views of scientists and science: Results from a national study. *Science and Children, 35* (1), 18–23.

Barman, C. R., & Ostlund, K. L. (1996). A protocol to investigate students' perceptions about scientists and relevancy of science to students' daily lives. *Science Education International, 4* (4), 16–21.

Barnes, C. P. (1978). *Questioning strategies to develop critical thinking skills*. (ERIC Document No. 169486)

Beaton, A. E., Mullis, I. V. S., Martin, M. O., Gonzales, E. J., Kelly, D. L., & Smith, T. A. (1996). *Mathematics achievement in the middle school years: IEA's third international mathematics and science study (TIMSS)*. Chesnut Hill, MA: Boston College.

Bennett, W. J. (1986). *What works*. Washington, DC: U.S. Department of Education.

Berger, C. F., Lu, C. R., Belzer, S. J., and Voss, B. E. (1994). *Research on the uses of technology in science education*. In D. L. Gabel (Ed.), *Handbook of research on science teaching and learning* (pp. 466–490). New York: Macmillan.

Bergman, A. B. (1993, February). Performance assessment for early childhood: What could be more natural? *Science and Children,* pp. 20–22.

Biddulph, F., & Osborne, R. (1984, February). Children's questions and science teaching: An alternative approach. *Learning in science project* (Working Paper No. 117). Hamilton, New Zealand: Waikato University, February. (ERIC Reproduction Document No. ED 252400)

Biddulph, F., Symington, D., & Osborn, R. (1986). The place of chil-dren's questions in primary science education. *Research in Science and Technological Education, 4* (1) 77–78.

Birnie, H. H., & Ryan, A. (1984, April). Inquiry/discovery revisited. *Science and Children,* p. 31.

Bloom, B. J. (1984). The 2 sigma problem: The search for methods of group instruction as effective as one-to-one tutoring. *Educational Researcher, 13,* 4–16.

Bloom, B. S. (1956). *Taxonomy of educational objectives: The classification of educational goals, Handbook I: Cognitive domain*. New York: Longmans, Green.

Blosser, P. E. (1985). Using questions in science classrooms. In R. Doran (Ed.), *Research matters . . . to the science teacher, 2*. (ERIC Document No. 273490)

———. (1993). *Using cooperative learning in science education*. Columbus, OH: ERIC Clearinghouse for Science, Mathematics, and Environmental Education. (ERIC Reproduction Document No. ED 351207)

Bruer, J. T. (1998). Brain science, brain fiction. *Educational Leadership, 56* (3), 14–18.

Bredderman, T. (1982, September). Activity science—The evidence shows it matters. *Science and Children,* pp. 39–41.

———. (1984). The influence of activity-based elementary science programs on classroom practices: A quantitative synthesis. *Journal of Research in Science Teaching, 21* (3), 290–303.

Brown, D. R. (1979). Helping handicapped youngsters learn science by doing. In M. B. Rowe (Ed.), *What research says to the science teacher* (Vol. 2, p. 85), Washington, DC: National Science Teachers Association.

Brown, I. D. (1986). Topic 4: Teacher questioning techniques. *Staff devel-*

opment project—*Science Grades K–6.* Jackson, MS: Mississippi Association for Teacher Education. (ERIC Document No. ED 285726)

Bruner, J. S. (1961). The act of discovery. *Harvard Educational Review, 31,* 21–32.

———. (1962). *The process of education.* Cambridge, MA: Harvard University Press.

Budavari, S., et al. (1989). *The Merck Index: An encyclopedia of chemicals, drugs, and biologicals* (11th ed.). Rahway, NJ: Merck & Co.

Bybee, R., & Hendricks, P. W. (1972). Teaching science concepts to preschool deaf children to aid language development. *Science Education, 56* (3), 303–310.

Bybee, R. W., Ferrini-Mundy, J., & Loucks-Horsley, S. (1997). National standards and school science and mathematics. *School Science and Mathematics, 97* (7), 325–334.

Charles, C. M., & Malian, I. M. (1980). *The special student.* St. Louis, MO: C. V. Mosby.

Chaille, C., & Brittain, L. (1991). *The Young Child as Scientist.* New York: HarperCollins.

Checkley, K. (1997). The first seven . . . and the eighth. *Educational Leadership, 55* (1), pp. 8–13.

Cheney, M. S., & Roy, K. R. (1999). Inclusive safety solutions: What every teacher should know about special education and laboratory safety legislation. *The Science Teacher, 66* (6), pp. 48–51.

Chivers, G. (1986). Intervention strategies to increase the proportion of girls and women studying and pursuing careers in technological fields: A West European review. *Journal of Engineering Education, 11* (3), 248.

*CHRIS: Hazardous Chemical Data.* (1989). U.S. Department of Transportation, Superintendent of Documents. Washington, DC: U.S. Government Printing Office.

Coble, C. R., Levey, B., & Matteis, F. (1985). *Science for learning disabled students.* (ERIC Document No. 258 803)

Cole, J. T., Kitano, M. K., & Brown, L. M. (1981). Concept analysis: A model for teaching basic science concepts to intellectually handicapped students. In M. E. Corrick, Jr. (Ed.),

*Teaching handicapped students science: A resource book K–12 teachers* (pp. 51–53). Washington, DC: National Education Association.

College Board. (1987). *Get into the equation: Math and science, parents and children.* (ERIC Document No. 295 785)

Cooper, H. H. (1979). Pygmalion grows up: A model for teacher expectation, communication, and performance influence. *Review of Education Research, 49,* 389–410.

Corporation for Public Broadcasting. (1995). *The Annenberg/CPB math and science project—the guide to math and science reform; EE toolbox, interdisciplinary education access (IDEA), parks as classrooms* (Computer disc). Available through the Corporation for Public Broadcasting.

Cremin, L. A. (1976). *Public Education.* New York: Basic Books.

Czerniak, C. M., & Haney, J. J. (1998). The effect of collaborative concept mapping on elementary preservice teachers' anxiety, efficacy, and achievement in physical science. *Journal of Science Teacher Education, 9* (4), 303–320.

D'Arcangelo, M. (1998).The brains behind the brain. *Educational Leadership, 56* (3), 20–25.

Dalton, B., Morocco, C. C., Tivnan, T., & Rawson Mead, P. L. (1997) Supported inquiry science: Teaching for conceptual change in urban and suburban science classrooms. *Journal of Learning Disabilities, 30* (6), 670–684.

Dean, R. A., Dean, M. M., & Motz, L. L. (1997). *Safety in the elementary science classroom.* National Science Teachers Association, Arlington, VA. Booklet stock number PB 30, ISBN 0-87355-117-6.

Decker, L. E. (1981). *Foundation of community education.* Charlottesville, VA: Mid-Atlantic Center for Community Education.

Denkla, M., in Kantrowitz, B., & Wingert, P. (1989, April 17) How kids learn. *Newsweek,* 53–54.

Dewey, J. (1916). *Democracy and education.* New York: Macmillan.

———. (1937). *Experience and education.* New York: Collier Books.

Dillion, G. (1977). Mimeograph. In D. L. Hager-Schoeny et al., *Community involvement for classroom*

teachers (2nd ed., p. 27). Charlottesville, VA: Community Collaborators.

Dixon, N. (1996). Developing children's questioning skills through the use of a "Question Board." *Primary Science Review 44,* October, 8–10.

Driver, R. (1983). *The pupil as scientist?* Milton Keynes, England: Open University Press.

———. (1994). *Making sense of science.* London: Routledge.

Driver, R., Guensne, E., & Tiberghien, A. (1985). *Children's ideas in science.* Milton Keynes, England: Open University Press.

Duckworth, E., in Kantrowitz, B., & Wingert, P. (1989, April 17). How kids learn. *Newsweek,* p. 55.

Dunn, R., & Dunn, K. (1975). Finding the best fit—learning styles, teaching styles. *NAASP Bulletin, 59,* 37–49.

Ediger, M. (1994). *Technology in the elementary curriculum.* U.S. Department of Education (ERIC Reproduction Document No. ED 401882).

*Education Week* (1999, October 7). Science group finds middle school textbooks inadequate.

Eggen, P., & Kauchak, D. (1992). *Educational psychology: Classroom connections.* New York: Macmillan.

Elfner, L. E. (1988). *Exemplars: Women in science, engineering, and mathematics.* Columbus, OH: Ohio Academy of Science.

Elliott, D. L., & Carter, K. (1986). *Scientific illiteracy in elementary science textbook programs.* Paper presented at the Annual Meeting of the American Educational Research Association, San Francisco, April. (ERIC Document No. 269257)

Elstgeest, J. (1985). The right question at the right time. In W. Harlen (Ed.), *Primary science: Taking the plunge.* London: Heinemann Educational Books.

ETS (Educational Testing Service). (1989). *A world of differences: An international assessment of mathematics and science.* Princeton, NJ: Center for the Assessment of Educational Progress.

———. (1992). *National assessment of educational progress.* Washington, DC: U.S. Department of Education.

Fathman, A. K., Quinn, M. E., & Kessler, C. (1992). *Teaching science* to *English learners, grades 4–8.* Washington, DC: National Clearinghouse for Bilingual Education. (ERIC Document Reproduction Service No. ED 349 844)

Fields, S. (1989, April). The scientific teaching method. *Science and Children,* p. 15.

Flick, L. B. (1989). Will the real scientist please stand up! *Science Scope, 13* (3), 6–7.

———. (1993). The meanings of hands-on science. *Journal of Science Teacher Education, 4* (1), 3–4.

———. (1995). *Complex instruction in complex classrooms: A synthesis of research on inquiry teaching methods and explicit teaching strategies.* Paper presented at the National Association for Research in Science Teaching, San Francisco (April 1995). (ERIC Reproduction Document No. ED 383563)

Fort, D. C., & Varney, H. L. (1989). How students see scientists: Mostly male, mostly white, and mostly benevolent. *Science and Children, 26* (8), 8–13.

FOSS (1990). *Full option science system.* Berkeley, CA: Lawrence Hall of Science.

Foster, G. W., & Heiting, W. A. (1994). Embedded assessment. *Science and Children, 32* (2), 30–33.

Funk & Wagnalls (1968). *Standard dictionary.* New York: Reader's Digest Association.

Gallagher, J. J., & Aschner, M. J. (1963). A preliminary report on analyses of classroom interaction. *Merrill-Palmer Quarterly, 9,* 183–195.

Gamrell, L. B. (1983). The occurrence of think-time during reading comprehension. *Journal of Educational Research, 75,* 144-148.

Gardner, H. (1983) *Frames of mind: The theory of multiple intelligences.* New York: Basic Books.

George, R., & Kaplan, D. (1998). A structural model of parent and teacher influences on science attitudes of eighth graders: Evidence from NELS: 88. *Science Education, 82,* 93–109.

Gerlovich, J. A. 1997. Safety standards: An examination of what teachers know and should know about science safety, *The Science Teacher, 64* (3), 46–49.

Gerlovich, J., & Hartman, K. (1990). *Science safety: A diskette for ele-*

mentary educators. Waukee, IA: JaKel.

———. 1998. *The total science safety system: Elementary, 4th edition* [computer software], Waukee, IA: JaKel, Inc.

Gerlovich, J., Hartman, K., & Gerard, T. (1992). *The total science safety system for grades 7–14.* Waukee, IA: JaKel.

Gerlovich, J. A., Wilson, E., & Parsa, R. (1998). Safety issues and Iowa Science Teachers, *The Journal of the Iowa Academy of Science, 105* (4), 152–157.

Glencoe Science Professional Series. (1994). *Alternative assessment in the science classroom.* (ERIC Reproduction Document No. ED 370 778)

Goldhammer, A., & Isenberg, S. (1984). *Operation: Frog* [Educational software]. New York: Scholastic.

Good, R. G. (1977). *How children learn science.* New York: Macmillan.

Good, R. G., Wandersee, J. H., & St. Julien, J. (1993). Cautionary notes on the appeal of the new "ism" (constructivism) in science education. In K. Tobin (Ed.), *The practice of constructivism in science education* (pp. 71–87). Washington, DC: AAAS Press.

Gorodetsky, M., Fisher, K. M., & Wyman, B. (1994). Generating connections and learning with Semnet, a tool for constructing knowledge networks. *Journal of Science Education and Technology, 3* (3), 137–144.

Graesser, A. C., & Person, N. K. (1994). Question asking during tutoring. *American Educational Research Journal, 31,* 104–137.

Guerra, C. J. (1988, March). Pulling science out of a hat. *Science and Children,* pp. 23–24.

Habecker, J. E. (1976). *An analysis of reading questions in basal reading series based on Bloom's taxonomy.* Unpublished doctoral dissertation, University of Pennsylvania, Philadelphia.

Hager-Schoeny, D. L., & Galbreath, D. (1982). *Utilizing community resources in the classroom: An in-service reference collection.* Charlottesville, VA: University of Virginia, Mid-Atlantic Center for Community Education.

Hallahan, D. P., & Kauffman, J. M. (2000). *Exceptional learners.* Boston: Allyn and Bacon.

Halloran, J. D. (1970). *Attitude formation and change.* Great Britain: Leicester University Press.

Hammrich, P. L. (1997). Yes, daughter, you can. *Science and Children, 34,* January, pp 21–24.

Hamrick, L., & Harty, H. (1987). Influence of resequencing general science content on the science achievement, attitude toward science, and interest in science of sixth grade students. *Journal of Research in Science Teaching, 24* (1), 16.

Haney, J. (1998, September). Concept mapping in the science classroom: Linking theory into practice. *The Agora, 8,* 1–7.

Hannaford, C. (1995). *Smart moves.* Arlington, VA: Great Ocean Publishing Co.

Hargie, O. D. (1978). The importance of teacher questions in the classroom. *Educational Research, 20,* 99–102.

Harlen, W. (1992). *The teaching of science.* London: David Fulton Publishers.

———. (1993). *Teaching and learning primary science.* London: Paul Chapman Publishing.

Harms, N. (1981). VIII. Project synthesis: Summary and implications for teachers. In N. C. Harms & R. E. Yager (Eds.), *What research says to the science teacher* (Vol. 3). Washington, DC: National Science Teachers Association.

Harris, R. (1981). An audio-tactile approach to science education for visually impaired students. In M. E. Corrick, Jr. (Ed.), *Teaching handicapped students science.* Washington, DC: National Education Association.

Haury, D. L. (1993, March). *Teaching science through inquiry.* Columbus, OH: Clearinghouse for Science, Mathematics, and Environmental Education (EDO-SE-93-4).

Hazen, R. M., & Trefil, J. (1992). *Science matters: Achieving science literacy.* (New York: Doubleday).

Hein, G. E., & Price, S. (1994). *Active assessment for active science: A guide for elementary school teachers.* Portsmouth, NH: Heinemann.

Holdzkom, D., & Lutz, P. B. (1984). *Research within reach: Science education.* Charleston, WV: Research and Development Interpretation Service.

Holt, J. (1971). *How children learn* (p. 52). London: Penguin Press.

Howard, P. (1994). *Owner's manual for the brain.* Austin, TX: Leornian Press.

Humrich, E. (1988). *Sex differences in the second IEA science study: U.S. results in an international context.* Paper presented at the annual meeting of the National Association for Research in Science Teaching. (Education Resource Information Center Document No. ED 292 649)

Hunkins, F. P. (1970). Analysis and evaluation questions: Their effects upon critical thinking. *Educational Leadership, 27,* pp. 697–705.

Hurd, P. D. (Ed.). (1968). *New directions in elementary science teaching.* Belmont, CA: Wadsworth.

———. (1982). Middle school/junior high science: Changing perspectives. *Middle/Junior High Science Bulletin, 5,* 12.

———. (1986, January). Perspectives for the reform of science education. *Phi Delta Kappan,* pp. 353–358.

Iatridis, M. (1981, October). Teaching science to preschoolers. *Science and Children.*

Iwasyk, M. (1997, September). Kids questioning kids: "Experts" sharing. *Science and Children,* pp. 42–46.

Jarrett, D. (1997). *Inquiry strategies for science and mathematics learning: It's just good teaching.* Northwest Regional Educational Laboratory. (ERIC Reproduction Document No. ED 413188)

Jegede, O. J., Alaiyemola, F. F. & Okebukola, P. A. O. (1990). The effect of concept mapping on students' anxiety and achievement in biology. *Journal for Research in Science Teaching, 27* (10), 951–960.

Jelly, S. (1985). Helping children raise questions—and answering them. In W. Harlen (Ed.), *Primary science: Taking the plunge* (p. 54). London: Heinemann Educational Books.

Jensen, E. (1998). *Teaching with the brain in mind.* Alexandria, VA: Association for Supervision and Curriculum Development.

Johnson, F. (1997). New standards show too many students know too little science. *NSTA Reports!, 9* (3), 1, 12.

Johnson, R. T., & Johnson, D. W. (1991). So what's new about cooperative learning in science? *Cooperative Learning, 11* (3), 2–3.

Jones, G. M., Mullis, I. V. S., Raisen, S. A., Weiss, I. R., & Weston, E. A. (1992). *The 1990 science report card, NAEP's assessment of fourth, eighth, and twelfth graders.* Washington, DC: U.S. Department of Education.

Jones, M. G., & Wheatley, J. (1988). Factors influencing the entry of women into science and related fields. *Science Education, 72,* 127–142.

Jones, R. M. (1985, May). Teaming up. *Science and Children,* p. 21.

Kahle, J. B. (1983). Do we make science available for women? In F. K. Brown & D. P. Butts (Eds.), *Science teaching: A profession speaks* (pp. 33–36). Washington, DC: National Science Teachers Association.

———. (1990). Why girls don't know. In M. B. Rowe (Ed.), *What research says to the science teacher. Vol. 6: The process of knowing.* Washington, DC: National Science Teachers Association.

Kahle, J. B., & Lakes, M. K. (1983). The myth of equality in science classrooms. *Journal of Research in Science Teaching, 20* (2), 131–140.

Kahle, J. B., & Rennie, L. J. (1993). Ameliorating gender differences in attitudes about science: A cross-national study. *Journal of Science Education and Technology, 2* (1), 321–333.

Kamen, M. (1996). A teacher's implementation of authentic assessment in an elementary science classroom. *Journal of Research in Science, 33* (8), 859–877.

Karplus, R. (1964). The science curriculum improvement study—Report to the Piaget conference. *Journal of Research in Science Teaching, 2,* 236–240.

Katz, L., in Kantrowitz, B., & Wingert, P. (1989, April 17). How kids learn. *Newsweek,* p. 55.

Kinnear, J. (1994). *What science education really says about communication of science concepts* (Report No. CS508-657). Sydney, Australia: Annual Meeting of the International Communication Association. (ERIC Document Reproduction Service No. ED 372 455)

Knuth, R. (1995). *Engaging learning through technology.* Paper presented at the IVLA/IAECT Conference, Chicago, October.

Koran, J. J., & Koran, J. L. (1973). *Validating a teacher behavior by student performance* (Report No. FSDE-730-063). Tallahassee, FL: Florida State Department of Education.

Kroot, N. E. (1976). *An analysis of the responses of four, six, and eight year old children to four kinds of questions.* Unpublished doctoral dissertation, Indiana University, Bloomington.

Kuhn, T. S. (1970). *The structure of scientific revolutions.* (1st edition published in 1962). Chicago: University of Chicago Press.

Langrehr, J. (1993). Getting thinking into science questions. *Australian Science Teacher Journal, 39* (4), 36.

Lederman, N. G., & Niess, M. L. (1998). 5 apples + 4 oranges = ? (Editorial). *School Science and Mathematics, 98* (6), 281–284.

Levin, T., & Long, R. (1981). *Effective instruction.* Washington, DC: Association for Supervision and Curriculum Development.

Levine, D. U., & Ornstein, A. C. (1983). Sex differences in ability and achievement. *Journal of Research and Development in Education, 16* (2), 62–66.

Lind, K. (1999). Science in early childhood: Developing and acquiring fundamental concepts and skills. In AAAS (Ed.), *Dialogue on early childhood science, mathematics, and technology education* (pp. 73–83). Washington, DC: American Association for the Advancement of Science.

Linn, E. (1994). Science and equity: Why it's important. *Mathematics & Science Education, 4,* (1), 1,4.

Los Angeles Unified School District. (1977). Title IV-D: Effects of teacher expectation on student learning project. In *The Reflector.* Los Angeles: Unified School District Office of Instruction.

Loucks-Horsley, S. (Ed.). (1990). *Elementary school science for the '90s.* Andover, MA: The Network.

Madrazo, G. M., Jr. (1997, March). Using trade books to teach and learn science. *Science and Children,* pp. 20–21.

Marek, E. A., & Cavallo, A. M. L. (1997). *The learning cycle: Elementary science and beyond.* Portsmouth, NH: Heinemann.

Martens, M. L. (1999, May). Productive questions: Tools for supporting constructivist learning. *Science and Children*, pp. 24–27, 53.

Martin, R., Wood, G., & Stevens, E. (1988). *An introduction to teaching: A question of commitment.* Boston: Allyn and Bacon.

Martin, R. E. (1984). *The credibility principle and teacher attitudes toward science.* New York: Peter Lang.

Marx, R. W., Blumenfeld, P. C., Krajcik, J. S., & Soloway, E. (1997). Enacting project-based science. *The Elementary School Journal, 97* (4), 341–358.

Matthews, M. R. (1998) In defense of modest goals when teaching about the nature of science. *Journal of Research in Science Teaching, 35* (2), 161–174.

Maxim, G. (1997). When to answer the question "Why?" *Science and Children, 35* (3), 41–45.

McCracken, M. (1986). *Turnabout children.* Boston: Little, Brown.

McIntyre, M. (1984). *Early childhood and science.* Washington, DC: National Science Teachers Association.

McKinney, W. J. (1997). *The educational use of computer based science simulations: Some lessons from the philosophy of science.* Boston: Kluwer Academic Publishers.

McLane. K. (1998, Fall). Integrating technology into the standard curriculum: Extending learning opportunities for students with disabilities. *Research Connections in Special Education*, p. 3.

McLeod, R. J. (1979, October). Selecting a textbook for good science teaching. *Science and Children*, pp. 14–15.

Mechling, K. R., & Oliver, D. L. (1983a). *Characteristics of a good elementary science program, handbook III.* Washington, DC: National Science Teachers Association.

———. (1983b). *Science teaches basic skills, handbook 1.* Washington, DC: National Science Teachers Association.

———. (1983c). *Activities not textbooks: What research says about science programs. Principal, 43.*

Meyer, L. A., Greer, E. A., & Crummey, L. (1986). *Elementary science textbooks: Their contents, text characteristics, and comprehensibility* (Technical Report No. 386). Champaign, IL: University of Illinois. (ERIC Document No. 278947)

Minstrell, J. (1982). Conceptual development research in the natural setting of a secondary school classroom. In H. B. Rowe (Ed.), *Science for the 80's.* Washington, DC: National Education Association.

Morgan, N., & Saxton, J. (1991). *Teaching, questioning & learning.* New York: Routledge.

Mullins, I. V. S., & Jenkins, L. B. (1988). *The science report card: Elements of risk and recovery.* Princeton, NJ: Educational Testing Service.

Mullis, I. V. S., Martin, M. O., Beaton, A. E., Gonzalez, E. J., Kelly, D. L., & Smith, T. A. (1997). *Mathematics achievement in the primary school years: IEA's third international mathematics and science study (TIMSS).* Chesnut Hill, MA: Center for the Study of Testing, Evaluation, and Educatinoal Policy, Boston College.

Munson, B. H. (1994). Ecological misconceptions. *Journal of Environmental Education, 24* (4), 30–34.

Murphy, N. (1994). Helping preservice teachers master authentic assessment for the learning cycle model. In L. E. Schafer (Ed.), *Behind the methods class door: Educating elementary and middle school science teachers.* Columbus, OH: ERIC Clearinghouse for Science, Mathematics and Environmental Education.

National Association of Biology Teachers. (1990). *NABT guidelines for the use of live animals.* Position Statement of NABT, January 1990.

National Curriculum Council. (1989). *Science: Non-statutory guidance.* London: NCC.

National Education Goals Panel. (1997). *The national education goals report: Summary.* Washington, DC: Author.

National Geographic Society. (1995). *National Geographic Kids Network.* Washington, DC: Author.

National Research Council. (1992). *National Science Education Standards: A sampler.* Washington, DC: Author.

National Research Council. (NRC). (1996) *National Science Education Standards.* Washington, DC: National Academy Press.

National Research Council. (1997). *Every child a scientist: Achieving scientific literacy for all.* Washington, DC: National Academy Press.

National Science Board Commission on Precollege Education in Mathematics, Science, and Technology. (1983). *A revised and intensified science and technology curriculum for grades K–12 is urgently needed for our future.* (ERIC Document No. 239 847)

National Science Teachers Association. (1982). *Science-technology-society: Science education for the 1980's: Position statement.* Washington, DC: Author.

———. (1983). *Conditions for good science teaching in secondary schools.* Washington, DC: Author.

———. (1991, October–November). *An NSTA position statement: Multicultural science education.* Washington, DC: Author.

———. *NSTA Handbook, 1996–97.* Arlington, VA: Author.

Nickerson, R. S. (1995). Can technology help teach for understanding? In D. N. Perkins, J. L. Schwartz, M. M. West, & M. S. Wiske (Eds.), *Software goes to school—teaching for understanding new technologies.* New York: Oxford University Press.

North Carolina Museum of Life and Science. (1992). Science in the classroom. In Triangle Coalition for Science and Technology Education, *A guide for planning a volunteer program for science, mathematics, and technology education* (p. 59). College Park, MD: Triangle Coalition.

Novak, J. D. (1979). *A theory of education.* Ithaca, NY: Cornell University Press.

———. (1991, October). Clarify with concept maps. *Science Teacher,* p. 45.

Novak, J., & Gowin, D. B. (1986). *Learning how to learn.* New York: Cambridge University Press.

O'Brien, G. E., & Lewis, S. P. (1999). Connecting to resources on the internet. *Science and Children, 36* (8), 42–45.

Osborne, R., & Freyberg, P. (1990). *Learning in science: The implications of children's science.* In S. Loucks-Horsley (Ed.), *Elementary school science for the '90s* (p. 49). Andover, MA: The Network.

Oskamp, S. (1977). *Attitudes and opinions.* Englewood Cliffs, NJ: Prentice-Hall.

Ostlund, K. L. (1992, March). Sizing up social skills. *Science Scope*, pp. 31–33.

O'Sullivan, C. Y., Reese, C. M., & Mazzeo, J. (1997). *NAEP 1996 science report card for the nation and the states.* Washington, DC: National Center for Education Statistics.

Padilla, M., Muth, D., & Lund Padilla, R. (1991). Science and reading: Many process skills in common. In C. M. Santa & D. E. Alvermann (Eds.), *Science learning: Processes and applications* (pp. 14–19). Newark, DE: International Reading Association.

Pearlman, S., & Pericak-Spector, K. (1992, October). Expect the unexpected question. *Science and Children*, pp. 36–37.

Pert, C. (1997). *Molecules of emotion.* New York: Charles Scribner's Sons.

Peterson, P., & Knapp, P. (1993). Inventing and reinventing ideas: Constructivist teaching and learning in mathematics. In G. Cawletti (Ed.), *Challenges and achievements of American education.* Alexandria, VA: Association for Supervision and Curriculum Development.

Petty, R. E., & Cacioppa, J. T. (1981). *Attitudes and persuasion: Classic and contemporary approaches.* Dubuque, IA: William C. Brown.

Phillips, W. C. (1991). Earth science misconceptions. *Science Teacher, 58* (2), 21–23.

Piaget, J. (1954). *The construction of reality in the child.* New York: Basic Books.

Piburn, M., & Enyeart, M. (1985). *A comparison of the reasoning ability of gifted and mainstreamed science students.* (ERIC Document No. 255 379)

Pollina, A. (1995). Gender balance: Lessons from girls in science and mathematics. *Educational Leadership, 53* (1), 30–33.

Prather, J. P. (1991, April). *Speculative philosophical analysis of priorities for research in science education.* Research report presented at the 64th Annual Meeting of the National Association for Research in Science Teaching, Fontana, WI.

Price, S., & Hein, G. E. (1994, October). Scoring active assessments. *Science and Children*, pp. 26–29.

Project Technology Engineering Application of Mathematics and Science. (1992). Tips for teachers working with volunteers. In Triangle Coali-

tion for Science and Technology Education, *A guide for planning a volunteer program for science, mathematics, and technology education.* College Park, MD: Triangle Coalition.

Puckett-Cliatt, M J., & Shaw, J. M. (1985, November–December). Open questions, open answers. *Science and Children*, pp. 14–16.

Raizen, S. A., & Kaser, J. S. (1989, May). Assessing science learning in elementary school: Why, what and how? *Phi Delta Kappan*, 718–722.

Rakow, S. J. (1986). *Teaching science as inquiry.* Bloomington, IN: Phi Delta Kappa.

———. (1989, November–December). Safety supplement. *Science Scope.*

Reichel, A. G. (1994). Performance assessment: Five practical approaches. *Science and Children, 32* (2), 21–25.

Reichert, B. (1989, November–December). What did he say? Science in the multilingual classroom. *Science Scope*, pp. 10–11.

Renner, J. W., & Marek, E. A. (1988). *The learning cycle and elementary school science teaching.* Portsmouth, NH: Heinemann.

Rennie, L., & Parker, L. (1986). *A comparison of mixed-sex and single-sex grouping in year 5 science lessons.* Paper presented at the Annual Meeting of the American Educational Research Association, San Francisco. (ERIC Document No. ED 273 443)

Rice, J. R. (1983, January). A special science fair: LD children learn what they can do. *Science and Children*, pp. 15–16.

Riley, J. P. (1986). The effects of teachers wait-time and knowledge comprehension questioning on science achievement. *Journal of Research in Science Teaching, 23* (4), 335–342.

Risner, G. P. (1987). *Cognitive levels of questioning demonstrated by test items that accompany selected fifth-grade science textbooks.* (ERIC Document No. 291752)

Risner, G. P., Skeel, D. J., & Nicholson, J. L. (1992, September). A closer look at textbooks. *Science and Children*, pp. 42–45, 73.

Roberts, R. M. (1989). *Serendipity: Accidental discoveries in science.* New York: Wiley.

Rodriguez, I., & Bethel, L. J. (1983). An inquiry approach to science

and language teaching. *Journal of Research in Science Teaching, 20* (4), 291–296.

Rogers, D. L., Martin, R. E., Jr., & Kousaleos, S. (1988). Encouraging science through playful discovery. *Day Care and Early Education, 16* (1), 21.

Rop, C. (1998, December–January). Breaking the gender barrier in the physical sciences. *Educational Leadership, 55*, pp. 58–60,

Rosenshine, B. (1976). Classroom instruction. In W. L. Gage (Ed.), *The psychology of teaching methods.* Chicago: University of Chicago Press.

———. (1979). Content, time, and direct instruction. In P. L. Peterson & H. C. Walberg (Eds.), *Research on teaching: Concepts, findings, and implications.* Berkeley, CA: McCutcheon.

———. (1986, April). Synthesis of research on explicit teaching. *Educational Leadership*, pp. 60–69.

Ross, M. E. (1997). Scientists at play. *Science and Children, 34* (8), 35–38.

Rothkopf, E. Z. (1972). Variable adjunct question schedules, interperson interaction, and incidental learning from written material. *Journal of Educational Psychology, 63*, 87–92.

Rowe, M. B. (1970). Wait-time and rewards as instructional variables: Influence on inquiry and sense of fate control. *New Science in the Inner City.* New York: Teachers College, Columbia University.

———. (1973). *Teaching science as continuous inquiry.* New York: McGraw-Hill.

———. (1974). Wait-time and rewards as instructional variables, their influence on language, logic, and fate control: Part I—Wait time. *Journal of Research in Science Teaching, 13* (2), 81–94; Part II—Rewards. *Journal of Research in Science Teaching, 13* (4), 291–308.

Rutherford, F. J., & Ahlgren, A. (1988). Rethinking the science curriculum. In R. S. Brandt (Ed.), *Content of the curriculum.* Alexandria, VA: Association for Supervision and Curriculum Development.

———. (1990). *Science for all Americans.* New York: Oxford University Press.

Sabar, N. (1979). Science, curriculum, and society: Trends in science curriculum. *Science Education, 63* (2), 257–269.

Sadker, D., Sadker, M., & Thomas, D. (1981). Sex equity and special education. *Pointer, 26* (1), 33.

Safran, D. (1974). *Preparing teachers for parent involvement.* Menlo Park, California: Center for the Study of Parent Involvement.

Sargent-Welch Scientific Co. *Equipment catalogue.* Skokie, IL: Author.

Schlichter, C. L. (1983, February). The answer is in the question. *Science and Children,* p. 10.

Schwartz, J. L. (1985). *Sir Isaac Newton's Games* [Educational software]. Pleasantville, NY: Sunburst Communications.

———. (1995). Shuttling between the particular and the general: Reflections on the role of conjecture and hypothesis in the generation of knowledge in science and mathematics. In D. N. Perkins, J. L. Schwartz, M. M. West, & M. S. Wiske (Eds.), *Software goes to school—teaching for understanding new technologies* (pp. 7–22). New York: Oxford University Press.

Scruggs, T. E., Mostropieri, M. A., Bakken, J. P., & Grigham, F. J. (1993). Reading versus doing: The relative effects of textbook-based and inquiry-oriented approaches to science learning in special education classrooms. *The Journal of Special Education, 27* (1), 1–15.

Shakeshaft, C. (1995). Reforming science education. *Theory Into Practice 34* (1), pp. 74–79.

Shapiro, B. (1994). *What children bring to light: A constructivist perspective on children's learning in science.* New York: Teachers College Press.

Shavelson, R. J., & Baxter, G. P. (1992, May). What we've learned about assessing hands-on science. *Educational Leadership,* pp. 20–25.

Shaw, K. L., & Etchberger, M. L. (1993). Transitioning into constructivism: A vignette of a fifth grade teacher. In K. Tobin (Ed.), *The practice of constructivism in science education* (pp. 259–266). Washington, DC: AAAS Press.

Shaw, K. L., & Jakubowski, E. H. (1991). Teachers changing for changing times. *Focus on Learning Problems in Mathematics, 13* (4), 13–20.

Shepardson, D. P., & Pizzini, E. L. (1992). Gender bias in female elementary teachers' perceptions of the scientific ability of students. *Science Education, 76* (2), 147–153.

Shrigley, R. L. (1987, May). Discrepant events: Why they fascinate students. *Science and Children,* p. 25.

Shymansky, J. A., Hedges, L., & Woodworth, G. (1990). A reassessment of the effects of inquiry-based science curricula of the 60's on student performance. *Journal of Research on Science Teaching, 27* (2), 127–144.

Shymansky, J. A., Kyle, W. C., Jr., & Allport, J. M. (1982, November–December). How effective were the hands-on programs of yesterday? *Science and Children,* pp. 14–15.

Silver, H., Strong, R., & Perini, M. (1997). Integrating learning styles and multiple intelligences. *Educational Leadership, 55* (1), 22–27.

Slavin, R. L. (1995). *Cooperative learning.* Boston: Allyn and Bacon.

Smith, D. D., & Luchasson, R. (1992). *Introduction to special education.* Boston: Allyn and Bacon.

Smith, P. G. (1995, September). Reveling in rubrics. *Science Scope,* pp. 34–36.

Snir, J., Smith, C., & Grosslight, L. (1995). Conceptually enhanced simulations: A computer tool for science teaching. In D. N. Perkins, J. L. Schwartz, M. M. West, & M. S. Wiske (Eds.), *Software goes to school—teaching for understanding new technologies* (pp. 106–129). New York: Oxford University Press.

Solomon, J. (1997, September/October). Is how we teach science more important than what we teach? *Primary Science Review, 49,* 3–5.

Spady, W. G. (1994). Choosing outcomes of significance. *Educational Leadership, 51* (6), 18–22.

Starr, M. L., & Krajcik, J. S. (1990). Concept maps as a heuristic for science curriculum development: Toward improvement in process and product. *Journal of Research in Science Teaching, 27* (10), 987–1000.

State of Iowa. (1988). *School code of Iowa.* Des Moines, IA: Author.

Staver, J. R., & Bay, M. (1987). Analysis of the project synthesis goal cluster orientation and inquiry emphasis of elementary science

textbooks. *Journal of Research in Science Teaching, 23* (7), 629–643.

Stead, B. R., & Osborne, R. J. (1980). Exploring science students' concepts of light. *Australian Science Teachers Journal, 26* (3), 84–90.

Stefanich, G. P. (1985). *Addressing orthopedic handicaps in the science classroom.* (Educational Resource Document No. 258 802)

Stone, C. L. (1982). *A meta-analysis of advance-organizer studies.* Paper presented at the Annual Meeting of the American Educational Research Association, New York. (ERIC Document No. 220476)

Styer, S. (1984, March). Books that ask the right questions. *Science and Children,* pp. 40–42.

Suchman, J. R. (1962). *The elementary school training program in scientific inquiry.* Report to the U.S. Office of Education, Project Title VII. Urbana: University of Illinois.

———. (1971). Motivation inherent in the pursuit of meaning: Or the desire to inquire. In H. I. Day, D. E. Berlyne, & D. E. Hunt (Eds.), *Intrinsic motivation: A new direction in education.* Toronto: Holt, Rinehart, & Winston.

Sumrall, W. J. (1995). Reasons for the perceived images of scientists by race and gender of students in grades 1–7. *School Science and Mathematics, 95* (2), 83–90.

Taba, H., Levine, S., & Elsey, F. F. (1964). *Thinking in elementary school children* (U.S. Office of Education Cooperative Research Project No. 1574). San Francisco: San Francisco State College.

Tobin, K. (1984). Effects of extended wait-time on discourse characteristics and achievement in middle school grades. *Journal of Research in Science Teaching, 21* (8) 779–791.

Tobin, K. G., & Capie, W. (1982). *Wait-time and learning in science. AETS Outstanding Paper for 1981.* (ERIC Document No. ED 221353)

Tobin, K., Tippins, D. J., & Gallard, A. J. (1994). Research on instructional strategies for teaching science. In D. L. Gabel (Ed.), *Handbook on research on science teaching.* New York: Macmillan.

Triangle Coalition for Science and Technology Education. (1991). *A guide for building an alliance for science, mathematics and technology education.* College Park, MD: Author.

———. (1992). *A guide for planning a volunteer program for science, mathematics and technology education.* College Park, MD: Author.

*USA Today* (1999, October 18). Teachers support standards and accountability.

U.S. Department of Labor, Occupational Safety and Health Administration. (1990). 29 CFR Part 1910, Occupational Exposures to Hazardous Chemicals in Laboratories. *Federal Register.* Washington, DC: U.S. Government Printing Office.

U.S. Department of Labor, Occupational Safety and Health Administration. (1991). 29 CFR Part 1910.1030, Occupational Exposure to Bloodborne Pathogens; Subpart Z, Bloodborne Pathogens: Standard Summary Applicable to Schools. *Federal Register.* Washington, DC: U.S. Government Printing Office.

U.S. Office of Education. (1977, December 29). Education of handicapped children: Assistance to the states: Procedures for evaluating specific learning disabilities. *Federal Register, Part III.* Washington, DC: U.S. Government Printing Office.

Van Horn, J., Nourot, P. M., Scales, B., Alward, K. R. (1993). Play at the center of the curriculum. Columbus, OH: Merrill.

Valentino, C. (1985). *Question of the week.* Palo Alto, CA: Dale Seymore Publications.

Victor, E. (1985). *Science for the elementary school.* New York: Macmillan.

Von Glaserfeld, E. (1993). Questions and answers about radical constructivism. In K. Tobin (Ed.), *The practice of constructivism in science education* (pp. 23–38). Washington, DC: AAAS Press.

Vygotsky, L. S. (1978). *Mind and society: The development of higher mental processes.* Cambridge, MA: Harvard University Press.

Wadsworth, B. J. (1996). *Piaget's theory of cognitive and affective develop-*

*ment.* White Plains, NY: Longman Publishers.

Watson, S. B. (1992, February). Cooperative methods. *Science and Children,* pp. 30–31.

Weiss, I. R. (1978). *Report of the 1977 National Survey of Science, Mathematics, and Social Studies Education* (SE 78-72). Prepared for the National Science Foundation Directorate for Science Education. Research Triangle Park, NC: Center for Educational Research and Evaluation.

Western Regional Environmental Education Council. (1992). *Project WILD and Aquatic Project WILD.* Golden, CO: Author.

———. (1994). *Project Learning Tree.* Golden, CO: Author

———. (1995). *Project WET.* Golden, CO: Author.

Wheeler, G., & Sherman, T. F. (1983). Readability formulas revisited. *Science and Children, 20* (7), 38–40.

Wilen, W. (1986). *Questioning skills for teachers.* Washington, DC: National Education Association.

Wilen, W. W., & Ambrose, A. C., Jr., (1986) Effective questions and questioning: A research review. *Theory and Research in Social Education, 14* (2), pp. 153–161.

Willert, M. K., & Kamii, C. (1985, May). Reading in kindergarten: Direct vs. indirect teaching. *Young Children,* p. 3.

Williams, C. K., & Kamii, C. (1986, November). How do children learn by handling objects? *Young Children,* p. 26.

Williams, I. W. (1984). Chemistry. In A. Craft & G. Bardell (Eds.), *Curriculum opportunities in a multicultural society* (pp. 133–146). New York: Harper & Row.

Williams-Norton, M., Reisdorf, M., & Spees, S. (1990, March). Home is where the science is. *Science and Children,* pp. 13–15.

Willis, S. (1995a, Summer). Reinventing science education. *Curriculum Update.* Alexandria, VA: ASCD.

———. (1995b, Summer). Reinventing science education: Reformers promote hands-on, inquiry-based learning. *Curriculum Update.* Alexandria, VA: ASCD.

Wilson, L. D., & Blank, R. K. (1999). *Improving mathematics education using results from NAEP and TIMSS.* Washington, DC: Council of Chief State School Officers.

Windram, M. P. (1988, March). Getting at reading through science inquiries. *Roeper Review,* pp. 150–152.

Wiser, M. (1995). Use of history of science to understand and remedy students' misconceptions about heat and temperature. In D. N. Perkins, J. L. Schwartz, M. M. West, & M. S. Wiske (Eds.), *Software goes to school—teaching for understanding new technologies* (pp. 23–28). New York: Oxford University Press.

Wolfe, P., & Brandt, R. (1998). What do we know from brain research? *Educational Leadership, 56* (3), 8–13.

Wolfinger, D. M. (1984). *Teaching science in the elementary school.* Boston: Little, Brown.

Wright, D. (1980). A report on the implications for the science community of three NSF-supported studies of the state of precollege science education. In H. A. Smith (Ed.), *What are the needs in precollege science, mathematics, and social science education? Views from the field.* Washington, DC: National Science Foundation.

Yager, R. E. (1983). The importance of terminology in teaching K–12 science. *Journal of Research in Science Teaching, 20* (6), 577–588.

———. (1984). The major crisis in science education. *School Science and Mathematics, 84* (3), 196.

Yager, R. E., & Penick, J. E. (1987, October). New concerns for affective outcomes in science. *Educational Leadership,* p. 93.

Yager, R. (1991, September). The constructivist learning model. *Science Teacher,* pp. 52–57.

Zimmerman, B. J., & Pike, E. O. (1972). Effects of modeling and reinforcement on the acquisition and generalization of question-asking behavior. *Child Development, 43,* 892–907.

# Index